Marketing Today

First Canadian Edition

Marketing Today

First Canadian Edition

F. Ross Crain
Seneca College
of Applied Arts and Technology

David J. Rachman
Baruch College
City University of New York

Holt, Rinehart and Winston of Canada, Limited
Toronto

Canadian Cataloguing in Publication Data
Crain, F. Ross, 1932–
    Marketing today
1st Canadian ed.
Includes bibliographical references and index.
ISBN 0-03-922792-8
1. Marketing.   I. Rachman, David J.   II. Title
HF5415.C72   1991   658.8   C90-095583-X

Acquisitions Editor: *Donna Muirhead*
Developmental Editor: *Brenda Hutchinson*
Editorial Co-ordinator: *Marcel Chiera*
Editorial Assistant: *Kerry Gibson*
Copy Editor: *Lenore d'Anjou*
Cover and Interior Design: *Q.E.D. Design Associates*
Cover Photograph: *Adrian Dorst/Western Canada Wilderness Committee*
Typesetting and Assembly: *Compeer Typographic Services Ltd.*
Printing and Binding: *John Deyell Company*
∞ This book was printed in Canada on acid-free paper.

1 2 3 4 5   95 94 93 92 91

Other titles available from Holt, Rinehart and Winston of Canada Limited

Preface

The purpose of the first Canadian edition of *Marketing Today* is to teach basic marketing principles by demonstrating the link between theory and practice. This text, however, goes a step further by reflecting the interests of today's students across Canada. Unlike most principles texts, *Marketing Today* captures the excitement and vitality of the modern marketing environment. Students will enjoy learning from this textbook because it speaks to them.

Organization of the Book

Marketing Today is organized into six parts. Each part presents basic marketing concepts and describes how these concepts relate to marketing decisions and activities. Part One, "Overview of Marketing," covers the scope of marketing, management and planning, and the marketing environment. Part Two, "Markets and Segmentation," focuses on marketing research and information systems and consumer and industrial buying behaviour. The next three parts discuss the marketing mix variables: Part Three, "Product and Pricing Strategy"; Part Four, "Placement Strategy"; and Part Five, "Promotion Strategy." The chapters in Part Six, "Special Marketing," cover international marketing and marketing activities in not-for-profit organizations. Three appendixes especially helpful to students are "Career Resource Guide," "Marketing Arithmetic," and "Marketing for Small Businesses."

Special Features of This Edition

Each chapter contains the following pedagogical aids designed to provide information that promotes learning.

- **Learning Objectives.** Each chapter begins with a list of learning objectives that highlight chapter concepts, guide individual study, and facilitate review of chapter material.

- **Opening Vignettes.** An actual marketing situation introduces students to the main theme of each chapter.

- **Contemporary Examples.** A criticism of many textbooks is that examples of concepts are not fully integrated into the text but instead appear "tacked on." In *Marketing Today*, current examples enhance students' understanding of key marketing practices and activities.

The examples focus on topics and events that students are familiar with, thus encouraging them to learn how marketing relates to their everyday lives.

- **Marketing Today Boxes.** These special features take a look at marketing principles in action. They give students the chance to relate concepts to actual marketing decisions and strategies.

- **Services Marketing Boxes.** Called "At Your Service," these boxes reflect the growing importance of services in our economy by providing a real-world application of the marketing of services as they relate to specific chapter topics.

- **Marginal Glossary Terms.** Key terms are defined in the margin of the page on which they are first dealt with in detail. Ready access to key terms and their definitions permits students to concentrate on each chapter without flipping back and forth to an end-of-book glossary. In addition, a complete text glossary of all definitions is included at the end of the book. Each glossary term and the page on which it is defined are highlighted in the subject index in boldface type.

- **Chapter Summaries.** The "Chapter Replay" summarizes key points that correspond to the learning objectives that begin each chapter.

- **End-of-Chapter Questions.** Two types of questions test knowledge of chapter content. Recall questions test concept recognition, while discussion questions present scenarios for applying these concepts and challenge the students to further thought.

- **End-of-Chapter Cases.** Two cases at the end of each chapter allow students to evaluate and apply marketing practices discussed in the chapter. Focal questions accompany the cases, which primarily deal with real-world situations in marketing.

Other Features

- **End-of-Part Cases.** These longer cases help instructors who use the case approach to integrate chapter concepts within each part of the book.

- **Career Resource Guide Appendix.** Particularly useful to today's career-minded student, this new end-of-text supplement serves as a resource guide for students to familiarize them with realistic entry-level job possibilities in the field of marketing.

- **Marketing Arithmetic Appendix.** This section will help students review basic mathematical techniques necessary for studying marketing principles.

- **Marketing for Small Businesses Appendix.** In today's economy, nearly 70 percent of the organizations are small businesses. This appendix, written by Peggy Lambing of the University of Missouri—St. Louis, discusses special marketing issues relevant to small businesses and presents an extended case study of a successful small company.

Ancillary Materials

A complete, carefully developed support package accompanies the first Canadian edition of *Marketing Today*. It includes a *Study Guide, Computerized Marketing Simulation Game, Instructor's Manual, Test Bank, Computerized Test Bank*, and *Videos*.

Instructor's Manual

The *Instructor's Manual* parallels the text and includes the following items in each chapter: a chapter synopsis that includes learning objectives; a chapter outline that indicates where the corresponding transparency masters can be used; lecture notes that include current event highlights; key terms and definitions; answers to end-of-chapter discussion questions; classroom projects and activities; and answers to the case questions.

Test Bank

Written by Neil Beattie of Sheridan College and Ross Crain of Seneca College, the *Test Bank* is organized by quiz-type and exam-type questions. True/false, multiple choice, mini-case, and essay questions are provided in each chapter along with the correct answer, text page reference, major subject area, and level of each question.

Computerized Test Bank

The questions on the diskettes are identical to those that appear in the printed version of the *Test Bank*. This system gives instructors the flexibility of entering the program and adding or deleting questions. The test bank is available for the IBM personal computer.

Study Guide

Written by Gerald Stephenson of Okanagan College, the *Study Guide* has chapters corresponding to the text chapters. Each *Study Guide* chapter contains a summary, learning goals, key concepts, programmed review, exercise, and self-quiz.

Videos

Videos are available upon adoption of *Marketing Today*. Ideal for classroom use, the videos are accompanied by a separate booklet of teaching notes that explains how to use them in teaching key marketing topics. The notes are written specifically to accompany *Marketing Today*.

Acknowledgements

This book is truly the result of a team effort. Many individuals devoted enormous amounts of time and energy to ensure that the first Canadian edition of *Marketing Today* is the best it can be. We extend our sincere thanks to these marketing educators who have provided ideas and suggestions for this first Canadian edition: Neil Beattie of Sheridan College, Mary Foster of Ryerson Polytechnical Institute, Bernard Friedman of Centennial College, Mark Haber of John Abbott College, Henry Klaise of Durham College, Wayne McIntyre of Algonquin College, and Dennis Sullivan of Fanshawe College. We would also like to thank the editorial and production professionals associated with Holt, Rinehart and Winston of Canada—Donna Muirhead, Brenda Hutchinson, Marcel Chiera, Kerry Gibson, and Lenore d'Anjou.

F. Ross Crain
Seneca College
of Applied Arts and Technology

David J. Rachman
Baruch College
City University of New York

Publisher's Note to Instructors and Students

This textbook is a key component of your course. If you are the instructor of this course, you undoubtedly considered a number of texts carefully before choosing this as the one that would work best for your students and you. The authors and publishers of this book spent considerable time and money to ensure its high quality, and we appreciate your recognition of this effort and accomplishment.

If you are a student we are confident that this text will help you to meet the objectives of your course. You will also find it helpful after the course is finished as a valuable addition to your personal library.

As well, please do not forget that photocopying copyright work means the authors lose royalties that are rightfully theirs. This loss will discourage them from writing another edition of this text or other books; doing so would simply not be worth their time and effort. If this happens we all lose—students, instructors, authors, and publishers.

Since we want to hear what you think about this book, please be sure to send us the stamped reply card at the end of the text. This will help us to continue publishing high-quality books for your course.

Contributors

Ross Crain— *General Editor*
Seneca College of Applied Arts and Technology
- Chapters 4, 5, 6, and 7

Bill Crowe
St. Lawrence College
- Chapters 11, 12, and 13

Bill Inglis
Capilano College
- Chapter 18

Peggy Miller
John Abbott College
- Chapters 1 and 2

Don Shiner
Mount St. Vincent University
- Chapters 3, 8, 9, and 10

Mark Siemonsen
Marketing Consultant
- Chapters 11, 12, and 13

Gerry Stephenson
Okanagan College
- Chapters 14, 15, and 16

Anne Watson
Capilano College
- Chapter 17

Contents in Brief

Contents

PART TWO Markets and Segmentation

PART THREE Product and Pricing Strategy

PART FOUR Placement Strategy

PART FIVE Promotion Strategy

PART SIX Special Marketing

PART ONE

Overview of Marketing

1

Chapter 1

The Importance and Scope of Marketing

In this chapter, you will learn:

- The definition of marketing, including some examples of marketing activities.

- The distinctions among products, goods, and services.

- How marketing adds value to a product.

- Three orientations to doing business.

- The nature of a seller's market and a buyer's market.

- Key ideas underlying the marketing concept.

- The four elements of the marketing mix.

- Issues critics have raised about the marketing concept.

- How marketing reconciles today's concern for social responsibility with company profit motivations and individual wants.

Music Stores Turn Up the Volume

"The old traditional record store with loud rock music and teenagers hanging out is out," says Brian Robertson, President of the Canadian Recording Industry, which represents most of Canada's record producers. "Retail stores are becoming entertainment centres to appeal to an older population." In November 1989, HMV opened a new downtown Montreal store fashioned after music super stores like HMV and Towers in London, England. HMV Montreal has 40 000 titles, a recording studio, listening booths, full-time disc jockey, and 66 video monitors. "It's the store of the 1990s — it makes shopping for music both fun and entertaining," says the HMV Quebec Operations Director.

Industry official Robertson said he's not surprised by the feverish expansion activity in Montreal and other North American cities in view of the healthy state of the retail music business. Retail sales of cassettes, compact discs, and records totalled $700 million in Canada in 1989, up by about 6 percent to 7 percent from 1988.

Sales of compact discs have nearly wiped out vinyl LPs, jumped by more than 30 percent, and have helped bring new buyers back to the market. The question on industry-watchers' minds is how many consumers will still be out there once this vinyl phase-out is complete and the added sales of this switch have flattened. About 10 percent of Canadian homes now have CD players and the penetration should approach the United States level of 19 percent within a few years.

Many of the issues raised by the situation in the music industry are common to all types of marketing. For example, what kind of products will appeal to consumers in the future? How does any organization let consumers know about its products? What is the best way to reach the intended target market for these products? This chapter begins our study of the field of marketing. This textbook explores these and many other questions as it defines marketing and describes the many activities involved in this exciting field.

Source: Craig Toomey, *The Gazette*, Montreal, January 27, 1990, p. C1-2.

A well-known management theorist, Peter Drucker, once noted, "Any business enterprise has two—and only two—basic functions: marketing and innovation."[1] Many of the world's largest and most successful organizations — Procter & Gamble, IBM, McDonald's and Toshiba among them—have built their businesses around this philosophy.

The trick to successful marketing appears to be quick adaptation to a changing marketplace. Consider that experts predict the next 20 years will see new products such as integrated household computers, holograms, and electric automobiles with compact batteries. The marketplaces *will* change, and successful marketers will change with it. Advances in biotechnology will create changes in our food and general health.

Some Basic Concepts

As a child, did you ever ask for a toy you saw on TV? Did you ever try selling lemonade on the street corner? Have you ever distributed flyers promoting a fund-raising event or a local day-care centre or school organization? Did you ever try a new pizza place or oil-change service because you had a discount coupon? If so, you have been involved in marketing. Advertising, personal selling, brochures, and coupons are all part of this broad field.

What Is Marketing?

Those who sell toys or lemonade or day care or oil changes need to find buyers. **Marketing** comprises the activities performed by individuals, businesses, and not-for-profit organizations to satisfy needs and wants. This satisfaction occurs through **exchange** —the process by which two or more parties freely give something of value to one another. For example, a student might exchange money for a textbook. Exchange is basic to all marketing. The academic discipline of marketing studies exchanges to find out how they can be made better or more efficient.

Marketing is an important but often misunderstood activity. Some of the confusion arises from the use of the word *marketing* to mean selling. For example, many companies call their salespeople marketing representatives. One commentator observed that the word may be "the most widely abused term in the business lexicon today."[2] In fact, much more than selling is involved in satisfying needs and wants through exchange. Some of these other activities are suggested by the American Marketing Association's definition of marketing:

Marketing is the process of planning and executing the conception, pricing, promotion, and distribution of ideas, goods, and services to create exchanges that satisfy individual and organizational objectives.[3]

Besides selling, marketing includes product development, market research, distribution, pricing, and many other activities. This course will show you how all the elements of marketing work together.

Over the past 50 years, the proportion of the work force involved in marketing has grown largely because of expanding marketing tasks and the ever-increasing number of goods and services being offered. Men and women are considered to be in marketing if they participate in a marketing exchange either directly (by selling) or indirectly. Indirect participation includes product delivery, communication of product availability, or research into demand for products. Under this broad definition, an advertising copywriter, a supermarket clerk, a long-distance truck driver, and Bill Cosby could all be engaged in a joint marketing venture —selling Jell-O pudding.

What Can Be Marketed?

Almost anything that people need and want can be marketed. And in a society as sophisticated as ours, people need and want much more than simple food and shelter. Consequently, the variety of things that can be marketed ranges from the most concrete, such as furniture, to the very abstract, such as investment advice.

The marketing term for anything offered to meet a want or need is a *product*. Products can be goods, ideas, or services.

Goods and Services

When you go into McDonald's and trade a couple of dollars for a hamburger and a Coke, you are engaged in a marketing exchange. You receive tangible items — food and drink. In marketing terms, tangible items received in an exchange are **goods**.

But what about when you deposit a token in the fare box of a bus and ride nine blocks? Or when a stylist trims your hair? Money is exchanged, but what goods do you have to show for the transaction? In these cases, instead of a tangible object, you receive a **service,** or intangible benefit.

Canada is rapidly becoming a service economy. The most important services that individuals and families purchase are:

1. Shelter: use of housing in exchange for rent or mortgage payments.

2. Transportation: automobile, air, bus, and train travel.

3. Household operation services: energy, water, telephone service, and interior and exterior maintenance.

4. Personal care services: hair and beauty care, use of exercise facili-

Goods
Tangible objects exchanged in marketing.

Service
Intangible benefit exchanged in marketing.

ties, weight control and smoking-cessation services, and so on.

5. Recreation and travel: theatre-going, eating out, vacationing.

6. Education: college and university tuition, and music lessons.

In addition to the money individuals spend on services, businesses expend billions more for such services as transportation, advertising, legal advice, and machine repair. If individual and business purchases are taken together, more money is now spent on services than on goods.

The expansion and export in the service sector is of primary importance to Canada in the 1990s. On the international scene, potential growth areas for Canadian service firms are in the engineering areas of communication and energy, management consulting, and computer technology. But when the value of export services is figured into the nation's balance of payments, the overall balance for 1989 was a troublesome *deficit* of $24 billion. Expansion in service exports is essential to overcome this deficit.

Impressions

Marketing is not confined to goods and services in the narrow sense of those words. Marketing is also used to create impressions about the following:

- People in the public view, from political figures to entertainers to sports celebrities.

- Places, using slogans such as "There's a world of difference in Newfoundland and Labrador" and "Spain: Everything under the sun."

- Charitable organizations, such as the Canadian Red Cross and the Canadian Cancer Society.

- Public service announcements, such as "Don't use it if you can't reuse it" from organizations, such as Alcan, that want to be viewed favourably by potential customers, employees, and shareholders.

Most marketing experts agree that a substantial part of any marketing exchange involves intangible elements, even when the item exchanged is as unmistakably solid as a car. The typical automobile purchaser, for example, buys not only an assemblage of rubber, steel, and glass, but also convenience, a feeling of independence, and perhaps a sense of prestige. GM's advertising slogan "the spirit of Cadillac" is based on selling these intangible benefits. (See Marketing Today 1.1.)

When you buy almost any product, you are buying certain symbolic or psychological benefits along with the product itself. For example, when you purchase Reebok shoes, you are also purchasing the psychological benefits of owning goods that are highly regarded by your peer group. A marketing exchange can therefore be much more than simply an exchange of goods or services for money.

Marketing Today 1.1

Cadillac's Hopes for Spirited Design

Why would car buyers who in the previous year refused to spend $25 000 on a car that seats six now want to pay $50 000 for one that seats two? General Motors is hoping that the Cadillac Allante's benefits will make the higher price worthwhile.

The Allante offers the features that consumers expect in a high-priced car, such as ten-way adjustable power seats, a leather-wrapped tilt and telescoping steering wheel, and a fancy sound system. But what makes the car unusual for Cadillac is its design. To give this Cadillac added prestige, GM hired an Italian designer, Pininfarina, to create a new model. The Allante they have created is a sleek convertible designed to appeal to young, wealthy car buyers who might otherwise favour imports.

GM expects the Allante to boost sales of its entire line of Cadillacs. The company's advertising emphasizes the Cadillac division over individual Cadillac lines. The theme of the advertising campaign is ''the spirit of Cadillac,'' with the Allante being called ''the new spirit of Cadillac,'' the Seville ''the elegant spirit of Cadillac,'' and so on. GM hopes that the prestige generated by the Allante's new design will make Cadillac's ''spirit'' seem like a desirable benefit to buyers of the entire Cadillac line.

Sources: Adapted from Ralph Gray, ''Cadillac Line, Led by New Allante, Refocuses on Spirit,'' *Adweek*, September 15, 1986, p. 4; Stephen Koepp, ''A Passion for Italian Bodies,'' *Time*, September 15, 1986, p. 46; Jim Mateja, ''Cadillac Gambling on Allante,'' *Chicago Tribune*, September 14, 1986, sec. 17, p. 1; Raymond Serafin and Patricia Strand, ''Financing Fallout: '87 Ads Facing Heavy Challenge,'' *Advertising Age*, September 15, 1986, pp. 3, 30.

Cadillac Motor Car Division

Intangibles

Some marketers have taken the question of what constitutes a marketing exchange one step further. They suggest that the objects of exchange might be entirely intangible and symbolic. One theorist maintains, for example, that a marketing exchange takes place when a person decides to watch a television program.[4] Figure 1.1 shows how this might work.

If you watch a television program with commercials, you exchange your attention and potential purchasing power for entertainment and information. This initial marketing exchange makes possible several other exchanges that happen to involve money. For example, suppose you see an ad for Diet Pepsi. Besides exchanging your attention for

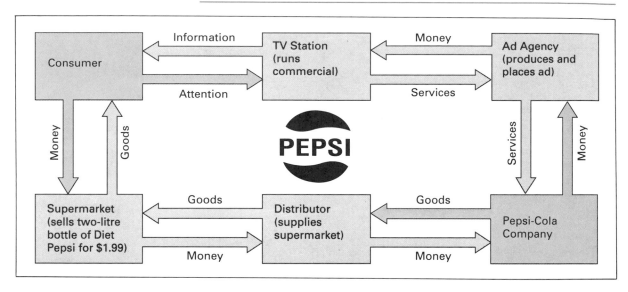

Figure 1.1 From Pepsi to the Consumer — A Marketing Exchange

information about the soft drink, you may decide to give a supermarket $1.99 or so for a two-litre bottle of the product. The supermarket, in turn, exchanges a certain percentage of that price with a distributor, who exchanges a portion of that with the Pepsi-Cola Company. Pepsi-Cola, in turn, exchanges a portion of its share of the purchase price with an ad agency for producing and placing a television commercial, and the ad agency exchanges a certain amount of that sum with the TV station for running the ad.[5] All of the transfers are marketing exchanges, from your initial viewing to your final purchase, because something of value (whether money, goods, information, or attention) is offered for something else in order to satisfy a need.

Marketing's Primary Activities

Estimates indicate that 40 to 60 cents of every dollar the consumer spends help to pay for marketing costs.[6] Figure 1.2 shows the breakdown of cost for an 11-ounce box of Ritz crackers, purchased for perhaps $2.00. Of this, $1.12, or 56 percent of the price, goes for marketing activities—advertising, packaging, shipping and warehousing, and paying both the Nabisco sales force and the grocer. Meanwhile, the cost of actually manufacturing the crackers accounts for only $.88, or 44 percent of the price.

In an age of heightened consumer awareness and scarce resources, critics have charged that such marketing costs are excessive. They maintain that manufacturing, not marketing, has produced the goods and services North Americans enjoy. They also claim that the North American genius for technology, not marketing, has brought us the wide variety of products that characterize our economy.

But the manufacturing process is only one of the many activities that

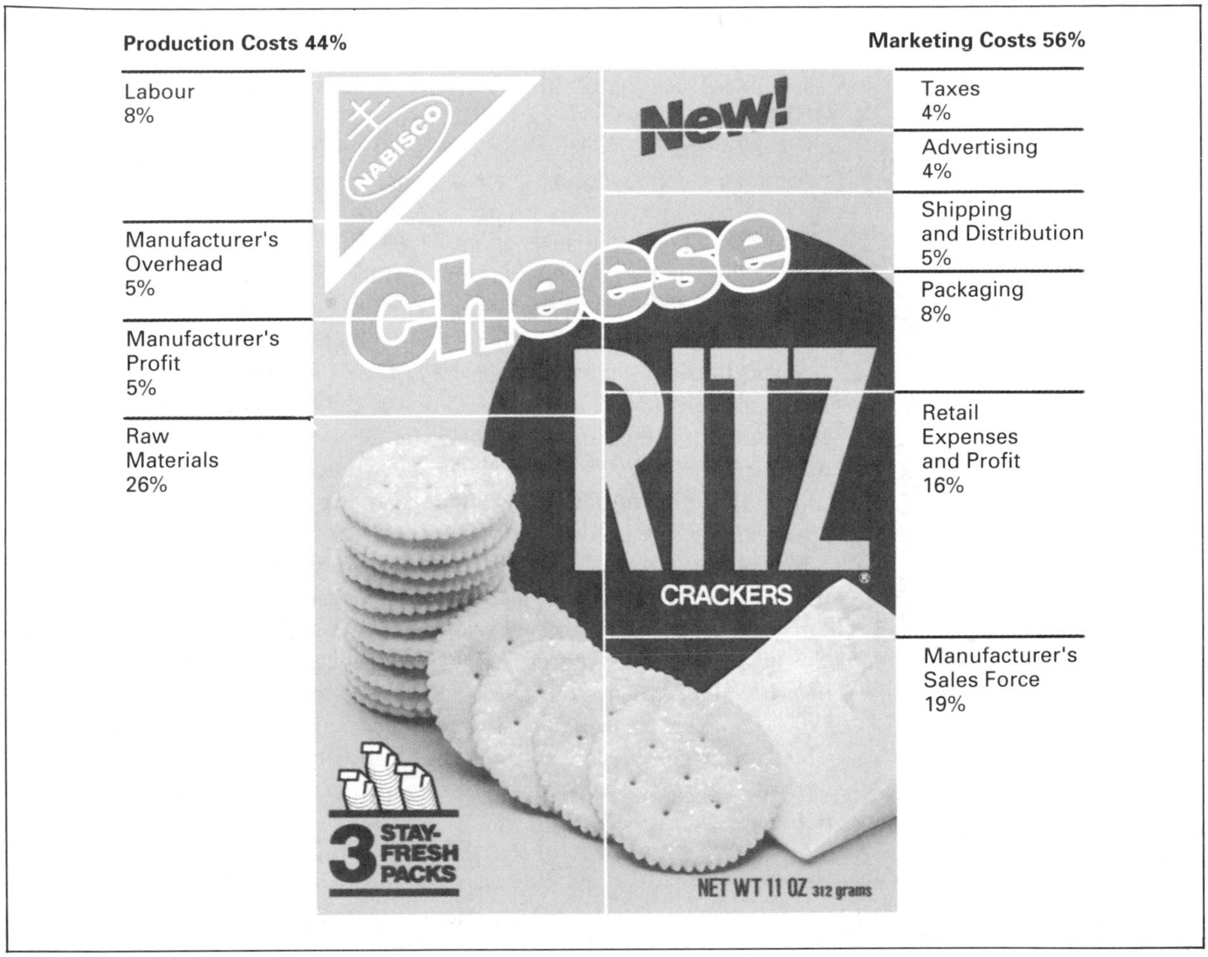

Production Costs 44%
Labour 8%
Manufacturer's Overhead 5%
Manufacturer's Profit 5%
Raw Materials 26%
Marketing Costs 56%
Taxes 4%
Advertising 4%
Shipping and Distribution 5%
Packaging 8%
Retail Expenses and Profit 16%
Manufacturer's Sales Force 19%
NABISCO
New!
Cheese
RITZ
CRACKERS
3 STAY-FRESH PACKS
NET WT 11 OZ 312 grams

Figure 1.2 Costs of Producing and Marketing Ritz Crackers

Source: Information from William J. Taylor and Roy T. Shaw, Jr., *Marketing: An Integrated Analytical Approach*, 3rd ed. (Cincinnati, Ohio: South-Western Publishing Company, 1975), p. 5.

bring a box of crackers to your pantry. The product must be developed to meet actual wants and needs, and it must be delivered to where the consumer can buy it. The consumer must know that the product is available. In sum, without the services the marketing sector provides, the product would simply pile up at the factory, languishing for lack of customers.

Values Provided by Marketing

Economists distinguish four kinds of utilities, or values, that can be added to a product. **Form utility** is given to a product by converting raw materials into a finished good. A shoe factory that transforms leather and rubber into a wearable item creates form utility. Creating form

Form Utility
Value added to a product by converting raw materials into a finished good.

Time Utility
Value added to a product by
making it available when
buyers need it.

Place Utility
Value added to a product by
making it available where
buyers want it.

Ownership Utility
Value added to a product by
giving consumers a way to
obtain ownership of it.

utility is the role of the manufacturing sector.

Marketing adds other kinds of utility. It creates **time utility** by making goods or services available when consumers want them. It creates **place utility** by making goods and services available where they are accessible to consumers. Marketing also creates **ownership utility** by giving the consumer a way to obtain the rights of owning and using a product, say, by mailing in payment with an order form or by using a charge account at a store. These utilities are necessary for a product to have value.

Consider the Ritz crackers again. Nabisco, the manufacturer, performs a service by converting flour, eggs, and other ingredients into an edible product, thereby creating form utility. When the firm packages and transports the crackers to a grocery store, it provides place utility. The retail grocer, also a marketer, helps satisfy the need for crackers by storing the product until the customer's regular shopping day, thus creating time utility. The grocer creates ownership utility by providing a place (the checkout counter) where money or a cheque is given in exchange for the product.

Marketing may increase demand for products to the point at which mass production (and savings in costs) may become possible. Before 1958, for example, toys were not widely advertised and were sold mainly through department stores. After that time, they were heavily promoted on television, and discount stores began to sell them as well. This additional marketing activity led to an increase in demand, a drop in manufacturing costs, and a consequent lowering of prices. Customers benefited directly by lower prices resulting from increased marketing activity.[7]

Functions of the Marketing Sector

Various experts disagree on the precise number of activities in which marketers engage, but they usually include some of the following:

1. Searching out buyers and sellers.

2. Matching goods, services, and other offerings to the needs of customers.

3. Finding an acceptable price in the marketplace.

4. Informing buyers and sellers of product availability and convincing them to purchase.

5. Transporting and storing goods.

6. Settling details for the final exchange (arranging credit, delivery, and so forth).

7. Assuming risks (absorbing losses for unwanted products or paying the cost of keeping products until wanted).[8]

Marketing people help create and bring about exchanges by performing certain functions. Some organizations may stress one function or another. Manufacturers take responsibility for transporting goods to convenient locations. Advertisers alert the public to the product's availability. Retailers are responsible for the details of the final exchange. Some functions — such as providing information, setting a price, and assuming risk — may be shared by many marketers. The point to keep in mind is that someone must perform these functions in order for an exchange to occur.

The History of Marketing

Marketing is probably as old as civilization itself. It's not hard to imagine a Stone Age person convincing a neighbour to trade food for a spare tool. By getting together and trading their respective surplus, both would benefit.

As occupations became more specialized, exchange became more regular. Towns grew, with central marketplaces where people could meet and exchange what they produced. Soon money became an acceptable substitute for goods. Trade among localities, kingdoms, and empires waxed and waned with wars, changes in transportation and navigation, and a thousand other factors, but for the most part it grew.

The Middle Ages brought increased trade among the kingdoms of the West and the development of brands and trademarks. A craftsman belonging to a guild (a trade organization for merchants and artisans) would put the association's distinctive mark on his product. Consumers would know from the mark that they were buying from a reputable craftsman. Thus the concept of buying "name brands" dates back to long before the promotion of designer jeans.

In the eighteenth century in the lands that became Canada, the principal industries were fishing and fur trading and trapping. Canada's first marketers were probably coureurs de bois like Pierre Radisson and Médard Chouart des Groseilliers who traded for furs on their own behalf, not on behalf of the French court. By the 1750s, the French had trading posts as far west as the Saskatchewan River.

In the late 1700s, the Industrial Revolution brought the beginning of modern marketing. Factories began turning out items in quantity, prices dropped, and it became more desirable to buy than to make many products. In the 1800s in Upper and Lower Canada, new settlers from the United States and Britain demanded manufactured products from Europe. This market demand led the government to support the expansion of the St. Lawrence water system through the building of canals. The development of railways made it easier to move goods to consumers, and the growth of larger cities made it easier to sell the products.

As modern marketing has developed, the philosophy of doing business has changed. Businesses were first based on a production concept, then on a sales concept; today they are based on a marketing concept. The following paragraphs explain the development of these philosophies.[9]

The Production Concept

In the 1800s and early 1900s, the industrialized world, especially North America, had a seemingly boundless supply of natural resources and of customers. The result was the first Industrial Age business philosophy —the production concept.

The **production orientation** emphasized the importance of producing goods. Three assumptions basic to this concept are:

1. Anything that can be produced can be sold.

2. The most important task of management is to keep the cost of production down.

3. A company should produce only certain basic products.

This way of thinking arose naturally from the state of North American business. Manufacturing, using specialized labour and complex machinery, was new. Industrialists had to focus on working out the bugs in the production process. Efficiency experts, not marketers, were the policysetters.

Probably the best representative of the production orientation was Henry Ford. By concentrating on production and simplifying it through assembly-line procedures, Ford was able to offer consumers a car for less than $300. Of course, he turned out only one type of car, the Model T, and he offered it to the public "in any color they wanted it, as long as it was black."

Businesses took a similar approach to other products. Consumers could purchase only a limited range of products, such as basic black telephones and white kitchen iceboxes. Until about 1920, businesspeople could ignore the problem of selling their goods because demand greatly exceeded supply. Figure 1.3 shows selected advertisements for products during this period.

The Sales Concept

After World War I, the business environment changed. Competition grew, and there were more goods to sell than demand warranted. Companies began thinking about how to stimulate sales of their products; thus they developed a **sales orientation.**

Sales-oriented businesses emphasize that:

1. Finding buyers for products is the chief concern.

Production Orientation
Business philosophy emphasizing that (1) anything that can be produced can be sold; (2) the most important managerial task is to keep the cost of production down; and (3) a company should produce only certain basic products.

Sales Orientation
Business philosophy emphasizing that (1) finding buyers for products is management's chief concern; and (2) convincing buyers to purchase a firm's output is management's chief task.

Figure 1.3 Selected Ads for Products, 1865–1920

2. Management's chief task is to convince buyers — through varying degrees of persuasion — to purchase a firm's output.

The sales orientation prevailed from 1920 to about 1950. Particularly during the Great Depression of the 1930s, businesses found it necessary to "push" products coming off the assembly line. Sales departments were started to oversee sales personnel. Advertising also grew in importance.

The Pillsbury Company, for example, became sales oriented in the 1930s. The firm spent millions of dollars advertising its limited line of baked goods. Pillsbury also trained a sales force to find out what grocers needed in order to sell the company's products successfully.[10] Characteristic of the sales orientation was the advertising campaign for Listerine used in the 1920s, described in Marketing Today 1.2.

Marketing Today 1.2

New Uses for an Established Product: Listerine

According to the sales concept, consumers must be persuaded to buy a product. When consumers haven't been interested in one use for a product, some advertisers have invented new uses.

A case in point is the advertisements for Listerine during the 1920s. For years, Listerine had been marketed as a general antiseptic. To sell more of it, advertising copywriters Milton Feasley and Gordon Seagrove, along with company president Gerard B. Lambert, set about to induce the public to discover a new need for Listerine.

They succeeded with an ad featuring a picture of a beautiful girl and a story titled "He Never Knew Why." The story was of a rising young businessman spurned by the beautiful girl after a single encounter. The young man had many advantages but a major handicap: "halitosis."

The copywriters had found the term *halitosis* in an old medical dictionary and chose it because of its scientific sound, which dignified the subject. The ad developed into a series patterned after personal interest stories and advice columns in the tabloids of the day. Soon, using mouthwash became an accepted part of one's daily routine.

But Gerard Lambert was not content to stop with this new need. He began to proclaim Listerine's virtues as a cure for dandruff. This claim was followed by ads promoting the use of Listerine as an aftershave, a cure for colds and sore throats, an astringent, and a deodorant.

Source: Adapted from Roland Marchand, "The Golden Age of Advertising: Two Legendary Campaigns," *American Heritage* 36 (April/May 1985), 74–77.

The Marketing Concept

The stage was set for a new way of doing business when, at the end of World War II, the economy shifted from a **seller's market** to a **buyer's market.** A seller's market is one in which there is a shortage of goods and services. A buyer's market is one in which there is an abundance of goods and services.[11] Companies occasionally adjust production to create a seller's market for their goods so they can keep prices high and make their product seem especially desirable, but a buyer's market is more common in the North American economy. Usually there is a greater supply of laundry detergents, hamburgers, pocket calculators, and four-door sedans than existing demand alone would warrant.

In the buyer's market of the 1950s, Pillsbury and many other companies realized that the sales-oriented approach was no longer effective. Customers had become both more affluent (better able to afford a wider range of products) and more sophisticated in taste (less willing to accept whatever was for sale). Competition for buyers' attention in the marketplace was keener. Once again, business needed a new philosophy to reflect important changes, and a new approach to business was formulated—the **marketing concept.** (See Figure Fig. 1.4.)

The marketing concept proposes three basic ideas:

1. Companies should produce only what customers want.

2. Management must integrate all company activities to develop programs to satisfy those wants.

3. Long-range profit goals rather than "quick" sales should guide management decisions.

Managers who adopt the marketing concept no longer support the idea that customers must be "sold" whatever the company produces. Instead, they seek to uncover desires through research and to design products as a result of that research. Marketing departments take on the overall responsibility for this work. Other departments work with marketing to satisfy customers and keep them loyal.

Pillsbury management expressed this concept when it stated, "We are in the business of satisfying needs and wants of consumers."[12] This is a far cry from using advertising to persuade consumers to find a need for a product, as Listerine did in the 1920s.

Key Elements of the Marketing Concept

Successful implementation of the marketing concept requires that a company pay close attention to three basic principles: (1) discover what customers want (a customer orientation); (2) mobilize the entire organization to meet those wants; and (3) pursue long-term profit.

Seller's Market
Market in which there is a shortage of goods and services.

Buyer's Market
Market in which there is an abundance of goods and services.

Marketing Concept
Business philosophy emphasizing that (1) companies should produce only what customers want; (2) management must integrate all company activities to develop programs to satisfy those wants; and (3) long-range profit goals should guide management decisions.

Era	Philosophy
Production Orientation (1869–1930)	"We are professional flour millers. Our basic function is to mill high-quality flour, and of course (and almost incidentally) we must hire salesmen to sell it." The company's first new product was middlings, the bran left over after milling. It was launched as a way to get rid of a by-product not because of marketing considerations.
Sales Orientation (1930s–1950s)	"We are a flour-milling company, manufacturing a number of products for the consumer market. We must have a first-rate sales organization which can dispose of all the products we can make at a favourable price." Pillsbury backed its sales force with advertising and marketing intelligence.
Marketing Orientation (1950s–1960s)	"We make and sell products for consumers." Pillsbury reorganizes the company so that marketing is at the centre of the corporation. The marketing department marshals the forces of the firm to study consumer wants and needs, conceives and develops new products to fill them, and translates those products into sales.
Marketing Control (1960s–present)	"We are moving from a company which has the marketing concept to a marketing company." Marketing sets the company's short-term policies and influences long-term planning. Marketing guides technical research, production, inventory control, advertising, and sales.

Figure 1.4 Changing Business Philosophies at Pillsbury

Source: Courtesy of The Pillsbury Company.

Customer Orientation

Companies that adopt the marketing concept organize their businesses around consumers' wants and needs. This may sound like an obvious idea. After all, what company would intentionally disregard what consumers want? North American automobile manufacturers did just that in the late 1970s when they failed to take changing consumer preferences for smaller, energy-efficient, high-quality cars into account in their planning. After years of losing millions of dollars in sales to the Japanese, Detroit and Windsor finally began to design cars more in keeping with what the marketplace was demanding.

While a marketing orientation benefits a company, it also makes marketing exchanges more complex. Customers must be sought out not only for their purchasing power, but also for their opinions about products. Often companies develop marketing research departments or hire firms that specialize in marketing research to keep them up to date about changing consumer preferences and activities of their competitors. Marketing research is a method of collecting information about a particular marketing problem or opportunity. (Chapter 5 discusses how marketing research works.)

Market researchers do more than simply analyze how consumers feel about particular products. They must also determine if consumers have needs that no product on the market currently satisfies. Often consumers themselves do not know exactly what they want. Few men, for example, actually demanded a twin-blade razor from Gillette. What they wanted, according to research, was a better shave. Gillette's marketers and engineers worked together to devise an improved product to meet that need. As one board member at Procter & Gamble noted, "We expect (our research people) to search for needs and desires that the consumer perhaps has not yet perceived, but that the consumer will regard as important, once recognized."[13]

Integrated Organizational Approach

When a company adopts the marketing concept, it often finds it must reorganize staff to reflect changes in the way it conducts business. For the marketing concept to work, many other aspects of a company must be co-ordinated with the plans and goals of the marketing department. Often the executive in charge of marketing oversees activities in departments as diverse as research and development, production, sales, distribution, and even personnel.

Commitment to the marketing concept requires top management to reorganize completely how the company works. As one marketing director put it:

> The true marketing concept guides a firm's progress by monitoring the needs and wants of the marketplace, enabling management to identify market segments . . . that will most profitably utilize available resources.[14]

Managers ideally take a flexible approach that emphasizes co-operation within the organization to meet the common goal of satisfying consumers.

An integrated effort requires more than just the co-ordination of a firm's departmental activities. The marketing department must also develop *a unified plan*, known as the **marketing mix**, which specifies what will be offered to customers and how. The marketing mix specifies the policies a firm intends to adopt with respect to the **four "Ps"** (Figure 1.5):

1. **Product:** the offering (a good, service, or idea) that embodies benefits consumers seek. Determining a product's packaging and name are among the decisions product designers must make. Apple computers, for example, combined a nonthreatening name with user-friendly technology.

Marketing Mix
Plan that specifies what will be offered to customers (the product) and how (its price, promotion, and placement).

Four "Ps"
Elements of the marketing mix, which are product, price, promotion, and placement.

Product
Anything that can be offered to a market for attention, acquisition, use, or consumption that might satisfy a want or need.

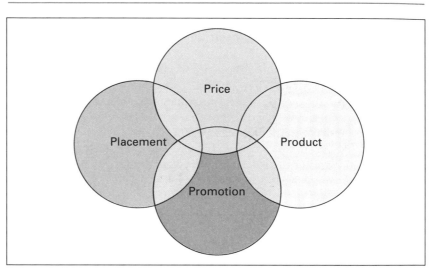

Figure 1.5 Elements of the Marketing Mix

Price
Value placed on a product.

Promotion
Marketing communication that attempts to inform and remind individuals and persuade them to accept, resell, recommend, or use a product, service, idea, or institution.

Placement
Means of delivering a product; also called distribution.

2. **Price:** the value placed upon the product by the firm. A product's price is often affected by competitors' prices for similar products. Price often is also influenced by psychological issues. Apple's early success was at least partially a result of its products' prices, which were low enough to be affordable to a nonbusiness market.

3. **Promotion:** the firm's communications with customers to inform, persuade, and remind them of the product's benefits. For example, when Apple introduced the Macintosh computer, its advertising and sales promotional efforts went into high gear. The computer was launched with a $50-million media blitz that included lavish 20-page, four-colour inserts in national magazines, a three-page ad in *The Wall Street Journal,* and TV spots during the Super Bowl and the Winter Olympics.

4. **Placement:** also called distribution — the means of delivering the product. This aspect ensures that a product is in the right place at the right time. Taking a path unlike that of IBM, which is building Product Centres to sell its computers, Apple's executives met with dealers to stress that Apple is committed to selling through them. The company also built a $20-million, highly automated factory to make sure that demand would not outpace supply.

These areas of decision making are known as the four "Ps." Each area is relatively complex. For example, advertising, personal selling efforts, publicity, and sales promotion are all part of the area of promotion. To master the whole field of promotion, or even a part of it, such as advertising, may take a lifetime. Nevertheless, marketing generalists are expected to know their way around not just promotion but the other three areas as well. Failure to plan any one of the four "Ps" can lead to

a costly error. The various aspects of the marketing mix are explored
further in Chapter 2 and at length in Chapters 8 through 16.

Long-Term Profit Goal

Besides requiring customer orientation and an integrated effort, the
marketing concept also stresses the importance of long-term **profit.** No
business can survive without making a profit. Businesspeople have
always recognized this, but they have sometimes misinterpreted what
it means. In a sales-oriented firm, the goal is often to make a quick profit,
an objective that can cripple the firm eventually. A pushy car salesperson
may pressure a customer into buying, but the customer, remembering
the experience, may never return.

The marketing concept says that businesses should think in terms of
the long run. They may have to sacrifice profits in the present for a
better return in the future. New products often lose money when they
are first introduced until they attract enough buyers. Lacking a long-
run outlook, many managers would never have marketed such products
as pocket calculators and instant cameras, which were not overnight
successes.

A long-term perspective also fits better with the idea of customer satisfaction. No company can afford to jeopardize the loyalty of its customers. According to one study, brands that have lost brand loyalty are the
ones that lose some of their share of the total market.[15]

Although brand loyalty has apparently remained steady during the
last 15 years, consumers' loyalty toward specific products rises and falls.
Shampoo, for example, is known for the brand *dis*loyalty of its buyers.
Research firms have discovered that a substantial percentage of adults
have a new favourite shampoo every year. Intense competition makes it
hard to achieve customer loyalty for a particular brand of shampoo, as
hundreds of brands are available. The challenge of competition extends
to many products; companies that compete for the consumer's dollar in
supermarkets must share shelf space with about 12 000 products.

Because the most brand-loyal consumers are thought to be those who
have purchased the product at least once, marketers try to keep their
current customers. This may mean spending some money and forgoing
some profits. Many companies find it worthwhile to spend dollars to
achieve loyalty if in the long term they may recoup their initial investment many times over. A customer orientation and a future orientation
are in many ways two sides of the same coin.

Issues Raised by the Marketing Concept

The marketing orientation is widespread in North American business.
A survey of chief executive officers in 30 major corporations disclosed

Profit
What remains for a business
after expenses are deducted
from revenues or income.

that those executives believe marketing is the most important management function in their business and will become more important in the future.[16] Despite its pervasiveness, however, the marketing concept has its detractors. Criticism has centred on three basic areas: consumerism, profit orientation, and long-term competitiveness.

Consumerism

Consumerism
Movement to increase the influence, power, and rights of consumers in their dealings with institutions of all types.

Consumerism has been defined as a movement to increase the influence, power, and rights of consumers in their dealings with institutions of all types.[17] Advocates of consumerism are sceptical about the sincerity of marketing's claim to be consumer oriented. They suggest that being consumer oriented means more than providing a product consumers ask for; it also includes accepting responsibility for the impact of that product on users and the general public.

Marketing analysts recognize the problem. Peter Drucker, who pioneered the marketing concept, has referred to consumerism as "the shame of marketing."[18] He believes that the consumer movement developed because many firms gave only lip service to the marketing concept, while remaining basically sales oriented.

The marketing concept, as we have seen, seeks to identify consumer wants and to satisfy them. You may prefer the lower price of leaded gasoline. But in meeting the demand for low-cost transportation, critics say, automobile and oil companies must also weigh the consequences to the public of breathing in lead from exhaust fumes.

In another vein, C. J. Rapp determined that some consumers prefer a soft drink that contains caffeine and sugar. But some people criticize him for making available Jolt Cola, a product containing the maximum caffeine allowed when this ingredient is considered harmful. Others contend that Rapp's approach is at least frank. Some of these people question whether it is really more in the public interest to make a pop containing 10 percent apple juice or added vitamin C and represent it as being nutritious.[19] Soft-drink manufacturers need to weigh both views in developing their products.

Unless marketers respond to consumer criticism, they may be subject to government regulation. Many businesspeople fear government regulation as a threat to the free enterprise system. But failure to examine ways to cope with the conflicting demands imposed by the marketing concept may force more government action.

Advocates of consumerism demand that companies respond to consumer needs in the broadest sense. This argument says that companies must bear in mind their social responsibility to make products that are safe and that do not harm the environment. Growing consumer interest in conservation, pollution controls, reduction of pesticides and contaminants in the food chain, and increasing demand for better labelling for consumer goods are key issues of the 1990s. How to achieve the company's goals while meeting the demands of consumers and fulfilling social responsibilities will continue to be one of marketing's greatest challenges.

Profit Orientation

Some observers contend that a contradiction is inherent in the marketing concept. It is the conflict between providing customer satisfaction and the basic goal of any business: to make a profit. For-profit or otherwise, organizations do not exist to satisfy the goals of others. In the words of one analyst:

> The initiators of a commercial venture do so to satisfy their own needs. The initiators of a public program, such as an infant immunization program or a myriad of other public policy efforts, do so for the benefit of the citizens of that political body. It is the goals of the membership which define the organization's purpose.[20]

Can an organization have a marketing orientation if it sees a consumer demand and then does not try to meet it? It can, because the marketing orientation includes evaluating the position of the organization as well as that of consumers. The organization must decide whether meeting certain needs is in line with the organization's goals — profitability in the case of a commercial organization. In some situations, an organization with a marketing orientation may choose not to design a product to meet a certain demand.[21]

A church, for example, may be sensitive to its members and their needs, but it generally would not base its teachings on what members want to hear. Or a manufacturer of disposable pens may decide that, even though people's hands are of different sizes, it is uneconomical to make pens in many different sizes to accommodate them.

Of course, businesses cannot ignore what customers want. Eventually, consumers will patronize the organizations that are sensitive to their demands. If businesses want profits for the long term, they must maintain customer goodwill.

Long-Term Competitiveness

Another concern with the marketing concept has centred around its implications for North American business in an increasingly competitive world market. Critics have accused the marketing concept of diverting attention from the product to advertising, selling, and promotion.[22]

An example of this diversion of attention is the automobile market of the late 1970s and early 1980s. While North American automakers were emphasizing selling, Japanese automakers were developing models that consumers demanded. By 1980, imported cars had captured 30 percent of the market.

The problem, according to analysts, is that by allowing marketing departments to direct research and development, companies tend to develop only low-risk modifications of existing products. However, real technological breakthroughs usually result from the ideas of scientists and engineers. Consumers, in contrast, may not have much insight into what they will demand years from now or what the significance is of some technological innovation. For example, few consumers of 20 years ago would have expressed a need for microchips, but most consumers now buy them as integral parts of numerous products, including watches, radios, and microwave ovens. Market research has even transformed the traditional campus bookstore into a supermarket of goods ranging from frozen food to videotapes. (See At Your Service 1.1.)

In fact, part of the marketing concept involves anticipating future wants and needs and drawing upon the insights of scientists and engineers. Marketing is not limited to meeting needs that are current and expressed. In the words of one observer, the marketing manager is an "orchestra leader" who brings into harmony all strategic thinking and planning across departmental lines.[23] When the marketing concept is used appropriately, it addresses both long-term and short-term concerns.

It is interesting to note that marketing goals of Japanese and North American executives apparently continue to differ. In a recent study, executives of major North American and Japanese companies reported the most important elements in their long-range strategic marketing operations.[24] The top sales concern for the Japanese executives was establishment of innovative sales channels. For the North American executives, the top priority was training of first-line salespeople. Note that neither group cited product development as being of primary importance. Only time will tell whether these objectives will lead to long-term competitiveness for Japan or North America.

Marketing and Society

One of the most difficult problems marketers will face in the coming years is striking a balance between the needs and wants of individuals and those of society at large. For example, people are strongly encouraged these days to return empty bottles and cans from beer and soft drinks. The purpose is to help prevent litter and to recycle valuable resources such as aluminum. Most people would agree that these are commendable goals. But as an individual, you may find returning bottles to the supermarket an annoying obligation. How can marketing reconcile such diverse positions?

Once more, marketing has proved the old adage, Necessity is the mother of invention. Several beverage manufacturers are now packaging their drinks in small cardboard containers that can be thrown away when the consumer is finished with them.

In a similar fashion, appliance manufacturers have responded to high energy costs by developing refrigerators and air conditioners that are energy efficient, and cereal manufacturers have begun to address concerns about excess sugar by promoting products with a diminished sugar content. Often these products prove to be profitable because they successfully integrate society's and individuals' needs.

This approach is the essence of a new marketing concept called **societal marketing,** which balances concerns for profits, satisfying individual wants, and meeting overall societal needs.[25] In some cases, these diverse goals have been happily reconciled, but in many industries resolving these issues is far more complex.

Societal Marketing
Concept that balances concern for profits with concern for satisfying individual wants and societal needs.

Social responsibility within a company involves three areas of concern: (1) philanthropic giving; (2) total compliance with international, federal, provincial, and municipal laws; and (3) moral and ethical standards under which the company will operate, stated in terms of what the company will and will not tolerate.[26] Specific issues companies address are as diverse as pollution control, pricing, and product safety.

A variety of factors—including a marketplace fragmented into many special interest groups, increased international competition, and rapid technological change—have combined to make marketing the top corporate priority. The future has never been brighter for people with marketing experience who understand how to develop a product strategy that can succeed in a highly competitive environment. A career in marketing offers not only many exciting personal challenges and opportunities but often the chance to have a significant impact on a company's future.

Chapter Replay

1. **What is marketing, and what are some examples of activities included in marketing?**
   Marketing consists of the activities that satisfy needs and wants through the process of exchange. It includes finding buyers and developing, pricing, promoting, and distributing products.

2. **What are products, goods, and services?**
   A product is anything offered to meet a want or need. Goods are tangible items received in an exchange; services are intangible items.

3. **How does marketing add value to a product?**
   Marketing adds value by creating time utility, place utility, and ownership utility.

4. **What three orientations to doing business have organizations used?**
   In the 1800s, businesses developed a production orientation. After World War I, the emphasis shifted to a sales orientation. During the 1950s, many businesses led the move to a marketing orientation.

5. **What is a seller's market? A buyer's market?**
   A seller's market is one in which there is a shortage of goods and services. In a buyer's market, there is an abundance of goods and services.

6. **What are the key ideas underlying the marketing concept?**
   The three basic ideas are that (1) companies should produce only what customers want; (2) management must integrate all company activities to develop programs to satisfy those wants; and (3) long-

range profit goals rather than quick sales should guide management decisions.

7. **What are the four elements of the marketing mix?**
The marketing mix consists of the four "Ps": product, price, promotion, and placement.

8. **What issues have critics raised about the marketing concept?**
Critics have contended that marketing is insensitive to the real needs of consumers, that the goal of providing customer satisfaction conflicts with the profit motive, and that the marketing concept causes long-term competitiveness to suffer.

9. **How does marketing reconcile today's concern for social responsibility with company profit motivations and individual wants?**
Societal marketing balances the objectives of increasing company profitability and satisfying individual wants with a concern for societal needs. Companies practise societal marketing when they give to philanthropic organizations, comply with all laws, and set moral and ethical standards.

Key Terms

buyer's market	placement
consumerism	price
exchange	product
form utility	production orientation
four "Ps"	profit
goods	promotion
marketing	sales orientation
marketing concept	seller's market
marketing mix	service
ownership utility	societal marketing
place utility	time utility

Discussion Questions

1. What is marketing? Are the people who prepare a mail-order catalogue engaged in marketing? The people who decide the prices of the products in the catalogue? The people who research what consumers would like to find in the catalogue?

2. Give an example of a good and of a service. Could either of these be considered products? Explain.

3. Mary and Martha went shopping for a coat for Mary. As they looked at the prices, however, Mary got increasingly irritated. "You know,

Martha," she complained, "I read that the actual cost of making a coat is only about one-third of what I'm paying for it. It's not right for the store to charge so much." Based on what you have read about the values provided by marketing, explain why a coat is worth more than the cost to manufacture it.

4. What functions are performed by the marketing sector? Do all organizations perform all the functions?

5. What assumptions are basic to the production concept? Does this concept work better when demand exceeds supply or when supply exceeds demand?

6. At Green Nursery, the main concern is finding customers for the company's products (chiefly decorative shrubs). Green Nursery's owner, Mr. Green, recently said to the sales personnel, "Our main task is to convince the people of our community that they need more decorative shrubs around their homes." Does Green Nursery have a production orientation, a sales orientation, or a marketing orientation?

7. What are the three basic ideas underlying the marketing concept? Did this concept emerge in a buyer's market or a seller's market?

8. Ellen Nelles just bought a concert hall. What product will she be selling? In developing a unified plan to sell her product, what elements of the marketing mix must she consider?

9. What is consumerism? Why should marketers be concerned about it?

10. Is a marketing orientation compatible with innovation? With social responsibility? Explain.

CASE 1.1

The Coca-Cola Company

The Coca-Cola Company is a symbol of refreshment, enjoyment, and relaxation around the world. Coca-Cola, which celebrated its hundredth birthday in 1986, is the world's best-selling soft drink, being consumed more than 355 million times per day. The entertainment business sector is a major producer and distributor of films and television programs such as *Ghostbusters* and *Who's the Boss?* The company's foods business sector has developed many new products around the popular Minute Maid trademark and also has introduced new categories in this growing segment.

Source: Adapted from The Coca-Cola Company's annual reports and information provided by the company.

Soft-Drink Marketing

Soft-drink products accounted for 76 percent of the company's net operating income in 1985. The company's soft-drink products include Coke, Coca-Cola Classic, Diet Coke, Fanta, Sprite, Minute Maid Orange and Lemon-Lime sodas, Tab, Fresca, Mr. Pibb, Mello Yello, and Ramblin' Root Beer. The company now has more than a 40 percent share of the U.S. soft-drink market and more than 30 percent in Canada.

The Coca-Cola Company manufactures soft-drink syrups and concentrates that it markets to bottling and canning operations and to approved fountain wholesalers. The bottling operations combine the syrup with carbonated water or combine the concentrate with sweetener and carbonated water, and package the final soft-drink product for sale to retailers. Packaged soft drinks are distributed to consumers in cans, returnable and nonreturnable glass bottles, and plastic packaging. Fountain wholesalers sell soft-drink syrups to fountain retailers, who in turn sell soft drinks to consumers.

During 1985, the company sold 67 percent of its soft-drink syrups and concentrate in the United States to approximately 475 bottlers. The remaining 33 percent was sold to nearly 3500 authorized fountain wholesalers. Outside the United States, soft-drink concentrate is sold to approximately 950 independently owned bottling and canning plants.

The following represent recent major highlights of The Coca-Cola Company:

- In 1985, the company developed a new taste for Coca-Cola, which continues to earn superior preference ratings. As a national launch of the new formula got underway in April of that year, many consumers came forward with unexpected loyalty to the original taste of Coca-Cola. Responding promptly, the company introduced Coca-Cola Classic in July—a new name for the original formula.

- In the major growth area of diet colas, Diet Coke achieved a volume growth of 33 percent in 1985. Including caffeine-free Diet Coke and Tab products, the company's diet colas command more than 50 percent of overall diet cola sales. In Canada, diet soft drinks represent 27 percent of all soft drinks consumed.

- Cherry Coke was introduced nationally in 1985 and quickly established itself as a top-10 soft drink in the United States. Cherry Coke enjoyed the highest consumer trial level of any new product ever in the history of the company. A diet version of the popular drink is currently in test market.

- In 1986 the company acquired Merv Griffin Enterprises, a producer of programming for network television and first-run syndication. Among the company's current programs are *Wheel of Fortune* and *Jeopardy!*—the top two syndicated shows. The entertainment business sector also includes Columbia Pictures, Tri-Star Pictures, and Coca-Cola Television.

■ The company formed Coca-Cola Enterprises in 1986 as part of an ongoing program to strengthen its bottling network. Coca-Cola Enterprises is the largest bottler of Coca-Cola in the world, distributing approximately 38 percent of the total bottle/can volume for the company in the United States. The Coca-Cola Company holds a 49 percent interest in this publicly held bottling entity. In Canada, Coca-Cola owns 49 percent of TCC Beverages Ltd., a bottling company.

Strategy for the 1980s

The following quotes have been extracted from the "Strategy for the 1980s," presented to the board of directors of The Coca-Cola Company by its chairman, Roberto C. Goizueta, on March 4, 1981:

> In order to give my vision of our Company for 1990, I must first postulate what I visualize our mission to be during the 1980s. I see our *challenge* as continuing the growth in profits of our highly successful existing main businesses, and those we may choose to enter, at a rate substantially in excess of inflation, in order to give our shareholders an above average total return on their investment. The unique position of excellence that the trademark Coca-Cola has attained in the world will be protected and enhanced as a primary objective. I perceive us by the 1990s to continue to be or become the *leading force in the soft drink industry* in each of the countries in which it is economically feasible for us to be so. We shall continue to emphasize product quality worldwide, as well as market share improvement in growth markets. In choosing new areas of business, each market we enter must have sufficient inherent real growth potential to make entry desirable. It is not our desire to battle continually for share in a stagnant market in these new areas of business.
>
> When we arrive at the 1990s, my vision is to be able to say with confidence that all of us in our own way displayed:
>
> ■ The ability to see the *long-term consequences* of current actions;
>
> ■ The willingness to sacrifice, if necessary, short-term gains for *longer-term benefits*;
>
> ■ The sensitivity to *anticipate and adapt to change*—change in consumer life styles, change in consumer tastes and change in consumer needs;
>
> ■ The commitment to manage our enterprise in such a way that we will always *be considered a welcomed and important part of the business community* in each and every country in which we do business; and

■ The capacity to *control what is controllable* and the wisdom not to bother what is not.

Focal Topics

1. In light of the material in this chapter, how would you respond to the question, Who needs The Coca-Cola Company?

2. To what do you attribute the success of The Coca-Cola Company over its almost 100-year history?

3. In what ways do you think The Coca-Cola Company might become even more marketing oriented?

Levi Strauss & Co.

CASE 1.2

Levi Strauss arrived in California in 1850 with a large supply of canvas that he hoped to sell to miners for use as tents and wagon covers. He quickly found that the miners' real needs involved pants that would hold up in the mines. Levi Strauss promptly took his roll of canvas to the nearest tailor and "those pants of Levi's" were born. Those extra-tough work pants, first of canvas and then of heavy denim, complete with copper rivets, became the "folk costume" of the American West. Eventually, however, the miners of pioneer days and the cowboys began to fade from the scene and the company considered liquidation.

To reposition the company, management started to redefine its markets and decided to concentrate on young males between 15 and 24 years old, and expanded from distribution only in the West to national and eventually international markets. Later, management continued to improve the product, expanded the variety of its line, and targeted new market segments such as young females, boys, and adult buyers of sportswear.

Current Situation

Today, Levi Strauss is the world's largest brand-name apparel manufacturer. It designs, manufactures, and markets a diversified line of apparel for men, women, and children, including jeans, slacks, shirts, jackets, skirts, hats, and accessories. The company's products are marketed principally under the Levi's® trademark in Canada and the United States and in numerous other countries throughout North and South America, Europe, Asia, and Australia.

Levi Strauss USA is organized into four operating divisions outlined below. Each division is essentially an integrated operation with its own

Source: Adapted primarily from Levi Strauss & Co.'s 1982 10 K Report; and D. C. Cleary, *Great American Brands* (New York: Fairchild Publications, 1981), pp. 211–216.

staff, manufacturing plants, distribution centres, and sales force, although overlap exists among products marketed as well as retailers and consumers served by the division.

■ *Jeanswear Division.* This division is the largest in the company in terms of sales and profits and is the leading manufacturer of jeans in the United States. In addition to basic and fashion jeans and slacks for young men, this division markets a broad line of western wear, knit and woven shirts, and casual jackets.

■ *Menswear Division.* This division primarily markets men's jeans, casual and dress slacks, sports coats, and vests. Additional products include participant and spectator sportswear, outerwear, and accessories as well as such items under the Oxford® clothes label for both men and women.

■ *Womenswear Division.* This division markets lines of casual sportswear, including jeans, slacks, knit and woven tops, blazers, and skirts. Sizes range from junior and miss to special sizes such as large, petite, tall, and maternity.

■ *Youthwear Division.* This division is one of the world's largest brandname manufacturers of children's apparel. Its products include basic and fashion jeans, slacks, skirts, knit and woven tops, jackets, blouses, vests, and active wear.

A new subsidiary company, Battery Street Enterprises, has been created to market the diversified brands of Koret of North America, Oxford, and Resistol. Battery Street Enterprises will also house any new brands that Levi Strauss & Co. acquires.

Additional Information

The following points provide some additional information about Levi Strauss and its marketing activities:

■ For the first time, beginning in 1982, the company's jeans were distributed in Sears and J.C. Penney stores, a move that expanded Levi's major retail outlets by 2600 units, or approximately 7 percent.

■ The company advertises on radio and television and in national publications. It also participates in local co-operative advertising programs under which it shares with retailers the costs of advertising its products. Levi's contracted with the U.S. Olympic Committee and the Los Angeles Olympic Organizing Committee to be the official outfitter and a major apparel sponsor of the 1984 Olympic games.

■ For the first time in its history, Levi's has collaborated with a name designer, Perry Ellis. The new company, Perry Ellis America, will be headquartered in New York and will function as an independent business unit within Levi Strauss USA. The Perry Ellis American collection for Levi's includes sweaters, shirts, and jackets as well as jeans. The new line will be more affordable than what Ellis had traditionally offered, but more expensive than the regular Levi's line.

■ Another new line of clothing, Frank Shorter Sportswear, has been acquired and will report to the senior vice-president of marketing for Levi Strauss USA. The line includes shirts, shorts, running suits, GoreTex® wind suits, and other runner's apparel.

Focal Topics

1. In light of the material in this chapter, how would you respond to the question, Who needs Levi Strauss & Co.?

2. To what do you attribute the success of Levi Strauss & Co. over its more than 150-year history?

3. In what ways do you think Levi Strauss & Co. might become even more marketing oriented?

2

Chapter 2

In this chapter, you will learn:

- The marketing manager's basic tasks.

- What is involved in strategic marketing planning.

- The elements of a marketing strategy.

- Some special challenges of marketing management.

- How to define a mission and objectives.

- What goes into a marketing plan.

- How marketers decide what segments of the total market will be the focus of their efforts.

- The role of marketing mix in the marketing plan.

Gardening — A Growth Industry

On a sunny Saturday in May, the line of parked cars outside Humber Nurseries Ltd. stretches a kilometre down the highway. Inside, 3000 gardeners are elbowing and kneeing each other for the choicest specimens. Humber Nurseries, located in suburban Toronto, is one of the largest gardening centres in Canada with an inventory of 1500 different perennials for sale, 1200 kinds of annuals and vegetables, and 1500 varieties of bushes, trees, and vines. Business is booming!

Tom Thompson, chief horticulturist at Humber, has noticed a big change in his customers in the last few years. The older crowd, most of them retired people, have been joined by affluent couples in their 30s and 40s who may not be able to tell a hosta from a heliotrope but are willing to open their wallets for the right effect. ''The bigger and more expensive it is, the more they like it,'' says one long-time employee about the purchasing decision.

Across Canada, many of the Baby Boom generation have turned to cultivating their gardens. Gardening is Canada's most popular hobby — a $2.5 billion a year trade encompassing nurseries, garden centres, commercial greenhouses, garden designers, architectural designers, and horticultural consultants.

Even reading about gardening is hot. Specialty stores devoted to gardening books have sprung up in Vancouver and Toronto, and a new magazine, *Canadian Gardening*, sold 40 000 copies of its first issue in 1990.

The marketers at Humber Nurseries are among the

many who have responded and adapted to a changing environment. This chapter shows how marketing professionals use the tools of marketing — beginning with planning — to identify opportunities and match their product offerings with consumers' changing tastes. Marketers use strategy in market planning to identify the target market and plan the marketing mix. To state the point more broadly, this chapter describes the job of the marketing manager.

Source: Marjorie Harris, *Report on Business Magazine*, June 1990, p. 60-63.

What Do Marketing Managers Do?

A marketing manager, or chief marketing executive, is the person who co-ordinates the work of a marketing department. Depending on the size and organization of the company, the marketing manager may be responsible for marketing planning, new product planning, distributor and dealer relations, sales promotion, advertising, marketing research, and many other areas.

While the scope of marketing managers' jobs is defined by the companies for which they work, every marketing manager engages in certain basic tasks. The most important are (1) *planning*, (2) *implementing*, and (3) *evaluating*. (See Figure 2.1.)

The job of marketing manager has been compared with that of a symphony conductor.[1] Both seek to bring harmony out of a potentially discordant situation by balancing the activities of the members they direct.

Planning

The marketing manager is responsible for strategic marketing planning. **Strategic marketing planning** is the process of establishing an organization's overall goals, assessing opportunities, and developing marketing objectives.[2]

The marketing manager should establish marketing goals in accordance with the rest of the company's objectives. For example, when Steven Rothschild, marketing director for General Mills, wanted his firm to buy the company making Yoplait yogurt, he had to work with General Mills executives to make sure that the acquisition was in line with his company's goals.[3]

Establishing goals also requires evaluating the marketing environment. The marketing environment includes the company's own resources, such as equipment and personnel; the competitive environment; relevant laws and regulations; and broad social issues, such as consumer safety and the environment. For example, in deciding whether to market Yoplait yogurt, Rothschild considered the existence of only one major competitor, Dannon, and whether General Mills had the resources to acquire Yoplait.

The next step in strategic marketing planning is to assess opportunities. When Rothschild weighed the opportunities in entering the yogurt business, he considered the rapid growth in yogurt consumption (3400 percent from 1954 to 1976) and the large proportion of the population that had not yet tried yogurt. Perhaps those who had not tried yogurt could be convinced to do so.

The final step in strategic marketing planning is to develop marketing objectives. **Marketing objectives** specify what the marketing depart-

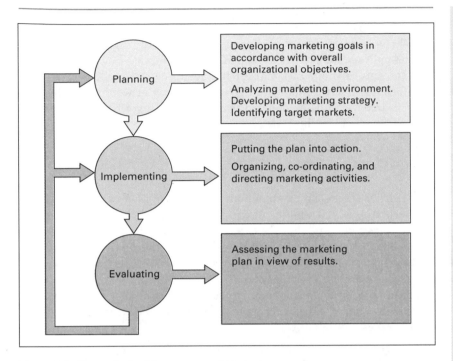

Figure 2.1 Stages in the Management of Marketing

ment intends to accomplish through marketing activities. These accomplishments should contribute to achieving the objectives of the organization as a whole. The manager should state the objectives clearly and set time limits for them. For example, Rothschild might have set the objective of being the best-selling yogurt in California by 1981 or of having 40 percent of the North American yogurt market by 1985.

Strategic marketing planning results in marketing strategies. A **marketing strategy** is a plan for achieving the marketing objectives. It describes the marketing mix that the company will use to reach a selected part of the market. For example, Rothschild decided to convince people who had not yet tried yogurt to try Yoplait. He targeted his efforts at "early adopters," people who like to try new products. To reach these people, he scheduled television ads for prime time and late-night shows rather than daytime shows. He also emphasized Yoplait's French origins, because French food has a positive reputation. Later in this chapter marketing strategies are discussed in greater depth.

Implementing

The second task of the marketing manager is implementing the marketing plan. To implement a plan is to put it into action. A plan for a new product may require many activities, from developing new manufacturing facilities to lobbying the government on issues that may affect the product.

Marketing Strategy
Concrete plan for achieving marketing objectives by using a specified marketing mix to reach a specified target market.

One would expect Apple Computer's marketing plans, for example, to rely heavily on the development of technologically sophisticated products. Apple's plans have not stopped with machinery, however. Its strategy to capture the youth market included, for example, lobbying the California legislature for a change in tax laws that would give the company a tax writeoff for donating computers to every elementary and secondary school in the state.

Evaluating

The third stage in the management of marketing is evaluating. This is the means by which a manager can ensure that the department is meeting its objectives, and that the department revises its plans if something goes wrong. One typical method of evaluation is the sales analysis, which measures actual sales against forecasts of sales. Other evaluation procedures are discussed in Chapter 16.

Broad responsibilities accompany the development, implementation, and evaluation of marketing plans. Marketing Today 2.1 describes the new marketing plan at CTV.

Is Marketing Management Different?

On one level, managers from various departments perform the same function: they are involved in a company's strategic planning and implementation of that planning. They set objectives, develop plans, execute those plans, and evaluate their success.

Marketing managers are unique in that they direct their department's activities toward the goals of maintaining demand for the firm's products. This goal sets the marketing manager apart from the production manager, whose responsibility is to oversee the manufacture of the product, and from the financial manager, who is concerned with the supply of funds that support production and marketing activities.

Despite the differences in their responsibilities, a company's managers work toward the organization's primary goals. In most marketing-oriented companies, marketing is equal, but not superior, to other departments. Nevertheless, the interests of key managers in other departments may seem to conflict with those of the marketing manager.

A marketer, for example, may want to produce many different products tailored to various customer needs. However, this plan could create problems for a production head, who would prefer to stick with the efficiency of mass producing similar goods. The plan might also antagonize inventory managers, who may want to keep warehousing costs down by stocking as few products as possible.

A marketing manager must know the problems and capabilities of the other departments in the company. Before mounting a major advertising campaign, for example, a marketing manager for an automobile manufacturer should know if the assembly line can produce enough cars to

Marketing Today 2.1

Can a Marketer Move CTV to the Top Shelf?

It was the bold stroke of a marketing wunderkind. No sooner had 37-year-old John Cassaday settled into his new job as president of the CTV Television Network Ltd. than the network moved its public affairs program, *W5*, from 8 p.m. on Sundays to 7 p.m. Cassaday's hunch? He thought, given the choice, Canadians would pick a homegrown show over a U.S. one (*60 Minutes*). The result? *W5* picked up 20 percent more viewers the next week.

Cassaday calls the move "indisputably brilliant." But for all the talk from the former president of Campbell Foods PLC about the likeness of selling soup to selling television, even Cassaday admits that changing the cream of leek display at a Loblaws supermarket isn't quite like fiddling with TV time slots.

Playing the Canadian television network game nowadays is no piece of cake, even for a food industry maven like Cassaday, whose task is to ease CTV's battle in the ratings war. Problems of scheduling seem like smooth sailing against the greater political and economic undercurrents. On the one hand, there's pressure from the Canadian Radio-television Telecommunications Commission (CRTC) to increase Canadian content on the airwaves. On the other hand, and of greater significance, is the shrinking share of the national television and market relative to other media, says Derrick Leach, an analyst at Deacon Barclays de Zoete Wedd Ltd.

Increasingly, according to Leach, advertisers are tuning to more specific markets. And only the larger of CTV's 24 affiliates, he claims, can afford the steep network fees for the 60 hours a week that CTV pipes to its local stations.

But even locally, CTV's flagship operation, Toronto-based CFTO, is feeling the pinch of a competitive market. Since 1983, CFTO's share of viewers in the rich Toronto market has dipped, while the rival Global Television Network has upped its share. Now, Global owner Israel Asper wants to create his own national television system through his Winnipeg-based CanWest Global Communications Inc. Unlike CTV's centrally run operation, however, independent CanWest stations would control programming locally.

So, what can Cassaday pull from his soup biz background to stay in the network game? "Vision, strategy, urgency," he says. Translation: quality shows. But what of the high cost of making quality Canadian shows alone? The answer is co-productions with foreign companies, says Cassaday. But the CRTC does not consider such ventures with U.S. broadcasters fulfil Canadian content requirements.

"The economics of Canadian network television aren't alluring," says Leach. And though he thinks Cassaday's background might be ideal for television, he's a tad sceptical. "Had he been an undertaker, he'd be even more suited to it."

Source: Christian Allard, "Can a Marketer Move CTV to the Top Shelf?" *Canadian Business*, June 1990, p. 15.

---

satisfy projected demand. Similarly, although a marketing manager need not necessarily know the ins and outs of corporate finance, he or she should know if current interest rates make it unwise to borrow large sums for new-product development. In sum, although company plans should be market-oriented, the marketing department's plans are not the plans of the whole company. If, however, the marketing manager is sensitive to the company's goals in general, as well as to the particular plans of the organization's other functional areas, the marketing department's plans can help establish the tone and direction for the whole company.

Because of the marketing department's special focus, the marketing manager faces unique challenges. Some of these challenges are:

1. *The highly changeable nature of the market.* This year's style may not be next year's fashion; competitors' new technology may make one company's product look outdated before it even gets a foothold in the market. Marketing managers must be alert to changing consumer preferences and new-product developments.

2. *Geographical complexities of the market.* Now that many companies are marketing their products across the country and around the world, marketing managers must be sensitive to local customs, language, and ways of doing business in a wide variety of locations.

3. *People variables.* A marketing department is much more dependent on people than are most production or financial departments. The quality of the sales force, the creativity of the advertising personnel, and the skills of the market researchers are subject to wide variations.

4. *The need to rely on people outside the firm.* Particularly in the distribution area, marketing executives need to deal with large organizations over which they have little authority. Supermarkets must be persuaded to allot shelf space, and department stores must be convinced that an item fits in with their merchandising plans.

5. *Wide number of alternatives.* No other department in a company faces quite so many choices as marketing does. What product should we sell to what market? At what price? Should we sell through department stores or discount outlets? The wide range of choices, any combination of which may lead to success or failure, is one of the things that makes marketing such a challenging field.

6. *Marketing's influence on the success of the firm.* Costs for new-product development, advertising campaigns, and market research can run into the hundreds of thousands, or even millions, of dollars. A successful promotion can provide rewards far in excess of these costs. An unsuccessful one could be disastrous for a firm's image and finances. This high degree of uncertainty coupled with the potential for large profits—or losses—make the executive marketing decisions critical to the success of the firm.[4]

Marketing Planning

Successful marketing planning takes into account everything from a company's broadest, most abstract goals to the final details of distribution to the consumer.

Establishing a mission and objectives is the first step in any plan—and for a very good reason. Unless an organization knows what it is and where it is going, it will waste its resources.

Defining Mission and Objectives

As Chapter 1 noted, marketing seeks to serve consumer needs. Therefore, marketing managers have an important role in establishing a firm's mission, or overall goals.

Companies usually define their mission in short, general statements. IBM's corporate mission, for example, is "to meet the problem-solving needs of business." That statement may sound too vague to give any real direction. In fact, it is a good one for two reasons. First, it is not too specific. IBM might have said that its mission is "to sell computers." However, that would have confined the company to marketing only a limited line of computer hardware instead of the broad line of problem-solving equipment and computer services it now sells.[5] Second, it defines a group of customers to be served—namely, business.

Too often firms forget to do this. One analyst claims that the chief reason Chrysler lagged behind General Motors and Ford was that its mission did not define a customer group. Chrysler had thought of its purpose as the manufacture of a well-engineered car. In contrast, Ford's stated mission was "to produce a workingman's car." Lacking a customer-oriented purpose like Ford's, Chrysler repeatedly changed direction without gaining on its competitors.[6] Despite the company's profitability beginning in the mid-1980s, Chairman Lee A. Iacocca has conceded that Chrysler will not catch up to the size of GM and Ford: "We can be a first-rate company as long as we respect our size and don't try to have any delusions of grandeur."[7]

A well-defined sense of mission is important, but it is not enough. The mission must be translated into specific objectives.

Organizational objectives specify goals for the organization to pursue as a whole. Many people think that businesses have only one objective—to maximize profits. Profit is important for business survival, but it is by no means the only objective that organizations pursue. General Foods once produced a line of gourmet foods to foster a quality image for the company's products even though the line lost money. Other common business objectives are to increase the company's share of the market, to achieve industry leadership, and to diversify the corporation's activities.

Organizational objectives are most helpful when they are linked with specific **goals.** Managers use the term *goals* to describe objectives that have been made specific in size and time. A possible organizational objective for IBM would be to increase long-term profitability. Using that objective, the corporate planners at IBM might set a goal of increasing profit by 5 percent each year for the next five years. Giving an organizational objective a numerical value and a time frame makes it more useful as a guide to action and a measure of performance.

Quantifying organizational objectives is only one way to make them more exact. Another way is to indicate what each department in the organization can do to achieve those goals. Since marketing sets the tone

Organizational Objectives
Overall goals a firm pursues, such as increasing sales or maintaining a quality image.

Goals
Organizational objectives that have been made specific with regard to size and time.

in many firms today, marketing objectives are especially important. To be effective, marketing objectives should be quantified as well. "To expand the market by 5 percent in three years" or "to develop two new products for the office in seven years" could be marketing goals that IBM might pursue.

Once a marketing department has set specific goals, it can then go about mapping a strategy for attaining them.

Creating a Marketing Plan[8]

An important distinction must be made between marketing planning and a marketing plan. Marketing planning is an ongoing, continuous process. Every day a marketing manager may be engaged in some form of planning, such as mapping out the dimensions of a marketing research project, designing an advertising strategy, setting up a network of dealers, or devising ways to motivate the sales force. In contrast, a marketing plan sums up the insights gained in the course of that process and focuses them on a particular course of action for a specific period of time.

Most businesses now require formal written marketing plans. Plans may be long-term, covering a period of several years, or short-term, detailing proposed activity for a year or less. Short-term plans should always be in harmony with long-term plans, and both should be in keeping with a firm's long-term objectives.

Although firms' requirements for the structure of a marketing plan may differ, certain topics are generally included. The following elements are in most marketing plans:

I. Market analysis

    A. Demand (see Chapters 5–7)

    B. Competition (see Chapter 3)

    C. Environmental climate (see Chapter 3)

    D. Resources of the firm (see this chapter)

    E. Distribution factors (see Chapter 13)

    F. Political and legal constraints (see Chapter 3)

II. Problems and opportunities

III. Marketing strategy

    A. Marketing objectives (see this chapter)

    B. Target markets (see Chapter 4)

    C. Marketing mix

        1. Product (see Chapter 9)

        2. Price (see Chapter 10)

        3. Promotion (see Chapters 14–16)

4.   Placement (see Chapters 11–13)

Market Analysis

In the mid-1980s, the housing market in Canada was thriving. Buyers were scrambling to make deals, and prices were escalating rapidly. Then mortgage interest rates began to climb almost as quickly as housing prices. By 1990, rates were so high that few people could afford to buy. Demand for housing evaporated, particularly in large cities where prices had escalated most rapidly. (See Figure 2.2.)

The housing market may constitute an extreme example, but it demonstrates one of the primary difficulties marketers face: planning in the midst of constantly changing conditions. It is not enough for a marketer to plan on the basis of what is. The more critical question is, what will be? Marketers must examine several areas to determine what the future might bring and how it is likely to affect the marketing strategy they plan to pursue.

Demand   The question basic to all marketing is, who are we going to serve? The answer determines the organization's **markets.** For businesses, markets consist of people who are willing to buy a firm's output and have the purchasing power to do so. For nonprofit firms, markets are made up of individuals who have an interest in a product offering (whether a tangible good or an intangible service or idea) and a willingness to exchange something (attention, support, change of habit, and so on) in return.

Consider some examples of markets. The market for rubber bands contains different kinds of rubber-band buyers—businesses of all types, students, crafts instructors who want to use them for projects, and children who want to use them as aerial weapons. But if you were a rubber-

Market
For business, those who are willing to buy a firm's output and have the purchasing power to do so. For nonprofit firms, those who have an interest in a product and are willing to exchange something in return (whether monetary or nonmonetary).

Brian Willer

Figure 2.2   Toronto Housing Market

band manufacturer, would this market diversity matter? Most likely not; you would probably get the best return from making rubber bands in a few different sizes and using inexpensive, functional packaging.

But what about the market for shirts? For starters, people need shirts in different sizes. And men and women often prefer different styles or colours. Different occasions — weddings and golf outings, for example — call for different styles as well. Furthermore, 16-year-olds and 46-year-olds often have different preferences. A shirt manufacturer will not be in business long if it sells one style and size for everyone, so the company has to consider the differences in shirt buyers.

Few organizations know the exact wants and needs of every potential customer. Instead, marketers learn about the market by dividing it into submarkets, called market segments. A **market segment** is a group of individuals, groups, or organizations in a market that share similar characteristics that cause them to have similar wants or needs. A shirt manufacturer might consider one market segment to consist of men aged 35 to 50 who earn $40 000 to $60 000 in white-collar jobs. In determining market segments, the shirt manufacturer also might take into account people's attitudes, say, toward clothing or toward trying new things.

In business, two broad market segments are the consumer and industrial markets. The **consumer market** consists of individuals who buy either for their own or their family's personal consumption. The **industrial market** is made up of purchasers who buy for business, government, or institutional use, mainly for the purpose of resale or re-exchange.

Within each of these broad categories are many subgroups that make up possible market segments. Customers can be grouped according to age, income level, interests, and a variety of other factors. The process of segmenting markets is investigated at length in Chapter 4.

Marketing managers cannot set realistic objectives without knowledge of the market they want to serve. Markets are an uncontrollable factor because customers have more influence in shaping marketing plans than managers have in shaping customer needs. Determining the extent to which consumers will want a firm's product or service is a key variable that marketers must address early in the planning process.

Demand is the one element on which much of the marketing plan hinges. It is often the least known, especially in the case of a new product, and the least predictable. But on it rests the weight of not only the marketing department's plans, but also those of production, finance, personnel, and other departments in the firm.

To assess the nature of demand for a product or service, marketers might ask such questions as: Who makes the purchase decision? Who influences the decision maker? How much brand awareness or loyalty does this product possess? Where is this product purchased? When? As well, is the consumer price sensitive? (If consumers of a product are price sensitive, lowering the price will influence demand positively.)

After assessing the nature of the demand for a product, marketers must examine the extent of the demand. Marketers might ask the following questions: What is the size of the market now, and what does the

Market Segment
Group of individuals, groups, or organizations in a market sharing similar characteristics that cause them to have similar wants or needs.

Consumer Market
Individuals who buy either for their own or for their family's personal consumption.

Industrial Market
Businesses, governments, and organizations that buy goods and services for resale or for use in producing other goods and services.

future hold? What is our current share of the market, and is that share growing or declining?

The answers to these questions give marketers a basis on which to predict the company's profit opportunities and to determine how much of the firm's resources should be allotted to marketing and production.

Competition   Demand is not the only key variable in a marketing plan. The number and types of competitors must also be analyzed.

Marketers view competition rather broadly. When marketers of RCA televisions evaluate their competitors, they not only think of Zenith, Panasonic, and Sony but also consider alternate forms of entertainment, including movies, museums, books, sports, and a variety of others. All represent competing ways for consumers to spend their entertainment money. Thus the RCA marketers' job is to lure customers away from other entertainment media as well as from other TV set manufacturers.

Competition both within and between industries is keener today than ever before, partly because of the increasing strength of foreign marketers at home and abroad. Three of the top ten television makers, for example, are Japanese (Sony, Quasar, and Panasonic). Competitors outside North America also are important in the markets for autos, steel, cameras, shoes, clothing, and chemicals.

Competition cannot be avoided, and the actions of competitors cannot be controlled. The effect of competition can be blunted, however, if marketers can convince customers that their product offers a clear advantage. Offering a product at a lower price than that of competitors is one source of advantage.

Managers also often try to establish customer preference by other means. Making a distinctive product is one way. In the highly competitive market for pocket calculators, Hewlett-Packard has survived by offering models with more functions than those of competitors, thus appealing to the professional end of the market. A distinctive means of distribution can also appeal to customers. Avon's direct selling to neighbours and co-workers of its sales representatives has proved effective in competing with well-established cosmetics firms that sell mainly in department stores and drugstores. Any element, or unique combination, of the marketing mix can help distinguish a company's products.

Environmental Climate   Suppose you know that your neighbourhood contains many pizza lovers but no pizzerias. Is this information sufficient for setting a goal of opening a pizzeria? No. The next step of your market analysis is to evaluate the environment. You might ask questions like these: What are the zoning restrictions that affect opening a restaurant in this neighbourhood? Are reliable suppliers accessible and reasonably priced? What laws apply to food service and liquor sales?

Marketing departments investigate questions such as these because a marketing department may succeed or fail for reasons unrelated to its effort. For example, workers at a supplying firm may go on strike. The government may decide to build a highway through your chosen pizzeria site. Or the economy may take a sudden downturn, so that consumers spend less.

Environmental Analysis
Examination of the environment and identification of the circumstances and conditions that can cause the greatest problems or offer the greatest opportunities.

Internal (Micro) Environment
Factors in an organization (such as financial resources and employees) capable of being influenced but not totally controlled by marketing managers.

Operating Environment
Individuals and organizations outside a firm (such as dealers and competitors) that help shape marketing plans and can, in turn, be shaped by them to some extent.

General (Macro) Environment
Economic, technological, legal, and social forces that are largely outside the control of marketers and that affect the success or failure of marketing plans.

Evaluating issues such as these is called **environmental analysis.** It involves examining the environment and identifying the circumstances and conditions that can cause the greatest problems or offer the greatest opportunities. An example of a potential problem is rumours that the truck drivers who deliver key supplies may go on strike.

Marketers often find it useful to divide the environment into the three environmental levels illustrated in Figure 2.3. The division is based on the immediacy and controllability of the circumstances and conditions within each level.

The most immediate and controllable environmental level is the **internal,** or **micro, environment.** This level contains factors that are outside the control of marketing managers but within the organization as a whole. For example, a marketing manager who sees an opportunity to increase revenues by expanding the sales force may run into problems if the organization's plans for that year include employee cutbacks or a hiring freeze. The next level is the **operating environment.** This level consists of individuals and organizations outside the organization that help shape marketing plans and can, to a limited extent, be shaped by them. Suppliers, distributors, and competitors are part of a firm's operating environment. The level least subject to marketing control is the **general,** or **macro, environment.** This level includes the national and global conditions that affect the success or failure of marketing plans. These conditions may be social, political, regulatory, economic, or technological.

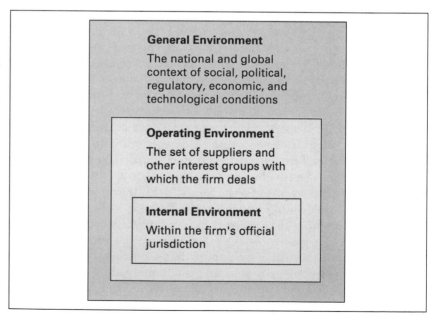

Figure 2.3 Environmental Levels

Source: Adapted from Philip S. Thomas, ''Environmental Analysis for Corporate Planning,'' *Business Horizons*, October 1974, p. 28.

Resources of the Firm   The success of marketing plans often depends largely on the resources of an organization. Resources can be both tangible and intangible.

Tangible Resources.   The most obvious organizational resources contributing to marketing success are tangible. These include:

1. *Physical plant:*   the land, buildings, and machinery owned by the organization. The location of the plant can be crucial to marketing.

2. *Financial reserves:*   the money needed for investment. More than one marketing department has discovered that it underestimated the amount of capital needed to market a new product—and failed as a result. Capital is especially important for capital-intensive industries—those requiring a large initial investment. Even large companies like RCA and Westinghouse had to pull out of manufacturing computers because of the heavy expenses incurred.

3. *Raw materials:*   the supply of basic products needed to produce a product. To ensure a steady supply of these, many large firms have bought a controlling interest in their source of supply. For example, the New York Times Company purchased a substantial share of a Canadian pulp supplier, the Spruce Falls Power & Paper Company. Small manufacturers who cannot afford this approach may suffer marketing disadvantages. They may attempt another approach—negotiating long-term contracts with their suppliers.

A firm can make use of any of these tangible resources to establish what marketers call a **differential advantage.** This is the special edge over competition a company may have or develop. A differential advantage may have a number of sources, including an organization's tangible and intangible resources.

Intangible Resources.   Intangible resources include a firm's public image with customers, shareholders, suppliers, and others. Other intangibles are its reputation, the quality of its products, the fairness of its prices, and its willingness to service products or to replace or repair products that are defective.

Some companies have made major marketing mistakes by ignoring their intangible assets, such as company reputation. The German car manufacturer, Volkswagenwerk AG, prospered in the North American market for years by producing homely but sturdy Volkswagen Beetles. Owners loved them because they were cheap to buy, cheap to operate, and remarkably reliable. Volkswagen owners also liked the idea that their car was a product of superior German engineering. But in an attempt to expand the market for its product, Volkswagen changed its character—with dire results.

The company built a plant in Pennsylvania and began manufacturing VW Rabbits. Quality control at the plant was poor, and VW's reputation for reliability suffered. The design was changed to "Americanize" the car, and the price climbed. Some prospective buyers came to view the Rabbit as a small, unreliable, overpriced North American car. Between

Differential Advantage
Special edge over competition an organization may have or develop by working with the elements of the marketing mix.

1970 and 1983, VW's U.S. market share fell from 7.2 percent to 2.6 percent.[9]

The recall of a product (a relatively common occurrence for auto manufacturers) may have a major impact on a firm's reputation but the effect need not always be adverse. Perrier, the French water producer, recalled its mineral water in Canada in 1990 when its quality-control department found trace amounts of benzene in the product. The firm organized a voluntary recall program to respond and communicate to the public what Perrier was doing to ensure product safety. This action probably ensured that its image and reputation was not damaged in the long term.[10] (See Figure 2.4.)

Perhaps just as important as a company's reputation are the people the organization employs. Sometimes organizations develop a reputation for attracting and training talent in special areas. General Mills, Procter & Gamble, and General Foods are known for their outstanding product management programs.[11]

Distribution Factors No marketing plan can succeed without the cooperation of the people who deliver the product from the producer to the consumer. Dealers, or intermediaries, are another element in a firm's operating environment. The grocery store, the wholesale outlet, and the

The imported bottled-water market:

Perrier (France) . . . . **1st ranking**

Evian (France) **2nd**

San Pellegrino (Italy) **3rd**

Naya (Canada) **4th**

Ramiosa (Sweden). **5th**

Montclair (Canada) **6th**

Figure 2.4 It's Perfect. It's Perrier.

travel agency are all examples of dealers. Occasionally dealers are wholly owned by manufacturers, but frequently wholesalers and retailers are independents. They must be dealt with as outside forces that can benefit or harm a business.

Marketers often have less control over dealers than they would like. Dealers' co-operation in meeting marketing objectives cannot be guaranteed. Furthermore, the wrong choice of a dealer can spell disaster for a firm because it can affect costs and revenues. But with careful planning, a company can establish and maintain good relations with dealers. Chapter 11 discusses this subject under the topic of Managing Channels: Problems and Solutions.

Political and Legal Constraints   Before 1978, U.S. airlines had little competition. As labour costs increased, they were passed on to consumers. Fares may have been high, but the airline profit picture was rosy. Then the American Congress passed the Airline Deregulation Act. The skies became an aerial free-for-all. Price wars broke out, profits plunged, and some large carriers found they could not cut costs enough to compete and ultimately filed for bankruptcy or merged with other airlines. In Canada, where deregulation has not gone as far as it has in the United States, the plunge in profits has not been so severe.[12]

Another example of how political and legal situations change industries is found in the pharmaceutical industry. Pharmaceutical patent rights had lasted for four years. Recently, Parliament voted to lengthen the period to ten to twelve years. In exchange for this extension of generic-free competition (see Figure 2.5), the major international organizations promised to do increasing amounts of research and development in Canada.

When developing a marketing plan, marketers today must take into account anti-combines legislation, antipollution, truth-in-lending and truth-in-advertising requirements, and many other laws and regulations. Not only must marketers keep current laws in mind; they also need to be aware of pending legislation that could drastically alter the way they do future business. Chapter 3 discusses ramifications of political and legal constraints in greater depth.

Problems and Opportunities

Once the market analysis is complete, the marketer is ready to list the problems and opportunities that have been uncovered in the course of developing the preliminary phase of the plan. Each of the different factors can then be assigned a weight equal to its importance.

Parker Brothers, the hundred-year-old producer of such board games as Monopoly and Clue, admits, for example, that it nearly missed the boat when playing games on the television set started to become popular. Realizing that it had to rethink its product and marketing strategy — and fast—the company moved to restructure its marketing staff into two groups: electronic and traditional. It then hired 20 software engineers

Brian Willer/Maclean's

Figure 2.5 Generic-Free Competition in the Pharmaceutical Industry

to develop video games centred around popular movie figures and what had been arcade games such as Q-Bert.

In addition, the company increased its marketing budget enormously. In 1983, Parker Brothers allotted $30 million to promote video games alone; in 1981, the company's total marketing budget had been only $15 million. But while Parker Brothers was willing to make the leap into new technologies, it was not about to neglect its traditional strengths. The company also decided to begin promoting its most popular board games to adults, with a campaign stressing how such games bring people together as a group.[13]

Parker Brothers analyzed its problems and found a way to turn them into opportunities. The process of developing a marketing plan is often an occasion for marketers to step back for a moment from handling day-to-day concerns and to assess the broader issues affecting the company.

Marketing Strategy

Having analyzed the market and explored the various problems and opportunities that it presents, a marketer is ready to develop a marketing strategy to achieve specific objectives. Such a strategy uses the elements of the marketing mix—product, price, promotion, and placement—to reach targeted market segments. Because the elements of the marketing mix are the means for achieving the marketing objectives, much of the remainder of this book is devoted to discussing each element in depth.

Marketing Objectives   This stage of the marketing plan involves translating broad objectives into specific, quantifiable goals for the marketing department. Generally, marketing objectives include (1) sales volume (in dollars or units), (2) market share (expressed as a percentage of the total market), and (3) profits (expressed as a return on investment). Each goal should specify size and time, so the marketing manager can measure results as the plan is put into action.

Target Markets   The marketing department can meet its objectives most efficiently by focusing on the part of the total market most likely to want or need the company's products. Marketers do this by referring to their previous analysis of demand. Remember that part of this analysis involves dividing the total market into market segments. The marketer evaluates which of these segments are most likely to demand the company's products or which segments demand something that the company can offer. When the company decides to concentrate on reaching these market segments, they become **target markets.**

The Body Shop followed this process in devising a strategy for selling its personal-care products. This firm decided to make the environmentally aware segment of the personal-care market its target market. On behalf of Friends of the Earth, a non-profit environmental group based in Ottawa, The Body Shop store windows displayed information about the danger of ozone-layer depletion. (See Figure 2.6.) In 1989, the stores sold $30 000 worth of Protect the Ozone Layer T-shirts and $45 000 worth of World Wildlife Friend T-shirts. Such campaigns have made The Body Shop—a chain of 72 franchised and corporate-owned cosmetic and accessory stores—a standard bearer for corporate social consciousness.[14]

The chapters in Part Two offer a more in-depth look at target marketing and the analysis of markets.

Marketing Mix   Chapter 1 discussed the four elements of the marketing mix: product, price, promotion, and placement (or distribution). A marketing plan comprehensively treats each of these elements:

1. *Product.*   Should we develop new products, change old products, or drop products from the line? How should our product(s) be positioned? How should they be branded — national brands, private, generic?

Target Market
Market segment an organization designs its marketing mix to reach because that segment is considered likely to demand the product being marketed.

PRESIDENT MARGOT FRANSSEN/PARTNER QUIG TINGLEY

Window displays and fundraising campaigns
for good causes have antagonized mall managers,
but they haven't hurt The Body Shop's profits

Figure 2.6   The Body Shop

The Body Shop decided to position its products in the ecologically conscious segment of the market — its facial cleansers, wooden brushes, and bath products are all made from natural, biodegradable materials. Its skin-care products, which are available for both males and females, are packaged in mostly recyclable containers and are not tested on animals.

2. *Price.*   Should our price be above, below, or at the rate currently charged for similar products? Should we allow prices to vary based on discount structures or geography? What profit margin do we seek?

The Body Shop priced its products in the middle to higher end of the personal-care cosmetics market.

3. *Promotion.*   What should be our mix of advertising, sales promotion, personal selling, and dealer incentives? How should our budget

be apportioned? What media should we use? What message do we seek to convey?

The Body Shop decided to sell its products without advertising, depending on window displays, word of mouth, and publicity. The windows display the products, but four months a year they are devoted to noncommercial human rights and ecological crusades. Co-ordinated from the head office in Don Mills, Ontario, the themes run in all 72 outlets in Canada.

4. *Placement, or Distribution.* Should our products be available in many locations or few? What type of wholesaler and retailer should we use? Should these distribution channels be long or short?

The Body Shop products are distributed through franchise stores, most of which are located in high-traffic malls or in the downtown core of major cities in Canada, the United States, and the United Kingdom. The cost of opening a Body Shop has risen from $75 000 to $190 000, and most of the Canadian outlets have profit margins of 20 to 25 percent with the annual growth in sales allowing for a two-year payback.

A marketing manager's job is to mesh product, price, promotion, and placement into a workable plan so that the final result is more than the sum of its parts—all the while keeping budget considerations in mind. At the beginning of this chapter, the job of marketing manager was compared with that of a symphony conductor. Perhaps it is now easier to see why the analogy is apt. In both cases the concerns are many and the chances of disharmony great, but the rewards may be equally great for a job skilfully done.

Chapter Replay

1. **What are the marketing manager's basic tasks?**
The marketing manager is responsible for strategic marketing planning, implementing the marketing plan, and evaluating the results of marketing efforts.

2. **What is involved in strategic marketing planning?**
Strategic marketing planning includes establishing an organization's overall goals, assessing opportunities, and developing marketing objectives. This process results in marketing strategies.

3. **What are the elements of a marketing strategy?**
A marketing strategy consists of the marketing mix selected to reach specified target markets in order to achieve marketing objectives.

4. **What are some special challenges of marketing management?**
These challenges include the highly changeable nature of the market, geographical complexities of the market, heavy dependence on people's skills, the need to rely on people outside the firm, the great

number of alternatives, and the marketing department's major influence on the firm's success.

5. **How does a company define a mission and objectives?**
First, the company defines its mission in short, general statements, which are ideally customer-oriented. The mission is then translated into specific objectives linked with measurable goals.

6. **What goes into a marketing plan?**
A marketing plan begins with an analysis of the market, including demand, competition, environmental climate, resources of the firm, distribution factors, and political and legal constraints. Based on this information comes an evaluation of problems and opportunities. The plan then sets forth a marketing strategy, using target markets and marketing mix to achieve marketing objectives.

7. **How do marketers decide what segments of the total market will be the focus of their efforts?**
Marketers divide the total market into market segments. They evaluate which segments will most likely demand what the company offers. Based on this evaluation, they select segments to be target markets.

8. **What is the role of marketing mix in the marketing plan?**
A marketing plan comprehensively treats these elements — product, price, promotion, and placement—in determining how each will help the company achieve its objectives in reaching target markets.

Key Terms

consumer market	market segment
differential advantage	marketing manager
environmental analysis	marketing objectives
general (macro) environment	marketing strategy
goals	operating environment
industrial market	organizational objectives
internal (micro) environment	strategic marketing planning
market	target market

Discussion Questions

1. What is the difference between strategic marketing planning and a marketing strategy?

2. What is wrong with the following marketing objectives?

a. Have 65 percent of the automobile owners in Midtown try our car wash.

b. Increase profits by 5 percent by the end of next year.

3. Why must marketing managers be aware of other departments' problems and capabilities?

4. Before a marketer can set objectives or devise a strategy for meeting them, he or she must analyze the market. What topics are typically included in a market analysis?

5. Researchers in the marketing department of A-1 Gloves, Inc., have divided the market for gloves into groups according to high, middle, or low income; region of the country; and high or low frequency of participation in winter sports. What is the marketing term for such categories?

   The marketing manager has learned of a new fabric that is expensive but has superior insulating properties. Gloves made of this fabric could keep hands warm at $-45°C$. How might A-1 Gloves use the categories of consumers to select target markets?

6. Which of the following market segments describe the consumer market? The industrial market?

   a. Customers of a hair salon

   b. People who have enrolled in a stop-smoking workshop

   c. A gas station that buys gas from a major oil company

   d. Customers of the gas station

   e. An apartment building manager who buys a snow-blower to clear the walks around the building

   f. A father who buys a balloon and then gives it to his child

7. How can organizations blunt the effects of competition? Who are the competitors of charitable organizations, such as the Canadian Cancer Society or the Foster Parents Plan? Do the same strategies for competing apply to these organizations?

8. What is a differential advantage? Give an example of a tangible resource and of an intangible resource that give a company a differential advantage.

9. John Doe and Ray Mead established a music school. John gives piano lessons, and Ray teaches guitar and voice. They have a steady stream of pupils, but after several years and much analysis of their local market, they have decided to expand. Together, John and Ray settle on a marketing objective: to double their business in three years. To achieve their marketing objective, what should John and Ray include in their marketing strategy?

Avon Canada

Colourful Corporate Makeover

"We were hit by a triple whammy," recalls John Novosad, former President of Avon Canada. "We suddenly woke up one day and discovered that the world around us had changed dramatically and our formula for success was outdated. In the past, we had always been able to come up with some magic pill that would solve any dilemma we had. But now we found we had long-term problems and there were no instant fixes. By the time we finally understood that, it had become a very major problem."

The symptoms of Avon Canada's problems were sagging sales and profits — sales slipped from $94 million in 1983 to $88 million in 1985 and profits were flat at $4 million during this period.

Company Background

Founded in the United States as the California Perfume Company in the nineteenth century, Avon was a success from the beginning, selling fine fragrances directly to women. As the door-to-door business increased, David McConnell, founder, added toiletries, shoe cleaners and cook books to his company's product line. By the 1920s, the name was changed to Avon, after William Shakespeare's birth place, and the new business expanded internationally to Canada, the United Kingdom, and continental Europe. Sales increased as more personal care products were successfully introduced, including bath products, make-up, skin care products, jewellery, small gifts and home accessories.

Economic and Social Trends

By the beginning of the 1980s, great changes were taking place in the lives of women — Avon's traditional customers. The Avon image became tired and old-fashioned to the growing numbers of baby boom generation women entering the work force. It became difficult for the firm to recruit sales representatives and for the first time, total sales of Avon went down.

Revised Marketing Plan

In 1985, Avon formulated a new plan to win back the consumer and position Avon as a leader in the beauty products industry. After much marketing research, the firm introduced Avon Colour to add cohesiveness to the hundreds of products Avon offered. Avon Colour, a co-ordinated collection of 185 shades of skin, lip, eye and nail colour, became the centre of Avon's new product strategy. Colour families of these products were emphasized to enhance skin tones and hair colour.

Source: Information provided by Avon Canada, Pointe Claire, Québec.

Sales representatives were trained fully in the new Avon concept and the direct selling effort was directed towards the workplace. A mail-in coupon, in popular English and French women's magazines, was used to generate sales leads. The catalogues were redesigned and the same models were used in the 18 campaigns. Fashion demonstrations of clothes accented by the Avon accessories, such as jewellery, were held. Panty hose were introduced. The post-Christmas sales period became a time of special sales promotions.

Issues of importance to women were identified and the firm responded. Avon became the first major cosmetics manufacturer to permanently stop using animals in the safety testing of its products. Childcare brochures developed with the YWCA were made available. Ecologically based packaging is now being designed. By 1990, all of these changes to the marketing mix brought about the desired effect of increased sales.

Focal Topics

1. Describe the elements of Avon Canada's 1985 market analysis.

2. Do you agree that this firm should expand its product lines to include new types of products like toys, gifts, clothing?

3. Should Avon Canada re-define its target market in the 1990s? If so, how will its marketing strategy change?

Franklin International (A)

Franklin International can trace its roots to 1935 when the company started with a single product — animal glues for furniture. Today, the company still produces that initial product, Liquid Hide Glue, but it has grown from that single item to a highly diversified list of adhesives and sealants for home and industry. Franklin was the first to develop a synthetic aliphatic resin glue as a substitute for animal glues. The company continues its role today as an innovator of new products through its research and development laboratory, which also provides technical assistance to industry users of Franklin's products.

With manufacturing and corporate offices in Columbus, Ohio, the company operates warehouses located strategically to service its customers. From its base of industrial wood adhesives, the company has integrated backward into the manufacturing of the polymers that serve as the raw material for the wood glues. The company has also expanded forward into the manufacture of adhesive, sealants, and caulking for the consumer market.

Company Organization

The company is divided into four primary businesses. The Industrial Division, the original business, sells adhesives to furniture manufacturers. The Polymer Division, originally created to produce raw materials for the Industrial Division, now sells two-thirds of its production to other adhesive users, such as label manufacturers. The remaining third is sold to the Industrial and Consumer divisions. The Plastics Division was created to ensure the Consumer Division a steady supply of bottles to package its products; 90 percent of its sales are now to outside customers.

The Consumer Products Division was created as a new natural extension of the Industrial Division to market wood glues to nonindustrial users. The current product line includes Titebond (the first aliphatic resin glue) and Franklin Construction Adhesive (the first construction adhesive sold to the consumer markets). These two products, in varying sizes, account for nearly 40 percent of the Consumer Division's sales. Other products include wood flooring adhesives, latex caulks, and panelling adhesives.

Marketing activities of the Polymer and Plastics divisions are directed to a relatively small number of potential customers. The Industrial and Consumer divisions, on the other hand, have a large number of present and potential customers.

Industrial Division

The Industrial Division sells directly through company salespeople to furniture manufacturers and cabinetmakers. The salespeople also provide a technical support function to the manufacturer. The superior technical ability of the salespeople is believed to be a key differentiating factor in comparing Franklin to the competition.

The Industrial Division had always positioned itself as the quality, premium-priced producer in the marketplace. Management determined long ago that it did not want to participate in markets that are only based on price and that if satisfactory margins were not available from a product, Franklin would not carry that product. With increased competition in the 1960s and 1970s, however, even products that had traditionally been only moderately price sensitive were being promoted and sold on the basis of lower prices by Franklin's competition as a means of gaining a foothold in the market. This was probably the key reason for the shrinking of the Industrial Division's market share in the 1970s. To counteract, or at least abate this erosion, the company decided to initiate a formal advertising program in 1978 that continues today.

With the decision to create some type of advertising program, several additional decisions were reached to maintain consistency of image. First, all advertisements were to reflect the quality image the company enjoyed in the furniture industry. Second, the advertisements were to highlight the technical capabilities and experience of the company as well as the different products. Third, to illustrate company commitment to quality and service, all advertisements would be full page and in full colour.

Consumer Products Division

The Consumer Products Division manufactures some private brands for major retailers and markets its own brands through a variety of channels such as:

- *Building material distributors*—which sell primarily to lumber yards, cabinet shops, and large contractors.

- *Hardware distributors* — which sell primarily to independent hardware retailers.

- *Building materials chains* — which act as purchasing agents for all the stores in a chain, usually home centres.

- *Hardware co-ops*—which act as purchasing agents for member hardware dealers; typical U.S. co-ops include True Value, Ace, and Trustworthy.

In the past, promotions normally took the form of a discount on specific sizes of a product and were usually introduced at a hardware or home centre show. Special discounts of $1 to $5 per case to the buyer were sometimes used as an additional incentive to purchase the sale merchandise. A co-op advertising fund was utilized as an aid to the hardware dealer in promoting Franklin products. Dealers were eligible for reimbursement of 50 percent of their advertising costs on Franklin products up to a maximum of 3 percent of their total purchases upon submission of the advertising copy and proof of purchase of Franklin products from their distributor or U.S. co-op. The division plans to make some major changes in its promotional strategies.

Focal Topics

1. What would you describe as the "real business" of Franklin International? From a marketing perspective, why does the firm exist?

2. How might the marketing concept be applied to a firm like Franklin?

3. Assume that the president feels that Franklin is too product or production oriented. How would you suggest that the firm become more marketing oriented?

3

Chapter 3

Environments for Marketing Strategies

In this chapter, you will learn:

- General categories of competitive markets.

- How marketers can respond to the competition in each of these markets.

- How the government protects fair competition.

- How the government protects consumers.

- Ways in which industries regulate themselves.

- Issues marketers must address in responding to the social environment.

- Responsibilities of producers and consumers.

- How marketers can respond to changes in the economic environment.

- How marketers can respond to changes in the technological environment.

Tobacco Advertising under Fire

The environment for cigarette advertisers is hardly a friendly one. In nations around the world, consumer and medical groups are pressuring governments to prohibit tobacco advertising. Opponents of tobacco advertising argue that if a product is harmful, it should not be promoted. The tobacco industry and advertisers respond that a product that is legal to sell should also be legal to promote.

Despite this argument, the worldwide trend seems to favour restrictions. According to James Neelankavil, a consultant for the International Advertising Association, ''In the last five years, there seems to be more clamouring. For every ten times people jump up and down, three or four restrictions pass, and that's much more than before.'' In 1986 alone, tobacco advertising was under attack in Canada, the United Kingdom, Singapore, the Netherlands, Argentina, Australia, South Korea, Hong Kong, Brazil, and New Zealand.

In countries that already ban tobacco advertising, governments are restricting other moves by marketers to promote cigarettes. In Italy, for example, legislation was proposed to ban promotions such as displaying cigarette brand names on clothing.

Some governments are considering other avenues to reduce smoking, such as anti-smoking advertisements and higher cigarette taxes. In Germany, the government increased the tobacco tax 39 percent. Cuba has instituted a nationwide antismoking campaign. The country's president, Fidel Castro, has taken a leadership role by giving up cigars and urging others to do the same.

Although the results of these efforts are unclear, there is no evidence that the pressure on tobacco advertisers will ease anytime soon. The pressure is

more severe than other advertisers typically face, but every marketer is affected in some way by consumer expectations and government regulations.

Chapter 2 introduced you to the variety of issues that marketers must consider when planning a marketing strategy. Many of those forces are outside a marketer's control but can, nonetheless, exert a powerful influence over the success or failure of a marketing plan. Taken together, those forces constitute the company's marketing environment. This chapter considers more closely the various forces that bear upon the way a company markets its products.

Sources: Adapted from ''Fidel on Cigars: 'No More,''' *Time*, September 8, 1986, p. 47; and ''Pressure is on for Tobacco Ad Ban Worldwide,'' *Advertising Age*, August 18, 1986, pp. 46, 48.

The Competitive Environment

The previous chapter discussed competition as an element of the operating environment that marketers have to take into account in market planning. But not all competition is alike. A marketing manager for Nova Scotia Power Corporation, which is the only supplier of hydro in its service area, has quite a different job from that of the marketing manager for Virgin Records Canada — in more ways than are immediately apparent. The Virgin manager, for example, must worry about the competition from Risque Disque and from Capitol Records, RCA, MCA, Arista, and A&M, not to mention the competition for young adults' spending money posed by movies, video games, and rock concerts. The manager of NSPC also may have many things to worry about, such as population shifts or consumer attitudes, but competition from other utilities is not among those concerns.

Types of Competitive Markets

The nature of the competitive market greatly influences a firm's marketing decisions, especially pricing decisions. Therefore, the marketing manager needs to understand the nature of the market in which the organization operates.

Competitive markets fall into four general categories: pure competition, oligopoly, monopolistic competition, and monopoly.[1] When deciding which category applies to a given situation, marketers should keep in mind that categories overlap, and a firm may actually operate in a combination of competitive markets.

Pure Competition

Pure Competition
Situation in which there are many sellers, no seller dominates a market, and the products sold are interchangeable.

The competitive market is characterized by **pure competition** when the following conditions exist:

- Products are uniform—for example, potatoes, coal, chemicals, or laundry services.

- There are many buyers and sellers.

In this environment, sellers can do little to influence price. If a seller charges more than the going price, buyers will take their business elsewhere. The seller has no reason to charge less than the going price. Marketers facing pure competition seek primarily to ensure a wide distribution of their product at a competitive price.

Agriculture is typical of pure competition (at least in theory). Few consumers can distinguish between apples offered by various growers in Nova Scotia, so each grower must set prices in line with supply. If a drought destroys the apple crop in British Columbia, the Nova Scotia grower may be able to raise prices. But if Ontario farmers have a bumper crop, farmers in Nova Scotia may barely be able to charge enough to recover their costs.

Oligopoly

An **oligopoly** exists when a few companies dominate an industry and make entry by other firms difficult. Two examples of oligopolies are the U.S. steel industry, which is dominated by ten large companies, and the Canadian brewing industry, which is dominated by two major firms.

When competition is oligopolistic, the dominant companies have great control over the product's price. The prices of competitive products tend to be similar because price competition would reduce firms' profits.[2] Instead, marketers use other elements of the marketing mix to distinguish their products from those of competitors.

Monopolistic Competition

The word *monopolistic* means having exclusive possession. In **monopolistic competition,** each firm tries to gain exclusive possession of a share of the market. Buyers perceive products as being diverse, so firms can gain differential advantages. Product diversity is one source of the competition in this type of market. Another source is the relatively large number of sellers, enabling dissatisfied buyers to find alternatives.

Under monopolistic competition, the role of marketing is to establish a brand difference in customers' minds. If these efforts succeed, the company may be able to influence the price at which it sells its products. Ray Ban sunglasses, for example, sell for premium prices because the company has carved out a distinctive style-conscious image in the marketplace.

Monopoly

A **monopoly** exists when one company is the exclusive provider of a product or service. A pure monopoly is rare but can exist in one of the following ways:

- *As a government monopoly, such as Canada Post.* The government sets prices to meet various policy objectives, such as encouraging or discouraging use.

- *As a private regulated monopoly, such as a cable-TV or phone company.* Under this arrangement, rates are subject to the approval of government regulatory bodies.

- *Temporarily as a private monopoly by holding a patent on a product.* In Canada, a patentholder is protected for 20 years from the date of filing of the patent and may charge whatever price the market will bear. Companies may charge less than full price for a variety of rea-

Oligopoly
Situation in which a few firms dominate the market, set similar prices, and make entry by other firms difficult.

Monopolistic Competition
Situation in which there are many sellers in a market who rarely engage in price competition but compete by trying to establish brand preferences among consumers.

Monopoly
Situation in which one company is the exclusive provider of a product or service.

sons, including fear of government regulation or desire to penetrate the market quickly.[3]

Marketing to Meet the Competition

The type of competitive environment in which a company operates dramatically affects its marketing strategy. Often, companies wage their competitive battles in the area of price. (Pricing to meet the competition is discussed in Chapter 10.) Some companies may choose to offer enhanced services to distinguish themselves from the competition. Others may offer a unique method of distribution.

In the case of pure competition, a company typically invests little in marketing because consumers view one company's products as being basically the same as another's. For example, laundromats in a given community provide about the same service at the same price, and they don't take out ads in magazines, rent billboard space, or give away coupons.

In an oligopoly, although companies may engage in price wars, they avoid price competition. In the automobile industry, for example, major advertising campaigns in the past focused on informing consumers about the benefits of various car models. It is only recently, with excess capacity in the global automobile industry, that price has been featured in advertising. Since 1988, automobile ads have featured rebates and new-car loans at low interest rates as often as they have featured the cars themselves.

Under monopolistic competition, companies look for a differential advantage. In the restaurant business, for example, each restaurant has many choices in devising a marketing mix to capture a slice of the total market. These choices include varying the atmosphere, menu, service, location, and prices. McDonald's has a large share of the fast-food market, but even though its prices are lower than those at elegant French restaurants, McDonald's will not sell to much of the market segment that consists of people who want a fancy dinner.

It might seem that a monopoly company would have no need of marketing, but such companies usually do market their products. For example, a patentholder might try to build a large base of loyal customers before its patent runs out. Or a utility might try to build goodwill to reduce consumer opposition to future requests for rate increases.

Sometimes the marketing environment changes, and organizations can help to bring about such change. For example, although produce has traditionally been sold in a purely competitive market, some large sellers have begun putting their name on prepared fresh vegetables. Pillsbury has tried distributing cleaned and trimmed asparagus, broccoli, cauliflower, and two vegetable mixtures under its Green Giant name. Kraft Inc. has introduced a line of cut and packaged vegetables it calls VegiSnax. One industry observer forecasts that branded produce will

Figure 3.1   Lipton Salad Sensations!

eventually account for half of all produce sales.[4] Figure 3.1 shows an advertisement for another product developed to appeal to the branding of salad items.

The Legal and Political Environments

One of the strongest forces that marketing decision makers must face is the **legal environment.** It consists of laws and interpretations of laws that compel business to operate under competitive conditions and to observe various consumer rights.

Legal Environment
Laws that compel businesses to operate under competitive conditions and to observe specified consumer rights.

Legislation Regulating Business

Procompetitive Legislation Laws that sustain and protect competition.

Political and economic thinking in Canada and the United States assumes that the economy benefits from competition among many firms. Presumably, then, the public benefits from laws that protect competition. These laws are called **procompetitive legislation.**

In the United States procompetitive laws date from the late 1800s. The Sherman Antitrust Act, passed in 1890, forbids monopolies or attempts to form monopolies. Other American legislation prohibits price fixing and bid rigging, as well as boycotts and mergers within the same industry that would lessen competition.

Procompetitive laws in Canada can be traced to earlier legislation in Great Britain. In 1889, the Canadian government passed the Combines Investigation Act to regulate monopolies. Today the Department of Consumer and Corporate Affairs (CCA) administers a wide range of legislation. The department was created in 1967 to bring under one roof all legislation relating to business and consumers. Table 3.1 lists the major legislation affecting business for which the department is responsible. Of particular interest here are those laws governing competition.

Within the CCA are four distinct bureaus. One, the Bureau of Competition Policy, has specific responsibility for the Competition Act. This act provides for the investigation and prosecution of combines in restraint of trade, mergers, and monopolies detrimental to the public interest, and anticompetitive behaviour such as price discrimination, misleading advertising, and price fixing.

Regulatory Forces

Marketing decisions are greatly influenced by the many laws affecting competition. The enforcement of the laws, in turn, is affected by the

Table 3.1 Major Canadian Legislation Relating to Competition and Consumer Protection

- Competition Act
- Canadian Corporations Act
- Canadian Cooperative Associations Act
- Bankruptcy Act (and bankruptcy rules)
- Bank Cost of Borrowing Regulations
- Boards of Trade Act
- Copyright Act
- Hazardous Products Act
- Industrial Design Act
- Foods and Drugs Act
- Canadian Care Labelling Program
- Consumer Packaging and Labelling Act and Regulations
- Textile Labelling Act and Advertising Regulations
- Canada Standard Sizes Program
- Weights and Measures Act

prevailing political climate and by public opinion. The priorities of governmental and nongovernmental regulatory forces are subject to change. Marketers must be constantly alert to subtle shifts in public and political attitudes toward business in general and their products in particular.

Governmental Regulatory Forces

Businesses in Canada have to contend with regulatory forces at all levels of government; federal, provincial, and municipal.

Federal regulations, for example, control access to the airwaves for radio and television, require bilingual labelling that makes various disclosures about the contents, and hazards of a product, and limit the advertising of products such as alcohol and tobacco (see Marketing Today 3.1). Provisions of the Competition Act guard consumers against a variety of practices:

- Misleading advertising.

- Unsubstantiated claims.

- Misleading warranties.

- Misleading price representations.

- Untrue and misleading tests and testimonials.

- Double ticketing.

- Pyramid selling schemes.

Marketing Today 3.1

Politics and the Sale of Liquor in Canada

The sale of liquor in Canada can, at best, be confusing as one travels across the country. In British Columbia, beer and wine are sold in private stores next to hotels, as well as in government-run outlets. In Alberta, hotel operators can sell cold beer on hotel parking lots. In BC and Ontario, licensed agents are allowed to sell liquor in general stores in remote communities, and wineries are permitted to open their own stores.

For years Canadians have had a limited selection of liquor as governments have collected hefty taxes. Quebec is well known for brisk sales of beer and wine in corner stores — an idea that can't seem to get off the ground in the rest of Canada. Today the various provincial regulators that control the sale of liquor have realized that with consumption of alcoholic drinks sliding, a major revamping of stores is needed to keep generating much-needed revenue.

In response, the government stores have adopted some marketing techniques from the private sector:

- New Brunswick and Nova Scotia allow liquor companies to hand out coupons, run contests, and discount products.

- Suppliers vie for the chance to get front-of-aisle displays.

- Tastings and even wine consultations are on the rise.

- A number of provinces offer free magazine-style publications, giving tips on cocktail recipes or wine and food combinations.

Source: Adapted from Marina Strauss, ''Time for Private Liquor Stores,'' *The Globe and Mail*, November 30, 1989, p. B8.

- Bait-and-switch selling.
- Sales above advertised prices.
- Promotional contests.

The Director of Investigation and Research of the Bureau of Competition Policy ensures that these regulations are enforced in a fair, effective, and timely manner. Compliance is encouraged by an extensive information and education program and by the fact that business has an advisory role in regulation-setting. Moreover, companies can seek an opinion from the Bureau as to whether proposed business plans would bring them into conflict with the Act—for example, they can request an assessment of promotional and advertising material before it is used.

In addition to the laws just discussed, many actions at the federal level have a profound effect on business. For example, Bank of Canada decisions determine interest rates and affect the economy as a whole. These fiscal initiatives affect the ability of business to obtain capital and the mood of consumer spending.

Political Influences Affecting Regulation

Many regulatory agencies are technically independent, but they are greatly influenced by the political party in office. Often, when a new government takes office, high-level members of various agencies resign. Since the cabinet or a ministry is responsible for appointing new members, it has a strong influence on the subsequent behaviour of government agencies.

Cost-Benefit Analysis
System for weighing economic costs against economic benefits.

Other political and economic factors also influence the power these agencies command. When Jimmy Carter was president of the United States, for example, spiralling inflation was one of that country's chief economic concerns. After listening to critics who claimed that regulations, like those enforcing standards for pollution control, added significantly to consumer costs, he initiated the use of **cost-benefit analysis** as a way of weighing economic costs against economic benefits. Such an analysis might seek to compare the cost of a factory's new air-quality equipment with the cost society might have to bear if it were not installed and workers subsequently became ill because of job-related pollutants. Under Carter's successor, Ronald Reagan, deregulation was a priority. In the different political climate of the Reagan administration, many laws were revised or revoked. As a result, marketers faced a different set of choices for developing and selling products.

To be aware of all marketing opportunities while avoiding the consequences of violating the law, marketers must keep a careful watch over government actions, both in and out of the courts.

Industry Self-Regulation

Many industries in Canada and the United States have formed self-regulatory bodies to oversee the activities of their members. The motives for forming such groups range from an attempt to ward off possible government regulations to the hope of establishing a favourable image for the industry in the public mind. The few named here are of special interest to marketers.

The *Canadian Advertising Foundation* was founded in 1981 with the goal of increasing public understanding of the role of advertising and supporting industry standards and codes of ethics. The Foundation is an umbrella organization that includes four other groups: the Canadian Advertising Advisory Board (CAAB), the Advertising Standards Council (ASC), la Confédération générale de la publicité (COGEP), and le Conseil des normes de la publicité (CNP). CAAB (nationally) and COGEP (in Quebec) administer guidelines on sex-role stereotyping, work with multicultural groups, lobby the Quebec government to lift restrictions on advertising, and generate media public relations programs extolling the benefits of advertising. ASC and CNP administer and publicize industry standards and codes of ethics, resolve consumer complaints about advertising, generate and administer guidelines for food commercials, and provide preclearance procedures for broadcast commercials in socially sensitive areas such as advertising to children.

The *Council of Better Business Bureaus* (CBBB) is an international association of national and local businesses whose goal is to ensure consumer confidence in the marketplace. The council has offices in more than 130 cities, where it tries to mediate between consumers and businesses. The bureaus operate largely through the voluntary co-operation of their members and have little real enforcement ability. Consumers may, however, contact their local bureau to determine if a particular business is known to be reputable.

The Social Environment

Social Environment
Climate of public opinion that affects marketers' practices.

You switch on your new stereo, only to discover that one of the speakers doesn't work. Your pants shrink two sizes the first time you wash them. You call three banks to find out where your savings will get the best return but can't make sense of what the bank's representatives tell you. How do you feel in situations like these? Many consumers have come to believe that they have a right to expect more from the suppliers of goods and services.

The Rise of Consumerism

Chapter 1 discussed the rise of consumerism, the social movement that increased the powers and rights of buyers. One of the major causes of consumerism was increased education and income in the 1960s; consumers bought more, were disappointed more often, and were better able to express their frustrations. Another cause was greater complexity of products, making an informed choice difficult. At the same time, consumers found it especially important to make informed choices as the inflation of the 1960s and 1970s eroded their buying power. Finally, writers and activists, such as Rachel Carson and Ralph Nader, drew North Americans' attention to environmental and consumer issues.

Many politicians were quick to sense a potential vote-getting issue. In 1962, U.S. President John Kennedy articulated a "consumer bill of rights." It noted the obligation of the government to protect the consumer's right to safety, information, freedom of choice, and the ability to be heard. The rights he listed corresponded closely to specific complaints consumers were voicing about marketing practices. Today, consumerism is less popular as a political issue, but it still carries weight.

Marketing Abuses — and Responses

Consumers voice most of their dissatisfaction in four areas. They are most concerned about (1) deficiencies in product quality, (2) lack of information, (3) unfair pricing practices, and (4) environmental pollution.[5]

Product Quality

Consumers are concerned about the quality of the goods they buy and the quality of the services that accompany those goods. They complain that many products are unsafe, impure, or defective. They complain that it is nearly impossible to get honest and competent repairs.

Many types of services have been the target of consumer complaints. Marketers have had to face the challenge of trying to balance price and service to find a satisfactory mix. For example, in the States the price cutting that has followed deregulation in the airline industry has led airlines to increase their overbooking of seats. As a result, passengers are more likely to be bumped from flights.

In stores, customers complain about the difficulty in finding helpful salespeople. Sears grouped its salesclerks around cash registers to speed up the check-out process, reducing the number of employees who were in store aisles to answer questions. The decline in service led Sears to reevaluate its decision, and it has since put more people on the sales floor. Other common complaints about service involve banks that discourage small accounts, gas stations that no longer sell service along with gas, and doctors who no longer have time to talk to patients.[6]

With regard to deficiencies in the quality of goods, Ralph Nader's report on defective cars was one of the first major exposés. But automobiles have not been the only culprits. At about the same time as Nader's report, one U.S. government agency reported that 20 million Americans each year required medical treatment for accidents resulting from faulty products. The news media have told many stories of product hazards: cancer-causing food additives, highly flammable children's clothing, radiation seepage from colour televisions and computer screens, and many others.

Both the federal and provincial governments have laws and regulations designed to protect the consumer's right to safe products, especially where individuals would find it difficult to judge for themselves the risk involved in using a product. The Food and Drug Act, for example, closely regulates the manufacture, distribution, and sale of food, drug, and cosmetic products. The Hazardous Products Act requires that the labelling and packaging of dangerous products be clear and as safe as possible. This law gives the power to remove or **recall** unsafe products from the marketplace. The power to recall is the government's ultimate weapon. Recalls are expensive. Therefore, most companies are now spending more money on product testing before marketing.

Recall
Power of certain government agencies to require manufacturers to notify customers that a product may be hazardous and may be exchanged or repaired.

Market Information

As our society grows ever more complex, the consumer's right to information needed to make intelligent buying decisions has been protected by both federal and provincial laws. This *right to be informed* is covered by various pieces of legislation including the Consumer Packaging and Labelling Act, the Textile Labelling Act, and the Canada Standard Sizes program.

Under the Consumer Packaging and Labelling Act, a comprehensive set of rules ensures that full and factual information is provided on product labels and limits packaging deception or fraud by restricting misleading descriptions and nonfunctional "fill" in packages. This legislation requires that all prepackaged products have, on the main panel of the package, in English and in French, a prominent display of the commodity's common name as well as a quantity declaration in metric units of weight, volume, or length.

The Textile Labelling Act requires manufacturers to label articles made from fabrics. These labels tell the consumer the types of fibres used and the percentage of each in the fabric; they also identify the company for whom or by whom the product was made. In addition, most textile products sold in Canada carry care labels to guide the consumer in cleaning items (see Figure 3.2). Children's clothing also requires labelling under the Canada Standard Size Program which ensures the consumer that different manufacturers use uniform sizing. The program is voluntary, so there is no guarantee that every textile product will be labelled.

Besides regulators, competitors give marketers a reason to be careful that their advertising is factual. In the makeup business, Maybelline has disputed Noxell's claim that its Cover Girl Clean Lash mascara is waterproof. Charging false advertising, Maybelline won a court order halting shipments and ads for the mascara. An appeals court then issued a temporary stay of the order, but Maybelline took the case back to court.[7] Court battles are expensive, so advertisers do well to avoid leaving themselves open to such challenges.

Pricing

It might seem that price is one element of the marketing mix that has to be clear to buyers. However, when financing enters the picture, consumers can become confused. Different ways of stating the interest rate

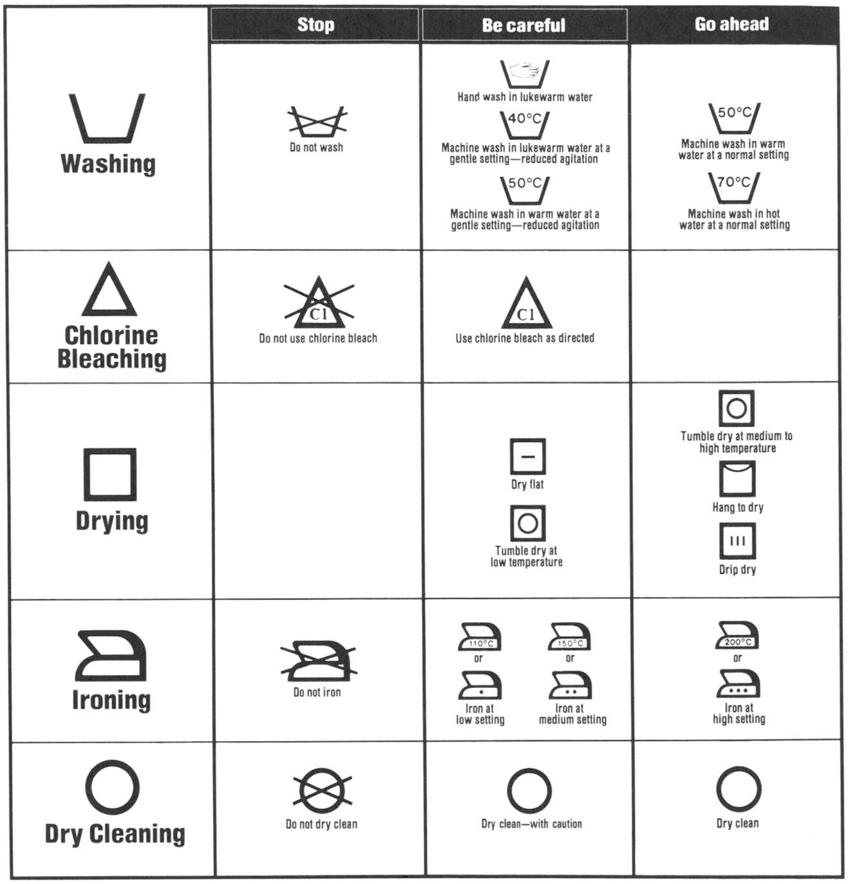

	Stop	Be careful	Go ahead
Washing	Do not wash	Hand wash in lukewarm water / 40°C Machine wash in lukewarm water at a gentle setting—reduced agitation / 50°C Machine wash in warm water at a gentle setting—reduced agitation	50°C Machine wash in warm water at a normal setting / 70°C Machine wash in hot water at a normal setting
Chlorine Bleaching	Do not use chlorine bleach	Cl Use chlorine bleach as directed	
Drying		Dry flat / Tumble dry at low temperature	Tumble dry at medium to high temperature / Hang to dry / Drip dry
Ironing	Do not iron	110°C or Iron at low setting / 150°C or Iron at medium setting	200°C or Iron at high setting
Dry Cleaning	Do not dry clean	Dry clean—with caution	Dry clean

Consumer and Corporate Affairs Canada

Figure 3.2 The Labelling of Textiles

for credit cards or credit plans can make it nearly impossible for someone who is not a financial expert to determine the actual cost of a product. A television purchased for a seemingly reasonable monthly interest rate could turn out to be outrageously expensive when the interest rate is stated on a yearly basis. Consumers' problems are compounded when businesses deny credit unfairly or debt collectors harass those who have fallen behind in their payments. When marketers are planning advertising messages, they must make sure that any information about financing complies with the truth-in-lending laws and regulations.

Environmental Pollution

Marketers have been accused of contributing to pollution in a number of ways. They have prepared advertising to bolster the image of companies that damage the environment by dumping industrial by-products into the air and water. They have introduced products with injurious environmental effects, such as fluorocarbon sprays that damage the upper atmosphere's ability to filter out certain harmful rays. Sometimes a product that is not harmful has damaging side effects. Plastic wrappings and nonreturnable bottles, for example, both contribute to the solid waste problem.

As the public has become more aware of the environment and the need to avoid dirty air, mountains of garbage, and depletion of the ozone layer, businesses have reacted by cleaning up their products. Companies cannot afford to ignore the problem. Indeed, marketers can contribute to the solution by weighing environmental concerns in product and packaging design.

This focus with the environment has resulted in a trend commonly referred to as *green marketing*. Gallup Canada asked 1000 adults a series of questions about their environmental concerns. The survey showed deep regard and a resulting willingness to change buying habits. This concern for the environment was highest among consumers aged 18 to 34 (90 percent said they'd pay more for environmentally safe products) and weakest among those ages 55 and older (85 percent).[8] The Lever Brothers ad for Sunlight detergent in Figure 3.3 reflects the use of environmental themes in advertising.

Special Interest Consumer Groups

In addition to the governmental agencies charged with the responsibility of protecting consumers, various special interest groups have arisen to inform the public of consumer issues and to exert pressure on business and government.

In Canada, the major organization representing consumers is the Consumers' Association of Canada (CAC). Dating back to 1947, the CAC represents the views of consumers to government. In the United States, the Consumers Union provides its subscribers and the public with product information on everything from antiperspirants to yogurt, and Action for Children's Television works to eliminate commercial abuses in programming targeted to children. Many other organizations lobby or disseminate information about particular areas of concern.

Beyond Laws: Social Responsibility

Marketing departments need to be aware of the company's reputation for responding to consumer and environmental issues. Heightened consumer awareness gives rise to a need for marketing that keeps consumers informed about the company's positive actions.

Another reason businesses must keep the concerns of consumer groups in mind is that they have a **social responsibility** for their actions. Managers must consider the effects of their decisions on the external world so as to accomplish social benefits as well as traditional economic ones.[9]

Social responsibility begins where the law ends. For example, the law requires fines for certain pollution-causing activities, such as dumping chemicals into waterways, but is silent about others, such as overpack-

Social Responsibility
Moral obligation of businesses to consider the effects of their decisions on society and to accomplish social benefits.

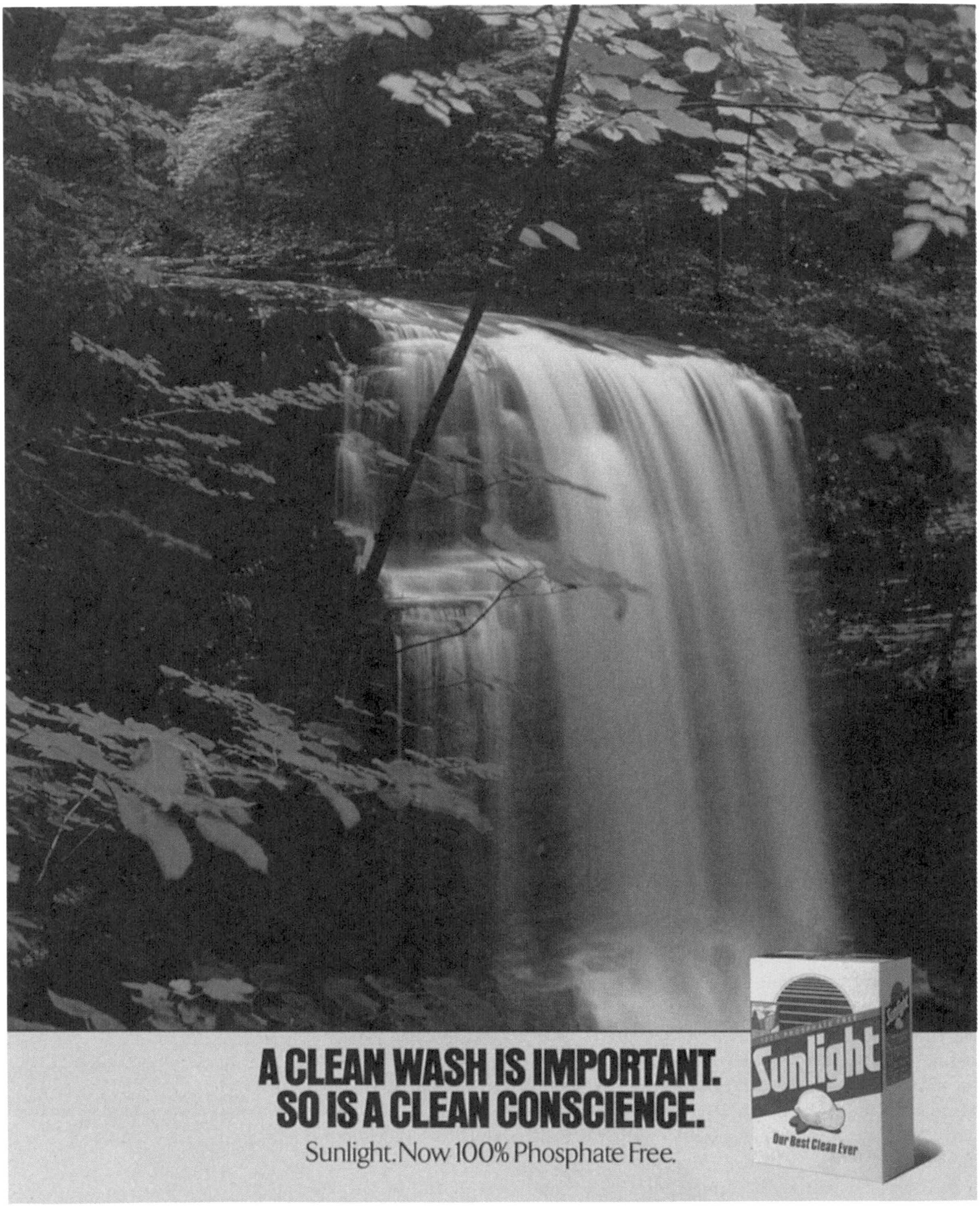
A CLEAN WASH IS IMPORTANT.
SO IS A CLEAN CONSCIENCE.
Sunlight. Now 100% Phosphate Free.
Sunlight
Our Best Clean Ever

Lever Brothers, Toronto

Figure 3.3 Sunlight Laundry Detergent

aging, which contributes to solid waste. A firm guilty of wasteful packaging is acting within the law, though some would question whether it is acting in a socially responsible way.

Like many business decisions, choosing to be socially responsible involves a trade-off. Social responsibility costs money, but it also creates goodwill, which can lead to more business.

Responses of Individual Firms

One organization that has committed resources to social responsibility is General Electric. Corporate officers are assigned responsibility for designing safety features into the products they want to market. To ensure that customers know about these features and the safe use of the firm's products, the company publishes safety tips for the home appliance user. The major complaint against appliance manufacturers is that repair service is difficult to secure. GE has removed many of the restrictions and clarified the legal language in its warranty statements.[10]

Other companies have instituted consumer hot lines with toll-free 800 numbers so that consumers with complaints or requests for information can be more readily in touch with the product's manufacturer.

Procter & Gamble claims to be a toll-free number pioneer, having experimented with the use of one in 1974 for Duncan Hines Brownie Mix. Today, nearly every P&G product has its own number. By 1983, P&G was logging more than 450 000 phone calls a year. (The question most asked: What makes Ivory soap float? The answer: All the air it contains.)[11]

While ingredient labelling is now required on all packaged foods, some companies have voluntarily chosen to furnish consumers with even more information than the law stipulates. The label on Sugar-Free Kool-Aid, for example, explains why each ingredient is included; it also gives information on the artificial sweetener it contains.

Other businesses sponsor consumer panels to alert them to the issues that concern their customers. The Bay, a large retail chain owned by the Hudson Bay Company, has operated a consumer panel for a number of years. It advises the store management in each local market area on a range of issues including changing consumer preferences and reactions to proposed merchandise selections.

These few examples show that socially responsible actions often pay for themselves. They also may generate a positive image in the public's mind. Good corporate citizenship is also good business.

Consumer Responsibility

Government can pass laws and businesses can supply product information, but eventually it is a **consumer's responsibility** to know his or her rights and to make an informed judgement based on the information provided. Mandating seat belts will not stop highway deaths if consumers do not use them. Instituting a cooling-off rule, which allows a consumer to change his or her mind after buying something from a door-to-

Consumer Responsibility
Buyers' obligation to know their rights and to make informed judgements.

door salesperson, has no effect if consumers do not know about it.

Consumer leaders such as Ralph Nader have suggested that instead of demanding more legislation to secure rights, consumers must now do more for themselves. The laws at present offer consumers substantial protection. According to consumer activists, citizens could take better advantage of those laws if they used the courts more frequently, were better educated about their rights, and participated more directly in

Table 3.2 How Well Do You Know Your Consumer Rights?

Answer true or false to each of these statements.

1. **False or Deceptive Advertising**
   A children's commercial for toy race cars that exaggerates the speed of the cars is *legal*.

2. **False or Deceptive Retail Advertising**
   It is *not legal* to advertise a low-priced item and then only stock enough for the first few customers who enter the store.

3. **Credit Regulations**
   It is *legal* to deny a female student a credit card on the basis of her sex.

4. **Credit Reporting**
   If you have been denied credit, you have the *legal* right to know the nature and substance of the information (except medical) collected about you by a credit reporting agency.

5. **Door-to-Door Selling**
   A door-to-door salesperson is *not legally* required to furnish the purchaser with a fully completed contract until 24 hours after the sale has taken place.

6. **Automobile Sales**
   When selling a car it is *not legal* to turn the odometer (distance meter) back on the car to show that the vehicle has fewer kilometres on it than it actually has been driven.

7. **Credit Cards**
   You are *legally* responsible for a credit card mailed to you that you did not request.

8. **Labelling**
   A manufacturer that produces merchandise subject to cleaning, such as clothing, is *legally* required to have a label in plain sight that tells the consumer how the product is to be laundered or dry cleaned.

9. **Truth in Lending**
   Retail stores are *legally* required to state the true interest rate and other costs of credit transactions.

10. **Deceptive Retail Practices**
    It is *legal* for a store to tell you that you have won a free gift of an oil painting if you have to pay $15.00 for the frame to receive the gift.

Correct Responses

1. False; 2. True; 3. False; 4. True; 5. False; 6. True; 7. False; 8. False; 9. True; 10. False

Source: William H. Cunningham and Isabella C. M. Cunningham, ''Consumer Protection: More Information or More Regulation?'' *Journal of Marketing,* April 1976, p. 65.

regulating businesses. How well do you know your consumer rights? Take the quiz in Table 3.2 to see how well you are informed.

The Economic Environment

Chapter 2 pointed out that the economy is an important factor in the marketing environment. In fact, an analysis of the general, or macro, environment is as important as an examination of the operating environment. One top corporate official noted, "The chief executive has to watch out for the killing variable in the external world that can change everything for his company."[12]

The killing variable can be any number of things. Many firms are keeping a close eye on the fluctuation of the dollar's value abroad. When the Canadian dollar rises in value, the price of Canadian exports also rises, making it more difficult to sell Canadian goods and services in foreign markets. A decline in the value of the Canadian dollar improves our ability to compete in international markets and makes Canada a more attractive country to visit, particularly for American tourists.

Other important variables in the macroeconomic environment are interest rates and inflation. When, for example, interest rates are low compared to inflation, students may be more likely to borrow money to pay their tuition. As a result, they might have more money available to spend on hamburgers or movies.

Such changes in economic conditions can dramatically influence business plans. Because the influence of the economy on marketing is so important, it will be considered more closely here to see how changes may affect market planning.

Economic Cycles

The economies of the industrialized nations go through a recurring cycle of boom and bust. The full cycle consists of four phases: **prosperity, recession, depression,** and **recovery.**

1. *Prosperity:* a period of generally high income, employment, and business growth.

2. *Recession:* a phase of decreasing income, employment, and growth rate.

3. *Depression:* a radical drop in business activity and consequent high unemployment and business failure.

4. *Recovery:* an upswing characterized by a gradual rise in business and consumer economic well-being.

Economic cycles rarely occur in a neat pattern. Even skilled analysts have trouble predicting how long any one cycle will last or what cycles will follow the current one. In the 1950s and 1960s, for example, both the Canadian and the American economies went through an extended

Prosperity
Period in business cycle of generally high income, employment, and business growth.

Recession
Phase of the business cycle characterized by decreasing income, employment, and growth rate.

Depression
Phase of the business cycle characterized by a radical drop in business activity and consequent high unemployment and business failure.

Recovery
Upswing in the business cycle characterized by a gradual rise in business and consumer economic well-being.

period of prosperity. Income rose nearly 70 percent, the unemployment rate was low, and the gross domestic product nearly doubled. In Canada, personal income per capita increased 90 percent over the period 1960 to 1970. Many economists expected that when the bubble burst in the early 1970s (with the oil crisis), the economy would slump into a recession and then a deep depression. In fact, throughout the decade, the economy fluctuated between recession and recovery without experiencing either prosperity or depression.

Although marketers cannot know exactly how long a phase will last or how to predict the onset of a new phase, they must plan to meet changes. Some economic indicators (such as the Wholesale Price Index and the rate of new construction) provide clues to the future. Marketing plans can be adjusted accordingly.

Economic downswings introduce a note of caution into marketing. In the recessionary 1970s, not only did the rate of new-product development slow, but the variety of products was cut back. For example, General Electric dropped the marketing of blenders, fans, heaters, humidifiers, and vacuum cleaners, and Philco eliminated 40 percent of its refrigerator models.[13]

The recession brought changes in other marketing areas as well. Some companies trimmed their sales forces and hired in their place less costly independent wholesalers. In other cases, advertising budgets were increased to stimulate demand, or the advertising messages themselves were changed to emphasize more economical products. (An old product, Bisquick, a multipurpose baking mix, made a major comeback.) Finally, some companies offered special low prices to encourage buying; for example, automakers and small appliance manufacturers offered rebates (or money back) for immediate purchase.

In periods of prosperity and recovery, marketing managers generally pursue growth-related objectives. They may introduce new products, increase advertising expenditures, hire additional salespeople, or add to the number of outlets through which products are sold. It was no accident that many of the goods and services we enjoy today — contact lenses, cassette recorders, one-hour dry cleaning, permanent press clothing — were commercialized in the prosperous 1960s. The era also saw a noticeable increase in the number of workers in marketing as well as in the number of retail outlets.

During the first half of the 1980s, the economy expanded much more slowly than in the 1960s. Companies had to pay special attention to the competition, because their own growth often had to come from competitors' share of the market. At one time it looked as if IBM couldn't lose in the rapidly growing market for personal computers, but in 1986 the company's earnings declined as it lost market share. One competitor making inroads was Compaq Computer Corp., which grew to Fortune-500 size in less than five years by making IBM-compatible computers with slight improvements and a lower price tag. Compaq introduced a personal computer that runs at twice the speed of IBM's AT and is as powerful as a minicomputer (a type of computer that costs considerably more). Slower growth in the microcomputer market means that the success of Compaq's new model can hurt IBM's performance.[14]

Consumer Spending

The state of the country's economic health greatly influences what marketing strategy a company might pursue. But it is not enough for a marketer simply to know when the country shows signs of slipping into a recession, or when it has finally moved over the arbitrary line marking the difference between recovery and full-fledged prosperity. More important than the economic cycle itself is how consumers are spending whatever funds they have during a given period.

Consumer spending has been called the nation's number one leading business indicator. Industries as diverse as metalworking, housing, and insurance keep a close watch on it because it accounts for nearly two-thirds of the spending power in the Canadian economy. Often the level of consumer spending is a barometer to industry of just what direction the economy is heading. For example, in October 1982, the U.S. was in the grip of a serious recession. Nonetheless, American consumers in that month outspent the rise in their personal incomes three times over. Analysts, noting the upturn in the consumer's willingness to spend, correctly began predicting that the recession was bottoming out.[15]

In addition to watching the amount of consumer spending, marketers must pay close attention to how those dollars are being used. Economists — and marketers — distinguish between two kinds of income. **Disposable income** is that amount of money remaining in a person's wallet after taxes are paid. A person's **discretionary income** is what remains after a person has paid for food, shelter, clothing, and other basic necessities. This money is what consumers use to buy furniture, automobiles, appliances, and vacations.

Changing Patterns in Family Income

Marketers need to know not only how much money consumers have but also how the income is distributed among families and who is spending it. Marketers use this information in targeting market segments and in planning how to use the marketing mix.

Between 1961 and 1986, the average household size in Canada decreased significantly, from just less than 4.0 persons per household in 1961 to 2.8 in 1986. (It is expected to fall to 2.4 by the year 2000.) This decline in the size of the average household was matched by a large increase in the percentage of one-person households: from 10 percent of all households in 1961 to 21.5 percent in 1986. Today Canadians live in a vast variety of family forms, and single-parent families are increasing at a faster pace than husband-wife families.[16]

Inflation has made it seem that almost everyone's income was rising quickly over the past 25 years, but the actual buying power of households has wobbled. For example, the average real income of a Canadian family with only one working parent did grow in the late 1960s and early 1970s

Disposable Income
Any money that remains after taxes are paid.

Discretionary Income
Any money remaining from disposable income that a family or individual is free to spend for luxuries or save.

but there was no real growth after 1975.[17] In 1988, a two-parent, one-earner family in Canada had virtually the same real income ($37 351) as it had in 1980 ($37 449).

To complicate matters, the gap between the haves and the have-nots is widening in Canada. In 1988, a family with two wage earners had an average income of $51 780, while the average for a single-parent family headed by a female wage earner was $19 740. Single Canadians averaged $19 608. Families headed by university graduates had an average income of $67 071. The upper 20 percent of Canadian families — those with incomes of more than $64 871 — received 39.2 percent of all family income, while the lowest 20 percent — those with incomes of less than $22 006 — received 6.5 percent. Overall average family income also varied considerably by province: from a high of $52 764 in Ontario to a low of $34 535 in Prince Edward Island.[18]

In marketers' minds, the key question is how households will choose to spend what income they have. Will they choose to live in the city or the suburbs? Will they spend their money on fast food or fast cars? What kind of furniture will they buy, and how will they outfit baby? The implications of buyer behaviour are explored in future chapters. To a marketer, economic and demographic changes are vitally important.

The Technological Environment

As recently as the 1970s, a student in a technical field might spend about $100 to buy a pocket calculator that could add, subtract, multiply, and divide. For the same price today, that student can purchase a small calculator that can automatically perform almost 100 functions and even be programmed for specialized tasks. Many students today also spend some time using a personal computer or the school's mainframe computer. And almost everyone has an inexpensive pocket calculator for balancing the chequebook or computing percentages.

Today we take for granted not only calculators but many products that were unimaginable only decades or years ago—stereos and compact disc equipment, videocassette recorders, watches that wake us up as well as tell time, and 24-hour access to cash through automated teller machines. These products are the result of technological developments—changes that even influence things from the past. (See Figure 3.4.)

Technology applies science to the solution of practical problems. It has enormous implications for our everyday lives, and its growth and direction are often unpredictable. This makes the technological environment vitally important for marketers but also extremely difficult to plan for. Companies have shot to the top of their industries or gone under because of changes in the state of technology. Bruce Culver saw a demand for people with technical expertise and started Lab Support, a business that provides high-tech temporary help: scientists, engineers, programmers, technical writers, and technicians. The business has grown three- to fivefold annually; by 1987 about 75 000 temporary employees were reporting to work at oil refineries, drug companies,

Technology
Application of principles of science to the solution of practical problems.

Figure 3.4 Today's Technology Influences Sounds from the Past

analytic chemistry labs, and other companies.[19]

There is no sounder way to gain a differential advantage over competitors than to come up with a technologically superior product. Photocopying is now synonymous with the name Xerox and instant pictures with Polaroid because those companies were the first to exploit an advance in technology. Product advances give a company only a temporary advantage, however. Kodak has challenged Polaroid in the instant picture market, and Canon, Hewlett-Packard, and Toshiba have gained a share of the market for photocopiers.

The most important technological advance of recent times has been the development of semiconductors — tiny silicon chips now found in everything from wristwatches to microwave ovens and space shuttles. Advances in this field turn largely on the development of ways of packing ever-greater amounts of information on the little chips and in devising ways to process that information more quickly.

At one time, the United States was clearly in the forefront of computer technology, but Japan has made inroads. In 1986, the U.S. Commerce Department became so concerned about Japanese companies' low prices and increasing sales that it negotiated a trade agreement with Japan's Ministry of International Trade and Industry. As a result of the agreement, prices of microchips rose rapidly.[20] One observer predicts that for the foreseeable future, U.S. companies will dominate the market for specialized microprocessors but will lose share to the Japanese in high-volume parts, where the Japanese benefit from greater production effectiveness.[21]

Computers are leading a revolution in the technological environment. By the year 2000 the electronics industry, which is already a $300-billion-a-year business, is expected to more than triple in sales to become the world's biggest business except for agriculture.[22] In addition, technology is bringing dramatic changes in the life sciences, the development of advanced materials, and the use of particles of light (called photons) to speed data processing.

While no one can be certain where these developments will lead, their influence is certain to extend beyond high-tech companies. Many students of today will be joining the work force as employees of the companies that bring about or are affected by technological developments. Those who enter the field of marketing will have a special role in bringing together new products and the users who can benefit from them.

Chapter Replay

1. **What are the general categories of competitive markets?**
   Competitive markets fall into four general categories: pure competition, oligopoly, monopolistic competition, and monopoly.

2. **How can marketers respond to the competition in each of these markets?**
   Marketers facing pure competition seek to ensure a wide distribution of their product at a fair price. In an oligopoly, marketers try to avoid price wars and use other elements of the marketing mix to distinguish their products. In monopolistic competition, marketers try to establish a differential advantage. In a monopoly, marketers establish strategies based on company or government objectives.

3. **How does the government protect fair competition?**
   The government protects fair competition through federal laws, beginning with the Competition Act, as well as through investigation and prosecution by the Director of Investigations, Bureau of Competition.

4. **How does the government protect consumers?**
   The Hazardous Products Act, the Food and Drug Act, and similar legislation provide the power to set safety standards and take action against companies that fail to meet those standards.

5. **What are some ways in which industries regulate themselves?**
   The member organizations of the Canadian Advertising Foundation prescreen sensitive advertising and monitor a code of ethics. The Council of Better Business Bureaus strives to ensure consumer confidence in the marketplace.

6. **What issues must marketers address in responding to the social environment?**
   Marketers must address consumer dissatisfaction about deficiencies in product quality, lack of information for making informed judgements, unfair pricing practices, and environmental pollution.

7. **What responsibilities do producers and consumers have?**
   Businesses have a social responsibility to consider the effects of their decisions on the external world. Consumers are responsible for knowing their rights and making informed judgements based on the information provided.

8. **How can marketers respond to changes in the economic environment?**
   Marketers can respond to economic downswings with cautious strategies and cutbacks, with advertising designed to stimulate demand, or with emphasis on low price. During more prosperous times, marketers can emphasize growth-related objectives. Changing patterns in disposable income also may affect marketing strategies.

9. **How can marketers respond to changes in the technological environment?**
   Marketers can follow technological developments closely in order to prepare for actions by competitors and to learn of opportunities for using new developments to gain a differential advantage.

Key Terms

consumer responsibility	**prosperity**
cost-benefit analysis	**pure competition**
depression	**recall**
discretionary income	**recession**
disposable income	**recovery**
legal environment	**social environment**
monopolistic competition	**social responsibility**
monopoly	**technology**
oligopoly	
procompetitive legislation	

1. Every day at supermarkets and convenience stores, many shoppers select breakfast cereals from among the wide variety offered. What term describes the competitive market for breakfast cereals? How do companies compete in this market? Name a few products besides cold cereal that provide competition for cereal makers.

2. In which types of competitive markets might a new competitor be able to influence the price of a product? Explain your answer.

3. What practices are prohibited by legislation in Canada? How does the Department of Consumer and Corporate Affairs help to protect competition?

4. In each of the following situations, how can industry self-regulatory bodies help you?

   a. You are planning to buy a television at a local discount store, and you want to know whether the business is reputable.

   b. You hear on the radio about a new brand of yogurt that contains twice the calcium of the major brands. You drive to the store, only to discover that this new brand contains twice the calcium merely because the carton is twice the size.

   c. You dislike getting advertising mail and want to have your name removed from as many mailing lists as possible.

5. The rise of consumerism has led the public to express dissatisfaction when companies fall short in four major areas. How can businesses respond to these consumer issues?

6. What is the role of the Director of Investigations and Research of the Bureau of Competition Policy?

7. How do marketers adjust their strategies to times of economic prosperity? To times of economic recession?

8. How does disposable income differ from discretionary income? Why is this difference important to marketers?

9. Al Goodman runs an amusement park about 30 kilometres from a metropolitan area in Saskatchewan. In the last couple of years, Al has noticed that business has fallen off somewhat. He wants to plan a marketing strategy to persuade more people to visit the park. What are some patterns of consumer spending and family income that Al should take into account in devising his strategy?

10. "Why are you reading about high technology in a marketing class?" Burt asked Lisa. "That's for engineers and computer programmers." Why do marketers need to keep abreast of technological developments?

Weight-Loss Schemes

In recent years the trend toward health and fitness has cut across most demographic and economic segments of our society. The Participaction program has seen average Canadians increase their participation in activities from power walking to yoga. Stores supply an amazing range of exercise equipment, and the number of service organizations catering to this trend has multiplied dramatically in the last five years.

Paralleling the physical fitness movement has been a significant change in our eating patterns. Canadians now want to "eat healthy." Eating for weight control is at the top of their list. Supermarkets have hundreds of new good-for-you foods ranging from light mayonnaise to light frozen pizza.

The Weight-Loss Industry

At the centre of this healthy Canadian movement is the phenomenon of seeking weight loss. With almost half of Canadians struggling with being overweight, a huge marketing opportunity has been identified and seized by a number of players including diet centres, weight-loss counselling centres, and exercise and fitness centres. The reality is that 95 of 100 who lose weight on a diet gain it back. This fact creates the marketing opportunity of the century: the chance to sell the same programs to the same people over and over again.

One result has been the wide range of weight-loss schemes that have been promoted across the country. Some relate to general weight loss, others to localized weight loss, and still others to toning of muscles for a firmer figure.

Complaints about Advertising

The weight-loss industry has aggressively marketed itself with a wide range of claims that have often brought firms into conflict with the law.

Source: Prepared by Professor Don Shiner, Mount Saint Vincent University, based on information contained in *Misleading Advertising Bulletin* no. 2, 1989, pp. 1–2.

The legal cases described here include *R.* v. *Allan Diamond*, Toronto, Ontario, unreported decision, February 7, 1983; *R.* v. *Nature Femme Inc. and Diane Pothier*, Montreal, Quebec, unreported decision, July 16, 1986, and *R.* v. *The Great Shape-Up Inch Loss Centre Inc., carrying on business as the Great Shape-Up*, London, Ontario, unreported decision, May 25, 1983; *R.* v. *Terence Filion, carrying on business as Professional Inch Loss Clinic*, Toronto, Ontario, unreported decision, April 24, 1985; *R.* v. *Heros Enterprises Limited, carrying on business as Lady Stauffer Figure Control Salons*, Montreal, Quebec, decision unreported, December 3, 1974; and *R.* v. *597721 Ontario Inc., carrying on business as Anatomy 2000 Clinic*, London, Ontario, unreported decision, August 8, 1988.

Most often this conflict has been with the Competition Act's general provisions against false or misleading advertising. In particular, there have been problems with false or misleading representations (which are prohibited by paragraph 52(1)(a)) and with representations not based on adequate and proper testing (which are prohibited by paragraph 52(1)(b)).

Reducing Devices

Among the devices that have caused problems are several forms of specialized clothing that, claim the weight-loss firms, will reduce the wearer's waist, hips, and thighs without dieting. In one instance, the claim was made that the device would remove weight while the wearer slept. A number of related claims have been made regarding toning and conditioning the body to control cellulite, usually with various types of body wraps and special creams. Some of the advertisements have gone as far as offering a possible loss of 4 to 18 inches on the first visit.

Passive Exercise

More recently, claims have been associated with passive exercise techniques, such as mechanical vibrating equipment and tables guaranteed to remove inches, tone and strengthen muscles, increase endurance, and reduce cellulite without physical effort on the part of the participant. In one case the claim was made that participants could "lose weight and inches permanently, no crash diets, no strenuous exercises." These programs usually consist of a motorized table that moves the client's muscle groups through a passive range of motion without exertion.

Electrical Muscle Stimulation

Another form of passive exercise involves electrical muscle-stimulator devices (EMS). During EMS treatments, a low-level electrical current causes certain muscles to contract. Expert medical evidence provided during court proceedings indicated that there was no cardiovascular benefit and, as a result, few, if any, calories were burned off.

Focal Topics

1. In the various schemes presented, were the companies in violation of the Competition Act? Why or why not?

2. Who should have the responsibility of supporting any claim made about a product or service?

CASE 3.2

Canadian Consumers and Products for the 1990s

The 1980s have been years of change for the average Canadian household. Our total population growth has been slow, and our real incomes have been eaten away by inflation. Consumer purchasing decisions have been difficult to predict, and they may be even more elusive in the first few years of the 1990s as new taxes, such as the Goods and Services Tax, influence people's choices.

One trend that emerged in the 1980s seems likely to continue, however. This is the desire of many Canadians to enhance their life-style and image. Much of consumer expenditure will focus on the home. And high-tech products will be important.

Product Proliferation

It wasn't so many years ago that the two-car family was unusual. Today, with many two-income families, two and even three cars in one family are much more common. Appliances and other major household products have also been proliferating. Households originally had one large radio; now they have several portables and a stereo. Recently, parents have been purchasing compact stereo systems for their own private use, giving over the family stereo to the teenagers in the house. One TV used to be adequate; today two or three are far more common.

Soon it will be the "two of everything" family. Next to become multiple items are probably VCRs and microwave ovens. (Already 5 percent of American households own two microwaves.) By the turn of the century, most families will own most home electronic products.

Estimated Household Penetration of Selected Products

	Canada		United States	
	1988	*2000*	*1988*	*2000*
Colour televisions	92%	96%	93%	96%
Projection televisions	1	7	3	12
Stereo televisions	10	40	20	50
Video cassette recorders	45	75	56	80
Lap-top and personal computers	15	35	17	40
Microwave ovens	55	85	70	90
Compact disc/digital tape equipment	3	75	4	85
Electronic home security systems	5	12	8	15
Three or more telephones	22	45	25	50

Source: Woods Gordon estimates, 1989.

While household growth will be more modest in the 1990s than in past decades, product proliferation will keep markets growing steadily, though not at the rates of the 1960s and 1970s. Major household items will be replaced more often than in the past, further stimulating demand. In many cases, replacements will be fancier and more sophisticated.

Source: Prepared by Donald Shiner, based on information compiled from: Ernst & Young, *Tomorrow's Customers*, 22nd ed. (Toronto, 1989) and an interview with the author by H. Dyck, *Halifax Mail Star*, January 6, 1990, p. 34.

Demand for household appliances and increasingly competitive world markets should continue to push down prices in real terms, making many products more affordable to a greater proportion of the population. As our ability to produce more varied products is enhanced by computer-aided manufacturing, more cost-effective production will be possible.

High Technology Products in Our Homes

In Canada, the 1990s will be the decade when sophisticated, high-technology products, such as facsimile (fax) machines, cellular telephones, and lap-top computers march out of the office and into our homes. As individuals, more of us will shift work from our offices to our homes, taking advantage of improved communications.

Another important factor will be our efforts to enhance our busy lifestyles by upgrading our homes as the centre of our leisure.

Taken together, these trends indicate that the Canadian home of the 1990s will feature a whole range of new electronics products that will be to this decade what radio and television were to earlier ones.

Products for the 1990s

Worldwide compact disc sales were about 400 million units in 1988, accounting for 12 percent of the recorded music market. Sales reflect acceptance of the CD player as a key component of the home entertainment system. Worldwide sales of CD players and a new generation of digital audio tape players will grow through the 1990s as they replace the current generation of record players and tape decks.

The other key area of home entertainment, the television and video cassette recorder, is also undergoing dramatic changes. Currently, digital high-definition TV sets with stereo sound are offering their quality images and sound to only a small segment of the population. But as prices drop, a new wave of trading-up is going to take place. In addition, the integration of the VCR and TV into small, portable units will create more opportunities for sales.

Focal Topics

1. It is clear that the market of the 1990s will be very different from that of the past decade. What do you see as the major forces that will determine consumer purchases in the next decade?

2. Do marketers respond to these forces with new products and services, or do the products and services marketers sell create these changes?

3. What single new product do you feel will have the most impact on the next decade? Why?

Case for Part One

Wendy's International, Inc.

"Does America need another hamburger chain?" was the question asked by R. David Thomas as he opened the doors to his first Wendy's Old Fashioned Hamburgers restaurant at 257 East Broad Street in downtown Columbus, Ohio, on November 15, 1969. At that time, many food industry experts and some sceptical observers had commented that the fast-food growth curve had already peaked during the late 1960s, ending the rapid expansion of the industry.

On March 21, 1978, after operating only eight years and four months, Wendy's opened its thousandth restaurant at 1000 Memorial Boulevard in Springfield, Tennessee. Never before had such an accomplishment been achieved in such a short period of time. During 1986, the company opened 300 new units, bringing the total number of Wendy's restaurants to nearly 3700. By the end of 1989 Wendy's operated 131 company and franchised stores across Canada as part of their 3800 outlets around the world.

Product Offering

Wendy's places primary emphasis on consistent quality in all areas of food preparation and presentation. The firm uses 100-percent pure domestic ground beef. The patties are cooked slowly to retain their natural juices and flavours. Whether the customer orders the 2-ounce junior, the quarter-pound single, or the Big Classic, the hamburger is served directly from the grill. By mixing and matching the nine available condiments, a Wendy's customer can specify one of 1024 different ways to have the hamburger served.

Chili, another menu item popular with customers, also serves a unique secondary purpose. To keep the hamburgers fresh for customers, no cooked patties are kept on the grill for more than four minutes. To eliminate the potential waste, hamburgers not served within that time period are steamed in a kettle and used for the

This case has been edited from an earlier one that appeared in *Cases and Exercises in Marketing*, by W. Wayne Talarzyk. Copyright © 1987 by CBS College Publishing. Reprinted by permission of Holt, Rinehart & Winston, Inc.; and updated with information from "Wendy's Battles Fast-Food Competition," by Richard Koenig, *The Wall Street Journal*, November 12, 1986, p. 6; "Marketing Strategy Looms Large in Wendy's Future," by Ann Hollifield, *Business First of Greater Columbus*, November 10, 1986, p. 7; and Wendy's International, Inc. Photo, p. 1, provided by Wendy's Restaurants of Canada Inc., Grande Prairie, Alberta.

next day's chili. Chicken sandwiches, baked potatoes, french fries, Frosties, coffee, tea, milk, and soft drinks round out the basic menu. The Frosty, a Wendy's exclusive, is a thick, creamy frozen dairy dessert—much like a very thick chocolate milkshake—served with a spoon.

In 1990, recognizing consumers' growing interest in nutrition, Wendy's introduced cholesterol-free french fries cooked in all-vegetable oil. They also introduced a grilled-chicken sandwich, made with a skinless, boneless breast of chicken topped with fresh lettuce and tomato, and served with a honey-mustard sauce.

Addition of Salad Bars

In 1979, seeking ways to improve customer traffic, Wendy's turned to a strategy that had worked fairly well for other food service organizations — an expanded menu. The company's desire to diffuse its dependence on beef products, yet not interfere with its extremely efficient in-store operating setup, led to salad bars as the first menu addition.

Salads represented a logical extension of the menu by being compatible with Wendy's operational system while enhancing the company's adult image. The salad bar also widened Wendy's appeal to families and increased its lunch and dinner business. Salads also helped attract the health- and weight-conscious and smaller-appetite consumers, both of which are growing market segments. In 1988, Wendy's expanded the salad bar by introducing the Super Bar, an expanded variety of hot and cold food.

Breakfast Menu

In May 1979, Wendy's began testing a breakfast menu that included omelette and scrambled egg platters, bacon, sausage, biscuits, hashbrown potatoes, and french toast. Breakfast is prepared primarily on the grill, with relatively minor additions to kitchen equipment, and is compatible with Wendy's system. It is designed to utilize the restaurants from 7 a.m. to 10:30 a.m., before the lunch service begins. Breakfast represents an attractive opportunity to increase sales and utilization of the restaurants. Customers view Wendy's offering as a superior product. By late 1983, the breakfast menu — narrowed down to omelettes, breakfast sandwiches, and french toast—was offered in about 200 restaurants. Breakfast was implemented systemwide in June 1985.

In March 1986, Wendy's decided to give individual restaurants the option of continuing a breakfast offering. By early 1987, the original breakfast menu was available in only about 15 percent of company-owned restaurants and in about 30 percent of franchised restaurants. Plans are now underway to develop a new breakfast menu.

Advertising Activities

Since 1982, the major hamburger fast-service chains have been fighting what the media have dubbed the Burger Wars. Wendy's, the world's third-largest hamburger chain, is outspent in advertising eight to one by its major competitors—McDonald's and Burger King. Accordingly, the company has been compelled to communicate by using creative treatments and media extension techniques that break through the clutter and dramatize product benefits in a unique and often humorous and exaggerated manner.

When the Burger Wars began anew at the start of 1984, Wendy's again found itself in this position. McDonald's promoted a very low-price hamburger. Burger King launched its "flame-broiling versus frying" campaign. At the same time, research findings showed the consumers perceived McDonald's and Burger King's hamburgers to be larger than Wendy's, although in reality Wendy's single hamburger contains more beef.

Seizing its hamburger-size advantage, Wendy's created the "Where's the Beef?" campaign, airing its first spots on January 9, 1984. Its goal was to create consumer awareness of its larger-size hamburger and leverage a comparatively small ad budget to extend the reach and frequency of the ad message beyond purchased media impressions. In other words, Wendy's planned to use public relations to do more with less — to bring the advertising theme into the North American vernacular, to create awareness of Wendy's larger hamburger, and to underscore the inherent value of all Wendy's menu items.

Recent Results

Wendy's sales were up slightly in 1986, following an 18-percent increase in 1985. While both years benefited from the additional company-operated restaurants that were opened, 1986 reflected an 8-percent decrease in average sales per restaurant and the elimination in the fourth quarter of sales from restaurants in the realignment program.

The realignment program involved selling, leasing, or closing 164 unprofitable or marginally profitable company-owned restaurants. One result, when the annual accounts appeared, was a book loss of nearly $5 million (U.S.).

In the 1986 annual report, management offered the following observations for the future:

> Looking into 1987, the first half of the year is expected
> to be difficult. However, we anticipate gradual improve-
> ment in the second half, based on a continuation of the
> current sales trends. Higher sales should alleviate the
> present pressure on margins over time. The company

has weathered difficult periods before and we have emerged stronger each time. We believe that we can do it again by laying a firm foundation for the future—not by quick fixes. We enter 1987 with a renewed determination toward long-term success.

Marketing Strategy

Company officials have told stock analysts that the challenge is to improve Wendy's price/value image with consumers. Slower inflation rates in recent years may have harmed the value image of the total fast-food industry.

Robert Barney, Wendy's chairman and chief executive officer, says he is confident "the worst is behind us." The firm's plan is to concentrate on a back-to-basics recovery plan. Two essentials of the strategy are better service and hamburgers. One of the largest Wendy's franchisees states, "I think our future hinges on our ability to do the best big hamburger in North America."

Some of the major elements of Wendy's marketing plan are:

- Concentrate on improving the company's price/value image by creating smaller products that can be sold for lower prices. Cutting prices on existing products may also be a possibility.

- Slow new-store development, and focus on the company's existing operations.

- Develop brand-name hamburgers, such as the Big Classic, that will be directly identified with Wendy's. Company officials believe that brand names will improve Wendy's product and company identification with consumers.

- Develop an "arsenal" of new products that can be rolled out at any time to spur customer interest.

- Focus advertising on the company's hamburger line-up.

- Concentrate on streamlining restaurant design to reduce construction costs and improve efficiency during operations.

- Streamline drive-through operations to improve delivery time.

Focal Topics

1. Discuss the environmental factors that have contributed to eating meals at fast-food restaurants rather than at home.

2. What do you see as the "real business" of Wendy's?

3. Why do you think Wendy's breakfast offering was withdrawn from many of its restaurants?

4. Based on your analysis of the case and your knowledge of the existing business environment, what are the basic problems facing Wendy's and the industry in the future?

5. Based on your response to question 4, what recommendations would you make to Wendy's at this time? Why?

PART TWO

Markets and Segmentation

4

Chapter 4

Market Segmentation and Sales Forecasting

In this chapter, you will learn:

- The differences between mass marketing and target marketing.

- Ways to segment the consumer market.

- Ways to segment the industrial market.

- The difference between concentrated marketing and differentiated marketing.

- Issues marketers consider in deciding how many market segments to target.

- What criteria make a market segment a good candidate for targeting.

- What types of forecasts marketers use.

- How marketers estimate demand.

Radio Stations Zero In on Baby Boomers

How do radio stations decide whether to play Madonna or Springsteen, the Beatles, or Rush? They start by deciding who they want to have listening.

According to radio-programming consultant John Parikhal, co-founder of Joint Communications Corporation (the largest company of its kind in Canada, as well as the largest in Australia and the second largest in the United States), ''If you don't serve the listeners, you're out of business. Number two, advertisers control all non-pay media and they control it by simply deciding what age groups they're going to buy.''

In many cases, the desired listeners are the Baby Boomers. As a target market this is the largest age group and has the most money to spend. Says Parikhal, ''Eighteen-to-34 (years of age) used to be the big buy because the baby boom was in it. Now the leading edge of the baby boom is 42, advertisers have all decided to buy 25 to 54 or 25 to 49. So it felt like, literally overnight, we had more (music) hits of the 1950s, 1960s, and 1970s than we could deal with.''

Other radio stations have found success by targeting less popular market segments. Parikhal points out that now there are ''jazz and new age stations on the air in the U.S.'' (JCC has 40 client stations in the States in addition to 25 in Canada.) He goes on, ''You can't have a 'new age' station in Canada because there aren't enough artists to meet the (government-regulated) content quotas.''

Like most companies, commercial radio stations in Canada find that they cannot appeal to everyone. Each radio station must evaluate, subject to federal government regulations on content, which group of listeners it can reach most effectively. As you learned in Chapter 2, such groups are called market segments. This chapter describes ways to segment a market. It also discusses how marketers decide which segment or segments to target, including how marketers estimate whether a segment will be profitable enough to warrant targeting.

Source: Adapted from Stan Sutter, ''Canadian Media Guru John Parikhal Talks about Radio Today,'' *Marketing*, March 13, 1989, pp. 19, 21, and 28.

Two Ways to Think of Markets

The market for a product consists of all the people who buy and sell it. As you learned in Chapter 2, some marketers find it most efficient to think of all the buyers of their product as being one great mass. Other marketers find it more effective to divide the market into segments and to target specific market segments. Because most marketers use this approach, it will be the focus of most of this chapter.

Mass Marketing

In **mass marketing,** all of the customers in a particular market are thought of as having the same, or homogeneous, needs. Those needs are easily satisified by a single product and a single marketing program or mix.

In the 1920s, the Ford Motor Company pursued a mass marketing approach by offering only one car, the Model T, in one colour, at one price, with no options. In fact, mass marketing was the basic approach to target marketing before the adoption of the marketing concept. A few companies today still adhere to mass marketing. Ace Playing Cards, for example, offers essentially the same product — laminated cards — to all customers in the playing card market at the same price and through the same outlets (variety stores).

Firms that opt for a mass marketing approach do so for one basic reason — to save money. These firms keep production, inventory, and transportation costs low by producing only one standardized product; administrative costs are lower because only one marketing program must be planned and executed.

Mass marketing works as long as consumers demand no variety. But few products can satisfy everyone's tastes. As consumers have become more affluent, they have come to expect a wider product choice. In the automobile market, some people buy a car for its styling and class distinction, others give priority to gas efficiency, and still others buy for price. No one car can satisfy all of these requirements.

Some staple food items such as sugar and salt still lend themselves to a mass market approach, but even these products are gradually being diversified for different markets. Sugar, for example, is available as regular granulated sugar; as only partially refined, blonde turbinado and dark demerara sugar for natural food lovers; as super-sweet fructose for dieters; as very fine crystals for bartenders; as icing sugar for bakers; and as light and dark brown sugar. It also comes in one, two and four kilogram bags, as cubes or tablets, and in packets. And we have not even started to mention the various sugar substitutes that now abound.

Farm products, such as meat, fruits, and vegetables, are also among the few items that may still be mass marketed. Faced with an apparent resistance to beef on the part of diet-conscious consumers, The Beef Information Centre launched an advertising campaign to mass market the meat, stressing its nutritional value. (See Figure 4.1.) Because consumers may not be able to distinguish items from different producers, marketers may use various promotional strategies to differentiate products from those of competitors. Oranges stamped "Sunkist," bananas with "Chiquita" stickers, and "Maple Leaf" turkeys are all distinctively labelled to distinguish them from everybody else's oranges, bananas, and turkeys.

Figure 4.1 A Refutational Advertisement

Source: Reprinted by permission of the Beef Information Centre.

Target Marketing and Segmentation

The increased acceptance of the marketing concept has resulted in the rapid adoption of **target marketing** as the most productive strategy for most companies to pursue. In contrast to mass marketing, target marketing to a market segment divides the market into groups of customers with different, or heterogeneous, needs. Each group requires a different product, a unique price, a suitable outlet, and a distinctive advertising appeal.

Target marketing is practised by firms in both the consumer and industrial markets. For example, the slogan for General Motors at one time was "a car for every price, purpose, and personality."

The main advantage of target marketing is that it usually results in more sales than mass marketing. Customers with no choice may simply drop out of the market. Given alternatives, more people may buy.

The chief drawback of target marketing is that it raises costs. General Motors, for example, must have special tools and limited runs for each automobile model it produces. Each different advertising campaign it plans costs extra. Thus the success of an organization that uses this approach depends on how well it identifies market segments and selects appropriate segments to target.

Different market segments are identified, depending on whether the marketer is considering the consumer market or the industrial market. As explained in Chapter 2, the consumer market consists of people who buy a product for personal use; when you buy milk at the grocery store, you are part of the consumer market. The industrial market is made up of businesses that buy products for resale or to operate their establishments. The purchasing agent at Kraft Foods who buys hundreds of tank cars full of milk to make Philadelphia cream cheese is part of the industrial market.

Segmentation Bases for the Consumer Market

A marketer can segment a consumer market in four primary ways: (1) by demographic factors; (2) by rate of product usage; (3) by perceived product benefits; and (4) by psychographic, or life-style, characteristics.

Some segmentation data, such as demographic information, are more easily obtained than others, such as psychographic information, which may require special research. No one basis for segmentation is best for all situations. In many cases, marketers resort to a combination of bases to obtain an adequate picture of their market target.

Demographic Segmentation

Demographic segmentation groups customers on the basis of geographic proximity or some shared socioeconomic trait (for example, age or social class). The theory behind demographic segmentation is that customers who live in the same locale or belong to the same age, income, or other grouping have common needs and will buy similar products.

Geographic Factors

Before the Industrial Age, local tradespeople produced goods to meet local needs. This was a kind of natural, or unplanned, geographic segmentation of the market. Today most consumer products sell to a continental or national market, but a growing number of firms tailor their products to regional or local needs or concentrate their marketing effort in one region or a few regions.

Companies can identify broad differences among people who live in different geographic regions by conducting research or by using consumer profiles developed by advertising agencies and consultants. For example, Hershey Canada launched a line of milder-flavoured milk chocolate bars after a survey indicated that Canadians preferred a light, creamy chocolate as opposed to the darker chocolate preferred in the United States.[1] Regional market segments can be reached in many ways, such as by differential distribution, through local radio and television stations, in regional editions of magazines, and through mailings to people in the targeted regions.

Socioeconomic Factors

General Motors was one of the first nationally known firms to use socioeconomic factors to distinguish segments for branded products. Alfred Sloan, GM's chief executive from 1923 to 1945, hit on the idea that cars could be sold as visible symbols of the climb up the social ladder. He produced different makes of cars to sell to different income groups at six price levels ranging from $450 to $3500. The models were positioned so that practically all of the buying public—from the most price conscious to the most affluent—was covered.[2]

Sloan's idea caught on. Soon other socioeconomic factors were used to describe market segments. Age, for example, has proved to be a successful way of dividing the market. Jordache jeans are advertised to consumers in their late teens and early twenties. (See Figure 4.2.)

Because many variables may be at work in a buying decision, marketers rarely use only one socioeconomic factor to segment the market. Sloan's exclusive use of income to distinguish segments of car buyers would not work today.

Automobile manufacturers now are likely to use multiple socioeconomic factors to identify buyers of specific brands and models. Saab, which calls itself "the most intelligent car ever built," has targeted a sophisticated, responsible, well-established man, probably the head of a family, who is interested in a car that combines sports-car virtues, such as performance and handling, with practicality. (See Figure 4.3.) In a few paragraphs of copy, the ad speaks to such diverse variables as age,

Figure 4.2   Jordache Advertises to a Specific Age Segment

sex, income, educational level, family size, family life-cycle, home ownership, and social class, and those only begin to suggest the various
appeals at work.

Socioeconomic factors, especially when used together, can help pinpoint a target market. These factors are widely used because they produce segments whose sizes can be measured easily (by the use of census
data). In addition, because the various advertising media (among them
magazines, television, and radio) use the same socioeconomic factors to
describe their audiences, marketers can easily find an appropriate
medium for reaching their target effectively.

But marketers cannot always relate product or brand choice to differences in age, income, sex, or family size. People with an identical demographic profile may still exhibit different tastes. Other criteria may
also be needed to zero in on the most likely buyers.[3] For that reason,
marketers also segment the market based on the use of products, the
benefits consumers seek, and consumers' life-styles and personalities.

Usage-Rate Segmentation

In addition to demographic differences, consumers also exhibit differences in the rate at which they buy and use products. Research results

IS IT POSSIBLE FOR SOMEONE WITH 3 KIDS, A MORTGAGE AND HEFTY ORTHODONTIA BILLS TO DRIVE A CAR HE ACTUALLY LIKES?

Congratulations. Here you are, an adult in contemporary America, with a full complement of domestic responsibilities.

And some years from now (after you've put the kids through college and after you've passed through much of your middle-age crisis) you figure you will be in a position to finally afford a car that will bring back the joys of driving you remember fondly from the days when you were irresponsibly single.

Except there is no reason for you to wait. Just by coincidence, there is a car with exceptional performance and handling that can liberate a person from the tedium of driving a boring car: the Saab 900.

Saabs start at about $11,000 which should be quite compatible with most commitments to real property, child rearing, and the correction of varying degrees of overbite.

So if you're concerned that you may grow old before you realize your ambition and that inflation and the necessities of family life have put you out of the car you want, take heart. They may well have put you right into a Saab.

Saabs range in price from $10,750 for the 900 3-door, 5-speed to $16,910 for the 900 4-door, 5-speed APC Turbo. Manufacturer's suggested retail prices. Not including taxes, license, freight, dealer charges or options.

SAAB

The most intelligent car ever built.

Saab-Scania of America, Inc. by Ally & Gargano, Inc.

Figure 4.3   Tarketing the Family Man Who Wishes for a Sports Car

have shown that in many product categories, a few consumers account for most of the sales. Figure 4.4 shows this graphically for several product categories. In the category of lemon-lime soft drinks, for example, 58 percent of the households sampled use the product. But half of these users (29 percent) did most of the buying. They purchased 91 percent of all lemon-lime soft drinks sold—ten times as much as the light users.

Usage-rate segmentation takes into account variations in demand among different groups and divides the market into heavy, light, and nonusers. Usually, marketers combine usage-rate segmentation with demographic segmentation; they look for demographic differences between heavy, light, and nonusers of a product.

Usage-Rate Segmentation
Division of a market into classes on the basis of the rate at which members buy and use products.

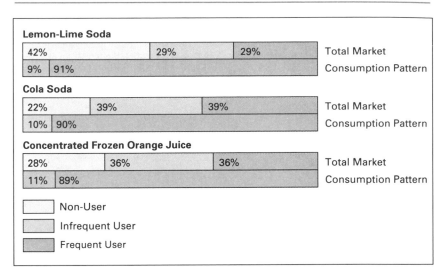

Figure 4.4 Variations in Demand for Three Beverages

Many marketers concentrate on the small number of consumers who buy in the greatest quantity. But if marketers in a field are catering to the heavy users, it may pay to appeal to the light-user or nonuser segments as well. Businesspeople, for example, may compose the largest share of the market for hotel rooms in downtown Montreal. But many hotels advertise special weekend rates to the tourist market to fill those rooms when businesspeople go home.

Monopolists are also often interested in nonusers or light users of their product or service. The Toronto Transit Commission, which runs the subways, buses, and streetcars in Canada's largest metropolitan area, conducts an annual survey permitting it to divide the public into heavy, medium, and light TTC riders and nonriders. Insight into the characteristics of light riders and nonriders helps the TTC to evolve marketing strategies to convert these groups into medium or heavy riders. Converting them is a difficult task as most of them habitually drive cars, and lifetime habits are hard to break. The typical nonrider is male, aged 25 to 54 with an income of $50 000 or more. The task is to promote the TTC to this group as being an attractive substitute for a car; doing so may involve product improvement as well as promotion.[4] (For details, see At Your Service 5.1 in the next chapter.)

Although many firms have benefited by employing usage-rate segmentation, the method does have limitations. Segmenting the market into heavy and light users and nonusers does not explain why consumers fall into one category rather than another. The labels may actually disguise the real subdivisions of the market and hide key information. The term "heavy coffee drinker," for example, actually describes two distinct types—compulsive coffee drinkers and those who drink for taste. The former usually buy cheap house brands, but the latter may prefer

Marketing Today 4.1

Hot Market Segment for Coffee Makers

Coffee drinking has declined over the past two decades, as young adults stick to soft drinks. However, the gourmet coffee segment has actually grown 15 percent. The consumers behind that growth are 25 to 49 years old and affluent. These consumers, who have been willing to spend as much as $15 to $20 for 500 grams of good coffee, have sparked a new industry of gourmet coffee roasters and retailers.

Having discovered this promising market segment, major coffee sellers have wasted no time moving in. In 1986, General Foods and the Great Atlantic & Pacific Tea Company both introduced lines of gourmet coffee, each featuring similarly exotic varieties. General Foods' line, called Maxwell House Private Collection, includes whole bean and ground roast coffee packaged in clear plastic bags. A&P's line, called Eight O'Clock Royale Gourmet Bean Coffee, is sold in gold-coloured bags. For both lines, the packaging includes a new innovation for longer shelf life: a one-way valve that allows the coffee to release gases without letting oxygen in.

Source: Patricia Winters, ''GF, A&P Grind It Out in Specialty Coffees,'' *Advertising Age,* July 21, 1986, pp. 3, 77.

premium products.[5] (Marketing Today 4.1 describes in greater depth the market segment of specialty coffee drinkers.) Often such differences within a segment become apparent only when the marketer considers other segmentation bases, such as those described below.

Benefit Segmentation

One way to discover possible hidden segments within the broad categories of light and heavy users and nonusers is to apply **benefit segmentation,** which attempts to identify the benefits people seek in a product as a basis for grouping them together. For example, in a study conducted in 1983, researchers were able to divide MBA candidates (the market for business schools) according to whether they were seeking quality, specialty programs, a degree, convenience, career flexibility, or a low-cost program involving minimal effort.[6]

The market for many products is divided quite naturally by the benefits people seek. Consumers usually want a combination of benefits, but they tend to stress one or two when deciding to buy. For example, you might want free chequing but would rather pay a small service charge if you can open an account that offers you the convenience of withdrawing cash on campus. Similarly, buyers of Timex watches seek a good product with a low price; buyers of Lean Cuisine frozen dinners seek a convenience food with reduced calories; and high-volume readers of romance or adventure novels may be seeking an inexpensive "escape" from their day-to-day lives.

Sometimes market researchers cannot immediately determine exactly what benefits different groups look for in a product. Could you, for exam-

Benefit Segmentation
Division of a market into classes on the basis of benefits that members of each class seek.

ple, explain the differences between how you decide which shampoo to use and how your parents make the choice? Often the researcher must apply sophisticated statistical tools to distinguish between the benefits people see in marketed products and the benefits they would ideally like to see. The techniques are complex but may reveal new product possibilities.

The classic study of benefit segmentation was performed by Russel I. Haley in the toothpaste market. He discovered that the market could be divided into four benefit segments, each with its own characteristics. One group in the study, composed primarily of large families, sought decay prevention. Another group, mostly teenagers and young adults, cared most about cosmetic features such as brightness and breath fresheners. Men looked for the brand with the lowest price, and children wanted a brand with the best taste or the most novel appearance. Each group could be linked with a brand demonstrating the benefits considered most important.[7] Although the research was completed in the 1960s, toothpaste companies still use the results of the study.

Psychographic Segmentation

The basic question left unanswered by demographic and usage-rate segmentation is *why* consumers purchase what they do. Benefit segmentation does not answer why people emphasize certain benefits. Psychographic segmentation tries to answer these questions by focusing on a potential consumer's life-style and personality traits.

The concept of **life-style** refers to a person's pattern of living in the world as expressed in his or her activities, interests, and opinions.[8] By examining a person's life-style, you can learn things that information about social class or other demographic data would fail to reveal. Two women of the same age and with the same family size and income might live next door to each other in an affluent suburb. One might be a top executive while her neighbour might be a traditional homemaker.

To determine the best approach to reaching either of these women, marketers might turn to psychographics. Using the methods and insights of motivation and personality research, **psychographic segmentation** seeks to divide the market according to people's life-styles, or distinct approaches to living.

Marketers identify different life-styles by measuring three factors: activities, interests, and opinions. (See Table 4.1.) To probe these areas, marketers administer lengthy questionnaires consisting of general statements (such as "I enjoy going to concerts") and product-specific statements (such as "Instant coffee is more economical than ground coffee"). Respondents must rate the extent of their agreement or disagreement with the statements on a seven-point scale. Usually, they are also asked to give information on their product usage and demographic characteristics. Marketers then group those with similar responses into

Life-Style
Person's pattern of living expressed in activities, interests, and opinions.

Psychographic Segmentation
Division of the market into classes on the basis of the life-styles of members.

Table 4.1 Life-Style Dimensions

Activities	Interests	Opinions	Demographics
Work	Family	Themselves	Age
Hobbies	Home	Social issues	Education
Social events	Job	Politics	Income
Vacation	Community	Business	Occupation
Entertainment	Recreation	Economics	Family size
Club membership	Fashion	Education	Dwelling
Community	Food	Products	Geography
Shopping	Media	Future	City size
Sports	Achievements	Culture	Stage in life-cycle

Source: Joseph T. Plummer, ''The Concept and Application of Life-Style Segmentation,'' *Journal of Marketing*, January 1974, p. 34.

psychographic categories and develop a profile of each group's demographics and product usage rates. Each group represents a different market segment.[9] The description of the teenage market in Marketing Today 4.2 includes psychographic as well as demographic information.

Using this method, the marketers at Colgate identified a new segment of the market for soap. After administering a psychographic questionnaire to a group, researchers were able to isolate three life-style categories among respondents. The first category, "rejuvenators," were other-directed, insecure, and in need of social reassurance. They sought the deodorant protection of a soap like Dial. The second group, "compensators," were pleasure seekers who liked to feel pampered by a beauty bar like Dove. But research uncovered another group distinctly different from these two. It was composed of self-assured, practical, rugged people —primarily men—who used a soap simply to get *clean*. Colgate, at the time, had no soap specifically targeted to this group, which was labelled "independents."

On the basis of this information, Colgate marketers tailored a marketing mix for the "independent" segment. The name given to the new soap, Irish Spring, was chosen to express the benefit that independents most desired—cleanliness. The distinctive black package was designed to catch the eye of the independent thinker. Commercials featured Sean, a rugged-looking guy, to stress the mood of outdoor "manliness." This strategy netted Colgate third place in the market for soap.[10]

The psychographic method is not infallible, however. It is costly, and information can be misinterpreted. Psychographics that richly describe a market segment do not always succeed in predicting how consumers will behave in the marketplace. Because research into the theory underlying psychographic segmentation has been limited, marketers lack a reliable procedure. Nevertheless, psychographic research provides marketers with descriptive detail that helps them in developing marketing strategies. Psychographic segmentation has therefore achieved widespread use.[11]

Marketing Today 4.2

Targeting Teenagers

According to Charles Mittelstadt, manager at the United States' Center for Advertising Services, today's teenagers differ a lot from teenagers of past years. ''You can't go back,'' says Mittelstadt, ''because the cultural differences between today and yesterday are so great.''

One difference is spending power. An estimate for 1986 predicted that U.S. teenagers would spend $30 billion of their own money that year. Many also do family shopping, because both parents work. As a result, they may be spending as much as $40 billion of family money, mainly on groceries. One study estimated that American teenagers make up to 20 percent of all supermarket purchases among families with teenagers. Canadian statistics would likely be similar.

In the U.S., this teenage group is estimated at 34 million, growing to 39 million by the year 2000. In contrast, the Canadian teenage group totalled 3.7 million in 1988 and is expected to remain virtually unchanged at 3.8 million by the year 2000.

Changing family patterns also affect teenagers' values. Because of high divorce levels, most teens rate family continuity as being extremely important. They tend to admire grandparents more than parents. Thus, ads including grandparents in family settings may appeal to teenagers. Mittelstadt summarizes teenagers' values this way: ''They are very disciplined about acquiring money, very goal oriented. But there's a major change in the work ethic. It's no longer work hard and save for a brighter future. Now it is work hard and get what you want today.''

Source: Adapted from Jeffrey A. Trachtenberg, ''Big Spenders: Teenage Division,'' Forbes, November 3, 1986, pp. 201, 204.

Segmentation Bases for the Industrial Market

Most of us are relatively familiar with the strategies companies use to reach consumer markets. But many marketing students may eventually find themselves employed by industrial firms whose target markets are not individuals but other industries.

Industrial buying behaviour differs in many ways from consumer buying. Although certain segmentation strategies are similar to those practised in consumer markets, others are unique to industrial marketing. The most common ways of segmenting an industrial market are by customer location, type of industry, company size, and end use of product.

Customer Location

As in consumer markets, industrial demand for products varies by geographic location. Companies seeking to market to oil-drilling firms would concentrate their efforts on Alberta. Similarly, firms targeting the automobile industry would make Windsor and Ontario's Golden Horseshoe area the focus of their efforts. But even when industries are highly concentrated, opportunities exist for smaller suppliers who may be able to provide superior service to local clients.

Industry Type

One of the most valuable tools for an industrial marketer is a Canadian government coding system called the **Standard Industrial Classification (SIC) Code**. SIC is a numbering system for categorizing businesses by economic activity. (See Table 4.2.) Each industry within these divisions has a distinct code number. The industry division E, for example, is divided into 30 major groups. (This division, representing manufacturing, is the one with the most subdivisions, reflecting the fact that it covers some 22 percent of the national income and also that a tremendous amount of detail is available.)

To continue the example, one of the 30 major groups under division E is clothing industries, which is given the two-digit code 24. The code of any group within this major group must begin with the two digits 24. One of these groups is men's and boys' clothing industries, which has the three-digit code 243. Within this group are five classes; each has a four-digit code of which the first three digits must be 243. For instance, the men's and boys' pants industry is coded 2433 (see Table 4.3).

Marketing managers can learn a great deal about potential customers by knowing their SIC codes. A number of government and private sources, including Dun & Bradstreet's *Market Identifiers,* and Statistics Canada's series from its *Census of Manufactures*, publish information about industries identified by SIC codes. By using these sources, marketers can acquire information such as where customers are located,

Standard Industrial Classification (SIC) Code Numbering system followed by the Canadian government for categorizing businesses by economic activity.

Table 4.2 The Standard Industrial Classification System

Industries Classified	Four-Figure Codes
A Agriculture and related services	0111–0239
B Fishing and trapping	0311–0339
C Logging and forestry	0411–0511
D Mining (incl. milling), quarrying, oil wells	0611–0929
E Manufacturing	1011–3999
F Construction industries	4011–4499
G Transportation and storage	4511–4799
H Communications and other utilities	4811–4999
I Wholesale trade	5011–5999
J Retail trade	6011–6921
K Finance and insurance	7011–7499
L Real estate operator and insurance agent	7511–7611
M Business service	7711–7799
N Government service	8111–8411
O Education	8511–8599
P Health and social service	8611–8699
Q Accommodation, food, and beverage services	9111–9221
R Other services	9611–9999

Source: W. Rupert Cook and Joan Mount, *Canadian Statistical Data: An Introduction to Sources and Interpretation*, (Toronto: Micromedia Limited, 1986).

how much of the market they control, and who the companies' key executives are. This information can then be used to identify target markets and to develop a marketing strategy.[12]

Customer Size

A marketer may want to segment the market further on the basis of the size of possible customers. Large buyers may have special requirements for purchasing procedures, delivery schedules, or price. While it may be worthwhile for some firms to service large and sometimes demanding

Table 4.3 Example of SIC System

Division E, Manufacturing Industries	Code
Major group: clothing industries	24
Group: Men's & boys' clothing	243
Classes: Men's & boys' coats	2431
Men's & boys' suits & jackets	2432
Men's & boys' pants	2433
Men's & boys' shirts & underwear	2434
Men's & boys' clothing contractors	2435

Source: Statistics Canada, *Standard Industrial Classification 1980*, cat. no. 12-501E, 4th ed., p. 32. Reproduced with the permission of the Minister of Supply and Services Canada, 1990.

customers, other companies might do well to concentrate on the smaller end of the market.

Richards Consultants, Ltd., for example, learned that small can be profitable when they first launched their executive search firm. The two founders originally thought large high-tech firms such as Digital Equipment Corporation (DEC) and Honeywell would be the best places to offer their services. But when they set out to investigate how they might develop a competitive edge over these companies' existing search firms, they realized there was a better way to approach the problem. Instead of fighting an uphill battle for the already well-serviced industry giants, why not target the many small, rapidly growing companies that were hungry for management talent? The two owners have since built a thriving firm serving the DECs and Honeywells of the next generation.[13]

In the industrial market, firms may also be segmented as to usage rate. Paper manufacturers, for example, may want to target book, newspaper, and magazine publishers who are heavy users of paper rather than companies who may occasionally use paper to print an in-house newsletter or brochure.

End Use of Product

Because an industrial product may be used many different ways, a marketer may want to segment the market by the way the product will ultimately be used. A paper manufacturer may decide to target companies that manufacture paper party goods, toilet tissue, greeting cards, or product packaging rather than publishers. Again, SIC data would be a valuable source of information about potential customers.

Selecting Markets to Target

After a marketer has divided a market into segments, the next step is to decide which segments to target. This decision involves weighing whether to pursue one segment or many, as well as selecting the market segments the company can target most effectively. American Express, for example, plans to expand its business by increasing its appeal to several target markets. (See At Your Service 4.1.)

One Segment or Many?

Marketers can target a single market segment, or they can diversify their efforts to try to appeal to several segments. For example, the CBC Newsworld cable-TV channel caters to television viewers who want news and information, whereas the CBC television network tries to schedule a variety of programs that will attract a broad audience.

Mark Snider

At Your Service 4.1

American Express Hopes New Services Will Appeal to Multiple Markets

When American Express wanted to target new markets, it revised its marketing mix. The company had selected several target markets; specifically, its objective was to increase the card's use among women, students, affluent elders, and empty nesters (parents whose children have grown up and left home).

The company adopted an advertising campaign promoting its new services, including 24-hour customer service, a 24-hour legal and medical referral hotline, and an innovative service called Buyers Assurance. Buyers Assurance doubles the repair period on manufacturers' warranties for merchandise charged on an American Express card. According to the company, this service is a first for the industry.

The company's advertising focuses on describing these services. American Express has, since introducing its card in 1958, made a practice of adding services to differentiate its card from competing credit services. Explains one senior vice-president for personal card marketing, "It's great to have services, but what we've found from time to time is we had to communicate those services in an intrusive way."

Source: Adapted from Sarah Stiansen, "American Express Drops 'Do You Know Me'; Shifts to Services," *Adweek*, August 18, 1986, p. 3.

Concentrated Marketing

Concentrated Marketing
Practice of dividing the market into market segments and selecting only one segment to serve with a marketing mix.

When an organization focuses all its efforts on one segment with a single marketing mix, it is engaging in **concentrated marketing.** Playschool, for example, concentrates its marketing on toys for preschoolers. In Los Angeles, the Wilshire House was built for people who could afford condominiums ranging in price from $1.5 million to $11 million — a specialized market indeed.

The advantage of concentrated marketing is that it allows a firm to know and understand its market thoroughly and thus to meet its specialized needs in a way that would not be possible with a more diversified strategy. Concentrated marketing may also be the best tactic for a firm with limited resources, since it may be able to serve its customers better than its larger competitors can.

Concentrated marketing does have drawbacks, however. By focusing efforts on one particular segment, a firm may be vulnerable if marketing conditions change and it has nothing to fall back on. When the bottom fell out of the housing market in the early 1980s, developers of the Wilshire House, for example, resorted to offering a free Rolls-Royce to anyone who would buy an $11-million condo.[14]

Another disadvantage of concentrated marketing is that a company's strength in one market may be a deterrent should it seek to expand its base. Disney Studios, for example, had trouble breaking into the market for young adult films because the company was so heavily identified with movies for children.

Differentiated Marketing

When an organization markets to many segments, each with a different marketing mix, it is practising **differentiated marketing.** The soft-drink industry provides good examples of this approach. Royal Crown, for instance, sells different colas to different market segments: RC for those who want the basic product, Diet Rite for weight watchers, and RC 100 for those who want to avoid caffeine.

A policy of differentiated marketing allows a firm to pull out of a segment that proves unprofitable and to rely on other segments. For example, nine years after Procter & Gamble entered the soft-drink market by purchasing Crush beverages, it pulled out of that segment by selling the division. The products, Crush, Hires, and Sun-Drop lemon-lime, not only failed to capture a following, their market share had declined from 1.3 to 0.8 percent. Earlier, Philip Morris Companies, with 7Up, and RJR Nabisco, with Sunkist orange soda and Canada Dry, had jumped out of the market.[15]

The production and marketing costs of servicing many different segments are very high. Marketers must weigh the risk of specialization against the cost of diversification. Three other questions relevant to deciding how many segments to pursue are:

1. *What is the financial condition of the firm?* Small firms with limited resources may need to restrict their marketing effort to one segment in order to survive.

2. *What is the competition doing?* If competitors are covering the major segments with a broad line of products, they may be ignoring smaller segments that can be pursued.

3. *Is the market new to the firm?* It may be better to concentrate on one segment when entering a new market and expand to other segments after a foothold is established.

Which Segments?

In deciding which segments to target, marketers evaluate which segments the organization can reach most effectively. A segment is a good candidate for target marketing if it meets three general criteria:

1. *A market segment is identifiable.* Marketers should be able to spot a common need or characteristic of some people that is different from that of other people in the market. It may be determined, for example, that when certain people are depressed, they become heavy consumers of snack foods. But how could a marketer reach people with just those tendencies? It is much easier to use a variable

Differentiated Marketing
Practice of marketing to many market segments, each with a different marketing mix.

like income as a way of distinguishing groups of people in a given market because a great deal of information on the composition of the North American population by income groups is available.

2. *A market segment is accessible.* Even if a marketer can identify a subset of consumers, segmentation may not be worthwhile if that market cannot be reached economically. A real estate office may recognize that the market for a five-bedroom, $375 000 house would most likely be a family earning more than $80 000 per year, with three or more children. But not all families with those characteristics in a given area are in the market for a house, and the potential buyer may even be someone who does not match those standards. The office may advertise in local papers knowing that most readers will not be interested in the offering. Compare that scattershot approach to the ability of marketers of expensive cookware to reach potential customers through such magazines as *Gourmet* and *Bon Appétit.*

3. *A market segment is large enough to be profitable.* There must be enough people in a potential segment to justify the high costs of marketing and production. While there may be a market in Toronto for romance novels written in Portuguese, it is likely to be too small for a marketer to justify the cost, especially since such novels usually are marketed in inexpensive paperback editions. Conversely, while the market for very specialized scientific books is also small, some publishers find this segment a worthwhile market. Scientific and technical books can command a premium price, and potential customers—usually professionals and libraries—are easily reached using highly targeted mailing lists. The determination of profit potential is so crucial to marketers that various techniques for measuring demand have been devised. They are explored at the end of this chapter.

Forecasting in Marketing

The strategy of target marketing is worthwhile only if the segments targeted have enough sales potential to warrant a special marketing program. To estimate the size of that potential, marketers engage in **forecasting,** which is the art of predicting demand in the marketplace over a given period of time. Forecasts may be short-range (one year or less), medium-range (one to five years), or long-range (more than five years).

Forecasting is complicated because demand can be expressed in a variety of ways. Sometimes demand refers to actual sales—the amount of money a company can expect to make in a given market segment. At other times demand refers to **market potential**—the total of all sales that might be generated in a market segment. If a company is the sole seller of a product in a certain segment, then the two meanings converge.

Forecasting
Predicting demand in the marketplace over a given period of time.

Market Potential
Total of all sales that might be generated in a market segment.

But because competition exists in most segments, a single company's sales rarely equal all that buyers are willing and able to purchase.

Properly speaking, the term **sales forecast** refers only to the prediction of actual sales a company can expect to make in a certain market or segment. But in order to arrive at this, marketers must first determine market potential, which sets an upper limit on what can be sold. Two other types of forecasts—economic and industry forecasts—enable them to gauge market potential.

Forecast Types: A Comparison

Economic, industry, and sales forecasts are distinct yet related. A general understanding of the economy underlies an accurate prediction of industry sales, which in turn serves as the foundation for predicting company sales.

Economic Forecasts

An **economic forecast** detects how changes in the national and international business climate will affect specific industries. As noted in Chapter 3, marketing activity varies with the phases of the business cycle (depression, recession, recovery, and prosperity). Marketers recognize that the general health of the economy may seriously affect sales in an industry. Hence, they pay close attention to variations in economic cycles before stepping into a new market segment or undertaking new programs in an established segment.

The gross domestic product (GDP) and the unemployment rate are two of the most widely used economic indicators. Researchers have found that sales in many industries are closely correlated to these measures. For example, when there is a rise in the GDP, auto sales usually increase.

Other, more specific indicators may successfully predict sales trends for various industries. The level of housing starts, for example, is an excellent indicator for companies that supply the construction industry. Businesses as diverse as lumber companies, appliance manufacturers, and real estate offices watch this indicator to help estimate what their sales might be in coming months. In the area of consumer products, an increase in average hours worked may signal a rise in sales, since overtime produces more income for discretionary buying.

The indicators needed to make an economic forecast are compiled by Statistics Canada. Two of the most useful government publications containing information are the monthly *Canadian Statistical Review* and the annual bulletin in the *Census of Manufactures* series. Many firms enter data from such sources in their computer banks for forecasting. Other firms depend on outside organizations (universities, banks, and brokerage houses) for economic forecasts. While the use of computers has made economic forecasting more accurate, unexpected world events can undermine even the most sophisticated predictions. For example,

Sales Forecast
Prediction of actual sales a company can expect to make in a certain market or segment.

Economic Forecast
Prediction of how the economy will fare as a whole in light of changes in the national and international business climate.

the 1974 Arab oil embargo and the drought of the summer of 1986 had widespread economic reverberations that could not have been anticipated in economic forecasts.

Industry Forecasts

Industry Forecast
Prediction of likely sales for a class of products.

Economic forecasts set an upper limit on potential demand in a given segment. They tell how much income may be *available* for purchase of a particular product. However, they do not indicate how much income people are *willing* to spend on that product (rather than save or spend elsewhere). For such information, marketers require an **industry forecast,** the prediction of likely sales for a class of products.

In addition to the economic climate, industry sales are affected by two factors: (1) the amount of industrywide marketing activity and (2) the prevailing social and legal climate.

Marketing activity by fellow industry members can increase or decrease demand for a product. The growth in sales of personal computers, for example, has created a boom market for manufacturers of software, disks, and terminal tables, as well as for publishers of computer books.

A marketing manager who must predict the sales of products must anticipate how the marketing activities of other companies may influence total demand. Also, as you learned in Chapter 3, marketers must take into account the current social and legal environment for their industry. For example, in 1989, some Canadian banks, despite lack of the long-promised revision of the federal Bank Act, began marketing home insurance products with the permission of provincial regulators (see Marketing Today 4.3).

Marketing departments can obtain information about social and legal issues for their industry from trade association publications, which report estimates of future patterns of industry growth and decline. Marketers in the energy business, for example, might be interested in supply and demand forecasts for natural gas given in *Petroleum Industry in Canada Report*; marketers in the computer industry might check the forecasts reported in *Canada's Electronic Market*.

Company Sales Forecasts

Market Share
Percentage of total industry sales that a particular firm can claim.

An economic forecast tries to set an upper limit on income available for purchases, and an industry forecast predicts how much of a specific product people may be willing to buy. A sales forecast is needed to determine how much of the market a company may expect to capture. This figure is known as a company's **market share,** the percentage of the total industry sales that a particular firm can claim.

A company's share of market demand is directly related to its marketing effort. Market share increases or decreases with changes in the marketing mix. A change in product formulation or design, price, distribution methods, or the amount of advertising may affect market

Marketing Today 4.3

Banks Market Insurance

In the absence of Ottawa's promised financial services reform, Toronto Dominion Bank is becoming even more aggressive in marketing insurance products. The bank plans to expand its marketing of home insurance products beyond Ontario while also working on sponsorship of an auto insurance program.

Having successfully launched marketing of home insurance products through its 450 branches in Ontario, TD next January will begin offering the service in its 45 Saskatchewan branches. That will be followed by Alberta, where TD has 105 branches, and Manitoba, with 54 branches, Mark Foerster, assis-tant general manager of insurance, said in an interview. The plan eventually is to offer the service in TD's 950 branches across Canada, and the bank is talking with provincial regulators in the rest of Canada to permit that, Foerster said.

Launched last March under the name Home Green Plan, the product is marketed by TD for Hamilton-based Simcoe & Erie General Insurance Co. TD was the first of the major banks to market home insurance through its branches this way.

"It got off to a slow start in the first couple of months against the backdrop of the media attention and the Commons Finance Committee hearings, which ultimately concluded that this service was within the purview of the Bank Act," Foerster said.

Last May, Bank of Nova Scotia announced it would market the property insurance products of Canada Life Casualty Insurance Co. in 21 Toronto branches. In October, the bank expanded that to most of its 440 branches in Ontario, a bank spokesman said. The bank will monitor the results for the province-wide service before deciding whether to expand it across Canada, he said.

Allstate Insurance Co. of Canada has also run successful direct marketing campaigns to Canadian Imperial Bank of Commerce Visa cardholders.

Source: Sonita Horvitch, "TD will market home insurance outside Ontario," *The Financial Post*, December 20, 1989, p. 4.

share. The relation between market share and marketing effort is a key point to remember. Some marketers mistakenly believe they must have a sales forecast before they can plan for marketing, forgetting that marketing strategy itself often affects how much is sold.

The forecast of company sales is arrived at by applying the company's historical share of the market — adjusted by marketing plans for the upcoming year — to industry forecast figures. The hardest part is determining the *expected* market share. The task is especially difficult when the forecast is for a new product with no track record. Even when past information is available, it is difficult to translate into hard figures how a change in strategy will affect demand. Various techniques for estimating demand are available to marketers.

Techniques of Demand Estimation

The methods for estimating demand can be simple or elaborate. Some involve merely a survey of opinion, others a manipulation of statistics, and still others a use of market tests. Marketers choose among them on the basis of market stability (whether the demand is changing), the number of potential customers, the availability of historical data, and the amount of money available for forecasting.[16] Sometimes a combination of methods is used to increase forecast accuracy. Table 4.4 summarizes the major techniques discussed below.

Survey Techniques

All of the survey techniques for estimating demand rely on soliciting the opinions of some of the people involved in the marketing process.

Executive-Panel Survey
Means for sales forecasting using opinions of company officials.

Executive-Panel Survey   An **executive-panel survey** is often used when funds are limited or when a new product is being introduced. Before introducing its line of heat- and cold-resistant glass cookware, Corning commissioned an economic feasibility study to determine if there was a market for such a product. Results of the study indicated there was not a market. But a panel of executives at Corning claimed that, based on their previous experience in marketing other types of cooking products, this line would succeed. The company chose to ignore the report and rely on its own managers' judgement. Corning has since gone on to become one of the leading manufacturers of this type of cookware.[17] Executive opinion is not always that reliable, however. The past experience of executives is often not a good guide to the future. Many times different executives come up with radically different figures, and an average of them all may be far off the target.

Table 4.4 Demand Estimation Techniques: A Comparison

Type	Use	Advantages	Disadvantages
Survey			
Executive panel	For new products in particular	Inexpensive; draws on marketing experience	Subjective and unreliable
Sales force	For few customers	Improved accuracy because of closeness to customers; provides psychological motivator	Often results in conservative, uninformed estimates
Customer sampling	For many customers	Relies on first-hand information	May not predict actual purchase; is costly
Statistical Methods			
Time-series projection	For products with stable demand; for firms with many products	Is more objective than survey methods	Requires years of data; cannot predict pattern changes
Correlation analysis	For products with stable demand over a long period	Can be quite reliable when many correlations are found	Associations are difficult to find, and sometimes unreliable
Market Tests	For new products	Provide information about actual, not just intended, purchases	Are expensive; can fail to be predictive if sample is poorly chosen

Sales-Force Survey   A **sales-force survey,** in which a company asks its salespeople to estimate sales in their territories in the upcoming year, may be more reliable. The sales force is closer to the market and may know customers better than executives do. In addition, if salespeople participate in estimating their own sales quotas, they may have more of an incentive to meet them.

However, marketers should exercise caution when estimating demand based on sales-force surveys. Salespeople often are not aware of planned changes in the company's marketing mix or of possible changes in the economic climate that may affect sales. When a salesperson's estimates are also to be used as a measure of performance, the potential demand may be underestimated so sales quotas can be easily exceeded. On the other hand, if money for sales promotions and advertising is keyed to a territory's potential sales, a salesperson may be tempted to overestimate demand. A sales-force estimate is useful, but only in concert with other estimates of demand.

Customer Sampling   Direct **customer sampling,** a survey of consumers' intentions to buy, may also provide useful information about the strength of market demand. The National Lead Company surveys its largest buyers each year to determine likely demand for its paint, paper, and rubber products; General Electric maintains a panel of consumers to keep the firm informed of their intentions to buy appliances.

Samples of customer intentions can be expensive to obtain, however. And an "intention to buy" often does not result in an actual purchase. Like all survey methods, a sampling of customers is subjective and can give inaccurate results. But in the case of new products, a survey of opinion may be the only feasible method.[18]

Statistical Methods

Although forecasting is not an exact science, some techniques are more objective than others. Statistical methods, which make use of past data, attempt to take some of the guesswork out of demand estimation.

Time-Series Projection   **Time-series projection** uncovers patterns of movement in past sales and projects these patterns into the future.[19] At least five years of past sales data are usually required for an accurate prediction.

Researchers look for four patterns of movement. Sometimes a product's sales move upward along a trend line, as light beer has done over the past few years. More often, sales patterns are cyclical, changing every few years with the general business climate. As previously noted, car sales are closely tied to economic conditions. The sales of some products exhibit a seasonal pattern of movement, soaring at one or more times of the year and trailing off at others. Sales of toys at Christmas and suntan lotion in July are typical examples. Finally, some products' sales move up and down randomly, exhibiting no apparent pattern.

When a past pattern is discernible, marketers can determine the rate of change mathematically and project a continuation of that rate. The

Sales-Force Survey
Means for sales forecasting using estimates of company salespeople.

Customer Sampling
Survey conducted to sample customers' intentions to buy.

Time-Series Projection
Statistical method for forecasting sales based on past patterns projected into the future.

Correlation Analysis
Statistical method of forecasting used to find factors that change in advance of changes in product demand.

Test Marketing
Trial marketing in a limited area chosen as representative of an entire market.

assumption is that the future will be like the past. Of course, that is not always so. Time-series projections cannot detect radical turning points, so they are generally more reliable when applied to the immediate, rather than the distant, future.

Correlation Analysis Another statistical technique, **correlation analysis,** is more sophisticated. It is used to find factors that change in advance of changes in product demand. One industrial packaging manufacturer found that changes in the Index of Industrial Production tended to precede a change in company sales by three months.

When many correlations are found, predictions of future demand tend to be even more accurate. However, finding correlations can be difficult and, at times, impossible.

Market Tests

Historical data for making time-series projections or a correlation analysis are not available for new products. Customers can be sampled, but, as noted previously, what customers say they will purchase and what they will actually purchase can be quite different. An alternative method is **test marketing,** during which a product is sold in a limited area chosen as representative of the entire market.

Test marketing is expensive. Moreover, if test cities are not properly chosen, the results can be deceptive. But small-scale tests are sometimes the only way to gauge demand. The advantages and drawbacks of this method are discussed in Chapter 9.

Combining Approaches

Since each of the methods for estimating demand has some disadvantages, many companies use two or more of the techniques as a check on accuracy. For example, the estimates of an executive panel are often weighed against estimates from the sales force. The executives supply the knowledge of long-term economic trends and marketing plans that salespeople often lack, and the sales force provides knowledge of local markets, customer reactions, and competitors' activities in the field.

Accuracy is important because companies use sales forecasts for many purposes other than marketing. Based on the sales forecast, production is scheduled, raw materials and equipment are purchased, inventory is planned, and the effectiveness of the sales force is monitored. Many managers strive for accuracy within 10 percent of the actual sales.

Chapter Replay

1. **What are the differences between mass marketing and target marketing?**
    In mass marketing, all the customers in a market are thought of as homogeneous. Target marketing divides the market into market

segments and develops a marketing mix to attract a particular market segment.

2. **What are some ways to segment the consumer market?**

A marketer can segment a consumer market based on demographic factors (including regional and socioeconomic factors), rate of product usage, perceived product benefits, and psychographic characteristics.

3. **What are some ways to segment the industrial market?**

A marketer can segment an industrial market based on location, industry type, company size, and end use of the product.

4. **What is the difference between concentrated marketing and differentiated marketing?**

Concentrated marketing focuses on one segment with a single marketing mix. Differentiated marketing uses different marketing mixes to reach many market segments.

5. **What issues do marketers consider in deciding how many market segments to target?**

Marketers consider the cost of diversification, the risk of specialization, the financial condition of the firm, the actions of competitors, and the firm's experience with the market.

6. **What criteria make a market segment a good candidate for targeting?**

A market segment is a good candidate for targeting if it is identifiable, accessible, and large enough to be profitable.

7. **What types of forecasts do marketers use?**

Marketers use economic, industry, and company sales forecasts.

8. **How do marketers estimate demand?**

Marketers use survey techniques, such as the executive-panel survey, the sales-force survey, and customer sampling. They also use statistical methods — including time-series projection and correlation analysis — as well as market tests.

Key Terms

benefit segmentation	forecasting
concentrated marketing	industry forecast
correlation analysis	life-style
customer sampling	market potential
demographic	market share
segmentation	mass marketing
differentiated marketing	psychographic
economic forecast	segmentation
executive-panel survey	sales-force survey

sales forecast	target marketing
Standard Industrial Classification (SIC) Code	test marketing
	time-series projection
	usage-rate segmentation

Discussion Questions

1. What assumptions does mass marketing make about customers and products? Three-ring binders are a fairly uniform product used for one basic purpose: to hold paper. Can marketers of three-ring binders use target marketing? If so, what market segments can they target and how?

2. In segmenting the consumer market, what demographic characteristics might a maker of air conditioners consider?

3. Middletown officials commissioned a study of who is using its public library, hoping to use that information to get more people to visit the library. According to the study, 15 percent of Middletown citizens — mostly students — use the library several times a week, 40 percent visit the library at least once a year, and the remaining 45 percent rarely if ever use the library. To convince more people to use the library, which of these groups might the library target? Suggest some ways in which the library might adapt the elements of the marketing mix — product, price, promotion, and placement — to reach the target market(s).

4. What is psychographic segmentation? How do marketers measure life-style?

5. Don Deluxe runs a word-processing business, Deluxe Word Processing. In deciding which companies to sell his services to, what segmentation strategies might Don use?

6. What are the advantages and disadvantages of concentrated marketing and differentiated marketing?

7. What criteria make a market segment a good candidate for target marketing? How do marketers evaluate whether a segment is likely to be profitable?

8. Marsha McCloud, who works in the marketing department of Best Consumer Products, is responsible for estimating the market potential for refrigerator sales. What kinds of information will help Marsha make this estimate?

9. How can Marsha use the information in question 8 to forecast company sales?

10. Acme Software Developers is planning to introduce a revolutionary new program for students that automatically does homework while

entertaining the user with video games. What techniques could the company use to estimate demand for this product? Describe the advantages and disadvantages of each technique you suggest.

Ernst & Young in Canada

Tomorrow's Customers is a report prepared by Ernst & Young (formerly Woods Gordon) each year as a service to clients. The firm offers comprehensive accounting, tax, management consulting, and insolvency services from 30 offices across Canada and worldwide through Ernst & Young International. The following information has been extracted from a recent report.

Population Trends

North America's population will continue to grow slowly to the end of the century, averaging less than 1-percent growth annually. By the year 2000, the population of Canada will be 29 million.

Changing Age Profile

The median age in Canada today — 32 years — is the highest in history. By the year 2000, more than half the Canadian population will be over age 37. While the predominant theme is that of ageing, there are, within certain age groups, some interesting developments, especially among teenagers, those 30 to 50, and seniors.

Teenagers: Consumers in Training

Teenagers have decreased as a proportion of the total population, but their economic power has increased. Children buy and influence the purchase of an increasingly wide range of products. One study concluded that teenagers make 20 percent of all their families' supermarket purchases. In total numbers, however, the Canadian teenage group was 3.7 million in 1988, and it is expected to remain virtually unchanged at 3.8 million in the year 2000.

The 30s to 50s

By the year 2000, 31 percent of the Canadian population will be 30 to 49 years of age. Marketers will face the challenge of a mature population, representing the most knowledgeable consumers in history. The older

Source: Adapted from Ernst & Young, *Tomorrow's Customers*, 22nd ed. (Toronto, 1989).

Baby Boomers (those born in 1946 to 1954) will control 40 percent of spending power, according to the (U.S.) Conference Board. A substantial portion of these funds will be spent on mortgages, children, and ageing parents. This group allocates more available income to housing (31 percent of expenditures) than does any other age group, but they will still be affluent enough to be major purchasers of discretionary products and services.

Over-65s

Seniors will represent 13.5 percent of the Canadian population in the year 2000 (compared to 10.7 percent in 1986). Of these, 1.7 million will be over age 75.

The whole North American population is "greying." The proportion now over 65 is 12 percent and is projected to grow to 13 percent by the year 2000. The fastest-growing segment is the over 85s.

To put the ageing of North American society into perspective for Canadians, the current group of U.S. seniors is larger than the entire population of Canada. By the year 2000, there will be 35 million American seniors, a group more than one-fifth larger than the total Canadian population. Canada's senior population is expected to increase fairly evenly across the country, but U.S. seniors will congregate in the Southeast and West. Many Canadians who can afford it will join them in these areas. These groups will be inclined to sell their family homes to move to seasonally occupied, maintenance-free, and secure accommodation in Canada, such as condominiums and retirement villages.

By 2006, Canada will have 25 percent more dependents over age 65 than it does now, and 25 percent fewer dependents under age 17, reversing the nature of dependency. Social support programs will change in response to this shift.

For marketers, it is noteworthy that today, 85 percent of the over-65s do not work and 80 percent are financially independent. They have more money, leisure time, and needs yet to be addressed than other age segments, presenting many marketing opportunities. More will work in the future, partly because of shortages of younger workers and partly because an increasing number of older people are disdaining conventional retirement-age thinking as they live longer and healthier lives.

Smaller Households, Slower Growth

The average size of households will continue to fall as the number of one-person households increases. Average Canadian household size in 1986 was 2.8 people; it will fall to 2.4 by the year 2000. The number of households is expected to grow but at a slower rate than in recent years. The number of households grew in Canada from 7.8 million in 1980 to 9.2 million in 1986 and should reach 11.6 million by the year 2000.

The "New" Family

The family unit came back into style in the 1980s as Baby Boomers began to form families. Many businesses that catered to the singles market in the 1970s and early 1980s must now adopt a more family-oriented approach. Witness Club Med's moves to transform its young single image to a more family-oriented image to attract Baby-Boomer families. Companies that do not adapt will lose market share to more astute competitors or new entrants.

Although the number of families is increasing slightly, the number of people per family has been declining. The typical family has also changed. In 1984, the participation rate of Canadian women in the labour force was 54.3 percent; mothers with young children had a lower participation rate but it was still very high. Participation rates for all women workers are expected to increase.

Focal Topics

1. Why is it important for a firm such as Ernst & Young to prepare a report on changing consumer needs?

2. What other types of information about consumers would be helpful?

3. How would you use the information given here if you manufactured baby products? Consumer foods? Household furniture? Children's toys?

Foodland Ontario

CASE 4.2

Foodland Ontario is the consumer promotion program of the Ontario Ministry of Agriculture and Food. The objective of the program is "to help producers achieve maximum penetration of the Ontario market by Ontario-produced fresh and processed agricultural products."

The program was developed during the 1970s to counteract the falling market share of Ontario foods, the increase in imports, and the constant surplus-stock situation at the end of the crop year.

Ontario is Canada's largest producer of agricultural food products, accounting for 26 percent of the country's total agricultural food production. Ontario's food and beverage industry is valued at $15.2 billion yearly.

Market Segmentation

All aspects of the Foodland Ontario program address a common target market, identified as the primary food shoppers: women age 25 and older,

Source: Adapted from news releases from Foodland Ontario, Ontario Ministry of Agriculture and Food.

with emphasis on mothers 25 to 49 years old with an annual household income of $15 000 or more.

The Component Programs

Foodland Ontario works in six areas: consumer advertising, retail merchandising, public relations, trade liaison, market research, and the shared-cost program.

Consumer Advertising

When the Foodland program began, its advertising message informed consumers of the wide variety and availability of Ontario-grown products. Both the theme line "good things grow in Ontario" and the Foodland Ontario symbol encouraged consumers to buy Ontario food by promoting and identifying quality Ontario products.

The message then changed to one of economic benefit by communicating to consumers how Ontario's economy benefits when they buy domestic products. The advertising message evolved further into specific commodity promotions of products that best represented Ontario's good food quality, given a number of selection criteria.

In 1986, the old slogan gave way to a more competitive one, "Ontario, there's no taste like home," to communicate better the single most important Ontario food benefit—taste.

Although this message is still communicated through specific product promotions, more advertising emphasis is currently being placed on generic Foodland campaigns and greater linkage of the Foodland Ontario symbol in media advertising and at the point of sale.

Foodland Ontario currently uses television as its primary advertising medium.

Retail Merchandising

Retail Merchandising identifies and promotes Ontario foods in grocery stores through the distribution of point-of-purchase material to 1700 stores across the province by Foodland retail representatives. Thanks to full retailer support, food stores continue to be the main source of awareness of the Foodland Ontario symbol.

Public Relations

Public Relations supports Foodland Ontario promotions through the development and distribution of media kits, radio and television interviews, recipe brochures, and other activities. This area also co-ordinates media and ministry functions featuring Ontario foods.

Trade Liaison

The Trade Liaison component of Foodland Ontario works closely with members of the food trade to invite their participation in promotions and encourages the placement of the Foodland symbol on packaging.

Shared-Cost Program

The Shared-Cost Program provides financial assistance to Ontario marketing boards and commodity groups for the promotion and research of Ontario foods. Participation in this program tripled during a 12-year period beginning in the 1977-78 fiscal year.

Market Research

Since its beginning in 1977, Foodland has conducted an annual research tracking study to measure the success of the program. The 1989 study shows that: 85 percent of target consumers recognize the Foodland Ontario symbol; 73 percent definitely or probably will try specifically to purchase Ontario-grown products in the future; 73 percent feel that the Foodland Ontario program is a worthwhile effort; and 63 percent believe the program is likely to succeed.

Focal Topics

1. What basis for market segmentation does Foodland Ontario use?

2. What other bases could it use?

3. Are there other market segments that Foodland Ontario might target? Explain why it should consider these segments.

5

Chapter 5

In this chapter, you will learn:

- How marketers get information for routine operations and for making nonroutine decisions.

- The kinds of information that go into a marketing information system.

- The steps in the marketing research process.

- Ways to conduct an exploratory investigation.

- Advantages and disadvantages of the basic methods of conducting research.

- Why researchers often use samples rather than trying to survey everyone.

- What types of samples are available to researchers.

- The role of analysis, intuition, and communication in interpreting data.

- Why marketing research is important to organizations.

People Meters Measure Television Audiences

How do marketers know that their television advertisements are reaching their target market? They rely on audience research data provided by firms such as Nielsen Marketing Research. In September 1989, Nielsen recruited 1500 Canadian households for its television People Meter Service, which reports on audiences for TV programs.

Nielsen has used a household meter to measure viewing in the United States for about as long as television has been around. Before that, it measured radio listening by meter. In Canada, however, Nielsen measured television viewing by means of a diary mailed to a selected sample. When Nielsen switched in the States from the household audimeter to the People Meter, Canada was not far behind.

The People Meter is a box attached to the television set with a remote control unit that works like those commonly used with VCRs and cable-TV converters. The difference in this remote unit is that respondents indicate their viewing by pressing buttons on the remote.

Unlike the old audimeter, which measured only whether the television set was on or off and to which channel it was tuned, the People Meter records viewing by each member of the household as well as by visitors. It is an improvement on the diary measurement system in that the sample is a panel — diary samples differ each week of the survey — and the respondent has less to do. Also, metered measurement is not subject to postal disruptions or lack of respondent co-operation.

The People Meter permits analysis of audience composition and response for even the smallest audience segments. Viewing can be analyzed by standard demographic data (sex, age, family size) and by addi-

tional socioeconomic factors such as education, employment, and income bracket. Data on prime-time programming are available daily by direct computer access. Published reports are released within ten business days following the survey week.

You will learn in Chapter 5 that Nielsen's People Meter is an example of a research method known as observation. Each of the three methods of research design — observation, experimentation, and survey — has distinct advantages and disadvantages depending on the situation. The chapter describes observation and other ways of collecting information for continuing operations and special marketing decisions.

Source: Adapted from Nielsen Marketing Research Information Package, December 1989.

Marketing can be risky. This is particularly true for new products, which fail about 80 percent of the time.

Imagine that you are an executive at a major consumer products company. The time has come to make a decision about a new product that could cost your company millions of dollars. The deadline for the decision is fast approaching. Your job — and your company's future profits — are on the line. Naturally, you want as much information as possible on which to base your decision. But you have no time to wade through oceans of data that may be only marginally useful. Clearly, having the right information at the right time is crucial.

Every day marketers in major companies face decisions like this. Since it can cost as much as $80 million or more to launch a new product continent wide,[1] marketers cannot afford to gamble with inadequate information. As the stakes have become higher, methods have been developed to accommodate decision makers' needs for critical information. The information generally can be broken down into two categories: (1) data important for staying on top of day-to-day operations and (2) facts on which to base important nonroutine decisions.

Consider, for example, the information needs of General Motors marketers. To plan for production and distribution, they must have continuous updates on which GM cars are selling, how many are in stock, and how many are on order by retail dealers. But to plan for the design of automobiles to be marketed in three years, they need a different kind of data. They must keep abreast of possible changes in consumer preferences by reviewing information such as trends in family size and the price of gasoline. They also must stay informed about new legislation that might be enacted affecting design — for example, requirements for seat belts or air bags and regulations concerning minimum fuel efficiency.

Major Sources of Information

To meet needs for information, marketers turn to marketing information systems and marketing research. These two sources of information are closely related, but they serve different purposes.

Marketing Information Systems

A **marketing information system,** or **MIS**, is an orderly system for collecting data from inside and outside the firm. The MIS converts the data into information that managers can use in making marketing decisions. A useful marketing information system meets three criteria:

1. *Data are collected regularly.* As conditions in the environment

Marketing Information System (MIS)
Orderly procedure for regular collection of raw data internally and externally and conversion of those data into information for use in making marketing decisions.

128

change, the changes are reflected in updated information. In a retail clothing store, for example, managers want to know which items are moving quickly and which are moving slowly, so that the store can order more of the popular items and put the unpopular ones on sale to move them out.[2] To learn this information, the store can set up an MIS using sales slips or data entered into a computerized cash register.

2. *The data collected from both inside and outside the organization.* Inside information could include figures on sales, costs, and inventory. Outside information could include figures on competitors' sales and costs, overall economic conditions, and changing consumer attitudes.

3. *The data are converted into useful information.* For example, a store manager might want to compare present sales of a line of gloves with past sales, with sales of a competing line, or with the store's goals for sales. This information could confirm that the store's activities are succeeding or could alert the manager that he or she needs to take corrective action. If the manager had to look at individual sales figures with nothing to compare them to, these data would provide little useful information.

Increasingly, managers who use an effective MIS view the available information as a *resource* for decision making.[3]

Marketing Research

In contrast to an MIS, **marketing research** involves collecting data in order to solve a particular marketing problem or take advantage of a particular opportunity. Marketing research differs from an MIS in three ways:

1. The researchers collect data once, not continuously.

2. The data collected are pertinent to a single problem or situation, such as developing a new product or preparing an advertising campaign.

3. Much of the data must come from outside the firm—from customers, competitors, or the government.

Marketing research and marketing information systems can involve collecting data in similar ways, but the data serve different purposes. Consider, for example, the electronic scanners commonly used in grocery stores today. The checkout clerk passes your cans and boxes over a glass scanner, which reads the black and white bars printed on the packages. Those bars tell the supermarket's computer what you are buying and how much it costs.

The store uses this information for inventory control—to decide when

Marketing Research
Method for collecting, on a one-time basis, data pertinent to a particular marketing problem or opportunity.

to order more of an item and which items to discontinue because they are purchased infrequently. When used this way, scanners are part of a marketing information system. The makers of the products you buy also use this information. These companies obtain scanner-collected data on a product to determine how well a new product is doing or whether a new promotion has boosted sales.[4] When the company uses the data to answer specific questions such as these, it is conducting marketing research.

A good marketing information system and good marketing research are essential to efficient management. This chapter concentrates on the information needs of companies that market to consumers. But keep in mind that whether an organization markets to consumers or industry, it needs up-to-date information to function successfully.

An Overview of MIS

Managers have always had some form of marketing information system to guide their decision making. In the past it was very informal. Some managers simply walked among their staff asking questions or talked to their customers firsthand. During this century, the following three developments have increased the need for more and better marketing information:

1. *From local to national marketing.* As a company expands its market area, its managers need more formal systems for gathering market information.

2. *From buyer needs to buyer wants.* As buyers' incomes increase, they become more selective in their choice of goods. Technological developments in production, communications, and distribution enable producers to make and inform consumers about a greater variety of products. Consequently, sellers find it harder to predict buyers' responses to different features, styles, and other attributes.

3. *From price to nonprice competition.* As sellers increase their use of branding, product differentiation, advertising, and sales promotion, they require information on the effectiveness of these marketing tools.[5]

Today, the informal collection of data is impractical and unnecessary. It is impractical because of the great amount of data that must be gathered; it is unnecessary because computers now do much of this work.

Most modern marketing information systems are computer based. The computerization of information needed for marketing started in the late 1950s at companies such as Pillsbury, Du Pont, and General Mills. Today, most firms whose sales number in the millions use some form of computerized MIS. Smaller companies and nonprofit organizations have been slower to adopt such systems because of the expense. But with the continued lowering of data processing costs and the price declines in smaller computers, even those organizations are finding that the increase in efficiency is well worth the investment.

At the heart of a computerized MIS is the **data bank** (also called a data base), which stores and selectively retrieves data gathered from the internal and external environments. A data bank typically stores such information as trade association data; census data; annual reports of customers, competitors, and suppliers; various market research reports; publication summaries; data on internal operations; and data from invoices. Data bank use has recently expanded with the high technology boom. Figure 5.1 shows the evolution of data management, and Marketing Today 5.1 gives an example of the kinds of use data management has in today's business environment.

Within an MIS, these data are organized into three subsystems of information. One is marketing research. Another is the internal accounting system, which provides data used for control of daily operations. The third is the marketing intelligence system, which analyzes data from outside the organization. Each system provides information important in making both short- and long-term decisions.

Data Bank
Marketing information system's storehouse of information gathered from internal and external environments and used to retrieve data selectively; also called a data base.

	Early Systems	**Recent Systems**
Hardware	• Limited on-line capacity • Slow, costly data manipulation • Hardware costs over 50% of data processing budget	• Enormous on-line capacity • Fast, cheap data manipulation • Hardware costs about 30% of data processing budget
Software	• Optimized machine resource usage • Batch processing oriented • Used files	• Optimizes human resource development • On-line, transaction processing oriented • Uses data bases
Systems	• Data management and applications built together • Data sharing and application enhancements difficult	• Data managed as a corporate resource • Multiple applications use the data base

Figure 5.1 Evolution of Data Management

Source: Direct Marketing Association, Database Marketing II (seminar)

Marketing Today 5.1

What Goes into a Data Bank?

Most organizations would agree that their customers are their most important assets. It makes sense, then, that the company would want to maintain a bank of information about customers, to make sure that the company is succeeding in its efforts to build up that asset.

One company that obtains such information is Benetton, the Italian textiles group. Benetton obtains a daily report of consumer purchasing patterns from its 2000 European shops. This information enables the company to adapt production to meet changes in market demand. In addition, the company conducts an annual audit; by comparing data for the current year with data from

Phyllis Woloshin.

the previous year, Benetton officials can establish whether its customer base is growing or declining.

In establishing a data base of customer information, a company can ask questions such as: How many customers do we have? How many of these customers are new since last year? Which are the top 20 customers? What is the average

purchase per customer?

What do customers consider important when buying the company's goods or services? How likely are customers to display similar purchasing patterns next year?

Source: Adapted from Alan Melkman, "Why the Customer Is King," *Management Today*, May 1985, pp. 43, 46.

Internal Accounting System

Before computers came into common use, companies laboriously compiled records of sales, costs, inventory levels, and accounts receivable and payable. While the information may have been available, it was often widely scattered throughout different departments in the company and frequently existed in a form marketing managers found difficult to use. Most companies now rely on the computer to process such information and to present it in a way useful for various departments, each with different needs.

In an internal accounting system, the chief source of data is the sales invoice, the record of a customer's order. The data on that form are invaluable. When data from all customers' sales invoices are totalled, they give a picture of how well a company is doing in sales. The total can then be put through **sales analysis**, which breaks down sales according to:

1. *Product* — to indicate which products or lines are in greatest demand.

Sales Analysis
Breakdown of a company's sales data by product or customer demand, territorial volume, and salesperson performance.

2. *Territory* — to show where products are selling best or most poorly.

3. *Salesperson* — to point out those who are meeting goals assigned them and those who are not.

4. *Customer* — to shed light on which customers are the largest buyers.

Sales analyses are important for spotting significant sales patterns. For example, Skil, second to Black and Decker in the sale of power tools, undertook a thorough sales analysis and discovered that too much of its sales representatives' time was devoted to serving small customers. By trimming accounts by 40 percent and concentrating its sales effort, Skil increased sales by 21 percent and cut market costs by 13 percent.[6]

In some companies, 80 percent of sales come from 20 percent of the firm's customers or from the purchase of a small part of the product line. A close watch on these key customers or products by the computer is crucial. At Time, Inc., the internal accounting system produces weekly circulation charts in colour to help management decide where to focus special marketing and promotion efforts.

Managers can apply the information in an internal accounting system in a number of ways:

- They can pinpoint reasons for a sales decline.

- They can evaluate the progress of a promotional campaign and, if necessary, reallocate funds to an area that is behind target.

- They can analyze sales by market segments.[7]

Managers and information specialists are continually refining new ways to use internal data.

Marketing Intelligence System

As demonstrated in previous chapters, to make wise decisions, marketers need information from outside their companies. Consequently, many firms supplement their internally generated information with data from external sources such as government agencies and private organizations. Data on total industry sales gathered from such sources can be helpful in evaluating a firm's standing in an industry.

The sales force can often provide information about competitors' activities. And business periodicals, trade journals, and trade shows can supply valuable intelligence about economic conditions and how developments in the social and legal environments might affect marketers. Companies may also purchase information from outside intelligence suppliers such as the A. C. Nielsen Company, which amasses data on retail prices and brand shares and evaluates television ratings, and ISL (International Surveys, Limited) which through its Consumer Panel of Canada, accumulates data from 4500 Canadian households. (See Figure 5.2 for an example of such information.)

As firms become increasingly aware of the need for up-to-date infor-

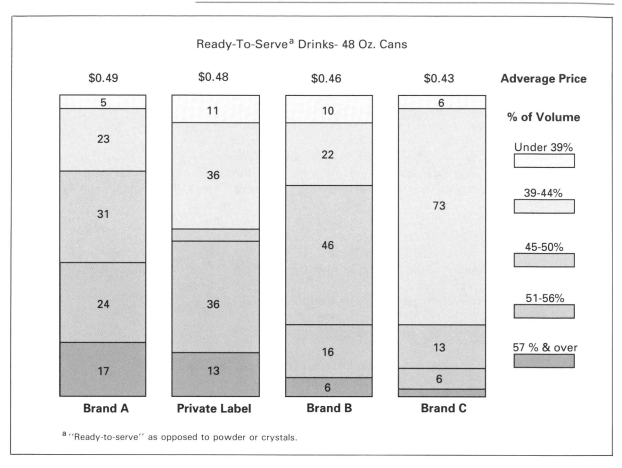

Figure 5.2 Data from a Consumer Panel

Source: ISL International Surveys Ltd., Consumer Panel of Canada.

mation, more and more are establishing company libraries. The key to the growth and management of all this information has been the data base, a computerized file containing information on specialized topics.

While great strides have been made in developing the technology for a sophisticated MIS, some problems remain in implementing such a system. Unless top management is committed to the development of a truly functional system, the design of the system may not adequately address the problems that its users ask it to solve. In some cases, the technical staff develops a system that provides impressive feedback, but not in a form that managers find useful for decision making. Thus it is important for managers to state their specific information needs clearly and to explain in what form that information should be presented.

If such issues are addressed in an early stage of system design, the resulting benefits can be enormous. For marketing managers, a system's potential to help design effective strategies, to oversee their performance, and to act quickly as the results emerge should prove an invaluable asset.

The Scope of Marketing Research

Marketing information systems are useful for controlling day-to-day activities and planning for the efficient use of people and money. But sometimes they uncover problems without giving any clear indication of solutions. In those cases, in-depth marketing research studies are needed to reveal the real causes of the trouble.

Tandem Computers Inc. enjoyed initial success by marketing a fault-tolerant computer—one in which parts could fail but the computer could keep on working. The reliable design attracted users who absolutely had to keep their computers running: banks, hotels, manufacturing plants, travel agencies, and the like. After several years, however, other companies were making fault-tolerant computers, and Tandem lost its technological edge. The company protected its position with extensive marketing research. Tandem learned that its customers were initially attracted to its product by the novelty of fault tolerance but actually bought Tandem computers because they had an efficient modular design. Tandem shifted its marketing message to emphasize this benefit and maintained its strong position in the market.[8]

Besides seeking the underlying causes of specific problems, marketing research can also be used to explore opportunities in the marketplace. Thus, when S. C. Johnson & Son Company decided to get into the hair-care market for women, it first conducted extensive marketing research to determine market sizes and trends. After having narrowed the growing markets to shampoos and creme rinses, it surveyed a national sample of women by mail to explore hair-care practices. The survey indicated that "oiliness" was the number one hair-care concern. To combat the problem, the company responded by developing a 99 percent oil-free shampoo and creme rinse. Advertising for its Agree brand claimed that the products would "help stop the greasies." Agree shampoo and creme rinse went on to become the most successful new products in the company's history.[9] (See Figure 5.3.)

Marketing research is most useful when marketing researchers work as partners with management. In this role, researchers help managers identify researchable issues and then conduct research or analysis to address these issues. Marketing researchers are best able to adopt the role of partner when three conditions are present:

1. Researchers do objective, professional work of the highest standard of integrity.

2. Management is receptive to the value of research.

3. Researchers and management share a sense of clearly identified research needs and issues. This requires researchers to be sensitive to the concerns of managers.[10]

When researchers work as partners with management, they try to solve problems, not merely gather data.

The usefulness of marketing research has been recognized for over a

Figure 5.3 Agree Shampoo and Conditioner

century. The first formal piece of research is credited to an advertising agency, N.W. Ayer and Sons. In 1879, the agency surveyed state officials about expected grain production. It used the results of the survey to plan the advertising schedule for a manufacturer of farm equipment.

Since then, the scope of marketing research has expanded considerably. More than two-thirds of all firms having sales over $5 million have marketing research departments of their own. In addition, the federal government through StatsCan conducts extensive research pertinent to marketing, and many nonprofit organizations are beginning to establish market research departments.

Not only has the number of firms engaged in marketing research grown, but the variety of research projects has also expanded. Table 5.1 lists the most common areas of research undertaken by businesses in North America. Most firms use marketing research to measure market potentials, determine market characteristics, and analyze sales and market shares.

A large national manufacturer of consumer packaged goods typically conducts research to provide information in the following key areas:

1. *Product category understanding.* This kind of research — seeking, for instance, an understanding of consumer acceptance and usage of laundry detergent — combines qualitative research and mass studies. Through sophisticated analytical techniques (such as multidimensional scaling), the company can obtain information about what kind of people use which products and how they purchase and use them.

2. *Product performance testing.* This kind of research is used in the development of new products and improvements to current products. Consumers are asked to use "blind" products in their homes for a few weeks, following their normal habits. At the end of the

Table 5.1 Research Activities of 798 Companies

Activity	Percentage of Companies
Measurement of market potentials	93%
Sales analysis	89
Competitive product studies	85
Short-range sales forecasting	85
New-product acceptance and potential	84
Establishment of sales quotas, territories	75
Distribution channel studies	69
Studies of advertising effectiveness	67
Packaging research	60
Export and international studies	51
Social values and policies studies	40

Source: Data from Dik Warren Twedt, ed., 1978 Survey of Marketing Research (Chicago, Ill.: American Marketing Association, 1978), p. 41. Table reprinted with permission from David L. Kurtz and Louis E. Boone, *Marketing*, 2nd ed., p. 134. Copyright 1984 by The Dryden Press.

period, they are asked to rate the product both overall and on its most important performance aspects.

3. *Concept testing.* Used mostly in researching proposed new products, this kind of research tells marketers if consumers, when presented with a concept, are likely to be interested.

4. *Brand tracking.* Measurements of market share and/or brand awareness over time are usually provided by syndicated services.

5. *Advertising testing.* Measurements of the effectiveness of a particular advertising message or creative approach are obtained by showing test ads to a sample of consumers. They are asked to interpret the main ideas of each ad and to record what they like and don't like about it.

According to one author, the purpose of all such research is "to find holes" — holes that may be fatal to an organization unless plugged or holes that provide an opening for a new venture.[11] The method for finding gaps in marketing knowledge is similar in all research situations.

Marketing Research Methods

Most definitions of marketing research note that it involves the methodic gathering of data. A method is an orderly way of proceeding. The order generally followed in marketing research studies is shown in Figure 5.4.

Problem Identification

Most experienced market researchers say that after the problem is identified, half the work is done. The reason is not difficult to understand. Most students soon learn when doing a term paper or special report that one of the trickiest problems is finding an area narrow enough to be handled in a few pages but broad enough to be of interest. In the case of market researchers, the most difficult task is defining underlying causes or areas of opportunities without so narrowing the definition that final recommendations for action are trivial.

Beginning researchers often mistake symptoms for the problem itself. Consider the hypothetical case of the soft-drink manufacturer who discovers a decline in sales. The problem for researchers is not the decline itself—a symptom—but the underlying causes.

The firm's MIS may give some clues as to which causes can be eliminated from consideration. Thus, if sales for the entire industry are up, the problem does not lie in the economy. Or if salespeople report no new competing products on the market, the problem probably does not originate there.

That leaves open for question some aspect of the firm's marketing mix.

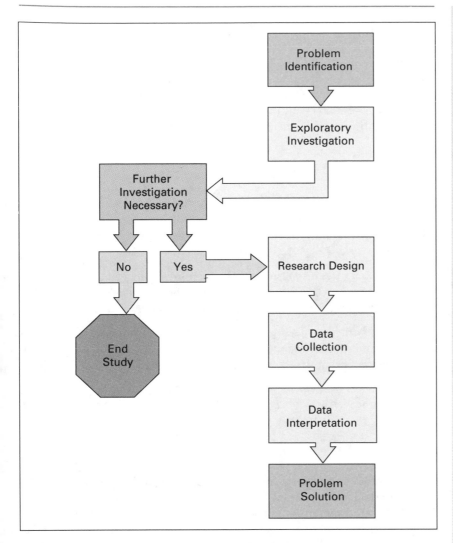

Figure 5.4 Stages of the Research Process

Again, some areas may be less promising for investigation than others. If the beverage is a well-established brand, the product formulation is an unlikely problem source. Similarly, if all pop on the market costs about the same, price too can be eliminated as the cause of declining sales.

By proceeding systematically, marketers can narrow down the source of the problem. However, during the first phase of problem identification, the problem is seldom clearly defined. The soft-drink researchers may know where the problem does *not* lie, but that is far from having a set of working recommendations on how to raise sales. After their preliminary narrowing of the problem, the researchers must search for a testable statement of the problem.

Exploratory Investigation

The purpose of exploratory investigation is to develop a **hypothesis**, or an educated guess about the relationship between things or what will happen in the future. This investigation, often called situation analysis, may involve either (1) talking to informed people in informal interviews or (2) investigating literature that may pertain to the possible problem areas.

Informal Interviews

Researchers talk to informed people to get their views on the source of a problem or on possible areas for research. For example, researchers for the soft-drink manufacturer might talk to at least some of the following people:

1. *Customers.*   A discussion with some users and perhaps nonusers of the company's brand may give researchers an idea of how customers view the product or how advertising messages are received.

2. *Intermediaries.*   This group might include franchised bottlers for the firm's product, some retailers who sell the product, and perhaps owners of restaurants who serve the beverage.

3. *The firm's own staff.*   Interviews with the sales force, for example, may uncover possible customer dissatisfaction or rumours circulating in the industry.

Focus Group Interview

One technique researchers have found useful for talking with customers is the **focus group interview**. In this approach, a group of people with something in common — such as owning a home or going to the movies at least once a month — assemble with a moderator or interviewer to discuss a topic. Usually the group exchanges views about a new product, an advertising approach, or some other marketing concern of the company sponsoring the interview. The moderator directs the interview based on a guide that indicates which subjects the group is to cover. This guide is not a questionnaire, however; the moderator uses it flexibly.[12] Often, observers watch from behind a one-way mirror.

Focus groups provide information relevant to a variety of situations. Newspapers, for example, use the groups as a guide in planning news features, improving graphic design, and deciding on how to approach certain stories. Universities use them in planning how to tailor their recruiting efforts and fund drives. A computer manufacturer used a focus group to find out why owners of businesses with sales of $2 to $5 million weren't buying its products. Participants in the group quickly made it clear that they weren't as technologically sophisticated as the company's marketers had assumed. They weren't buying the computer systems because they didn't understand them and were afraid of them.[13]

Hypothesis
Educated guess about the relationship between things or what will happen in the future.

Focus Group Interview
Method of determining customer attitudes by interviewing a relatively homogeneous group assembled to discuss a topic.

Focus groups can consist of in-house personnel as well as potential customers, an approach that may be particularly suitable for those who sell to the industrial market. The researcher gathers all company personnel who have contact with users of the company's product; these people might include product managers, accounting personnel, repair workers, and secretaries. The discussion in such a group would cover customers' expressed or hidden problems. For example, in one in-house focus group, it became evident that company maintenance people needed more training.[14]

While focus groups provide helpful information, this approach has limitations. The people chosen for focus group interviews are seldom scientifically selected; therefore, the results can be biased and should not be taken as conclusive. Researchers observing the interview are susceptible to preconceived notions and to hearing only what they want to. Because the groups are small and not randomly selected, what group members say is not necessarily representative of the total market. Nevertheless, when interpreted properly, the results of focus group interviews can give important clues for further research. Examples of some clues uncovered in actual focus groups are described in Marketing Today 5.2.

Literature Reviews

Researchers can save time and expense when they can find relevant **secondary data**, information that already exists somewhere, having been collected for another purpose.[15] Because such information is relatively inexpensive to gather and because there is no point in repeating work already done, researchers often investigate secondary data before turning to other sources of information.

Secondary Data
Information that exists before a particular study is conducted and that was collected for another purpose.

The firm's own internal data might be classified as secondary data if they were collected for purposes other than the study. Such internal data might include sales call reports, product performance reviews, company profit and loss statements, or analyses of marketing expenditures. In addition to internal data, the secondary data of most interest to researchers at this stage of the investigation are found in the published material of other organizations.

Some of the more useful publications for marketers are listed in Table 5.2. The organizations chiefly responsible for such publications are:

1. *The federal government*, through Statistics Canada, provides marketers with data including the size and composition of markets, the sales volume of industries, and the types and locations of wholesalers and retailers.

2. *Provincial and local governments*, which provide information such as traffic on roads, retail sales tax revenues, and consumption of various taxed products.

3. *Trade associations*, such as the Canadian Automobile Manufactur-

Marketing Today 5.2

The Marketer As Detective: Using Clues from Interviews

A diner in a lunch counter is obviously experiencing stomach distress. As a musical rhythm section plays in the background, he makes his way to the counter and mumbles to a concerned waitress, ''Bubbly . . . bubbly . . . bubbly?'' She shows him the Eno; with a smile of recognition, the customer sings, ''Bubbly, bubbly, bubbly Eno.'' As the man drinks the effervescing Eno solution, the two continue singing, without words, the rest of the Eno jingle.

This television commercial, launched in July 1989, marked Eno's first advertising campaign in more than ten years. The commercial, developed by Grey Advertising, was the result of some research performed by parent company Smith, Kline, Beecham Canada, Inc. The marketing problem was that the effervescent antacid segment of the market had been declining slightly, with most of the activity in antacid tablets and liquids.

Ellen Turner, Beecham's senior product manager, says that when Beecham turned to market research, it had some hypotheses about why product use was slightly down. Perhaps consumers found the effervescing tablets inconvenient. Or maybe people were wary of the sodium content in such products. In focus group interviews, however, neither of these reasons was given for lapsed use. Many could not remember why they stopped using the product. Others said that they had just forgotten about the product.

The real surprise was what focus group participants did remember. ''We were amazed,'' says Turner, ''at all the people (80 percent) who started singing the jingle as soon as we mentioned Eno. We are using the commercials to build on our heritage. This campaign is not really a relaunch of the brand but a reemphasis. We intend to continue advertising on TV as long as we see a positive impact on the business.''

After the launch of the commercial, sales picked up for Eno, which now enjoys the largest share of the effervescent antacid market.

Source: Adapted from Martin Mehr, ''Back to the Bubbly with New Campaign,'' *Marketing*, October 30, 1989, p. 2.

```
CLIENT:   BEECHAM CANADA INC.
PRODUCT:  Eno
TITLE:    "Lunch Counter"
LENGTH:   :30 sec.
```

MUSIC THROUGHOUT NATURAL SOUNDS

MAN: Ooooh. Bubbly, bubbly, bubbly.

WAITRESS (SINGS): Da, da da da da.

MAN (SINGS): Bubbly, bubbly, bubbly Eno!

WAITRESS (SINGS): Eno... da, da, da.

MAN (SINGS): Ta da da da da.

MAN AND WAITRESS (SING): Ta da da ta da.

ENO MUSIC IN MAN AND WAITESS (SING): Ta da da ta da.

ANNCR (VO): Good tasting Eno...

...soothes heartburn...

...and relieves acid indigestion...in seconds.

SINGERS: BUBBLY, BUBBLY, BUBBLY. MUSIC CONTINUES.

MAN AND WAITRESS (SING): Bubbly, bubbly bubbly Eno.

SmithKline Beecham Consumer Brands, Weston, Ontario

Table 5.2 Secondary Data: Some Useful Publications

Statistics Canada Publications

Canada Year Book. A record of developments in Canada's economic, social, and political life.

Canadian Statistical Review: A monthly publication containing current statistical information retrieved from CANSIM, the Statistics Canada computerized data bank, including economic indicators, population statistics, and data on labour, prices, manufacturing.

Census of Canada: Reports of a count conducted once each decade, with certain categories checked every five years. It provides demographic data on all residents of Canada by province, city or town, and census tract.

Census of Manufactures: A series providing annual coverage of major industries. Data include the value of products produced by an industry, cost of materials and equipment, number of establishments, and wages paid.

Statistics Canada Catalogue: A list of major data published by the agency.

Statistics Canada Current Publications Index: A listing of the agency's numbered publications released up to June 30 of any given year.

Private Publications

Business Periodicals. Publications dealing principally with marketing, including the Canadian weekly, *Marketing*, and the U.S. *Advertising Age* and *Sales and Marketing Management*.

Professional Journals. Especially *Journal of Marketing, Journal of Marketing Research, Journal of Advertising, Journal of Advertising Research*, and *Journal of Retailing*.

Indexes to Periodicals. Especially *Canadian Periodicals Index, Canadian Business Index, Canadian News Index*, and *Business Periodical Index* (U.S.).

Standard and Poor's Industry Surveys. Updated statistics and analyses of industries.

Private Marketing Guides

Canadian Markets. Estimates and forecasts for population, households, personal disposable income, and retail sales for markets nationwide. (Annual publication by Financial Post Information Service.)

Handbook of Canadian Consumer Markets. A compendium of data on population, labour force, employment, income, expenditures, production, retail trade, and price indexes. (Biennial publication of Conference Board of Canada.)

Sales Management Survey of Buying Power. Market data on population, income, and retail sales for counties and census divisions and other statistical areas in Canada and United States. (Annual.)

Source: M. Dale Beckman, David L. Kurtz, and Louis E. Boone, *Foundations of Marketing*, 4th ed. (Toronto: Holt, Rinehart and Winston of Canada, 1988), appendix B, pp. 158–175.

ers' Association, which sponsors special studies for members.

4. *Magazine and newspaper publishers*, who report on business trends, report the results of periodic surveys, and provide news of important legal developments and technological trends that may affect a marketer's business.

5. *Computer-assisted literature searching,* which is the computerized version of thumbing through a card catalogue. An increasing number of libraries—both public libraries and those in most postsecondary schools—have computer terminals that contain information on whether the library has a book and whether or not it has been checked out. In addition, computers that can hook up to a telephone with a modem can be used to obtain information from bibliographic data bases. The user enters the desired topic, and the computer lists the publications available on that topic.

6. *Commercial market researchers,* such as Canadian Facts, Market Facts, International Surveys Ltd., and A. C. Nielsen Company, which sell marketing information gathered from consumer and trade surveys on the rate of product usage or turnover in stores, the amount of advertising by brand, market share by product, and other vital indicators.

7. *Consumer attitude and public opinion research,* such as that provided by Environics and by the U.S. *Yankelovich Monitor,* an annual census of changing social values and how they can affect consumer marketing.[16]

The soft-drink manufacturer's researchers might benefit by consulting some of these sources. If the firm is a member of a trade association, data on the kinds of distributors used by other firms may reveal inefficiencies in the researching firm's distribution policies. Or information from A. C. Nielsen may suggest a link between increased advertising outlays by other companies and the firm's declining sales. One industry that relies on secondary data is the public transportation industry. At Your Service 5.1 describes how the Toronto Transit Commission has responded to such information.

All information from secondary sources must be interpreted carefully. The reasons for caution are related to the nature of secondary information. Because it is collected for purposes other than the specific study, it can be faulty. The information may be unreliable because it is biased. Because trade associations often act as boosters for their members, they may put data in a highly favourable light. Another problem with secondary data is that they may not be completely relevant to the problem at hand.

An interesting example of the last problem arose when Skippy introduced a new brand of peanuts to compete with Planters. Based on reports purchased from a commercial firm, Skippy brought the brand to market at what was supposed to be the height of the snack sales season—around the holidays in November and December. When heavy sales for the product failed to materialize, the brand was pulled from the market. A postmortem examination showed that the original information was misinterpreted. Retailers stocked up heavily in November and December, but sales of the product remained the same throughout the year. The secondary data had shown only heavy movement from factory to warehouses during the period, not heavy sales.[17]

At Your Service 5.1

TTC Regularly Surveys Riders and Nonriders

You may not realize it, but organizations serving the general public frequently research users of their service. The Toronto Transit Commission, which provides public transportation for Canada's largest metropolitan area, surveys the public each year throughout the year.

In the TTC's most recent Public Attitude Survey, Environics Research Group, using central computer-assisted telephone facilities, interviewed a random sample of 1608 respondents age 15 or older, representative of the population of Metropolitan Toronto (which includes six separate municipalities).

For the purpose of analysis, respondents were divided into four major groups according to their use of public transit:

- *Nonriders*, who rode the TTC not at all or no more than three times in a typical month.

- *Light riders*, who on average travelled on the TTC one to three times per week.

- *Medium riders*, who typically made four to nine trips per week on the TTC.

- *Heavy riders*, who used the TTC ten or more times per week. They generally made two peak-period trips each weekday getting to and from work or school.

From the survey results, it was easy to discern the demographic profile of each rider group (see the accompanying table).

Note that medium and heavy riders of the TTC are predominantly female, whereas nonriders are predominantly male. Not surprisingly, 99 percent of nonriders have access to a car, and they tend to own houses while the other groups are apartment dwellers. The light-rider group seems to be a mixed bag in terms of employment status and income. Although it is not shown in the table, a disproportionate number (36 percent) of light riders are 55 years of age or older.

Armed with these profiles, the TTC can initiate marketing strategies to accommodate the frequent riders better and to convert more of the light and nonriders to mass transit. The analysis by "product" usage not only reveals why certain people do not use the TTC (access to cars) but also the demographic characteristics of each group and thus how they can be reached.

Source: Adapted from information provided by the Toronto Transit Commission, January 1990, on its Annual Public Attitude Survey, performed by Environics Research Group.

TTC Rider Group Profiles

	Nonriders	Light Riders	Medium Riders	Heavy Riders
% of total population	36%	16%	15%	32%
Sex	Male	Both	Female	Female
Age	25–54	Over 25	Over 65	15–34
Income	$50 000 +	$20 000–$30 000, $50 000 +	$20 000–$30 000	Less than $40 000
Municipality	Scarborough, North York	Toronto, North York, Scarborough	Toronto, North York	Toronto, North York
Employment	Full-time	Full-time, retired, student	Retired, part-time	Full-time, student, part-time
Occupation	Professional/ technical, sales/ clerical	Professional/ technical, sales/ clerical	Professional/ technical, sales/ clerical	Sales/ clerical, professional/ technical
Access to a car	99%	93%	77%	78%
Marital status	Married	Married	Married, single	Single
Dwelling	Single, detached	Apartment	Apartment	Apartment
Own/rent home	Own	Own	Rent	Rent

Source: Information provided by Toronto Transit Commission

Hypothesis Formation

The preliminary investigation should have produced enough information for researchers to develop a hypothesis about the problem. The hypothesis must be carefully worded to avoid possible errors in future research.

Let us assume in the case of the soft-drink manufacturer that the preliminary investigation strongly indicates that the reason for declining sales is ineffective advertising. The researchers believe that sales are down because competitors are spending heavily on new advertising. Their hypothesis might read: "Sales will increase by at least 40 percent if the advertising message is changed to emphasize a new plastic bottle." This is only a hypothesis. It may or may not be true. Only further research will reveal whether the problem lies there or elsewhere.

Further Investigation?

The organization's research objectives, plus the amount and quality of information gained from exploratory research, help the marketing manager decide whether to continue researching. Sometimes the company needs more precise and reliable information than it can obtain from exploratory research. In many cases, however, research may be concluded after the inspection of secondary sources. If several studies report similar findings, the problem may be solved without further research and with a considerable cost saving. Or, if secondary sources hint that the problem can be solved only after more comprehensive and costly study, researchers may decide that further study is not worth the expense.

The high cost of marketing research often leads researchers to end the investigation at this stage. For example, it would not make sense for the soft-drink manufacturer to spend $1 million to learn how to increase sales by $500 000. But if the company were planning to spend $50 million to launch a new product, an additional $1 million spent to avoid a marketing catastrophe might sound like a bargain. In that case, the marketing department would be more likely to continue on to the next stage of research design.

Research Design

At the third stage of marketing research, marketers prepare to collect **primary data** — original information produced specifically for the present study. While primary data are almost always more costly and time consuming to gather than secondary data, any doubt about the reliability of published sources or accuracy of the hypothesis must be resolved by primary research.

Research design refers to the procedures of carrying out the study, using one of three methods — observation, experimentation, or survey. The correct method for doing research depends on the project. As one author has noted, "A research method for a given problem is not like the solution to a problem in algebra. It is more like a recipe for beef stroganoff; there is no one best recipe."[18]

Observation

Data collection by **observation** involves either the personal or mechanical viewing of subjects or physical phenomena. There are many varieties of observational studies. One common observation technique is the traffic count — of pedestrians or cars — used, for example, to determine the site of a new gasoline station or the popularity of a display. Another staple observation method used by marketing researchers is the Nielsen People Meter (see the vignette at the opening of the chapter). A third is supermarket scanners, which are now in all major grocery chains.

An advantage of mechanical observation is that it records exactly *what* people do, not what they *say* they do. For example, a group of electric utilities hired a researcher to find out why their fuel-use projections, based on poll-takers' reports of customer interviews, were falling short of reality. The researchers set up television cameras trained on the thermostats in 150 homes. Homeowners had claimed to keep them set at 20C°, but other people in the house—teenagers, older relatives, visitors,

Primary Data
Original information gathered for a specific research project.

Research Design
Method for carrying out a marketing study.

Observation
Research method that involves either the personal or mechanical viewing of subjects or physical phenomena.

and cleaners—fiddled with them throughout the day.[19]

The problem with observational research is that it reveals only *what* is happening, not *why*. To overcome this limitation, observation may be used in conjunction with one of the other methods.

Experimentation

Experimentation
Research method that establishes cause-and-effect relationships.

In recent years, **experimentation**, which establishes cause and effect relationships, has attracted more interest. Market researchers have conducted experiments both in laboratory settings and under real field conditions. In this technique, two matched groups of subjects are exposed to situations that are identical except for one or two elements called variables. The subjects' responses to the differences in those variables can then be measured.

The soft-drink manufacturer might commission a field experiment to test the hypothesis regarding advertising the new bottle. Researchers could run a television commercial stressing the new packaging in one city and simultaneously run the regular commercial in another city. (This technique is referred to as a *split run*.) Researchers might then contact viewers for their reactions to the commercials and compare the results. The small-scale test marketing of new products in different cities uses a similar approach.

A somewhat different approach is the laboratory experiment, in which researchers try to duplicate market conditions in an artificial setting. One example is testing TV commercials in a theatre situation.

Experimentation is an increasingly important marketing tool. The method does have some shortcomings, however. Experiments can be very expensive and time consuming. (Test marketing often goes on for about a year at a cost sometimes of more than $1 million.) Experiments are also difficult to control. Competitors have been known to sabotage field experiments by running heavy advertising of their own in test cities or lowering prices drastically. For example, when Campbell Soup Company tried to test market a dry soup mix, salespeople from Lipton, the market leader, stormed into stores and pasted high-value coupons on Lipton soups.[20] Another shortcoming of experimentation is that in laboratory settings consumers may behave differently because they know they are being observed. But despite these drawbacks, marketers will continue to use experimentation because they want to discover cause-and-effect relationships.

Surveys

Survey Research
Study using direct or indirect interviews.

The most widely used and useful method for marketers is **survey research**, which involves interviewing people. Surveys may range from the most informal—perhaps a few questions from an interviewer in the supermarket—to elaborately designed, computer-read questionnaires.

The survey may directly ask consumers their reasons for buying or not buying, or it may use questions to uncover motives indirectly. Mason

Haire used indirect questioning in a classic piece of marketing research almost 40 years ago. Instant coffee had just been introduced, and Haire wanted to investigate why consumers resisted buying it. When he had asked homemakers directly, they had replied that they disliked the flavour; however, in blindfold tests, they could not tell the difference.

So Haire prepared two shopping lists that were identical, except that one included Nescafé instant coffee, and the other Maxwell House drip-grind coffee. Haire asked the homemakers to describe the kind of women who would compile such lists. They replied that the instant-coffee buyer was lazy, a spendthrift, an inefficient manager, and a poor wife. Haire concluded that consumers were avoiding instant coffee because they feared that serving it would project a negative image of themselves.[21]

The popularity of survey research stems from its flexibility.[22] Surveys can be used to obtain a variety of kinds of information in a variety of situations. However, respondents may be unwilling to respond or unable to supply accurate information.

Additional advantages and limitations apply to each of the three basic survey methods. These methods are personal interviews, mail surveys, and telephone interviews.

Personal Interviews   The most favoured method for conducting a survey has been the personal interview. It may be conducted either in the home or at the offices of a research company. In the latter case, a group of individuals, constituting a panel, may be interviewed. Marketers prefer the personal interview for several reasons. It can be long, so a good deal of data can be secured. Doubts about the meaning of questions can be clarified, and visual aids can be used to increase understanding. In addition, the interviewer can report on the social and economic status of those interviewed — an aid for interpreting results.

But fears of loss of privacy (and, in urban areas, of admitting a stranger into a home) now limit the effectiveness of personal interviews. The high cost of hiring personal interviewers and then training them so they do not bias results by inappropriate remarks is another disadvantage.

Mail Surveys   Researchers may avoid some of the problems of personal interviews by conducting a mail survey. Mail surveys are less costly than personal interviews and can reach working people who might otherwise be missed. People seem to prefer mail surveys because they can answer at leisure and often remain anonymous.

But mail surveys also have limitations. The response rate may be only 25 percent or even less.[23] Questionnaires tend to be answered only by the better educated, so that the survey may be unrepresentative. (The section on sampling later in this chapter illustrates the importance of representativeness.) Also, since 20 percent of the population move yearly, an accurate mailing list may be impossible to obtain. Finally, respondents in mail surveys often misunderstand questions or skip them altogether.

Researchers can improve mail surveys to reduce or overcome some of these limitations. For example, researchers can test surveys on a few people to see whether they understand the questions. Testing is an inexpensive, trouble-shooting technique that applies to other kinds of surveys as well. In addition, researchers can try to improve response rates by making it easier to respond, say, by including a stamped return envelope and even a pencil. Including a small gift, such as a dollar bill, also can improve response rates; often people feel uncomfortable about accepting even a small gift without doing something in return.

Telephone Interviews For many research purposes, a good compromise between the face-to-face interview and the impersonal mail survey is the telephone interview. The telephone allows some probing by the interviewer and still permits some privacy for the respondent. Because organizations can shop for lower-than-normal long-distance rates, the expense of personal interviewing may be cut. Finally, telephone interviewing allows immediate response. The soft-drink researchers could get same-day reaction to a particular commercial by using this method.

Telephone interviews do raise a few problems, however, that researchers should keep in mind. People tend to be more impatient over the phone than in personal contacts. Therefore, questions must be brief. Also, many people now have unlisted phones, though through a technique called "random digit dialing" researchers can get around this limitation.

The advantages and disadvantages of each form of survey are summarized in Table 5.3. The survey method selected depends ultimately on the nature of what must be probed. In-depth questions about motivation for purchasing a product are best handled through personal interviews. A simple knowledge of fact ("Did you see our ad?") may be secured over

Table 5.3 Advantages and Disadvantages of Three Survey Methods

Personal Interview	Mail Survey	Telephone Interview
Advantages		
Obtains detailed information.	Covers widespread area cheaply.	Reaches wide area inexpensively.
Allows interviewer to probe.	Eliminates interviewer bias.	Speeds data collection.
Obtains socioeconomic data on respondent.	May reach otherwise inaccessible people.	Allows respondent some anonymity.
Permits use of visual aids.	Allows respondent to answer anonymously and at leisure.	
Disadvantages		
Can be expensive.	Can lack representativeness.	Difficult to reach those with unlisted numbers.
May introduce interviewer bias.	May produce low rate of return.	Must use short questions.
May raise fears for privacy.	Does not allow probing or follow-up questions.	

the phone. Whatever the form of survey, however, almost all methods employ a questionnaire.[24]

Questionnaire Design

All surveys, including personal interviews, require a data collection instrument, or form, so that all participants answer the same questions. People unfamiliar with research tend to think that almost anyone can write questions for a questionnaire. Researchers know that constructing a questionnaire requires genuine skill. Many kinds of mistakes can be made in questionnaire writing, but most are errors either of bias or of communication.

Errors of bias are common but not always obvious. Experienced researchers know that one source of bias is placement of an answer at the head of a list. Thus, the seemingly innocent question:

Which soap do you prefer?

- Ivory

- Dove

- Dial

- Irish Spring

will collect some votes for Ivory that it would not ordinarily receive if it were not listed first. The ongoing struggle among politicians to secure the first line on the ballot provides evidence of such a bias. To overcome it, market researchers sometimes rotate the order in multiple-choice questions or leave the question open-ended so that the respondent can supply an answer.

Perhaps the greatest source of error lies in faulty communication, or a misunderstanding of what the question means. In a survey for a new detergent, one question asked respondents where they might use the product in their homes. One specific reference was to "germ-ridden" areas. "I want a germ-ridden kitchen," one woman responded. "What do you mean by that?" asked the surprised interviewer. The woman answered, "Well, I want to be ridden of all my germs."[25]

Can you spot the problems with each of the questions in the "questionable" questionnaire in Figure 5.5?

Data Collection

Regardless of the research design chosen, researchers must decide from whom they want information and how they want to go about collecting it. One way to proceed is to collect data from every member of a population under study. Such a complete canvass is called a **census.** An alternative way is to collect information from only a part of the population. The theory is that the part of the population that is selected,

Census
Complete canvass of every member of a population under study.

Imagine that a university (we'll call it Gradgrind U.) developed this questionnaire to get information from the parents of its incoming first-year students. Can you detect any problems with these questions?

1. What was your total family income last year?

People often balk at giving such personal information. If this question were necessary, it should appear later in the questionnaire when a spirit of co-operation has been established, and in a less threatening form, such as: "Check one: $15,000–19,999; $20,000–24,999, etc."

2. How many postsecondary institutions did your son/daughter investigate before choosing Gradgrind U.?

Who can remember this? Besides, what does "investigate" mean? Look at the brochure, or visit the campus?

3. Don't you think the government should give financial assistance to all bright students who want to attend postsecondary institutions?

Biased question. What parents, faced with a hefty tuition bill, would answer "no"—especially since all parents fondly assume their kids are very bright?

4. Is your son/daughter eager to attend Gradgrind U.? yes (   ); no (   )

Who's to say what "eager" means? And can it be answered "yes" or "no"? The kid may be eager to get away from home, less eager to leave his or her girlfriend or boyfriend, and not eager at all to take English Comp I. Besides, what useful information does this question provide?

Figure 5.5 Test Your Skills as a Questionnaire Writer

Source: Based on Don A. Dillman, "Writing Questions," in *Mail and Telephone Surveys* (New York: Wiley, 1978), pp. 79–118.

Sample
In research: Limited canvass of a representative part of a population under study.

called a **sample,** may yield information about the larger group.

Most people are familiar with sampling as it is used to predict the outcome of elections. Major television networks have developed this technique to a high degree, and they have been criticized for "calling" elections even before polling places on the West Coast have closed.

Market researchers prefer to sample, rather than take a census, for several reasons. First, complete counts are usually time consuming and prohibitively costly. Second, it is sometimes physically impossible to check all members of a population. For example, researchers simply could not count everyone who had his or her television set on last night between nine and ten o'clock.

Types of Samples

Just as there is no one best research design, there is no ideal sampling method. Researchers recognize two broad types of samples—probability and nonprobability.

Probability Sample
Sample in which each member is selected from a given population on some objective basis not controlled by the researcher.

In a **probability sample,** each member of the sample is selected from a given population on some objective basis not controlled by the researcher. This is called random selection. In a **random sample,** each member of a population under study has an equal chance of being selected from a list. A firm wanting to sample automobile owners in Manitoba might obtain a registration list from the provincial ministry of transport and select every tenth name on the list.

If a population has subgroups that differ markedly, random sampling may produce inaccurate results. For example, corporations vary tremendously in size. If a sample of corporate attitudes toward social responsibility is taken, results may differ if all corporations are considered together, rather than if they were polled in groups according to size. In **stratified sampling,** important subgroups are identified and then randomly sampled.

Both random and stratified sampling work best when there is a precise list of the population being studied. Sometimes, however, no such list exists. There is no list of soft-drink consumers, for instance. In such cases, people may be divided by geographic area and then parts of the area (such as city blocks) may be sampled. This is known as **cluster sampling.** Note that such area sampling upholds the principle of probability sampling: all residents within the blocks selected have an equal chance of being chosen.[26]

Nonprobability samples are less objective than probability samples since they involve personal judgement in the selection of sampled items. The researcher, rather than chance, decides who will be chosen to participate in the study. In a **convenience sample,** such as an on-the-street interview, members are selected because they are close at hand. In a **judgement sample,** the kind often used in award nominations, experts who are thought to be specially qualified in the area of interest are chosen. Participants in **quota samples** are singled out by researchers on the basis of characteristics thought pertinent to the study. For example, the soft-drink manufacturer may instruct researchers to sample an equal number of men and women, half between the ages of 15 and 24 and half between 25 and 34.

In some circumstances, nonprobability samples are the preferred way of collecting data—for example, when special expertise, such as knowledge of an award category, is important. Frequently, however, researchers resort to nonprobability samples because they must collect data quickly or work with limited funds. In those cases, the results of such samples must be interpreted cautiously because those selected may be unrepresentative. Merely stopping someone on the street, for instance, is no guarantee that the opinion volunteered is representative of the population's. The nature of the street itself may seriously bias the answers given. For instance, we would expect different responses from people sampled on a street in a fashionable shopping area and people sampled on skid row. There may be less pronounced, but still significant, differences among various neighbourhoods in any city. In short, the unknowns in nonprobability sampling frequently make the results uncertain.

Random Sample
Probability sample in which each member of a population under study has an equal chance of being selected.

Stratified Sampling
Probability sampling in which subgroups are identified and then randomly sampled.

Cluster Sampling
Probability sampling in which the population under study is divided into subgroups and then parts of the group are chosen at random to be sampled.

Nonprobability Sample
Sample that involves personal judgement in the selection of sampled items.

Convenience Sample
Nonprobability sample in which subjects are chosen on the basis of convenience to the researcher.

Judgement Sample
Nonprobability sample composed of subjects who are specially qualified in the area of interest of a study.

Quota Sample
Nonprobability sample composed of subjects chosen on the basis of characteristics thought pertinent to a study.

Errors in Collecting Data

Probability samples are more objective than nonprobability samples because they avoid subjective judgements that may lessen the representativeness of the sample. That does not mean that probability samples are free of error. Sampling is done by people, after all, and people do make mistakes. The human factor is an important source of error in both probability and nonprobability samples.

In random sampling, for example, an interviewer assigned to canvass randomly selected homes may substitute a home because residents of the chosen home were out. The effect is to substitute subjective judgement for objective criteria of selection. Canvassers may also introduce errors by misreading a question or recording an answer incorrectly. Or they may bias results by asking questions in a certain tone of voice or by altering the wording.

The training of people who collect samples therefore becomes very important. Most companies use the services of outside polling firms or market research companies, which have highly trained professionals who can handle any research design from a simple count to an in-depth interview. In fact, although companies may design their studies themselves, almost all of those conducting research hire outside marketing research firms to do the field work (interviewing). Error can never be completely eliminated, but by using professionals it can be minimized.

Data Interpretation

Good market researchers, like efficient marketing information systems, must convert raw data into usable information. This is the critical step in the research process. At this stage, a researcher must draw upon many talents, including analytical skills, intuitive understanding, and an ability to communicate.

Role of Analysis

Data can be analyzed in a number of ways. Analysis may simply involve reviewing the data. Even if the amount collected is not large, it may be sufficient to produce conclusions and recommendations.

In most cases, however, researchers confront a mass of data. For example, researchers for the soft-drink manufacturer we have been following might have statistics on audience awareness of commercial messages in test cities. This information must be sifted to determine if there is a relationship between a particular kind of message and rising sales.

Various statistical techniques can be applied to yield information. The tools of analysis are too numerous to mention here, but skilled researchers must be aware of all of them.[27] They are the means of distinguishing the forest from the trees.

Role of Intuition

Statistical techniques by themselves cannot ensure reliable research results. Intuition—the ability to see what is relevant in the data—plays an important part. For example, the failure of researchers at two food companies to see the relevance of information they had collected cost their companies millions of dollars. The companies had seen an opportunity in the dry-soup market, which had barely been tapped at the time. They conducted extensive marketing research, and researchers recommended a go-ahead on the basis of their findings. But they chose to ignore an important piece of information they had learned: that consumers used existing brands of dry soup mainly as a flavouring for gravies and snacks. The companies produced dry-soup flavours that were unsuitable for non-soup uses. Consequently, sales were small and the companies pulled out of the market.[28]

Intuition is not infallible. But without it, statistical analyses may produce totally useless information.

Role of Communication

After the researchers have interpreted the data, they must write a report. Frequently, the decision makers who read the report are unskilled in research and statistical methods. The job of the researcher is to translate highly technical material into understandable English.

A good research report must be readable, objective (based on evidence revealed by the data), and pointed (answering questions important to managers).

It is usually best to start the report with the conclusions and recommendations—parts that most interest executives. Details of the research process can be included in an appendix or in a separate technical report.

Problem Solution

All the efforts of the marketing research process lead to the final step: solving the problem. Often, the person who decides how to solve the problem and the person who conducts the research are different people. However, the researcher typically recommends possible solutions.

Marketing Research Prospects

Good marketing researchers need the abilities to think mathematically and to write clear English. Researchers who combine those skills are prized by both business and nonbusiness organizations.

The marketing concept emphasizes attention to customer needs. Marketing research is the key to carrying out that purpose. Researchers are usually staff members who feed marketing managers information about customer reaction to the four "Ps." On the basis of this information, managers plan for the markets they serve. As long as firms continue to practise the marketing concept, there will be a need for marketing research. For that reason, the field offers excellent career opportunities.

The risks of conducting a business today are greater than ever before. Fluctuating economic conditions, increased competition, more government regulation, and less consumer confidence are all factors that contribute to this uncertainty. Advance information on changing conditions is a must for survival. Since marketing researchers can supply this information, their position in the organizational world of the future seems secure.

Chapter Replay

1. **How do marketers get information for routine operations and for making nonroutine decisions?**

   Marketers get information for routine operations from an ongoing marketing information system. They get information for making nonroutine decisions by conducting marketing research.

2. **What kinds of information go into a marketing information system?**

   A marketing information system comprises an internal accounting system, a marketing intelligence system, and marketing research reports.

3. **What are the steps in the marketing research process?**

   The steps in the marketing research process are problem identification, exploratory investigation, decision on whether to conduct further research, research design, data collection, data interpretation, and problem solution.

4. **What are the basic ways to conduct an exploratory investigation?**

   An exploratory investigation may consist of informal interviews with customers, intermediaries, or staff. These interviews might be focus group interviews. In addition, researchers review the literature for secondary data.

5. **What are some advantages and disadvantages of the basic methods of conducting research?**

   Observation records actual behaviour but does not give reasons for it. Experimentation discloses cause-and-effect relationships, but it is expensive and can be difficult to control. Surveys are flexible but subject to low response rates and inaccurate answers.

6. **Why do researchers often use samples rather than trying to survey everyone?**

   A census is time consuming, costly, and sometimes impossible. Samples are often more accurate because fewer errors are made.

7. **What types of samples are available to researchers?**
Researchers can use probability samples, such as random, strati-fied, and cluster samples, or they can use nonprobability samples, such as convenience, judgement, and quota samples.

8. **What is the role of analysis, intuition, and communication in interpreting data?**
Analysis involves reviewing the data and deciding how to organize it and calculate statistics that will yield relevant information. Intu-ition gives the researcher insight into the implications of the data. Communication skills are necessary to make the results meaning-ful to management.

9. **Why is marketing research important to organizations?**
Research enables the company to meet the marketing objective of paying attention to customer needs. Greater risks involved in run-ning a modern business make advance information crucial.

Key Terms

census	observation
cluster sampling	primary data
convenience sample	probability sample
data bank (data base)	quota sample
experimentation	random sample
focus group interview	research design
hypothesis	sales analysis
judgement sample	sample
marketing information system (MIS)	secondary data
	stratified sampling
marketing research	survey research
nonprobability sample	

Discussion Questions

1. What is the difference between a marketing information system and marketing research?

2. Jack Crabmeat of Crabmeat Cable Services has called in a computer consultant, Bea Brilliant, to put the company's sales invoices onto the company's computer. He has called a meeting of Bea; himself; Hal Roe, the company's marketing manager; and Lynette Flax, the accounting manager, to plan how to set up the system.

   At the meeting, Bea says, "I can set up the system to prepare reports in any format you'd like." Jack turns to Hal and asks, "What information would you need from a marketing standpoint?" How can Hal use the data on the sales invoices as a source of marketing information?

3. What conditions should be present for marketing researchers to work as partners with management?

4. Hotel manager Jill Waverly telephoned marketing consultant Phil Sunderby. "Phil," she said, "we just aren't filling up our rooms like we used to. We need to do a survey and plan a good advertising campaign." In light of what you know about the marketing research process, does Jill seem to be starting at the beginning? How might Phil suggest she go about solving her marketing problem?

5. Why do marketers sometimes decide *not* to proceed beyond the stage of exploratory investigation?

6. Master Mayonnaise Makers is planning to introduce its popular brand of mayonnaise in a plastic squirt bottle. The company's marketers estimate that the new container will capture 50 percent of the mayonnaise market. To predict whether the product will succeed in reaching that goal, Master Mayonnaise will conduct marketing research. Suggest how the company could design a study to make this prediction. Give three suggestions: one using observation, one using experimentation, and one using surveys.

7. Deluxe Video Creations is a company that develops and sells video games. The company has plans for a new game, but before spending any more development money, management wants to see whether enough people seem interested in playing it. Ted Tremendous, marketing consultant, has drafted a questionnaire to explore interest in the new game. Trained callers will randomly call students on a local campus. Following are the first three questions. For each question, indicate any shortcomings you see and suggest ways to improve the question.

   a. How many times have you played video games during the past year?

   b. Do you agree that the self-righteous people who castigate video games as being excessively violent just don't understand the many advantages attributable to playing the games, such as developing co-ordination and decision-making skills?
      [ ] yes [ ] no

   c. Which video game do you prefer?

      (1) Double Dragon

      (2) Tetris

      (3) Space Harrier

8. Under what conditions might stratified or cluster sampling produce

more accurate results than random sampling?

9. Marianne Hitek entered the office of her boss, the vice-president of marketing, who started in sales and rose through the ranks. "Marianne!" cried the boss, "We hired you because of your brilliance in statistics, but I can't make any sense of this report of yours. What's the conclusion? What do you recommend?" "The conclusion is at the end of the report," replied Marianne, pointing to the last sentence, "Conjoint analysis predicts the attribute utilities shown in table 14, which support the null hypothesis as described on page 3."

What aspect of data interpretation has Marianne failed to provide her boss? Suggest some ways she can improve her report.

Whirlpool Corporation

CASE 5.1

Whirlpool Corporation, a leading manufacturer of major home appliances, has corporate roots that go back to 1911. During the more than 70 years the firm has been making appliances, the variety of consumer products and services has grown dramatically. At the same time, competition for the consumer's dollar has become fierce. Whirlpool has always placed quality first in its products and services.

In an attempt to understand more about consumers today, Whirlpool commissioned the marketing research firm, Research and Forecasts, to conceive and execute a study that would uncover new information about the desires, expectations, and judgements of the consuming public, with emphasis on — but not limited to — an exploration of quality-related issues. The following material relates to that study.

Overview of Research

As more than a generation of marketing research has demonstrated, different perspectives on the consumer are much like the reports of the proverbial blind men who touched different parts of one elephant and came to radically different conclusions about the animal. *The Whirlpool Report,* however, deals with the broad topic of quality and the consumer. Rather than detailing specific profiles of markets for particular products or services, it outlines for the "postconsumerist" era what it means today to be a quality consumer. Some of the key questions explored in the research include:

- Do consumers feel surrounded by junk and poor-quality goods and services, or are they satisfied?

- Do consumers think quality is becoming scarce, or do they think the

Source: Adapted from *America's Search for Quality: The Whirlpool Report on Consumers in the 80's*, published by Whirlpool Corporation in 1983.

quality of goods and services has improved in recent years?

- Do consumers feel they have an adversary relationship with manufacturers and service providers?

- Are they more or less demanding about quality than they have been in the past?

Research Methodology

A multistage research design was used in conducting this study of attitudes toward quality in goods and services.

Phase One

The first phase consisted of qualitative and background research undertaken to generate hypotheses and develop topic areas for the general public survey stage of the project.

Phase Two

The second phase consisted of a series of interviews with 50 representatives of the print and broadcast media from throughout the United States between May 24 and June 18, 1982. These media representatives were specialists in the areas of consumer interest, business and finance, and home/life-style reporting. In these interviews topic areas for the general public survey were discussed at length in an open-ended interview format, and suggestions as to issues of consumer concern were solicited.

Advisory Panel

During phase one and phase two of the project, the advice of experts in the consumer relations and consumer research fields was actively solicited through numerous telephone and face-to-face interviews. The research staff invited a number of experts to act as an advisory panel for the general public survey stage of the project.

Phase Three

The third phase of the project was a general public survey. Twenty trained interviewers conducted phone interviews for a period of five weeks in late 1982 and early 1983. The interviews were conducted on weeknights between 6 p.m. and 10 p.m. and on weekends between 10:00 a.m. and 11:30 p.m. Each interview took an average of 34 minutes to complete. In order to ensure that the respondents interviewed represented a random sample of the total population, at least four callbacks were made to each telephone number that had neither yielded a complete interview nor had been disqualified. A final response rate of 63 percent was obtained.

Phase Four

In order to make projections valid for the entire population, the sample should match the total population on key demographic variables. Because of sampling fluctuations, it was necessary to weight the data to match census figures on four characteristics: age, race, gender, and education. The final weighted sample matched census figures very closely. The weighting produced a total weighted sample size of 1002.

Statistical Analysis

The bulk of analyses reported in the text are illustrated with cross-tabulation data. Relationships between variables were confirmed by reference to the chi square and Pearson's R statistics where applicable. Several three-way crosstabs were computed to test further for relationships among variables. The accompanying table shows a few of the research results.

Selected Research Results

	Very Satisfied	Somewhat Satisfied	Just Barely Satisfied	Unsatisfied	Very Unsatisfied
How satisfied are you with the manufactured goods you can purchase in your area? (992 respondents)	33%	52%	10%	3%	2%
How satisfied are you with the services you can get in your area? (998 respondents)	23%	59%	15%	2%	1%
	Significantly Improved	Somewhat Improved	Stayed about the Same	Somewhat Deteriorated	Significantly Deteriorated
In general, do you think the quality of goods has improved or deteriorated over the last ten years? (998 respondents)	13%	35%	24%	21%	7%
In general, do you think the quality of services in your area has improved or deteriorated over recent years? (979 respondents)	11%	36%	36%	13%	4%

Focal Topics

1. From the perspective of Whirlpool and recipients of the research (other businesses, academia, and the public), why is this type of research of value?

2. What is your evaluation of the research methodology used in the study?

3. What changes or additions would you recommend in the method of gathering data, in the types of topics explored, and in the data analysis?

CASE 5.2

Environics Research Group Limited: AdTrend Advertising Awareness Tracking

Environics is one of Canada's leading marketing and opinion research firms. Established in 1970 as a private, independent Canadian company, it is a full-service research firm experienced in nationwide telephone, in-home, and mail surveys, Environics clients include business, the media, industry associations, and departments and agencies at all three levels of government.

Since its inception, the research group has undertaken custom research studies on a wide variety of sociological and public policy issues. In recent years, the firm has developed syndicated studies that enable business and government to understand and track major public policy issues and consumer trends.

AdTrend

In 1988, Environics inaugurated the AdTrend Advertising Awareness Tracking study to measure consumer awareness of corporate and brand advertising. Special emphasis has been placed on brand awareness within specific product categories.

The Basic Study

Every three months, 1500 telephone interviews are completed with a sample of Canadians aged 18 and over. Interviews are conducted in the months of February, May, September, and December. Household telephone numbers are randomly selected; then a systematic procedure is used to select respondents in multiperson households.

The sample is stratified by province and five levels of community size with proportionate sampling by province for all communities that con-

Source: Environics Research Group, brochure, December 1989.

tain populations of more than 10 000. Communities with less than 10 000 population are selected randomly.

Measures of Advertising Awareness

The study measures four levels of awareness over 9 media and 20 product categories. Respondents are asked the following questions:

1. *Top-of-Mind Awareness of Advertising.*   "Of all the advertising that you have seen, heard or read in the past month, which one specific ad sticks in your mind the most?"

2. *Share-of-Mind Awareness of Advertising.*   "What other advertising that you have seen, heard or read in the past month sticks in your mind? Any other advertising?"

3. *Top-of-Mind Awareness of Advertising in 9 Media.*   "For each of the following media, which one specific ad or commercial that you have seen, heard or read in the past month, sticks in your mind the most?

    - Radio ad
    - Television commercial
    - Newspaper ad
    - Magazine ad
    - Outdoor billboard
    - Ads on public transit (for example, in or on buses, streetcars, transit trains and stations, and so on)
    - Direct mail advertising
    - Flyers or inserts that come with your newspaper
    - Movie theatres

4. *Top-of-Mind Awareness of Advertising in Specific Product Categories* [Product categories are defined by subscribers' needs.]   "Of all the advertising you have seen, heard or read in the past month that deals with each of the following, which one specific ad sticks in your mind the most?

    - Beer
    - Soft drinks
    - Automobiles
    - Fast-food restaurants
    - Retail stores which sell things for your home or car
    - Airlines

- Financial institutions
- Auto service
- Oil and gas companies
- Cheese
- Butter
- Shampoo
- Liquor or spirits
- Grocery stores
- Insurance companies
- Computers

Subscribers can add their own questions to the survey. For instance, a client may want to probe specific commercial/advertisement recall or product use. Also, in each wave, a special advertising issue is explored. Some of these have included federal election advertising, awareness of and participation in sales promotions, and attitudes toward advertising and advertising at Toronto's SkyDome.

Results

AdTrend data are available in printed form within three weeks of completion of interviewing. Data are also available on microcomputer diskettes. The data are valuable to a marketer because they make it possible to determine brand awareness within each of the following demographic breaks:

- Sex
- Age
- Marital status
- Family size
- Employment status
- Occupation
- Household income
- Education
- Language
- Ethnic group
- Political preference
- Media consumption

(See the accompanying table for a typical page of an AdTrend report.)

AdTrend Sample, Winter 1988
Of all the advertising you have seen, heard, or read in the past month that deals with each of the following, which one specific ad sticks in your mind the most?

■ Headache and cold remedies

	Total		Gender		Age					Marital Status		Children at Home		Employment Status						Occupation				
	N	%	Male	Fe-male	18 to 24	25 to 34	35 to 44	45 to 54	55 or more	Sin-gle	Mar-ried	Yes	No	Full Time	Part Time	Home-mak-er	Un-empl-oyed	Ret-ired	Work-ing Women	Prof., Adm., O.L.B.	Tech., S.P. O.S.B.	Office, Sales Serv.	Skilled/ Semi-skil.	Un-skilled Worker.
Total Responses	1505	1505	724	781	213	453	334	168	309	357	871	630	852	811	154	165	79	188	422	194	154	302	225	106
Tylenol	337	22	17	27	26	24	23	21	18	24	22	26	20	21	27	28	28	23	27	22	22	24	20	19
Anacin	297	20	19	20	23	22	19	20	16	21	21	21	19	22	15	22	11	15	21	19	23	20	19	23
Aspirin	126	8	10	7	8	9	7	7	10	7	9	7	10	8	10	5	12	9	7	7	8	7	13	6
Dristan	82	5	5	6	7	5	6	7	4	5	6	6	5	5	8	7	3	4	6	8	9	3	4	5
Bayer Aspirin	53	4	4	3	1	2	3	7	6	2	4	3	4	3	3	3	2	7	2	3	1	3	4	5
Contac C	49	3	4	3	3	5	2	2	3	4	3	3	3	4	1	3	4	2	3	3	3	2	5	3
NeoCitran	36	2	2	3	3	2	3	2	2	3	3	3	2	2	4	3	1	2	3	2	1	3	2	4
Sinutab	23	2	2	2	*	3	2	1	1	1	1	1	2	2	1	1	3	2	2	3	3	1	2	1
Triaminic	22	1	1	2	3	1	2	1	1	3	2	2	1	2	2	2	4	—	2	2	3	2	1	3
Nyquil	16	1	1	1	1	2	1	1	*	1	1	1	1	1	2	1	2	—	1	2	—	2	*	—
Dimetapp	11	1	*	1	*	1	1	1	*	1	1	1	1	1	1	1	2	1	2	2	1	1	*	—
Excedrin	11	1	1	1	1	1	1	1	—	1	1	1	1	1	1	—	—	1	1	1	2	1	1	—
Vicks	11	1	1	1	1	1	1	—	1	*	1	1	*	1	1	1	—	1	*	*	—	*	2	1
Children's Tylenol	7	*	*	1	—	1	1	1	—	1	1	1	*	1	1	1	—	—	1	1	1	2	—	1
Advil	2	*	—	*	—	*	—	1	—	*	*	*	*	*	*	1	—	—	—	*	—	*	—	—
Other	113	8	8	7	10	6	8	8	7	9	7	7	8	7	5	5	12	8	7	6	9	8	6	9
Don't know/no answer	308	20	25	17	10	16	21	21	31	17	19	16	23	21	18	16	18	26	15	22	16	21	20	23

Note: *sample not large enough to permit reporting of percentage—no response

Source: Environics Research Group Limited.

Focal Topics

1. Why do you think Environics uses telephone interviewing in conducting this study?

2. How do you think a marketer might use the information in the AdTrend study?

3. What other information do you think might be useful?

Chapter 6

Consumer Buying Behaviour

In this chapter, you will learn:

- Why cultures and subcultures are important to marketers.

- The kinds of groups that can influence buying.

- The order in which human needs arise.

- How people filter information.

- Why marketers are concerned about attitudes and personality.

- Ways in which consumers learn.

- How life-styles influence buyer behaviour.

- The stages of the buying process.

College-Level Consumption Attracts Marketers

Canadian college and university students represent a young, affluent, well-educated market segment. Students have large discretionary incomes — one study shows that they control as much as one-half of all discretionary purchasing power. Their special needs and life-styles lead students to spend more money per month on discretionary items than the average family of four.

Furthermore, college and university students are at a stage in their lives in which they are building brand loyalty. Finally, they are highly concentrated on campuses, enabling marketers to target them geographically.

Compared to the general population, college and university students spend little time watching television or reading newspapers. Magazine publishers reach this market by offering special student subscription rates and using on-campus subscription agents. In addition, Canada has its own student lifestyle magazine.

Campus Canada distributes 100 000 copies of its magazine to universities and community colleges from British Columbia to Newfoundland. It is published four times during the school year, offering reading on everything from new rock bands to new fashion to sports and campus issues. In addition to the four regular issues, two souvenir magazines are printed and distributed: one in the fall for the Vanier Cup, another in the spring centred around the national hockey championship.

Advertisers who target students use *Campus Canada* as an effective advertising medium to reach this audience. These advertisers range from manu-

Rene Ostetto/Campus Canada

facturers of computers and calculators, like Texas Instruments, through food and beverage advertisers and banks to tape and film companies, such as Fuji Film.

College and university students represent an attractive group for some marketers. Other segments of the population have different patterns of spending. The differences arise from variations in family structure, values, life-styles, and many other characteristics. This chapter looks at influences on buyer behaviour and at ways marketers can put that information to use.

Source: Adapted from Canadian Controlled Media Communications, *Campus Canada* press kit, 1990.

The Scope of Buyer Behaviour

Your attitudes and personality influence whether you spend your leisure time skiing, taking in a movie, or attending a party. Your friends and financial resources may affect this decision as well. And these are only some of the influences.

Knowing about these kinds of influences helps the managers of ski resorts, movie theatres, and potato chip manufacturers to plan successful marketing strategies. Therefore, marketers study **buyer behaviour.** Buyer behaviour is the discipline that provides marketing managers with an understanding of what is behind the decision to spend money, time, and effort on consumption-related items. It probes not only what is exchanged, but also why, where, when, and how often.[1] Without such knowledge, marketers do not know why their products are selling or failing to sell.

Contributions of the Social Sciences

The systematic study of consumer behaviour is relatively new. Pioneers in the field have therefore borrowed heavily from other, more established disciplines, particularly the social sciences. The fields that have been of most use to marketers are anthropology, sociology, demography, and psychology. Anthropology studies the culture of a society or part of a society. Sociology studies human behaviour as influenced by groups. Demography uses statistics to analyze various population characteristics such as residence, age, education, occupation, and income. Psychology studies the human mind and individual behaviour.[2]

Except for psychology, each of these fields treats individuals as part of a group. Every person belongs to several groups. One group membership might include teenager, suburban resident, high-school graduate, Anglophone Canadian, middle-class, single, and fraternity member. The first three labels (teenager, suburban resident, high-school graduate) are demographic categories and provide marketers with some very useful information. They indicate, for example, that a member of the group is much more likely to buy a stereo than bifocal glasses.

Demographic categories paint a portrait of a group by numbers. The supplied information is sketchy. To add colour to the numbers, anthropological data (the label "Anglophone Canadian" or "European") and sociological information (middle-class, fraternity member, and single) must be added. To marketers, these labels indicate, for example, that a group member would probably value leisure time and have the interest and income to fill some of that time with music. Such information would be of great value to a stereo manufacturer.

If there are enough people matching those characteristics, marketers

Buyer Behaviour
Study that provides marketing managers with an understanding of what is behind the decision to spend money, time, and effort on consumption-related items.

are likely to identify the group as a promising market. It is no mystery, then, why there are often many stores specializing in stereo equipment, records, and cassettes in university and college towns.

Users and Uses of Consumer Behaviour Data

As the chapter on market segmentation points out, few manufacturers can afford to sell to the whole North American market. It is simply too vast, and money would be wasted appealing to those who have neither the interest nor the income to buy. It is usually more profitable to specialize—to appeal to one group or, at most, a few. But such specialization requires knowledge of buyer categories, what interests them, and how they can be influenced.

In addition to businesses, nonprofit organizations are major users of buyer behaviour information, because they must understand demographic trends to plan facilities. Charities must learn what groups in society are most likely to heed appeals. Any organization that requires the support of a group (or the public) can benefit from knowing that group better.[3]

Cultural Influences on Consumer Behaviour

Anthropologists study **culture,** which refers to a people's shared customs, beliefs, values, and artifacts (housing, works of art, and so on) that are transmitted from generation to generation. The word *anthropology* brings to mind images of scholars in pith helmets digging up bones and taking notes on the behaviour of remote tribes. But those interested in consumer behaviour are primarily concerned with the study of today's culture. (See Marketing Today 6.1.)

> Most North Americans know how to handle money, turn on a television set, tie a shoelace, shake hands, write letters, dance a waltz, hold a fork, pay income tax, shop in a supermarket, and drive a car. These seem easy and natural. Yet people from another culture would be confused by these customs.[4]

Culture
A people's shared customs, beliefs, values, and artifacts that are transmitted from generation to generation.

Canadian Culture

In turn, Canadians represent a cultural group which is distinct and different from that of the U.S.[5] Indeed, given the definition of culture, it can be argued that the country has two distinct cultural groups: Anglophone and Francophone. English-speaking Canadians have a set of beliefs, values, and artifacts that mark them apart from people in the United States, the United Kingdom and other English-speaking countries. Similarly, French-speaking Canadians have their own set of char-

Marketing Today 6.1

Free Trade May Lead to a Clash of U.S. and Canadian Cultures

Most U.S. firms, especially those with Canadian subsidiaries, understand Canadian culture including bilingualism and regulations governing labelling. With the beginning of Canada–U.S. free trade, however, the number of U.S. products on supermarket shelves that fail to meet Canadian bilingual, nutritional, and other labelling requirements has increased significantly.

In 1989, the year the free trade agreement came in, the Grocery Product Manufacturers of Canada, which represents about 140 food firms, conducted a random check of stores around the country. It found 100 products, mostly from the United States, with improper labelling. The group's president, George Fleischman, explained that U.S. companies were gaining an edge by not labelling everything in English and French as required. That leaves a lot more space on containers for promoting the product's benefits.

Another problem is that in the United States companies can claim their products improve health and reduce the risk of disease a lot more freely than can be done in Canada. The same containers have been ending up on supermarket shelves here, looking better to consumers than competing domestic foods that adhere to Canadian labelling regulations.

"For instance," Fleishman said, "you can't say in Canada that an all-bran cereal will lower blood cholesterol."

The food manufacturers group insist that many of the illegally labelled products have entered Canada because of lower tariff barriers with the advent of the Canada–U.S. trade deal. A federal government spokesperson said the government is working with the food industry and customs officials in an effort to improve enforcement of Canadian labelling regulations.

Source: Adapted from "Firms Cite Free Trade for Mislabelled Goods," *The Toronto Star*, July 20, 1989, pp. D1, D2.

acteristics marking them as different not only from their Anglophone compatriots but also from people in France and other French-speaking countries. Information on the nature of each cultural group and their dominant subcultures helps marketers identify and serve customers in these groups.

English-Speaking Canadians

A majority of Canadians, including many ethnic subcultures, belong to the Anglophone cultural group. Because of its pluralistic tradition, geographic vastness, and similarities to other English-speaking countries, Anglophone Canada is difficult to describe in terms of a mainstream culture. There are, however, certain key cultural values.

Conservatism and Tradition

Most Anglophones still reflect their culture's colonial origins with considerable respect for institutions and authority. For example, the tradition of "dressing for work" is quite evident in English-speaking Canada.

Rather than discarding old products for new ones, Canadians prefer using products that they know work and last. This is why the Canadian government has set rust guidelines for all cars sold in Canada: it is an attempt to limit planned obsolescence.

Such a cultural environment does not encourage risk-taking, which is fundamental for entrepreneurial initiative. Nevertheless, marketers can use this value to their advantage by appealing to consumers on a conservative basis.

Materialism

Conspicuous consumption and the "more-is-better" mentality are common cultural values throughout Anglophone Canada. The acquisition of certain products and brands is often equated with status and prestige. Marketers have taken advantage of these values by offering products that provide instant gratification and are associated with the "good life." However, resource shortages, consumer debt, and wage restrictions have begun to discourage consumption.

Activity, Health, and Fitness

Emphasis on working hard and playing hard is evident in most areas of English-speaking Canada. In recent years, shorter work weeks, smaller families, and greater discretionary income have resulted in a boom for products related to hobbies, sports, leisure, and travel. Time poverty (having many activities and too little time in which to do them) has led to the expansion of many convenience-oriented retail concepts, such as 24-hour shopping and superstores.

Canadians take a great interest in maintaining their health. More than 40 percent of the federal government's annual budget is spent by Health and Welfare Canada, the largest federal department. Canadians also enjoy a long life expectancy. Universal medical insurance is a tangible sign that Canadians believe health to be a cultural value. In the mid-1980s, close to 8 percent of the total gross national product was spent on health-care services.

The federal government is also encouraging Canadians to become fitter. Some ten years ago, Fitness Canada, a federal government agency, launched the Participaction campaign to encourage participation in physical exercise. It has been a huge success. In 1989 almost 8.5 million Canadians took part in activities marking Sneaker Day, the kickoff for the annual Canada Fitweek.

The marketing of health and fitness in Canada has created new opportunities for manufacturers, distributors, and retailers of fitness and sports equipment. This emphasis on being fit and slender has led to increased demand for diet products and diet-control companies. Moreover, with a higher level of health care and concern about nutrition, seniors' longer life expectancy makes a growing market for products tailored to their needs.

Conformity

Although both Anglophone and Francophone Canadians aspire to the fostering of other cultures, neither group readily accepts departures from societal norms. In fact, it is sometimes claimed that Canadians' insistence on conformity makes them appear dull. Marketers can make this an opportunity by stressing traditional values of Canadian life.

Education

In Canada, education is a primary value in upward mobility. However, education as a cultural value is not evenly accepted across the country. A resident of Alberta, British Columbia, or Ontario is more likely to acquire a university education than someone from Atlantic Canada and Quebec.

Provincial departments of education spend hundreds of millions of dollars. The importance of education as a cultural value relates closely to skills and productivity, and many educational institutions market their programs on this basis.

French-Speaking Canadians

The close to seven million Canadians who are French-speaking represent a sizeable and distinct market. Federal regulations, following the national bilingualism policy, require marketers to provide labels and packaging in both French and English. In Quebec, the provincial law states that any sign visible externally (a billboard, a shop sign, and so on) must be in French only.

Marketers in Canada are aware that all forms of advertising must be altered to fit the Francophone market. Several studies have compared the consumption, buying, and media patterns of French-speaking Canadians with those of their English-speaking counterparts. The major findings are that Francophones:

- Spend more per capita on food than do Anglophones.

- Consume more soft drinks, instant/decaffeinated coffee, cake mixes, molasses, packaged soups, meat sauces, and sandwich spreads.

- Consume less canned fish, frozen foods, pancake mixes, potato chips, pickles, tea, chocolate chips, canned milk, dietetic foods, and convenience foods.

- Buy more cosmetics and headache and cold remedies.

- Have the highest per-capita consumption of maple syrup and molasses in Canada and prefer chocolate and butterscotch flavours to lemon.

- Watch more television and listen to more radio but read less. Premiums and coupons are also more popular.

- Prefer to shop in smaller, independent retail stores and also like door-to-door sales.[6]

Further evidence suggests that the life-styles of Francophones differ from those of Anglophones. These life-style differences affect consumption patterns and behaviour:

- Francophone women are more home- and family-oriented and like to cook. They are more fashion conscious, more concerned about personal and domestic cleanliness, and more receptive to product innovation.

- Francophones prefer their main meal at lunch and serve lighter meals in the evening. They prefer better-quality clothing and more expensive cars. They are becoming more mobile and exhibit leisure behaviour that differs from that of English-speaking Canadians (for example, French-speaking Canadians attend more movies, plays, and ballets).[7]

It has been argued that Quebec society can be characterized by a set of values that is traditional, consistent, and relatively static. For instance, in the 1960s, an ad appeared in many magazines in Quebec showing a woman dressed in shorts, playing golf with her husband. The copy indicated the woman could enjoy her day on the course and still prepare a good meal from canned tuna fish. Almost every aspect of the ad violated some component of Québécois life. At the time, women in Quebec were not likely to be golfing with their husbands, and women in shorts on a golf course were considered socially unacceptable. Further, the Québécois, who were light users of canned tuna at best, did not serve it as a main course for the evening meal.

One study has found that since the 1960s changes in Quebec life have become evident. Although predominantly Catholic, Québécois women are now consuming more birth-control pills per capita than women elsewhere in Canada, and the province's birth and marriage rates are both below the national average. University enrolments are rising. The study also found that the Québécois are changing their media habits and are reading more than ever.[8]

Some researchers have even questioned as to whether culture is the reason for differences between French-speaking and English-speaking Canadians in consumption and buyer and media habits. Some argue that demographics may help explain the differences, but many studies refute this argument. Others think that provincial regulations may be the reason. Commercial advertising to children is prohibited in Quebec, and there are, particularly severe restrictions on alcohol and tobacco advertising.

Acadians and Other Francophones

Marketers, who must alter their strategies for the French-speaking market, must be aware that Francophone culture extends beyond the boundaries of Quebec. Although 88 percent of French-speaking Canadians live in that province, 8 percent live in Ontario, and 4 percent are in New Brunswick.

Many Anglophone Canadians assume that all Francophone Canadians are basically alike. Yet there are distinct subgroups of French-speaking Canadians outside Quebec.

The Acadians, most of whom live in New Brunswick, are often referred to as the "forgotten French market." They are proud of their heritage and wish to be viewed as distinct from the Québécois. They want marketing communications directed to them to be in Acadian French, not Quebec French. Acadians are very fashion conscious and tend to dine out more often than their Quebec counterparts. Acadians are more aware of price, and marketing strategies directed toward this subculture should take this fact into account.

Ethnic Subcultures

Subculture
Subgroup within a larger culture that has distinctive lifestyles, values, norms, and beliefs.

Within a larger culture are often **subcultures** — subgroups that have distinct lifestyles, values, norms and beliefs. Consumers in a particular national, religious, or racial group are considered part of a subculture when their common heritage or environment influences values and consumption patterns.

Although Canada is often thought of as being made up of Francophones and Anglophones, these groups account for only seven out of every ten Canadians. The rest are members of groups that may be more or less part of the surrounding mainstream but have distinct cultural characteristics. Many of these subcultures in Canada are ethnically based, and the language of the home may be neither English nor French.

Marketers in Canada recognize that most ethnic Canadians are found in such major metropolitan areas as Toronto, Vancouver, Hamilton, and Montreal. Certain areas of the country are associated with specific ethnic groups. For example, Kitchener/Waterloo has a large population of German heritage. Winnipeg has many people with origins in the Ukraine. Toronto has the world's largest number of Italians outside Italy.

Social Influences on Consumer Behaviour

Although population can be segmented in a variety of ways, not all segments are of equal use to marketers. "Maritimers," for example, represent a demographic category. But people in this group do not interact with one another on the basis of shared geography, and individual buying behaviour is not directly affected by membership in that category. Members of a social group like the family do exchange views or act in ways that may influence what is purchased. Besides the family, the social groups of greatest interest to marketers are social classes, reference groups, and opinion leaders and innovators. Other social factors, such as the current age mix of the population, also affect the goods and services that are in demand.

Social Classes

If asked to identify themselves by **social class,** most people would probably respond that they are part of some vague "middle class." Marketers, however, recognize distinctions among social classes, which differ from one another in several ways.

Social Class
Group distinguished by characteristics such as occupation, education, possessions, and values.

Distinguishing the Classes

People commonly consider income to be the characteristic that differentiates the classes, but in fact it is a poor measure. A college professor and a factory floor supervisor may both earn $40 000 per year, but most people would agree that the professor has higher social status. Occupation is the most important basis for determining a person's social class. Other criteria include education, possessions (including type and location of home), and values.

Researchers have tried many methods for distinguishing among the social classes, including asking people to rank the social positions of others or to estimate their own position. Commonly used categories are those developed by Lloyd Warner and other sociologists: upper-upper, lower-upper, upper-middle, lower-middle, upper-lower, and lower-lower. The largest of these are the upper-lower class and the lower-middle class. These groups make up the primary market for mass consumer goods. Many marketers target the upper classes, however, because their higher-status occupations often pay well.

Importance to Marketers

Certain products are more likely to appeal to one class than another. For example, marketers of adult education courses would probably have more success recruiting among those in the lower-middle class, who are interested in getting ahead, rather than among the lower-upper class, whose members think they already have made it.

Even when members of different classes purchase the same product, the kind and quality of product selected may vary. Consider home furnishings. "Old money" families of the upper-upper class, secure in their fortunes for generations, tend to shun ostentatious displays of wealth. Their homes may be grand but are rarely decorated in the up-to-the-minute styles promoted by glossy magazines. The lower-upper and upper-middle classes, whose money, while substantial, is more recently acquired, tend to favour a more stylish approach to decorating and are the group most likely to employ the services of an interior decorator. Middle-class families tend to prefer do-it-yourself decorating with good-quality items purchased from local department and furniture stores. The lower classes may pay little attention to decorating trends, opting instead for functional, rather than stylish, furnishings.[9]

Differences among classes also can be demonstrated in other marketing areas. For example, the classes have different preferences in where they shop. The lower classes do much of their shopping in neighbourhood "mom and pop" stores that give them credit or in discount houses. The middle classes feel "safer" purchasing highly visible goods (like furniture and clothing) in department stores, although they shop in discount houses for appliances and other, less socially risky goods. The upper classes enjoy shopping in prestige stores like Holt Renfrew or in exclusive "to-the-trade-only" shops.

One other difference that affects marketing is class variation in media habits. The upper and middle classes read more newspapers and magazines that report on news, fashions, and hobbies than the lower classes. All classes watch television, but the different groups watch different shows. Advertisers who want to market to a particular class must consider these media habits when placing their messages.[10]

Reference Groups

Marketers have discovered that **reference groups** also strongly influence buying. These are groups that serve as a model for an individual's behaviour and as a frame of reference for decision making. A reference group may influence a decision to buy in one of three ways:

1. By reason of being a member of the group (called a **membership group**—family, friends, neighbours). You may buy a pair of Reebok aerobics shoes because your friends have them.

2. By reason of wanting to belong to the group (called an **aspirational group**—sports figures, cultural heroes, various occupational categories). A management trainee may purchase an attaché case to look like a successful manager.

3. By reason of not wanting to belong to the group (called a **dissociative group**—lower social classes, cults, recently arrived immigrant groups). A first-generation student may avoid restaurants reflecting his or her ethnic heritage as a way of dissociating from Old-World customs.

Some products can be sold by an appeal to reference groups, and others cannot. Researchers have shown that people tend to seek reference group approval when products are high-risk, that is, when an individual has little previous experience with them, or when they are highly visible in use.[11]

Purchasing usually involves a twofold decision: (1) whether to buy the product at all and, if so, (2) what brand to buy. Reference groups may influence either, neither, or both of these choices.

Reference Group
Group that serves as a model for an individual's behaviour and frame of reference for decision making.

Membership Group
Reference group to which a person may belong — for example, family, friends, neighbours.

Aspirational Group
Reference group with which a person may want to be identified.

Dissociative Group
Reference group from which a person may want to dissociate himself or herself.

Reference groups have been shown to have a strong product and brand influence on purchases of cars and colour TVs. There seems to be little reference group influence on purchases of such things as canned peaches and soap. Given this information, advertisers for products showing little or no reference group influence may want to stress product features like price and quality. To encourage product purchases demanding strong reference group approval, advertisements might show the kinds of people who use the product.

Many companies use celebrities from entertainment and sports to promote their products. Presumably, the marketers hope that these famous people serve as an aspirational group for many consumers.

Opinion Leaders and Innovators

While studying reference groups, researchers became curious about the way influence is exerted on members. They found that members of a group do not generally act as individuals. Rather, certain members act as influencers. Moreover, information spreads slowly, and not everyone absorbs it or chooses to act on it at the same rate. **Opinion leaders** are those capable of influencing others in a group, and **innovators** are those who are the first to find out about and use new products.

Role of Opinion Leaders

People become opinion leaders in a given area because they possess certain characteristics. Opinion leaders have been found to be (1) more interested and better read in the area they influence, (2) more self-confident and sociable, (3) slightly higher in social status, and (4) slightly more innovative.[12]

Study of opinion leaders has shown marketers how important word of mouth can be in spreading product information. At one time, many marketers thought that everyone received information directly from ads or salespeople. Researchers then showed that information travels in a two-step flow of communication: Ads or salespeople supply information first to opinion leaders, who then pass it on to followers.[13]

In some cases, marketers have been able to harness the power of opinion leaders to spread the word. The Cuisinart food processor, for example, gained initial acceptance not by massive advertising but by winning over professional cooks. Sometimes opinion leaders in a given category are hard to identify. In those cases, marketers may try to create such leaders. In exchange for a special discount on a pool or encyclopedia, for example, a family may agree to talk up the product in its neighbourhood.

Role of Innovators

Besides opinion leaders, marketers are interested in innovators — the ones who are the first to try something new. Researchers discovered

Opinion Leader
Member of a group who is capable of influencing others in it.

Innovator
Person who is first to find out about and use a new product.

innovators while looking for the way new ideas are adopted. Not everyone is receptive to novelty immediately. In fact, people appear to fall into one of five categories depending upon how soon they adopt new trends: innovators, early adopters, early majority, late majority, and laggards.[14] (See Figure 6.1.)

Innovators (the speedy adopters) and laggards (the last to change) are poles apart in more ways than just their psychological profiles. In comparison with laggards, innovators tend to be younger, wealthier, and more educated, and they have higher-status jobs. They also know more people outside their immediate circle of friends and read more magazines.

For their new products to succeed, marketers must catch the attention of innovators. One way is to advertise in special-interest magazines. Fashion marketers may rely on *Vogue, Flare,* or *Gentlemen's Quarterly,* for example, and automakers in *Motor Trend* magazine. Innovators may then be seen and imitated by early adopters. Since many opinion leaders come from the class of early adopters, word-of-mouth communication can play an important role.

The Family Group

Did you ever wonder why you use Hellmann's mayonnaise rather than Miracle Whip or vice versa? The chances are that you learned to use one

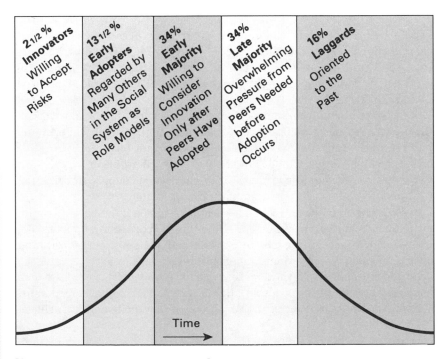

Figure 6.1 Characteristics of Adopter Groups

Source: Everett M. Rogers, *Diffusion of Innovations* (New York: Free Press, 1962).

or the other while growing up. Your family, in effect, steered you into the market for one product rather than the other. Buying behaviour is often shaped by the family. Two concepts—the family life-cycle and the role of family members—help explain such influence.

Traditional Family Life-Cycle

The stages of traditional family formation and change constitute the **family life-cycle.** These stages start with the unmarried state and continue through the rearing of children and loss of a spouse.

The family life-cycle concept considers four factors that influence buyer behaviour: (1) marital status, (2) age of family members, (3) size of family, and (4) work status of the head of household. On the basis of these factors, the family life-cycle specifies a series of stages through which families pass and the purchase behaviour of families in each phase. Table 6.1 divides the traditional life-cycle into nine stages.

Consider two young persons who recently graduated from college, have married, and have begun new jobs. The partners in the new marriage (stage 2 of the life-cycle) have a good deal of discretionary income but not a great deal of shopping experience. They will probably concentrate on purchasing moderately priced, basic furniture for an apartment or house, and they may be susceptible to ads or sales pitches that offer advice in an unfamiliar area. In contrast, parents (perhaps in stage 5) already have a furnished home and a great deal of shopping experience. If they are interested in household goods, they are likely to purchase better furniture or nonnecessary appliances (such as microwave ovens or food processors) and be guided by their own experience.[15]

Changing Family Patterns

The family life-cycle concept has been used in segmenting markets and targeting product and promotional appeals for more than 20 years. During that time, however, changes have occurred that may affect some generalizations. For example, the traditional family group of a working father, a homemaking mother, and one or more children accounted for less than one-fifth of the population as of the beginning of the 1980s.[16]

During recent decades, the rate of marriage (nuptiality) has been declining in Canada, with Quebec now having the lowest rate. Despite this trend, marriage and family remain important institutions in Canada. The percentage of adults getting married has remained relatively constant; the change is in the age at first marriage, which is rising.

Although most Canadians belong to a family and do not live alone, single households are increasing in Canada because of later marriage and increases in divorce and the percentage of women who work outside the home. Single households account now for more than 20 percent of all households in Canada. Interestingly enough, after 14 years of annual increases in divorce, decreases are starting to be seen. However, there has been a significant rise in common-law marriages, which may par-

Family Life-Cycle
Traditional stages through which families pass, from the unmarried state through child rearing, empty nest, and loss of a spouse.

Table 6.1 An Overview of the Family Life-Cycle and Buying Behaviour

Stage in Family Life-Cycle	Buying or Behavioural Pattern
1. Bachelor stage: Young single people not living at home	Few financial burdens. Fashion opinion leaders. Recreation-oriented. Buy: basic kitchen equipment, basic furniture, cars, equipment for the mating game, vacations.
2. Newly married couples: Young, no children	Better off financially than they will be in near future. Highest purchase rate and highest average purchase of durables. Buy: cars, refrigerators, stoves, sensible and durable furniture, vacations.
3. Full nest I: Youngest child under six	Home purchasing at peak. Liquid assets low. Dissatisfied with financial position and amount of money saved. Interested in new products. Like advertised products. Buy: washers, dryers, TV, baby food, chest rubs and cough medicines, vitamins, dolls, wagons, sleds, skates.
4. Full nest II: Youngest child six or over	Financial position better. Wives work outside the home. Less influenced by advertising. Like larger-sized packages, multiple-unit deals. Buy: many foods, cleaning materials, bicycles, music lessons, pianos.
5. Full nest III: Older married couples with dependent children	Financial position still better. More wives work outside the home. Some children get jobs. Hard to influence with advertising. High average purchase of durables. Buy: new, more tasteful furniture, auto travel, nonnecessary appliances, boats, dental services, magazines.
6. Empty nest I: Older married couples, no children living with them, head in labour force	Home ownership at peak. Most satisfied with financial position and money saved. Interested in travel, recreation, self-education. Make gifts and contributions. Not interested in new products. Buy: vacations, luxuries, home improvements.
7. Empty nest II: Older married couples, no children living at home, head retired	Drastic cut in income. Keep home. Buy: medical appliances, medical care products that aid health, sleep, and digestion.
8. Solitary survivor, in labour force	Income still good but likely to sell home.
9. Solitary survivor, retired	Same medical and product needs as other retired group; drastic cut in income. Special need for attention, affection, and security.

Source: Philip Kotler and Gary Armstrong. *Marketing: An Introduction* (Englewood Cliffs, N.J.: Prentice-Hall 1987), p. 157.

tially explain the drop in the divorce rate.

These changes in marital and family status are important for many marketers. Divorce has created a new market for furnishings, professional services, and social clubs. Smaller family sizes have implications for product sizes and housing. For some marketers, the number of families is more important than size of family (because of the effect on the demand for housing and furnishings). By delaying marriage until later in life, people may be better off financially and have more income to spend on travel and entertainment.[17]

Family Roles

The sociological concept of roles also has implications for marketing. A **role** refers to a kind of specialization of task. Many families divide household tasks by role: a wife cooks, a child sets the table, and a husband takes out the garbage. Research has shown a similar specialization in buying.

Most studies have concentrated on the relative influence of a husband or wife in a particular product category. One study indicated that purchase decisions should be classified as:

1. *Wife-dominated decisions.* Those in which the wife is the most influential in selecting a product in the majority of households (such as food, health care).

2. *Husband-dominated decisions.* Those in which the husband exerts the greatest influence in most households (such as insurance).

3. *Autonomous decisions.* Those in which either spouse may decide, though one may slightly dominate (such as appliances, alcoholic beverages).[18]

More recent studies have shown that roles in purchasing decisions have shifted somewhat over the years. As more women join the work force and contribute to the family income, they are gaining more influence on purchase decisions formerly reserved for men. As women have become a greater share of that market, automobile companies have taken a closer look at their buying behaviour; Figure 6.2 illustrates one effort to do this. Conversely, as men share more in child-care and housekeeping duties, they are beginning to influence purchasing decisions previously reserved for women.

The role of children in decision making has been studied much less frequently. But anyone who has ever brought a child along on a shopping trip knows that children do have a say. Children apparently have a great deal of influence in the selection of toys and fast-food restaurants (McDonald's spends millions advertising on Saturday morning television). However, when it comes to nutrition, mothers often veto a child's choice that is felt to be unsound.[19] That is why the makers of Cocoa Puffs, a chocolate-flavoured cereal, also advertise their product's vitamin content—to overcome mothers' doubts.

Role
In sociology, a kind of specialization of task. Family roles include those concerning decisions that may be wife-dominated, husband-dominated, or autonomous (either spouse may decide).

Value seekers—These women want it all. They are aggressive drivers and like cars with great pickup, yet they will watch the price. Japanese name plates score well with them, although they do like Dodges. Most are single, average age 29, working fulltime and have attended college.

Driving enthusiasts—Life in the fast lane: These women like sports and gambling, and are keenly interested in their cars. They are single, 30-35 and prefer American performance cars such as Pontiacs, Chevys and Dodges.

Voluntary minimalists—These women choose to spend as little time as possible thinking about cars. Most are married, well-educated, white-collar workers with an average age of 40. They prefer Chevys, Fords, Plymouths and AMCs.

Source: 1986 Conde Nast Report

Conde Nast puts the pieces together

Comfort seekers—The oldest purchasing group, these women are very conservative when purchasing an automobile. Most are retired, and few attended college. They try to save money and look for rebates. They prefer larger domestic-cars, including Oldsmobiles and Buicks

Affluent luxury seekers—With household incomes $20,000 higher than the average, these women are the big spenders. They will not hesitate to spend money on an expensive European import. Most are married and work fulltime in a professional position. Average age is 41. They don't buy as many American cars as Detroit could wish.

Budget-minded—These consumers are family-minded homemakers. Their average age is 43 and very few have attended college. If they work, they hold clerical or factory positions. They love American cars—Fords, Chevys and Oldsmobiles—and stay away from foreign models.

Figure 6.2   Conde Nast Researches the New Female Car Buyer

Source: Christy Ellis

Teenagers, too, seem to be involved in many shopping decisions. One study found teenage boys responsible for brand decisions on home computers in 49 percent of the homes surveyed. As you learned in Chapter 4, teenagers do an increasing amount of the family's grocery shopping and also spend millions per year of their own money.[20]

Age Mix Changes

Besides stages in the family life-cycle, marketers are interested in how the population breaks down by age. We are an ageing society. While the number of teenagers and people in their early twenties will continue to decline through the first half of the 1990s, the number of people over 65 is projected to increase dramatically. Part of the reason for this trend is increased life expectancy.[21]

Already, people over 50 make up about 25 percent of the population, but they have nearly 50 percent of the nation's disposable income. Because people in this age segment have typically finished rearing children and paying for a home, they have money to spend on travel and luxury items. At Your Service 6.1 describes ways the travel industry has attempted to appeal to this attractive market segment.

It is worth remembering, however, that income growth has become sluggish and is no longer an accurate measure of spending power. In the future, wealth — measured by the value of net assets accumulated by households in the form of housing, financial securities and deposits and pension assets — will play an even larger role in determining how much people spend and what they buy.

As concentration of wealth in the older age groups continues to gain importance in setting consumption patterns, our society will be characterized by a growing gap in living standards between generations. The

At Your Service 6.1

Over-50s Are on the Road

The travel industry is discovering customers over age 50. Several airlines have formed travel clubs for older passengers. The clubs offer fare discounts, with no limitations on flight times or destinations. Eastern Airlines and TWA are also offering their older travellers passes for a year of travel.

Hotels, too, are interested in the over-50 market. At Marriott Corporation, a promotion called Leisurelife provides room discounts of 50 percent and restaurant discounts of 25 percent to guests over age 62. Quality Inns International is offering Prime Time discounts. Hotels see attracting retired travellers as a way to fill rooms during normally slow seasons.

Tour operators are diversifying their offerings to attract repeat business. One of the first companies to rediscover the older market was Insight International. John R. Peckham, the company's North American president, observes, "This is an adventurous, well-heeled group." Insight International has even redesigned its brochures to show more grey hair and glasses.

Source: Adapted from Linda Lehrer, "More Marketers Seek to Target People over 50," *The Wall Street Journal,* February 18, 1986, p. 35.

current adult working population can be divided into three groups, which are marked by their relationship to the Baby Boomers, that unusually large North American generation born between 1946 and about 1963.

The Pre-Boomers

Born before the end of World War II, members of this group are now 45 to 60 years of age and entered the labour force in the prosperity of the 1950s and 1960s. Early in their careers, they enjoyed low housing costs and modest personal tax burdens. Later they saw a rapid rise in their equity in housing, with housing prices boosted by the demands of the larger generation behind them.

They are in an excellent position to continue to enhance their wealth. Many pre-Boomers will inherit significant sums over the next decade or so. In Canada, nearly 80 percent of households now headed by someone 65 and over own their own home; 90 percent of these homes are mortgage-free.

The Early Boomers

Born between 1945 and 1955, members of this group are now between ages 34 and 44, entering their prime asset-accumulation years. They will benefit from the higher labour force participation of women: families with two-income earners have average incomes 43 percent higher than single-income families.

The Late- and Post-Boomers

During the next two decades, people born after 1955 will be in a much weaker position to accumulate wealth and will therefore find it more difficult to increase their consumption. Across North America, market forces and government policies will contribute to this wealth generation gap.

The late- and post-Boomers should find greater wealth-accumulation opportunities relatively later in life as increased labour scarcity affords them higher incomes. Nevertheless, their main opportunity for asset growth will be inheritance. Since most are from smaller families, their share of parental wealth will be larger than today's typical inheritors.

Throughout the 1990s, the "grey market" will be one of the key niches that consumer marketers will have to address in order to thrive in an economy with modest overall real growth in consumer spending. Forecasters believe that growth will be largely in products and services that enhance life-styles and image.

Figure 6.3 spotlights some significant life-style trends. We are witnessing a return to the family focus of the 1950s and 1960s, with increased spending on home renovations. In particular, home entertainment products and travel services are expected to be at the top of the list of consumer growth areas for the rest of this century.

Life-Style Trends	
Tradition	The 1950s and 1960s are back in style. So are marriage and family life.
Back to the Home	Consumers are spending more on their homes and doing more entertaining there.
Adventure	Excitement and fantasy are in vogue—adventure vacations and exciting sports.
Individuality and Style	Consumers want to make a personal statement through what they wear, how they live and work, and what they eat and drink.
Indulgence	Consumers want to indulge in affordable luxuries. The fact that a product is imported, or has the aura of being imported, still has a cachet.
Quality	Consumers want top-quality products and will pay for them.
Convenience	Easy to buy and easy to use are the criteria for the 1990s.
Fitness	The desire for good health is creating a new way of life for many.

Figure 6.3 Life-Style Trends

Source: Ernst & Young, *Tomorrow's Customers*, 22nd ed., Toronto, 1989, p. 14.

Overall, the emphasis will be on quality, service, and convenience.[22] For an example of how age mix changes have affected one industry, see Marketing Today 6.2.

Psychological Influences on Consumer Behaviour

Up to now, we have concentrated on the kinds of things that influence a consumer as part of a group. But marketers know that individuals are unique and their behaviour can only partially be explained by such factors as age, social class, and family role. Consequently, marketers use many concepts borrowed from psychology to explain what goes on in a consumer's mind during the buying-decision process.

The consumer's mind is often referred to as a "black box" because what goes on inside is largely hidden from market researchers. Two men, who seem very much alike, walk into a supermarket. One picks up a frozen TV dinner and the other heads for the fresh meat and produce sections. Why? The answer lies in the workings of their individual black boxes.

Motivation, perception, attitudes, personality, and learning are concepts familiar to psychologists that marketers have also found of enormous value.

Motivation

Motivation
Inner state that activates or moves people toward goals.

Human behaviour is complex, and the phenomenon of motivation is one of its most perplexing aspects. Psychologists define **motivation** as an inner state that activates or moves people toward goals. To be motivated, individuals must feel pushed by an inner need or driving force, but they must also feel pulled toward a goal outside themselves.

Marketers are interested in discovering what motivates people to buy everything from chocolate chip cookies to condominiums and in influencing people to meet needs with the marketers' products. Needs must be understood if marketing goals are to be established correctly. Psychologists have shown marketers that needs can be classified and that people are often unconscious of the needs that motivate them.

Needs Hierarchy
Theory of Abraham Maslow that there is an order in which human needs arise. When one need is at least partially satisfied, the need at the next highest level arises.

Maslow's Hierarchy

A number of psychologists have proposed lists of needs considered basic to all humans. Abraham Maslow was the first to suggest a **needs hierarchy,** or order in which human needs arise. Maslow proposed five basic levels of motivating needs and believed that when one need is at least partially satisfied, the need at the next highest level arises (Figure 6.4).[23]

The first two levels of needs are physical in nature. The most basic need is for the necessities of life—food, clothing, and shelter. Only when the need for these is partially satisfied do humans start feeling the need for physical safety, perhaps to protect the things gathered to fulfil the first need.

The next three levels are psychological. The need for love, affection, and belonging arises first. When people are secure with family and friends, they may then seek to enhance their own self-esteem, or sense of personal worth. Some try to do this by achievement (on the job, at a hobby), while others direct the need outward in search of prestige and recognition by others (collecting status symbols). After achieving some sense of personal worth, they may then feel the need for something even higher—to become fully developed as a human. This need may be satisfied by such activities as learning to play the piano, travelling, reading, or even running in a marathon.

Significance to Marketers   Maslow's hierarchy is useful to marketing strategists in a number of ways. Understanding motives gives clues to the appropriate design of products. For example, a coat aimed at the low-

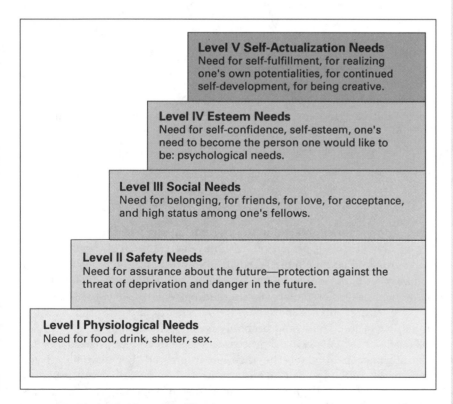

Figure 6.4 Maslow's Hierarchy of Needs

income consumer who is concerned with satisfying basic physical needs would be designed differently from a coat for the high-income consumer who probably dresses for prestige and social status.

Some goods and services can be marketed only in societies that have reached a level at which physical needs are satisfied and psychological needs can be indulged. In relatively affluent societies like Canada and the United States, needs for affiliation, esteem, and self-actualization tend to dominate consumer behaviour.[24]

Perception

An individual will buy a product if motivated by a need. But to buy a specific product, the person must be aware of it, and that is where perception becomes important. **Perception** has been defined as the process by which an individual becomes aware of the environment and interprets it so that it fits into a frame of reference.[25] This definition recognizes that perception involves both an objective component (information brought by the sense of sight, hearing, touch, smell, and taste) and a subjective element (interpretation, in light of a person's experience).

The subjective component explains why people perceive as different things that are objectively the same. Researchers using blind taste tests, for example, have shown that most people cannot tell the difference between various colas. Tests of cigarettes and beer have produced similar results. Yet many people are loyal to one product or another and insist that these products are superior to others.

People tend to read their subjective feelings into a product, insisting qualities are "there" for everyone to see. Marketers, of course, play a role in encouraging such interpretations. When products are indistinguishable to the senses, marketers try to differentiate them by packaging, advertising, and other marketing tools.

Selective Exposure

Every day you are barraged with information about goods and services. If you drive to work or school, you may hear ads on the radio or see billboards and signs along the road. If you take public transportation, you may see signs inside your train or bus, as well as advertisements in the magazine or newspaper you are reading. When you watch television in the evening, you see more ads. If you tried to pay attention to all of this information, you would probably be overwhelmed.

Consequently, people use a process called **selective exposure** to filter out information in which they are not interested. For example, if you don't drink coffee but you are planning to buy a stereo, you probably would find yourself flipping past the coffee ads in a magazine and stopping to pore over the stereo ads.

Perception
Process by which an individual becomes aware of the environment and interprets it so that it fits into his or her frame of reference.

Selective Exposure
Process of filtering out information that is not of interest.

Selective Perception

People also filter out information that conflicts with their ideas and beliefs. This is called **selective perception.** For example, if you believe that compact discs are overrated but decide to ask the stereo dealer about them anyway, you probably will pay less attention to the positive attributes he cites than to the negative ones.

Selective Retention

Finally, people have a selective memory filter that causes them to remember mainly information that supports their ideas and beliefs. Filtering conflicting information from our memory is called **selective retention.** When you tell your friends about your conversation with the stereo dealer, you probably will remember only the dealer's arguments against buying a compact disc player.

Implications for Marketers

Over the years, marketing managers have devised strategies to bypass the consumer's mental filters. Advertisers in particular have succeeded somewhat in penetrating the attention barrier.

Repeating messages has been found to work both in increasing awareness and in reducing forgetfulness. Ralston-Purina, for example, uses cats in TV commercials to repeat again and again the brand name of its cat food, Meow Mix.[26]

Advertisers have other techniques for penetrating perceptual barriers. Breaking with expectations can cause people to take notice. When Joe Namath pulled Hanes Beauty Mist pantyhose over his legs and gnarled knees, people noticed.

Attitudes

Each one of us holds attitudes that affect our buying behaviour. An **attitude** is a state that includes a person's beliefs about and feelings toward some object, coupled with a tendency to behave in a certain way with respect to that object.[27] Of particular interest to marketers are attitudes that include a predisposition to buy the marketer's product.

Marketers are very concerned about consumers' attitudes toward their products, since favourable attitudes often lead to higher usage rates and unfavourable ones are difficult to change.

Attitude Measurement

Marketers use several techniques to measure attitudes. Probably the most widely used method is the **attitude scale.** In this technique, consumers are asked to indicate the intensity of their agreement or disa-

Selective Perception
Process of filtering out or modifying information that conflicts with one's ideas or beliefs.

Selective Retention
Memory of only what supports one's ideas or beliefs.

Attitude
State that includes a person's beliefs about and feelings toward some object, combined with a tendency to behave in a certain way with respect to that object.

Attitude Scale
Technique for measuring consumer attitudes that poses statements about which respondents are asked to indicate the intensity of their agreement or disagreement.

greement with certain statements posed by the researcher. For example, a researcher might state, "Cigar smoke is offensive." Consumers would then respond either "strongly agree," "agree," "no opinion," "disagree," or "strongly disagree." (This set of choices is called the Likert scale.) Researchers would then tally the answers to get an indication of the strength of consumer opinions.

Changing Attitudes

Reversing a negative attitude is perhaps the marketer's most difficult job. Sometimes it is impossible, and a product may have to be scrapped. When change is possible, promotion often plays a large part in the process.

Marketers are quick to react to changes in consumer attitudes. Procter & Gamble, for instance, has implemented a solid waste management policy as a solution to waste management problems cited by ecology-conscious consumer groups. In 1989, P&G entered the "green" market with Enviro-Pak (see Marketing Today 6.3). Lever Brothers has followed

Marketing Today 6.3

Changing Attitudes Change Marketing Strategy

Canadians are changing the way they live. As a result, adapt or die is the cry among consumer products companies in the 1990s, according to Doug Grindstaff, president of Procter & Gamble Inc.

Seven of P&G's products — Liquid Tide, Mr. Clean, Spic and Span Liquid, Ivory Liquid, Joy, Downy Liquid, and Scope Mouthwash — are offered in a gusseted refill pouch, called an Enviro-Pak, whose contents can be emptied into the product's original plastic bottle. P&G claims this system reduces the number of discarded plastic bottles by 7 million annually and reduces its own plastic use by 7 percent. The price at which pouches are sold to the retailer should also mean a cost saving of up to 15 cents for consumers.

Said Grindstaff, "Procter & Gamble wants to be part of the solution to waste management problems. It's a practical way for consumers to make a difference by reducing the amount of plastic they throw out. We recognize that the management of solid waste is an enormous problem for which there are no easy answers and no single solution. We're making every effort to find a range of innovative solutions that can be applied to P&G products."

Sources: Adapted from Philip DeMont, "Heed Changing Consumer, Companies Told," *The Toronto Star*, February 2, 1990, p. C3; and Laura Medcalf, "P&G Goes 'Green' with 'Enviro-Pak'," *Marketing*, September 11, 1989, p. 2

Courtesy of Procter & Gamble Inc.

suit with environmental themes in advertising (see Chapter 3, Figure 3.3).

Also, "natural" products from soft drinks to makeup are flooding the market. Clothing is more casual, and furniture styles more basic. Figure 6.5 shows an ad emphasizing the "natural" aspect of Hälsa Shampoo.

Personality

Personality is one of those terms that everyone seems to understand, but few can define. For our purposes, **personality** is the sum of char-

Personality
Sum of characteristics that make a person what he or she is and distinguish each individual from every other individual.

BRING OUT YOUR NATURAL HIGHLIGHTS WITH HÄLSA.

Your hair has its own special glow. Make it come alive with Hälsa.

CHAMOMILE
Warms the glow of ash blonde, light brown or light chestnut hair.

GINGER ROOT
Lights the fire of red, reddish brown or auburn hair.

WALNUT LEAVES
Deepens the natural shine of brown, dark brown or black hair.

MARIGOLD
Brings out golden highlights in natural blonde or lightened hair.

HÄLSA SWEDISH BOTANICAL SHAMPOOS AND CONDITIONERS

Figure 6.5 Hälsa Emphasizes Tie to Nature

Source: Courtesy of S.C. Johnson & Son, Inc. Photograph courtesy of Nancy Brown.

acteristics that make the person what he or she is and distinguish each individual from every other individual.[28] It is a broader concept than those discussed thus far and may even be said to include them.

Marketers are interested in the connection between an individual's personality and product or store choice. Most of the attempts to relate personality to products or store type have tried to link certain personality traits with the heavy use or loyal buying of a product.

Researchers select traits they feel may influence choice of the product in question. They then conduct studies to see if the hypothesized relationship exists. The results have been somewhat promising. For instance, the makers of Black Label beer, through research, were able to link personality to beer drinking. Marketing Today 6.4 explains how they identified a distinct group of independent, artistic, and trendy beer drinkers.

Marketing Today 6.4

Research Links Personality to Beer Drinking

When trying to sell a "me-too" product in a crowded marketplace, it's important to have the right, if somewhat offbeat attitude, a leading Canadian advertiser says.

Karen Palmer, vice-president of Palmer Bonner, told a group of advertisers in Toronto that unconventional or outlandish marketing appeals based on consumer attitudes and values are often more effective and less risky than traditional sales pitches.

"It's particularly important in today's media environment, where there is so much clutter, to stand out," Palmer told the 1990 annual meeting of the Canadian Advertising Research Foundation. "We'd like to dispel the myth that audacious ads are inherently risky."

Palmer said her firm developed the provocative and successful

Black Label beer advertising from psychographic surveys of consumers' attitudes and values. They identified a potential market for the languishing brand that conventional surveys missed.

"Psychographics are particularly useful in mature markets, like beer, where there is no 'news' or product innovation occurring," Douglas Snetsinger, of the University of Toronto's faculty of management, said. "They enable marketers to pinpoint more emotive, high-impact messages to their target group."

In the Black Label case, Palmer said, psychographics enabled demographic marketers to identify a distinct group of independent, artistic, and trendy beer drinkers.

Most Black Label drinkers were over 55, but an unexpected group of followers turned up. "These people are the hippies and old beatniks of the 1990s," said Paul Hains, Palmer Bonner's creative

director. "They were rebellious against the establishment, but in a thoughtful, nonviolent way."

But Hains said targeting a hip, independent, rebellious clientele must be done with great care.

"With this group, as soon as something becomes commercial, it becomes establishment, and establishment was out," Hains said. "In this case, they hated regular beer advertising and they drank Black Label precisely because it wasn't advertised."

Further research showed that many of the same attitudes were shared by large numbers of mainstream beer drinkers and Palmer Bonner targeted them with a subtle, moody, black and white campaign that sells beer without showing the product or even mentioning its taste.

Source: Adapted from Bob Papoe, "Advertiser Tells How Black Label Found Its Fans," *The Toronto Star*, February 28, 1990, p. F1.

Learning

Learning, like personality, is a concept that underlies several others that have been discussed. It is defined as any change in an individual's response or behaviour resulting from practice, experience, or mental association.[29]

Studies have shown that learning usually involves three basic steps: drive, cues, and response.[30] (See Figure 6.6.) A drive is the force that motivates an individual. Hunger, for example, is a particularly powerful drive. A hungry person who sees a sign for a pizza shop — a cue — might satisfy the drive by buying a pizza — the response. If the person likes the pizza, the response is reinforced. Hence, the next time the person is hungry, he or she might choose to seek out a pizza shop, and the cycle would begin again. Of course, the person may not like the pizza and may ignore pizza signs and look instead for a place to buy a hamburger.

Marketers can take a lesson from this cycle. Often they have only one opportunity to demonstrate a product to a consumer. If the product is good and satisfies the person, they may have a customer for life. But if a product is poor or fails to live up to expectations created by its advertising, a marketer may not get a second chance.

There are many theories about how learning takes place. Two are particularly helpful to marketers who want to influence consumer behaviour. Ivan Pavlov's famous experiments with dogs led to the **theory of conditioned learning,** which holds that learning takes place by association. The Russian psychologist presented hungry dogs with food while a bell rang in the background. Invariably, the dogs salivated. After several trials, the food was omitted; only the ringing bell was heard, but the dogs still salivated. The dogs had learned to associate one stimulus (food) with another (the bell's sound) and to link both to the same response (salivation).

Advertisers often use the model of conditioned learning. In a long-running commercial for Nestea, for example, consumers are taught to associate iced tea with a cooling plunge in a pool on a hot day. When warm weather arrives, the commercial implies, Nestea is a good substitute for a cool dive. The surge of iced-tea sales in the summer points to the effectiveness of the simple association.

Learning
Any change in an individual's response or behaviour resulting from practice, experience, or mental association.

Theory of Conditioned Learning
View holding that learning takes place by association.

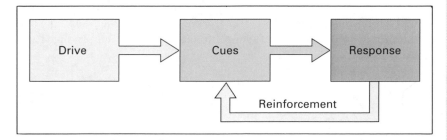

Figure 6.6 The Learning Process

Theory of Instrumental Learning
View that people learn to act in a certain way when some responses are rewarded (or reinforced) and others are punished.

Although often confused with conditioned learning, the **theory of instrumental learning** works with the response rather than the stimulus. This theory maintains that people learn to act in a certain way when some of their responses are rewarded (or reinforced) and others are punished. Reward strengthens the link between stimulus and response and increases the chances that the response will be repeated.

The instrumental model of learning is also valuable to marketers. Companies launching new food products often include a cents-off coupon in the package. They hope an early encouragement of repeat business will shape buying habits that will continue once the price incentive stops.

Applications of Learning Principles

Over the years, a large body of data about conditioned and instrumental learning has developed. Principles of practical value to marketers include:

1. *Learning cannot be conditioned or reinforced in the absence of a felt need.* Consumers are not robots. They learn best when they are experiencing an intense need. No amount of ads for Nestea in the wintertime could increase sales significantly because consumers are not motivated by a physical need for cooling. Similarly, if a product is terrible, no amount of couponing will spur sales.

2. *Learning is fastest and most complete when people are actively involved.* Department stores often use demonstrations at cosmetic counters to involve consumers in a trial of their products. Advertising cannot involve consumers physically, but it can engage their minds and emotions. Jingles are an attempt to get people to carry the message away with them by repeating the song.

3. *People learn to generalize more easily than they learn to discriminate.* Marketers find it easier to teach consumers to transfer what they already know to a new situation. That is why many new products are introduced under the same brand name as an old product. For example, Dannon retained its brand name for a line of frozen yogurt products because consumers would be able to transfer the quality reputation of the original to the new product.

The ease with which people generalize their learning also explains why successful new products are widely imitated. Other companies quickly followed Dannon into the frozen yogurt market hoping that consumers would generalize favourable feelings from the product they already knew to other brands.[31]

Life-Styles

Some of the influences on buyer behaviour that you have been reading about—attitudes, personality, and group characteristics—are related to consumers' life-styles. As you learned in Chapter 4, a person's life-style consists of his or her pattern of living as expressed in activities, interests, and opinions. Marketers are interested in life-styles because consumers tend to buy goods and services that are compatible with or appeal to their life-styles.

A major scheme for classifying according to life-style is the Stanford Research Institute's Value and Life-Styles (VALS) program.[32] This system classifies adults as integrated, achievers, emulators, belongers, societally conscious, experientials, I-am-me's, and need-driven. Each group behaves differently in the marketplace.

People who are classified as integrated value maturity, individualism, tolerance, and a world view. Their buying styles focus on ecology, quality, esthetics, uniqueness, and high standards. Achievers are leaders in business, professions, and government. They value efficiency, fame, status, comfort, and materialism; as buyers, they look for luxury and high technology. Emulators strive to attain the life-style of achievers; they are ambitious, upwardly mobile, status-conscious, and competitive. They look for products that are conspicuous and fashionable. Belongers are traditional, conservative, and home-centred. They look for popular products and brand names.

People who are societally conscious support social causes and are attracted to simple living. As buyers, they look for conservation and authenticity. Experientials value direct experience and vigorous involvement; they are heavy consumers of products that involve crafts and sports. I-am-me's are dramatic, self-expressive, impulsive, and individualistic. As consumers, they tend to favour products that are faddish and striking.

Sustainers are struggling to survive, and they value instant gratification. They buy to satisfy basic needs and shop at local outlets. Survivors are typically older and poor; they value security and are authoritarian, rigid, and followers. They are cautious shoppers, seeking low prices, familiar brands, guarantees, and reassurances.

Because consumers make different buying decisions based on their life-styles, marketers can use a classification such as this to tailor a product, advertising campaign, or distribution system to reach a certain segment of the population. For example, experientials might be more inclined to buy a car that is fun to drive, whereas emulators would be more attracted to a car that is associated with high status.

Consumer Buying: A Dynamic View

Previous chapters have shown, in a sense, still photos of the influence of various groups on purchase behaviour and the inner mechanisms of the consumer's mind. But buying is an activity—a dynamic process. To understand it, the still shots must be spliced to make a motion picture.

Researchers have proposed various models, or ways of representing how concepts from the social sciences fit together to describe consumer behaviour. Most of the models recognize that buying involves problem solving. The problems vary in difficulty. For example, people put more time and effort into buying a car than purchasing a litre of milk. But whether the item is expensive and seldom purchased or cheap and bought frequently, some problem solving is involved.

Figure 6.7 presents one model of consumer problem solving. The model shows that buying involves three stages — input, processing, and output.[33]

Input

Input
Facts not in a consumer's control that may affect decisions to buy.

Input consists of all those facts not in the consumer's control that may affect a decision to buy. Any element of a firm's marketing mix (such as a special warranty, a newspaper ad, a sale, or the opening of a new outlet) may influence a person to think about buying.

Equally influential as a spur to buying is the input a consumer receives from social or cultural groups. The comment of a friend considered an opinion leader, the example of reference group members, or usage by a family member exposes an individual to products he or she might consider buying.

Processing

Inputs will have no effect unless the consumer chooses to act on them. Generally, action is triggered by recognition of a problem — an unsatisfied need.

Consider a hypothetical problem. Suppose that after attending a party at a friend's house, you decide to have a party. But a good party requires music, and you have no stereo. You have a social need (in Maslow's words) that you think can be satisfied by purchasing a stereo.

At this point, you may begin an active search for more information. The process of selective exposure lets in some of the information previously screened out. Ads for Sony, Panasonic, and Technics products now seem to appear everywhere. To learn how to evaluate these brands, you may look for more objective information (such as from *Consumer Reports*) or seek out the opinion of family and friends. (If the purchase had been of a more routine item like a record, you might have eliminated much of this prepurchase search and relied solely on past experience.)

In the next stage of problem solving, the alternatives must be evaluated. The criteria used in evaluating products vary. In the case of a stereo, you may want to consider sound quality, styling, brand name reputation, and cost. To decide which qualities have the most weight, you may fall back on previously formed attitudes. For example, you may prefer to pay a high cost for goods that will last a long time. Personality may also influence the evaluation. Recall that if you lack self-confidence,

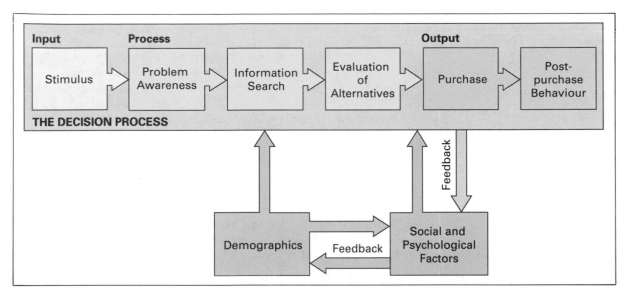

Figure 6.7   A Model of Consumer Problem Solving

you may shop at a department store and look for well-known brands.

At the end of the evaluation stage, you are ready to buy. However, a purchase is not always made at this point. If you decide to give the most weight to price, for instance, you may have to wait until you have enough money to buy an expensive model or until the store you frequent has a sale.

Output

The model shows that **output** consists of the actual purchase and post-purchase evaluation.

In the case of new food or drug products, consumers are often encouraged to buy with an offer of a free or inexpensive "trial" package. In the case of the stereo, no such trial period is possible. The decision to purchase is equivalent to a full commitment to the product, and that is why, after buying major products, people often feel anxious about their decisions.

You may turn to friends for assurance that you made the right choice. You will probably also rely on your own judgement to evaluate the product. In both cases, instrumental learning is involved. Every time the stereo receives a compliment or performs up to par, your initial decision to purchase is reinforced or rewarded. What you learn will become part of your experience and serve to influence future decisions.

Much of what has been said here about buying by consumers applies to industrial purchases as well. The next chapter explores the similarities and differences between industrial and consumer buying.

Output
Actual purchase and postpurchase evaluation by a consumer.

Chapter Replay

1. **Why are cultures and subcultures important to marketers?**
   The values of consumers' cultures and subcultures help shape what they buy. In Canada, with two dominant cultures, Anglophone and Francophone, and many subcultures, marketers can look for opportunities to market products and services to individual groups.

2. **What kinds of groups can influence buying?**
   The kinds of groups that can influence buying include social classes, reference groups (especially innovators and opinion leaders in these groups), the family, and age groups.

3. **In what order do human needs arise?**
   According to Maslow's needs hierarchy, physiological needs emerge first, then safety needs, social needs, esteem needs, and self-actualization needs.

4. **How do people filter information?**
   People use selective exposure to filter out information they are not interested in. When they listen to a message, they use selective perception to filter out information that conflicts with their ideas and beliefs. They also tend to forget conflicting information; this is called selective retention.

5. **Why are marketers concerned about attitudes and personality?**
   Marketers are concerned about attitudes because favourable attitudes often lead to higher usage rates, and unfavourable attitudes are difficult to change. Marketers are concerned about personality because certain traits may influence the choice of a particular product.

6. **What are two ways in which consumers learn?**
   The theory of conditioned learning holds that learning takes place by association. Consumers may learn to associate a product with something pleasant and therefore learn to like the product. The theory of instrumental learning holds that people learn to act a certain way when their responses are rewarded, for example, through a product that delivers desired benefits.

7. **How do life-styles influence buyer behaviour?**
   Consumers tend to buy goods and services that are compatible with or appeal to their life-styles.

8. **What are the stages of the buying process?**
   The stages of the buying process are input (stimulus), process (problem awareness, information search, and evaluation of alternatives), and output (purchase and postpurchase behaviour).

Key Terms

aspirational group	output
attitude	perception
attitude scale	personality
buyer behaviour	reference group
culture	role
dissociative group	selective exposure
family life-cycle	selective perception
innovator	selective retention
input	social class
learning	subculture
membership group	theory of conditioned
motivation	learning
needs hierarchy	theory of instrumental
opinion leader	learning

Discussion Questions

1. What are some current trends in Anglophone and Francophone cultural values? Would you say that Canada is bicultural or multicultural? Why?

2. What characteristics differentiate the social classes? John and Jake both got jobs within a week of graduating from high school. John went to work in a factory for $5 an hour and moved into an apartment with a friend. Jake became a bank teller at $4 an hour and saved money by living at home so that he could study for a business degree in the evening. Does the difference in wages mean that John has higher social status than Jake? Why, or why not?

3. What is a reference group? What kinds of products can be sold by an appeal to a reference group?

4. How does the family shape buying behaviour? How do marketers use this information?

5. When Terry Travis opened Terry's Tune-Up Shop last September, he had flyers distributed to all the homes in the neighbourhood. The announcement read: "Terry's Tune-Up Shop Now Open on Main Street. Come in and get your car tuned up today!" During the next few weeks, business was so slow that Terry made phone calls to local homes to ask people whether they had seen the flyers or heard of his business. To Terry's dismay, most people could not recall seeing or hearing anything about Terry's Tune-Up Shop.

   How can you explain this situation in terms of perception? How might Terry overcome the perception problem?

6. "Above all, be polite to our customers," restaurant manager Myrna

Byrd lectured the serving staff. "We can't afford rudeness here. If you are surly to a customer, we may never see that customer again."

How does learning theory support Myrna's concern? How does your understanding of attitudes support her concern?

7. What personality type might be most interested in each of the following products?

   a. Ski equipment.

   b. An obviously expensive home entertainment system.

   c. A membership in a consumerist group.

8. How do marketers try to influence a buyer's choice during the input, processing, and output stages of the buying process?

CASE 6.1

CKO, The All-Canada News and Information Network (A)

On July 1, 1977, radio stations of the All-Canada News and Information Network, with the call letters CKO, went on the air across Canada. This was the country's first radio network to broadcast news and information on a continual 24-hour basis. The Canadian Radio-television and Tele-communications Commission had granted licences for FM frequencies in major Canadian centres as well as a transfer of licence of an existing AM frequency in Montreal.

Network Coverage

In 1977, CKO covered the 1-million-plus English-language population areas of Toronto and Vancouver, English-speaking Montreal, and most Canadian cities in the 300 000-to-600 000 size. It began broadcasting in most of the major markets licensed with an understanding that the network would expand to include Regina, Winnipeg, Saint John, St. John's, and Halifax. As it happened, the network did add Halifax and Winnipeg in the 1980s, but it was unable to include the others.

Setting Up Operations

On the granting of the licences, CKO's founders (Saskatoon-based Agra industries were controlling shareholders) hired a U.S. consultant, Frank George. It had been decided to follow a well-established American model of all-newsradio formats, and Mr. George had designed news and infor-

Source: Adapted from David Spencer, "The Death of CKO: What Happened?" *Broadcaster*, January 1990, pp. 27–29.

mation formats for NBC (the National Broadcasting Company) in the States.

Mr. George designed what he knew best: what is called a "rotating clock format," which had proved successful in reaching car-bound commuters listening to an AM radio who took at least one hour to get to work in a large American city.

Rotating Clock

The format was designed to build on a series of special interest groups, which, in combination, would supposedly provide the network with relatively high audience shares. It was thought that it would work the same way here, as it had in, say, the New York metropolitan area: sports addicts would be added to stock market junkies, gold speculators, and anyone else who wanted to know how long it was going to take to drive from Long Island to Manhattan.

Rotating-clock encourages quick tune-in and tune-out. For instance, at a certain point during any given hour of programming, sports fans will tune in to get the latest scores. Other special interest groups will tune in when they know their particular news is on. As a result, over a given hour, a station with this format will attract a sizeable audience—the sum of all these listener groups—although most of each group spends only a short time listening to that frequency.

The Canadian Market

In the 1970s in what was then CKO's listening area, most car drivers took less than half an hour to get to work, and one out of four commuters chose public transit. FM had not significantly penetrated the auto market. Furthermore, the CBC had implemented a noncommercial news/talk format in drive time on its AM stations across Canada. Its use of veteran announcers and reporters contrasted with the relatively inexperienced on-air staff hired by CKO.

It was thus not surprising that for about the first ten years of its operation, CKO failed to attract a large audience. With the exception of a bump in the early 1980s, when part of the network carried NHL hockey, audience figures remained virtually stagnant.

Major Changes in the 1980s

In 1982, CKO scrapped the rotating clock in favour of a news-talk format parallel to that of the CBC. Tayler Parnaby, who had put Toronto AM station CKEY's news operation on the map, was hired to improve the standards of news gathering and reporting. By the spring of 1989, according to the Bureau of Broadcast Measurement, CKO attracted a respectable cumulative audience of 623 000 total persons nationally. Unfortunately, by that time, the radio network had lost about $55 million.

Focal Topics

1. What cultural differences between Canada and the United States do you think led to Canadians' lack of acceptance of the American news format?

2. To what social class do you think an all-news radio format would appeal? Why did CKO fail initially to reach sufficient members of this group?

3. What would you say about the effect of selective exposure, selective perception, and selective retention on listening to a station like CKO?

CASE 6.2

Town Pharmacy

Susan Clack is the owner and manager of Town Pharmacy. She purchased this business immediately after receiving her degree in pharmacy eight months ago. As a student, she had worked for the previous owner of Town Pharmacy for the last two summers. She had no other business experience prior to graduation.

Town Pharmacy is one of only two pharmacies located in a small community in an agricultural region of eastern Canada. This community has a minor retail centre serving primarily the farmers in the immediate area. There are several other small retail centres in the surrounding towns, and two major retail centres are located within an hour's drive.

Sources of Revenue

Susan has discovered that about 25 percent of her revenue and 30 percent of her profit come from the dispensary. The rest is from the front store, where a selection of general merchandise is sold: nonprescription medications, candy, soft drinks, photographic supplies, hunting supplies, and seasonal items, such as Christmas decorations. The front store is the growth sector of most pharmacies.

Like most Canadian pharmacists, Susan sells cigarettes, although she has mixed feelings about selling tobacco products. She believes that the sale of cigarettes is inconsistent with a pharmacist's health-care role, since the products themselves are harmful not only to their users but to nonusers as well. Susan also believes, however, that cigarettes are extremely profitable. They generate a great deal of revenue and profit from very little floor space. They turn over about 30 times a year in her store and seem to create a great deal of floor traffic. Cigarettes are

This case, written by Professor Richard Sparkman, Acadia University, 1988, appeared in a slightly different form in T.K. Clarke and F.G. Crane, *Consumer Behaviour in Canada Theory and Practice* (Toronto: Harcourt Brace Jovanovich, 1990), pp. 308–309.

expecially useful as traffic builders on Sundays, when they cannot be purchased elsewhere in town. The exact importance of floor traffic is not known for Town Pharmacy, but Susan has read that most drugstore purchases result from in-store decisions and that 40 percent are impulse buys.

The Competition

The competing drugstore has recently discontinued the sale of cigarettes. This resulted in favourable publicity in both the local press and in the trade press. The opinion of most pharmacists is that this action was noble but unprofitable. Susan had not questioned this opinion until recently.

Attitude Survey on Cigarette Sales

A journal editor has given Susan a copy of a two-year-old manuscript that reports the results of an experiment that studied the relationship between consumers' perceptions of pharmacists and the sale of cigarettes in drugstores. The results were based on 200 telephone interviews conducted in a large metropolitan area about 100 kilometres from Town Pharmacy.

One hundred people were asked about pharmacists in drugstores where cigarettes were sold, and the other 100 were asked about pharmacists in drugstores where cigarettes were not sold. Selling cigarettes had no effect on smokers' attitudes toward pharmacists. However, nonsmokers thought that pharmacists in stores where cigarettes were sold were less professional, less knowledgeable, less trustworthy, and more hypocritical than their counterparts in stores not selling cigarettes. The results for nonsmokers and for the combined sample of smokers and nonsmokers are given in the accompanying table.

Average Attitude Scores for Retail Pharmacists

	All Subjects (n = 200)		Nonsmokers (n = 133)	
	Cigarettes Sold	Cigarettes Not Sold	Cigarettes Sold	Cigarettes Not Sold
Professionalism	5.44	4.49	5.68	4.79
Expertise	4.76	4.37	4.88	4.23
Trustworthiness	5.87	5.01	6.17	4.95
Hypocrisy	5.72	4.82	5.98	4.73

Note: Scales have been reversed where appropriate so that a lower score always reflects a more positive attitude. All differences are significant at alpha = .05. Maximum possible score is 10; minimum possible score is 2.

Overall, most of the respondents and most of the nonsmoking subjects said that they preferred to shop in drugstores that did not sell cigarettes. Most of the smokers preferred to shop in drugstores that did sell cigarettes.

Smoking or Nonsmoking?

Susan is not sure to what extent the experimental results apply to her drugstore. She does know that some of her customers seem to come in primarily to buy them. She also knows that consumers' attitudes toward pharmacists have an effect on their choice of drugstore. The perceived expertise of the pharmacist seems to be very important when consumers need advice on nonprescription medications.

Susan doesn't know what to do. She has always been uncomfortable about selling cigarettes and other tobacco products in a health-care business. She has done so in the past because she thought that it was economically necessary. She has checked her books and learned that the tobacco category of merchandise contributed $20 000 to profit and overhead the year before she purchased the store. This represents half of her profits and will continue to do so until she can reduce her debt load. She feels that she cannot afford to drop tobacco for ethical reasons. She must decide what to do based on economic considerations.

Focal Topics

1. What consumer behaviour concepts do you feel are important in helping Susan make a decison?

2. What is your general evaluation of the attitude survey?

3. What would you advise Susan to do? Why?

Organizational Buying Behaviour

In this chapter, you will learn:

- How the industrial market is important to the economy.

- Differences between the industrial and consumer markets.

- Major classes of industrial products.

- The nature of demand in the industrial sector.

- What influences buyer behaviour in the industrial sector.

- Types of buying decisions in the industrial sector.

- Principal roles in industrial buying situations.

- Why some companies lease rather than buy certain products.

Selling Computer Systems to Real Estate Firms

North America's largest business-forms supplier, Moore Corporation, is moving into a new field — developing a computer sales system for real estate brokers.

Called Photo-Trieve, the system puts colour pictures of listed houses on computer screens. Combined with information about the listing, it should help cut down a potential buyer's searching time.

The new technology can be used with other real estate computer systems developed by Moore over the past decade.

In Canada, Photo-Trieve is being tested by the 65 member offices of the Guelph, Ontario, real estate board.

It is already in use in 10 U.S. cities. The system, created by Moore's research and development unit in Grand Island, New York, has copyrights and patents in Canada and the States, according to Thomas Gregorich, president of Moore's data management services division.

It can produce up to 16 views of a property, each within 30 seconds.

Moore is selling the complete software for $30 000 and expects sales and training to contribute substantially to the bottom line — as much as $75 million.

Revenues from the Guelph pilot project alone are expected to total $1.5 million.

Securities analysts point out that with Moore reporting revenues of $2.3 billion (Cdn.) for the first nine months of 1989, Photo-Trieve is just a drop in the bucket.

Corie Fisher, president of the Guelph and District Real Estate Board, says Photo-Trieve is the way of the future for real estate listings.

"It's like going from radio to television," she says. "It's just a quicker, more accurate system."

One private real estate company in southern California says Photo-Trieve helped it capture 35 percent more listings in the 18 months it has been in use.

Some real estate industry observers are not convinced, including Eric Daly, vice-president of information services, Royal LePage, Canada's biggest nonfranchise home broker. He says his company does not believe clients would rather look at pictures on a computer screen than actual properties.

"We're trying to listen to what the consumer wants and needs," he says. "Clients are not telling us they want computer pictures."

Daly points out that much of the decision to buy a home is emotional and made quickly — usually 15 to 20 minutes after a buyer enters the home. "The issue is, how will picture technology help our client select a home?"

Moore's Gregorich has further plans for the technology. He hopes to market it to law-enforcement agencies and security systems, among other businesses. Police officers, in particular, could get computer photos of suspects on their car screens without driving back to the office. Agencies that seek lost children could also benefit.

Marketing to the real estate industry uses many of the same techniques as marketing to consumers, but organizations do not always make buying decisions in the same way consumers do. Marketers to organizations therefore must understand organizational buying behaviour. This chapter looks at the industrial market and describes how organizational purchasing decisions are made.

Source: Adapted from Alanna Mitchell, "New Computer Program Has Real Estate in Focus," *The Financial Post*, December 20, 1989, p. 13.

A s buyers of consumer goods, we are often only dimly aware of the bustle of purchasing activity that preceded an item's appearance in the local supermarket, shopping mall, or dealer's showroom. Consider, for example, the many buying decisions that went into assembling the components of the family car: one company supplied the glass for the windows, another the steel for the body, still others the carpeting for the floors, the vinyl for the seats, the bulbs for the lights, and the locks for the doors. (See Figure 7.1.) Even before these parts could be purchased, however, they too had to be manufactured, necessitating even more buying decisions. The steelmakers bought barges of iron ore, the vinyl manufacturers purchased truckloads of petroleum products, and the glass producers shopped around for a good price on silicon. In addition, manufacturing equipment had to be purchased to turn these raw materials into finished goods.

Besides the obvious products used in manufacturing, consider the many other supplies a company needs to buy in order to function: soap for workers' hands, cardboard cartons for shipping, office forms for invoices, and filters for the coffee machine. Depending on the company, it may have purchased anything from paper clips to a Lear jet to enable

Figure 7.1 Selected Suppliers of Component Parts for a Ford Automobile

Source: Data from "Are U.S. Cars Really Getting Better?" *U.S. News & World Report*, August 29, 1983, p. 57.

it finally to manufacture that car in the driveway. From the first crude lump of iron ore to the final squirt of rustproofing, someone in the industrial sector had to make a buying decision.

What Is the Industrial Market?

The **industrial market** is composed of businesses (manufacturers, wholesalers, and retailers), governments (federal, provincial, and local), and organizations (colleges and universities, hospitals, nursing homes, and others) that buy products and services for resale or for use in producing other products and services.

This market is much larger than the consumer market. The scope of the industrial market is illustrated in Table 7.1. In the manufacturing sector alone, there are nearly 36 000 establishments and they employ more than 1.2 million people. The significance of this market is dramatized by the amount of materials and supplies used in operations—more than $112 billion worth! In total, the industrial market accounts for some 50 percent of purchases of manufactured goods in Canada.

One measure of industrial output is the **value added** by manufacturing—the increase in the value of input material when transformed into semifinished or finished goods. For example, value is added to a tonne of iron ore when it is made into steel plate, and more value is added when the plate is stamped into refrigerator bodies. In 1982, the value added by manufacturing in Canada totalled approximately $69 billion (Table 7.1).

Industrial marketing accounts for well over half the economic activity in the United States and Canada, and more than half of all business school graduates enter industrial product or service firms.[1] Given these

Industrial Market
Businesses, governments, and organizations that buy goods and services for resale or for use in producing other goods and services.

Value Added
The increase in value of input material when transformed into semifinished or finished goods.

Table 7.1 Manufacturers in Canada, 1982

Province or Territory	Number of Establishments	Total Employees	Materials and Supplies Used (in Thousands of Dollars)	Total Value Added (in Thousands of Dollars)
Ontario	14 822	589 649	56 020 076	35 188 820
Quebec	10 753	348 333	28 208 448	18 745 836
British Columbia	3 919	103 653	9 073 549	5 917 997
Alberta	2 490	54 834	9 058 291	3 801 812
Manitoba	1 279	39 130	2 863 844	1 859 175
Nova Scotia	781	24 967	2 248 815	1 123 255
Saskatchewan	749	14 075	1 640 905	777 615
New Brunswick	591	21 479	2 140 961	938 432
Newfoundland	295	13 764	661 468	549 475
Prince Edward Island	127	2 253	169 569	75 559
Northwest Territories and Yukon	19	219	23 651	9 761
Total	35 834	1 212 424	112 120 148	68 990 447

Source: Data from 1982 *Census of Manufactures*, presented in Statistics Canada, *The Daily*, May 1, 1984, cat. no. 11–001E, p. 6.

figures, it becomes clear how important it is to include this vast range of activity in our study of marketing.

Differences between Consumer and Industrial Markets

While many of the issues discussed concerning consumer buying behaviour also hold true for the industrial market, there are some important differences between the two markets.

Fewer Buyers

The scope of industrial buying is vast, but it is startling to realize how few buyers actually account for the enormous sums. Although the 1982 *Census of Manufactures* revealed a total of approximately 36 000 firms in Canada, a small proportion of firms—those with 500 or more employees—were responsible for approximately half of the total dollar value added by manufacturing.[2]

These numbers are not so surprising when one considers that a company such as de Havilland need only sell a few jets, worth a few million dollars each, to a handful of customers in order to have a profitable year. By contrast, McDonald's must sell a few million hamburgers to a few million people to do as well.

Geographical Concentration

Not only are there fewer buyers in the industrial market, but their numbers are greatly concentrated in certain areas of the country. The largest markets are in Ontario and Quebec. However, industrial markets for specific items often do not follow the general pattern. For example, the market for marine engines and fishing gear is concentrated on the Atlantic and Pacific coasts. The market for oil-drilling equipment is in Alberta, British Columbia, and to a lesser extent Saskatchewan; recently, East Coast oil discovery has caused it to expand eastward.[3]

This concentration of activity has important implications for marketers. Companies that sell to the industrial sector can effectively concentrate their efforts in areas of high market potential. Often companies will locate a full-time personal sales force in these markets. In addition, they may locate distribution facilities in large-volume areas so that major customers can be assured speedy delivery.[4]

Nature of Demand

Another important difference between industrial and consumer markets is the nature of the demand for goods. The demand for products in the consumer market is direct: if consumers want houses, they buy houses, and the number can be easily measured. But demand in the industrial market is not so simple. If consumers buy houses, builders buy plumbing supplies, lumber, roofing shingles, and nails. If consumers stop buying, the need for all these goods may decrease. Thus, the demand for industrial products is a *derived* demand—it depends ultimately on how much consumers are willing to buy.

Industrial marketers therefore watch changes in consumer buying patterns carefully. Economic factors, changes in consumer tastes, and new government regulations all have important effects on industrial markets. For example, when the military cuts spending, Canadair may have less business. (Marketing Today 7.1 describes how one aerospace firm is adapting to defence cutbacks.) When consumers demand better gasoline efficiency, automakers buy lighter materials to use in making cars.

Industrial Products and the Marketing Mix

Another difference between consumer and industrial markets rests in the kinds of products that each buys. An earlier example showed that automotive manufacturers need everything from sheet metal to paper clips to get a car to a dealer's showroom. While companies may buy large quantities of each of these products, the way in which each company acquires them may be quite different.

Planning a marketing strategy for the tens of thousands of industrial products sold would be impractical without some way of classifying them.

Marketing Today 7.1

Aerospace Firm Reacts to Defence Cutbacks

When its Zurich-based parent company announced cutbacks in production of guns and ammunition because of the shrinking defence business, Oerlikon Aerospace, Inc. of St-Jean, Quebec, began looking for civilian applications for its defence technology. The company was created to build sophisticated defence machines for the Canadian Forces, but early in 1990, Marco Genoni, the president, suggested that Oerlikon start courting civil contracts. Said Genoni, although "we want to keep a foot in defence, if the world keeps moving toward space we want to play a major role there." The company will specialize in communications uses for the space industry.

The federal government is providing funds for research and development depending on export sales, jobs created, and the company's own investment. The last is considerable, with plant expansion valued at $35 million and a five-year research budget at $100 million.

Besides space, the Oerlikon's technology can be applied to land surveying, city traffic control, and the monitoring of remote electrical power stations.

Source: Adapted from Canadian Press, "Aerospace Firm Charts New Horizons," *The Toronto Star*, July 20, 1989, Business Section.

One of the most practical classification systems is based on their use. There are six major classes: (1) raw materials, (2) manufactured materials and parts, (3) installations, (4) accessory equipment, (5) supplies, and (6) business services. (See Figure 7.2.)

Raw Materials

Raw Material
Natural resource such as crude oil or a cultivated product such as wheat used in the production of finished products.

All manufactured products are composed of **raw materials,** which are natural resources, such as crude oil, iron ore, and other minerals, or cultivated products, such as wheat, cotton, and timber. Raw materials can be very important to food processors like General Mills. Consequently, the initial buying of raw materials may be in the hands of a top executive, though the regular purchase thereafter can be handled by company purchasing agents. Raw materials may be bought directly from

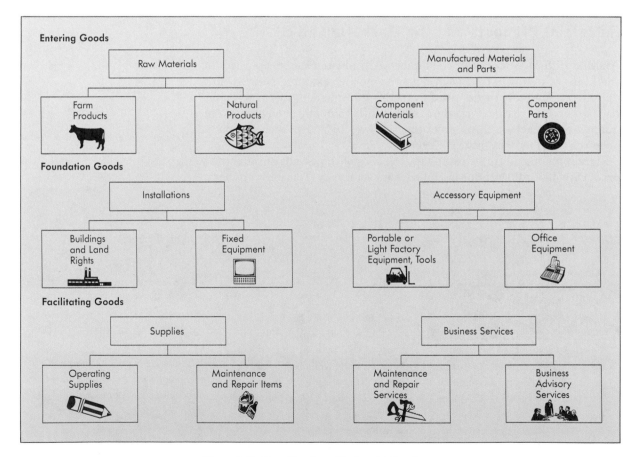

Figure 7.2 Classification of Industrial Goods

Source: Phillip Kotler, *Marketing Management: Analysis, Planning, and Control*, 4th ed., © 1980, p. 172. Adapted by permission of Prentice-Hall, Inc., Englewood Cliffs, N.J.

producers, or they may be purchased through co-operatives like Sunkist (which markets oranges grown on numerous farms) or through distributors like Shell and Exxon (which transport and sell petroleum for many of the oil-producing nations of the world).

The price of raw materials rarely varies from producer to producer, so purchasing agents often make up their minds on the basis of who can supply a steady flow of quality material. To guarantee the supply, agents may negotiate long-term contracts, or they may buy from many suppliers.

Manufactured Materials and Parts

Goods that have in some way been shaped or finished and incorporated into another product are known as **manufactured materials,** or **manufactured parts.** As shown in Figure 7.1, such parts and materials are especially important to the manufacture of automobiles.

The marketing strategy for selling manufactured parts and materials is similar to that for selling raw materials. In both cases, purchases are frequent, and a steady supply — not price — is often the primary consideration. Contracts are negotiated between the purchasing agents of a company and the sales representatives of a supplier. One difference is that design considerations can win the supplier a long-term contract if the supplier can promise to build to the specifications requested by the buyer.

Manufactured Materials (Manufactured Parts)
Industrial goods that have in some way been shaped or finished and are incorporated into another product.

Installations

Large, expensive goods necessary for the production of final products, although they do not become a part of those products, are known as **installations.** Factory sites, such as the steel mills of Hamilton, Ontario, and major equipment, such as machine tools, fall into this category.

The purchase of installations is a major decision, and sales negotiations usually take place over long periods of time. The top personnel of the buyer company and the technical experts and high officials of the selling company often conduct negotiations for installations. Decisions on factory sites can take years. Negotiations over major equipment can last equally as long because machinery sometimes has to be made to engineering and production specifications. The final decision to buy is usually made less on price than on the installation's expected performance. Obviously, a relatively cheap computer that keeps breaking down would prove a very expensive item for a company. Because price is not often the major consideration, sellers must attract buyers in other ways, such as providing leasing or rental arrangements and service guarantees. IBM business computer equipment, for example, may require too much capital for a small company to buy outright and may be too complex to be maintained by the company's personnel. Therefore, IBM often rents

Installation
Large, expensive, industrial product necessary for the production of final products but not a part of those goods — for example, industrial plants and major equipment.

equipment to companies and sends in technicians to set up a system for a client.

Accessory Equipment

Like major equipment, **accessory equipment** does not become part of the final product, although it is necessary to the final product's manufacture. Included in this category are hardware of all sorts, such as hand tools and drills, and office equipment, such as photocopiers and fax machines.

Because accessory equipment is less expensive and needs replacement or parts on a regular basis, responsibility for purchase is generally given to a company purchasing agent who specializes in equipment and can follow up on any purchases. Companies that manufacture accessory equipment may depend upon **industrial distributors,** wholesalers who sell to the industrial market, to sell their products. To supplement the efforts of the wholesalers, manufacturers sometimes advertise equipment in such trade magazines as *Canadian Industrial Equipment News* and *Plant Engineering.* Purchasing agents generally shop around for the best price, so extras like rental arrangements and service guarantees can be important.

Supplies

Products needed for the maintenance or repair of equipment or for the operation of a business are classified as **supplies.** Light bulbs, lubricating oil, paper clips, and adding machine tape may not be part of a finished product, but they are often essential to its manufacture or sale.

Supplies are regularly used up and must be purchased constantly. Purchasing departments have informal or contractual supplying arrangements with wholesale intermediaries. Computer systems greatly reduce reordering chores that were once done by clerks. When supplies are first purchased, price is the primary consideration, and price competition among wholesalers for a contract can be fierce. Thereafter, price may play a relatively insignificant role, since purchasers are unwilling to spend time searching out bargains for small, inexpensive items. For the seller, therefore, the basic strategy is to get in early and maintain good relationships.

Business Services

Organizations often turn to specialists outside the firm to perform specific functions. Services may include maintenance and repair support (for example, window cleaning, copier repair) and advisory support (for example, management consulting, legal counsel, advertising, and public relations services).[5] At Your Service 7.1 describes a company that provides personnel services.

Industrial Demand

Derived Demand

As discussed earlier, one of the essential differences between industrial and consumer marketing is that in industry, demand for a product is based on what a buying organization's customers want — **derived demand** — not what the organization itself wants. Because consumers ultimately determine industrial demand, occasionally an industrial marketer will develop a campaign directed at a product's final buyer. An ad for canned food (see Figure 7.3) encourages consumer demand for this form of packaging.

Derived Demand
Demand by industrial users that depends on consumer demand for the finished product.

Fluctuating Demand

Because demand in the industrial sector is derived from consumer preferences, it may fluctuate widely in response to changing economic conditions or when consumer tastes change. Since **fluctuating demand** influences not only inventory levels and warehousing needs, but also has serious effects on production, many industrial marketers have diversified their product lines.

Fluctuating Demand
Demand in the industrial sector that may vary widely in response to changing economic conditions or changes in consumer tastes.

At Your Service 7.1

Temporary Employees, New Employees, Transferred Employees

The Dunhill Personnel System provides business services in a variety of ways, including temporary help, searches for new employees, and employee relocation.

Dunhill Temporary Systems provides temporary help to business. This is a service that many businesses are turning to these days. The U.S. Department of Commerce reports that temporary help services are one of the United States' fastest-growing industries, and they are thriving in Canada too. Dunhill Temporary Systems meets this demand with a network of franchises serving local markets. A computerized accounting system enables the franchisees to promote their ability to provide individualized billing.

The Dunhill Personnel System also offers franchises to those who want to provide personnel recruitment services. These services include senior- and middle-management search, technical recruiting, and office personnel. In addition, the company offers a Relocation Management Program, which includes selling a transferred employee's home and helping him or her find a new home. The relocation service also arranges for the employee's move to the new location.

Source: Brochures from Dunhill Personnel System, Inc., including "A Dunhill Personnel Franchise," "A Dunhill Temporary Systems Franchise," and "The Dunhill International Search & Relocation Program."

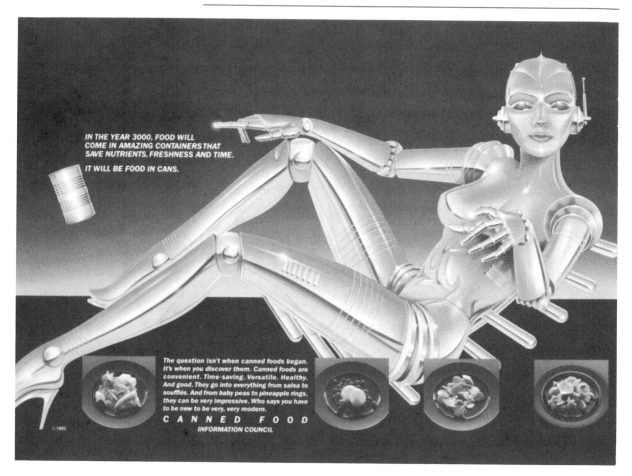

Figure 7.3 Advertisement from the U.S. Canned Food Information Council
Source: Courtesy of U.S. National Food Processors Association.

Joint Demand

Joint Demand
Market condition when demand for one product will be affected by the availability of another product with which it is used.

In some cases, demand for one product will be affected by the availability of another product with which it is used. This is called **joint demand.** For example, record manufacturers need vinyl for records and cardboard for slip cases. If petroleum shortages affect the supply of vinyl, resulting in diminished record production, then industrial buyers may cut back on the amount of cardboard they purchase.

Inelastic Demand

Inelastic Demand
As it relates to consumer behaviour: Demand that remains relatively constant despite price changes.

Although demand for a manufactured product may be seriously affected by changes in the consumer market, within the industrial market, demand remains relatively constant despite price changes. This is known as **inelastic demand.** Since most industrial products are composed of many parts, price increases on one or two of the parts may result in a slightly higher cost to the consumer but will not seriously affect how much of that item a manufacturer purchases. If consumer demand for products containing NutraSweet remains high, manufacturers will continue to buy it instead of saccharin despite the product's higher cost.

Buying Behaviour in Industrial Markets

In many ways, the industrial buying process is similar to that of families. For everyday items (for example, ketchup or paper clips), one member may routinely buy a preferred brand. On the other hand, major decisions —a new refrigerator or computer installation—may involve a lengthy search for information and long deliberations over size, price, and features among a family or organization's decision makers.

Just as marketers must understand what influences consumer buying behaviour, they also must recognize the factors that affect buying decisions within an organization.

Criteria for Industrial Purchases

Because businesses are motivated by profit considerations and governments and institutions must be accountable for their budgeted expenses, economic considerations such as price, quality, features, and service are often the primary considerations of industrial buyers. Unfortunately for marketers, various members of the buying organization may place different emphasis on these factors. A company's engineers, for example, may stress quality, and the purchasing agent may value maximum price economy. The weight of each of these factors and the influence of each participant may vary with the organization and the type of product being considered.[6] The challenge for marketers is to determine who among the participants has the final say—and what that person values most.

Continuity of supply is also an important consideration for an industrial marketer. Because interruption in the flow of materials can bring the production process to a grinding halt, industrial buyers are often reluctant to rely on a single source for supplies. This is especially true when there are few alternative suppliers.[7]

Emotional Influences on Buying Behaviour

Although industrial buying decisions are often less whimsical than those in consumer markets, they are not necessarily free from emotional influences. Human beings, with all their strengths, faults, and frailties, still make the big decisions. (See Marketing Today 7.2.)

The same needs for esteem, affiliation, and security that were explored

Elco Industries, Inc.

Marketing Today 7.2

What Hidden Forces Motivate the Machine Tool Buyer?

Can marketers use psychographic research in industrial advertising and sales? One of the few attempts to answer that question was a study of 200 industrial buyers done by psychologist Bruce J. Morrison.

Morrison studied four groups of industrial buyers: managers, purchasing agents, design engineers, and production engineers. Each group, he found, had distinct personality traits that influenced the way in which they perceived advertising and selling appeals.

Design and production engineers, for example, tend to have low anxiety levels and a sense of personal control over their environments. They prefer advertising that shows solutions to problems and specific engineering information.

Managers and purchasing agents tend to be more anxious than engineers and feel controlled by their environment. They also tend to have authoritarian personalities.

The best way to reach managers, Morrison suggests, is to design advertising around "modern, aggressive, idea presentations — the big picture approach." Managers are anxious to succeed and willing to take risks to move their companies ahead.

Purchasing agents, on the other hand, like facts and figures, and are fond of wheeling and dealing. Morrison found that purchasing agents are "subjective fellows striving for status." Ads geared to them should stress quality, reliability, delivery, and company image.

Based on this information, Elco Industries, Inc., a manufacturer of specialty metal components, felt confident that its advertising strategy was on target. Advertising directed at design engineers, for example, stressed the full range of

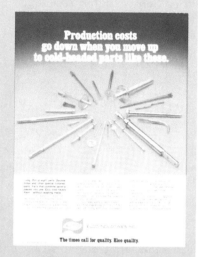

capabilities of Elco's custom-engineered metal components. When the company advertised the same product to purchasing agents, however, it emphasized delivery, quality, reliability, and company image.

Sources: Adapted from "Know the Buyer Better," film by B. J. Morrison; and Marianne Paskowski, "Psycho-Marketing," *Industrial Marketing,* July 1981, pp. 41–42.

in Chapter 6 are also at work in the industrial marketplace. In business, a buyer may be motivated by a desire for status within the organization, a promotion, or a salary increase. Industrial salespeople need to understand this reward system in order to compete effectively with other suppliers.[8]

In one case, a manufacturer of sophisticated graphics computers was puzzled by its unimpressive record in selling to large potential customers. Instead of following the industry practice of quoting high list prices and giving generous discounts for quantity purchases during negotiations with buyers, this company had simply offered the lowest net prices in the industry. Sales had failed to materialize. The reason? Purchasing agents and their bosses evaluated their performance on how much of a price break they had managed to negotiate from suppliers, not on the net price actually paid.[9]

Fear plays a role, too. A purchasing agent may be insecure because of uncertainty about decisions, about status within a firm, about executive approval, and about job security.[10]

Many analysts attribute IBM's success in selling personal computers to industry at least partially to this factor. With more than 150 different computer manufacturers pounding on corporate doors, many purchasing agents began suffering "option shock." As a result, for many, "the low-risk decision was to buy IBM."[11]

Friendship may also influence buying decisions. While many companies require competitive bids on purchases, a buyer may work closely with a friend to ensure the friend's competitiveness on price and product specifications.[12]

Industrial marketers who recognize the various emotional factors that influence buyers may be able to design strategies that can subtly address the unspoken issues in a purchasing decision.

The Importance of Personal Selling

In the industrial market, personal selling is much more important than advertising. The opposite is often true for the consumer market. Another distinction is that intermediaries are seldom used in the exchange of goods between supplier and industrial buyer. Because large industrial purchases often rest on the skill and quality of a company's sales force, the larger firms often spend substantial amounts of time and money training their salespeople. Table 7.2 shows the results of a poll in which 300 purchasing managers were asked to identify what characteristics they liked—and disliked—in salespeople.

Many firms find that an efficient way to generate high-quality sales leads is to attend trade shows of the industries they serve. Trade show selling is less expensive than paying visits to buyers and often requires

Table 7.2 Buyers Rate Salespersons: Likes and Dislikes

What Buyers Like	What Buyers Dislike
Thoroughness and follow-through	Hard-selling, high-pressure tactics
Complete product knowledge	Talking too long about unrelated matters
Willingness to pursue the best interests of the buyer within the supplier firm	Exhibiting little interest in meeting the buyer's "real needs"
Sound market knowledge and willingness to keep the buyer informed	

Source: Based on a survey of 300 purchasing managers conducted by *Purchasing* magazine and reported in Larry Giunipero and Gary Zenz, "Impact of Purchasing Trends on Industrial Marketers," *Industrial Marketing Management*, February 1982, pp. 17–23.

fewer follow-up calls. Furthermore, the visitors to a trade show tend to be well motivated to buy. The results for marketers can be impressive. For example, Acco International, manufacturer of a full line of office products, has made trade shows the focus of its marketing strategy. During one three-day show, the company wrote $700 000 in sales.

Continuing Contact between Buyer and Seller

Unlike consumer markets, buyers and sellers in the industrial sector often build relationships that span years. This is partly the result of fewer buyers for a given industrial product. In addition, sellers may extend credit to buyers for large purchases and provide follow-up service and technical assistance for their products.

Often two industries are so inextricably bound together that the vitality of one is closely tied to the other. Depending on the industries, there may even be trade possibilities between them. In such cases, they may choose to make an arrangement between them based on **reciprocity**. Such an arrangement may be stated as, "I'll buy from you if you buy from me." A relationship involves reciprocity when the buyer-seller arrangement, rather than economic or performance factors, influences the purchase decision.[13] Such arrangements are legal as long as they do not involve coercion or seriously limit the competition in one of the industries involved.

Types of Buying Decisions

Industrial buyers make decisions differently, depending on whether the purchase is routine or complex. To understand these buying decisions better, marketers classify them into three types: the straight rebuy, the modified rebuy, and the new task.[14]

Straight Rebuy

A **straight rebuy** involves reordering something without any modifications. For example, office supplies are routine purchases. Typically, a purchasing department handles straight rebuys. Suppliers try to maintain quality and may propose that the organization use an automatic reordering system.

Modified Rebuy

A repurchase in which the buyer wants to modify product specifications, prices, terms, or suppliers is called a **modified rebuy.** Employees other than purchasing agents may take part in such decisions. Companies that wish to become suppliers try to make a better offer than current suppliers. Current suppliers must work harder to keep the business.

Reciprocity
In industrial marketing, the relationship between buyer and seller that influences purchasing decisions rather than economic or performance factors.

Straight Rebuy
Repurchase without any modifications to the product, terms, or suppliers.

Modified Rebuy
Repurchase in which the buyer wants to modify product specifications, prices, terms, or suppliers.

New Task

A **new task** involves buying a product or service for the first time. If the cost and risk are great, many people may participate in making the decision. Machinery and computer systems are often purchased this way. Marketers in this situation may have to supply a great deal of expertise and make a favourable impression on a number of decision makers.

A Profile of Industrial Buyers

Those who have studied the industrial buying process refer to the group of people who are involved in purchasing for an industrial market as the **buying centre.** The members of a buying centre, like the members of a family, tend to assume certain roles. According to one system of classification, the five principal roles in industrial buying situations are:

1. **Users** — those in the organization who work with the products purchased.

2. **Buyers**—individuals, often called purchasing agents, with the formal responsibility of placing orders.

3. **Influencers**—those who can affect the decision process by assisting in evaluating alternative products.

4. **Deciders** — managers with the authority to make the final choice.

5. **Gatekeepers** — organizational members who control the flow of information into the buying centre.[15]

Sometimes an individual may assume more than one of these roles. For example, for relatively routine buys such as the ordering of office paper supplies, the purchasing agent may have full authority to buy without consulting others, in effect becoming gatekeeper, influencer, decider, and buyer.

Many purchases are much more complicated than a simple reorder. This is why other people are called in to consult or decide. Consider what might happen if a firm decides to order new carpeting for an office. Along the way, a variety of people take on the roles described above, but only two decisions are being made—the decision about whether to purchase at all and the choice of what to purchase.

The role of gatekeeper for the first decision may be played by the company receptionist, who makes others aware of the need. Various divisional heads may influence the decision to act on the receptionist's suggestion, but the plant manager may be the person who makes the final decision.

Once the decision to purchase is made, a whole different set of people becomes involved. The gatekeeper this time may be the supplier who selects the sample to be shown. Engineers and a secretary may act as influencers in viewing the samples and giving opinions on the durability

New Task
Purchase of a good or service for the first time.

Buying Centre
Group involved in purchasing for an industrial market.

User
Member of a buying centre who works with the products purchased.

Buyer
Person, often called purchasing agent, with the formal responsibility of placing orders.

Influencer
One who can affect the decision process by assisting in evaluating alternative products.

Decider
Manager with authority to make the final choice.

Gatekeeper
Organizational member who controls the flow of information into the buying centre.

and beauty of the selections. Ultimately, the chief factory engineer and company co-owner may make the final selection. In a decision such as this, the purchasing agent may play only the minor role of buyer or order taker.

Distinguishing the persons in a buying centre and the roles they play is crucial to making a sale. If the salesperson in the carpet decision (the supplier) had assumed that the purchasing agent had full authority in the buying decision, he or she would have wasted time trying to sell to someone whose decision power in the case at hand was minimal. In fact, while the composition of a buying centre for a new computer would differ from that for new carpeting, research has shown that for many buying decisions key influencers are outside the purchasing department. Many firms conduct extensive marketing research to identify buyer roles. The research guides them in tailoring a sales message that addresses the concerns of each participant.[16]

By anticipating the needs of each department involved in the decision and developing a strategy that takes individual concerns into account, a marketer can greatly increase the chances of closing a sale. At Your Service 7.2 explains how a supplier of transportation services developed a strategy to serve a marketing niche in the industrial sector.

At Your Service 7.2

Freight-Forwarding Company Fills Industrial Marketing Niche

The conventional method of long-distance freight transportation is for a truck to first pick up a cargo of goods and, second, take it to the local railway yard where it is, third, shipped across the country. Delivery generally requires six to eight days. This is the cheapest method; urgent cargoes go by air and are much more expensive. Regular freight forwarders call a half-dozen carriers to see who can handle their shipments and then are left at the mercy of the service that the one willing carrier provides.

Enter "road express" or "expedited freight," in which a team of two drivers will pick up, move, and deliver the shipment across the country in just three days. The service is priced somewhere between rail and air transportation. It works best if the forwarding company has control over its own "line-haul."

Jetrans Freight Systems, Inc. became the first such company to gain this kind of control by linking up with an existing transportation firm. Jetrans is a relatively small operation, and its four founders — Walter Civiero, Garry Linn, Chris Creed, and Brian Nash — explain that their larger-size competitors are not able to react with the speed required to make expedited freight work the way it must. Also, the four are not afraid to "get their hands dirty" by pitching in and, for instance, helping to load cargo.

The four founders are well known in the industry; they all worked for large transportation companies before forming Jetrans. "I can't believe some of the running times we have been able to perform," Linn says. "You tell us when you have to have it and we'll make sure it's there."

Source: Adapted from Herve DeJordy, "On Your Own: Fired Employees on the Road Again with a Freight Service of Their Own," *The Toronto Star*, August 7, 1989, p. B3.

Leasing versus Buying

A growing pattern in industrial buying behaviour is leasing products instead of buying them. Organizations may sign leases for products as diverse as data-processing equipment, delivery trucks, and machine tools.

Among the benefits of leasing rather than buying are that the user has money free for other uses, and that lessors often service the products they lease. Companies that lease may also enjoy tax advantages, including deductibility of rental expense. For companies that use equipment only part of the year, leasing can be particularly attractive.

Chapter Replay

1. **How is the industrial market important to the Canadian economy?**
   The industrial market is much larger than the consumer market. Industrial marketing accounts for well over half the economic activity in the country.

2. **What are some differences between the industrial and consumer markets?**
   The industrial market contains relatively few buyers, and their numbers are geographically concentrated. Demand in the consumer market is direct, but demand in the industrial market is indirectly influenced by consumer demand.

3. **What are the major classes of industrial products?**
   The major classes of industrial products are raw materials, manufactured materials and parts, installations, accessory equipment, supplies, and business services.

4. **What is the nature of demand in the industrial sector?**
   Demand in the industrial sector is derived, fluctuating, and inelastic. Also, in some cases demand for one product is affected by the availability of another product with which it is used.

5. **What influences buyer behaviour in the industrial sector?**
   Industrial buying behaviour is affected by economic considerations and emotional factors. Personal selling is very important in the industrial market, with buyers and sellers typically maintaining long-term relationships.

6. **What types of buying decisions are made in the industrial sector?**
   Buying decisions in the industrial sector include straight rebuys, modified rebuys, and new tasks.

7. **What are the principal roles in industrial buying situations?**
    The principal roles are users, buyers, influencers, deciders, and gatekeepers.

8. **Why do some companies lease rather than buy certain products?**
    Leasing frees up money for other uses. Suppliers of leased products often service what they lease. Companies that lease may also benefit from tax advantages, including deductibility of rental expense. Companies that use equipment for only part of the year can pay for it only when they need it.

Key Terms

accessory equipment	joint demand
buyer	manufactured materials
buying centre	(manufactured parts)
decider	modified rebuy
derived demand	new task
fluctuating demand	raw material
gatekeeper	reciprocity
industrial distributor	straight rebuy
industrial market	supplies
inelastic demand	user
influencer	value added
installation	

Discussion Questions

1. What are three major differences between consumer and industrial markets?

2. Give an example of each of the following categories of industrial products.

    a. Raw materials.

    b. Manufactured parts.

    c. Installations.

    d. Accessory equipment.

    e. Supplies.

    f. Business services.

3. What is inelastic demand? Why is industrial demand relatively inelastic?

4. Bernice Bliss is a sales representative for Industrial Janitorial Service, Inc. In preparing to sell her company's services to a potentially large client, she has decided to list the factors that might influence the customer's decision to buy. What criteria could Bernice put on her list?

5. Tim Treemont is a sales representative for Perfect Packaging Products. He likes to use a friendly approach, so when he called on Rob Freemont of Yummy Foods, he spent 20 minutes discussing the recent World Series. When Tim turned the subject to the previous year's World Series, Rob looked agitated and exclaimed, "I thought you wanted to talk about why we should start putting our chocolate frosting in aerosol cans." "That's right," replied Tim quickly, "Listen, I'll give you a deal on your first 500. Trust me; it'll be the best move you ever made. Can I count on your order?"

   Why do you think Tim didn't get the sale? What traits do buyers like in a salesperson?

6. Describe the three types of buying decisions. Which type of decision is likely to involve the greatest number of decision makers?

7. Eileen Green, secretary, reported to her boss, Sue Blue, that the service rep had told her that fixing her typewriter any more was probably hopeless because it was so old. "Well," replied Sue, "get some information on typewriters, narrow your choice to one or two, and then show me what you found."

   Eileen looked through a couple of catalogues she got from the company's purchasing agent. She also called her friend, Jack Black, to discuss how he liked his new electronic typewriter. The next day she described her first choice to Sue. Sue approved Eileen's choice, and Eileen requested the purchasing agent to order the typewriter.

   In this scenario, who played each of the roles as members of the buying centre? How could a marketer have influenced the buying decision?

8. Why might a company prefer to lease its sales representatives' cars rather than own them?

CKO, The All-Canada News and Information Network (B)

On July 1, 1977, CKO, Canada's first national all-news radio network hit the air. From the beginning, the network had difficulty attracting a sufficient number of listeners. Even when audiences eventually grew to a respectable 630 000, as a result of format changes, the radio stations

Source: Adapted from David Spencer, "The Death of CKO: What Happened?" *Broadcaster*, January 1990, pp. 27–29.

still had trouble attracting advertisers — almost their sole source of revenue.

The Buying and Selling of Advertising

Most daily newspapers and small radio stations obtain the largest share of their advertising revenue from retail advertisers. On the other hand, consumer magazines and television networks and stations derive most of their revenue from national advertisers.

The key decision makers in the purchase of national advertising are the media buyers at advertising agencies, who buy time or space for clients. What these purchasers are constantly seeking is the most cost-efficient buy—that is, they want to get an ad exposed to the most number of people in a target group at the lowest possible price.

Calculating Cost Efficiency

The traditional calculations of cost-efficiency in advertising are based on the kinds of TV audience data produced by the Bureau of Broadcast Measurement and A.C. Nielsen. Each purchase is measured in terms of gross impressions (the number of people exposed to an advertising medium multiplied by the number of times they are exposed). A similar measure is gross rating points (GRP): the percentage of the target group exposed multiplied by the number of times exposed.

Cost efficiency is measured in terms of cost per thousand impressions (CPM) or cost per rating point. The CPM is the total cost of the campaign divided by gross impressions and multiplied by 1000 to yield the cost of 1000 exposures to the ad medium. Cost per rating point is calculated by dividing the total cost of the campaign by the GRP to yield the cost of exposure to 1 percent of the population of the target group.

New Data Bases for Print Media

Such calculation of a cost-efficient buy obviously requires accurate information on the number of people exposed to an ad. In the late 1970s and early 1980s, television drew by far the most dollars from national advertising budgets. Some people suspected that one reason the share was so huge was the availability of extensive audience data from BBM and Nielsen. Firms from other media started banding together, trying to fight television's dominance of national advertising by gathering the information media buyers seemed to demand.

The print media, which had previously depended primarily on circulation data, were fairly successful in their efforts. Through the Print Measurement Bureau (PMB), consumer magazines began to provide media buyers with an audience data base. So did daily newspapers when the Newspaper Marketing Bureau launched the Newspaper Audience Data Bank (Nad Bank). Media selection experts accepted the new data bases which permitted them to analyze advertising buys by assessing their efficiency of exposure to an infinite number of target groups, as well as by relating these groups to product purchase.

Radio Measurement

BBM has long measured radio station audiences in Canada. Because of the way it surveys listeners, the basic unit of measurement is the "average quarter-hour." It measures radio listening by means of a diary completed by the respondent. Over a week, each person in the sample fills in the diary by writing the call letters of the radio station listened to in each of the 15-minute time blocks provided.

The manner in which the data from these surveys are presented has not always been satisfactory, but Canadian radio stations have been largely unsuccessful in getting together as a group to provide advertising agencies with a computerized data base. Broadcasters did attempt to gain recognition for a data base of their own—Radio Product Measurement (RPM). It failed, however, to gain universal acceptance among influential media buyers, many of whom questioned its validity.

The Struggle To Sell Advertising on CKO

Unfortunately for CKO, it was a station for which the BBM surveys were particularly unhelpful. The typical listener to the station's original rotating clock format—someone listening to an FM car radio who tuned in and out frequently—could not be expected to record this listening in a BBM diary with much accuracy, if at all. What listening was recorded resulted in a low quarter-hour average audience figure, especially if broken down by geographic listening area, but a reasonably high cumulative audience over a week (weekly reach) nationally. Unfortunately, most media buyers preferred high average audience figures, which yielded large GRPs, the latter expressed market-by-market and not nationally.

CKO, then, was a national medium. But because of the demands of organizational buyers at ad agencies, sales personnel wrote GRP-driven presentations that allowed the agencies to break the network into its component parts. Thus, CKO was attempting to market low audiences in an era when media buyers had relegated all radio to third place on the advertising industry's influence scale. (There were continued threats that more national radio dollars would be switched to the medium of direct promotion.)

Change of Marketing Strategy

With the release of the broadcasters' first RPM study, CKO switched its strategy. With the RPM data, the network demonstrated that it was strong in reaching users of more than 200 product categories and thus attractive to advertisers of these kinds of products. Unfortunately, the data applied only to the Toronto area. CKO tried to compensate by suggesting a buy in combination with other stations that were also strong in these product groups.

New Studies

Convinced that the diary measurement seriously underestimated its audience, CKO commissioned a number of studies in the Toronto market to examine the premise. The first series was conducted in the early 1980s by Brock University professor Ronald Rotenberg. His results showed that CKO had an audience roughly 80 percent higher than that reported in BBM. Two day-after-recall studies conducted with the sanction of BBM in 1988 demonstrated a wide variance in ballot and phone-call reporting, all of it in CKO's favour.

Yet both marketing efforts were flatly rejected by most media departments. Repeatedly, they regarded the Rotenberg report as invalid because it had been commissioned by CKO. Faced with presentations driven by the BBM-sanctioned DAR studies and RPM data, a majority of media buyers dismissed them because they were based on circulation (cumulative audience). CKO and the radio industry generally were confronted with a secular fundamentalism that recognized only those presentations including cost-efficiencies based on GRP analysis.

Low Revenues, High Costs

In part, then, the inability to market commissioned research and RPM had a rippling impact on CKO's revenue prospects. CKO's chief executive officer, Stanley Stewart, pointed to his cost problems, approximately 400 percent more for an hour of programming than a music and news outlet. Since the stations were "narrowcast," by nature they attracted smaller audiences than typical mass-media radio outlets. Continuing money shortages led to intense pressure to produce, constant turnover of staff, and unionization. Stewart was never able to instil a sense of mission at CKO, although he never stopped trying.

On Friday, November 10, 1989, CKO pulled the plug on its transmitters across Canada. A little more than a dozen years and $55 million in losses later, the experiment was ended. The network fell silent, and more than 200 staffers were out of work.

Focal Topics

1. What are the criteria for purchases of advertising time and space by media buyers?

2. Were there emotional influences on buying behaviour that worked against CKO? What were they?

3. How do you think CKO could have marketed itself better to media departments of advertising agencies?

Jefferson Manufacturing

One of the major components of Jefferson Manufacturing is its rivet division. In recent years, the overall demand for rivets has declined as other fastening systems have replaced them. Rivets, however, still remain the best buy for their strength-to-weight ratio, ease of application compared to welding, and speed compared to nuts and bolts. Adhesives have replaced them in some applications in appliances and automobiles. Welding, however, is providing more competitive pressure than adhesives.

Markets for Rivets

The four key markets for rivets are construction, aircraft, automotive, and consumer. In the automotive industry, rivets are selectively used to assemble certain interior parts. Unibody construction with automotive welding has virtually eliminated rivets from other automobile assembly processes. Huge rivets — 25 to 50 millimetres in diameter and 10 to 15 centimetres in length — are used to fasten structural steel in high-rise construction. Since the early 1970s, this market has been declining as rivets have been replaced by welding and high-performance steel bolts.

Because aircraft are formed from smaller sections of plates or frames, rivets are used to hold the structures together. The number of rivets per aircraft has not changed, but the number of aircraft produced has declined since its peak in the late 1960s and early 1970s. There is strong pressure from structural adhesive companies and a high interest by aerospace engineers to replace rivets. If an aircraft could be fabricated with adhesive, its cost could be reduced by as much as 20 percent, largely because of labour savings.

At the consumer level, sales are primarily to do-it-yourselfers, various types of assembly contractors in the construction business, and welding shops. A pop rivet system sold to these customers is used with a gun that compresses the rivet in one step. Small contractors and shops find the pop rivet system a definite time saver. Most of the customers purchase rivets and guns from distributors that service them with other tools, primarily with imported products from the Far East.

Jefferson's Marketing

A customer survey indicates that the Rivet Division of Jefferson Manufacturing has an image of a high-quality supplier that meets delivery

Source: Much of the material in this case was developed by Jim Staneluis. Appreciation is expressed to him for his assistance and co-operation.

schedules on time and is, in general, a good company with which to do business. The division also has a fine reputation for the degree of technical services it provides customers. As shown in the accompanying table, however, total sales have been declining in recent years.

The consumer side of the rivet market is serviced by 50 salespeople calling on hardware stores, lumber yards, large chains, discount stores, contractors, and manufacturers. The total market is divided into 5 regions and 25 sales territories and involves almost 20 000 individual accounts. Because the product here is used by contractors and small manufacturing firms, some technical service is provided via telephone using a toll-free number. Advertising for the consumer side of the business is through trade journals, along with special promotions involving prizes and trips for dealers.

Ten application engineers work as the field sales force and five technical service people in the home office provide marketing activities for the industrial side of the rivet business. Three of the engineers are in San Francisco and handle the aircraft companies, and three more are in the Detroit area to help service the automotive industry. The other four engineers cover the balance of the United States.

The process of selling means calling on the research and development groups of existing and potential accounts every few weeks to help identify new applications for rivets and ways in which current applications might be improved. The emphasis of the marketing effort on the industrial side is to manage programs that introduce new products to keep up with the changes in fastening technology plus specific changes in the technology of the automotive and aircraft industries. The industrial group also has a number of accounts in the appliance industry.

Focal Topics

1. What recommendations do you have for Jefferson Manufacturing in the area of applying market segmentation strategies to the rivet market?

Jefferson Manufacturing: Annual Sales (in Millions of Dollars)

	1984	1983	1982	1981
Consumer Markets				
Retail stores	$ 1.23	$ 1.51	$ 1.64	$ 1.52
Construction contractors	7.45	6.92	7.59	8.12
Welding shops	1.01	1.39	1.45	1.51
	$ 9.69	$ 9.82	$10.68	$11.15
Industrial Markets				
Aircraft	$ 3.47	$ 3.59	$ 3.91	$ 4.31
Automotive	2.98	2.80	2.70	2.95
Others	3.75	3.97	4.52	4.91
	$10.20	$10.36	$11.13	$12.17

2. Discuss the techniques that the firm could use to forecast its rivet sales for 1985 and 1989.

3. Given the information in the case, what is your best estimate for Jefferson's 1985 rivet sales?

Case for Part Two

Jolt Cola

In recent years many beverage manufacturers, in addition to trying to satisfy consumer wants for low-calorie, low-sodium, and no-caffeine products along with "regular" soft drinks, have tried to develop more sales with products that contain vitamins, minerals, and real fruit juice. Then along comes a maverick, contrary product called Jolt Cola.

Jolt offers "all the sugar and twice the caffeine" of mainline colas. Developers of the product state, "Our product is naughty and bold, and we don't mind that image." The label carries the claim, "Inspired by the Need for a Better-Tasting Soft Drink!"

The Soft-Drink Industry

North Americans are drinking more soft drinks than ever before. According to *Beverage World*, U.S. consumption reached 43 gallons (163 litres) per capita in 1985 compared to 37 gallons (140 litres) in 1981. Canadians consumed more than 2.2 billion litres in 1988. Viewed somewhat differently, the average American consumed 500 12-ounce (355-millilitre) units of soft drinks in 1985, according to the National Soft Drink Association, with consumption growing at about 7 percent annually. In Canada, the growth rate is 4 percent.

One percentage point in the soft-drink industry translates into an average of $300 million (U.S.). Other trends and information on the industry include:

- Coca-Cola, with all of its products, has 38.6 percent of the U.S. market, while Pepsi-Cola products account for some 27.4 percent. In Canada, the shares are 32.9 percent and 26.1 percent respectively.

- Dr Pepper brands and Seven-Up brands account for 7.1 percent and 6.3 percent (of the U.S. market), respectively. In Canada, 7Up accounts for 9.3 percent.

Source: Material presented here has been adapted from Stephen W. Bell, "Jolt Offers 'All the Sugar, Twice the Caffeine'," *The Columbus Dispatch*, September 9, 1986, p. 2F; Richard W. Stevenson, "Jolt Cola's Contrary Strategy," *The New York Times*, August 20, 1986, p. D19; "100 Leading National Advertisers," *Advertising Age*, September 4, 1986, pp. 66 +; Alvin Ng and Ann Sandy "Who's on First? Fifth Annual Report on Market Share," *Financial Times of Canada*, December 4, 1989, p. A3; "Jolt Cola gives jolt in Ontario," *Marketing*, August 29, 1988, p. 20.

- Brand Pepsi (with 17.4 percent) moved into the number-one brand spot by default in the United States because of the splitting there of former number-one Coke with Coke Classic (14.2 percent) and regular or new Coke (7.0 percent), a multibrand strategy that whether planned or not gave Coca-Cola a higher corporate share. Diet Coke has 6.7 percent and Cherry Coke has 1.6 percent. Pepsi-Cola's Slice brands have achieved a 2.1 percent share with about 60 percent national distribution.

- At least six companies have rolled out or announced plans for 14 soft drinks with "value-added" ingredients such as fruit juice or vitamins and minerals. Examples of these brands include Pepsi's Slice, Del Monte's Diet Sunkist Plus, Squirt's Diet Squirt Plus, Crush's Crush with Juice, Coca-Cola's Minute Maid sodas with vitamins C and B-6 and folic acid added, and Coca-Cola's Tab with calcium.

Development of Jolt

C. J. Rapp and his father, Joseph F. Rapp, Jr., who retired in 1985 after 40 years of operating a Canada Dry bottling operation in Rochester, New York, decided to buck the trend of less sugar, less caffeine, and fruit juice and vitamin additions to soft drinks. The Rapps invested $100 000 and spent six years testing 114 formulas before arriving at the one they liked for Jolt.

Jolt has 5.9 milligrams of caffeine per fluid ounce (29.6 millilitres), which is just less than the 6.0 milligrams allowed by the U.S. Food and Drug Administration. The level of caffeine in Jolt is about twice the amount in leading soft drinks but only one-fifth the amount in regular coffee. The product's sugar content is just slightly higher than other sugared colas. The only difference is that Jolt is made with 100 percent sugar compared to the less expensive corn syrup sweetener that is used by the rest of the soft-drink industry.

In personal interviews, C. J. Rapp has stated, "Soft drinks were never really created for people who wanted to lose weight. What the big companies did was try to gain soft-drink consumers that otherwise were not. In our opinion, what they did was they abandoned those that had been drinking soft drinks for years." He also said, "Soft drinks were created for sheer enjoyment and pleasure, but the industry has become awfully serious. They've saturated the negative selling aspects, and they've drastically changed their products. We're trying to bring back the fun."

Industry Response

A spokesman for Pepsico Inc., Stuart Ross, said that today's Pepsi tastes the same as it did 15 or 20 years ago. He added, "Soft drinks today are so popular, there's a niche for everyone." Ronald Coleman, a Coca-Cola spokesman said, "We've been in the business for 100 years; we're the world's most popular drink, and I think that speaks for itself."

The National Action Health Letter, a publication of the Center for Science in the Public Interest in Washington, D.C., has assailed the product as unhealthy because of its caffeine content. The organization nominated Mr. Rapp for a "personal niche in the nutrition hall of shame."

Jesse Meyers, editor and publisher of *Beverage Digest,* commented on Jolt by saying, "The hallmark of the soft-drink industry from word one has been innovation. Word two has been filling a market niche. The industry has seen fragmenting over the last few years . . . so they certainly have a shot at a market."

Future Directions

Jolt is seeking a market across the continent by signing up franchised bottlers and distributors. The company is planning on spending more than $1 million in introducing advertising nationally as the product begins appearing in more areas. Jolt will be sold in Western Canada under licence by Vancouver-based International Beverage Corporation. Future plans include entering the Ontario market. The company is confident that it can obtain a 2 percent share of the market where Jolt Cola is available. The objective is to achieve a 4 percent share.

Many consumers have tried the brand either out of curiosity or because the product appeals to them. C. J. Rapp realizes that Jolt's real challenge is to sustain its momentum and grow into more than just a novelty.

Focal Topics

1. In your opinion, why has the soft-drink industry become so segmented in recent years?

2. What market segmentation strategy would you use to position Jolt?

3. What problems would you anticipate in trying to get distributors and retailers to carry Jolt?

4. What types of marketing research would be helpful to Jolt at this time?

5. What overall marketing strategy would you recommend to Jolt management at this time?

Product and Pricing Strategy

Chapter 8

Product and Service Concepts

In this chapter, you will learn:

- Why new-product development is risky.

- Three dimensions of products.

- How consumer products are classified.

- How industrial products are classified.

- Some pros and cons of branding.

- Issues marketers face in planning for branding.

- Advantages of nationally branded, private label, and generic products.

- Characteristics of services that distinguish them from goods.

- Special issues that arise in the marketing of services.

Lauren Respects the Past but Has a Flair for the Present

Polo matches in Palm Beach. A safari in Kenya. Tea in a London hotel. A life of hand-tailored clothes, manor houses, sports cars, fine horses, manicured lawns. These are the images conjured up by the name Ralph Lauren.

Ralph Lauren has built a sportswear empire based on selling what his advertising calls "originality, but always with integrity and a respect for tradition." His products are comfortable, durable, and elegant and not too shocking. They are designed to appeal to those who think fashion is too faddish but traditional business clothing is dull.

While Ralph Lauren's most famous item may be his Polo shirt, his products extend to an entire line of menswear with the Polo label, another called Chaps, a line of women's wear, clothing for boys and girls, fragrances, luggage, eyeglasses, handbags, and home furnishings. What the products have in common is a link to classic design. Describing his sources of inspiration, Lauren says, "I love jeans, cowboy boots, tweed jackets, pinstripe suits, old race cars, Porsches, Indian blankets, and baskets."

All these tasteful products come at a price. But many consumers are willing to pay a high price for the prestige that accompanies the Ralph Lauren name. In particular, the image of prestige attracts upwardly mobile consumers who want to display their success.

Lauren reinforces the image of his products in the way he displays them. His Madison Avenue store features handcarved mahogany woodwork, custom-forged brass trim, Oriental rugs, orchids, saddles, trophies, and other paraphernalia. A side table in a

Brenda Hutchinson

Lauren display contains rows of framed pictures evoking comfortable, traditional surroundings.

All this image making is intended to generate an appeal for the many products that bear the Lauren name. Someone who likes the feel of a Lauren blazer might want to carry that image further with a suitcase or sofa. So far, the strategy seems to be working. Between 1981 and 1986, sales rose fourfold.

Selling a variety of products linked by a brand name such as Polo or Ralph Lauren is only one of the strategies marketers can adopt. Other marketers find advantages in lower-cost approaches that enable them to charge lower prices. This chapter describes some of these choices. It also looks at some of the special issues that arise in marketing to industrial buyers and in marketing services.

Source: Adapted from Stephen Koepp, "Selling a Dream of Elegance and the Good Life," *Time*, September 1, 1986, pp. 54-61.

Defining a Product

What do a compact disc from the group New Kids on the Block, a Benetton T-shirt, tickets to *Phantom of the Opera*, a rerun of *Cheers*, a house baby-sitting service, and a flight on the Concorde have in common?

They are all **products**. A product is anything that can be offered to a market for attention, acquisition, use, or consumption that might satisfy a want or need. It includes physical objects, services, persons, places, organizations, and ideas.[1] Physical objects offered in the marketplace are as diverse as record albums and machine tools. Services, too, are varied, including haircuts and legal assistance. Persons include the performers and athletes you pay to watch. Places include those where people choose to vacation or set up a new business. When you buy a membership in an organization, such as the Canadian Wildlife Federation, that organization is a product. Ideas offered to the marketplace include anti-smoking messages.

In today's world, developing new products is difficult and expensive. Marketers must find a niche in an ever-changing marketplace. Government agencies check many aspects of the marketing mix, including contents, claims to effectiveness, and possible side effects of packaging material. Competitors are working on innovations of their own. For product managers to navigate these shoals, they must find ways of getting the public to notice their products amid shouts of competitors all promoting better, faster-acting, new, and improved products.

As shown in Chapter 5, it can cost enormous amounts of money to launch a new product nationally. Nonetheless, in recent years new-product introductions in North America have been estimated at more than 5000 a year.

At the 1990 Food Institute Marketing Convention more than 1000 exhibitors competed for wholesale buyers' attention with a whole range of new-product ideas. New products displayed included iced coffee in a can, french fries in a canister, chocolate-coated frozen yogurt bars, and ready-to-eat cereals based on organic ingredients and sweetened only with pure fruit juice and barley malt.

This furious pace continues even though, according to one industry source, only a hundred or fewer new products a year top $1 million in sales in their first 12 months.[2] In spite of this daunting record, few companies can afford to rest on their previous successes. Some marketing experts have responded to the difficulty and expense of new-product development by creating specialized services that help companies with this task. (See Figure 8.1.)

Clearly, new-product development is critical to any company's success. This chapter explores some of the decisions marketers must make as they transform a new product from an idea in someone's mind to an item

Figure 8.1   Product Initiatives

in a consumer's shopping cart. (See Marketing Today 8.1 for a description of one new product that has proved successful.)

Three Dimensions of Products

Products serve human needs in various dimensions. We may think of a product as being similar to an apple. It has several layers, each of which contributes to the total product image. At the heart, or core, of the apple is the basic need-satisfying aspect or benefit of the product or service. It answers the question, What problem does this product solve? Passengers flying to Paris on the Concorde, for example, are not simply seeking transportation. Many other airlines offer that service for less. In fact, according to officials at Air France, Concorde passengers are not even primarily interested in luxurious surroundings and service. After all, for a fare significantly less than that of the Concorde, passengers flying first class on a regular wide-bodied Air France 747 have much more leg room and comparable amenities. What Concorde passengers are chiefly buying is *speed*. In the fast-paced world of international business, those few hours gained are often worth the premium price. When developing a product, a marketer must always ask, What is it that people are *really* buying when they purchase this product or service? The answer will affect the other dimensions of the product.

Once the basic benefit offered by the product or service is defined, a

Marketing Today 8.1

Who Would Have Thought You Could Build a Better Whistle?

In 1984 Canadian Ron Foxcroft tried to blow the whistle on a foul in a tight basketball game in São Paulo, Brazil, but the wave of noise from 25 000 screaming fans drowned out the initial sound. And then the whistle jammed. Foxcroft had a few tense minutes as the fans almost rioted. On the plane back to Canada, he decided to take the pea out of the whistle.

Three years and $150 000 later, Foxcroft and fellow referee Joe Forte had their pea-less whistle — the Fox 40. Based on three inner chambers that give a piercing shrill sound that penetrates even the noisiest game, the Fox 40 has become a massive success and

consigned the old pea whistle to the record books of sports history.

Success did not come overnight to the whistle. It took three years of development work and 14 prototypes before the final version was unveiled. Then distributors and sporting goods stores showed no interest in carrying the new product. At $6 a whistle, they thought it would never sell.

Foxcroft went right to the refe-

rees themselves and by blowing his whistle got their attention. After the 1987 Pan-Am Games, Foxcroft came back to Canada with 20 000 orders. Today the Fox 40 is the official whistle of the Canadian Football League and the National Basketball Association.

Source: Tony Martin, "The Whistleblower," *Report on Business (Globe and Mail)*, February 1990, pp. 50–53.

product planner can begin developing physical or functional features of a product. Disposable diapers, toothpaste, sports cars, and running shoes are all tangible products. They all include physical characteristics such as packaging, product features, and distinctive styling. They may also include a brand name that may give the product additional value because of the manufacturer's reputation for quality or because of an image created through advertising.

Additional benefits and services often added to a product make up the outer skin of the apple. These may include after-sale service (such as a warranty on a new car), installation, credit, or delivery. Many products or services that are otherwise indistinguishable physically become preferred products of consumers because of these added features. For example, tax consultants perform essentially the same service, but H&R Block has captured an important share of the market by offering extras such as free estimates of the cost of preparing forms and back-up assistance in case of a Revenue Canada audit. Product managers who ignore this dimension in defining a product miss an important marketing opportunity.

Marketing by Product Types

The 3M Company—Minnesota Mining and Manufacturing—sells more than 27 000 products ranging from Scotch tape to copying machines and fabrics coated with Scotchguard. Each of these products requires a different marketing strategy. Scotch tape is sold through many small outlets, such as grocery and stationery stores, and is promoted through advertising. Copying machines are sold through office machine stores staffed by personnel who carry on the main sales effort. Scotchguarded fabrics are sold to upholsterers, furniture factories, and clothing manufacturers through sales representatives of the 3M Company.

If 3M's marketing managers had to devise separate strategies for each of the 27 000 products, their task would be time consuming, if not impossible. Fortunately, their job has been simplified because it is possible to group products into categories according to the markets served and to develop generalizations about products in each category.

As discussed in Chapter 7, industrial products are goods bought by an organization's purchasing agents, or by intermediaries, to make other goods, to resell them, or to carry on some other exchange-related activity. Scotchguarded fabric, IBM computers, and GMC trucks are industrial products. By contrast, **consumer products** are those goods sold to individuals or households for their personal use. Scotch tape, Kellogg's Rice Krispies, and Sony Walkmans are familiar examples.

Some goods can be classified as either consumer or industrial products. A GE light bulb can be used in a home, office, or factory. But a marketing manager would vary product strategy according to the market for which the product is destined.

Each of these two broad classes of products can be further divided into groups whose shared characteristics lend themselves to similar marketing strategies.

Consumer Products
Goods sold to individuals or households for their personal use.

Consumer Products

Although there is no reliable estimate of the number of consumer products available, it is known that the average retail grocery store contains between 7000 and 10 000 different items. It is safe to say, then, that consumer products number in the hundreds of thousands. Effective market planning requires a system for classifying the vast number of consumer products.

Since consumers buy goods and services not only for their functional value but also to satisfy a variety of emotional needs, a classification system based on use would be of little value. Consumer products are usually grouped according to the manner in which consumers buy them: convenience goods, shopping goods, or specialty goods. A closer look will show why each requires a different marketing strategy.

Convenience Goods

Convenience Goods
Products that individuals buy quickly and often.

Staple Items
Products bought through habit — for example, milk.

Impulse Items
Products bought on the spur of the moment.

Emergency Items
Products bought when an unexpected need arises.

Products that individuals buy quickly and often are **convenience goods**. Candy, drug products, food, snacks, cigarettes, and almost any ordinary household item may be included in this category. Such products may be **staple items** bought through habit (such as milk), **impulse items** bought on the spur of the moment (a copy of *Canadian Living* magazine bought while standing in the checkout line with a bottle of milk), or **emergency items** bought when an unexpected need arises (a bag of rock salt bought when one discovers it has begun snowing while standing in the line with a bottle of milk reading *Canadian Living*).

Ordinarily, convenience goods are low priced. Because these items cost so little, few people will bother to shop around for them. The tobacco industry, for example, has discovered that people will rarely go more than a block or two to pick up a pack of cigarettes. Consequently, they must supply many retail outlets — including food stores, candy stores, taverns, gasoline stations, vending machines, and drugstores — with their products.

Although consumers will not make a special effort to purchase a convenience good, they can be persuaded to buy a particular manufacturer's product regularly. This is done by building a brand name for a product and advertising the brand heavily. Procter & Gamble, probably the foremost user of this tactic, ranks first in the selling of detergent (Tide), shampoo (Head and Shoulders), and toothpaste (Crest). Other successful brand names include Kraft cheese, Scotch tape, and Kleenex tissues. Retailers sometimes draw customers to their stores by marking down the price of such widely advertised, popular convenience goods. Such marked-down goods are often referred to as *loss leaders* because store owners may take a loss on those items in exchange for the many additional customers drawn into the store by the low price.

Convenience goods are the fastest-growing category of consumer goods. This results in part from the increase in the number of working women outside the home, who have little time to comparison shop. In addition, more goods are now considered convenience goods by consumers. Even drugstores now stock such items as radios and wristwatches in addition to cheaper, small items traditionally classified as convenience goods.

Shopping Goods

Shopping Goods
Products that a consumer buys only after making comparisons among competing stores.

Homogeneous Shopping Goods
Products that a consumer buys only after making price comparisons among sellers — consumers see them as essentially the same.

Heterogeneous Shopping Goods
Products that a consumer will buy only after making a comparison of the style or quality of brands — for example, a dress or suit.

Products that individuals buy only after making comparisons in competing stores are known as **shopping goods**. If the basis of comparison is price, those products are known as **homogeneous shopping goods** because consumers see them as essentially the same except for price. For example, one would probably shop around for a desk lamp on the basis of price. If the basis of comparison is quality or style, the products are called **heterogeneous shopping goods**. Shoppers looking for a dress or suit would probably go from store to store until they hit upon an appealing style.

Shopping goods are usually more expensive than convenience goods. Because consumers are willing to make an effort to locate these more expensive goods, manufacturers need fewer stores in which to sell their products. Some manufacturers (Zenith, for example) sell their merchandise mainly through major department stores. Stores carrying shopping goods are often clustered together, a pattern different from that of stores selling convenience goods. Rarely are two supermarkets on the same block, but a row of shoe stores or automobile dealers is not uncommon. (See Figure 8.2.) Clustering makes comparison shopping easier.

Advertising can be important in the case of shopping goods, especially to lure customers into stores where the goods are sold. But at the point of purchase, the most important means of promotion is the personal selling effort of salespeople. Appliance manufacturers recognize this point and frequently offer salespeople bonuses to reward sales of their brands.[3]

Specialty Goods

Specialty goods are so named because consumers are willing to make a special effort to obtain them. Included in this category are such items as Ray-Ban sunglasses, Gucci handbags, Porsche sports cars, gourmet coffee, and Rolex watches. Specialty-goods buyers differ from shopping-goods buyers in that the former know what they are looking for and have a particular brand in mind. They are unwilling to settle for substitutes and will go out of their way to find an outlet handling the product.

Specialty goods are usually high priced. But because they are so highly

Specialty Goods
Products that a consumer is willing to make a special effort to obtain.

Phyllis Woloshin

Figure 8.2 A Cluster of Auto Dealers

valued by the consumers who seek them, few sales outlets need to carry such items.

Specialty goods are a growing category of products. Many Canadians have more leisure time and are willing to spend more on such goods. Hobbyists are typical shoppers for specialty goods. For instance, stamp collectors from around the world will make a special effort to find a Canadian 1851 three-pence beaver stamp. People who enjoy gourmet cooking may travel a substantial distance to find a store that carries fresh basil or a particular brand of copper skillet.

Limitations of Consumer Product Classification

As noted earlier, a particular product can be classified as a consumer or an industrial product depending on its use. Similarly, within the consumer product category, a particular good may be a convenience, shopping, or specialty good depending on the buying habits of a certain shopper. A student living on a tight budget may feel obliged to shop around for an occasional steak dinner. But high-income families may treat it as a convenience good, settling on a Porterhouse steak when they need a quick dinner. A consumer interested in taking snapshots of the family might shop around for a camera, while a tourist who discovered she had left her camera at home might buy a disposable camera (a convenience good). A serious amateur photographer might insist on a high-quality Nikon (a specialty good).

The categories are not neatly marked off from one another. The more effort consumers are willing to expend to obtain it, the more a product resembles a shopping or specialty good. For the product manager, of course, the important point is how the *majority* of buyers view the company's product. This information is integral to the marketing approach — selecting target markets and drawing up policies on price, promotion, and distribution.[4]

Industrial Products

The most practical way of classifying industrial products is by their use. The six major classes of industrial products are:

1. *Raw materials:* natural resources, such as crude oil and iron ore, or cultivated products, such as wheat or cotton, that become part of the final product.

2. *Manufactured materials and parts:* semi-finished or finished items, such as headlights or buttons, that are incorporated into the final product.

3. *Installations:* large, expensive goods, like machine tools or manufacturing plants, necessary for the production of final products.

4. *Accessory equipment:* smaller items, such as tools and office equip-

ment, that do not become part of the final product but are necessary for its manufacture.

5. *Supplies:* those items needed to operate a business but not part of the final product. Supplies are sometimes called MRO items because they can be divided into three categories: (1) maintenance items, (2) repair items, and (3) operating supplies.

6. *Business services:* specific functions, such as copier repair and legal counsel, performed by specialists outside the firm.

While industrial products are not customarily classified into convenience, shopping, and specialty goods, many of the same principles apply. In an industrial buying decision, "staple" items such as office supplies may be solely the responsibility of an office manager or purchasing agent; in highly automated offices, they may be ordered by one computer "talking" to another. "Specialty goods," such as major new pieces of machinery, may require months of planning and negotiations, in which large numbers of people have input. Each of these categories of products requires a specialized type of marketing strategy.

The Question of Branding

A major decision, particularly for consumer goods manufacturers, is whether to produce a product with a recognizable brand name or market the product without such identification. The various terms marketers use when discussing branding are defined in Figure 8.3.

The practice of attaching a brand name or symbol to a product is very old. Some say it began when ancient Greek artists carved their names in sculptures. Branding became commercially significant in the Middle Ages when guilds (the precursors of unions) required handcrafters to put their mark on the goods they made. The guilds did this for two reasons: to be able to trace poor workmanship and to limit output and thereby prevent prices from falling. The practice faded in some fields at the end of the Middle Ages but was generally revived a century ago with the start of mass production. Some hundred-year-old brand names are still around, including Ivory soap, Quaker Oats, and Vaseline.

Branding Pros and Cons

Branding has clearly caught on since its reintroduction a century ago. Nearly all consumer products today are branded, and even some industrial products (Mack trucks, NutraSweet aspartame, IBM computers) carry brand names. A decade ago, marketers believed that shopping goods such as women's ready-to-wear apparel could not be branded. They assumed that women bought dresses because of fit or styling that could not be duplicated by other dresses sold under the same brand name.

Today, apparel manufacturers — as well as manufacturers in a wide

Trademark
A name, term, sign, symbol, design, or some combination used to identify the products of one firm and to differentiate them from competitor's products. The golden-arch symbol and the word *McDonald's* in its distinctive typeface combine to identify a certain brand of fast-food restaurant.

Logo courtesy of McDonald's Corporation

Brand Name
The most common form of trademark is the brand name that can be expressed verbally, including letters, words, and numbers. Atari, Ultima II, and A&W Root Beer are examples.

Brand Mark
The part of the brand that can be recognized but not spoken. It may consist of symbols, designs, or distinctive lettering or colours. Coca-Cola's red and white colours and script lettering are recognized worldwide. The Playboy bunny, Ralph Lauren's polo player, and the owl symbol on the spine of this book are all brand marks.

Trademark Rights
A brand name, slogan, or fanciful design becomes a trademark with use in connection with a product or commercial service. The trademark created and used is sometimes referred to as a "common law" trademark, but it is a valid, protectible trademark nonetheless. Registration of a mark with the Canadian government gives the owner of a mark important procedural rights. *Xerox,* a coined word, is a trademark of the Xerox Corporation to identify its copiers and other equipment. The title *Realtor,* which applies to companies only, is a trademark of the Canadian Real Estate Association. A trademark protects a firm's exclusive rights to use a brand name and/or brand mark.

Logo courtesy of the Xerox Corporation

Figure 8.3 The Terminology of Branding

Source: Committee on Definitions, *Marketing Definitions: A Glossary of Marketing Terms* (Chicago: American Marketing Association, 1960), pp. 9-10.

Licensing
As it relates to business in general: Process by which designer or character names or identities are leased to businesses for use on their products in exchange for royalties.

variety of other industries—practise a kind of branding called **licensing.** Licensing is a process by which designer or character names or identities are leased to businesses for use on their products in exchange for royalties. Millions of consumers now seek out jeans, sportswear, sunglasses, wallets, handbags, and other items bearing the brand names of fashion designers such as Alfred Sung, Calvin Klein, and Perry Ellis.

Why do businesses favour branding? Primarily because it permits a company to distinguish its products from those of others. The company does not have to compete with others directly on the basis of price. Many consumers buy Coca-Cola even when cheaper substitutes are readily available because they have built up a certain loyalty to the brand.

Another important reason for using a brand name is the value it creates and lends to other products the company produces (called the company's product line). For example, after watching its profits plunge along with the North American birth rate, Binney & Smith, the manufacturer of Crayola crayons, revamped its marketing strategy. It created a consistent "family" look for the other products in its line by using the familiar yellow and green graphics that distinguish its crayon boxes. As a result, many products, particularly felt marker pens, showed dramatic sales increases.[5]

The transfer of goodwill from one product in a company's line to another is known as the **halo effect.** Ralph Lauren benefits from the halo effect in selling its broad range of products. Similarly, Benetton is planning fragrance, cosmetics, and skin-care items in the hope that consumers who like its apparel will be attracted to these items as well.[6]

Consumer groups sometimes complain that branding is detrimental to their interests. Establishing a brand name involves heavy advertising costs that are inevitably passed on to consumers. Marketers counter that while establishing a brand name is expensive, consumers do benefit from the practice. They are guaranteed consistent quality because brand-name companies have a reputation to maintain. Moreover, brand-name merchandise allows a consumer to comparison shop for value. Cuisinart food processors, for instance, are the same everywhere they are sold, so potential buyers can compare prices in various stores. Further, some branded products are perceived as conferring status or prestige.

Despite advantages for both the seller and the buyer, some companies decide not to seek national brand awareness for their products. The cost of promoting a national brand may be too great for them. Or they may deal in a standardized product (such as lettuce or nails) that does not readily lend itself to differentiation and brand recognition. Sometimes branding can limit marketing opportunities. Estée Lauder, for example, ordinarily keeps its cosmetics out of discount stores because it wishes to maintain a quality image for the brand.

Halo Effect
Transfer of goodwill from one product in a company's line to another.

Planning for Branding

If a company's product is unique and it has the resources to promote the product, the advantages of branding far outweigh the disadvantages. Once the decision to brand has been made, two other important questions must be answered: What type of brand should be used? What name should the product carry?

Brand Type

Family Brand
Brand that covers many products under one brand name.

Individual Brand
Distinct name given to each product a company produces.

Marketers generally distinguish two types of brands. A **family brand** covers many products under one brand name. For example, the name Heinz is used for ketchup and soups as well as for baked beans, pickles, and relishes. By contrast, some companies treat their products as **individual brands,** giving each product a distinct name. General Mills, for example, produces Gold Medal flour, Nature Valley granola bars, Cocoa Puffs, Chef Saluto pizza, Wheaties, Bisquick, and Betty Crocker cake mixes.

Family brand names are commonly used when products are essentially similar or sold in the same market. The Heinz products cited are obviously related and might be bought together. Products sharing the same brand name also share promotional costs, thus cutting down on that expense. Moreover, new products can take advantage of the halo effect.

Sometimes a company produces products that are essentially dissimilar, so no halo effect could occur. Allegis Corporation's Hertz rental cars, United Airlines, and Westin hotels may be examples of such products. Another example is the Coca-Cola Company, which uses the Columbia Pictures name on its movies and video services.

Occasionally, one product may actually detract from the sales of another if marketed under the same name. Consumers would probably just as soon not know that the company that produces Purina Cat Chow also makes Rice Chex. Markets, too, may be so dissimilar that individual brand names are essential. Chevrolet and Cadillac, both produced by General Motors, appeal to very different market segments.

Multiple Brand Strategy
Corporate practice of promoting individual brands that compete with one another.

Some companies promote individual brands that compete with one another. Procter & Gamble produces two toothpastes under individual brand names — Crest and Gleem. Marketers call this tactic a **multiple brand strategy.** Procter & Gamble maintains that this policy promotes efficiency within the company by encouraging competition between individual brand managers. Also, since there is competition for supermarket space among companies, P&G thus keeps its competitor (Colgate-Palmolive) from having more room to display its products. And, if consumers decide to switch from Crest, they might switch to Gleem, thus retaining sales for P&G. Finally, a multiple brand strategy increases a firm's total market share.

Naming a Brand

For a company that decides on an individual brand name, the next problem is to find a distinctive name around which to build a marketing program. While many companies continue to pick names based on brainstorming sessions, employee contests, or bosses' inspiration, some analysts believe that such unscientific methods pose great risks. Marketing Today 8.2 describes another approach. Some of the things a company must keep in mind when choosing a brand name are:

Marketing Today 8.2

Computer Company Gets a Name

As head of a computer company, Ben Rosen wanted his new product to have widespread recognition. For help he turned to NameLab, a company that specializes in coming up with names for products and organizations.

Ira Bachrach, president of NameLab, scheduled meetings with the computer company's officials to determine what they wanted their product's name to project. They wanted a new word that indicated "small integral object which is a computer."

Next, NameLab's computer sifted through a list of 6200 morphemes (the smallest meaningful element of a word). The computer prepared a list of every word combination possible using morphemes that suggested small objects and computers. The potential choices included Cortex, Cognipak, Suntek, and Compod. None of these sounded quite right.

Eventually, the computer company and NameLab personnel agreed on "com," which suggested a computer, and "pac," which indicates smallness. To make the printed name more visible, they changed the final *c* to a *q*. The company had a name: Compaq Computer Corporation.

Source: Adapted from Mike Sheridan, "Naming Names," *Sky,* November 1986, pp. 11–12.

- The name should be easy to pronounce, recognize, and remember.
- The name should have impact.
- The name should be relevant and suggest product benefits.
- The name should suggest positive images to the consumer.
- The name should be appropriate to the product category.
- The name should be available for use.

Many firms fight legal battles to defend their names from encroachers. The Coca-Cola Company has set a record for persistence in defence of a brand name. Coke, the product's trademark, is clearly identified as a registered name by both the word "trademark" and the symbol ® whenever it appears. Typically, the company will initiate 50 cases a year against soft-drink firms who use the name Coke. In addition, the firm sends warning letters to print media when Coke is not capitalized or is used in the possessive form.

Apart from the harmful impression left by the misuse of brand names, companies seek to protect their trademarks because they can lose legal protection and market share if the name comes into common use. Such names as cellophane, escalator, yo-yo, and ping-pong can now be used freely because the companies that once owned those names allowed them through usage to become common words describing a product class.

Parker Brothers lost the trademark to its game Monopoly in the United States. That country's Supreme Court ruled that it had become the generic term denoting a kind of game. That decision cleared the way for a San Francisco State University professor to market a game called Anti-

Monopoly. Many analysts expect that the court's action in this case will result in more companies' protecting their trademarks by carefully distinguishing the product's brand name from its generic name.[7]

The Battle of the Brands

The term *brand* has been used here mainly in connection with those branded items distributed by national manufacturers. Such items are called **national brands.** In addition, there are products sold under the name of a retailer or wholesale intermediary called **private** (or **distributor**) **brands.** Some private brands have a national reputation even though they are not promoted by a national manufacturer. Perhaps the best known retailer-produced private brands are those of Sears (Kenmore, Craftsman, and DieHard) and Loblaws (President's Choice).

The "battle of the brands" refers to the competition that exists between owners of national and private brands to win retail outlet shelf space and consumer loyalty.[8] The competition is intense. In 1985, about seven new products were introduced each day, compared to only three a day in 1980.[9]

"House," or private brands, often mimic the formula, specifications, and taste of national brands. In many cases, even the shape of the container and the label imitate the better-known national brand. One obvious advantage that private brands have over national brands is that they are generally less expensive. Because most private brands are not advertised nationally, they can be marketed more cheaply.

The consumer appeal of private brands is matched by their appeal to retailers and wholesalers. Many store owners maintain that such brands allow them greater freedom to sell what they and their customers need. Selling private brands, moreover, allows intermediaries to build up a faithful clientele that prefers such brands. Finally, intermediaries prefer private brands because they earn higher markups on them.

Manufacturers may oppose private brands because they believe their quality is inferior. They also maintain that it is nationally advertised products, not private brands, that tend to bring customers into stores. Despite their objections to private brands, many manufacturers of nationally advertised merchandise also produce private-brand products for retailers. For example, Michelin Tires produces tires for Sears Canada under that store's brand name (Sears sells them for competitive prices), and Sears' Kenmore washers and dryers are manufactured by Whirlpool.

Because of their advantages for both consumers and retailers, private brands appear to be gaining in the battle of the brands. Thirty years ago, most Canadians bought national brands. According to an American study, private brands account for 60 percent of the annual sales of department stores. They also represent an important share of the grocery business—as much as 16 percent of total sales and up to 35 percent in some categories.[10]

National Brand
Branded item distributed by a national manufacturer.

Private (Distributor) Brand
Product sold under the name of a retailer or wholesale intermediary.

Some supermarkets hope to increase profits by offering an even cheaper alternative to private brands—**generic,** or no-name, **products.** These are unbranded goods that receive little advertising, are sold in plain packages (often white or yellow with black lettering), and may be slightly lower grade. In Ontario, Loblaws refers to its stark yellow-labelled products as "no-frills" goods. According to supermarkets that carry the goods, the lower grades, plain packaging, and lack of advertising allow them to sell the products for 15 to 40 percent less than national and private brands.[11]

When generic products were first introduced in 1977, certain national manufacturers predicted that they would be nothing more than a fad. In recent years the growth of generics has levelled off, but they still command about an overall 2 percent market share in supermarkets. Although generics command only a small share of the grocery business, many stores claim they will continue to carry them in order to offer consumers a three-tier price choice. (See Table 8.1.)

Some marketing experts have suggested that a significant market segment may comprise buyers who have a "generic mentality"—that is, they want products that offer simple, basic value. Buyers of generic grocery products tend to be price-conscious members of middle-income, large households.[12] One study, conducted in Toronto in the late 1970s,[13] found that the most likely purchasers came from four- to five-member families with parents 30 to 39 years old. Less likely users came from the lower income groups and lowest education levels. (This finding supports the view that information search plays a key role in the purchase decision, and the level of education of any individual determines to a great extent the amount of information gathering and comparing of generic products to brand leaders.)

In the hotly contested area of prescription drugs, the total market for generic equivalents is expected to reach $8 billion by 1990. One success story is Zenith Laboratories, whose sales of generic drugs in the United States soared 115 percent from 1984 to 1985.[14]

Brand-name manufacturers maintain that drug products are not always interchangeable. They say generic drugs may vary in the speed

Generic Product
Product that is unbranded and marketed with minimal advertising.

Table 8.1 Price Comparison of Generic, Private Label, and Nationally Branded Products

Item	Size	National Brand	Private Label	Generic Product
Peanut butter	1 kg	$6.29	$5.19	$3.99
Spaghetti Sauce	700 ml	2.59	2.49	1.89
Applesauce	796 ml	2.49	2.29	1.89
Olive Oil	1 L	10.49	6.39	5.39
Apple Juice	3 × 250 ml	1.99	1.59	.89
Soda Crackers	450 g	2.39	1.99	1.39
Facial tissues (2 ply)	150	1.19	1.09	.99
Barbeque Potato Chips	200 g	2.19	1.89	1.29

at which they are released into the body or in their capacity to produce side effects. Nonetheless, this segment of the market is likely to remain strong, thanks in part to an increasing number of regulations and guidelines encouraging pharmacists to substitute generic drugs for brand-name medications when appropriate. A case in point is diazepam, the generic equivalent of Valium. In diazepam's first year on the market, Valium's share fell from 100 to 50 percent.[15]

Marketing Services

Most of the products discussed so far in this chapter have been tangible items. Products also include services: financial advice, sales services at a store, a taxicab ride, research assistance from a librarian, and entertainment by a singer. Together, services are a large and growing part of the world economy.

The Goods-Services Continuum

When you pay for legal advice, it is clear that your product is intangible —a service. But when you pay for dinner at a restaurant, you are buying something to eat along with the service and something to drink along with the atmosphere. Thus, some products are clearly goods or services, while others fall somewhere in between.

One way to describe the nature of products is to place them on a continuum. At one end are products that are purely tangible; at the other end are purely intangible products. In general, the products on the continuum fall into four major categories of offerings:[16]

1. *A pure tangible good.* Masking tape, margarine, mothballs, and mousetraps are all such goods; no services accompany the product.

2. *A tangible good with accompanying services.* Toaster ovens, calculators, home computers, and microwave ovens usually come with warranties. They may also come with users' manuals, cookbooks, and maintenance tips. Automobile manufacturers offer many customer services with their products. In fact, promoting the quality of a company's postpurchase service has recently become an important aspect of the marketing strategy.

3. *A major service with accompanying minor goods and services.* On an airline flight, a passenger usually accumulates a variety of minor items in addition to the major item (transportation). A trip on the Concorde might net one a rose, an in-flight magazine, a direct-mail catalogue of Concorde-inspired accessories, and other items. The airline may also offer additional amenities: earphones for the stereo system, a wheelchair for the disabled, or help in securing a limousine on arrival.

4. *A pure service.* A doctor's advice, a trip to the movies, or a haircut are pure services. Penicillin, popcorn, or shampoo would be additional product purchases.

Characteristics of Services

Four characteristics are unique to services and influence the way they are marketed: intangibility, perishability, simultaneous consumption and production, and lack of control.[17]

Intangibility

A service is intangible—a deed, a performance, or an effort. This is true even if providing the service requires equipment. For example, a landscaping service must purchase lawn mowers to do the job, but the company's customers are buying efforts at lawn beautification, not the lawn mowers. Similarly, a bank that offers chequing account services may buy automatic teller machines to help it deliver those services more economically.

Perishability

Sellers of tangible goods can generally stock some inventory to meet demand during peak periods or order less when sales are slower. For services, however, there is no inventory. This makes it especially important for services providers to anticipate and respond to changing levels of demand.

Perishability of their product has been an issue for many colleges and universities as the 18- to 23-year-old population has shrunk. The schools simply cannot put their faculty into cold storage and wait for the environment to change. In Halifax, Nova Scotia, Mount Saint Vincent University has responded by providing courses in the evenings, on weekends, and over television. These offerings, combined with a mature-students admissions policy, have resulted in a rise of the average student age to 27 years. Not only has enrolment grown considerably, but these mature students bring their practical point of view to the classroom, enlivening the discussion for all faculty and students.

Simultaneous Consumption and Production

Sadly enough, you simply cannot get your cavities filled unless you accompany your teeth to the dentist. You also cannot be transported to Paris unless you show up at the dock or the airport. Services are used at the same time that they are produced. This typically puts the supplier of services into close contact with customers.

It also means that customers cannot test products before they buy them. As a result, consumers of services tend to perceive relatively greater risk when they are shopping for a service. They rely more heavily on the recommendations of others.[18] Perhaps the best example of reducing this risk is the attention that movie-goers pay to reviews.

Lack of Control

To maintain a standard of high quality, makers of tangible goods can discard defective products before they reach the consumer. The quality of service delivered is harder to control. On an airplane, a passenger's flight may be ruined by a thunderstorm or an irritable flight attendant. Such experiences can alter a passenger's perception of an entire airline.

Marketers of services try to compensate by controlling where they can. Some companies go to great lengths to standardize their services. It is no coincidence that McDonald's restaurants are nearly identical whether they are in Moscow or Regina. Another approach to control is to invest in high-quality employees. For example, Nordstrom department stores pay their sales clerks about 20 percent more than the clerks of competitors. Nordstrom trains them thoroughly and encourages them to do almost anything within reason to satisfy customers. The store also has a policy of replacing any item on demand.[19]

Marketing Strategy Decisions

To market services effectively, a company must perform many of the same basic functions it would do if its product were a tangible good, but often with significant differences. (See At Your Service 8.1.) For example, a service company must analyze the market to determine consumer needs and preferences, but it must also consider whether the concept it has in mind will be understandable and attractive to consumers. Often, this must be accomplished without the same kinds of test marketing and marketing research that usually accompany new product introductions.

A service provider must also analyze its abilities to deliver the service. If a restaurant has limited seating, for example, it could do itself more harm than good by mounting a large promotional effort that might generate demand it could not satisfy.

In addition, a service company must analyze the competition. This process is also trickier for services than it is for products. The competition is not just other service businesses, but what people can do for themselves. A person who wants a well-kept lawn, for instance, can do it alone, see that the family's children do it, or hire a lawn service. Service industries must keep consumers' options in mind when designing a marketing strategy.

Once a market analysis is completed, a service company must identify the market segments it wants to reach and investigate ways to reach them. Because services may mean different things to different people, more initial research may be required to determine how the public really

At Your Service 8.1

Diapers Hot Business

Two young Canadian entrepreneurs, Beth Malloy and Christine Pensa, saw the growing concern with environment and the debate over disposable diapers as a golden business opportunity to provide an old service in a new way. Malloy and Pensa acquired the Canadian rights to Stork Diaper Service, which had been providing reusable cloth diapers for 50 years to the Toronto area.

In 1988 the company went out of business when the original owners retired. The company had seen a steady decline in business over the years as consumers moved away from the traditional cloth diaper to the more convenient disposable diaper.

The average baby has seven diaper changes in a day. By the time he or she is toilet trained at age two, the average child has gone through 5000 diaper changes. By 1988, many consumers were showing negative reactions to this huge volume of waste, which was not readily biodegradable and contained fairly dangerous contaminants. The first response was a chemical-free, biodegradable diaper, developed in Boulder Colorado, but even this did not satisfy many consumers.

The secret to the success of disposable diapers was their convenience. The problem for diaper services like the resurrected Stork Diaper Service was to provide the same convenience at a reasonable price. The solution was to incorporate new technology with old-fashioned delivery service. Today's cloth diaper is held in place by waterproof cotton pants with handy Velcro fasteners. In the home, the messy diapers do not need to be rinsed; they are stored

Stephen Kennedy

in deodorized hampers provided by the service. Pick-up and delivery is arranged to suit the customer's schedule.

The complete diaper service that Stork offers has proven very attractive to the environmentally conscious consumer and the business continues to grow.

Source: Adapted from Margret Bream, "Diapers: Back to the Basics, Baby," *Marketing*, November 27, 1989, p. 10.

views a proposed service. Service marketers must rely more heavily than product marketers on the tools and skills of psychology, sociology, and other behavioural sciences to uncover the public's perception of their offering and to determine how those markets might be segmented.[20]

Finally, because a service is essentially abstract, it becomes very important to pay attention to the tangible elements surrounding the service. In a restaurant, this may include making sure the tablecloths are spotless, the restrooms immaculate, the menus attractively printed, and the bar well stocked. It may also extend to dismissing a surly bus boy or recooking a dissatisfied customer's steak.

To the extent possible, management of the physical environment should be one of a service marketer's highest priorities. In a similar fashion, even the quality of a firm's letterhead may influence a consumer's perception of the company's service. A cheaply duplicated, non-personalized letter contradicts any words about service quality in the text.

Special attention should also be paid to creating advertising and promotion that gives the service a concrete image in the public's mind. Merrill Lynch's herd of bulls is a clear, visible symbol for its abstract financial services.

A service's price often determines how people perceive its quality. Because comparison shopping is often difficult, customers will pay what they think the service is worth. Thus, pricing in many service businesses is based on whatever the market will bear. Rarely, for example, will you hear businesspeople boast that they have just hired the cheapest consultant available.[21]

As the service industry becomes more competitive, more companies are offering guarantees as a way to differentiate themselves from the competition. Certain services, such as those offered by hairdressers, are so personal that guarantees of satisfaction would be difficult to fulfill, but others, among them Federal Express—and even Canada Post—are now willing to guarantee fulfilment, such as overnight delivery of a package or letter.

The service sector accounts for two-thirds of the U.S. and Canadian gross domestic product, and three of four nonfarm jobs.[22] As this sector of the economy continues to grow, marketers will be increasingly expected to respond to the unique challenges posed by service marketing.

Chapter Replay

1. **Why is new-product development risky?**
   Customer needs, government regulations, and competitor offerings continually change. Launching a new product can be enormously expensive. One marketer's new products must compete for attention with many other new offerings.

2. **What are three dimensions of products?**
   Three dimensions of products are a basic benefit, physical or functional features, and additional benefits or services.

3. **How are consumer products classified?**
   Consumer products may be (a) convenience goods, which include staple items, impulse items, and emergency items; (b) shopping goods, which may be homogeneous or heterogeneous; or (c) specialty goods.

4. **How are industrial products classified?**
   Industrial products may be installations, accessory equipment, raw materials, component parts or materials, supplies or business services.

5. **What are some pros and cons of branding?**
   Branding permits a business to distinguish its products from those of others so that it does not have to compete directly on the basis of price. Brand names lend value to other products the company pro-

duces and guarantee consistent quality. Consumer groups sometimes complain that branding is detrimental to their interests
because the costs are passed on to consumers.

6. **What issues do marketers face in planning for branding?**
    The marketer must decide whether to use a family brand or indi-
    vidual brands, including, possibly, a multiple brand strategy. The
    company also must find a distinctive brand name around which to
    build the marketing program.

7. **What are some advantages of nationally branded, private
    label, and generic products?**
    Nationally branded products, according to their manufacturers,
    bring people into stores and are of higher quality. Private label
    products resemble national brands but at a lower cost. Accord-
    ing to store owners, they allow stores to stock what customers want
    and to build up a faithful clientele. Generic products are the least
    expensive.

8. **What characteristics of services distinguish them from
    goods?**
    Services are intangible, perishable, simultaneously consumed and
    produced, and difficult for marketers to control.

9. **What special issues arise in marketing services?**
    Some concepts may be difficult for consumers to understand. Pro-
    viders must have the capacity to deliver the product. The competi-
    tion for services includes customers who can provide the service
    themselves. Service providers may find it more difficult to uncover
    public perceptions and to segment the market. Marketers must pay
    special attention to the tangible elements surrounding the service
    and to the promotional message. Difficulty in comparison shopping
    may affect how consumers view a service's price.

Key Terms

consumer products	**individual brand**
convenience goods	**licensing**
emergency items	**multiple brand strategy**
family brand	**national brand**
generic product	**private (distributor)**
halo effect	**brand**
heterogeneous shopping	**product**
goods	**shopping goods**
homogeneous shopping	**specialty goods**
goods	**staple items**
impulse items	

Discussion Questions

1. Products may be thought of as having three dimensions. Read the following scenario and identify which features of the product purchased fall into each of these three dimensions.

   Marianne Matrix wanted to spend less time writing term papers, so she bought a word-processing software package for her personal computer. Included with the diskette containing the software was an instruction manual. On the first page of the manual, Marianne found the phone number of a toll-free hotline for customer questions.

2. Identify each of the following as a convenience good, a shopping good, or a specialty good. For convenience goods, state whether they are staple, impulse, or emergency items. State whether shopping goods are homogeneous or heterogeneous.

   a. The boots Marge bought when they were on sale.

   b. The bottle of ASA Jim bought when his head began to ache.

   c. The rare Bordeaux wine Alicia bought for a special dinner she was planning.

   d. The newspaper Philip bought when the headline caught his eye.

3. What is the difference between a brand and a trademark?

4. What are some advantages of using branding? Why do some consumer groups object to the practice? Why do some companies choose not to use branding?

5. Under what circumstances would a company use a family brand? Under what circumstances would it use individual brands?

6. In the Sears catalogue, microwave ovens, refrigerators, and vacuum cleaners carry the brand name Kenmore; tool chests, hammers, tractors, and ladders carry the name Craftsman. What type of brands are these? What benefits does Sears derive from selling such brands?

7. Marge McClain is a real estate broker; her product is the service of bringing together buyers and sellers of real estate. Explain why her product can be described as perishable. How might the perishability of Marge's product affect the way she markets it?

8. Last March, Max Mustard decided to open a generic tax preparation company. He thought that a lot of people would want to cut costs, especially considering how painful it is to pay taxes anyway. So Max signed a lease for a plain storefront office, bought a couple of chairs and a second-hand steel desk, and moved in. His only advertising was a black-and-white sign that read in plain block letters, "Tax Preparer, Cheap. Open 8 a.m. to 4 p.m."

   Based on what you have read about marketing services, why do you think Max's business failed?

9. Because a service is intangible, marketers need to pay attention to the tangible elements surrounding the service. What tangible elements do you look for when selecting a restaurant?

Cheryl's Cookies

Cheryl's Cookies enters 1991 with plans to open two to five stores during the year and to position itself not just as a place to buy a cookie or brownie, but also as a gift shop. In a little over four years since the firm was founded, Cheryl's has grown from a single shop to a mini-network of stores in Ohio, Indiana, Pennsylvania, Missouri, and New Jersey. The company would like to have a hundred stores open by 1995.

Company Background

People in Bellevue, Ohio, probably best remember Cheryl Krueger as the little farm girl who made cookies for various church groups. As the eldest of three children, Krueger was always baking. The aroma of cookies, cakes, brownies, and other baked goods always seemed to fill the family home.

A 1979 graduate of Bowling Green University, Krueger gained some of her early business experience as a buyer for Burdines, one of the Federated stores, and The Limited, based in Columbus. "Through my travels I saw David's Cookies and Mrs. Fields' Cookies, which operate on both coasts," she said. "We lived on a farm when I was a child, and I was always baking things at home. I thought it would be great to bring something like David's or Mrs. Fields' to Columbus." At first, Krueger weighed the advantages and disadvantages of bringing one of those franchised operations to Columbus. "But it would always be their store, and I didn't really want that," she said.

The first Cheryl's Cookies was opened in September 1986. In January of the next year, the second store was opened. Sales for 1987 reached $250 000. By the end of 1990, the company had 14 stores with total sales of $2.5 million. Krueger estimated average monthly sales at about 280 000 cookies and more than quadruple that to 1.2 million during the 1990 Christmas season. Overall, the company has some 130 to 150 full- and part-time employees. Krueger estimates that sales from 15 to 18 units will top $4 million during 1991.

Product Description

The stores feature about ten varieties of cookies, including chocolate chip and chocolate chunk, peanut butter, oatmeal, macadamia coconut,

Source: This case has been edited from an earlier one that appeared in W. Wayne Talarzyk, *Cases and Exercises in Marketing*, copyright © 1987 by CBS College Publishing.

oatmeal raisin, white chocolate pecan, and others. Through product development, Krueger keeps the assortment current with demands of the consumers. She is currently developing her line of brownies by adding more chips and switching varieties of pecans, finding that the brownies sell better than chocolate chunk cookies. When Cheryl's first started, the cookies were priced at $4 per pound ($8.80 (U.S.) per kilogram). Today they sell for $4.95 per pound ($10.90 (U.S.) per kilogram). Competitors' prices range up to $6.95 per pound ($15.30 (U.S.) per kilogram).

In addition to over-the-counter business, Cheryl's operates a good-sized mail-order service, especially around Christmas. Orders can be placed at the store or by phone, charged to Visa or MasterCard, and mailed anywhere in the continental United States. Cheryl's also has a corporate gift service that assists organizations in arranging gifts for corporations, fund-raisers, or any group purchase. Discounts for quantity purchases are available. In some of Cheryl's market areas, the firm will deliver free of charge orders of $3 or more in designated downtown areas.

Cheryl's has recently introduced several new cookie packages, as well as packages that combine cookies with nonedible items like oven mittens and coffee mugs. Cheryl's offers three different sizes of cookie tins and two sizes of gift boxes. Four sizes of "gourmet dessert baskets" have been created and are priced from $39 to $75 each. In addition to brownies or cookies, the baskets contain such items as dessert sauces, gourmet coffee, imported chocolates, nuts, napkins, kitchen mittens, and coffee mugs.

Additional Information

All of Cheryl's cookie and brownie dough is prepared in Columbus, Ohio, and shipped frozen in 30-pound (13.5-kilogram) boxes via the company's own refrigerated trucks. "We're trying to have control of a highly perishable product," Krueger explains. Each location gets a four-week inventory per trip. The dough is thawed and baked as needed in each store. The centralized preparation enables the company to ensure consistent quality. There is no difference in taste between cookies baked from fresh and frozen raw dough.

To help use the additional retail space, the firm is introducing some gourmet innovations. For example, at the Columbus store, the firm is testing new ideas like muffins, croissants, and freshly squeezed orange juice in the morning, and different kinds of coffee. The store opens at 7 a.m. to capture the didn't-have-time-for-breakfast trade Monday through Friday. If there is a special evening event in the downtown area, the store will stay open for after-theater customers. For this group there will be espresso, cappuccino, and perhaps some gourmet desserts. Unlike the other Cheryl's Cookies, this store has tables at which to sit.

Focal Topics

1. What is the "real business" of Cheryl's Cookies? What do you see

as the marketing problems it is likely to face in the future?

2. What are the benefits sought in a product like Cheryl's Cookies by each of the following market segments: (a) consumer (personal use), (b) consumer (gift-giving), and (c) organization (gift-giving)?

3. What recommendations do you have for Cheryl's in terms of the firm's product and service offering?

Campbell Soup Co. Ltd. of Canada

CASE 8.2

In 1984, in the United States, the Campbell Soup Company introduced a line of breakfast foods called Great Starts under its Swanson's label. Within the first year the line had captured 15 percent of the American market of $330 million. The manager of marketing research for Campbell Soup in Canada was given the task of determining if Canadian consumers would respond to the idea of a microwavable breakfast. (Campbell Soup Co. Ltd. of Canada is 70 percent owned by its parent, but operates independently.)

Market Research

Campbell Soup had experimented with different kinds of breakfast entrees over the years, beginning with a line packaged in aluminum trays that came out in the early 1980s. This line bombed as people weren't willing to wait 40 minutes for the product to heat up in a conventional oven. But the rapid spread of microwave ovens quickly changed the market potential; by 1987, the U.S. market had 766 microwavable products, including the Swanson's Great Starts.

The first market research task in Canada was to determine if this market had a similar potential for microwavable breakfasts. Focus groups were set up to test the American product. Groups of eight people, screened to include only those who normally bought frozen foods and who ate breakfast, sat around a table and tasted the products. The consensus was that they loved the product.

Next research moved to the concept stage. Kiosks were set up in two Toronto-area shopping malls. Researchers buttonholed passing shoppers and interviewed more than 350 of them. They gathered information on their family makeup, breakfast eating habits, work schedules, their kids' breakfast habits, and whether those habits changed on the weekends — the who, what, when, where, and why of their lives as they related to breakfast. They even handed 250 of the interviewees sample boxes of the U.S. products and asked them to try them at home.

Source: This case was prepared by Donald Shiner, based on information compiled from Pat Davies, "The Soul of a New Instant Breakfast," *Report on Business (Globe and Mail)*, September 1988, pp. 78–92, and "Where They Are Now," *Report on Business (Globe and Mail)*, December 1989, pp. 101–111.

The results showed that 80 percent were interested in buying the product before they tried it but only 50 percent would buy again after sampling. Canadians wanted changes in the American product too. The sausages had to be spiced up; the texture of the scrambled eggs was too grainy; English muffins, not biscuits, had to be used. And Canadians definitely preferred fried eggs in the sandwiches, not the omelet-style filling of the U.S. product. There was a high level of acceptance among a broad range of people, including working mothers, teens, and children. Customers said they would be willing to pay about $2 per breakfast.

Product Development

Based on the positive conclusions of the market research, Campbell's Canada proceeded to the prototype development stage of Swanson's Breakfast. The eight-item line was to include French toast with sausages; blueberry pancakes; scrambled eggs with sausage and hash-brown potatoes; and two English muffins, one with egg and cheese and the other with sausage and cheese.

The R&D group proceeded to break each product down into what Campbell calls components. An egg-and-cheese sandwich has a muffin component, a cheese component, and a fried egg component. The R&D staff then built a blueprint of the finished product with components of a particular size, shape, taste, and cost. For instance, R&D specified desirable qualities for each of the components of a fried-egg sandwich, dealing with matters such as diameter, thickness, how much salt, how much spice, how bland or bright the colour should be, what the texture (or "mouth feel," in Campbell talk) should be like.

The development process did not run smoothly. Major problems emerged with several of the products. The English muffins proved a problem: they heated up so quickly in the microwave that they tasted like hockey pucks when the rest of the ingredients were barely warm. The scrambled eggs were too grainy, and the blueberries leaked colour into the pancakes, turning them a dark grey.

Despite these problems, six products emerged from the process to the factory floor and ultimate production on time. The final two followed several months later. The R&D people never did solve the problem of the leaking blueberries and had to settle for a packet of blueberry sauce.

Focal Topics

1. What is your evaluation of Campbell's new product strategy?

2. What questions would you ask your fellow students if you wanted to design a perfect breakfast food?

3. What is your evaluation of the new microwavable breakfast line and the chances of success?

Chapter 9

In this chapter, you will learn:

- What makes a product new.

- The stages of a product's life-cycle.

- What is involved in the incubation of a new product.

- How companies delegate responsibility for developing new products.

- How marketing proceeds during the introduction of a new product.

- How marketers take advantage of the growth phase.

- The marketing emphasis during a product's maturity.

- How marketers manage the decline phase of the product life-cycle.

Test Audiences Vote for Happy Endings

If you saw the movie *Risky Business*, you might have envied the way that Joel Goodsen (Tom Cruise) seemed to have it all. Joel gets a practical experience in free enterprise when a young hooker named Lana (Rebecca De Mornay) helps him turn his parents' fancy suburban home into a bordello for a night. After that big party and an unorthodox university interview, he gets into Princeton. He feels great.

The movie's author isn't so happy. The ending you saw is not the original one Paul Brickman wrote for *Risky Business*. In the original ending, Joel Goodsen doesn't get into Princeton, he and Lana don't walk off into a starry night, and when Joel describes his money-making scheme at the end of the movie, his voice is grim.

Why the change? Movie makers conduct audience research, and this research shows that moviegoers want the story to make them feel good. Hollywood has found that there's more money to be made in a happy ending. In the case of *Risky Business*, test audiences watched the movie with the original ending and with the happier ending that was ultimately used. The test audiences preferred the version that didn't teach a lesson.

Test audiences also influenced the ending of *Pretty in Pink*. The first version had Andie (Molly Ringwald) attend the prom with her faithful pal Duckie (John Cryer). In the final version, however, she ends up with handsome, preppie Blaine. The paperback novelization of the movie uses the original ending.

Another movie influenced by test audiences was *First Blood*. Three endings were planned for the movie: the original, in which Rambo dies; one in which

Jeff Slocumb/The Picture Group, Inc.

he is wounded and carried off on a stretcher; and one in which he breaks down and is led away crying uncontrollably. Of these endings, two were filmed, and the one in which Rambo is carried off was not. Test audiences saw the two versions, but their preferences for the endings were split 50-50. The final decision — to let Rambo live — enabled the subsequent filming of *Rambo: First Blood Part II* and *Rambo III*. Says director Ted Kotcheff, "It's a good thing we didn't kill him. Everybody would be a lot poorer."

Planning and selling new movies and other new products is a complex process. Marketers want to develop products that will have a strong and enduring appeal. This chapter describes the development of new products, as well as strategies for marketing them as their popularity grows, matures, and declines.

Source: Adapted from Pat H. Broeske, "Hollywood's Change of Art," *Rolling Stone*, February 12, 1987, pp. 24ff.

P eople all over the world have become fascinated with newness. Innovations like the facsimile machine, cellular telephones, and digital television appear to come to the market from nowhere.

The business world shares this fascination with novelty. Many companies invest heavily in the development of new products. One study predicted that new products would account for one-third of all profit by 1986. The same study predicted that new products (those less than one year old) would account for 40 percent of all product sales by the same year.[1] By all appearances this level of new product activity has been exceeded by the 1990s.

A case in point is 3M Company, where products less than five years old account for one-quarter of the company's sales.[2] According to Robert Adams, 3M's senior vice-president of technical services, management considers just about anything related to coated products to be a possible 3M line. This tradition dates back to the 1950s, when one of the company's technicians thought of making an extra-wide sheet of adhesive that could be used as a drape during surgery. Today, the technician is chair of 3M's board, and health-care products and services account for a significant part of the company's sales. One of the company's best-known innovations of the 1980s is Post-It notes, developed as a result of research into a new type of adhesive.

3M actively encourages innovation within the company. Salespeople try to obtain one-fourth of their revenue from items that were not in the product line the year before. Engineers are encouraged to spend 15 percent of their time working on new ideas of their own. In this way, 3M encourages **intrapreneurship** — entrepreneurial activity within an organization.[3] 3M hopes that its intrapreneurs will enable the company to continue bringing out successful new products.

New Products

What is a new product? According to Consumer and Corporate Affairs Canada, a company can call a product "new" for a period of one year in the region in which it is made. In planning a marketing strategy, however, companies need a broader definition of newness.

In general, a **new product** is a good or service new to the company producing it. This may include a technological breakthrough, such as digital audio tape machines. Or it may be merely an existing product to which the company has made major or minor revisions, such as Pillsbury's calcium-enriched flour.

When the new product has a function differing from that of existing products, marketers must not only tell consumers that the product exists, they must also educate them about the use of the product. For example,

Intrapreneurship
Entrepreneurial activity within an organization.

New Product
Good or service new to the company producing it.

268

the managers of the first tanning salons had to generate publicity about what was involved in visiting a tanning salon. Then they could encourage customers to visit their particular establishment.

More commonly, a new product is an improvement on an existing product. A product improvement can be a relatively minor change in packaging, formula, or design. For example, when consumers indicated concern about the cholesterol content of foods, several potato chip manufacturers stamped "cholesterol free" on their packages. (All the words indicated was that the product had never contained cholesterol. The actual product, potatoes, have always been cholesterol free.) Pillsbury added calcium to its flour and indicated this fact on its package.[4] A product improvement can also be a major change in the product itself, such as the development of disposable cameras.

Improvements on a product already manufactured by a company qualify as new when they involve a shift in the firm's marketing effort. For example, even though the "cholesterol free" message on a bag of chips does not change what is inside the bag, the company has changed part of the total marketing mix (in this case, promotion).

To maintain a competitive edge, companies invest much time and effort in improving upon and developing new products. These investments are necessary to the firm's survival. To understand why, we must investigate the concept of the product life-cycle.

The Product Life-Cycle

William Shakespeare spoke of the seven ages of man from birth to death. Like humans, products also pass through several phases. The **product life-cycle** is composed of five phases: (1) incubation, (2) introduction, (3) growth, (4) maturity, and (5) decline. Figure 9.1 depicts the product life-cycle in terms of the sales and profit of a typical product. It also gives examples of a product at each phase of the cycle.

In the **incubation phase,** a company conceives, develops, and tests a product before bringing it to the marketplace. Figure 9.1 shows the profit line sinking below the axis because research and development drain money from the company. For example, companies working on development of holographic television are not yet bringing in any money from this product.

After testing, a product enters the **introductory phase,** during which a company brings the new product to the marketplace. Sales begin to build as potential buyers learn of the product from advertising. But profits are still generally low because the company must recoup some of its losses incurred in developing the product. Digital stereo TVs represent a product at this stage of the life-cycle.

As buyer interest expands, a product moves into its **growth phase.** Other firms, sensing a marketing opportunity, introduce similar products at this phase. Both product availability and marketing efforts expand, and sales and profits surge upward. Products in the growth

Product Life-Cycle
Five phases through which a product passes: (1) incubation, (2) introduction, (3) growth, (4) maturity, and (5) decline.

Incubation Phase
Stage of product life-cycle during which a product is conceived, developed, and tested.

Introductory Phase
Stage of product life-cycle during which a company brings a new product to the marketplace.

Growth Phase
Stage of product life-cycle during which product availability and marketing efforts expand and sales and profits surge upward.

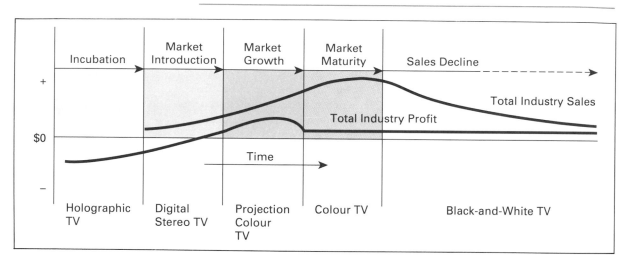

Figure 9.1 Product Life-Cycle

phase include non-ASA pain killers, granola bars, compact disc players, health clubs, and financial planning. In Figure 9.1, projection colour TV illustrates a product in this stage of relatively rapid growth and high profits.

Maturity Phase
Stage of product life-cycle during which the number of buyers continues to grow, but more slowly, until sales level off.

In the **maturity phase,** the number of buyers continues to grow, but more slowly, until a levelling-off occurs. So many competitors have entered the field that supply exceeds demand. Competition becomes more fierce, money is spent to lure customers from one brand to another, and profits may begin to decline. Most products now on the market are in this phase of the life-cycle. Colour televisions are at this stage. Similarly, owners of video stores have struggled to keep up in a maturing market. (See At Your Service 9.1.)

Decline Phase
Stage of product life-cycle during which products start losing a significant number of customers without replacing them.

When products start losing a significant number of customers without replacing them, they enter the **decline phase.** Both sales and profits drop steadily, and new products begin to take the place of declining products. Black-and-white televisions are an endangered species since the introduction of colour television. And you probably don't ever have to worry about learning how to use a slide rule now that pocket calculators are so inexpensive. Producers of slide rules must turn to other products.

Length of the Product Life-Cycle

In diagrams of product life-cycles, the vertical axis indicates the dollar amount of sales and profit and the horizontal axis shows the amount of time for each phase. In general, it is much easier to specify sales and profits than time span because the length of the product life-cycle varies greatly from product to product. Generalizations are risky, though some have been made.[5]

During the early 1980s, the video-cassette rental business was hot. Such a business was relatively easy to operate and relatively inexpensive to enter, and customer demand for home videos was booming. Many new businesses opened during that time, and, as a result, the competition had become stiff. Today, owners of video stores are competing with video rental services at car washes, grocery stores, and even in vending machines that accept credit cards. In addition, video superstores stock as many as 10 000 movies compared to 2000 titles in a typical neighbourhood shop.

The owners of small rental shops are having a particularly difficult time competing against giant chains such as Kmart, Zellers, and grocery chains. The competition has cut prices by 50 percent or more. Because the big chains can get quantity discounts, the competition is especially hard on the small shops.

While many mom-and-pop operations are closing down, others are trying to find a niche in the market. Some offer more personal service. Others specialize in a narrow market segment. Video Adventure attracts an upscale clientele with foreign titles and movies featuring dance and opera. The Original Kids' Video Store stocks only carefully chosen material for youngsters.

Brenda Hutchinson

Source: Adapted from Stephen Koepp, "Clash of the Video Merchants," *Time*, November 17, 1986, p. 74.

One study has found a 40-year life-cycle for many industrial products. For grocery products, the product life-cycle may be as short as 12 to 18 months. For most types of products, because of the increasing pace of technological innovations and the rapid rate at which new products are being introduced, the life-cycle is shrinking.[6]

Some products, called **fads,** have extremely short life-cycles, usually no more than two years. Fads have shorter lives because they do not require much development time and they usually skip the maturity phase. Pet Rocks, Silly Putty, Hula Hoops, Rubik's Cubes, and Cabbage Patch Dolls were all products extremely popular for short periods of time and then settled to the bottoms of toy boxes where they languished until exhumed for yard sales.

Fad
Product with a short life-cycle, usually no more than two years.

Importance of the Product Life-Cycle

Although it is extremely difficult to predict when the sales and profit of a particular product will peak, the life-cycle concept is a useful tool for marketing managers. Earlier we indicated that companies must continuously create new products and recreate the image of their older products. The life-cycle concept explains why.

The product life-cycle reminds management that sooner or later a product will die. If a business is to be an ongoing concern, it must develop new products or improve on those already established. Microwave ovens, for example, will probably replace many gas and electric ranges within the next 20 years, just as colour televisions have now replaced most black-and-white sets. Appliance manufacturers that have not already entered the microwave market may be too late and may have to drop out of the market for stoves altogether.

The product life-cycle also indicates that a firm's products must compete with the products of other companies for consumer attention. By knowing the phase through which a particular product passes, marketers can plan a strategy to meet that competition. A declining product may have to be replaced; a mature product may simply need more advertising. In the remainder of this chapter, we will investigate each phase of the product life-cycle.

The Incubation Phase

Even the simplest products require a large amount of work. An example is the development of dust-free Kitty Litter. To maintain its leadership in the market for cat litter in the face of competition from Clorox, Lowe Industries, the makers of Kitty Litter, decided to try to make a product with less dust. First, Lowe Industries developed a machine that used vacuum vents to shake the dust out of the litter before packaging. The device didn't work; more dust was generated during shipping.

So the company quadrupled its research and development spending from $1 million to $4 million. Months passed, the researchers kept sending the marketing committee dust-free products, and the committee kept sending them back. Meanwhile, Clorox's Fresh Step was gaining on Kitty Litter. Finally, two years later, Lowe Industries had developed a successful dust-control additive. The company introduced 99 percent dust-free versions of its two products, Kitty Litter and Tidy Cat 3.[7]

This example shows that the incubation of a product involves several important steps. First, a product idea must be conceived. Next, the idea must be developed; it must be shown to be feasible technically and from a business perspective. Finally, marketers must demonstrate in some way that the public will buy it. The process is the same whether the product is a television show, a new toy, or a textbook.

To keep up with today's rapid pace of product development, many companies are seeking ways to bring out new products faster than before. Some marketing experts suggest replacing the traditional sequential approach with a holistic approach. In this approach, product development is the responsibility of a team of people with many areas of expertise, such as marketing or research and development. The team members share information throughout the development process, revising plans as research and testing increase their information. Canon, for example, developed its Sure Shot camera using this approach.[8]

Conception

According to one marketing wit, the "perfect product" is one that is (1) cheaper than any possible competitor's product, (2) not reusable, and (3) guaranteed to be habit forming. Needless to say, perfect products are scarce. Companies generally settle for far less in their search for new-product ideas. They look mainly for ideas that seem technically feasible.

Where do technically feasible product ideas originate? They can come from almost any source. In general, however, companies usually derive new-product ideas from one of three sources: (1) their work force, (2) customers, or (3) competitors.

Company Work Force

Many firms maintain research and development departments that look for product ideas related to the technology the company has already developed. Bell Northern Research, which specializes in communications research related to telephones, fibre optics, and data communication, is an outstanding example. Another is Eastman Kodak, which has more than 600 Ph.D.s on its staff, who turn out thousands of scientific papers each year.

Not all product ideas originate with a company's research staff. For example, an assembly-line worker for the Lewyt Company, a manufacturer of industrial cleaners, came up with the idea for a home vacuum cleaner. One of Pillsbury's greatest successes, Crisp Crust Pizza, was based on an old family recipe of a company vice-president, and the now classic green-plastic garbage bag for consumers was developed from a Canadian salesman's suggestion.

Customers

Feedback from customers is also an important source of new-product ideas. Sometimes companies send out questionnaires or set up interviews to ask customers for their complaints or suggestions. As a result of questioning more than 2000 people, for example, Gillette discovered consumer demand for a roll-on deodorant that goes on dry. The product, Dry Idea, was launched a few years later.[9] Consumers' complaints about having to run down to their washing machines at the rinse cycle to pour in fabric softener led Procter & Gamble to develop Bounce, a rayon softener sheet that goes in the dryer.[10]

Competitors

Perhaps the major source of product ideas for a company is the new products of competitors. Copying competitors' ideas can save a company a great deal in research and development costs; by looking at competitors' results, marketers can gauge what works and what doesn't. It can also save the imitating company the expense of building initial demand.

For example, Ed Lowe came up with the idea of labelling five-kilogram bags of dirt Kitty Litter and selling them in pet stores and supermarkets. Once this idea became practical, Clorox moved into the market with a similar but improved product.[11]

One of the most publicized cases of all times was that of the stainless steel blade. The Wilkinson Sword Company, manufacturer of swords and garden tools, produced a small quantity of stainless steel razor blades for the U.S. market and sold them through garden shops. There was an immediate demand for the blades because of their superiority over those then on the market. The Wilkinson Company did not have the production capacity to keep up with demand, so the Gillette Company jumped into the market. Gillette soon surpassed Wilkinson in production and thereafter retained the largest share of the market.

Development

A company must sift through ideas that flow in, gear up for production, and conceive a workable marketing program for each new product. This is the second step of the incubation phase—development.

Organizational Arrangements

Almost all company departments—research and development, finance, marketing, and production — have some say in new-product development. Many large and medium-size companies with diverse products have found that assigning their marketing managers the duty of co-ordinating input from many other departments becomes too burdensome. They cannot efficiently handle both new-product development and the management of existing products, which is their primary responsibility. Some firms have tried to resolve this dilemma by creating the post of new-product manager. In practice, however, this arrangement also has serious drawbacks. New-product managers rarely have authority over members of other departments, so they must rely on persuasion to implement their decisions.

Many companies now delegate responsibility for new-product decisions to a group rather than an individual. Three types of groups have been used:

New-Product Committee
Group of top-level executives and representatives of several departments that meets regularly to consider new products.

1. The **new-product committee.** This group is composed of top-level executives and representatives of several departments. At the Gerber Company, for example, the board chair, president, vice-president, and other officers representing diverse interests meet once a month to consider new-product ideas.[12] Their high standing in the company guarantees that disputes over authority will seldom arise.

   This type of organization usually serves a company well when only a few product ideas must be considered. The major disadvantage of the new-product committee is that, since it meets only occasionally, it cannot handle a large volume of ideas efficiently. Meeting more frequently would be a costly use of time for a company's highest-paid executives.

2. The **new-product department.** This form of organization is, in effect, a permanent committee that works on new-product ideas on a day-to-day basis. It is usually responsible directly to the chief operating officer and is staffed with researchers and experts in production, marketing, and finance to avoid conflict over authority. Both General Mills and S. C. Johnson and Company (makers of household waxes) employ this type of organization for product development.

   The new product department solves the problem of working with many new product ideas, but it has one major drawback: the department's responsibility for the product usually ends after test marketing. The product's success after that may depend on a product manager who does not fully understand the potential of the product.

3. The **new-product venture team.** Like new-product departments, venture teams are staffed by experts from various fields. The small team of employees that begins a project grows as the project progresses. Unlike new-product departments, however, venture teams usually assume total responsibility for a new product from its conception through its decline. Another distinction is that venture teams often operate apart from the firm's headquarters. The venture team has several advantages. One is that it inspires an enthusiastic team spirit. In addition, it encourages greater creativity, speed, and flexibility. Studies have shown, however, that the venture team concept is not the ideal solution it once appeared to be. Venture teams have been accused of being too expensive and unproductive and of developing ventures too unrelated to existing business capabilities.[13]

New-Product Department Permanent committee that works on new-product ideas on a day-to-day basis.

New-Product Venture Team Group that usually assumes total responsibility for a new product from conception through decline.

The Developmental Process

Product committees, product departments, and venture teams perform three important functions during the developmental process: screening, business analysis, and planning for the production and marketing of the product.

Screening refers to the first attempt to separate those ideas worth pursuing from those that are not. If properly done, screening can save companies time and money. But firms often make two types of errors in the screening process.[14]

Sometimes companies commit drop-errors, which occur when potentially profitable ideas are eliminated. Lack of vision is the most common cause of drop-errors. Eastman Kodak, for example, dismissed Edwin Land's self-developing camera as "a toy with limited commercial appeal." Kodak then spent years trying to regain the significant share

Screening First attempt to separate ideas worth pursuing from those that are not.

of the amateur photography market it lost to Polaroid. Almost every publishing company has a list of books it has rejected that later went on to become enormous hits. George Orwell's *Animal Farm* was rejected by many publishers who complained either that its writing was "too cerebral" or that the pigs in the book were "offensive characters."[15]

By contrast, some companies commit go-errors in screening. They let poor ideas proceed. The Ford Motor Company's Edsel was one of the costliest new product failures in history. The car was introduced in 1957 and discontinued by 1959. Ford lost $350 million on the project.

Often companies develop products that are not complete failures, but are not successful enough to continue producing. A good example is the Concorde aircraft. Some products may cover their costs but make no profit. Others may earn a profit, but one that is smaller than a company's normal rate of return.

Marketers estimate that as many as 70 percent of the new consumer products that enter the marketplace fail. Obviously, many of these failures could have been prevented by eliminating poor ideas from the start.

How are poor ideas detected? One way is to subject them to careful **business analysis,** which involves estimating the future sales and profit potential of the new product. Most firms, before seriously entertaining a new-product idea, have certain criteria that must be met. For example, one major oil company insists that all new-product ideas return 20 percent of the cost of investment by the second year. In addition, the firm insists that this return on investment must increase to a minimum of 30 percent by the fifth year.

After management has demonstrated a product's financial feasibility, it must convert the product idea into an actual physical product. That task involves the co-operation of experts in both production and marketing. If a product is complex, engineers may develop a model first and take the product through a limited production run. Even with such precautions, bugs may show up in the product.

While production managers work out the physical dimensions of the product, marketing managers develop the image of the product. Branding and packaging decisions must be made at this time, as well as decisions regarding pricing, promotion, and distribution. Just as flaws in the physical product may show up despite careful planning, so too can flaws in the marketing program. Because of this possibility, market planners have developed a kind of dry run for the product, the next step in the incubation phase.

Test Marketing

Most major firms test their products in some way before launching a full-scale marketing effort. In large companies with sophisticated electronic hardware, computers may simulate market conditions to determine consumer demand. More commonly, firms may do in-home testing,

Business Analysis
Process of estimating future sales and profit potential of a new product.

during which potential buyers use the products and then evaluate them on a questionnaire. Or they may test their products by marketing them through retail outlets under controlled conditions in selected cities — a process called **test marketing.**

Test marketing is not practical for all products. For example, it would be difficult for an automaker to produce a car before introducing it because of the tremendous cost of the operation. But for technically simple products, especially those that represent a major product innovation, test marketing is a good idea. It can save a company a multimillion dollar loss by uncovering errors in the marketing program. Green Giant, for example, once thought it had a sure winner in Oven Crock baked beans, which came already sweetened in the can. In blind taste tests, people loved them. But the beans bombed in a test market. Research later showed that people who ate heavily flavoured baked beans added their own seasonings to the bland variety and did not want anybody doing it for them.[16]

Test marketing presents some difficulties, however. The most severe problem is that it informs competitors of a company's new product. The competitor can then jump into the market without a similar investment of time and money.

General Foods, for example, spent more than $600 000 to test its fruit-filled waffles, Toast'em Popups, in the 1960s. Immediately after General Foods finished testing, Kellogg introduced its own line of toasted waffles, Pop Tarts. Kellogg skipped the testing, but Pop Tarts reached first-place standing in the market. Marketing people believe that Kellogg decided to make Pop Tarts only after seeing the success of General Foods' test.[17]

Another serious drawback to test marketing is that it sometimes produces what is referred to as the "laboratory effect." Those in charge of the testing programs usually pay very close attention to details in the test market. Displays are fully stocked, price tickets are prominently displayed, and all decals and banners are positioned advantageously. In effect, test marketing managers create an unreal situation. When the product is actually marketed, it will never receive the same amount of attention from the retailer.

In addition, new-product managers, eager to get their products distributed nationally, have been known to bias factors (such as test-city location) in their product's favour. People in Atlantic Canada, for example, generally buy more canned condensed milk than consumers in other areas of the country. Test marketing a new condensed milk in Newfoundland would probably yield results that could not be duplicated nationally.

Test marketing, then, provides no guarantee of product success. In fact, a product that survives test marketing may have just a 50-50 chance of becoming a commercial success. Faulty test marketing partly accounts for that failure rate. Another important factor is the strategy employed after the incubation phase to bring the product to the consumer's attention and to keep attention focused on it. One way to do this is to develop an effective product positioning strategy.

Test Marketing
Trial marketing in a limited area chosen as representative of an entire market.

Product Positioning

Regular readers of *Rolling Stone* may have noticed a change in the magazine a few years ago. The counterculture publication, which documented the latest trends on the rock music scene, suddenly seemed to change. The magazine's format was streamlined, its graphics updated, and the paper on which it was printed was of a different quality. More importantly, its editorial coverage changed. The space devoted to music was cut back, and there was more talk of politics and entertainment. The magazine was clearly being redesigned to meet the needs of a changing market.[18] Marketers would say that the product had been repositioned.

Product Position
Image that a product has in consumers' minds, especially in relation to competing products.

Product Positioning
Decisions marketers make to create or maintain a certain product concept in consumers' minds.

A **product's position** is the image that a product has in consumers' minds, especially in relation to competing products. **Product positioning** refers to the decisions marketers make to create or maintain a certain product concept in consumers' minds.[19]

Product positioning is a natural outgrowth of market segmentation. Once a market segment has been identified and its characteristics understood, marketers may decide to position the product to appeal to the specific wants and needs of a particular segment. If that target market changes, the product may need to be redesigned to keep up with the market's new needs and interests. In the case of *Rolling Stone,* the magazine's editors found that their target market had aged and had become wealthier and more conservative in their music tastes. The company pointed out this change to potential advertisers by using a series of ads comparing the image of typical *Rolling Stone* readers with the reality. (See Figure 9.2.)

But as *Rolling Stone* evolved into a publication with a different orientation, it left a gap in the marketplace. That position was soon filled by *Rockbill,* a new magazine whose intent was to cover the new music for the consumers who are 18 to 34.

Products can be positioned in two ways. Marketers may choose to position the products in head-to-head competition with the industry leader. This strategy may be effective if the product's performance characteristics are similar to those of its competitors, but its price is lower. Automobile manufacturers are particularly fond of this strategy, since cars can be compared on the basis of so many different features. In ads for the Thunderbird Turbo Coupe, for example, Ford boasts that its car surpasses the BMW 633 CSi in handling but not in price. And ads for Volkswagen claim, "German engineering is either expensive or Volkswagen."

If a product's performance characteristics are superior to those of the competition, a marketer may choose a head-on position even if the product's price is higher. For example, in its advertising for running shoes, Puma USA promotes its 40 years of experience: "New shoes are introduced almost daily. They come from companies that have experience . . . in just about every activity except performance walking."[20]

Not all marketers wish to position their products against the compe-

Figure 9.2 Advertisement from *Rolling Stone's* Perception/Reality Campaign

Source: *Rolling Stone*, 1986, Straight Arrow Publishers, Inc. © 1986. All Rights Reserved. Reprinted by permission, Agency: Fallon McElligott.

tition, however. If a product's characteristics do not differ substantially from those of competitors, marketers may seek another positioning strategy. Thus, when makers of athletic shoes began to target the market for walking shoes, Lowell Shoe, maker of more conservatively styled "comfort shoes," chose to focus on a different market segment. "There are 60-year-old grannies wearing Reeboks," explained Lowell's marketing director, "but they'd rather be wearing a traditional shoe." And after seeing Canada's appeal starting to slip with American tourists, Tourism Canada decided to reposition the country's image as a tourist destination by focusing on its key regional strengths, such as the French flavour of Quebec.

Companies that have several similar products may also wish to position a new product so that it does not erode sales, or **cannibalize,** those of earlier brands. Pepsi Free, Pepsi Cola's caffeine-free cola, for example, has been considered only a qualified success since most of its sales have come at the expense of regular or Diet Pepsi. Typically, manufacturers differentiate brands on the basis of size, features, quality level, or price.

To decide how to position a product, marketers sometimes use a map such as the one shown for automobiles in Figure 9.3. Chrysler Corpo-

Cannibalization
Process by which a company's new product takes sales away from existing products in the same company's line.

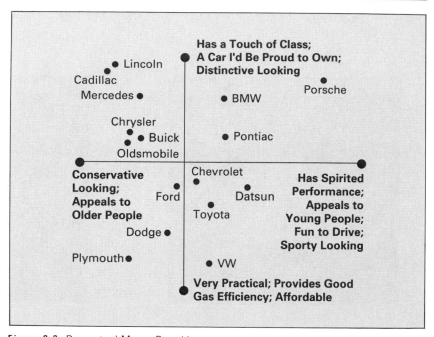

Figure 9.3 Perceptual Map — Brand Images
Source: Adapted from John Koten, "Car Makers Use 'Image' Map as Tool to Position Products," *The Wall Street Journal*, March 22, 1984.

ration uses this map to determine whether consumers see its cars as relatively stylish or practical and relatively appealing to young or old drivers. In other industries, marketers may map whatever characteristics are relevant to their products. Based on the information in the map, marketers may decide to revise their choice of target markets or their marketing mix.

Once a positioning strategy has been determined, marketers use the various elements of the marketing mix to reinforce that product's image in consumers' minds. The success of a positioning strategy can be evaluated by several tests (discussed in Chapter 15). If the product's position has failed to make an impact on consumers, marketers may choose to reposition it. This strategy should be used with caution, however, since an inconsistent positioning strategy can create consumer confusion.

Following positioning decisions — the last stage in the incubation phase—a product is ready to be launched. Each phase of the product life-cycle requires a different marketing strategy. The remainder of this chapter focuses on effective strategies for the other phases. Table 9.1 summarizes the basic strategy for each phase.

The Introductory Phase

Risks are highest during the introductory phase when a product first becomes available nationally. Marketing managers' aims during this

Table 9.1 Marketing Strategy over the Life-Cycle

	Price	Promotion	Placement	Product Changes
Introduction	High, to recover development costs; or low, to capture large market share	Heavy, emphasizing information on product benefits	Generally, many outlets to assure wide public access; however, access to outlets may be limited	None
Growth	As high as possible, because consumer demand is high	Heavy, emphasizing brand name to win consumer loyalty	Additional outlets	New sizes, packages, and styling features; service extras
Maturity	Lower, to draw remaining potential customers	Heavy, emphasizing superiority over competitors and reminding consumers of benefits	Additional outlets	New uses, new users, flanker products, major modifications
Decline	Low, to liquidate inventory quickly	Moderate, discouraging product use	Decreasing number of outlets	Major modifications, if not already made

phase are really twofold: (1) to make the general public aware of the product's benefits and (2) to recover some of the costs incurred during the incubation phase. To accomplish these objectives, managers must work with the elements of the marketing mix—product, price, promotion, and placement.

Marketing Mix Strategy

Product Often when a product is first introduced, it will be available in limited quantities, reflecting a manufacturer's reluctance to invest substantial sums in production equipment until there is evidence that enough of a demand for the product exists to warrant such an expenditure. In the food industry, a company may even contract with another company to produce the product initially. If sales go well, the sponsoring company may then decide to invest in the necessary equipment.[21]

Price A firm may charge a very high price in the introductory phase or price the new product extremely low. When videocassette recorders first came on the market, they were expensive (about $1500), but they have been coming down in price ever since. Bic disposable razors were first marketed at practically a giveaway price (25 cents). High-technology products are priced high initially to recover developmental costs quickly. Low-technology, convenience products are priced low to capture a large market share as quickly as possible.

Promotion A company seldom makes a substantial profit when introducing a product, because the company must spend huge amounts on promotion to inform the public of the product's virtues. Many analysts believe that home computer marketers missed this first step when they introduced the machines. Initial advertising, they say, stressed RAM, keyboards, and screen resolution. The problem was that people did not know what to do with a computer. By the time the industry stepped back and addressed the more important issue of product benefits, several companies had already filed for bankruptcy.[22]

Placement   The manufacturer must also convince retailers and wholesalers of the merits of carrying the product. The placement (or distribution) strategy for most new products, with the exception of specialty goods, is to find as many outlets as possible. Thus, much of the promotion and advertising at this stage is aimed at the reseller market. Manufacturers may promise intermediaries high profit margins or special sales aids.

Timing   A product priced correctly, promoted heavily, and distributed widely can still fail because of improper timing. Timing is crucial in the introductory phase. With careful attention to the marketing mix and proper timing, some of the risks of new product introduction can be reduced. A product that survives introduction stands a good chance for rapid sales growth in the next phase.

The Growth Phase

The growth phase is sometimes referred to as the market acceptance phase. The product may have gained a reputation by word of mouth. New customers raise the level of sales, though not necessarily the firm's market share (since other firms' sales may be growing more rapidly). In general, profits start to take off, but rising profit is a mixed blessing, since it attracts more competition. Marketing managers must adjust the elements of the marketing mix to the new competitive situation. They must also begin the process of recreating the product, that is, adding features to distinguish it from others.

Marketing Mix Strategy

Product   In the growth phase, a firm must begin to increase the desirability of its product to counteract competition. It can do so by making minor product modifications that would strengthen its position or broaden its appeal.

Radical product changes in the growth phase would be unwise because they would confuse the public. But minor changes can help give the product a unique image in the consumer's mind. The most common types of minor modifications are:

1. *The addition of new sizes.*   When Pepsi-Cola introduced its new soft

drink, Pepsi Light, it offered only individual cans and bottles. When sales started growing, it introduced larger sizes.

2. *The introduction of new packages.* In the growth stage of Head and Shoulders shampoo, Procter & Gamble offered the product in unbreakable plastic bottles, plastic tubes, and jars to satisfy consumer preferences.

3. *The addition of new product features and models.* In the growth phase of the life-cycle of blow dryers, Gillette added a swivel handle to its stylers.

Price As greater production leads to cost savings, marketers may lower an initial high price, which may also be an effective way of discouraging potential competitors. On the other hand, if the product's initial price was low, marketers may choose to raise it to take advantage of heavy consumer demand.

Promotion The major change in marketing strategy occurs in the product's promotion. Expenditures for advertising are likely to remain high, but the content of messages changes. The emphasis shifts from informing consumers of a product's benefits to persuading them to buy and to continue purchasing a particular brand. Thus, in the early 1970s, most advertising for microwave ovens stressed the product's cooking speed and tried to dispel fears of potential dangers from high-frequency waves. Today, manufacturers build advertisements around such slogans as "If it isn't an Amana, it isn't a radar range." These slogans build brand recognition among consumers.

Placement As demand for the product increases, marketers may continue to expand the number of distribution outlets. As competitors enter the market, a company may want to pay particular attention to keeping dealers happy by ensuring prompt delivery of merchandise, allowing credit for damaged goods, or making service adjustments. To forestall competition, managers may try to persuade retailers to sell only their products.

The Maturity Phase

The maturity phase is sometimes referred to as the saturation point in a product's marketing because most potential buyers have already adopted the product. Sales growth continues very slowly, if at all, during this phase, so new, competing products do not enter the market. The competition is set. A few companies generally divide the market among themselves. Market share, not sales, is the key figure to watch. The only way marketing managers of mature products can succeed is to capture a larger share of the market by luring customers away from competitors. To accomplish this, managers again adjust the elements of the marketing mix. They must also rework the consumer's image of the product.

Marketing Mix Strategy

Product Theodore Levitt has shown how the life-cycle of mature products can be extended almost indefinitely by reworking the product. He cites the example of Du Pont's nylon.[23] The product was used primarily by the military in the 1940s for parachutes and ropes. After World War II, military use of the product fell off sharply. Du Pont then entered the consumer textile market. The company convinced women to switch from silk to nylon stockings. It later expanded the market by persuading teenagers to wear nylons, then further increased sales by introducing stretch socks, nylon rugs, tires, and many other nylon-based products. The effect on the life-cycle is illustrated in Figure 9.4.

The Du Pont experience shows some of the ways in which managers can increase a product's market share by reworking its image. The four most common methods are (1) to find new uses for the product; (2) to discover new users; (3) to add flanker, or related, products to the company line; and (4) to make major product modifications.

New Uses From the standpoint of a marketing manager, the best way to keep a mature product's sales growing is to convince consumers of the product's versatility. Du Pont developed a variety of products made from

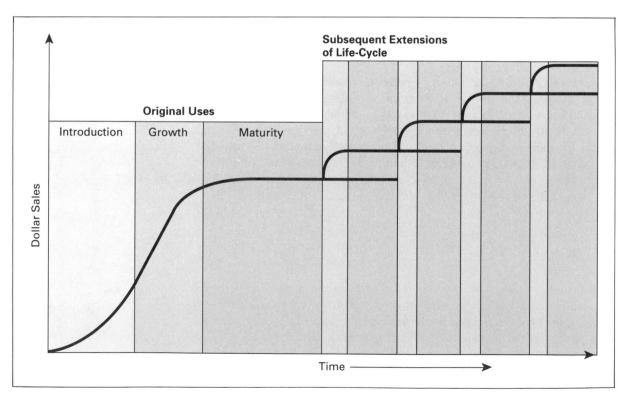

Figure 9.4 Hypothetical Life-Cycle

Source: Adapted from Theodore Levitt, *Marketing for Business Growth*, 2nd ed. (New York: McGraw-Hill, 1974), p. 163.

nylon. Doing so required a major effort by its research department, but finding new product uses need not be costly at all. New uses for food and other convenience products are relatively easy to find. Orange growers have conducted a major advertising campaign to persuade North Americans that "orange juice isn't just for breakfast anymore." Arm & Hammer has persuaded the public to use baking soda as a refrigerator deodorant and drain cleaner as well as an ingredient in baked goods.

Consumers are an especially good source of ideas for new product uses. Many companies conduct research and sponsor contests to learn of possible product extensions from consumers. Bisquick's product manager ran a golden-anniversary recipe club for the brand's fans to launch the baking mix into its second half-century.[24]

New Users   The search for new users involves finding unexplored market segments. As noted in Chapter 4, through segmentation managers develop marketing programs for subgroups rather than the mass market. As time passes, subgroups that provided the original markets for the product may offer no new sales potential. In that case, a firm must look to other segments to increase sales.

The most radical shift in markets occurs when a firm goes from the industrial to the consumer market, or vice versa. Du Pont made the move when it shifted production from nylon parachutes to nylon stockings. The move is radical because it involves entirely new methods of distribution, promotion, and pricing. A firm rarely drops out of one market altogether. Instead, it operates in both until one shows itself to be more profitable. Arm & Hammer, for example, also sells baking soda to commercial bakers and to the manufacturers of deodorants and powders.

More frequently, a firm looks for a new subgroup of buyers within the consumer or industrial market. For example, Dannon yogurt, which was positioned as a diet food in the 1950s, expanded its market in the 1980s by promoting yogurt as a wholesome food for people interested in keeping fit, with or without dieting. Its advertising campaign, "Get a Dannon Body," never mentioned the word "diet."[25]

Flanker Products   Items related to an already established product and bearing the same brand name are termed **flanker products.** Pepsodent toothbrushes are a flanker product to Pepsodent toothpaste. Marketing managers sometimes succeed in boosting sales of a mature product by the introduction of other use-related products. For example, Clairol's main product is hair colouring. In recent years, Clairol has added a number of other products, including conditioners, shampoos, and hair dryers. These flanker products support sales of the main product by encouraging home hair care.

Flanker products sometimes serve as cheap giveaways to encourage the sale of the more profitable mature item. For years the Gillette Company has sold razors at comparatively low prices in the hope of hooking customers into coming back for profitable blades. Some computer manufacturers have extended that concept to their own markets.

Major Modifications   Many companies wait until products show definite signs of decline before introducing major product changes. They do

Flanker Product
Item related to an already established product and bearing the same brand name.

this because they fear that a modified product will cut deeply into the sales of the old product before the latter is ready to be retired.[26] Most marketing experts, however, think such a policy is a mistake. The problem with a don't-rock-the-boat approach to product improvement is that changes in the market are inevitable, and the penalty for being second with an innovation is a permanent loss of customers.

The steel industry's experience with canning shows how disastrous delay can be. The industry thought that no one could challenge its dominant position in canning and failed to improve its basic product. Aluminum and plastic manufacturers then entered the field with a lighter can that was easier to ship. The steel industry was then forced to develop a lighter product, but it never succeeded in winning back lost markets.[27]

Major product improvements should be planned well in advance of a product's decline. The introduction of an improved product may indeed cut into the sales of an already established product, but it is far better for a company to lose ground to itself than to an innovative competitor. The makers of Coca-Cola, for example, hope that the combination of Coke Classic and regular Coke will maintain their position as the number one cola.

Price   Because of intense competitive pressures at this point in the life-cycle, marketing managers often lower the price of their products. The lower price draws the remaining potential buyers who could not previously afford the product. For example, colour TV sets now outsell black-and-white models because the colour sets are less expensive than ever before. Sometimes marketing managers deliberately engage in price wars to draw away consumers from other brands. In the short run, this can be an effective technique, but in the long run it usually fails because competitors retaliate.

Promotion   Instead of competing directly with other companies on the basis of price, most marketing managers prefer to compete indirectly through new promotional programs. Advertising may feature competing products and show their supposed faults. This technique is known as "comparative advertising." Much of the advertising in the maturity phase is also geared to reminding customers of product benefits in order to keep them loyal users of a brand.

Placement   Firms also compete indirectly by trying to place products in more outlets than competitors. Food producers may offer supermarket owners more services in exchange for more display space. Appliance manufacturers may offer their products in discount stores to appeal to a wider segment of the market.

The Decline Phase

All products eventually outlive their usefulness. The telltale signs are poor sales performance and profit declines that cannot be traced to a slump in the industry. There may be many reasons for the decline. Consumers may simply be tired of the product. A competitor may introduce a superior product. Or the company itself may have wisely implemented a major product improvement that makes a particular product outmoded. Whatever the reason, management must face the problems of eliminating one of their offerings. (See Marketing Today 9.1.)

The decision to withdraw a product can be difficult, especially if the product has had a long life-cycle. Internally, the company faces the problem of managerial resistance to the withdrawal of an old favourite and employee demoralization at the prospect of job loss. This happened, for example, when Westinghouse decided to discontinue production of most major appliances. A firm's external relations may also be negatively affected by product elimination. When RCA announced its withdrawal from the manufacture of computers, the company generated ill will among customers, who wondered who would service the equipment in which they had invested millions.

Another interesting phenomenon occurs when all of the producers in a developed country such as Canada stop producing a product in the decline phase. For example, when Canadian companies stopped manufacturing glass radio vacuum tubes, some Canadian military equipment continued to need these tubes. The only source of supply was Czechoslovakia, which provided the needed parts at a very high price.

Despite such problems, if a company decides after analysis that a product is no longer profitable, it must make plans for the product's elimination. A change in the marketing mix will again be necessary to accomplish this new goal.

Marketing Today 9.1

Corning Cookware: Premature Decline?

For generations, consumer demand for Corning Glass Works' bowls, casserole dishes, and dinnerware was so strong that Corning's management seemed to think it had a perpetual franchise in North America's kitchens. But the company was wrong.

First, the company failed to see the attraction of lower-cost but good-quality imports from Japan and Taiwan. Consumers found that they could get an equivalent foreign-made set of dinnerware for

half the price of Corning's product. Many of the imports were more stylish as well. In 1982, Corning was selling dinnerware that had been designed in the early 1970s.

Furthermore, Corning had managed to overlook the boom in microwave cooking. Even though Corning's products are suitable for use in a microwave oven, the company didn't get around to informing consumers of this until early in 1985. And Corning failed to introduce a product line specifically targeted for microwave users until 1985. While competitors were profiting from microwave cook-

Phyllis Woloshin

ware, Corning was losing share.

Although Corning has now embarked on a strategy to regain share, it is finding that losing business is easier than regaining it.

Source: Adapted from Jeffrey A. Trachtenberg, "Too Little, Too Late," *Forbes*, March 24, 1986, pp. 172–173.

Marketing Mix Strategy

Product   At this point in the life-cycle, many of the product's original competitors may have dropped out of the market or introduced products that are so similar that consumers fail to distinguish between them. A product now need not be available in all sizes, colours, and styles. A company may continue producing only models or styles that retain a certain level of demand.

Price   The main objective of the decline stage is to gain as much profit as possible. Since demand for the product is declining, however, prices cannot be raised. During decline, a product's price usually reaches a low point so that the company can liquidate its stock as quickly as possible.

Promotion   Relations with the public may suffer unless customers are prepared for the prospect of the product's eventual elimination. Promotion can help ease the shock. Marketers have developed a special type of promotion, called **demarketing,** to persuade the public that there are valid economic reasons for withdrawing the product. Demarketing is especially important for concerns such as telephone, gas, and electricity companies, which are eager to maintain customer goodwill. Thus, when Bell Canada decided that it could no longer afford the expense of a large staff of operators to handle long-distance calls, it sponsored a series of educational commercials. The ads stressed that it was cheaper to make a long-distance call by dialling directly.

Placement   To keep profits at an acceptable level, costs must be cut. This usually involves cutting back on the number of intermediaries who handle the product. Retail outlets that are unprofitable must be phased out.[28] Sometimes a new marketing channel, such as a factory outlet, will be used to liquidate the remaining inventory of an obsolete product. As the product becomes harder to find, it may become a specialty item and loyal users will seek out dealers who still carry it.[29]

The decision to lower prices, eliminate distributors, and promote the idea of the product's elimination should be made only after careful analysis of the product's future in the marketplace. Some product managers have later regretted their decision to kill a product. *Life* magazine, Ipana toothpaste, and even the television program *Cagney and Lacey* have all made successful comebacks after being withdrawn from the market. Product management in the decline phase is a balancing act. Managers must have the courage to pull the plug on an obviously ailing product and the perception to see when the reports of a product's demise have been greatly exaggerated.

Demarketing
Promotion aimed at persuading the public that there are valid economic reasons for withdrawing a product.

Chapter Replay

1. **What makes a product new?**
   A new product is a good or service new to its producer; its newness may result from a technological breakthrough or from major or minor modifications.

2. **What are the stages of a product's life-cycle?**

   The product life-cycle consists of incubation, introduction, growth, maturity, and decline.

3. **What is involved in the incubation of a new-product?**

   In the incubation phase, new product ideas are proposed, and the better ones are developed and produced. Often a new product is test marketed before it is made widely available. A product positioning strategy is also usually developed at this stage.

4. **How do companies delegate responsibility for developing new products?**

   Input comes from almost all company departments, including research and development, finance, marketing, and production. Many companies delegate responsibility for new-product decisions to a group. Such a group may be a new-product committee, a new-product department, or a new-product venture team.

5. **How does marketing proceed during the introduction of a new product?**

   In the introductory phase, managers may set high or low prices, seek out as many distributors as possible, and spend heavily on promotion to acquaint the public with the product.

6. **How do marketers take advantage of the growth phase?**

   In the growth phase, marketers begin improving and expanding upon the product and use promotion to build brand recognition and preference.

7. **What is the marketing emphasis during a product's maturity?**

   In the maturity phase, marketers focus on winning market share by making major product improvements and by increasing promotion and distribution channels.

8. **How do marketers manage the decline phase of the product life-cycle?**

   In a product's decline phase, marketers reduce the number of styles and models of a product, eliminate distributors, cut prices, and may even demarket the product.

Key Terms

business analysis	intrapreneurship
cannibalization	introductory phase
decline phase	maturity phase
demarketing	new product
fad	new-product committee
flanker product	new-product department
growth phase	new-product venture
incubation phase	team

product life-cycle   screening
product position   test marketing
product positioning

Discussion Questions

1. When Dairy Delights Company came out with a line of sugar-free, calcium-enriched ice cream, its cartons carried the message, "New! You'll Love This Stuff!" According to Consumer and Corporate Affairs Canada, how long can Dairy Delights call its new product new? From a marketing perspective, when do changes to a product make the product "new"?

2. Describe the stages of the product life-cycle. Why is this cycle important to marketers?

3. Which stage of the product life-cycle is generally most profitable? During which stage are sales likely to peak? Why don't sales and profits peak at the same time?

4. Marge Watercress owns the Sleepy Time Motel. When two new motels started going up just down the street from hers, Marge realized that she would have to offer something extra, or the competition would take away all her profits. Where can Marge get suggestions for new services to offer?

5. Distinguish the following: new-product committee, new-product department, new-product venture team.

6. Would it make more sense to test market a dishwasher or a new kind of candy bar? An improved version of a cassette tape or a revolutionary new detergent that washes clothes without water?

7. What is a product's position? In the map in Figure 9.3, identify a car that is positioned to appeal to young drivers who are willing to spend extra for style and status. Identify a make that is positioned to appeal to conservative drivers who value economy.

8. During a product's introductory phase, what do marketers typically emphasize in their promotional messages? What do they emphasize during the growth phase?

9. Belweather Credit Union operates in a mature market. To enhance its opportunities in this market, the credit union has hired a marketing manager. What general strategies might the marketing manager suggest for winning market share?

10. What is demarketing? When might a company want to use such a strategy?

International Dairy Queen, Inc.

"It's certainly the biggest thing that has happened to Dairy Queen in the last 25 years," according to Harris Cooper, International Dairy Queen's president and chief executive. He was referring to Dairy Queen's Blizzard, a new, flavoured, frozen dairy dessert product introduced in the spring of 1985. Company sales in 1985 were $159.1 million (U.S.), compared to $132.3 million in 1984, and net income increased to $9.7 million from $7.7 million. Much of these increases were attributed to the introduction of the Blizzard.

Company Background

In 1938, near Moline, Illinois, J. F. McCullough and his son Alex developed the product millions have come to know as 'Dairy Queen' soft-serve. The McCulloughs' innovation was the beginning of what was to become a system of more than 4900 Dairy Queen and Dairy Queen/Brazier stores in the United States, Canada, and 12 other countries.

The McCulloughs made an arrangement with Sherb Noble, owner of an ice cream retail shop in Kankakee, Illinois, to test their new product in his store. Noble held an "All You Can Eat for 10¢" sale, and more than 1600 people lined up to try the new treat. Based on this success, the McCulloughs knew they had an exciting business opportunity.

The first Dairy Queen store opened in Joliet, Illinois, in 1940 and was owned by Sherb Noble. Early growth of the system progressed through a network of territory operators, individuals who were granted territory rights to develop Dairy Queen stores in a specified geographic area. In 1962, several territory operators pooled their assets and formed International Dairy Queen, Inc. and its wholly owned subsidiary, American Dairy Queen Corporation. In 1968, the Dairy Queen system adopted a new food system, the Brazier system, which teamed soft-serve treats with a hot food line consisting of hot dogs and hamburgers. One of the system's goals is to continually live up to the slogan, "We Treat You Right!" and to offer customers uniform quality, value, service, and cleanliness.

Product Description

The Blizzard consists of Dairy Queen soft-serve ice cream blended with a variety of cookies, fruit, and nationally branded candy and cookies (such as Snickers, Butterfinger, Heath bars, and Hydrox cookies). No

Sources: International Dairy Queen Inc.'s *1985 Annual Report,* and Stephen Phillips, "Dairy Queen's Blizzard Is Hot," *New York Times,* August 31, 1986, Business Section. Additional information courtesy of International Dairy Queen, Inc.

milk is added. It is blended in seconds in a $500 machine called the Blizzard Blender. Served with a spoon rather than a straw, the Blizzard comes in some 35 flavours.

According to Dairy Queen, the butterfat content of the Blizzard is 5 percent, compared with 10 to 12 percent for many ice creams and 15 percent for premium ice creams. This allows Dairy Queen to sell the Blizzard for a lower price — $2.25 for 350 millilitres and $3.39 for 600 millilitres.

Dairy Queen officials credit Samuel J. Temperato, a franchise holder of 67 Diary Queens in the St. Louis area, with developing the Blizzard. Although Temperato agrees to having introduced the Blizzard to Dairy Queen officials, he says that credit for the invention should go to Ted Drewes, Jr., also of St. Louis and associated with two frozen custard stores.

According to Dairy Queen, the success of the Blizzard has been spectacular. At the end of 1985, over 80 percent of all Dairy Queen stores in the United States and Canada had included this product in their line of frozen dairy desserts. Interest in the Blizzard generated increased consumer visits to Dairy Queen stores, which favourably affected other product sales.

One stock analyst called the Blizzard a "signature item." He added that if Dairy Queen can introduce new flavours, the Blizzard can be as long-lasting as the ice cream cone. Company officials stated, "The successful and quick introduction of the Blizzard reflects the strength of the Dairy Queen system." The organization plans to " . . . take advantage of other opportunities to expand the company's business and profitability."

Focal Topics

1. Discuss other ways in which Dairy Queen might build on the success of the Blizzard.

2. Based on the information in this chapter, discuss ways in which Dairy Queen might engage in new product development.

3. Discuss other product strategies that could be used to strengthen the Dairy Queen system.

CASE 9.2   Newman's Own, Inc.

Paul Newman's lines of spaghetti sauce, salad dressing, and gourmet popcorn have been major successes since his company, Newman's Own, Inc., was formed in 1982. It is estimated that as of 1986, Newman's spaghetti sauce had about 1.6 percent of the market, his salad dressing had a 3 percent share of the market, and his gourmet popcorn may have owned as much as 10 percent of the market. Most recently the company has introduced microwave popcorn and lemonade.

Company Background

Newman's Own, Inc. started as a lark when Newman and his friend, author A. E. Hotchner, decided to market the homemade salad dressing Newman gave his friends each Christmas. The product was marketed locally in Connecticut under the Newman's Own label. In a few months, requests for the product were being received from all parts of the United States. A chance meeting with a food broker led to national distribution. Newman's Own products are now sold in about 80 percent of the supermarket chains in the United States.

In 1983, the company introduced its Industrial Strength Venetian Spaghetti Sauce. Newman explained that he chose that name because he thought it signified that the sauce was "the real thing." Later the company brought out its gourmet popcorn.

At the outset, the two partners never expected to make any money. After a year of phenomenal success, they decided to give away the profits. So far the company has given away over $7 million to some 200 groups including the Sloan-Kettering Center for Cancer Research, Catholic Relief for Ethiopia, and Recording for the Blind. Overall, about 20 percent of the price of a jar of Newman's spaghetti sauce goes to charity.

Marketing Strategy

When they first started the company, the partners sought marketing advice. After receiving estimates of $500 000 for test marketing and a probable loss of $1 million in the first year, they decided to go it on their own. Each partner put up $20 000 to set up the company and had his investment back in six weeks.

The company's sales philosophy can probably best be described by a small banner that reportedly hangs above a ping-pong table in the three-room corporate headquarters furnished with patio furniture: "'If we ever have a plan, we're screwed'—Paul Newman to himself at the Stork Club urinal, 1983." The company does not advertise and only occasionally distributes coupons.

Newman's smiling face does appear on the label of each product. He has explained the products' success by saying that people first try the products because of his name, but because they are good food, customers buy again. The label on the spaghetti sauce states: "La stella della salse

Source: Materials presented here have been adapted from "Paul Newman Is Packing 'Em in at the Supermarket," *Business Week,* November 4, 1985, p. 38, and a product review in *Consumer Reports,* October 1985, p. 630. This case originally appeared in a slightly different form in W. Wayne Talarzyk, *Cases and Exercises in Marketing.* Copyright © by CBS College Publishing. Reprinted by permission of Holt, Rinehart and Winston, Inc.

e la salsa delle stelle." Translated, that means "The star of the sauces, the sauce of the stars."

Focal Topics

1. From a marketing perspective, how would you explain the success of Newman's Own?

2. In what ways might marketing be of help to the company?

3. What sort of marketing strategy would you recommend for Newman's Own?

Pricing Concepts and Practices

In this chapter, you will learn:

- Basic considerations consumers and businesses weigh in accepting a price.

- Typical steps involved in price setting.

- Objectives companies try to achieve in price setting.

- General characteristics of demand.

- Types of costs sellers must cover.

- Some pricing policies companies might choose.

- Methods companies use to set prices.

- Kinds of discounts a company might offer.

- How companies can adjust for location in setting prices.

- How companies can adjust prices to meet consumer expectations.

Sweet Satisfaction at a Premium Price

Godiva Chocolatier, Inc.

Back in 1960, ice cream was pretty much all the same. Despite marketing research that showed consumers considered quality more important than price, dairies continued to churn out inexpensive two-litre boxes of ice cream as a sideline to the milk business. Then Reuben and Rose Mattus changed all that.

The Mattuses developed a premium-quality ice cream and invented the foreign-sounding name Häagen-Dazs. They sold their ice cream in small gourmet shops in New York for the then-outrageous price of 75 cents for 500 millilitres. Despite the high price and minimal promotion their ice cream was a hit. Says Reuben Mattus, ''The only problem we ever had with Häagen-Dazs was keeping up with demand.''

Today, Häagen-Dazs sells for $3.65 per 500 millilitres. In addition, consumers can choose from many other superpremium brands, including Alpen-Zauber, Frusen Glädjé, and Ben & Jerry's. That's not to mention the ice cream sold by Godiva, the famous candy maker, which commands a steep $3.75 for 500 millilitres.

In California, ice cream lovers are lining up to spend $1.50 a *scoop* for Robin Rose ice cream. The price is justified by the quality: Robin Rose ice cream averages 20 percent butterfat, compared to 14 to 16 percent for Häagen-Dazs. The factory cuts up its own fresh fruit and nuts and buys raspberry puree from an Oregon supplier for a sky-high $120 per four litres.

Costs for prime-quality cream, nuts, and other ingredients often come to half the product's retail price. In fact, the best-selling flavour, Raspberry Chocolate Truffle, is so expensive to make that the company sells it for less than its cost as a way to attract customers.

High prices on superpremium ice cream don't seem to deter customers. While sales of regular ice cream were projected to grow at not much more than half a percentage point a year from 1985 to 1990, sales of the superpremium brands were expected to grow by 13 percent a year to more than $3 billion.

As the example of ice cream illustrates, determining a price for a product is more complicated than setting it as low as possible to attract buyers. This chapter explores some of the choices companies make in setting prices for their products.

Sources: Adapted from Michelle Bekey, ''Empire Building with Ice Cream,'' *Working Woman*, August 1986, pp. 37-39; and Lynne Morgan Sullivan, ''Ice Cream's Cold Wars,'' *Sky*, August 1985, pp. 40–42 + .

Basic Considerations in Price Setting

You are a price setter, though you may never have thought of yourself in those terms. As a consumer, you set prices by deciding what you are willing to pay for something and then finding a seller who agrees with that estimation. Of course, finding the point of agreement—the right price—is complicated by many subjective factors.

Have you ever passed up an item in the supermarket because it was 10 cents more than you expected but spent an entire week's budget getting scarce tickets to a concert? Why was one not worth the extra dime, but the other worth purchasing at any price? To a buyer, price reflects the value of the total product, which includes both tangible and intangible benefits. The concert tickets had more **utility,** or want-satisfying power, than the supermarket product and were therefore worth the extra sacrifice of money. Similarly, customers willing to spend $2 a scoop for Robin Rose's ice cream may be satisfying a variety of needs: taste, status, or simply the thrill of wild extravagance on an affordable scale.

Businesspeople see prices from a different perspective. They cannot ignore the want-satisfaction dimension, especially if they belong to a market-oriented firm. But for them, price represents **profit** — what is left over after expenses are deducted from revenue (income). Like consumers, businesspeople must weigh many factors before arriving at the "right price."

In the late 1970s, for example, the major North American automakers decided to lower the prices of some cars on the West Coast and raise the prices of large cars throughout the country. They made these decisions for several reasons. Lower prices on compact cars on the West Coast seemed necessary because the auto market there was particularly over-supplied, especially with Japanese imports. The decision to raise the price of big cars stemmed from government rules regarding gas efficiency. Manufacturers had been forced to make cars smaller and lighter to get better efficiency. But smaller cars did not produce as much profit as did the big gas guzzlers. To offset decreased profit from smaller models, companies made big cars more expensive. They also began offering luxury small cars—compacts with many options—to boost profits.

This example and that of the gourmet ice cream illustrate several important pricing factors. In setting prices, firms must consider: (1) buyer demand; (2) supply and costs; (3) competition; (4) government regulation; and (5) other elements of the marketing mix. Before we discuss these factors, consider first who in a firm is responsible for setting prices.

Who Sets Prices?

Because so many factors must be considered, a number of specialists participate in setting prices. Marketing managers play an especially

Utility
Want-satisfying power of goods or services.

Profit
What remains for a business after expenses are deducted from revenues or income.

important role. Aside from estimating marketing costs, they may also co-ordinate information from other department heads. The controller and production engineer supply cost estimates. The company's attorney and public relations head indicate possible legal and consumer reactions to a proposed price. The economist collects information on how demand will fluctuate in response to various price levels.

In highly centralized companies like General Motors, this information is then given to top executives who make the major pricing decisions. In companies like Du Pont, with many large product divisions, price decision making may be more decentralized.

Top management makes the major decisions, and lower-level employees carry out, or administer, the prices. The latter often have a great deal of freedom in the prices they quote. For example, a clothing manufacturer's sales representative may be allowed to negotiate a final wholesale price with retailers.

Recent studies have shown that pricing is the main source of concern for many top marketing officers in a highly competitive environment, surpassing such obvious areas of anxiety as new product introduction and the competition provided by rapidly changing technology.[1] Price is the only element in the marketing mix that produces revenue; the other elements represent costs.[2] As price is the one variable in the mix that can be changed quickly, it becomes increasingly important that a company's price setters be sensitive to changes in the marketplace. Marketing Today 10.1 describes how the price for lobsters from Nova Scotia plunged dramatically in response to changes in the marketplace.

The Price-Setting Process

The process of setting a price may be compared to the way a sculptor makes a statue. First, the broad outlines appear, and then details are added. The broad outlines are the responsibility of top managers. Their tasks are twofold: (1) to state the company's pricing objectives and policies and (2) to translate these goals into specific prices. Salespeople and others then adjust prices in specific competitive situations. Figure 10.1 shows the main steps most companies follow when setting prices. This pattern is far from rigid. While certain factors—such as fixed costs and

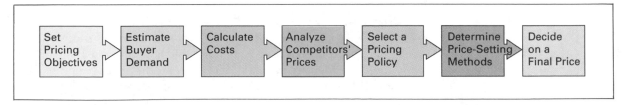

Figure 10.1 The Price-Setting Process

Marketing Today 10.1

Lobsters, Japanese Emperors, and Price

In the 1980s, lobster from Nova Scotia became a delicacy for many parts of the world. In France, the red crustacean from Nova Scotia is the number one food for the family Christmas celebration, and in Japan, fish lovers have added Nova Scotian lobsters to their list of favourites.

In response to this steadily growing demand, the lobster industry became more efficient and perfected technologies to store live lobster for long periods of time in saltwater storage systems. At Clearwater Fine Foods, Canada's largest lobster dealer, some 500 000 kilograms of live lobster are always available in storage tanks located in the Bedford Basin, less than six kilometres from downtown Halifax.

In the spring of 1990, lobster was selling for about $13 a kilogram. By Mother's Day in May of that year the price plummeted to $5.97 a kilogram. Canners — lobsters weighing less than about 450 grams — which had fetched $30 a dozen dropped to $22 a dozen with a free lobster for Mother's Day. One major retail chain, Real Atlan-

Clearwater Fine Foods

tic Superstores, went so far as to sell canner lobsters for $1.39 each or $16.68 a dozen.

What brought about this dramatic fall in prices? In 1989, the death of Emperor Hirohito of Japan put the Japanese into an official state of mourning; as a part of it, the Japanese stopped entertaining and buying gifts and that dramatically reduced the export sales of lobsters from Nova Scotia. At the same time, the lobster fishers had good weather and record catches in the fall of 1989 and the spring of 1990. This filled all of the lobster pounds around the Maritimes to capacity and raised consumers'

expectations for lower prices. The third event was an American law, passed in early 1990, that increased the minimum size of lobster allowed into the United States.

Together these three events led to the dramatic drop in prices. On the Mother's Day weekend, Nova Scotia retailers of lobster saw sales increase by 400 to 600 percent as thousands of local customers lined up to buy the tasty crustaceans at bargain-basement prices.

Source: Adapted from "Halifax Gourmets Pinching Themselves as Lobster Prices Hit Rock-Bottom," *The Globe and Mail*, May 12, 1990, p.A1.

competitors' prices—are usually taken into consideration, setting a final price is often somewhere between an art and a best guess. When a researcher asked a variety of businesspeople how they set their prices, many could not identify anything more formal than "meeting the competition" or "making a fair profit." The process in reality is far from being scientific.[3]

While in practice price setting may not adhere to neat formulas, this chapter explores the various factors that most marketers weigh when determining a price.

Step One: Set Pricing Objectives

As Chapter 2 pointed out, most organizations formulate marketing objectives before devising a marketing program. These objectives give the firm direction but in themselves are not sufficient. Marketing managers should also specify related objectives for each of the four "Ps."

Setting objectives is an especially important step in the area of pricing. Products have failed because managers have neglected to state clearly how pricing should work to support a marketing objective. For example, a food processing firm once set as a marketing objective the production of goods of superior quality. A new product, mustard, was packaged in a crock jar to convey a quality image. But the product failed in test marketing. Its price—49 cents—was the same as that of ordinary mustard. When the price was raised to $1, it finally succeeded in winning consumer acceptance as a quality product.[4] While there is some evidence that high price does not correspond to high quality, consumers do tend to perceive such a relationship.[5] Management could have avoided the initial trouble by specifying pricing objectives consistent with the overall marketing objectives.

Pricing objectives are the long-range goals that managers wish to pursue in their pricing decisions. Most pricing objectives can be grouped into categories relating to profit, sales, maintaining the status quo, or pursuing social goals.

Pricing Objectives
Long-range goals that managers wish to pursue in their pricing decisions.

Profit-Related Goals

Profits are important to a business. They show that a company is doing something right because revenues (money taken in) exceed costs (money paid out).

Economists say that the main objective of business firms is to maximize profits. According to this view, it pays for a company to raise its price just to the point at which a decline in sales begins to have a negative effect on revenue. For example, when Hershey raised the price of its candy bars from 15 to 20 cents, the price hike was a wise move that helped Hershey maximize profits. Sales dropped (that is, fewer people bought at the higher price), but profits remained the same or were slightly better. Why? To make $30 at 15 cents an item, Hershey has to sell 200 candy bars; at 20 cents, it has to sell only 150. As long as the firm sells at least 151 bars at 20 cents, it is better off than selling 200 bars at 15 cents, according to this analysis.

Although profit maximization makes sense economically, it is a difficult objective to pursue. It requires a knowledge of how much demand will fall in response to price increases, and that is difficult to predict.

Also, a firm may find it worthwhile not to maximize profits in the short run as a strategy to gain a large and loyal clientele.

For these reasons, many firms reject profit maximization as an explicit goal. Instead, they speak of gaining a "satisfactory" profit, or a "fair rate of return." The specific level of profits pursued may be expressed as a **target rate of return.** The target is stated as a certain percentage of return on sales or investment. When firms fail to meet their targets, they have some measure of by how much they failed and can take steps to improve their profit. Figure 10.2 shows strategic planning for price.

Target Rate of Return
Goal stated as a certain percentage of return on sales or investment.

Sales-Related Goals

At one time, many firms preferred to state their pricing goals in terms of maximizing sales, not profits. The theory was that high sales inevitably led to high profits. But if the costs of doing business increase more rapidly than sales, profits will decline.

Today, when businesses tie their pricing objectives to sales, they do so more indirectly. A common pricing objective is to increase market share (a company's sales in relation to those of its competitors). A case in point was the competition in the American home computer market during the early 1980s. Texas Instruments tried to gain market share from Atari, Commodore, and Mattel by dropping the price for its 99/4A computer from $950 to $199. Sales soared, and TI took another $50 off the price. But Commodore cut the price of its competing model to $99 and began outselling TI ten to one. TI again cut its price to match Commodore, but its profits had evaporated. In 1983, TI pulled out of the home computer market after sustaining losses of half a billion dollars.[6]

Studies have generally correlated large market share with bigger prof-

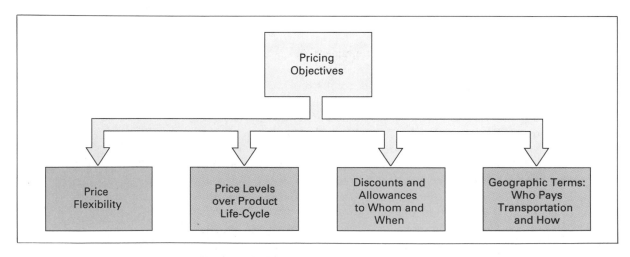

Figure 10.2 Strategic Planning for Price

its. Consequently, firms continue to pursue market share as an objective. At Your Service 10.1 describes how a dry-cleaning business has pursued such a strategy.

Status Quo Objectives

The objective of maintaining the status quo can take two distinct directions. In one sense, firms that maintain a status quo pricing objective merely reflect management's keen interest in avoiding the type of pricing battle in which Texas Instruments found itself. Usually a firm in such a situation finds it is dealing with a market that is not growing. It presumes that an aggressive policy will take market share from competitors and provoke an instantaneous reaction.

By contrast, a firm can maintain a status quo pricing policy but at the same time focus on an aggressive marketing policy that does not include price. Franchises such as Midas Muffler or Mr. Transmission, for example, emphasize their warranties, numerous outlets, and large selection of replacement parts for both domestic and foreign autos. Both firms combine these offerings with a strong advertising program. In this case, these firms may choose to emphasize, in an aggressive manner, one or more of the four "Ps" other than price.

Social Objectives

A number of pricing objectives relate to social goals. Examples include being regarded as fair by customers or trustworthy by rivals. A fair price wins customer loyalty. Repeat sales may ultimately be more profitable than a highly lucrative one-time sale. Similarly, gaining a reputation as trustworthy among rivals may pay off in the long run by avoiding

---

At Your Service 10.1

One Place That Won't Take You to the Cleaners

At Clean 'N Press of Phoenix, Arizona, customers can have any garment dry cleaned for only 99 cents (U.S.). On the opening day at the company's first outlet, so many people were lured by the low price that most of them had to wait at least half an hour.

"I never thought people would wait in line for *dry cleaning*," says owner Robert Gottschalk. His stores provide the same services as other dry cleaners but at prices two to three times lower. When the chain runs its Clean Your Closets promotion, prices drop even further, to 79 cents per garment — and the cleaning load triples.

So far, Gottschalk is optimistic about his low-price strategy. He has expanded his business from one store to nine and plans to open more franchises around the United States. Says Gottschalk, "Discount pricing is powerful."

Source: Adapted from Laurie Freeman, "In Arizona, They'll Stand in Line To Be Taken To the Cleaners," *Advertising Age,* July 21, 1986, p. 44.

market share squabbles that damage the profits of all concerned.

Social considerations are very important in setting prices for some service businesses and for many nonprofit organizations. Universities and provincial governments subsidize the price that many students pay for their education by offering scholarships and student loans. More is said about these pricing situations in Chapter 18.

Step Two: Estimate Buyer Demand

The price a firm may charge for a product depends to a large extent on demand. At the beginning of the chapter we noted that automakers lowered prices on the West Coast because demand decreased. The car manufacturers' response illustrates the **law of demand,** which states that, in general, more goods are sold at a lower price than a higher one. The law of demand holds true only if buyers have a genuine need for a product and the income to satisfy that need. Thus, no matter how low the price of microwave ovens in the Brazilian jungle, demand is not likely to increase where few homes have the electricity or the discretionary income necessary to justify the purchase.

Figure 10.3 illustrates the law of demand. It shows some prices at which a hypothetical automobile manufacturer might offer one of its models and the number of cars people might buy at those prices. For example, at $7500, people would be willing to buy 1 million of these cars. If the company lowered the price to $6000, it could sell twice as many cars. Because the number of cars purchased increases as prices decrease,

Law of Demand
Economic rule that states more goods generally are sold at a lower price than at a higher one.

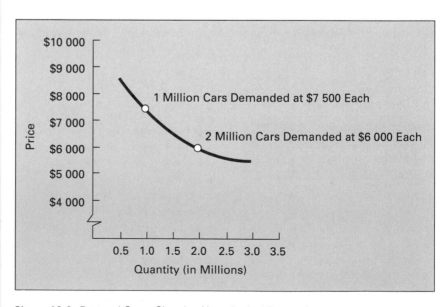

Figure 10.3 Demand Curve Showing Hypothetical Demand

the demand curve slopes downward as it moves to the right. Most demand curves follow a similar pattern.

Marketing managers are not just concerned with the absolute level of demand at each price. They also want to know about the **elasticity of demand** — how fast demand changes in response to price changes. In some cases, the quantity demanded changes very little or not at all when price changes. For example, if a person needs a drug for which there is no substitute, a price increase will not affect demand. In other cases, demand fluctuates a good deal in response to price changes. The market for compact disc players has been growing steadily since the price has spiralled downward. Despite price cuts, manufacturers have increased total revenue.

Chapter 7 discussed demand inelasticity in industrial markets. Variations in a product's price cause relatively little change in demand for the product, because a company buys numerous products for use in producing a good or service. If, for example, car manufacturers have to pay more for upholstery, they can raise the price of cars a little, or they can cut other costs involved in making cars. In either case, the change in the price of upholstery will not have much influence on how much of it the automaker buys. This means that if the upholstery company increases its prices, its revenues also will increase. In general, demand is **inelastic** if an increase in price also increases total revenue or a decrease in price decreases total revenue.

In contrast, **elastic demand** means that a decrease in price will increase the seller's revenues, while a price increase will decrease revenues. Compact disc players are an example of demand elasticity. When the manufacturers of CD players reduced prices, demand rose; the lower price actually increased revenues. Elastic demand can also work in the opposite direction. If tuition at a given school were to double suddenly, many of its students might look for a less expensive alternative. Just as stretching an elastic band causes a pull in opposite directions, so elastic demand causes price and total revenue to move in opposite directions.

In general, the more substitutes for a product, the more elastic is its demand, and vice versa. If frost wipes out an orange crop, causing prices of juice to double, consumers might switch to grape, apple, or cranberry juice until orange juice prices come down again. But the demand for pro football tickets has not fallen off despite price hikes because there are no close substitutes. Keep in mind, however, that demand is inelastic only over a certain range. If football fans had to pay a very steep increase, demand for such tickets would no doubt start falling off.

Step Three: Calculate Costs

Demand is only one of the factors that affect price. Equally important are costs, or how much money producers need to pay out to supply goods or services. Virtually every consumer in Canada would be willing to buy a car at $100. However, no manufacturer could supply them at that price

Elasticity of Demand
Rate at which demand changes in response to price changes.

Inelastic Demand
As it relates to price setting: Relationship that holds between price and revenue if total revenue increases with price rises or decreases with price cuts.

Elastic Demand
Relationship that holds between price and revenue if total revenue increases with a price drop or decreases with a price rise.

because of the costs of steel, labour, machinery, and other elements.

In general, supply curves are mirror images of demand curves. They slope upward as they move to the right. The supply curve for the prices in Figure 10.3 may look like that in Figure 10.4. Figure 10.4 shows that at a price of less than $5000, few cars would be produced because costs would be prohibitive. But at prices above that figure, the number of cars produced steadily increases. At higher price levels, more and more car manufacturers can cover their costs and make a profit.

Costs set a floor on how much will be offered for sale. Producers must cover them over the long run, or they will not market a product. Marketers are concerned with two types of costs—fixed and variable. **Fixed costs** are those that do not vary with a firm's output. Also referred to as *overhead*, these costs include all contractual payments (such as interest, rent, and associated property taxes) and executive and clerical wages. A firm must pay property taxes or make mortgage payments on its facility regardless of whether there is any output.

Variable costs, as the name implies, are costs that increase or decrease with the amount of output. Examples include direct labour costs and the costs of materials and utilities used in the production of goods or services. A restaurant owner who wants to increase business by staying open later will have to buy more food and pay staff for working longer hours (or hire more people). These costs are variable because they change with the number of customers served.

In the long run, businesses must cover all their costs in setting prices or face bankruptcy. As Marketing Today 10.2 illustrates, this is sometimes difficult to do. Besides setting prices high enough, businesses can look for ways to keep their costs under control. To keep up with competitors, most companies try to do both.

Fixed Costs
Costs that do not vary with a firm's output; also called overhead.

Variable Costs
Costs that increase or decrease with the amount of output.

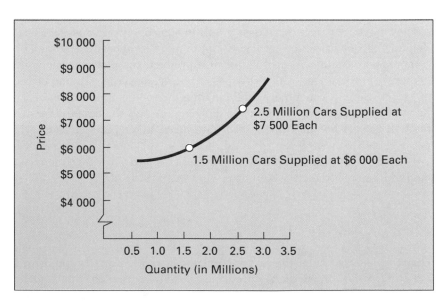

Figure 10.4 Supply Curve Showing Hypothetical Supply

Marketing Today 10.2

Keeping Costs below Profits Is a Struggle for Some

Between 1981 and 1985, costs in the tire industry rose 4 percent, but the prices charged by tire companies *declined* 7 percent. Because buyers are willing to switch among brands of tires, one company cannot charge a higher price than other companies selling similar tires.

To earn a profit in this difficult environment, Firestone tried cutting costs wherever it could. The company closed ageing plants and slashed the number of sizes and brands of Firestone tires. The company also sold off a profitable polyvinyl chloride resins business when it appeared that the business would never become a force in the industry. And Firestone executives pruned management ranks and reduced the number of employees almost by half.

Despite these efforts, Firestone ended its 1986 fiscal year with a profit considered paltry for its revenues.

Stiff competition forced Firestone to pass its savings along to customers, and by 1988 the Firestone company had been acquired by the Japanese tire firm, Bridgestone. By the beginning of 1990 the global tire industry was dominated by six firms, only one of which was North American. Many other producers of commodities — products such as steel and semiconductors that seem indistin-

guishable from one maker to another — experienced this problem during the 1980s.

Source: Ralph E. Winter, "Many Companies Find They Can't Pass Along Rising Costs to Buyers," *The Wall Street Journal,* April 28, 1986, pp. 1, 19; and Jonathan P. Hicks, "Decreasing Demand and Global Competition Propel Consolidation," *New York Times,* February 11, 1990, p.8.

Step Four: Analyze Competitors' Prices

Ideally, companies set prices based on the interaction of supply and demand. Digital watches provide a good example of how action in the marketplace influences price setting. In the early 1970s, digital watches sold for more than $2000. Many companies, seeing a profit opportunity, began producing the watches. As demand for the product increased, supply also increased because more companies entered the field. In the face of increased competition, price cutting began in earnest. The price slipped to below $10. Many companies dropped out of the market because they could not produce at the low cost required.

The digital watch market in the early 1970s exemplifies the workings of pure, or perfect, competition. As noted in Chapter 3, pure competition exists when there are many sellers, no seller dominates the others, and the products sold are interchangeable. In pure competition, any increase in supply results in lowered prices until supply just equals demand. Similarly, increases in demand call forth new suppliers who cover the demand. (Supply and demand reach an "equilibrium point.")

Today, most firms operate in markets in which imperfect competition is the rule. In some cases monopolies exist — one seller has absolute control over the price. More often, firms operate as oligopolies or partial monopolies. An oligopoly, as defined in Chapter 3, is a market controlled by a few firms that tend to set similar prices and make entry by other firms difficult. The five largest cereal companies (Kellogg, General Mills, General Foods, Ralston-Purina, and Quaker) produce most of the cereals consumed in North America and market them at similar prices. In the case of partial monopolies (or more commonly, monopolistic competition), there may be many sellers, and entry into the market may be easy. However, the sellers have more control over the market than under pure competition, and they rarely engage in direct price competition. Most businesses are characterized by this form of competition.

Firms can avoid price competition in partially monopolistic markets because they are able to make their products distinctive in the eyes of consumers. Hewlett-Packard can charge a premium price for its calculators because its models offer special features, the company has a quality reputation, and the target market is mainly professionals who are relatively insensitive to price. Advertising is another way to establish a unique product image and avoid direct price competition. Recall from Chapter 2 that this tactic establishes a differential advantage.

Thus, a company may or may not have to pay attention to a competitor's pricing, depending on the structure of the market. Today, however, even industries with very few domestic competitors are being forced to look at price as a competitive tool as foreign competition becomes more intense.

Step Five: Select a Pricing Policy

Pricing Policies
Pricing plans for dealing with situations in the future that generally recur.

Pricing policies are more specific than objectives and deal with situations in the future that generally recur.[7] A firm whose dominant pricing objective is to maintain an established prestige image may make it a policy to offer goods for sale at only one suggested retail price. Unlike objectives, pricing policies may not be stated explicitly, but they are generally known throughout the organization.

Three important policy-making issues are: (1) whether to offer a product at a single price or many different prices; (2) whether to price at, above, or below the market; and (3) how to price a new product. Government regulations regarding pricing policies must also be considered.

One Price or Many?

One-Price Policy
Policy of offering goods purchased at the same time and in the same quantity at a single price to all.

Before the beginning of the century, almost all prices were determined by bargaining. In many weekend flea markets and garage sales, one can still haggle with sellers to get a price. But, for the most part, shoppers are likely to trade in stores with a **one-price policy.** They offer goods purchased at the same time and in the same quantity at a single price to all.

George Fox, founder of the Society of Friends (Quakers), is credited
with first advocating this policy. He believed that bargaining created
opportunities for deception, which violated his religious principles.[8] His
policy has been adopted not only by retailers, but also by many manufacturers. The major advantages of the one-price policy are that it simplifies transactions, creates customer trust, and simplifies bookkeeping
and forecasts of earnings. One disadvantage is that once a price becomes
well known, competitors may try to undercut it.

A **variable-price policy** allows special prices for different customers.
It is often followed in pricing expensive consumer shopping goods or
industrial products. No two customers are likely to pay the same price
for a new car or a new home. Automobile salespeople try to assess each
buyer's desire to own a particular model. Some customers are ready to
bargain for days, while others cannot be bothered. The salespeople use
this information to make the sale at the highest price they can.[9]

The major advantage of variable pricing is its flexibility. Sometimes
only a little negotiation will result in a major sale. The chief limitation
is government regulation against price discrimination.

Heeding Government Regulations

The government has a powerful impact on pricing. One example of its
indirect influence is gas-efficiency regulations, which have influenced
automotive prices. Government also affects pricing directly, primarily
by outlawing various kinds of variable pricing and other pricing practices believed unfair. Much of this regulation is through the federal
Competition Act. For example, one section of it forbids the sale of articles
of similar quality and quantity to different customers at different prices.
Another section of the Act regulates predatory pricing — setting prices
unreasonably low to reduce or eliminate competitors. A third section
requires that promotional allowances be granted proportionately to all
competing customers.

Another important section of the Competition Act was specifically
designed to prevent **price collusion**, or the joint fixing of prices by
competitors.

Some of the other pricing practices directly affected by this legislation
are:

1. *Continuous sales.* Promotions that involve a continuous sale for a
   substantial length of time have been the subject of prosecution. The
   issue is, what is the regular price if a sale price is advertised for
   several months? In one such case, the T. Eaton Company had advertised mink coats at sale prices for 114 days of the year. The court
   found that the coats were not sold ordinarily at the higher, regular
   price.[10]

2. *Manufacturer's suggested list price.* One means retailers use to
   promote the sale of a product is to compare the price at which they
   are offering it with some other higher price that presumably reflects

Variable-Price Policy
Policy that allows special
prices for different customers.

Price Collusion
Joint fixing of prices by
competitors.

the product's real value. The manufacturer's suggested list price is a price that a manufacturer has indicated may be a proper price at which to list the product for sale. U.S. law permits its use as the advertised comparison price in many cases. The Canadian Competition Act states, however, that "a representation as to price is deemed to refer to the price at which the product has been sold by sellers generally in the relevant market."[11] Thus, the manufacturer's suggested list price may be advertised as a higher comparison price only if most retailers really do use it for that product.

Bait Pricing
Illegal practice of advertising a "special" at a cut-rate price with no intention to sell at the price advertised.

Also forbidden is price deception, which means any false advertising of prices. An example is **bait pricing,** whereby a seller advertises a "special" but has no intention of selling it. That practice, like many others, is also forbidden by the U.S. government, which at one time complained that Sears was following that policy in advertising home appliances. Consumers, lured to the store by bargain prices, were discouraged from buying the specials and talked into purchasing higher-priced appliances.[12]

Price Discrimination
Price cuts that are not offered equally to every buyer.

The issues surrounding **price discrimination** are complex. Basically, the government outlaws price cuts that are not offered equally to every buyer.

Price At, Above, or Below the Market?

In devising a pricing policy, firms have three choices with respect to a competitor's price: they can meet it, undercut the going rate, or price at a higher level.

Price Leader
Dominant member of an industry that announces pricing policies other companies often follow.

In the past, meeting a competitor's price was very common in oligopolistic industries such as steel, automobiles, and oil. Products were very similar and competitors' prices were well known. Any variations set off price wars that lowered profits for all. To avoid the charge of price collusion in such industries, one company usually assumed the role of **price leader,** setting a price that other companies matched. In the flour milling industry, for example, a price rise announcement by Robin Hood Multifoods usually led to similar announcements by other companies. Although price leadership discouraged active price competition, in a way it protected smaller firms by guaranteeing a price at which they could compete. (Leadership pricing is therefore often called "umbrella pricing.")

All this has changed in today's competitive market. For one thing, the United States has extended its definition of price collusion, throwing into question the concept of price leadership in that country, and by extension, in Canada. For another, a recession early in the 1980s meant slower sales and a consequent emphasis on price variations to encourage buying. According to one expert, a firm "should either price above or below the competition—anything to set it apart."[13]

Pricing below the market has become common. For example, small steel companies have cut prices independently of the traditional price leaders.

Pricing above the market is an effective alternative, provided a firm can distinguish its offering in some way. First-run movie houses often charge a premium price. Some convenience supermarkets, such as 7-Eleven and Green Gables, can charge higher prices because they offer round-the-clock shopping. Brooks Brothers shirts are more expensive because the name is associated with superior quality. Godiva could charge — and receive — a premium price for its ice cream because its chocolates had already established the company as a producer of prestige products. (See Figure 10.5.) An identical ice cream by Sealtest probably would not command the same price.

Price hikes have actually increased demand, contrary to the law of demand. In the face of deteriorating sales, Fleischmann's raised the price of its gin $1 a bottle. Sales picked up dramatically.[14] Many customers associate high price with quality, although the relationship does not always exist. One researcher found that there was a positive relationship between price and quality for only 51 percent of the products analyzed. For 14 percent of the products, higher prices actually meant poorer quality. Some of the product categories for which consumers paid more and received less were electric hair dryers, eight-track tape decks, microwave ovens, and electric blankets.[15]

Despite such evidence, many buyers still rely on price as a guide, especially for intangible services. Most consumers, for example, find it difficult to distinguish a poorly prepared tax return from a well-prepared one, or to judge whether one lawyer or dentist is better than another. Because criteria to guide the purchase of services are often lacking, people tend to judge on the basis of fees charged.[16] Just as with goods, though, price is not always a reliable guide to quality. As long as people think such a relationship exists, however, pricing above the market will continue to be used by marketers of goods and services.

Price New Products High or Low?

The previous chapter noted that new products are often priced high, and their price is gradually lowered as they mature. This pricing policy is referred to as **skimming.** The cream of the profit is "skimmed off" at the very beginning.

Sony routinely follows this policy. The company claims to have the largest engineering staff in the consumer electronics industry. It also maintains that only one product in twenty that are developed ever becomes commercial. To support this costly process, the company "sells the first run at the highest price [it] can get without pricing itself out of the market," according to one Sony vice-president.[17] Sony has followed this policy with the Walkman, CD, and Handicam products.

Skimming has three advantages. First, it allows a firm to recover its initial investment quickly. Second, it gives the company a chance to

Skimming
Pricing policy under which new products are often priced high, and their price is gradually lowered as they mature.

Figure 10.5 A Prestige Product at a Premium Price

work out flaws in production before having to meet maximum demand. Third, by establishing an initial high-quality image, skimming leaves consumers with the impression that they are getting a good buy when prices go down. The chief disadvantage is that the high price exposes the product to cut-rate imitators.

Occasionally, to prevent competitors from rushing in, a company will follow a **penetration pricing** policy. The initial price for a new product will be very low to achieve the largest possible market share quickly. Penetration pricing is very popular among retailers, who may offer special low prices at a "grand opening." Their purpose is to build traffic and store loyalty. Manufacturers who expect costs to go down as production increases may also follow this policy. For example, transistor manufacturers foresaw that the most profitable course was in mass production and set an initial low price to stimulate the largest possible demand quickly.

Penetration pricing may discourage competitors from entering a market and builds brand loyalty. But there is one problem. Demand may build so quickly that a firm may be unable to keep up.[18]

Penetration Pricing
Policy of setting initial price for a new product very low in order to achieve the largest possible market share quickly.

Step Six: Determine Price-Setting Methods

Objectives and policies serve as a framework for determining prices. Table 10.1 provides three examples of how objectives and policies mesh to form a pricing structure. Working within this framework, an organization's price setters apply various methods to arrive at a basic price. If the price will be variable, the basic price will serve as a point of departure for negotiating with a buyer.

Table 10.1 Possible Combinations of Pricing Objectives and Policies

Objective	Policy	Advantages	Disadvantages
Maximize short-term profit	Skimming Pricing above the market	Provides funds quickly to cover costs Limits demand until production is ready Suggests higher value in buyers' minds	Attracts competition Discourages some buyers from trying the product
Stabilize prices	Pricing with the market	Requires less analysis and research Causes no competitive ill will	Limits flexibility
Increase market share	Penetration pricing Pricing below the market	Discourages competitive inroads Allows maximum exposure in minimum time	May create more business than production capacity can handle Requires significant investment Small errors may result in large losses

Price-setting methods vary from firm to firm just as objectives and policies do. Some are simple to apply and are used mainly by firms with status quo objectives. Others may require a computer to determine costs and to analyze statistical data regarding demand. The latter methods are more likely to be used by large, multiproduct companies with aggressive objectives. Three methods are discussed here. The first two — cost-plus and markup—determine price solely on the basis of costs. The third —breakeven analysis—can be used in combination with demand projections to arrive at a price figure.

Cost-Plus Pricing

Cost-Plus Pricing
Policy of setting prices by totalling costs and adding a margin of profit.

Firms that use **cost-plus pricing** set prices by totalling their costs and adding a margin of profit. This method is used by contractors, public utilities, most service businesses (such as exterminators and restaurants), and companies whose objective is to secure a target rate of return. In all of these cases, certain conditions prevail:

- Cost figures—but not demand figures—are relatively easy to secure.
- The firm seeks a fair rate of return, rather than maximum profits.
- Price competition within the industry may not be very keen.

Cost-plus pricing may be a poor method when rapid inflation is expected. Costs may rise so fast that a fixed rate of return on investment or a rigid markup may be insufficient to guarantee a profit.

A simple case, showing how costs enter into target return pricing, will demonstrate how cost-plus pricing works. Suppose a company produces only one product — an alarm clock. It will first determine how many clocks it can expect to produce in a year's time and the total costs of that output. Those figures may be 100 000 alarm clocks at a cost of $1 million. The company may hope to reach a target of 20 percent profit over costs (a figure arrived at by looking at industry averages, the company's past profit performance, or some combination thereof). If so, it will calculate 20 percent of $1 million (or $200 000) and add that to its total cost figure.[19] The result ($1.2 million) represents what the firm must take in to operate at its desired level of profit. At 100 000 units, each alarm clock must be priced at $12 ($1 200 000 ÷ 100 000 units) to achieve that target rate of return.

Some Complications

Under the assumptions made in the clock example, cost-plus pricing is simple to apply. In the real world, however, the costs that serve as the basis for price setting are not always easy to specify. For instance, if the clock company manufactures many products — electric as well as mechanical alarm clocks, pocket watches, and wristwatches—total costs for each can be difficult to figure. Remember that total costs are made up of variable costs (labour, materials, and so on) and fixed costs (overhead costs, such as insurance, salaries). If the factory is producing all four products at once, determining the fixed overhead costs for each is a problem. If the company's president is making $95 000, for example, how much of that should be assigned to the making of alarm clocks as opposed to wristwatches? Companies usually have formulas for assigning fixed costs, but the figure can be arbitrary. However, that figure directly affects the final price of each product.

Another complication in cost-plus pricing is that companies occasionally produce a product even though they cannot cover *all* their costs in doing so. The theory is that as long as a company will run up fixed costs, whether it is manufacturing or not, it may as well produce any good that covers variable costs and contributes even a small amount to paying overhead.

Assume a company manufactures three products — tennis rackets, squash rackets, and skis. Only the first two items are profitable. The skis are unprofitable because they cost $50.40 to make ($36 in variable and $14.40 in fixed costs), but they sell for only $40. However, the company may decide to continue producing them because the $40 is enough to cover variable costs and make a contribution of $4 to fixed costs or overhead ($40 price − $36 variable cost). The assumption here is that ending the manufacture of skis will free no additional resources for the production of tennis or squash rackets.

This special type of cost-plus pricing, which allows companies to produce unprofitable items to cover variable costs, is referred to as **contribution,** or **incremental, pricing**. Airlines use this method of arriving at prices when they offer half-price fares at off-peak hours. Rarely do they cover all costs on such flights. However, merely keeping a plane in a hangar adds to costs. Therefore, they will offer the flight as long as they can cover the costs of fuel, flight crew, and other variable costs.[20]

The airlines have encountered some problems in following this pricing method, however. Selling at lower prices in off-peak hours has drained some customers from full-fare flights in peak hours. In effect, the airlines may be merely shuffling customers about rather than gaining new customers by offering lower fares. During the first years of airline deregulation in the United States, from 1978 through 1984, the proportion of airline passengers using discount fares rose from 33 percent to more than 80 percent. Profits suffer from contribution pricing as long as markets cannot be kept isolated.[21]

Other problems with contribution pricing and cost-plus pricing will be considered after looking at another pricing method based on costs.

Markup Pricing

Markup has traditionally been defined as the difference between the cost of an item and its selling price. In modern merchandising, firms generally express this difference as a percentage — the **markup per-**

Contribution (Incremental) Pricing
Special type of cost-plus pricing that allows companies to produce unprofitable items to cover variable costs.

Markup
Difference between the cost of an item and its selling price.

Markup Percentage
Markup expressed as a percentage.

centage. If, for example, an item costs a firm $50 and is sold for $75, the markup is $25; the markup is 33⅓ percent of the selling price. The markup percentage has two purposes. It must cover all the expenses of the firm, including the cost of the item and the cost of selling it to the public. It must also contain an allowance for planned profit.

Figuring a Markup Percentage

A markup percentage is usually expressed in terms of the retail selling price. To determine the markup percentage of the retail price, divide the markup by the selling price. For example, a paperback that sells for $3.00 and costs $2.25 per copy to make has a markup of $.75, or 25 percent of the retail price:

$$\text{Markup Percentage} = \frac{\text{Markup}}{\text{Selling Price}}$$

$$= \$.75/\$3.00$$

$$= 25 \text{ percent.}$$

Sometimes the markup is figured as a percentage of the cost to make the item, rather than as a percentage of the retail price. In the preceding example, the markup would be 33⅓ percent:

$$\text{Markup Percentage} = \frac{\text{Markup}}{\text{Cost}}$$

$$= \$.75/\$2.25$$

$$= 33⅓ \text{ percent.}$$

Whether a firm uses retail price or cost as the base depends on its accounting procedures. The accounting procedures, in turn, depend on the type of merchandise sold. In general, the cost base is used by stores that sell a limited variety of merchandise, such as furniture stores, and those that have a wide range of markup percentages, such as jewellery shops. In any case, a marketing manager should be familiar with both methods of determining markups to set prices.[22]

Choosing a Markup Rate

Unlike manufacturers, wholesalers and retailers seldom attempt to determine fixed and variable costs for each product they sell before setting a price. The reason is simple. A large department store may carry more than 100 000 items. It would be almost impossible to determine such costs for each item. Instead, such businesses use an **average markup**; that is, the same markup percentage is used for each item in a given product line. Hats may have a high average markup (such as 50 percent), whereas books may be marked up only 20 percent. Different types of stores also have different markups. The same bottle of ASA may

Average Markup
Single percentage used to determine the selling price of each item in a given product line.

be found at widely varying retail prices depending on whether it is being sold in a small convenience store or a large discount drugstore chain.

Why do some categories of goods carry higher markups than others? One reason is **turnover,** the number of times average inventory is sold during a given period.[23] Generally, the slower an item moves off the shelf, the higher its markup. A slow-moving item, such as a high-priced necklace, occupies the same selling space and requires the same investment as a fast-selling item such as a book. Thus a higher markup is required on jewellery if it is to contribute an equivalent share to profit. In stores carrying a homogeneous assortment of merchandise, the rate of turnover can also be expressed as an average. For example, if a firm's average inventory is $10 000, and sales for a month (or some other specific time period) amount to $30 000, the turnover is three. A furniture store with a turnover of three times a year, therefore, must make more profit on each item than a grocery store with a turnover of thirty times a year.[24]

Other factors also influence the markup rate. The price level of competition is important. Most intermediaries are aware of what their competitors charge and adjust their markups accordingly.

Markups that vary with competition and other factors are termed "flexible." A cake that normally sells for $1.79 may go for $1.59 on Saturday and $1.99 on Wednesday. Saturday specials are meant to attract price-conscious customers. When an item is priced below cost to attract customers, it is called a **loss leader.** A slightly higher than normal markup for other items or for the same item on a slow day makes up for the loss. The trend among businesses that use markup pricing is to treat the average percentage of markup as a guide only, not as a rigid formula.

Turnover
Number of times average inventory is sold during a given period.

Loss Leader
Item priced below cost to attract customers.

Evaluation of Cost-Plus and Markup Pricing

The chief merit of setting prices on the basis of costs is that the method is convenient. The technique is also easy to apply, even by an unskilled business owner.[25] Buying a product for a dollar and selling it for two dollars is a tempting way to price a firm's products.

Despite its advantages to users, pricing based solely on costs is flawed. Cost-based pricing fails to recognize that there is a two-way relationship between costs and price. The law of demand states that more goods are sold at lower prices. It is also true that the more goods produced and sold, the less the cost of production. It follows that if prices are lower, more goods will be sold, and thus costs should be lower. Price indirectly affects cost.

In effect, both cost-plus and markup pricing ignore demand. Basing a high price on high costs is wrong if costs can be lowered by increasing demand through lowering the price. Marketers, therefore, often use another method of pricing, breakeven analysis, which attempts to consider both demand and costs.

Breakeven plus Demand Pricing

Breakeven Analysis
Way for price setters to determine what will happen to profits at various price levels.

Breakeven analysis is a way for price setters to determine what will happen to profits at various price levels. It, too, is cost based and, when used alone, suffers from the same weaknesses as other pricing methods. However, it is possible to combine figures obtained from breakeven analysis with demand estimates, thereby avoiding the difficulty mentioned earlier. Figure 10.6 explains how breakeven analysis is figured.

Step Seven: Decide on a Final Price

List Price
Selling price quoted to buyers.

By applying the techniques described earlier, firms arrive at a **list price,** the selling price quoted to buyers. However, as anyone who has ever

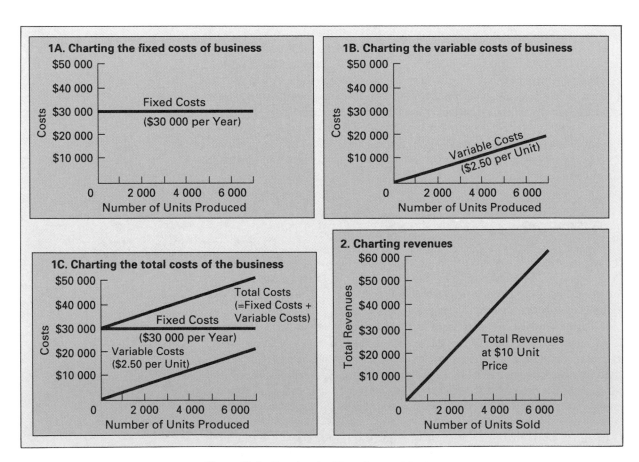

Figure 10.6 Charting the Fixed Costs of Business

Source: David J. Rachman and Michael Mescon, *Business Today* (New York: Random House, 1982), p. 288. Reprinted with permission by Random House.

Figure 10.6 (Continued)

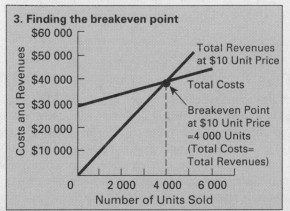

3. Finding the breakeven point

Costs and Revenues

Total Revenues at $10 Unit Price

Total Costs

Breakeven Point at $10 Unit Price =4 000 Units (Total Costs= Total Revenues)

Number of Units Sold

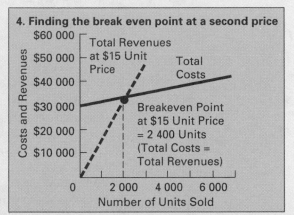

4. Finding the break even point at a second price

Costs and Revenues

Total Revenues at $15 Unit Price

Total Costs

Breakeven Point at $15 Unit Price = 2 400 Units (Total Costs = Total Revenues)

Number of Units Sold

One of the basic questions all businesspeople need to answer is, How many units of my product (or service) will I have to sell in order to break even—that is, to cover costs? And, of course, the question that goes along with that one is, How many units will I have to sell in order to make a reasonable profit? If you don't have a basic estimate of these two figures, you may be out of business before you know it.

The best way to attack these questions is through a method known as a breakeven analysis. Here's how it's done.

1. Charting the costs of the business We have seen that marketing managers have to take two different kinds of costs into consideration: fixed costs (rent, taxes, etc.) and variable costs (supplies, labour). In a small beauty salon, for example, fixed costs might amount to $30 000 a year. Variable costs, such as labour and shampoo for one haircut (with wash and set) might be $2.50. So 10 units would cost $25, 20 units would cost $50, and so on.

To figure out the total costs of operating the business, simply add the variable costs to the fixed costs. Total costs increase with the number of units produced.

2. Charting revenues The next step is to chart the revenues, or payments, the company will receive as it sells more and more units at the price the manager plans to charge. If the beauty salon charges $10 per haircut, its revenues are $1000 for 100 units, $2000 for 200 units, and so on.

3. Finding the breakeven point Next, we put the two graphs together, to show costs *and* revenues. Notice that there is a point at which the line representing revenues crosses and goes over the line representing costs. The point is the **breakeven point**—*the point at which revenues will just cover costs*. Now, to find the number of units the business must sell to reach the breakeven point, just look along the "number of units produced" line at the bottom. Any additional units sold will produce profit for your business.

4. Finding the breakeven point at a second price What if you charge a higher price for your product or service? You will break even after selling a smaller number of units. To find out exactly how many units you will have to sell to break even at your second price, simply repeat steps 2 and 3 using the second price. Here, we have charted revenues and breakeven point at a unit price of $15.

Making a final decision on a price Clearly, each of the two prices offers you certain advantages. The higher price, which allows you to break even after selling fewer units, may be attractive if you suspect that the market for your product or service is limited in your geographic area. At the lower price, you will have to sell more units, but your price may bring in more customers. Which price do you decide on? Here you have to make an "educated guess" about your customers and your product.

bought a new car knows, the price is often negotiable. In general, prices may be modified in response to consumer expectations, or they may be adjusted to gain wholesaler or retailer co-operation.

Discounts

Discount
Deduction made from the list price and offered to wholesalers and retailers.

Discounts are deductions made from the list price and offered to wholesalers and retailers. Discounts come in many forms. Some are special promotional allowances, like free advertising to gain dealer support (see Chapter 15). Others — trade, cash, quantity, and seasonal discounts — mean a reduced purchase price. In theory, discounts are simply cost savings realized by manufacturers and passed on to intermediaries. In practice, they may be special treatment offered to big dealers because of their size. The Competition Act attempts to curb unfair discounting practices.

Trade Discounts

Trade Discount
Reduction to "the trade" (wholesalers and retailers) from list price.

Manufacturers offer **trade discounts,** reductions from list price to "the trade" (wholesalers and retailers), in return for services performed. For example, McCain's wholesalers save the manufacturer the trouble of dealing with the many small grocers who carry the brand. In exchange, the wholesalers, and their retail customers who also perform services for the manufacturer, buy at lower prices.

A typical manufacturer's price quotation to the trade is "list $10 less 30 percent less 10 percent." The price to the wholesaler and retailer is calculated as follows:

$$
\begin{array}{ll}
\$10.00 & \\
-3.00 & (30\ \text{percent}) \\
\hline
\$\ 7.00 & \\
-\ \ .70 & (10\ \text{percent}) \\
\hline
\$\ 6.30 & \\
\end{array}
$$

The wholesaler pays $6.30 and sells to the retailer for $7, who in turn sells to the consumer for $10.

Discounts to the wholesaler and retailer vary according to the function they perform and their profit needs. Retailers, because they perform more functions than wholesalers, tend to require most of the discount. In this example, more than 80 percent of the $3.70 trade discount is given to the retailer.

The Competition Act makes clear that discounts offered to one reseller must be made available to all similar resellers. But interpreting the Act presents some difficulty. Some retailers (such as large chain stores) perform wholesaler tasks such as storage and transportation. Should they be given the wholesaler's as well as the retailer's discount? The answer seems to be yes, provided smaller firms are offered proportional discounts.

Cash Discounts

Reductions from list price made for early payment are called **cash discounts**. A typical cash discount is "2/10, net 30." In this case, the buyer may deduct 2 percent for paying within 10 days of billing, or may pay in full in 30 days. Both the buyer and the seller benefit from cash discounts. A savings of 2 percent on a regular basis can add up for the buyer, and early payment means more cash on hand for the seller. No legal problems arise in offering cash discounts as long as all buyers have an equal opportunity to save. The practice is widespread in business transactions.

Cash Discount
Reduction from list price made for early payment.

Quantity Discounts

Manufacturers sometimes offer **quantity discounts**, a reduction in list price to intermediaries for buying in large volume. Large purchases save the manufacturer money. Less inventory must be stored, and it costs less to do the paperwork for one large order than several smaller ones. Sometimes these savings are passed on to consumers. One merchant in New York, for example, sells Ted Lapidus silk ties for $6.99. (The same tie in the swank Ted Lapidus boutique on Fifth Avenue sells for $55.) How does the merchant do it and still make a profit? "I buy in huge quantities and I pay immediately," the merchant says.[26]

There are two types of quantity discounts. **Noncumulative discounts** are one-time reductions for larger-than-usual orders. (Group fares on airlines are a form of noncumulative discount for consumers.) **Cumulative discounts** permit a customer to total consecutive orders to qualify for the discount. Manufacturers encourage the use of cumulative discounts because it tends to tie buyers to them in the hope of securing a discount.

Quantity discounts are legal as long as the manufacturer can prove that costs are reduced by selling in quantity. Savings are much harder to prove in the case of cumulative discounts because consecutive orders do not lower storage or order-processing costs. Manufacturers may claim that they offer such discounts in good faith to meet an equally low price of a competitor. In the United States the courts have upheld this defence.[27]

Quantity Discount
Reduction in list price to intermediaries for buying in large volume.

Noncumulative Discount
One-time reduction for larger-than-usual order.

Cumulative Discount
Policy that permits a customer to total up consecutive orders to qualify for the discount.

Seasonal Discounts

Manufacturers of boats, air conditioners, and other such goods offer **seasonal discounts,** cash savings for buying out of season. Airlines, hotels, and other service businesses may also offer seasonal discounts for out-of-season periods. The special price helps spread production (or usage of facilities) throughout the year, which can mean savings for the seller as well as the buyer. For example, a retailer who buys a boat in the winter allows the manufacturer to reduce storage costs rather than borrow money at high interest to finance the inventory.

Seasonal Discount
Special price for buying out of season.

Seasonal discounts may come in the form of extended payments. Purchases made in December may not have to be paid for until May, which represents a kind of cash advance to the buyer. Seasonal discounts are legal—provided they are offered equally to all.

Geographical Adjustments

Prices may also have to be adjusted upward or downward, depending on who picks up the transportation tab. Consumers who have shopped in a furniture warehouse know how much prices may differ when the transportation charge is an option. Transportation fees are an important factor in pricing bulky goods like machinery or goods that must travel a long distance. Several alternative price strategies are available to sellers.

FOB Pricing

FOB Pricing
Practice of having the buyer choose and pay for transportation at some point (''free on board''). The buyer takes title at that time.

Manufacturers who send goods FOB ("free on board") follow one of two **FOB pricing** policies—FOB destination or FOB origin. In the first policy, the manufacturer pays freight to the destination. Title and responsibility for the shipment do not pass until the merchandise reaches the buyer. Buyers, of course, prefer the FOB destination terms.

More common terms, however, are FOB origin — the buyer pays for transportation and takes title to the goods from the time they are loaded on board a carrier. The recipient then pays for the freight and makes any claims for goods damaged in transit. Cars and other heavy goods are shipped this way.

Strategically, the choice of destination or origin pricing policies can greatly affect the manufacturer's market range. For example, manufacturers who ship FOB origin may find that buyers will tend to deal with local vendors in order to save freight costs. When freight costs are a large fraction of the final selling price, this may be an important consideration for the buyer of the product.

Uniform-Delivery Pricing

Uniform-Delivery Pricing
Practice of quoting a single price to all sellers regardless of location, reached by averaging the transportation charges of all buyers and adding that figure to the selling price.

For national marketers, one way to compete with local producers is to quote a single price to all sellers regardless of location. Such **uniform-delivery pricing** works by averaging the transportation charges of all buyers and adding that figure to the selling price. Buyers feel that they are getting shipments "free" because they are not aware of transportation costs; however, a Peterborough buyer is actually subsidizing a Vancouver buyer if they both purchase from a Toronto seller. Canada Post engages in uniform-delivery pricing of letters, which is why the practice is sometimes called "postage-stamp" pricing. In business, the practice is followed when transportation is only a small part of the price of goods.

Zone-Delivery Pricing

A variation of uniform delivery is **zone-delivery pricing.** Manufacturers divide the country or their market into two or more zones, charging the same rate within a zone but different rates among zones. The closer a zone to the manufacturer, the lower the price.

Catalogue retailers in Canada all tend to use zone pricing. Catalogues are printed with different prices for at least the main geographic zones of Canada: Atlantic Canada, Quebec and Ontario, and Western Canada. Thus if you happen to move from Toronto to Halifax and try to use your Ontario Sears catalogue to order a dishwasher from your new home, you would be surprised at the higher price you pay. The extra represents the additional freight cost of moving the dishwasher to Nova Scotia from Ontario. There are no restrictions on zone pricing in Canada, even though some buyers end up subsidizing others.

Zone-Delivery Pricing
Policy under which sellers divide the country or market into two or more zones, charging the same rate within a zone but different rates among zones.

Consumer-Related Price Adjustments

Discounting and geographical adjustments affect the prices paid by intermediaries, but sometimes prices must also be modified to meet consumer expectations. The same person who thinks $3.95 is too much to pay for a paperback novel may think $3.75 is acceptable for half a litre of Godiva ice cream. To appeal to consumer preconceptions or needs, price setters use several forms of "psychological pricing."

Price Lining

Sporting goods stores typically sell athletic shoes at prices of $39.95, $59.95, and $79.95. This practice is an example of **price lining,** grouping merchandise into classes by means of price. Wholesalers often use the same tactic in pricing the goods they sell.

According to its users, price lining simplifies decision making for consumers. For example, if standard markups on cost are used, two ties may be priced at $3.39 and $3.85. The range is not wide enough to indicate a difference in quality, so consumers may become confused. By pricing one at $3 and the other at $5, a retailer can establish clear lines of distinction.

Price lining also benefits sellers. It simplifies accounting procedures by reducing the number of prices. Also, retailers do not have to train clerks to deal with quality differences among a wide variety of prices.

One drawback is that price lining may limit the kinds of merchandise a retailer can carry. When a manufacturer's costs go up, so does the price to retailers. A retailer who wants to maintain current price lines may have to look elsewhere for suppliers. However, if a retailer is large

Price Lining
Practice of grouping merchandise into classes by means of price.

enough (like the Sears chain), a manufacturer may tailor its output to match the retailer's price lines.

Customary Pricing

Customary Pricing
Pricing some types of products — usually small-value items — at a certain level to avert consumer resistance at higher levels.

Some types of products must be priced at a certain level or consumer demand drops off rapidly. Such **customary pricing** is common for small-valued items such as candy bars, gumballs, and newspapers. When manufacturers become locked into customary prices, they may try to adapt by changing the size or quality of their products.

Candy manufacturers have become ingenious at this. From 1949 to 1983, Hershey changed the price of its standard milk chocolate bar only seven times, gradually raising it from $.05 to $0.35. During the same time, the weight of the candy bar was altered 32 times within a range of ¾ and 1⅞ ounces. In general, the size of the candy bar at a given price gradually declined. Eventually a larger candy bar would be introduced at a higher price.[28]

Some producers redo the packaging rather than the product itself. Aluminum cans have fallen 35 percent in weight since the 1960s and have become much thinner-walled.[29] The change in packaging may also involve a switch in materials, such as replacing glass bottles with plastic ones or with aseptic packages (which are, in effect, paper bottles; see Figure 10.7).

Manufacturers insist they are not trying to deceive consumers or to squeeze more profit from the items they sell. Inflation drives up their costs. As long as buyers insist on certain prices, the temptation to pare quantity and quality will remain.

Odd Pricing

Odd Pricing
Retail practice of adjusting prices to end with an odd number or just under a round number (for example, $7.99).

Prices are sometimes adjusted to end with an odd number (1, 3, 5, 7, 9) or just under a round number (98, 99). This practice, called **odd pricing,** is common among retailers. One study showed that most retail ads contained such prices.[30]

The custom started years ago among retailers. To prevent clerks from pocketing money from a sale, retailers set odd prices, which forced salespeople to ring up a sale to get change. The practice continues today because most retailers believe that consumers do not round off to the next highest dollar figure and thus think they are getting a bargain. Marketers using odd prices assume they have a jagged demand curve — slightly higher prices reduce the quantity demanded. (See Figure 10.8.) There is little experimental evidence to prove or disprove this assumption. In fact, some merchants think that customers are no longer fooled by prices ending in .99 or .98, so they set even stranger prices. A factory outlet, for example, prices its jeans at $9.86. Why the 86 cents? "When people see $9.99 they say, 'That's $10,'" says the sales manager. "But $9.86 isn't $10. It's just psychological."[31]

THIS IS A ^Recycled JUICE BOX.

So are some park benches we could show you. And road pylons. Pallets. Tree planters. And a whole list of other useful items, now made mostly from wood.

The fact is, juice boxes can now be recycled.

Through a proven new technical process, sponsored in part by Tetra Pak – the leading manufacturer of juice boxes in Canada – empty juice boxes, along with their straws and wrap can now be combined with waste plastics and turned into a sturdy new material called Superwood® lumber. And Superwood lumber can be used to make anything from picnic tables to picket fences.

The Town of Markham, Ontario has already taken the initiative, by adding juice boxes and all plastics to their Blue Box collection program. And Tetra Pak is working to get similar programs adopted in other municipalities right across Canada.

We all have to do our part to improve the environment. It's a commitment we at Tetra Pak have made to ourselves and to Canada.

Juice boxes – because they use so little raw materials to begin with – have always produced less waste than other forms of packaging. Now that they can be recycled, they will produce even less waste. And help conserve our forest resources at the same time.

That means that juice boxes now make even better sense for your family and for your children.

And for your children's children, too.

Get all the facts about juice boxes and our environment. Write Tetra Pak Inc., 200 Vandorf Road, Aurora, Ontario L4G 3G8.

Figure 10.7 A Recycling Advertisement

Conversely, many merchants have adopted an opposite but related tactic to give the impression of quantity or luxury. To connote this image, a quality store may price its offerings at even dollar figures. For this reason, a diamond ring may be priced at $3000 rather than $2999. Whether either approach has the desired effect is a topic for further research.

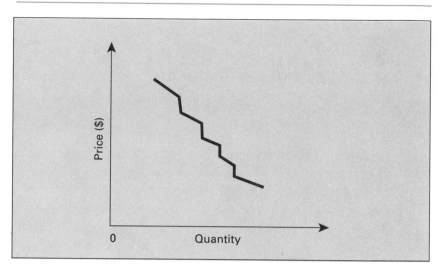

Figure 10.8 Demand Curve When Psychological Pricing Is Appropriate

Chapter Replay

1. **What basic considerations do consumers and businesses weigh in accepting a price?**
    Consumers weigh the utility of a product to them. Businesses consider a variety of objective factors, including demand, supply, costs, competition, government rules, and other elements of the marketing mix.

2. **What steps are typically involved in price setting?**
    In the price-setting process, management sets pricing objectives, estimates buyer demand, calculates costs, analyzes competitors' prices, selects a pricing policy, determines price-setting methods, and decides on a final price.

3. **What objectives do companies try to achieve in price setting?**
    Pricing objectives may include achieving a certain level of profits or sales or a certain market share. They may also include maintaining the status quo and achieving social objectives, such as being regarded as fair or trustworthy.

4. **What are some general characteristics of demand?**
    Demand for a good generally increases as the price falls. In addition, demand may be inelastic (if an increase in price increases the seller's total revenue) or elastic (if an increase in price decreases the seller's total revenue).

5. **What types of costs must sellers cover?**
    Sellers must cover fixed costs, which do not vary with the firm's output, as well as variable costs, which do vary with output.

6. **What are some pricing policies companies might choose?**
    A firm must decide whether to charge one price or several; whether

to price at, above, or below the competition; and whether to price new products high or low.

7. **What methods do companies use to set prices?**
A firm may choose from a variety of price-setting methods, including cost-plus pricing, markup pricing, and breakeven plus demand pricing.

8. **What kinds of discounts might a company offer?**
A manufacturer might offer wholesalers and retailers trade discounts in return for services performed. Reductions for early payment are called cash discounts. Manufacturers may offer intermediaries quantity discounts, which may be cumulative or noncumulative. Companies may also offer seasonal discounts for products used primarily during certain times of the year.

9. **How can companies adjust for location in setting prices?**
Companies can use various price strategies, including FOB pricing, uniform-delivery pricing, and zone-delivery pricing.

10. **How can companies adjust prices to meet consumer expectations?**
Companies can appeal to consumer preconceptions or needs by using psychological pricing. This may take the form of price lining, customary pricing, or odd pricing.

Key Terms

average markup	odd pricing
bait pricing	one-price policy
breakeven analysis	penetration pricing
cash discount	price collusion
contribution	price discrimination
(incremental) pricing	price leader
cost-plus pricing	price lining
cumulative discount	pricing objectives
customary pricing	pricing policies
discount	profit
elastic demand	quantity discount
elasticity of demand	seasonal discount
FOB pricing	skimming
fixed costs	target rate of return
inelastic demand	trade discount
law of demand	turnover
list price	uniform-delivery pricing
loss leader	utility
markup	variable costs
markup percentage	variable-price policy
noncumulative discount	zone-delivery pricing

Discussion Questions

1. Who helps set a company's prices? What role do these people play in the price-setting process?

2. Roger Stonewall is a salesperson at Jake's Furniture Outlet. One day he complained to Jake, "If you would lower the price of these chairs, I could sure sell a lot more of them." What are some disadvantages of Roger's pricing objective? What other kinds of pricing objectives can a business pursue?

3. When the Olympia movie theatre doubled the price of chocolate-covered raisins, sales fell so much that the theatre actually made less money. When the dentist down the street from the Olympia raised her fees, her patient load declined somewhat, but her revenues increased. Other things being equal, what can you infer about the elasticity of demand for chocolate-covered raisins compared with the elasticity of demand for dental care?

4. While he was looking in the newspaper for a summer job, Ray Montana found an ad for delivering phone books. He called and learned that he would have to provide his own car and would be paid a fixed amount for each address to which he delivered a phone book. Ray does not own a car, but his friend Jay will sell him one for $500. What fixed and variable expenses must Ray cover before he can make a profit on this undertaking?

5. What pricing practices are forbidden by law? Describe these practices.

6. Deluxe Software Inc. is planning to introduce a new tax-planning package. What pricing policies might Deluxe use for this new product? Which do you recommend? Why?

7. Under what conditions might a company use cost-plus pricing?

8. At Martha's Bargain World, the markup on a pair of pants is 40 percent. Shoppers at Martha's can buy one brand of pants for $20. What did the store pay for the pants?

9. What is the difference between a trade discount and a quantity discount?

10. Classic Catalogue Creations advertises that it ships its handwoven rugs "anywhere in Canada at no additional charge." Is the shipping really free? Wondrous Office Furniture has a different policy. It ships desks and file cabinets to offices throughout the East Coast. Its terms are FOB origin. What does this mean?

CASE 10.1

Franklin International (B)

In addition to producing plastic bottles for other divisions of Franklin International, the firm's Plastic Division is an extrusion blow moulder and decorator of plastic containers, primarily for the health and beauty-aid market. The division has one Hayssen and five Bekum blow-moulding machines, operating 24 hours a day, seven days a week. The division is capable of producing plastic containers out of high-density polyethylene (HDPE) or polyvinylchlorine (PVC). Customers of the division can buy a completely finished product since the division has equipment to silk screen, hot stamp, or use the Therimage process to decorate and print information on the plastic containers.

Division Promotion

The following information from a promotional brochure for the division describes its marketing offer:

> The Franklin Plastic Container Division is a very specialized custom manufacturer, providing packaging services to cosmetic, drug, and industrial marketers. From one manufacturing location, both containers and decorative requirements are produced in response to specific orders. A collection of standard and custom plastic container configurations and sizes is in continuous production for promotional packaging and market testing of your products. From this standard collection, Franklin provides custom-labelled containers within very short lead times.
>
> Franklin creative structural and graphic design services can also produce unique container shapes and decoration to co-ordinate with your national distribution requirements. Here, Franklin offers a practical range of production options: single and multiple colour silkscreening, hot stamp decoration in metallic colours, and economical multicolored pre-printed Therimage labelling for long production runs. And personal service is part of the Franklin tradition of product excellence in doing business.

Market Segments

There are two product/market segments of the business: private label and national brand. The national brand segment consists of products or a family of related products that go into a well-defined and unified market. National brand accounts consist of nine products, all of which are within Franklin's effective freight area. Products are custom blow-moulded in sizes ranging from 300-millilitre to 2-litre containers with various decorating applications. As a result of research and development, quality, and service, more specialty blow-moulding and new business can be expected in the future.

The private label segment of business consists of products that are close in image to the national brands and also offer a no-frills package emphasizing low prices. Private label accounts consist of 13 products. The division has been able to utilize the distribution department to be cost effective in freight. Stock moulds are used for this segment of the business. Sizes range from 230 millilitres to 1 litre with various decorating applications. Because of multiple-cavity moulds in HDPE, a larger stock line of containers, and conversion to PVC, increased volumes are expected in the future.

Therimage Decorating

One process of imprinting and decorating plastic containers is Therimage. Multicoloured preprinted labels are applied to the containers with special equipment involving heat and a cooling-down process. As part of its marketing planning, management has been reviewing pricing procedures and strategies for the Therimage process.

The fixed costs of running the Therimage equipment, such as salaries, indirect labour, fringes, depreciation, taxes, and transfer costs were estimated at $107 000 per year. Various costs for the process, over and above the cost of the bottle, such as direct labour, fringe benefits, materials, utilities, and supplies, were estimated to be $16 per 1000 bottles printed. Allowing for set-up time, maintenance, and other operating factors, it was estimated that the Therimage process could print up to 20 million containers per year. In checking with prices charged by competitors, division management found that the range was from a low of $17 to as much as $25 to $30 per thousand bottles printed.

Focal Topics

1. What issues and pricing alternatives should Franklin take into account in pricing its plastic containers?

2. Why do you think Therimage prices range from $17 to more than $25 per thousand bottles printed?

3. On average, what prices do you think Franklin should charge for Therimage printing on plastic containers?

CASE 10.2   Hewlett Enterprises (A)

It all began on a cold winter night in eastern Ontario. Scott and Trish Hewlett were playing one of their favourite board games with their two children—Andy, who was 14 years old, and Rosy, who was 12. The family had always enjoyed playing board games together; Scott and Trish both came from families for whom board games and weekends were synonymous. Scott claimed that when he was about ten his family once started a Monopoly game on a Friday evening that he did not finally win until 10 p.m. on Sunday evening.

Problem or Opportunity?

For years Scott had talked about developing and marketing his own board game. He had even sketched out a few ideas and discussed them with other board game fans. As Andy won the game on that winter evening, he remarked: "Dad, maybe you ought to invent your own game, with your own rules. Then you might have a better chance of winning." The whole family laughed, but little did they realize that future events would lead to such an activity.

With a degree in chemical engineering, Scott had worked for 15 years as a laboratory researcher for an adhesive manufacturing firm. A few days after his son's suggestion, Scott found himself out of a job for the first time in his adult life. The company he worked for had lost a major account, and layoffs became necessary. Although his employer was reluctant to lay him off, even temporarily, Scott was let go. A family meeting was held that evening.

There were not many opportunities for Scott in town, given his rather specialized experience. He would receive unemployment benefits, which would help ease the loss of his job somewhat, and Trish still had her part-time position as a special-education instructor with the local school system. The family would be able to get by for a while, but eventually something would have to be done. It was Rosy who came up with the obvious suggestion: why not take this time to develop one of her father's board game ideas?

Making It

Scott had spent the most time on a game idea in which players would move around a board filled with businesses and life situations. The first person to land on one of the businesses could buy it and then collect payments from other players who subsequently landed on it. The business could be expanded by building branch locations, which meant that players would have to pay more if they landed on a business with one or more branches. Each time players moved completely around the board, they received a salary of $7000.

The objective of the game was straightforward—avoid going bankrupt. The payments from people who landed on your business and the salary received from going around the board would be enough, one hoped, to cover expenses as one landed on opponents' businesses. There was one other dimension to the game—life opportunities and problems. Not all spaces on the board had businesses; some contained other activities such as investments ($500 paid to the person landing on the space), contests ("You just won $300"), medical expenses not covered by medicare ("You owe $200"), and postsecondary school tuition ("You owe $100").

Summing the points on two dice determined how many spaces a player would move each turn. If doubles were thrown, the player would select a card from the Life's Little Situations piles. Those cards instruct the player to do such things as: "Your faucet leaks, call the plumber and pay $200," "Your United Way pledge is due, pay $100," "You won a scholarship, take $500," and "You received an income tax refund, take $300."

Scott decided to name the game Making It. The idea was that the winners made it in life; the losers did not make it and went bankrupt.

Pricing Considerations

In its final form the game consisted of a full-colour playing sheet attached to a folded cardboard backing, 500 pieces of play money, deed cards for the 25 businesses, 50 small plastic pieces for "branches," 6 player pieces, a pair of dice, and 50 Life's Little Situations cards. A sheet of playing instructions and a box to hold all of the game items completed the package.

Scott was now faced with the problem of what price to charge for Making It.

Initially, Scott decided that he would do the selling himself and call on local retail stores to get them to carry the game. Obviously, he was concerned about how many sets of the game to produce at the outset, but he realized that economies of scale are such that to produce just a few would be almost as expensive as to produce a thousand. After talking with several printers, plastic companies, and other suppliers, he came up with the numbers in the accompanying table. Several of the people he talked with indicated that they were giving him very special prices in the hope that the game would catch on and that larger orders would come in the future.

Estimated Costs for Producing 1000 Games

Component	Cost
Play money	$140
Plastic pieces	325
Game boards	815
Deeds	115
Situation cards	120
Instruction sheets	45
Dice	110
Boxes	735

Focal Topics

1. What basic pricing strategies could Scott use in establishing his price for Making It?

2. What other "expenses" beyond manufacturing costs should Scott consider?

3. What price do you recommend that Scott charge retailers for Making It? Please support your recommendations.

Case for Part Three

Dylex Ltd.

What stops you dead is the look. The Fairweather store in Toronto's Eaton Centre fairly breathes serious money and haute class. The broad, black-and-grey marble aisle and elegant Greek columns evoke the cold glamour of art deco mansions; the lavish folds of burgundy velvet suggest a film star's boudoir. The mannequins have such a devastatingly icy presence that you scarcely notice what they're wearing. "It's gorgeous," sighs one woman. "It looks like Holt Renfrew."

Welcome to Fairweather, the next generation. The 130-store chain, owned by troubled retail giant Dylex Ltd., used to sell fun fashion; hip, low-priced, seasonal throwaways snapped up by trend-conscious teens and style-hungry secretaries. But there are 600 000 fewer teens today than a decade ago. The boomers — the original Dylex clientele — are getting older, and all of them want to dress *up*. The executives at Dylex finally got the demographic message: Fairweather needed a new image.

The result is a $1 million facelift, a fantasia of marble, chrome, velvet and gleaming wood. And the clothes? Well, call them *material working girl*. "It's the same cheap stuff they've always sold," says a woman passing through. "The buttonholes are frayed and these seams are puckering. And the cloth on these blazers is really thin."

New Product Strategy

In retailing, as in other businesses, the product is much more than the merchandise being sold. The product includes store location, interior decor, the sales staff, and the quality of service, as well as the items offered for sale. The Fairweather strategy of combining uptown decor with middle-rent fashion is deliberate. Secretaries read Danielle Steel and yearn to be rich but their paycheques don't stretch very far. Fairweather will give them their dreams, at least for the half-hour they go shopping. "Why can't the working girl making $20 000 or $30 000 a year be surrounded by the luxury of the very wealthy woman?" asks Lynn Posluns, the highly stylish 32-year-old president of Fairweather.

Source: Material presented here has been adapted from Michael Salter, "On the Rack," *Report on Business Magazine*, February 1990, p. 54; and Jan Matthews and Greg Boyd, "Can Lionel Robins Rescue Dylex?" *Canadian Business*, November 1990, p. 106.

Lynn Posluns understands the very wealthy woman. She is one. Her father is Wilfred Posluns, the tough, secretive multimillionaire who is the chairman, chief executive officer, president, and co-founder of Dylex. Lynn is the rising star of her father's company. She's overseeing the Fairweather repositioning and she's gambling that lots of secretaries will fall for those velvet drapings, that rich marble, those cool columns—that look.

Dylex has more than money riding on Lynn Poslun's expensively padded shoulders. The Fairweather revamp — coming soon to a mall near you—is designed to show that Dylex can still conjure a retail miracle, just as it used to do. But if the miracle fails, one thing is certain: Lynn Posluns won't be the one out of a job.

The Dylex Family

Wilfred Posluns is an intensely private man dedicated to two things: his family and his company. His two loves are closely intertwined. Posluns and his elder brother Irving, who runs one of the Dylex clothing manufacturing companies, own the majority of Dylex's voting shares. Poslun's three children, Wendy, Lynn, and David, are all involved in the company. Wendy, the eldest, is a lawyer and sits on the board of directors. David, 30, is president of the Club Monaco chain in the United States. The way Wilf Posluns sees it, any threat to Dylex is a threat to his family's well-being.

Problems and Opportunities

Wilfred Posluns has a whole plateful of problems. He's locked in a bitter court battle with Jimmy Kay, his former friend and partner, for control of the company they co-founded in 1966. And Posluns and Kay's disastrous acquisitions in the United States—the worst moves in Dylex's history—continue to bleed money. Before the red ink is stanched, the company will have lost well over $200 million. But what galls him most is that Dylex, once Canada's red-hot retailer, has lost its touch. And it will be years before the picture improves. "They don't have much momentum at all," says a retail consultant. "They had their best year in 1985. Since then, they seemed perplexed about what to do next." If his family didn't control the company, Wilfred Posluns would probably be history.

Dylex is still king of the mall, with 1350 stores in Canada under such names as Braemar, Town & Country, Tip Top, Harry Rosen, Thrifty's, and Bi-Way. About $1 in every $10 that Canadians spend on clothes goes into a cash register in a store in one of the 15 retail chains owned by Dylex. But the profits are slipping. In 1988, Dylex earned $30 million on revenue of $2 billion, compared with a profit of $47 million on revenue of $1.6 billion three years earlier. The market segmentation Dylex pioneered—separate chains for different age, style, and mass market income groups—is old hat. This is the age of high-concept retailing, where stores project a picture of a way of life consumers would like to enjoy, and consumers buy image, shopping environment, and merchandise in equal parts.

The competition is stores such as Randy River and Willow Ridge, which sell a hip, global-traveller image, and the clothes to match. Dylex is stuck with Suzy Shier, a retrograde *bimboesque* name from the '60s. The competition is Brettons, a hugely successful chain that sells Ralph Lauren-style clothes for the whole family with terrific service. Dylex is still pushing unisex at Thrifty's, years after the concept went the way of shag haircuts.

The mass market for retail clothing is fragmenting fast. The new buzzword in the rag trade is *micromarketing*. "That," says retail researcher Len Kubas, "means designing the store and stocking merchandise to appeal to customers in the immediate neighbourhood. That works against the mass-market chain retailer. The big chains are just not geared to buying that way."

Company History

It was so much simpler back in the 1960s and 1970s, when Kay and Posluns made retailing magic through potent blend of entrepreneurial dynamism and corporate organization. The two men brought up a raft of chains operating in different segments of the mass market. They left in charge the people who had started them, with huge performance bonuses as incentives. Dylex was a silent partner offering efficient, centralized services such as warehousing, shipping, computers, financing, and real estate. Its 10 manufacturing divisions made many of the clothes the chains sold.

Together Posluns and Kay saw the future of retailing and its name was *shopping mall*. With their dozens of specialty stores, the malls broke the stranglehold the department stores had on shoppers. "We made the decision right from the start we'd go into every regional mall in Canada that had two department stores, no matter where it was, with all our chains," Posluns says. In return for renting so much space, Dylex got long leases at good rates, prime locations, and financial help in building the stores. "Essentially, we were a department store with our departments spread down the spine of the mall," says Kay.

For years, Posluns and Kay relied on the market smarts of their chain operators to keep the company nimble. Dylex was an association of partners; it was never as tightly directed as outsiders believed. "Our roles were to communicate with the chains and watch the bottom line," Posluns says. "My attitude was, 'You've built the chain, you run it.' I never got involved."

Problems in the 1980s

The formula worked, until the mid-1980s, when retailing hit the skids. Mall rents skyrocketed, the competition among the increasing number of specialty stores got ugly, and the women's apparel market, where Dylex does 40% of its business, dissolved into confusion. The company got stuck in a rut, unable to react to the changing mass market. There were fewer young women buying clothes, yet Dylex had three chains—Fairweather, Suzy Shier, and B.H. Emporium—competing for the same shrinking market.

Dylex fumbled new ventures. Harry Rosen Women flopped. Dylex then bought Rubys, which operated 54 high-fashion shoe stores for women under four different names. That, too, was a disaster, and the stores were sold.

As its chains matured and retailing grew more complex and less profitable, Dylex failed to respond. Success had bred complacency. Added to that, the men at the top had their minds on other matters. Posluns admits that Dylex has fallen behind in computer technology, merchandising, marketing strategies, even advertising techniques. "There are a lot of things we've recently started looking at that we didn't pay enough attention to before," he says.

Expansion to the United States

Like most partners who were once close, Kay and Posluns were loath to call it quits. If they gave it one more shot, maybe things would work out. In this atmosphere of hope and mistrust, the two men took their biggest gamble: they announced that Dylex had run out of expansion opportunities in Canada and would go south of the border. That was only partly true. "By going into the United States, Jimmy and I were trying something new," Posluns says. "It reminds me of a couple that has a child to save a marriage."

Posluns and Kay started off cautiously, buying control of two small retail chains in 1984. Then, only months after entering an intensely competitive market in which adventurous Canadian retailers have invariably lost their shirts, Posluns and Kay jettisoned their financial conservatism. They borrowed heavily to buy into a $450 million joint acquisition of Brooks Fashions and T. Edwards, two medium-priced women's clothing chains. The following year they purchased a 600-store chain called Foxmoor aimed at the teenage market, and became the proud co-owners of 1500 stores across the United States.

It was a high-risk move, quite out of character for the two men. They may have been dazzled by their big-name partners. Posluns and Kay had teamed up with AEA Investors Inc., a high-powered acquisitions and leveraged-buyout firm whose funds came from a group of very wealthy executives, men such as the former chairmen of American Express and RCA. "They were supposed to be the leveraged-buyout experts," grumbles Posluns. Kay allows that "we didn't spend enough time taking a close enough look. The management of the chains looked good, but it wasn't. We didn't do enough homework."

And so they failed. Soft sales across all three chains meant that interest costs were impossible to meet. Posluns was soon spending part of every week in New York trying to turn things around. In 1987, after two years of losses, Dylex wrote off its $118 million investment in Brooks and T. Edwards and placed the two chains in bankruptcy. Posluns spent two more years and another $100 million trying to turn around Foxmoor. He gave up in the summer of 1989 and announced that these stores would be sold or shut. "It was a terrible five years," Posluns says, "A fiasco." Dylex's U.S. stores were a black hole into which more than $200 million had disappeared.

The fiasco cost Dylex's Canadian operations their momentum, and Posluns knows it. "We should have started changing things in Canada four or five years ago, because the old way wasn't working anymore," he says. "Part of the reason we didn't was that I was so busy trying to make things work in the United States. Then there was the fighting between me and Jim. Things started happening to us, instead of us being in charge of our own destiny."

New Management Structure

Posluns was too distracted to recognize that if Dylex was going to regain its former glory, it needed a new management structure. It took a beating in the U.S. market to make him realize that he's not a retailer (something Posluns's senior managers have known all along) and Kay's departure to show him that he can't direct a $2-billion conglomerate by himself. Until 1989, Dylex didn't even have a squad of merchandisers to chart the company's course. The vice-presidents in charge of the chains ran their own shows and reported directly to Posluns. "Jim and I were the only people doing strategic level thinking," he says.

Posluns broke the logjam at the top, freeing key chain-store executives from day-to-day operations and forming a nine-member executive committee of vice-presidents and heads of divisions in charge of strategic planning. Top managers like Don Evans, Gord Edelstone, and Irving Teitelbaum immediately set to work on repositioning Dylex's stores and forcing up profits. Dylex's new president, Lionel Robins, was promoted from his position as executive vice-president of womenswear to run this committee. Chairman and majority owner Wilfred Posluns has handed Robins the task of utterly transforming the way Dylex does business.

Focal Topics

1. What do you see as the basic marketing problems facing Dylex Ltd.?

2. What type of marketing research would be helpful to Mr. Posluns and his management team in marketing their stores?

3. What kinds of product extensions and product expansions should Dylex consider?

4. Do you think it is wise for Dylex to change the marketing of their Fairweather stores? Please support your recommendations.

PART FOUR

Murphy's

Placement Strategy

Chapter 11

Channels and Wholesaling

In this chapter, you will learn:

- How marketers make a product available to users.

- How intermediaries serve consumers and producers.

- The decisions marketers make in designing marketing channels.

- What marketers consider in deciding on a channel length.

- Reasons some companies use multiple marketing channels.

- The basic kinds of channel members.

- A firm's choices for how much market exposure a product should have.

- How conflict in channels is controlled.

- Why organizations create vertical marketing systems.

Channel Decisions: The Evolution of a Channel System

Unox Foodservice of Weston, Ontario, manufactures the Shopsy's and Hygrade brands of frankfurters. Refrigerated meats have a shelf life of just over 28 days. Since foodservice distributors were not able to work within the time constraint posed by the short shelf life, direct shipping from plant to each restaurant became necessary.

By 1987 Unox was shipping directly to over 10 000 foodservice establishments in Ontario and Quebec. The escalating costs of fleet-truck operations combined with low volumes per outlet forced Unox to offer frozen frankfurters and convert their customers to distributors. In Quebec, however, they encountered strong resistance to a frozen product. Thus, in 1987, in an attempt to satisfy both the needs of the manufacturer and those of the restaurant owner, the Shopsy's frozen product was introduced to Quebec as the distributor brand, while the fresh Hygrade product remained the direct delivery brand.

Within a few years 100 percent of the Ontario foodservice frankfurters were reaching the restauranteur through distributors in a frozen state. In Quebec, 60 percent of the two brands were sold through distributors. Plans are for the remaining direct business in Quebec to be converted to distributors since they are quickly improving their effectiveness in handling

refrigerated meats with a short shelf life. By the end of 1991 foodservice distributors will handle 100 percent of distribution for Unox Foodservice.

Marketers are faced with decisions like this every day. Every product must follow some path from the producer to the consumer. This chapter discusses some of the decisions marketers make in planning for and managing such paths.

Source: Unox Meats Canada Inc., Foodservice Division, Weston, Ontario.

P roviding goods and services when and where they are needed is the subject of the next three chapters. This business activity is known in marketing as **distribution**.

Consumers often take distribution for granted because the goods and services they desire are usually readily available. It is no longer unusual to find kiwis, fresh strawberries, or even roses in the local supermarket during the cold Canadian winters. The consumer rarely considers the complex route Japanese television sets, Italian leathers, and Norwegian wools take to reach the Canadian marketplace. But marketers must design strategies that efficiently link buyers with sellers.

What Is a Marketing Channel?

The individuals and organizations involved in making a product available to a user form a **marketing,** or **distribution, channel.** (The channel of distribution is also called *channel* or *trade channel*.) It is the route that a product or service travels as it moves from the manufacturer to the ultimate consumer. Apples, for example, follow a marketing channel from apple growers to apple eaters. Even services have marketing channels. Airlines and resorts use travel agencies to sell tickets to travellers.

Notice that both producer and consumer are members of any marketing channel. In fact, the minimum marketing channel is one seller and one buyer. More typically, a marketing channel also includes various intermediaries. **Retailers** are intermediaries who sell directly to consumers while **wholesale intermediaries** sell to other sellers *or* industrial users.

The basic transaction in a simple marketing channel is the exchange of ownership, or title, of goods. The physical movement of goods is often involved in a transaction, but it is not necessary — think of real estate purchases. Return payment is usually in the form of money, but this is not always the case. Pizza Fantasy Inc., of Toronto, which markets pizza in the Soviet Union, uses a form of barter to realize profits. Soviet customers pay for pizza using rubles. But the ruble is a nonconvertible currency, one that cannot be exchanged into another currency. So PFI purchases hotel rooms using its ruble profits and then resells the accommodations to Canadian and American travel agencies and travel wholesalers in return for hard (convertible) currency such as dollars.

The activities described in Table 11.1 must be performed by someone in the channel system. A manufacturer may choose to do them all internally and maximize control. Alternatively, the producer may employ the services of intermediaries to perform some or all of these functions. The selection of marketing specialists to get the product efficiently to one's target market is an important decision.[1]

Table 11.1 The Functions of Intermediaries

Transactional Activities
- Buy products from sellers and create assortments for buyers
- Promote products to customers in various ways
- Absorb risks of product ownership (inventory, obsolescence)
- Price products for resale
- Standardize transactions

Physical Activities
- Store the products
- Transport products from producers to consumers
- Sort and package products
- Break bulk products into smaller quantities
- Service and repair

Facilitating Activities
- Assist with customer financing
- Grade product quality and label accordingly
- Provide market information
- Counsel customers on product use and maintenance

Source: Adapted from Kenneth G. Hardy and Allan J. Magrath, *Marketing Channel Management: Strategic Planning and Tactics* (Glenview, IL: Scott Foresman and Company, 1988), p. 4.

Are Wholesale and Retail Intermediaries Useful?

From time to time, a public cry goes up to "eliminate the middleman." When the price of coffee skyrocketed in the mid-1970s because of crop failures in Latin America, intermediaries were accused of making a bad situation worse by raising their prices. The basis for such views is not hard to understand. Goods that go through marketing channels are in no way physically changed as they pass through several intermediaries, and yet these intermediaries add to the cost.

Are Channels Really Necessary?

If intermediaries did not exist and it was necessary to purchase all goods and services directly from the producer, consumers would have to give up a great deal of what they have come to expect. Many functions must be performed as goods move from manufacturer to ultimate consumer. They can be grouped into three types of activities—transactional, physical, and facilitating—which are reflected in Table 11.1.

To understand how useful these activities are to consumers, consider a case in which they have not been performed. A student taking a marketing course has to buy this textbook directly from the publisher because all the local bookstores have gone out of business.

Unless our student lives in Toronto, where the publisher is located, he or she must fly, drive, or take a train there. Unfortunately, the publisher sells only the marketing book needed, not the textbook required for an accounting course—or notebooks or pens. Our student pays cash for the textbook and heads back to campus. On arrival in class, the instructor announces that students should have purchased study guides to go with the textbooks. This means another trip to Toronto to obtain the study guide.

Our consumer has had to perform many of the jobs that intermediaries usually assume. Marketing intermediaries, particularly retailers, serve consumers by:

1. Bringing together a wide assortment of goods. A typical campus bookstore sells textbooks for all classes, other books of interest to students, notebooks, pens, and other supplies.

2. Placing that assortment in a convenient (that is, time-saving) location. A campus bookstore is located in or near the school it serves. (See Marketing Today 11.1.)

3. Providing credit, and therefore the use of goods or services at the time they are needed. If our student had not had the cash to buy the required books, most stores would have accepted a credit card.

4. Offering money-saving services (such as delivery, alterations, sales help, and so on). A campus bookstore could have special-ordered the study guides the professor had neglected to mention.

5. Giving consumers the desired product in the desired quantity. Our student needed only one copy of this textbook, not ten copies, which might be the minimum order quantity supplied by the publisher.

Creating Utility for Consumer and Producer

Producers as well as consumers benefit from the existence of intermediaries. First, wholesaling intermediaries and retailers help simplify

Marketing Today 11.1

Who Pays for Convenience?

Convenience does not come without added cost. John Winter Associates of Toronto reported after a recent survey that 60 percent of the basic commodities found in convenience stores cost at least 10 percent more than in supermarkets and that 20 percent of these items cost at least 25 percent more.

The study identified the typical convenience store customer as

- A poor person. Poor people do not have ready access to transportation and so may have difficulty getting to a supermarket.

- A rich person. The wealthy have the money but lack the time to shop where it's cheaper.

- Someone who likes to pick up things in small quantities and so would save less in supermarkets.

Source: Adapted from "Who Pays for Convenience?" *Small Business*, July/August 1990, p. 44.

contacts between producers and consumers. Figure 11.1 represents a simple market consisting of four buyers and four sellers. In the upper panel, each buyer contacts each seller, so sixteen contacts must be made. The lower panel illustrates the efficiency of having an intermediary: the number of necessary contacts is reduced to eight. The full impact of the efficiency principle does not show in this trivial example. Imagine the chaos that would exist if intermediaries were not present in large urban centres such as Montreal, Edmonton, Calgary, and Vancouver.

Intermediaries also help producers financially. In some cases, they save manufacturers the cost of carrying inventory in warehouses, thus

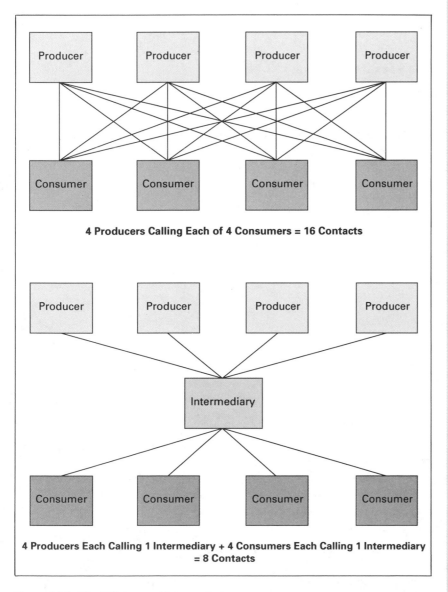

Figure 11.1 The Efficiency of Intermediaries

freeing funds that can be used for other business purposes. Some intermediaries finance the operations of producers of seasonal goods, such as air conditioners or skis, by ordering and paying for goods during slack times. Finally, intermediaries who purchase goods relieve manufacturers of some of the financial risk they might suffer if their goods did not sell.

One other function that intermediaries perform for producers is the communication of marketing information. Cities with convention bureaus often serve as intermediaries for the hotel industry. They solicit convention business and then let industry members know that a group will be in town so hotels can make arrangements. Retailers offer the same service to manufacturers (and wholesaling intermediaries to retailers) by letting them know what items are selling well.

The Transfer Principle

Transfer Principle
Principle that all functions of the marketing channel are vital and when not performed by one channel member must be taken over by another.

The **transfer principle** states that all of the functions of the marketing channel are vital and when not performed by one channel member must be taken over by another. In a two-channel system involving just a producer and a buyer, the producer absorbs some functions (such as financing or providing marketing information) and passes others to buyers (such as transporting goods or providing services for themselves). The use of one or more intermediaries allows the burdens to be shared by more parties.

Channels of distribution bridge gaps (see Table 11.2) to create the four kinds of utility discussed in Chapter 1:

1. Form utility.

2. Time utility.

3. Place utility.

4. Ownership utility.

In today's competitive global marketplace, producers of goods and services are becoming more and more specialized. Focusing on the production of fewer items improves efficiency. The firm has fewer resources available for the activities needed for direct exchange of goods and services with the consumer. It is more efficient to use intermediaries that specialize in the services which they provide. This is the theory of *efficiency of exchange*.[2]

The major tasks facing marketers specializing in distribution are to design marketing channels that ensure goods reach a market efficiently and to manage problems that arise within the channels.

Forward and Backward Channels

Most channels organize the forward movement of goods — from manufacturer to end user. Yet there are also backward channels directing the

Table 11.2 How Channels of Distribution Create Utility, Filling Gaps between Producers and Consumers

Form Utility	Time Utility	Place Utility	Ownership Utility
Quantity Gap ▪ bulk breaking ▪ packaging Assortment Gap ▪ grading ▪ providing assortments	Time Gap ▪ storage ▪ inventories ▪ warehousing ▪ financing ▪ order taking ▪ expediting	Spatial Gap ▪ transportation ▪ materials handling ▪ delivery	Knowledge Gap ▪ promotion and information dissemination ▪ feedback and information gathering Ownership Gap ▪ buying and selling ▪ credits ▪ collections ▪ financing ▪ passing title ▪ servicing

Source: Adapted from Kenneth G. Hardy and Allan J. Magrath, *Marketing Channel Management: Strategic Planning and Tactics* (Glenview, IL: Scott Foresman and Company, 1988), p. 5.

movement of goods from the consumer to the producer. They are necessary for products that may require regular servicing, such as automobiles. Any defective merchandise returned to a factory for repair or replacement moves through a reverse or backward channel.

Firms' adoption of the societal marketing concept has introduced some new backward channels. For example, the issue of environmental protection, combined with increases in raw material costs, has created opportunities for recycling companies such as Superwood Ontario Ltd., which collects multimaterial Tetra Pak drinking boxes discarded through the Blue Box program. Here we see waste products from the consumer being returned to the manufacturer, where they are combined with a mixed-plastics waste stream in a mould to form Superwood a plastic "wood" product used in benches and highway markers.[3]

Designing Marketing Channels

Why does Revlon sell its products through retail stores, while Avon has representatives who sell directly to neighbours and co-workers? Why can you buy a Michelin tire in an auto supply store and the same tire, under a different brand name, in a Sears store? Why can Hanes panty hose be found only in department stores, while L'Eggs are available in almost every supermarket and drugstore? The answer to all of these questions is that marketers have made certain decisions about the way a product can best be distributed. The manufacturer often controls these

Channel Length
Number of links (intermediary types) in a particular marketing chain.

Channel Number
Quantity of different marketing channels used to reach buyers.

Channel Member Type
Kind of wholesaling intermediary and retailer in a marketing channel.

Channel Width
Number of outlets or individual firms employed at each level in a channel.

decisions, but as discussed later in the chapter, other channel members can also take on the role of policy maker for the channel. The four principal decisions concerning channels are:

1. *Channel length:* whether to use wholesaling intermediaries, retailers, or some combination.

2. *Channel number:* how many different marketing channels to employ.

3. *Channel member types:* what kinds of wholesaling intermediaries and retailers to bring in.

4. *Channel width:* how many outlets or individual firms to employ at each level of the channel.

None of these decisions can be made without considering the other elements of the marketing mix. A closer look at the four principal channel decisions will make clear that product and price are not the only factors that determine how a product will be distributed.

Channel Length

There are important differences between the channels of distribution used for consumer and industrial products. Industrial products usually move through fewer channels than do consumer goods. Figure 11.2 displays the typical channels involved in distribution for each market.

Each intermediary that performs one or more functions in the distribution channel bringing the product to the ultimate consumer is known as a channel level. The producer and the ultimate consumer are part of every channel. The number of intermediary levels defines the length of a channel. There are four different channel lengths for consumer goods and three different channel lengths for industrial goods. The latter involve two different kinds of channels each having one intermediate level.

Channels for Consumer Goods

Consumer goods commonly go through a two-level channel employing both wholesalers and retailers. Almost all convenience goods—including food, tobacco, and nonprescription drugs—come through such a channel. Imperial Tobacco, for example, uses wholesaling intermediaries to distribute its cigarettes to the thousands of candy and grocery stores, newsstands, and vending machines that carry them. The same wholesalers also distribute other firms' cigarettes, saving retailers the bother of having to deal with sales representatives from each company.

Occasionally, consumer products go through a three-level channel. Retailers are supplied by two wholesale links, only one of which takes title to the goods. For example, some frozen foods are first handled by a food broker whose job is to find other wholesale buyers for the products.

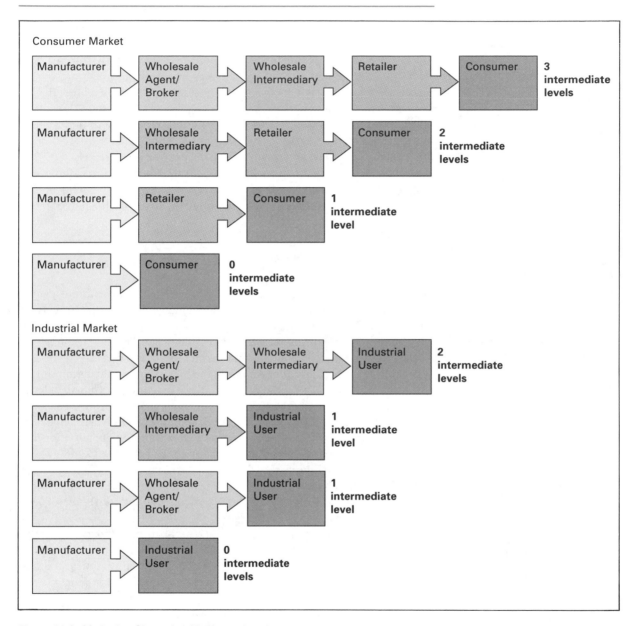

Figure 11.2   Marketing Channels of Different Levels

Source: Adapted from Richard R. Still, Edward W. Cundiff, and Norman A.P. Govoni, *Sales Management: Decision, Policies, and Cases*, 3rd ed. (Englewood Cliffs, N.J.: Prentice-Hall, 1976), p. 44; and from Philip Kotler, Gordon H.D. McDougall, and Gary Armstrong, *Marketing*, Cdn. ed. (Toronto: Prentice-Hall, 1988), pp. 299–300.

Brokers specialize in selling to other intermediaries who transport and warehouse the goods.

Another important channel is the one-level consumer channel that uses only retailers. Automobiles are sold through this channel arrangement because dealers also provide service. Clothing and other goods that may quickly go out of fashion also require this short channel.

An increasingly popular route delivers goods directly from the producer to the consumer. For example, Creative Kids, of Mississauga, Ontario, which manufactures educational toys, reaches the consumer with a direct selling approach in the form of parties (the kind pioneered by Tupperware).[4] This level of personal service cannot be matched by stores.

Direct selling is also characteristic of manufacturers with factory outlets and small businesses such as bakeries. In addition, almost all banks, insurance companies, and other sellers of services deal directly with the consumer, although that is changing. For example, banks now use employers as intermediaries for the direct deposit of pay cheques, and insurance companies such as Allstate sell insurance through department stores such as Sears.

Channels for Industrial Goods

Most industrial goods go through fewer channels than consumer goods. In fact, direct selling is by far the most common channel in industrial marketing. Almost all the components of an automobile, for example, are sold directly to car manufacturers. In general, all high-volume transactions between large suppliers and large buyers are direct.

A wholesaler, usually called an *industrial distributor*, may be employed when the unit price of a product is small. For example, Century Tools and Machinery, of Scarborough, Ontario, has grown since 1981 to become the largest stocking distributor of tooling components in North America. By specializing, rather than becoming a general industrial supplies distributor, Century Tools is able to offer a huge selection backed by engineering support with same-day delivery. With an inventory of more than $1 million in drill bushings in its Scarborough warehouse, Century Tools has expanded its coverage of the Canadian marketplace with new offices in Quebec and British Columbia.[5]

Occasionally, wholesaling intermediaries who do not physically handle or purchase goods may be used instead of industrial distributors or in addition to them. Such intermediaries act as a manufacturer's sales force. Some of them specialize in selling highly technical products, such as large industrial machine tools, that require a lengthy marketing effort. Others work for small manufacturers that cannot afford their own sales force.

Factors Influencing Channel Length

The discussion here has hinted at some of the factors that influence the decision on channel length. Four main factors must be considered:

1. Product factors.

2. Market factors.

3. Producer factors.

4. Environmental factors.

A company that makes only a few simple, durable, low-priced products (such as screws or paper clips), for which there are many intermediaries, will probably choose to distribute its goods through long channels. Conversely, a company that produces many complex, high-priced products (such as computerized office systems) for a relatively small number of customers will probably favour shorter channels. A few examples may clarify the circumstances that influence the channel length decision.

Product Factors The characteristics of a product are an important influence. Crest toothpaste, which is a simple, low-priced, standard consumer item that has remained on the market more than 25 years, can be sold through a long chain of wholesalers and retailers. Procter & Gamble's strategy with Crest, which involves the producer's own appeals to consumers to raise demand, means intermediaries need make little effort to reach them. (It is important to note that consumer products such as Crest are likely to be marketed directly to the consumer in the future.)

By contrast, the machine tool that makes the auto body of a Buick is custom-made, complex, and high-priced, and it may be discarded with the next model change. The sales force must make a direct effort to sell it. There are consumer goods that resemble the machine tool in characteristics (such as a custom-made Rolls-Royce), and there are industrial goods that resemble Crest toothpaste (such as a wrench). In such cases, the consumer good would go through a shorter channel than the industrial good. The products' characteristics would be the determining factor.

Market factors Channel length is also influenced by characteristics of the particular market. A snack-food company such as Christie Brown, which markets nationwide, must use wholesalers to reach thousands of grocery stores and vending machine operators. (Technological advances and the introduction of the Loonie coin have made the vending machine a very attractive channel for many types of goods, including disposable razor blades, tooth brushes, condoms, and pain relievers, as well as the traditional snack foods and pop.)

Special customer needs might also favour a short channel. For example, the manufacturers of highly technical custom equipment must have close contact with the ultimate consumer since on-site servicing (setup) and training are likely to be necessary upon delivery. Computer systems are a good example of a product for which long channels are inappropriate.

Producer Factors Company characteristics — particularly financial condition and depth of the product line—might influence channel length as well. At IBM, for example, personal selling is a major component of the marketing program. The company earns enough on its sales to support direct marketing costs and has the resources for direct distribution[6] (although it also chooses to use intermediaries such as MicroAge). By contrast, most new companies have neither the money nor the product assortment to follow a similar strategy of direct marketing; Amstrad Computers, for example, employs dealers including the Brick furniture chain.

Environmental Factors Finally, a variety of considerations help determine channel length. The most important are:

1. *Manufacturer's resources.* Lack of capital and marketing expertise may force producers to use distributors, rather than hiring their own sales force.

2. *Product factors.* Products that receive regular servicing or on-site selling typically move through shorter channels.

3. *Market factors.* The size and location of the target market, the shifting needs of the consumer, and the channels employed by competitors will affect the channel selection. A small number of buyers concentrated in a small geographic region suggests a direct marketing approach.

Although the factors considered here have been treated separately, in practice they must be weighed against one another to determine the proper channel length. Because most cases require a weighing of a variety of factors, channel length decisions are complex.

Channel Number

In contrast to the length of a channel, channel number refers to the number of channels an organization uses to sell its products. For example, IBM uses a sales force to make personal calls on large customers. The company also reaches smaller customers by selling through stores such as MicroAge and ComputerLand. Similarly, hotels take reservations directly from consumers, or they may accept reservations made through airlines, tour operators, or travel agents.

Companies might use multiple channels for four basic reasons:[7]

1. They may be selling to entirely different markets. For example, novels are sold to the general trade market through bookstores by way of wholesale intermediaries and to other markets (such as public libraries) by a more direct route.

2. They may be selling to different market segments. Esso Petroleum Canada Limited supplies Mr. Lube with oil, targeting those consumers who require the oil change service, as well as its own retail outlets, which service consumers who need gas and oil fill-ups. (See At Your Service 11.1.)

3. Different geographic regions may require different channels. A manufacturer may sell through its own sales force locally but gain marketing presence by utilizing wholesale intermediaries in other provinces or markets with lower population densities.

At Your Service 11.1

Mr. Lube: A New Concept Creates a New Channel for a Major Player

Mr. Lube is a franchise company specializing in oil changes, oil and air filter replacement, and chassis lubrication in Canada. In its multiple-bay drive-through centres, Mr. Lube offers a selection of 18 brands of warranty-approved oil and the convenience of ten-minute service time without appointment. Started by Clifford Giese in Edmonton, Alberta, in 1976, the company was a natural progression in the trend toward increased specialization in the automobile maintenance market evidenced by muffler, transmission, and radiator franchises. By 1979, Mr. Lube had four outlets operating in the Edmonton area, and it quickly expanded to other parts of Canada with some 70 stores open in 22 cities by June 1990.

Mr. Lube's key success factors are identified as site selection, convenience, professional service, selection of national brands at competitive prices, standardization, and franchisee support. The Canadian passenger-car oil market, for 1990, of 220 million litres is divided as shown in the accompanying table.

The success of Mr. Lube did not escape the notice of Esso Petroleum Canada Limited, which quickly recognized this new channel's potential for its petroleum products. Using a "pre-empt" strategy to assure presence in this

Mr. Lube Canada Inc.

Canadian Passenger-Car Oil Market, 1990 (220 Million Litres)

Outlet	Market Share
Car dealers	33.0%
Service stations	25.3
Quick oil-change shops	14.6
Repair shops	8.8
Canadian Tire	8.6
Discount stores	1.4
Auto parts stores	0.7
All other	7.6

developing market, Esso negotiated an agreement in 1985 to supply Mr. Lube's "house oil" in return for necessary capital for further expansion and for access to real estate owned by Esso. On December 10, 1987, Esso purchased the company, which is now a wholly owned subsidiary.

That other oil giants are following the same strategy is scarcely surprising. The Canadian market for passenger-car oil is sizeable. With customer acceptance of the convenience concept of retailing and with well-operated and well-

promoted stores, fast oil-change retailers are expected to increase their market share to 30 percent by the year 2000. There are approximately 200 fast oil-change stores in Canada today, and the number is expected to reach 600 when the market is mature. Mr. Lube Canada plans to have 125 stores in operation by 1995, with Esso Petroleum Canada supplying most of the oil.

Source: Adapted from Connie Bryson, "Mr. Lube Catches the Eye of a Giant," *The Globe and Mail*, April 17, 1989, Report on Business.

4. Different-size buyers may be reached through different channels. Alcan sells to its large-volume buyers directly but advises its smaller buyers to purchase through service centres.

Although using multiple channels may solve a producer's problems, it may also cause conflict by creating competition. For example, local retailers of IBM computers may lose business because IBM allows customers to buy directly from the company. This situation, which is known as *horizontal competition*, is discussed later in this chapter.

Channel Member Types

The manufacturer that has chosen one channel or a number of them has already, in a way, selected the type of intermediary to use — whether wholesale, retail, or some combination. But the choice must be further specified because there are many categories of retailers and wholesaling intermediaries. The wide variety of retail outlets is well known. Less familiar, but even more varied than retailers, are the types of wholesaling intermediaries.

Merchant wholesalers are independents who buy goods from manufacturers, take physical possession of them, and sell them to other intermediaries. By contrast, **agents** (also called brokers and commission merchants) merely arrange for the buying and selling of goods but never actually acquire ownership or physical possession of goods. **Wholly owned wholesalers,** often called manufacturers' sales branches and offices, are, as their name implies, the distribution arm of manufacturers who set them up. The term "wholesaler" is usually reserved for the first and third categories; "wholesaling intermediary," however, covers all three types.

Each of these three types has several subcategories, as illustrated in Figure 11.3.

The various kinds of intermediaries perform various functions, choosing the right one for a product can be a key marketing decision.

Full-Service Merchant Wholesalers

Of the three categories of wholesalers, merchant wholesalers are the most numerous and account for more than half of all sales by wholesalers. Based on the number of marketing functions they perform, merchant wholesalers are classed as full-service or limited-function wholesalers.

Full-service merchant wholesalers perform a wide variety of distribution tasks, including (1) assembling goods from manufacturers, (2) storing and delivering them, (3) financing retailer purchases, and (4) providing marketing information for both manufacturers and retailers. Marketers commonly distinguish three types of full-service wholesalers — wholesale merchants, industrial distributors, and rack jobbers.

Wholesale merchants supply mainly retailers and some institutions (hospitals, schools, and so forth). Those that service small department

---

Merchant Wholesaler
Independent who buys goods from manufacturers, takes physical possession of them, and sells them to other intermediaries.

Agent
Wholesale intermediary who merely arranges for the buying and selling of goods but never actually acquires ownership or possession of them.

Wholly Owned Wholesaler
Distribution arm of manufacturer that sets it up. Can be manufacturers' sales branches or sales offices.

Full-Service Merchant Wholesaler
Wholesale intermediary who performs a wide variety of distribution tasks such as assembly, storage and delivery, and financing, and may provide market information.

Wholesale Merchant
Full-service merchant wholesaler who supplies mainly retailers or institutions.

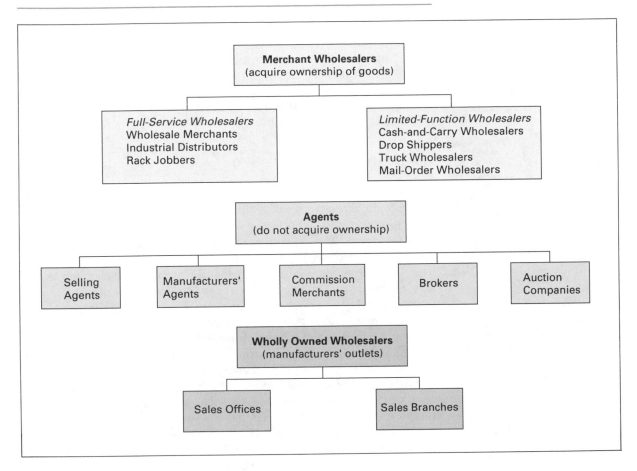

Figure 11.3 Types of Wholesaling Intermediaries

Source: Adapted from Eric N. Berkowitz, Roger A. Kerin, and William Rudelius, *Marketing* (St. Louis, Mo.: Mosby, 1986), p. 356. Reproduced by permission from Times Mirror/Mosby College Publishing.

stores carry many lines of goods, including hardware, furniture, and appliances. More commonly, however, they specialize in one line. For example, Drug Trading Inc., is one of the country's largest wholesalers of drugs and cosmetics for small retailers and institutions.

Industrial distributors are the counterparts of wholesale merchants in the industrial market. They are often used to sell small items, such as power tools and workshop equipment. Industrial distributors are best suited to companies that have a large base of potential customers, have a product that is relatively easy to stock, sell in small quantities, and sell to customers at a low level in their organization. IBM, for example, uses industrial distributors to sell its typewriters.[8]

Rack jobbers emerged in the 1950s as a special category of full-service wholesalers. They supply grocery and other retail stores with nonfood items such as housewares, toys, and health and beauty aids. The racks they set up and supply gave them their name. In a sense, rack jobbers

Industrial Distributor
Wholesaler who sells to the industrial market.

Rack Jobber
Full-service merchant wholesaler who supplies grocery and other retail stores with nonfood items on display racks and who owns the goods and racks.

are themselves small retailers who sell from space given them by a merchant. The merchant takes no risk (title belongs to the jobber) and is not billed for unsold goods left on the rack. Yet merchant and jobber split profits from sales according to a percentage agreed upon ahead of time. (Usually a special cash register key records the sale of such merchandise.) Because retailers risk so little in such an arrangement, they welcome the rack jobbers' business.

Limited-Function Merchant Wholesalers

Full-service wholesalers perform many functions for the retailer. Some retailers do not require all of these services. They often use **limited-function merchant wholesalers**, which provide only a few services for their customers. Typically, they extend no credit, and some do not even store or deliver goods, although they all assume ownership or take title. They became popular mainly because full-service wholesalers are expensive, and some manufacturers do not need the full range of services. The four principal types are cash-and-carry wholesalers, drop shippers, truck wholesalers, and mail-order wholesalers.

The **cash-and-carry wholesaler,** as the name implies, does not provide financing or delivery services. In dealing with such wholesalers, it is customary to pick up the merchandise at their place of business. Traditionally, these firms service small retailers who are constantly in need of fill-in items. Larger stores also use them, however, to cover temporary out-of-stock situations. For example, larger department stores might call on cash-and-carry drug wholesalers to keep the store stocked with the many hundreds of drug items carried in their cosmetic and drug departments. Many of these wholesalers flourish in the grocery field.

A new form of cash-and-carry wholesaler is the warehouse club, a cut-rate variety wholesaler that operates on a low margin (10 percent is typical) with a high inventory/turnover ratio. A good example is Titan Warehouse Club Inc. which opened its first outlet in 1986 in London, Ontario and had expanded to ten outlets across Canada by 1988. Memberships are granted to small businesses, which must show a commercial licence, for an annual fee of $25. The selection of goods varies widely, from fresh produce to automotive supplies. The attraction to a small business is that it can get lower wholesale prices at a warehouse club than its individual buying power can command elsewhere. Industry observers have noted that warehouse clubs are increasingly focused away from the original concept of cash-and-carry toward the price-sensitive consumer goods market.

In direct contrast to cash-and-carry wholesalers are **drop shippers.** They neither maintain warehouses nor carry inventories. They do, however, take title to the goods and are responsible for billing a customer and collecting payment. All orders to the manufacturer are shipped directly to a drop shipper's customer. Drop shippers operate in the lumber, building materials, coal, and other industries in which the costs of

Limited-Function Merchant Wholesaler
Merchant wholesaler who provides only a few services for customers.

Cash-and-Carry Wholesaler
Limited-function merchant wholesaler who does not provide financing or delivery services.

Drop Shipper
Limited-function merchant wholesaler who neither maintains a warehouse nor carries inventories but who takes title to goods and is responsible for billing and collecting payment.

hauling and transportation are high in comparison with the final price of the product.

Truck wholesalers perform all the functions of full-service organizations except financing. They may maintain a warehouse, but they operate by selling and making deliveries directly from a truck. Ordinarily, truck wholesalers handle nationally advertised food specialties such as potato chips, bakery products, fruits, vegetables, and many other similar items. Most of these firms call on retailers daily, and usually they demand cash on delivery. Truck jobbers also aggressively promote their products, which adds to their appeal to a manufacturer. They are expensive because of the high costs associated with operating a delivery truck.

Mail-order wholesalers do not engage in personal selling. Instead, they send catalogues to retail firms or other wholesalers, with instructions on how to order goods. Many of these firms are found in the cosmetics, jewellery, printing, and stationery fields. Although they do not push products actively as truck wholesalers do, mail-order wholesalers are an attractive distribution alternative because they are relatively inexpensive. Small manufacturers who cannot afford their own catalogue get needed market exposure by offering their products, with those of other small manufacturers, in the mail-order wholesaler's catalogue.

Agents

Unlike full-service and limited-function merchant wholesalers, agents do not take title to goods, and only rarely do they warehouse them. Their principal function is to buy and sell goods for others in return for a commission. There are five classifications of agent wholesalers: selling agents; manufacturers' agents; commission merchants; brokers; and auction companies.

Selling agents handle the entire output of small manufacturers, especially in the textile, canning, and lumber industries. They may combine the outputs of several small manufacturers of the same products and serve as their sales force. A manufacturer, particularly one just starting out, may have committed all its human and financial resources to production. Selling agents serve the producer by handling all of the marketing functions. A problem sometimes associated with selling agents is lack of effort devoted consistently to the selling task. Their loyalty may be divided when they handle competing accounts, as they often do.

Manufacturers' agents have far less power because they handle only part of a producer's output. Usually they take over the selling functions in areas that it does not pay manufacturers to cover with their own sales force. Manufacturers' agents may represent several manufacturers of noncompeting but complementary products, such as roofing, siding, and paint supplies in the building trade or tires, batteries, shock absorbers, and engine parts in automotive supplies. Manufacturers' agents provide instant access to new markets at a lower cost to the manufacturer than the alternative of hiring sales personnel to develop a new market.

Truck Wholesaler
Limited-function merchant wholesaler who performs all the functions of full-service organizations except financing; operates by selling and making deliveries directly from a truck.

Mail-Order Wholesaler
Company that provides a wide range of goods ordered by customers from catalogues and shipped directly to them by mail.

Selling Agent
Agent wholesaler who handles marketing for the entire output of small manufacturers.

Manufacturers' Agent
Agent wholesaler who handles marketing in areas a manufacturer chooses not to cover with its own sales force.

Commission Merchant
Agent wholesaler who markets the output of small farmers for a commission; may store goods but does not take title.

Broker
Agent wholesaler who brings buyers and sellers together, acting on behalf of one or the other and used on a one-time basis.

Auction Company
Agent wholesaler that works on a one-time basis for a commission; may send catalogues to prospective buyers and take bids at time of auction.

Sales Office
Headquarters for a sales force away from a company's plant.

Sales Branch
A manufacturing firm's service centre and stock storehouse.

Commission merchants play an important role in selling the output of small farmers. Unlike most other agents, commission merchants may store the goods they handle until enough is gathered for a sale, though they do not take title to the goods. They are given full power to negotiate price and are paid a commission on the proceeds of the sale.

Brokers are common in fields like real estate and agriculture in which there are mainly buyers and sellers and no central marketplace for exchange. They bring buyers and sellers together, acting on behalf of one or the other. Unlike most other wholesale agents, brokers are used on a one-time basis. After completing a sale, they receive a commission and may or may not act in the future for the party they represented.

Fast-talking auctioneers who sell tobacco, flowers, or other farm products at a frantic pace have made **auction companies** familiar to most Canadians. Artwork, antiques, used industrial equipment, and other products that vary widely in quality—and thus must be sold individually—are also handled by them. Auction companies often send catalogues to prospective buyers and take bids at the time of the auction. Like brokers, auction companies work on a one-time basis for a commission.

Wholly Owned Wholesalers

A manufacturer that wishes to have greater control of the movement of goods to the consumer can achieve it through sales offices or sales branches. Highly specialized products that require careful installation or servicing are marketed this way. The outlets may be either sales offices or sales branches.

Sales offices act as a headquarters away from a company's manufacturing plants for the sales force. As a general rule, they do not carry stock. They are effective in reducing selling costs and improving customer service. **Sales branches** differ in that in most cases they do carry stock and, more important, they act as servicing centres. Sales branches and offices are often used in the sale of farm equipment, electrical and plumbing supplies, elementary school textbooks, and chemicals.

Industry trade exhibitions, such as the Plastex exhibition held annually in Toronto, offer manufacturers a place to display their products to the various wholesalers. These trade shows bring buyers and sellers together to facilitate transactions and also to provide the opportunity to view the current state of technology in their industry.

Channel Width

Besides the length, number, and types of channels to use, marketers must determine the number of wholesalers or retailers to use within each channel. This is called channel width. A manufacturer that has decided to use, say, three different channels must still determine how many wholesalers or retailers to use in each of the channels.

Another way of stating the problem of channel width is, how much market exposure should a product have? A firm has three choices: intensive, exclusive, or selective distribution.

Intensive Distribution

When goods and services are sold in as many wholesale or retail outlets as possible in order to maintain market share, the producer is adopting a strategy of **intensive distribution.** The effective use of advertising, publicity, and sales promotion has led to brand awareness and preference for many products. Items such as cigarettes, disposable razor blades, soft drinks, and breath mints need little personal selling if they are readily available. Thus they are found in many traditional and nontraditional retail locations. In fact, an intensive distribution strategy is used for almost all branded convenience items in the consumer market. The objective is maximum product exposure because shoppers will switch rather than go out of their way to buy a particular brand. In the industrial market, office supplies, small tools, and all other standardized, low-unit-cost products purchased in quantity are sold this way.

Intensive distribution results in a large volume of sales. But it also costs a great deal — for advertising or maintaining a sales force. Companies using an intensive distribution strategy may find it difficult to motivate intermediaries to sell a particular product more aggressively than a competing item, because intensively distributed items are usually low-value, low-profit ones. Nevertheless, this strategy is more or less essential for items of small unit value.

Exclusive Distribution

Selling a product through only one wholesaler or retailer in a given area is known as **exclusive distribution.** Mercedes Benz automobiles are sold through only one or two dealerships in a city. Appliance manufacturers also use this strategy in the consumer market. Industrial marketers might use it in distributing expensive installations or special parts.

In return for exclusivity, the intermediary is often prohibited by contract from marketing a competitor's product. The intermediaries' profits are tied directly to the success or failure of the product they represent. From a manufacturer's point of view, there can be risks associated with granting exclusivity to a retailer. First, the product will be exposed to only one sector of the market. Second, if the retailer does not market the product effectively, the sales expectations of the manufacturer may not be met. Moreover, exclusive distribution gives intermediaries some incentive to build sales in their assigned territory because they alone will profit. Also, the selection of fine retailers can contribute to the

Intensive Distribution
Selling a product through almost all available wholesale or retail outlets.

Exclusive Distribution
Selling a product through only one wholesaler or retailer in a given area.

quality image of a product and justify a higher price.

Selective Distribution

Selective Distribution
Use of more than one but fewer than all firms that might carry a product.

In between intensive and exclusive distribution is **selective distribution**, a nonexclusive arrangement in which a product is carried by more than one outlet but fewer than all those that might offer it in the area. (See Marketing Today 11.2.) In the consumer market, shopping and specialty goods such as name brand clothing and sporting goods are often distributed selectively. These products are usually well known to the consumer, who is willing to spend some time and effort in locating a retailer that carries them. Industrial products such as accessories and parts may also be handled by a limited number of wholesalers.

Marketing Today 11.2

Get Hip or Get Out!

Winnipeg-based Chip Foster Inc. manufactures Chip & Pepper Wetwear, a line of teen's casual clothing. Owners Chip and Pepper Foster want to maintain a sense of exclusivity, which is reflected in their pricing and distribution policy.

Fleece sweatshirts retail for $56, and the company sells only to those boutiques and chain stores that fit the Chip & Pepper image. Old Firehall Sports of Toronto and Village Streetwear of Winnipeg are two examples of the more than 800 outlets across Canada that carry the lines.

Chip and Pepper Foster are always innovating. Says Pepper, "We set the trends. I figure as long as we're on the cutting edge, we're okay."

The Fosters introduced their own line of barbeque sauce, which is selling in boutiques that carry their clothes. They've sold 50 000 cases in their first year. Now they are considering a line of jewellery, and endorsing other products.

Whatever the Fosters try, their exclusive image will likely remain. After all, "If you can get Chip and Pepper anywhere, then it isn't the hippest, is it?"

Source: Lindor Reynolds, "Twin Ambitions," *Small Business*, July/August 1990, pp. 12-14.

Gerard Kwiatkowski

Manufacturers see three advantages to selective distribution:

1. It costs less than intensive distribution because there are fewer clients to call on.

2. It lessens the possibility of price cutting because competition is less intense.

3. It promotes close co-operation between the selected channel members, who feel that they have an important stake in selling the product.

The last point is very important. Many sources of friction within channels work against a spirit of co-operation.

Managing Channels: Problems and Solutions

The potential for conflict often exists between a manufacturer and its distributors. Two types of conflict can develop—horizontal and vertical. Horizontal conflict occurs between intermediaries at the *same* level in the distribution channel, such as competing retailers. Vertical conflict occurs between intermediaries at *different* levels—for example, a manufacturer may attempt to bypass a wholesaler and sell direct to the consumer.[9]

Conflicts arise because channels involve many independent businesses, and they can end up working against each other. For example, although the manufacturer and the distributor of a product share the goal of reducing costs to improve profitability, their methods may be mutually defeating. The manufacturer needs large production runs to reduce setup costs and improve efficiency, whereas the distributor wants to place small orders with short lead times in order to reduce the costs associated with carrying inventories.

Goal conflict may also arise when a manufacturer attempts to introduce a new product version at a higher price. At the wholesale and retail level, new models at higher prices are often not welcome. Intermediaries worry about how they are going to get rid of the old models they now stock. They anticipate that consumers will resist higher prices, resulting in lost sales. New technology implemented by the manufacturer also puts a strain on the intermediaries' service departments. Dealer service personnel must have ongoing training in order to keep up with technology.

Not all complaints originate with intermediaries. Manufacturers sometimes feel that other channel members do not put forth a sufficient sales effort. Intermediaries who handle competing products may have neither the time nor the interest to sell one product aggressively. Some companies may even force intermediaries to sign contracts specifying that they cannot handle competing lines. The Warehouse clubs' increasing focus on the consumer goods market has upset many retailers; some who have earned rebates as long-standing customers have threatened to abandon suppliers that offer the same volume rebates to clubs.[10]

Some conflict is desirable in a channel system because it reveals flaws that can be remedied. For example, resistance to a price increase may mean that intermediaries have not been shown how they too can profit. Such faulty communication is a system weakness that can be eliminated. But not all conflict is beneficial. That is why formal means of controlling it have evolved.

The Channel Captain

Conflict can be controlled to a certain extent if the channel has one strong member with either the power or the leadership ability to set policy. That member is referred to as the **channel captain.**

In the early nineteenth century, the wholesale intermediary was the channel captain.[11] Manufacturers were small producers of only one product, and retailers were widely scattered. They depended on wholesale intermediaries to forge a link between them. Toward the end of that century, however, manufacturers assumed leadership. They had grown larger, were able to mass produce a multiproduct line, and could reach their markets readily because of transportation improvements. Advertising also enhanced their power. Manufacturers could create consumer demand that could force an intermediary to sell their products. For example, no grocery store today can resist stocking Campbell's soup or Kellogg's corn flakes because consumers' brand awareness has reduced the sales effort required from the retailer.

For the most part, manufacturers still dominate channels. The reason is simple. Generally, the broader the base of a channel member's financial resources, the less it has to share power with other members.

Some retailers, however, are now challenging manufacturer leadership. The chain style of organization (discussed more fully in Chapter 12) has given some retailers enormous economic power. Some Canadian chains are showing their ability to insist on products that are environment-friendly. For example, Provigo Inc., the country's second largest supermarket chain, announced in 1989 it would phase out the sale of produce that had been treated with pesticides—particularly those with cancer-causing chemicals. It was also among the first retailers to boycott aerosol products with ozone-damaging chlorofluorocarbons (CFCs) as propellants. Canadian Tire no longer carries the cooling fluid used to recharge air conditioners because it too damages the ozone layer. Canadian Tire and Provigo, as well as Sears and The Bay, are examples of retailers that are channel captains. Many marketers predict that retailers will take over dominance of marketing channels in the way manufacturers once took leadership from wholesale intermediaries.[12]

Power within the Channel

A channel captain, whether a manufacturer or a retailer, can force its will on other channel members or use methods to win their voluntary

Channel Captain
Member of a marketing channel with power or ability to set and enforce policy.

co-operation. The power base has eight possible sources, each of which can be used to gain leverage during negotiation.[13]

1. *Coercive power*—from the threat of economic punishment. A group of discount retailers may refuse to buy from a manufacturer that has been giving larger discounts to catalogue store owners.

2. *Legitimate power*—from contractual arrangements between channel members. Franchisees have obligations under contract. McDonald's, for example, dictates service standards, procedures, and hours of operation to the franchisee.

3. *Referent power*—from the perceived attractiveness of associating with a specific channel member. A clothing manufacturer whose products are sold through Harry Rosen gains power through the retailer's market image.

4. *Expert power*—from expert or specialized knowledge that can benefit another channel member. A manufacturer could provide a retailer with sales and service training in a certain product line.

5. *Reward power*—from the offering of rewards such as sales incentives or volume discounts.

6. *Connection power*—from personal relationships developed with key contacts in senior management.

7. *Persuasion power*—from communication and personal selling skills so effective that they can gain the support of others.

8. *Information power*—from access to privileged information.

Suppliers can exercise control in a distribution channel by one of four methods[14] (some of which have already been mentioned briefly):

1. Dealer selection—selecting customers with which to deal and refusing to deal with others.

2. Exclusive dealing—prohibiting a dealer from carrying a competing product.

3. Tying contracts—agreeing to sell a product to an intermediary provided it also buys another (possibly unwanted) product.

4. Exclusive territories — restricting an intermediary to sell *only* to consumers within an assigned territory.

Whether exercised by suppliers or intermediaries, some coercive techniques may be so annoying as to be counterproductive. Others may be illegal if competition is lessened as a result of their use (see Table 11.3). Thus channel captains often rely on voluntary co-operation, using a variety of techniques to foster it. One way is to aid resellers in carrying out their tasks by providing advertising materials, training an intermediary's sales force, or giving financial advice.[15] Retail channel cap-

Table 11.3 Criminal Offences in Relation to Competition

Part VI of the Competition Act prohibits, under criminal sanction, certain trade practices. Some of those specified are:

1. **Combines**   Conspiracies, combinations, agreements, or arrangements to lessen competition unduly in relation to the supply, manufacture or production of a product (section 45).

2. **Bid-rigging**   An agreement by two or more parties that one will refrain from bidding in a call for tenders or that they will collude in the submission of bids — unless such actions are made known to the tendering authority (section 47).

3. **Price discrimination**
   a   Knowingly engaging in a practice of discrimination against competitors of a purchase of an article by granting a discount or other advantage to a purchaser that is not available to competitors purchasing articles of like quality and quantity (paragraph 50 (1) (a)).
   b   Engaging in a policy of selling products in any area of Canada at prices lower than those exacted elsewhere in Canada, where the effect or design is to lessen competition substantially, or eliminate a competitor (paragraph (1) (b)).

4. **Predatory pricing**   Engaging in a policy of selling products at unreasonably low prices where the effect or design is to lessen competition substantially or eliminate a competitor (paragraph 50 (1) (c)).

5. **Discriminatory Promotion Practices**   Granting to a purchaser an allowance for advertising or display purposes that is not offered in proportionate terms to competing purchasers (section 51).

6. **Resale price maintenance**
   a   Attempting to influence upward or discourage the reduction of the price at which another person supplies or advertises a product or refusing to supply or otherwise discriminating against anyone because of that person's low pricing policy (subsection 61 (1)).
   b   Attempting to induce a supplier to refuse to supply a product to a particular person because of that person's low pricing policy (subsection 61 (6)).

Source: Director of Investigation and Research, Competition Act, Consumer and Corporate Affairs Canada, *Annual Report*, March 31, 1989, chapter 5, p. 21.

tains can aid manufacturers by keeping them current on what products consumers are buying.

As in most conflict situations, open communication between the parties is an important step to resolution of any channel difficulties. "Win-win" solutions often result when channel members search for solutions that are mutually beneficial. Point-of-purchase electronic scanning equipment is, however, providing valuable order information that the distributor and manufacturer can share for better communication to improve the channel efficiency.

Vertical Marketing Systems

Statesmanlike measures to control conflict do not always work. Consequently, more and more firms are trying to guarantee the smooth operation of channels by curbing or eliminating the independence of channel members. When they succeed, the result is a **vertical marketing system (VMS),** in which one channel member owns, controls, or co-ordinates the operations of other channel members. Besides lessening channel friction, a VMS also saves money. For example, a centralized accounting system may be instituted to eliminate duplication of paperwork on two or more levels.[16]

A vertical marketing system may be administered, corporate, or contractual. These three types of VMS are illustrated in Figure 11.4.

Administered Systems

Administered systems are really only one step removed from the channel captain approach of traditional marketing systems. The main difference is that in an **administered system,** such things as what a product will sell for, how it will be displayed, and how much money will be spent on its advertising are included in a detailed plan that the channel leader submits to other members. The co-ordination of channel activities is achieved through the economic power of one of the channel members. For example, retailers are very willing to co-operate with Procter & Gamble regarding pricing, displays, and shelf space policies.[17]

Corporate Systems

Corporate systems develop when one channel member owns or at least partially owns the business operations of two or more channel levels.

Vertical Marketing System (VMS)
System in which one channel member owns, controls, or co-ordinates the operations of other channel members.

Administered System
Vertical marketing system in which one member secures agreement from other members of a channel on certain plans concerning price, display, and advertising.

Corporate System
Vertical marketing system in which one channel member fully or partially owns the business operations of two or more channel levels.

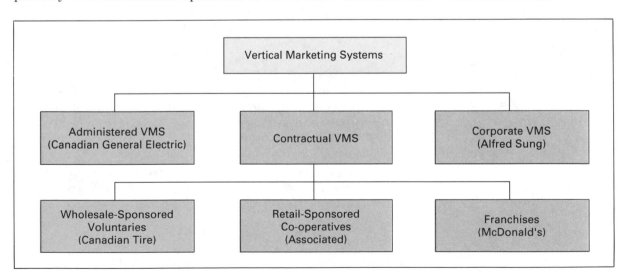

Figure 11.4 Types of Vertical Marketing Systems

Source: Adapted from Eric N. Berkowitz, Roger A. Kerin, and William Rudelius, *Marketing* (St. Louis, Mo.: Mosby, 1986), p. 360. Reproduced by permission from Times Mirror/Mosby College Publishing; and M. Date Beckman, David L. Kurtz, and Louis E. Boone, *Foundations of Marketing*, 4th ed. (Toronto: Holt, Rinehart and Winston, 1988), p. 434.

There are two ways that such ownership can come about. First, a manufacturer may buy wholesaling or retailing operations and market its products through them. Alfred Sung takes this approach to selling its clothing.[18] Second, and more frequently today, retailers and wholesalers may buy out or buy a controlling interest in manufacturers who supply them, as in the case of Dufferin Cue (see Marketing Today 11.3).

From the retailer's point of view, the major advantages of an integrated corporate system are a lower cost for goods purchased and guaranteed access to supplies. For the manufacturer, the integrated corporate system like the administered system, means greater control over price and quality. The major disadvantage is that government is taking a sterner look at vertically integrated companies. For example, on December 12, 1986, Canada Safeway Limited announced its intention of acquiring 23 food outlets of Woodward Stores. The Director of Investigation and Research of the Competition Act ruled that the transaction was likely to prevent or substantially lessen competition in six market areas in Alberta and British Columbia. Only after Safeway agreed to divest 12 stores in these markets within a 24-month period, to satisfy the director's concerns, was the merger allowed to proceed.[19]

Contractual Systems

Contractual System
Vertical marketing system based on a formal agreement among channel members to co-operate on such matters as buying, advertising, accounting practices, and other functions. Forms are franchises, retail-sponsored co-operatives, and wholesale-sponsored voluntaries.

Contractual systems are really a middle ground between administered and corporate systems. They involve a formal legal agreement (or contract) between channel members to co-operate on such matters as buying, advertising, accounting practices, and other functions. Members of a contractual system are not owned, but the relationship that exists between them is defined with more legal precision than in administered systems.[20]

Contractual systems are familiar to most Canadians today under such names as Canadian Tire, IDA, and McDonald's. Those companies represent, respectively, three different forms of contractual systems — wholesale-sponsored voluntaries, retail-sponsored co-operatives, and franchises. All three are an important part of retailing today, accounting for about 40 percent of sales to consumers. A detailed description of them is given in Chapter 12.

Contractual systems — and in general all vertical marketing systems — are expected to continue to grow in the future. If the trend continues, independent wholesalers and retailers will find it increasingly difficult to survive in the future.

Chapter Replay

1. **How do marketers make a product available to users?**
    Marketers use marketing channels, which typically include buyers, sellers, and some combination of retailers and wholesaling intermediaries.

Marketing Today 11.3

Dufferin Cue: Growth Strategy through Integration

Dufferin Cue Ltd. began in 1967 on a mission to "make the best cue possible at the best price possible." New owners Al and Elizabeth Sellinger risked everything to purchase Dufferin Patterns and Wood Specialties Ltd., which manufactured billiard cues in Toronto, Ontario.

The first problem facing them was to redesign the manufacturing process to become "the first company in the world with a straight cue." Today Dufferin Cue invests approximately $50 000 annually to keep its production machinery up to date, and production rates approach 2000 cues daily.

With almost all of the Canadian-made cue market secured, export opportunities quickly developed for Dufferin products. But raw material supply became a concern. The raw material for a cue is white maple. Only wood with straight grain and without defects — about 5 percent of a tree — is suitable for quality cue production. Goderich Manufacturing Inc., a producer of bowling lanes and maple products, had been shipping the unused "short ends" of its maple bowling lane planks to Dufferin Cue where they were made into billiard cues. Then demand for bowling lanes softened, and Goderich began to have financial difficulties. Dufferin Cue assured its raw materials source by acquiring Goderich, which was renamed Sellinger Wood Ltd.

The U.S. market represented

Tim Leyes

about two-thirds of Dufferin's sales by 1981. Consistent with its integration strategy, the firm established a subsidiary near Chicago to handle its American sales. A company-owned subsidiary offered more control than a network of distributors.

With forward and backward integration established, the next move was horizontal. In 1984, Canada's largest billiard-table-maker went bankrupt. Riley World of Billiards was bought and renamed Dufferin Leisure Ltd. Now Sellinger Wood had another customer to supply.

In 1985, Edward Billiard Supply Ltd., of Winnipeg, Manitoba, sold its table-making operation (which was closed after the buyout) and its three retail outlets to the Sellingers. The retail outlets were renamed Game Room Stores.

Dufferin Leisure was having difficulty carving out market share against competitors. The solution was to launch a chain of stores committed to selling its products. In 1986, outlets were opened in Mississauga, Ontario, and Clear-

brook, British Columbia. Since then 25 outlets have opened across the country.

The chain now channels more than 70 percent of Dufferin Leisure's billiard tables and about 25 percent of its pool cues to the Canadian consumer. Sales across the Dufferin Game Room outlets grew from $5 million in 1988 to $8.3 million in 1989. This success has fuelled demand for Dufferin's cues, Dufferin Leisure's tables, and lumber from Sellinger Wood.

Integration allowed the organization to react quickly to changing market conditions. Resources can be reallocated to the division which needs them most. The Sellingers are very optimistic about the future with five franchises opening in 1990 and another five to ten scheduled to open in 1991.

Source: Adapted from Cathy Hilborn and Philip Mathias "Dufferin Racks Up Sales through Integration," *Small Business*, July/August 1990, pp. 18–20; and "Integration: Making It All Add Up," *Small Business*, July/Aug 1990, p. 21.

2. **How do intermediaries serve consumers and producers?**
Intermediaries serve consumers by bringing together a wide assortment of goods, placing that assortment in a convenient location, providing credit, offering money-saving services, and giving consumers the desired product in the desired quantity. Intermediaries serve producers by helping to simplify contacts between producers and consumers, by reducing costs or bearing financial risk, and by communicating marketing information.

3. **What decisions do marketers make in designing marketing channels?**
Marketers must select channel length and width. They must decide whether to use a single channel or multiple channels. And they must decide what types of intermediaries to include in the channels they use.

4. **What do marketers consider in deciding on a channel length?**
Marketers consider the specific characteristics of the product, the market, the company, and the environment.

5. **Why do some companies use multiple marketing channels?**
Companies might use multiple channels when they are selling to entirely different markets, different market segments, different geographic regions, or buyers of different sizes.

6. **What are the basic kinds of channel members?**
The basic kinds of channel members are merchant wholesalers, agents, and wholly owned wholesalers. Merchant wholesalers may be full-service or limited-function wholesalers. Agents include selling agents, manufacturers' agents, commission merchants, brokers, and auction companies. Wholly owned wholesalers include sales offices and sales branches.

7. **What are a firm's choices for how much market exposure a product should have?**
A producer can use intensive distribution, selling goods and services through most available outlets; exclusive distribution, selling through a single wholesaler or retailer; or selective distribution, which involves using only some of the firms that might carry the product.

8. **How is conflict in channels controlled?**
If the channel contains a channel captain, that member can control conflict by setting policy. Coercive techniques to achieve control are limited by law, so channel captains often try to encourage co-operation.

9. **Why do organizations create vertical marketing systems?**
By owning, controlling, or co-ordinating the operations of other channel members, an organization may be able to guarantee the smooth operation of channels. A vertical marketing system may also reduce costs.

Key Terms

administered system
agent
auction company
broker
cash-and-carry
  wholesaler
channel captain
channel length
channel member type
channel number
channel width
commission merchant
contractual system
corporate system
distribution
drop shipper
exclusive distribution
full-service merchant
  wholesaler
industrial distributor
intensive distribution

limited-function
  merchant wholesaler
mail-order wholesaler
manufacturers' agent
marketing (distribution)
  channel
merchant wholesaler
rack jobber
retailer
sales branch
sales office
selective distribution
selling agent
transfer principle
truck wholesaler
vertical marketing system
  (VMS)
wholesale merchant
wholesale intermediary
wholly owned wholesaler

Discussion Questions

1. What is the difference between a retailer and a wholesaling intermediary? Can a marketing channel exist without either of these intermediaries?

2. How do intermediaries add value to the products consumers buy?

3. Ron Masters is planning a new business manufacturing his Masterful Chili. He is trying to decide whether to arrange for intermediaries to distribute his chili or to sell it himself from a chili wagon on Main Street. What advantages might the use of intermediaries offer Ron? What are some disadvantages of using intermediaries?

4. Under what circumstances is a marketer likely to prefer a long channel? A short channel?

5. When Renée Fielding decided to start selling her popular accounting software directly to businesses as well as through computer stores, her profits improved. What problem could result from this arrangement? Why should Renée be concerned about that problem?

6. Stuart Participle runs a grocery store. He keeps all the profits from the fish he sells from the frozen food case in the back of the store,

but he keeps only a part of the profits from the magazines he sells from the rack near the checkout counter. Nevertheless, Stuart is glad to carry the magazines. Why? What kind of intermediary supplies the magazines to the store?

7. How do agents differ from merchant wholesalers? What is the difference between a selling agent and a manufacturers' agent?

8. Imogene Crumpet sells her hand-painted ties through a few prestigious stores. Imogene's friend Pam Sparks told her, "You could sell a lot more ties if you tried to get them into every store in town." What are some advantages of this recommendation? Why might Imogene be better off with the present arrangement?

9. What are some sources of conflict between manufacturers and distributors? How can conflict be controlled?

10. Ed Strump, owner of Strump Furniture, has decided that he wants to make the marketing channels for selling the company's furniture operate more smoothly. He is investigating ways of using vertical marketing systems for obtaining greater control over the process. What are some ways Ed might do this?

CASE 11.1

Burcan Industries

How does one man cover a sales territory of 72 countries overnight? That's the question that faced Clem Brodeur.

Since graduating from the civil engineering program at Queen's University, Kingston, Ontario, in 1949, Brodeur had spent his entire career in soils and foundation engineering. While vacationing in Sweden, he noticed an unusual operation underway at a highway intersection. He was witnessing a test installation for a new kind of soil-stabilization technology. It was a method of removing water from moist, soft earth, thereby strengthening the soil so that it would be able to support the foundation of a new highway or heavy building without settling.

Brodeur immediately saw the system's vast potential and secured the North American rights for Burcan Industries, the company he founded in 1973.

Organization

Research revealed that the concept was sound, but a redesign of the drainage material was necessary. Brodeur came up with a new design that solved all of the technical problems of the original one.

Source: Case developed by Bill Crowe, St. Lawrence College, Kingston, Ontario, and Mark Siemonsen, marketing consultant, based on information supplied by Burcan Industries Ltd., Whitby, Ontario

He spent the next 18 months travelling to several countries searching for a process capable of manufacturing the product. A Toronto-based company came up with the solution. During the next six months, it built a production line to manufacture the new drainage material, which was named Alidrain. In tandem, a Swedish equipment manufacturer developed the rig required to put the material in the ground.

Test installations proved successful, and Brodeur had a worldwide market awaiting him. Immediately, Burcan secured patents for the Alidrain system in 42 countries. Without the financial and human resources necessary to serve a market of that size, he looked to Alimak, a Swedish firm with a worldwide reputation for quality, custom construction equipment, that had representation in 72 countries. An agreement was reached whereby Alimak, which used a distributor system, had the exclusive rights to market the Alidrain system worldwide except in North America.

Sales Launch

Burcan personnel conducted a two-month training program for the Alimak managers. With a distribution network now in place, the Alidrain system was introduced at the International Soils Conference at Tokyo, in 1976, where more than 4000 geotechnical engineers were in attendance. The system was instantly on the international scene.

A licensee was established in the United States. Burcan Industries felt that Alimak was not aggressive enough in pursuing projects in its territory. Eventually, an agreement was reached whereby Burcan bought out Alimak's entire soil-stabilization division. An office was set up in Germany to market the Alidrain system throughout Europe and the Far East. The venture proved very successful. The market eventually declined in Europe, because of a reduction in construction activity, but it shifted to the Far East where a licensee was immediately established.

Licensees

Licensees are technically capable of selling the Alidrain system; the task includes estimating, design, and installation. They purchase equipment and materials for a previously agreed upon price and take ownership once a shipment leaves the manufacturing plant. A licensee in this business must:

- Be very knowledgeable in geotechnical engineering and soil mechanics.

- Have excellent contacts with engineering and contracting firms and with governmental agencies.

- Be financially stable.

■ Have sound marketing skills.

Particularly in the Far East, government contacts are very important since most of the major projects there are government controlled.

The Situation Today

Since 1976, more than 27 000 000 metres of the Alidrain system have been installed in some 24 countries around the world. To this day, it is recognized as the premier prefabricated vertical drainage system available.

Southeast Asia is expected to be the "hot spot" in this industry during the next ten-year period. Alternative channels to serve this market better are already being considered.

Focal Topics

1. What program would you recommend for serving the Southeast Asian market?

2. What other channels could Burcan Industries have utilized for its product launch in 1976?

3. What problems do you foresee in locating proper representation and negotiating business deals in other countries?

CASE 11.2

Hewlett Enterprises (B)

After six months of attempting to market his board game, Making It, Scott Hewlett was, in fact, not making it. He had great difficulty in developing contacts with the buyers at the major retail stores in his area. Some of the stores were part of large chains and indicated that he would have to work through the home offices. Other buyers said that they were simply too busy to see "another entrepreneur with the world's next great product."

Scott had achieved placement of his game in only three variety stores, two toy stores, and one small department store. Actual retail sales had amounted to only 40 units. The retail selling price varied from $11.95 to $14.95 among the three stores. Scott had sold the games to all the stores at a wholesale price of $6.25. He had also given away almost 50 games as samples to various stores hoping that they would try the game, like it, and stock it. Another 20 sets of Making It had been given to friends to help get the game played and talked about in the community.

For background information on the company and its product, see Case 10.2, Hewlett Enterprises (A).

Distribution Issues

From all indications, people who had played Making It enjoyed the game and planned to continue playing it. The retail stores had received no returns, and Scott's friends all said the game looked like a winner to them. But Scott was clearly running out of time. He had invested almost all of his savings in producing 1000 sets and in travelling to retail stores. His unemployment benefits would expire soon, and he had few prospects for a job in his town. He had to do something.

Scott began to think about alternative channels of distribution for his game. In talking about some of his ideas with friends and business acquaintances, he assembled the following possibilities:

- Sell the game directly to the consumer through mail order. Hewlett Enterprises could run advertisements for the game or try to get catalogue companies to place Making It in their publications. Hewlett Enterprises could fill the orders in either case, or it could send the games directly to the catalogue firms, which could stock and ship them.

- Try to find a toy distributor who would represent the company and carry Making It as part of its product line.

- Personally go into the present stores handling the game and give demonstrations to help boost interest in Making It. This gets into the whole area of a variety of types of promotional and personal selling activities that could enhance sales once distribution is achieved.

A Different Approach

As he thought through his options, Scott came up with a smashing new idea. Instead of putting fictitious businesses on the board, why not sell positions to local firms? Hewlett Enterprises would receive additional revenues from selling the spaces, and the firms and organizations involved would receive advertising exposure. This would mean that someone would have to sell the advertisements, that the present inventory of games would be of little value, and that the game would have only local appeal.

But, on the other hand, he could produce specialized games for other markets, maybe even involve some national companies. In addition, if local firms were on the Making It board, they might be willing to help sell the games, perhaps at a lower cost than regular retail stores, since they would be receiving some advertising value from the game.

With these new ideas, Scott began to check around again to see how businesses might respond. Several firms — a bank, a restaurant, and a radio station — showed immediate interest. A couple of larger retailers said they might carry Making It, especially if the game started getting publicity in the community. He now had another option to think about

—to get local businesses to help distribute the game, since their advertisements would be on it.

Focal Topics

1. If Making It stays in its present form, what are the relative advantages and disadvantages of alternative channels of distribution open to Hewlett Enterprises?

2. What are the strengths and weaknesses of changing the game by selling advertising on the board?

3. Based on your overall evaluations, what channel of distribution would you recommend to Scott? Support your recommendation.

Chapter 12

Retail Marketing: Structure and Management

In this chapter, you will learn:

- The kinds of retailers that emphasize product mix.

- Types of retail establishments that specialize in offering low prices.

- Where retailers locate their stores.

- Ways of retailing without stores.

- Ways of organizing retail establishments.

- How retailers create an image for their store.

- How the wheel-of-retailing theory and the life-cycle hypothesis attempt to explain

  changes in retailing.

Challenges This Decade

Dynamic retailers view strategic planning and precise execution of their business plan as a necessity in the 1990s. Merchandisers face numerous opportunities and negative business forces that will significantly affect their profit performance.

Canada's moderate growth in population combined with aggressive commercial development has produced a situation in which each retailer already has fewer customers. Domestic and foreign competition will pose a further management challenge to find ways of creating store traffic and transactions. Foreign retailers will follow the example set by firms such as Marks and Spencer, Toys ''Я'' Us, and Lenscrafter. The characteristics and the regionalization of Canada will cause many of these foreign firms to modify their operations to suit our marketplace.

Today's more educated consumer has increased the importance of finding a unique selling proposition that can be included in a firm's positioning strategy. The Canada–U.S. Free Trade Agreement will increase supplier choices, making unique product offerings viable through competitive and beneficial pricing.

The increase in consumers who demand time-saving goods and services has resulted in many enterprises' offering more flexible shopping hours, including Sunday shopping. These time-poor customers also want rapid access to top management. Many retail stores have responded by placing photographs of their executives in much of their promotional materials and advertising and pictures of their unit managers in visible locations throughout the retail store. The profile of unit managers on the sales floor and in the community has become a component in the review of managements' quarterly and annual performance.

Organizations must continually respond to customer needs and prove to the marketplace that their societal marketing concept considers all the pertinent issues of the day. The emerging concern for the environment is a force that decision makers must continue to address. The stocking of biodegradable

Brenda Hutchinson

products and environmentally friendly products is sure to rise dramatically in the 1990s. Provigo, Canada's second largest supermarket chain, has joined with environmentalists in a campaign to phase out the use of pesticides, especially cancer-causing chemicals.

Many Canadian retailers are pessimistic about the economic outlook for Central Canada but optimistic about the B.C. economy, according to a Touche Ross survey of 171 chain store retailers. Planning marketing strategies executed with precision in the retail environment will be crucial for an enterprise's survival and growth in the current decade. In brief, the challenge for retailers in the 1990s is to meet customer needs and to achieve financial objectives through effective production and marketing.

This chapter looks at the development of retail institutions, the organization of retailing today, and some important trends in the retail business.

Sources: Anthony Stokan, ''The 1990's — A Tough Time for Retailers,'' *Marketing*, p. 8, October, 1989; Mark Evans, ''Marks and Spencer Battles On,'' *Financial Post*, p. 32, December 11, 1989; Jim McElgunn, ''Survey Says Retailers Pessimistic about 1990,'' *Marketing*, p. 25, November 20, 1989; Jim McElgunn, ''Retail Council Conference Outlook — Canada Headed for Retail Invasion,'' *Marketing*, p. 2, October 2, 1989; Ian Bailey, ''Loblaws Introduces Re-Usable Bags,'' *Whig Standard* (Kingston, Ont.), p. 16, January 6, 1990; and Canadian Press, ''Retailers Assail Move To Phase Out Pesticide-Treated Produce,'' *Whig Standard* (Kingston, Ont.), p. 3, September 12, 1989.

The Scope of Retailing

Total Canadian retail sales will exceed $200 billion early this decade. Table 12.1 segments recent Canadian retail sales by province.

Large or small, the retailer must offer the ultimate customers what they want, when they want it, at the price they are prepared to pay. Restaurants, hotels, boutiques, street vendors, car dealers, and department stores are all part of the vast spectrum of the Canadian retailing industry. Many firms in these categories and many others are members of the Retail Council of Canada (see Figure 12.1). **Retailing** can be said to include all the activities involved in selling goods or services directly to final consumers for their personal, nonbusiness use.[1]

Table 12.1 Retail Sales in Canada

	1986	1987	1988	1989
British Columbia ($ million)	15 567	17 116	18 609	20 370
Annual % change	+8.8%	+10.0%	+8.7%	+9.5%
Alberta ($ million)	14 338	14 885	15 954	16 970
Annual % change	+6.0%	+3.6%	+7.4%	+6.4%
Saskatchewan ($ million)	4 999	5 254	5 502	5 590
Annual % change	+6.3%	+5.1%	+4.7%	+1.6%
Manitoba ($ million)	5 444	5 769	5 972	6 230
Annual % change	+4.7%	+6.0%	+3.5%	+4.3%
Ontario ($ million)	53 412	59 039	63 584	66 530
Annual % change	+9.0%	+10.5%	+7.7%	+4.6%
Quebec ($ million)	34 593	38 866	41 616	42 700
Annual % change	+8.8%	+12.4%	+7.1%	+2.6%
New Brunswick ($ million)	3 482	3 794	4 120	4 340
Annual % change	+9.8%	+9.0%	+8.6%	+5.3%
Nova Scotia ($ million)	4 796	5 225	5 606	5 800
Annual % change	+4.7%	+8.9%	+7.3%	+3.5%
Prince Edward Island ($ million)	577	641	704	735
Annual % change	+5.4%	+11.0%	+9.8%	+4.5%
Newfoundland ($ million)	2 407	2 755	3 074	3 260
Annual % change	+6.8%	+14.5%	+11.6%	+6.1%
NWT & Yukon ($ million)	393	417	451	475
Annual % change	+4.6%	+6.0%	+8.2%	+5.3%
Canada ($ million)	140 009	153 733	165 190	173 000
Annual % change	+8.2%	+9.8%	+7.5%	+4.7%

Note: Data for 1989 are estimates.

Source: "Report on the Nation," *Financial Post*, Winter 1989.

Figure 12.1 Retail Council of Canada Advertisement

Retailers are intermediaries who represent the only contact with the countless distribution channels that make up the national economy. They are the final testing ground for an entire marketing campaign. Table 12.2 lists the six rights of merchandising that willing retailers bear in mind every day.

The Development of Retailing Institutions

Consumers buy from a variety of retail institutions. Department stores, supermarkets, discount houses, and specialty stores are the kinds of

Table 12.2 The Rights of Retailing

''A Balancing Act''
■ The Right Product
■ The Right Price
■ The Right Time
■ The Right Quantity
■ The Right Appeal
■ The Right People

firms that constitute the more traditional retail field. But constant innovations in the industry—the development of catalogue showrooms, off-price shopping malls, video-game vending machines, and electronic shopping—continue to make retailing an exciting and fast-paced field.

Because the industry is changing so rapidly, it is difficult to categorize. Traditionally, retailing institutions were grouped into the categories of general merchandisers and limited-line merchandisers. For example, department stores and discounters were considered general merchandisers because they carried many different product lines—clothing, furniture, appliances, and so on. Supermarkets and specialty stores, on the other hand, were thought of as limited-line stores because they carried only one or two lines—food, shoes, or clothing. That classification has lost ground. Today retailers are also now classified as:

■ *Product retailers*—enterprises that purchase tangible products and sell them with a markup but otherwise no modifications. An example is Mac's Milk convenience stores, which merchandise milk, bread, and similar items.

■ *Service retailers*—enterprises offering service activities to the ultimate consumer. An example is firms that provide lawn maintenance.

■ *Converter retailers*—enterprises that modify items before offering them to the customers. Examples are restaurants and night clubs.

Another way to look at the classification of retailers is to realize that this is the era of **scrambled merchandising:** retailers who previously specialized in a particular line now sell many nontraditional lines as well.

Scrambled Merchandising
Practice, by previously specialized retailers, of selling many unrelated lines of goods.

Thus almost all retail classifications have become untidy. To clarify the marketing aspects of the retailing industry, this discussion focuses on how the various elements of the marketing mix are manipulated to give each retailing firm its unique character. The following sections look at several kinds of businesses:

■ Retailers that emphasize product mix.

■ Retailers that stress price.

- Retailers that carve out a niche by offering unique distribution approaches.

While many of the categories overlap, the main challenge for marketers is to appreciate the scope of retailing and to understand the opportunities available.

This approach also permits emphasis on the role of the retailer in the marketing system. That role is to

- Bring together manufacturers' products and potential consumers (provide form utility).

- Co-ordinate customer feedback to suppliers.

- Assume much of the distribution risk (help with possession utility).

- Offer accessible locations for the buying public (provide place utility).

- Offer time utility.

Emphasis on Product Mix

Businesses categorized by emphasis on product mix are best described by the kind of merchandise they offer. On a continuum, they may range from extremely focused specialty stores to large operations offering a wide variety of product lines.

Specialty Stores

In pre-Confederation times, bootmakers, druggists, bakers, and others opened shops in cities. On the frontier, peddlers settled down and opened similar shops. Today, **specialty stores,** which concentrate on selling a large selection of only one line of merchandise, predominate in retailing. Most are independently owned, but a few are chains. In some cases, these stores carry specialization to an extreme, selling only mystery books, women's tennis clothes, or some other narrow product line.

Specialty Store
Store that concentrates on selling a selection of only one line of merchandise.

Compucentre is an example of a product retailer operating with a specialized format. Compucentre responded to the initial explosion of the home computer market by offering an assortment of name brands that satisfied the consumer need for personal computers. Capitalizing on a category of goods or services before the growth stage of the market lifecycle can result in that merchant's capturing a significant market share.

Superstores

Specialization enables small retailers to thrive by targeting a narrow segment of the market. Specialty stores can also succeed in the marketplace by carrying a broad selection. Large stores that carry a broad selection of one type of product at low prices are called **superstores.**

Superstore
Large store that carries a broad selection of one type of product at low prices. Sometimes called "category killer."

Retailers such as Footlocker and Leon's Furniture are sometimes referred to as "category killers" because their inventory assortment and value pricing can devastate competitors.

The 1990s will bring more examples of *outboarding*. In this diversification strategy, the retailer spins off a store related to the firm's original concept. For example, Footlocker now has Ladies' Footlocker and Kids' Footlocker units.

Department Stores

Department Store
Store that brings together a number of items under one roof.

A **department store** is an establishment that brings together a number of product lines under one roof. Many department stores originated as specialty stores, but they took on new lines as demand increased among a growing urban population. The distinguishing characteristics of Eaton's and other such stores is their organization by departments. In a department store, responsibility for stocking a particular line (or "department") of goods is delegated to a buyer. Sears Canada and The Bay are examples of stores that have invested significant funds to design, renovate, and place fixtures in their units to merchandise goods by category. Firms in this retailing category departmentalize by carrying a wide variety of merchandise lines and rarely specialize in merchandise categories.

Some department stores have taken this concept one step further. They have arranged merchandise into boutiques of similar goods. One area might be targeted to working women and another to teen-age users of cosmetics.

The boutique concept is growing in popularity because it allows retailers to provide a clear focal point for consumers. It is also very flexible. Colours, display decor, and graphics can be altered to feature new merchandise without disrupting the entire floor.[2]

Three other characteristics of modern department stores are important. First, they offer many augmented services, including delivery, credit, and money-back guarantees. Their operating expenses are as high as 40 cents for every dollar's worth of goods sold. Second, the Christmas season is crucial to their financial performance (see Marketing Today 12.1). Third, department stores appeal mainly to the upper and middle classes.

Today, the major challenge is the low prices offered by superstores, discount houses, off-price retailers, and manufacturers that are now becoming retailers. Sears startled the U.S. market in 1989 by announcing the elimination of specific sales and beginning an everyday low price strategy. It is interesting to note that the Canadian organization did not follow the lead of its U.S. parent.[3] To survive, many department stores are dropping lines that yield relatively low profits. Some department stores have eliminated hardware and paint departments. Instead, stores emphasize fashion goods and are expanding into the sale of services. For example, customers of Sears Canada can now purchase insurance,

Marketing Today 12.1

November and December Can Be the Chips!

Retailing managers must organize their programs on an annual basis. For many retailers, the volume of business completed in November and December emphasizes the necessity of being prepared.

Bill Turner, vice-president of merchandising for Sears Canada says of these two months, "It is a nervous time. It does not matter whether you are in good shape or bad shape for the year."

November and December can make or break a retailer's annual performance. For department stores, those two months' sales represent approximately 26 percent of a year's revenues. The accompanying table shows similar figures for other types of retailers. (If sales were constant throughout the year, each month would see 8.8 percent of the annual amount and a two-month total would, of course, be 17.6 percent.)

The importance of the Christmas selling season has resulted in many stores' modifying their year-end from December or January 31 to September 30. This shift provides more accurate projections, since the numbers for November and December often are indicators of the outcome for the remainder of the year.

Source: Adapted from "Sears Very Optimistic about Make or Break November and December," *The Financial Post*, November 21, 1988.

Christmas Season Sales, 1988

Store Category	Nov. and Dec. as % of Annual Total
Men's clothing	28.8%
Women's clothing	22.4
Household furniture	20.3
Book and stationery	29.3
Jewellery	33.1

Source: Statistics Canada, *Retail Trade*, cat. no. 63-005, Sept. 1988, pp. 54–55.

arrange vacations, order flowers by telephone, and have their eye-glass prescriptions filled.

Supermarkets

The idea of a **supermarket,** dividing a food store into areas carrying dry goods, dairy products, and fresh produce and allowing customers to make their own selection, was introduced in the 1920s. It caught on, however, only in the 1930s when people became more price conscious. Alert retailers recognized that if they could sell in large volume, costs — and prices — would go down. Technological advances (such as better refrigeration) and marketing advances (including consumer-sized packaging and brand acceptance) also aided the development of supermarkets.[4]

Although their sales are large, most supermarkets have trouble maintaining even the industry's normal 1-percent profit margin. The market for groceries is saturated in many places. Inflation and increased labour costs resulting from demographic shifts and unionization[5] also explain some of the increases in supermarkets' operating expenses, which have made it a challenge to generate the desired profitability.

Supermarket
Retail food store that carries dry groceries, dairy products, and fresh produce and allows customers to make their own selection.

In addition, supermarkets face stiff competition from fast-food establishments, whose share of the Canadian food dollar was substantial in the early 1980s. Grocery stores have thus adjusted their product assortment with new offerings, such as bakery goods, fresh pizza, and flowers.

An increasingly segmented population is now demanding many, often contradictory, things from supermarkets. As one analyst observed, "We want expansive displays of the provender of the land in brilliantly illuminated, air-conditioned, hangar-size buildings; we want low prices and unlimited selection; generic paper towels and genuine French Roquefort; a comfortably small store around the corner, open cartons on steel shelves, one-stop shopping, all-night banking, and a place to park the car."[6]

Supermarkets are responding to the challenge of higher costs and lower profits in different ways.[7] Scrambled merchandising is one of them. Setting up delicatessens and salad bars with high-profit carry-out items is another.

In addition, stores are expanding to achieve even greater savings through volume sales, and many are automating the checkout stand. The adoption of electronic point-of-sale cash register systems ("point and shoot") has increased significantly over the years and has resulted in an improvement in quality and timely management information while improving operating productivity. On the horizon is debit purchasing — a shopper can have the store automatically deduct the purchase amount from his or her bank account — which will improve the cash flow of the enterprise and provide a convenient payment option for many customers. The Royal Bank recently tested this payment program in the London, Ontario, area with considerable success.[8]

Supermarkets are also taking a variety of new approaches to attract customers. Many are open longer hours, including Sundays, and offer a variety of customer services such as cheque cashing. To attract customers, some stores have even hosted events such as singles nights. Other developments are described in Marketing Today 12.2. The field of grocery marketing has also given rise to several new species of stores — some larger and some smaller than conventional supermarkets.

Convenience Stores

Convenience Store
Small retail outlet that provides snack food and staple groceries quickly and conveniently.

The small stores attracting today's consumers are called **convenience stores** — small retail outlets providing snacks and staple goods quickly and conveniently. Their convenience includes short lines, parking close by, long hours, and locations near busy streets and intersections. Originally concentrated in the suburbs, which lacked local food markets, and in warmer climates (where people are more apt to run to the store at night), convenience stores today are located throughout North America. Major chains include Mac's Milk, Beckers, and Hasty Market.[9]

Marketing Today 12.2

Supermarket Update

The hottest growth areas in today's supermarkets are delis and in-store bakeries. Supermarket owners are attracted to them because deli and bakery food is more profitable than other products sold in supermarkets. Industry experts are recommending that supermarkets offer product samples at the deli and bakery counters and that they suggest other grocery products consumers can use with deli and bakery items.

Taking this approach one step further, many supermarkets are turning to ready-to-eat foods, such as barbecued ribs, chickens, pastas, soups, and salad bars. Some stores even provide sit-down areas for eating these products.

Supermarket owners are also struggling with limited shelf space during a time of rapid product development. With food compa-

Phyllis Woloshin

nies introducing 20 to 30 products a week, supermarkets must either bump slower-moving products or refuse to stock the new ones. As a result, the new products that make it onto store shelves are often those of the largest companies with the most clout. And one survey shows that over half of shoppers are unhappy that they cannot find certain items anymore.

Sources: Lynn Asinof, "Business Bulletin," *The Wall Street Journal*, February 5, 1987, p. 1; Doreen Higgins, "The Power of the Supermarket," *Advertising Age*, August 18, 1986, p. 18; Robert Johnson and Betsy Morris, "Food Companies Fight to Display More Products on Less Shelf Space," *The Wall Street Journal*, April 10, 1986, p. 35; and "Supermarket Delis Striving to Attract Shoppers with Quality, Convenience," *Marketing News*, July 4, 1986, p. 1.

Besides groceries, cold pop, and baked goods, convenience stores offer a growing array of services that complement the life-style of many working Canadians. There are approximately 30 million gasoline transactions per week in Canada. Filling up one's car is not an optional activity, and it has become a suitable product extension for retailers offering convenience goods.[10]

Industry observers explain the popularity of convenience stores as reflecting the rise in the number of two-income, two-career households and the greater number of single-person households. Today's consumers value time and convenience. Many convenience store operations provide banking services from automatic teller machines, video rentals, prepared foods, and postal services. Such product- and service-line extensions have created an increase in convenience store traffic that has benefited operators. Canada now has more than 5000 convenience stores with annual sales of more than $6 billion.[11]

The challenge for owners of convenience stores is to find a way to attract women and upscale consumers. Many are trying to do so by making their stores safer and more attractive.

Combination Stores and Hypermarkets

Combination Store
Combination of a supermarket and a drugstore under a single roof.

Hypermarket
Giant mass merchandiser that offers a broad selection of hard and soft goods and grocery items at discount prices on a self-serve basis.

A "combo" store, as a **combination store** is called in the retail trade, is what results when a drugstore is crossed with a supermarket. Combo stores profit by exposing food shoppers to general merchandise.[12]

Hypermarkets are even larger mass merchandisers that offer a broad selection of hard and soft goods and grocery items at discount prices on a self-serve basis. Hypermarkets keep costs down in a variety of ways. They typically resemble warehouses more than specialty shops. Their volume allows them to cut the prices of certain products. They also spend a relatively low amount on labour. Even so, to break even, most hypermarkets must move at least $1 million worth of merchandise each week. This makes hypermarkets a risky kind of retailing.[13]

Service Retailers

Many retail establishments offer activities to their target market with or without tangible products. Landscapers, rock concert organizers, movie theatres, and hotel operators are all part of the growing service economy. Often these service retailers are just beginning to tap the potential of full-scale marketing.[14] Tridont, for example, has a chain of dentist locations in shopping malls that offer evening and weekend access for individuals requiring dental work.

Many service retailers are acquiring an understanding of the way marketplace needs shift with changes in the environment (social, demographic, natural, legal, and so on). The importance of customer service must be in the forefront of the retailer's mind; some general observations about this rule of thumb are listed in Table 12.3.

Emphasis on Price

Pricing is a critical component in any marketing strategy. Nowhere has the battle over prices been as hard fought as in the retailing industry. While price cutting may have the retailing industry in an uproar, it has been a bonanza for consumers. A significant group of customers will often sacrifice some of the amenities of full-price, full-selection stores in return for a chance to buy anything from apples to zippers at discounted prices.

Table 12.3 Winning and Losing in the Retail Service Game

Winning Service Retailers
- Are noticeably more friendly, courteous, and really care about customer satisfaction
- Go out of their way to understand customer needs
- Consider the smallest detail as critical
- Know the business exceedingly well: its products, its services, its procedures, and how to get things done quickly and accurately
- Shine under pressure, especially in solving customer problems
- Adopt integrity as their byword
- Exhibit genuine appreciation for patronage

Losing Service Retailers
- Dehumanize the service delivery interaction by inattention or plastic professionalism
- Regard questions or service requests as interruptions or nuisances
- Often do not keep promises
- Are poor trouble shooters and unskilled in rectifying problems promptly
- Appear disorganized, inefficient, and waste the customer's time without noticeable regret
- Communicate in vague language

Source: George A. Reider, "'Show me': The Secret To Building a Service-Minded Culture," *Retailing Issues Letter* (Center for Retailing Studies, Texas A&M University), June 1986, p. 1.

Discount Stores

Discount stores, which sell fast-moving merchandise at cut-rate prices, have capitalized on the strategy of manufacturers that promote products directly to the ultimate consumer. Firms such as Campbells, Kelloggs, and Heinz have created not only brand acceptance, but brand insistence! Discount stores were created when retailers who understood the opportunity reacted by developing locations that provided low prices for brand-name products, stores that could generate high volume with reasonable operating expenses. When the recession of the early 1980s forced much of the buying public to become more price aware, one result was the coming of age of discount retailing.[15]

To guarantee low prices, the discounters had to keep costs low. They set up stores in low-rent places, kept interiors plain, and eliminated traditional retail services such as sales assistance, credit, and delivery. The discounters did offer extended shopping hours and ample parking.

Discounters soon added many other products, such as toys, cameras, luggage, and housewares. At the same time, separate discount outlets specializing in apparel sprang up, among them Zayre and Shoppers Fair. The older stores followed their lead and added clothing. Discount houses became full-line discount department stores. Other established retailers, noting the success of discount operations, started discount operations of their own.

In recent years, discounters have found that simply offering low prices does not guarantee success. In the mid 1980s shoppers began to focus on

Discount Store
Store that sells fast-moving branded merchandise at cut-rate prices.

value rather than on price. Many were willing to pay a little more to get a quality product.[16]

Some discounters met the challenge successfully by improving their decor, expanding services (taking charge cards, offering "rain checks" for out-of-stock merchandise, and improving their return policies), and carrying more attractive lines of merchandise. Discount stores, such as Willie Wonderful, selling designer clothing are another attempt to meet the demand for quality products at low prices. Today, many shoppers get information at more expensive stores, then try to find the products they are interested in at discount stores. Of course, selections at the discount stores are often limited.

One of the most influential trends in the field has been the rise of the specialty discounter. The Home Economist sells gourmet foods at a discount, and the Linen Factory sells discount linens. Barnes and Noble and Coles Books sell all their books at less than list price, and establishments such as 47th St. Photo in Manhattan do a thriving business in cameras and computers.

Warehouse Stores

Warehouse Store
No-frills store that emphasizes lower prices over atmosphere and customer service.

Warehouse stores were born in the early 1970s as no-frills operations that sacrificed atmosphere and customer services in order to offer consumers the lowest possible prices. In food warehouses, items are typically displayed in original packing cases, the selection of merchandise is usually limited, and customers bag their own groceries in boxes or pay extra for shopping bags. Prices are often from 10 to 30 percent less than in traditional supermarkets.

Many warehouse stores are adding features unknown to their more primitive ancestors. At Ikea furniture stores, shoppers can select from thousands of different household articles stacked on flats. Each metropolitan area is served by only one retail outlet. Toronto's store, which cost some $20 million to locate in suburban North York, is one of the largest in North America at 23 000 square metres.[17] The store provides customers with little sales help—just a tape measure, a catalogue, and a map of the store. Customers hoist their own merchandise onto carts and then assemble the furniture themselves when they get home. For many customers, this extra work is justified by low prices. Ikea targets a narrow customer base (Baby Boomers and young singles) with clean-line modular furniture that has a reasonable price tag.[18]

Home Improvement Centres

Home Improvement Centre
Large-scale hardware store that offers one-stop shopping for around-the-house needs at prices that may be somewhat lower than those at smaller hardware stores.

Home improvement centres are really large-scale hardware stores for do-it-yourself customers. The stores stock building materials, paint, garden supplies, and tools. Their prices may be somewhat lower than traditional hardware stores, but their main attraction is one-stop shopping for around-the-house needs. Canadian Tire is an example of a retailer that is serving this market segment.

Catalogue Showrooms

Catalogue showrooms combine the low prices of discount stores with catalogue promotion. Retailers such as Consumers Distributing sell a variety of brand-name hard goods, such as small appliances, jewellery, and luggage, at substantially reduced prices. Consumers receive colour catalogues in the mail or travel to the showroom to page through them. The showrooms display a limited selection of the items in the catalogue. Customers choose what they want, fill out an order form, and pick up their goods from an adjacent warehouse.

Catalogue showrooms cut costs by buying in bulk, stocking brand-name items, leasing stores in low-rent areas, and hiring few salespeople. Customers must travel farther and receive little service, but the low prices make catalogue showrooms attractive. However, with increasing competition from discount stores and sales in department stores, catalogue showrooms have had to struggle to maintain sales and profits.[19]

Emphasis on Location

At the turn of the century, little variety stores and small shops accounted for much of the retail business in North American towns. In the cities, department stores and specialty shops clustered together to create thriving central business districts. In the 1950s, suburban growth led to the rise of the shopping centre, which took sales from small-town and big-city retail businesses. Nonstore retailing is now on the rise, with many consumers responding to the direct marketing programs offered by retailers through catalogues and electronic shopping (television, telephone, and computer).

The location of a retail business — the corner grocer or the computer terminal in the living room — has always been of critical significance. Consider now some of the issues facing retailers in traditional locations and what the future of retailing might bring.

The Importance of Retail Store Site Selection

The location decision has always been important, but today more so than ever. There are two major areas in which stores locate — in the central business district and in shopping centres.

The Central Business District

The **central business district** is the downtown shopping area of most cities, and it consists of large department stores and specialty stores.

Catalogue Showroom
Retail discount business based on catalogue promotion and showrooms that display a limited selection of the items in the catalogue. Customers receive goods from an adjacent warehouse.

Central Business District
Downtown shopping area of most cities, consisting of large department stores and specialty stores.

Downtown areas have been in decline over the past quarter century as population growth shifted to the suburbs. However, efforts to revive them are now under way, usually by reconstructing them around a central shopping mall.

Shopping Centres

A **shopping centre** is a group of stores planned, owned, and managed as a unit and with ample parking facilities, usually located in a suburban area. The owner plans not only the location and size of the stores, but also the types of stores. The three types of shopping centres, which are distinguished by size and types of store, are shown in Figure 12.2.

The strip mall serves up to 20 000 customers and has between 5 and 15 stores — usually a supermarket and small specialty shops. A community shopping centre is larger — 15 to 35 stores, including both a department store and a supermarket, and it may serve 100 000 customers. The largest of all is the regional shopping centre. An extreme example is Alberta's West Edmonton Mall, which contains more than 800

Shopping Centre
Group of stores planned, owned, and managed as a unit and with ample parking, usually in a suburban area.

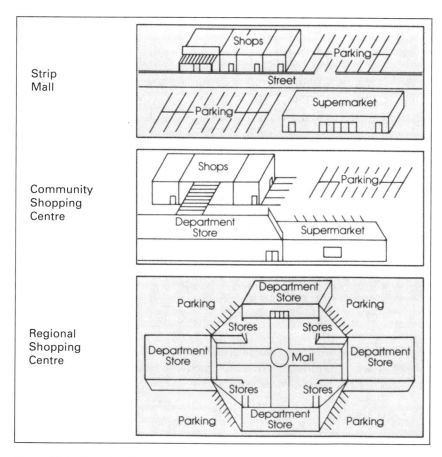

Figure 12.2 Shopping Centre Types

shops, several dozen restaurants, 34 theatres, an 18-hole miniature golf course, a four-hectare water park for swimming and sunning under tanning lamps, two dozen amusement rides, and a 360-room hotel for extended stays. All these attractions are housed under a single roof.[20]

Centre-City Marketplaces

Shopping centres have traditionally been a suburban phenomenon, dependent, as they were, on vast expanses of cheap land. But inner cities are now fighting back. To lure shoppers into town again, many cities have turned decaying slums or waterfront warehouse districts into fashionable shopping centres. Downtown merchants, via business associations, along with municipal governments, are driving programs, many of which include parking expansion to attract customers to the area.

Off-Price and Factory Outlet Shopping Centres

Until recently, factory outlets and off-price retailers generally operated out of stripped-down, single-unit facilities in out-of-the-way locations. It was only a matter of time before several would decide to band together into shopping centres. Lured by the promise of bargains in a large grouping of such stores, out-of-town shoppers from an eight-state region regularly converge on Reading, Pennsylvania. One of Orlando's most popular adult attractions, besides Disney's Epcot Center, is Factory Outlet Mall, a 32 500-square-metre extravaganza of 67 off-price and factory outlet stores and 13 kiosks. There are about 100 off-price centres in the United States.

Outlet malls tend to differ from their more traditional counterparts in a significant way: studies have shown that from 50 to 60 percent of the shoppers live outside the centre's metro area. Notes one developer, "Be sure to provide parking for bus tour use, and [locate] close to major road access."[21]

Nonstore Retailing

What do a soft drink machine, a weekly newspaper, and a neighbourhood ice cream vendor have in common? They are all forms of nonstore retailing.

The idea for selling merchandise independent of a store site is not new. Itinerant peddlers travelled the land long before bulk postal rates were invented. While some forms of nonstore retailing are thriving, others are suffering as the demographics and life-styles of consumers change.

Door-to-Door Selling

When farmers were far from a central marketplace, peddlers were the suppliers of wares that could not be made on the farm. Travelling salespeople brought knapsacks or saddlebags full of tools, buttons, medicines, and wooden utensils — and they brought the news as well. Today, the leaders in the direct-sales business include Tupperware, Michelle-Lynn Jewellery, and Amway.

Some modern door-to-door salespeople are paid commissions of 50 to 100 percent on the products they sell by the companies for which they work. Others are independents who own the merchandise they sell (merchant wholesalers). Most still prospect for customers by canvassing houses. A few, such as those who work for Tupperware and Mary Kay, arrange in-home parties to demonstrate goods and take orders.

Recently, however, this type of selling has been experiencing some serious problems. Some companies are having trouble finding recruits. Women who demonstrated cosmetics, for example, are taking steadier jobs in other fields. Once in the full-time work force, those same women are often reluctant to spend leisure time on selling parties, and they can afford to buy cosmetics in department stores. In addition, increased divorce rates and mobility have broken down the extended networks of relatives, friends, and neighbours that such salespeople used to rely on.[22]

Direct Marketing

Mail-Order Firm
Company that provides a wide range of goods ordered by customers from catalogues and shipped directly to them by mail.

While department stores were developing to meet the needs of city dwellers, a new type of firm began servicing the rural countryside. The **mail-order firm** provided customers with a wide variety of goods ordered from catalogues and shipped by mail. When Sears was founded in 1886, it started putting out a store catalogue. In Canada, Eaton's started its catalogue in 1884. In rural areas, the arrival of the catalogues was a regular social event.

Many of the early mail-order houses later became chain department stores, but much of their business is still conducted through the mail. About one-quarter of the business at Sears comes from mail-order business.[23]

Many specialty and traditional department stores send out catalogues as well. One of Ikea's strongest marketing strategies is mailing a 3000-item catalogue annually to more than 2 million Canadians.[24] The promotional program of Intertan Canada Limited (Tandy products) includes direct marketing targeted at large employee groups, such as employees of financial and educational institutions.

The American Direct Marketing Association has predicted that by the year 2000, one-fourth of consumer expenditures will be for mail-order sales.[25] A major reason for the popularity of catalogues is that the decline in the number of full-time homemakers means that fewer people have time to spend in stores.

Marketers have taken note of the interest in mail-order shopping, and the number of catalogues produced has soared. As a result of this competition, it has become more difficult to start a new catalogue business.

Along with direct-mail marketing, other forms of direct marketing are growing in importance. These include newspaper inserts, direct-response ads in magazines, 800-number advertising on radio and television, and telephone selling.

Telephone selling, in which salespeople phone potential customers, is often referred to as **telemarketing.** Some marketers are using computers to recite prerecorded messages or to dial phone numbers automatically. Consumers often object to the computerized phone calls, and some jurisdictions regulate their use. Marketers who are considering this approach must therefore first investigate consumer attitudes and legal requirements.

Telemarketing
Direct selling in which salespeople telephone potential customers.

Automatic Vending Machines

Vending machines, which dispense goods automatically after money is inserted, are not new. The ancient Egyptians had such machines to sell sacrificial water 2200 years ago. Vending machines became widespread in Canada only in the 1960s. Improvements, such as reliable change makers and machines to refrigerate and heat products, spurred their growth. The development of this industry in Canada is illustrated in Figure 12.3. Since the date of the latest data there, the federal government's introduction of the loonie to replace one-dollar bills has been another positive environment force for the vending machine industry.[26]

Vending Machine
Device that dispenses products automatically after money is inserted.

The four big items dispensed are candy, coffee, cigarettes, and cold drinks. Food and nonfood items such as stockings, newspapers, stamps, and railroad tickets are also sold through vending machines. Vending machines that sell services include coin-operated photocopiers, telephones, juke boxes, and skate sharpeners.

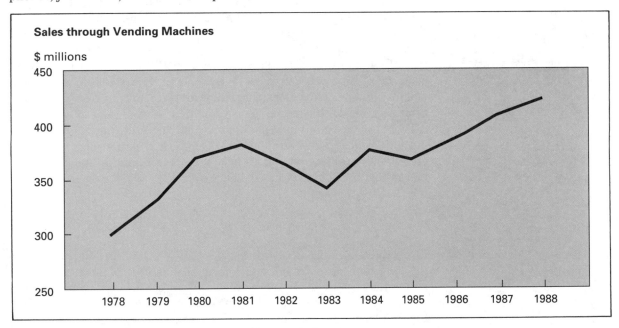

Sales through Vending Machines

Figure 12.3 The Growth of the Vending Machine Industry in Canada

Source: Statistics Canada, *Vending Machine Operators*, April 1990, cat. no. 63-213, p. 6.

Debit cards issued at vending machine sites by a cashier or a currency machine are being tested by Toronto-based Versa Foods, Canada's largest vending machine retailer. Bell Canada has introduced payment by generic credit cards to supplement its own credit card. The most common examples of vending machines that use cards are automatic teller machines, which dispense cash or perform other banking services when the user inserts a banking card. Similarly, travellers can use credit cards to buy airline tickets and travellers cheques through vending machines.

Marketers are also experimenting with computer terminals that display various gift items. The terminals are located in kiosks in airports, colleges and universities, supermarkets, office buildings, and industrial parks. Customers can select an item and order from a warehouse linked to the terminal. The success of these machines has so far been mixed; many consumers miss the interaction with a human salesperson and the immediate gratification of carrying away what they buy.[27]

The growth in the use of vending machines has been steady, but there are some problems. Mechanical breakdowns and a high pilferage rate make them an expensive way of retailing; nevertheless, they will continue to be used because of customer demand.

The Organization of Retailing

Sears, Roebuck and the little neighbourhood mom-and-pop shop represent two distinct forms of organization for retail stores—the chain and the independent. Sears is a classic **chain store,** which may be defined as a group of stores centrally owned and managed that sell similar goods. By contrast, an **independent store** is usually a one-unit operation owned and managed by a single person, partnership, or corporation.[28] Not all chains are large, as is the case with the Dylex group, which consists of Big Steel, Fairweather, Suzy Shier, Harry Rosen, and so on. Chains can have only a few stores and can be in just one area or region. Similarly, not all independents are small, at least in sales volume.

There are also giant merchandising conglomerates that may own several different types of retail chains. Moreover, another form, the franchise (which represents a cross between a chain and an independent), has gained in popularity in the last 25 years.

Independents

Firms that specialize in certain services, such as landscaping, dry cleaning, and hair care, are often independent businesses. Such stores are numerous because of the advantages they offer the owner and the consumer. They are relatively easy to establish, requiring little capital. Independents offer customers three important benefits:

1. *Convenience in shopping.* Independents are often neighbourhood or territory stores.

Chain Store
Group of stores centrally owned and managed that sell similar goods.

Independent Store
Store owned and managed by a single person, partnership, or corporation, usually a one-unit operation.

2. *Service extras.* Most independents stay open long hours, give credit, cash cheques, deliver, and offer personalized service.

3. *Timely goods.* Independents purchase frequently and in small quantities; thus they can keep abreast of rapidly changing styles and customer preferences.

Small independent retailers suffer from some limitations, however, such as deficiencies in management specialization and lack of volume purchasing, that affect their pricing structure. To alleviate the bulk buying issue problem, some independent retailers form buying groups, such as the Toronto Culinary Purchasers Society, which can pass on to members as much as 15-percent savings on a variety of products.[29]

Independent stores frequently fail because of a lack of management experience and poor execution of the retailing mix elements. The major reason is often related to the proprietor's lack of experience in retail management. One disadvantage of independents is the difficulty they experience in accessing suitable professional development. The association described in Figure 12.4 provides professional training to many family enterprises in Canada.

Chains

Chain stores developed in the 1920s, first among grocery stores and then in other retail areas. Today, chain stores (regional, national, and international) account for most of the sales of department stores, discount stores, and food stores, as well as for a large proportion of the sales of shoe stores and drugstores.

The main characteristics of chain stores are centralized buying and centralized management. The chain's main office buys much the same merchandise (with some regional and other variations) for all stores and receives discounts for large purchases. The main office ordinarily sets prices and creates advertising that stores run locally. Store layout may be standardized. Much of the effort of management and staff focuses on delivering a consistent product and service offering in each location (see Figure 12.5). The presence of standardized systems is evident where regular quality assurance evaluations are performed by regional and divisional management members. Marketing Today 12.3 describes the key role that employees have in the overall effectiveness of the firms for which they work.

Centralization allows chains to overcome the drawbacks of independents. Prices are lower because costs can be spread over a large number of stores. Management can hire specialists to handle advertising, window display, warehousing, and other business functions.

In the past, independents had a clear advantage in the number of services they offered, but now most stores extend credit and stay open long hours. Chains are still often at a disadvantage, however, in offering timely goods. Centralized buying requires ordering in advance and in

Canadian association of family enterprise
Association canadienne des entreprises familiales

Objectives and Brief History

CAFE's Objectives are:

* To educate, inform and encourage its members in areas of unique interest to the family business, through a stimulating program of activities that brings to its members the best sources of information and professional advice available.
* To foster greater awareness and understanding of governments of family enterprise and of its function in the present and future economic community of Canada.
* To provide the nucleus for meaningful exchange of ideas and help between individuals involved in family enterprise at all generation levels.
* To build a network of aquaintanceship and information-sharing between participants in family business throughout Canada.

In brief, CAFE's purpose is to provide the kind of personal and business support for family members that you simply can't obtain elsewhere in Canada at any price.

A Brief History

In mid 1983, a small group of family business owners found their conversations frequently turning to the desirability of forming a communications network of fellow owner/participants in Family Enterprises.

All agreed that many of their business problems and opportunities were unique to this form of business structure, but usually common to them as a group. Often, on an informal basis, they had helped one another over some of these special hurdles through the exchange of present knowledge and past experience. They were also aware that outside Canada, formal associations of "family business" had been actively operating for many years. There was no such formal association in Canada.

Casual conversation turned to planning, and in October, 1983, two founding luncheons were held, culminating in the election of 17 founding directors. CAFE itself was formally constituted on December 12, 1983, as a federally chartered, non-profit association, fully owned and operated by its members through its Board of Directors.

Figure 12.4 Support for Family Businesses: CAFE

Exterior	Interior
• Sign	• Lighting
• Parking lot maintenance	• Cleanliness of restrooms, floors
• Window signage	• Signing
• Window displays	• House music
Merchandise Presentation	**Customer Service**
• Display quality	• Appearance
• Condition of merchandise	• Product knowledge
• Pricing	• Selling skills
• Point-of-purchase items	• Appearance

Figure 12.5 Retail Is Detail: Store Checklist

massive quantities. Sears cannot afford to be a leader in new tennis fashions or evening wear because a misjudgement of public taste may mean a huge loss.

Associations of Independents

Among independents, the trend today is to take advantage of some of the benefits of group membership without giving up freedom and flexibility. Several types of organizations have been tried.

Ownership Groups

Among department stores, the **ownership group** is common. In this organization (1) stores are owned by a corporation, (2) some management functions (research, recordkeeping, finance) are performed centrally, and (3) some centralized buying for nonfashion goods may be practised. But stores keep their separate names and do most of their buying and planning independently.

Franchising

The franchising concept is both a distribution strategy for franchisors and a means for entrepreneurs to launch into business. Franchising as a business format exploded in the 1970s and 1980s. A **franchise** is a

Ownership Group
Type of department store organization in which stores keep their separate name but are owned by a corporation that centrally provides some buying and management functions.

Franchise
Agreement whereby an independent businessperson sells the products or services of another company, uses its name, adopts its policies and otherwise operates it in accord with the methods prescribed by the head office.

Marketing Today 12.3

Managing Human Resources in Retail

In the 1980s, many retailing firms began to realize that they could gain a competitive edge with the recruitment and development of quality staff. Productivity has improved with the introduction of internal training programs and with a commitment from senior management to life-long learning. Extensive professional development programs are now preparing service personnel to communicate and deal with the public better.

Compensation programs have become more systematic, and remuneration has moved ahead of the provincial minimum wage in many outlets. The growth of the Retail, Wholesale, and Department Store Union which now has more than 225 000 members, has also increased management's awareness of high quality leadership. Reductions in employee turnover have been achieved through training, career development, and motivating management. These human resources management approaches are now priorities for segments of the Canadian food service and hospitality industry and others.

Retailing can expose individuals to the marketing, production, and operations components of a business. The ability to design a needed product and service and then to deliver it effectively to the target market will always require human resources! People skills in retailing now include customer, supplier, and employee relations.

legal agreement whereby an independent businessperson sells the products or services of another company, uses its name, adopts its policies, and otherwise operates it in accord with the methods prescribed by the head office (franchisor). Table 12.4 describes some of the advantages and disadvantages of franchising.

Table 12.4 Franchising: Advantages and Disadvantages

Advantage	Disadvantages
Best chance of success	High cost to enter
Total business package	Ongoing royalty for the support
Acquisition of a proven package	Little or no deviation from set business standards
Volume discounts	Limited scope for growth without purchase of a second franchise location
Management training and development	
Market analysis territory protection	

Source: *Starting a Small Business*, Ontario Ministry of Industry, Trade and Technology, (Toronto, 1989), p. 20.

Franchise owners are neither independent operators nor mere store managers. In most cases they have the right to sell their businesses, but they operate under the rules of the parent company. They receive training from the parent company and assistance in recordkeeping and operating the business after that. The company sets prices, creates advertising programs, and may require owners to buy inventory and supplies from it.

Many store owners are glad to be relieved of these responsibilities, but some resent their lack of decision-making power, and others complain about abuses by franchisors.

Partly because of troubled relations, many parent companies are trying to gain more control by buying back franchises and turning them into company-owned outlets. Several companies, including McDonald's and Radio Shack, are expanding overseas to avoid more competition in the saturated North American market. However, franchising opportunities still exist in Canada and the United States, especially in business areas long dominated by independents—among them real estate, travel services, accounting, and home remodeling.[30]

Industry experts predict that 55 to 60 percent of retail sales will be generated from franchise organizations by the end of the 1990s. Expansion of this retailing sector will include casualties, most falling because various franchising concepts have been mismanaged or inadequately tested before being packaged. The idea that all franchisors will catch a struggling franchisee is a myth.

Before beginning a formal relationship with a franchisor, prospective franchisees should acquire experts' opinions if they lack experience in franchise law, accounting, or marketing. Because of past problems, some U.S. jurisdictions now have legal requirements for the selling of franchises. So does Alberta, whose Franchise Act requires franchisors to register with the Alberta Securities Commission prior to selling franchises.[31] Such full disclosure is likely to be a legal requirement in other provinces as casualties continue to increase.

Creating an Image

Once retail proprietors have decided on a product line, pricing strategy, location, and ownership, they must consider the type of image they want their stores to project. (See Figure 12.6.)

Evidence suggests that consumers shop at stores that match their own self-images. A study was made of how three stores in New York were viewed by their shoppers. The profiles of the three stores closely matched the customers' views of themselves. The lower-income shoppers at one store saw the store as "plain, rugged, economical." The trendy upscale shoppers described their store [Bloomingdale's] as "modern, sophisticated, extravagant." The study concluded, "The more widely separated the store image and the self-image, the less likely the shopper will find the store attractive."[32] Some shoppers will go to a prestige store to improve their own self-images, however.

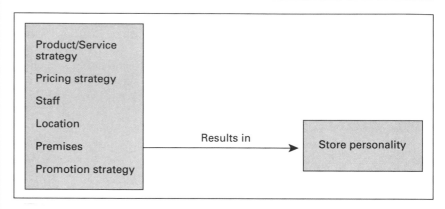

Figure 12.6 The Retailing Mix

Store Location

Often the most important decision in the planning of a store is where to locate the unit. Location is more crucial to a retail enterprise than to many other types of businesses. The quality of the location affects, among other things, the amount of advertising that a firm must allocate to generate store traffic.

When selecting a site, management must consider the following:

- Is the location available?

- Is the location suitable?

- Is the location accessible to customers?

- Is the location affordable?

Store Design

Store design plays an important role in presenting the proper message to customers. Customers often judge a retail store by external appearance. Store fixtures, lighting, carpeting, and merchandise displays all contribute to the impression that a store makes on a customer. No one design is best. What works for a supermarket might be a disaster in a specialty store and vice versa. However, studies have shown that some patterns are better than others for different categories of stores.

The first task any store designer faces is layout. Some establishments, such as supermarkets and discount houses, are laid out in a grid pattern with straight aisles. This forces customers to move in a certain direction and makes maximum use of selling areas. Modern specialty shops and department stores are more likely to use a free-form layout. Counters or racks of merchandise are placed like islands in a sea. Customers are free to roam, which encourages buying on impulse. When People's Jewellers modified its stores, it emphasized its diamond line; the result was an overall sales increase and profit improvement.[33]

Besides layout, other design elements that contribute to a store's image are lighting, fixtures, music, videos, and even scents. The term **atmospherics** has been used to describe the marketing task of creating certain effects in buyers by designing store environments.[34]

Marketing Mix Factors

Consumers fashion their image of a store from the elements of the marketing mix as well. Pricing definitely affects store image. Discount stores, for example, often use odd pricing (pricing below even dollar amounts) to give consumers the impression of a bargain. Quality stores, on the other hand, believe their image is portrayed best by even amounts.

Advertising also affects a store's image. Newspaper ads help distinguish stores to a certain extent. The ads of stores with a low-price emphasis feature few illustrations and a lot of type. Quality stores, in contrast, may use elegant models, little type, and a good deal of white space.

The salespeople a store employs further its image as well. Salespeople are especially important for retailers of services, such as banks and airlines.[35]

Explaining Retail Changes

It has been said that the only thing that is constant in life is change. Retailing certainly bears out that observation. Marketing specialists in retailing have long tried to find patterns in retail changes and the causes of change. Two explanations have been forwarded—the wheel of retailing theory and the life-cycle hypothesis.

The Wheel of Retailing

According to Malcolm McNair, changes in retailing are cyclical. At first, a new store type challenges an existing institution by cutting prices, using simple facilities, giving few services, and offering only a limited merchandise selection. Once the store is established, however, it starts trading up its merchandise, offering more services, and improving appearances. Prices follow costs upward. The store then suffers the fate of its old competitor as a new store type develops, using cost-cutting tactics. The wheel will have turned full circle.[36]

McNair's **wheel of retailing** theory explains many changes in retailing. For example, it describes how supermarkets challenged old-fashioned grocery stores and are in turn being challenged by superstores today. But not all changes in retailing result from an effort to cut costs. Vending machines and convenience stores, for instance, are high-cost innovations that nevertheless succeeded.

Atmospherics
Marketing task of creating certain effects in buyers by designing store environments.

Wheel of Retailing
Theory that all retail innovators start as low-cost, low-price stores, improve services and raise prices at maturity, and decline when new types of low-cost stores challenge them.

The Life-Cycle Hypothesis

Retail Life-Cycle
View that retail stores, like products, have life-cycles that consist of phases: innovation, accelerated development, maturity, and decline.

A different hypothesis is that stores, like products, have **retail life-cycles** that consist of phases: innovation, accelerated development, maturity, and decline. The movement to a new phase is brought about by competitive pressures, but they are not necessarily related to cost cutting. Maturity sets in when there are so many stores of a certain type that no room remains for new entrants.[37]

The theory has led to insights about retail change. It holds, for example, that retail life-cycles are accelerating. Although it took department stores a century to reach maturity, catalogue showrooms matured in less than ten years. The speed-up of the life-cycle development means that businesspeople going into a new type of retailing have less time than ever to recover their initial investments. Retailing is becoming risky business.

The theory also suggests that just as in the case of a product, a retail store's maturity phase can be extended. This requires adjusting operations to meet the times. Woodward's, for example, has introduced a purchase-protection plan — automatic 90-day insurance against breakage, loss, or theft — for merchandise that is purchased on its charge cards.[38]

Chapter Replay

1. **What kinds of retailers emphasize product mix?**
   Retailers that emphasize product mix include specialty stores, which may be superstores; department stores; and supermarkets. In addition, retailers have responded to changing needs with new species of supermarkets: convenience stores, combination stores, and hypermarkets.

2. **What types of retail establishments specialize in offering low prices?**
   Retailers that focus on price include discount stores, warehouse stores, home improvement centres, and catalogue showrooms.

3. **Where do retailers locate their stores?**
   Retailers primarily locate stores in central business districts and in shopping centres. Shopping centres may vary in size and may include factory outlet malls.

4. **What are some ways of retailing without stores?**
   Nonstore retailing includes door-to-door selling, direct marketing (including telemarketing), and automatic vending machines.

5. **What are some ways of organizing retail establishments?**
   Retailers may be independents, chains, or associations of independents (ownership groups or franchises).

6. **How do retailers create an image for their store?**

   Retailers create an image through store design, including layout and atmospherics. They also use the elements of the marketing mix to create an image.

7. **How does the wheel of retailing theory attempt to explain changes in retailing?**

   According to the wheel of retailing theory, changes in retailing are cyclical. First, a new store type challenges an existing institution by cutting prices, using simple facilities, giving few services, and offering a limited selection. Gradually the store trades up in these categories, and prices follow costs upward. Eventually, a new, lower-priced type of store develops to replace this one.

8. **What is the life-cycle of stores?**

   The retail life cycle consists of innovation, accelerated development, maturity, and decline. The movement to each new phase is brought about by competitive pressures.

Key Terms

atmospherics	mail-order firm
catalogue showroom	ownership group
central business district	retail life-cycle
chain store	retailing
combination store	scrambled merchandising
convenience store	shopping centre
department store	specialty store
discount store	supermarket
franchise	superstore
home improvement	telemarketing
centre	vending machine
hypermarket	warehouse store
independent store	wheel of retailing

Discussion Questions

1. What are two strategies that specialty stores can use to gain a marketing advantage?

2. How do department stores compete with the lower prices of superstores, discount houses, and off-price retailers?

3. Kevin Killroy is interested in entering the retail business. He learns that a new subdivision, Happy Acres, does not yet contain any stores. Kevin decides that a good market exists for an establishment where residents can shop for groceries. Which would you recommend that Kevin open—a supermarket, a convenience store, a combination store, or a hypermarket? Support your choice.

4. Sonya Slocum's job at an advertising agency pays just enough for Sonya to support herself and her two children in a comfortable lifestyle. Although Sonya sometimes has to stretch to pay all the bills, she almost never shops at discount or warehouse stores. Why might someone choose to pay full price elsewhere when discount stores are cheaper?

5. For each of the following products, indicate whether you would recommend selling it through direct-mail marketing or through telemarketing. Explain your choice.

   a. A line of cheeses, fruits, and chocolates packaged in fancy containers for gift giving.

   b. Subscriptions to a local newspaper.

   c. A stress-management and physical fitness program at a neighbourhood recreation centre.

   d. Donations to the local orchestra in the form of $30 memberships.

6. What is the major advantage independent stores offer their owners? What are some drawbacks of independents?

7. Nancy Nonesuch is thinking of buying a car-rental franchise. What drawbacks of this retailing arrangement should she be aware of? Would she be better off starting an independent operation? Why, or why not?

8. What are some of the elements retailers consider in store design?

9. What are the stages in the retail life-cycle? Based on what you read about convenience stores, at what stage of the life-cycle is this type of establishment? At what stage of the life-cycle are catalogues?

CASE 12.1

Early Country Pine

Walter Elliot has owned and operated Early Country Pine since 1981. The firm's recent mission statement is "To provide solid wood furniture with a strong emphasis on quality." It purchases unfinished furniture components from various producers and then assembles and finishes the items.

Since 1981, the firm has made regular changes in its retailing mix (see the accompanying history). The current merchandise lines are

- Dining tables.
- Chairs.

Source: Case developed by Bill A. Crowe, St. Lawrence College, Kingston, Ontario and Mark Siemonsen, marketing consultant.

History of Early Country Pine

Date	Event and Comments
September 1981	Established to produce small gift items, wooden bowls, lamps, and so on.
October 1983	Began wholesaling finished furniture.
November 1984	Begin retailing solid furniture and accessories assembled and finished by the firm.
September 1985	Product line diversified to include waterbeds, brass beds, and wooden chairs. Firm was operating with two locations in the city (an industrial location for production purposes and a retail location).
August 1986	Expanded to another city with a population of approximately 70 000.
January 1987	Began an expense-reducing program and consolidated from three locations to one.
1988 — present	Operating exclusively out of an industrial/business park location. Elliott is considering the addition of an employee or partner to be responsible for marketing.

- Bedroom furniture.

- Mirrors.

Because Early Country Pine has access to key manufacturers of solid wood furniture and can produce a variety of custom finishes, it offers consumers a large selection of furniture "looks." The visual presentation of the merchandise selection is, however, difficult in the leased 185-square-metre showroom and production facility. The firm cannot display all of its product lines, a fact that often makes the buying decision overwhelming for prospects who lack vision. Moreover, the "showroom" has bare cement walls and neither carpeting nor vinyl on the floor.

The primary direct competition comes from three other retailers of solid wood furniture located in the same city, which has a population of about 112 000. (See the accompanying list of competitors.)

Direct Competition for Early Country Pine

Firm	Comments
All Pine	A quality firm that has just announced that it is going to close down operations in Early Country's market and relocate to a small city an hour's drive west.
Furniture Plus	A firm with professional displays and a good store image. It carries many quality lines and has a large on-site inventory of finished products almost identical to Early Country Pine's. Its prices are higher.
Pine Plus	A low-profile operation located in a different industrial park. Its furniture is of lower quality than Early Country Pine's.

Financial Situation

An analysis of the firm's 1981–1989 financial performance, concentrating on the revenue, reveals symptoms of the following:

- Rapid growth during the early stages of company development.
- Fluctuating sales performance (partly because of the consolidation of the multiple locations).
- Problems with store locations.
- Problems with merchandising.
- Lack of store awareness.
- Lack of diversified management expertise.

In the fiscal year ending August 31, 1990, the firm generated a moderate profit, which was attributed to a sales increase of 101 percent over 1989. (The figure is somewhat misleading, however, since sales had dropped by 44.7 percent from 1988 to 1989.) The business had not generated a profit since 1984, and it has accumulated a deficit that is a negative influence on any potential new marketing direction. Inventory turnover has been a major problem for the company since 1987; even with its large sales growth in 1990, it is operating substantially below the national average for the furniture industry. Specific data on which lines are contributing what to the revenues have not been maintained.

Walter Elliott is becoming frustrated with the whole situation. He is particularly annoyed by a trend he has noticed in the last 18 months: customers are trying to negotiate price at his store.

Focal Topics

1. To what do you attribute the trend of prospects wishing to negotiate on the basis of price?

2. What do you see as the major opportunities and problems likely to face Early Country Pine in the future?

3. Develop a list of key objectives for Early Country Pine and a program on how to achieve them.

CASE 12.2

Fashion Focus

In the fall of 1987, Kim Webber opened Fashion Focus, a store specializing in casual and dress clothing for men in Vancouver. Since then she has added women's clothing, some of it under a private label.

The store's typical customer is upwardly mobile middle class, between

Source: Case developed by Bill A. Crowe, St. Lawrence College, Kingston, Ontario and Mark Siemonsen, marketing consultant.

20 and 40 years old, fashion conscious, very career oriented, and involved in some sort of individual sport. Approximately 16 percent of annual sales are to tourists, who often ask what plans Fashion Focus has for expansion.

The Store's History

Before opening Fashion Focus, Kim was a national sales manager for a chain of footwear stores. Tired of constant travelling, she turned to entrepreneurship, a natural choice, given her experience. She realized that many Canadian markets have considerable potential for high-quality fashion, and she felt able and willing to commit herself to providing top-flight customer service. Establishing her own fashion retail shop seemed logical, and Vancouver seemed an attractive place to live and work.

Choosing a Location

Kim decided to open Fashion Focus in Vancouver's central business district. She found an existing building in a cluster of fashion retailers, trendy restaurants, and bars, the sort of neighbours that seemed appropriate. The location became even more interesting when she learned that the city's largest restaurant and nightclub complex would open in the immediate area by the following spring. She felt intuitively that it would bring additional foot traffic to the area, creating more exposure for Fashion Focus's merchandise in attractive window displays.

Kim purchased the 300-square-metre property, even though it was larger than she needed initially.

Opening and Growth

Kim opened Fashion Focus in 140 square metres of the building. The high-quality merchandise, dynamic displays, and professional sales staff provided a unique selling proposition.

Within two years, Kim felt ready to expand. In October 1989, she increased the store size to 270 square metres of selling space and, after considering and rejecting a variety of product line extensions, expanded the product mix to include women's clothing.

Just as Kim decided to add women's clothing, she met a small manufacturer who suggested that he and she develop private-label garments for the shop. Fashion Focus has since operated a women's private-label program at a solid sales level, and the items bring a margin higher than the store's average.

Competition and Promotion

Kim has noted that most of her competition focuses on brand names (as she does herself except for the private-label line) and appears to spend more on advertising than she does. Customer service seems superior at Fashion Focus. Kim has devoted much energy to selecting staff and training them to serve customers properly, and she is proud of her employees' skill and expertise.

She is also proud of a detailed information base on Fashion Focus clientele that she has had on her personal computer since 1988. Once someone has purchased an item from the store, a significant effort is made, by telemarketing and mailings, to entice that customer to return. Award-winning displays of the quality merchandise, supplemented by staff product-knowledge and solid customer service, have often resulted in sales to this repeat customer traffic. The data base has proven particularly worthwhile for promoting specific categories of merchandise and special events such as Fashion Focus's spring and fall anniversary sales.

Since the introduction of these programs, the average transaction has been $285! Sales have grown steadily. The 1990 total for men's clothing was $635 000 and for the women's line $210 000. Kim's projections indicate that by 1994 men's and women's sales will be equal.

In brief, Fashion Focus is showing itself to be a store that has the ability to promote intelligent fashion to its target market.

More Expansion?

When Kim conceived Fashion Focus, she was aware that being in business would present her with many challenges. Now she faces another major decision: should Fashion Focus expand? If so, how?

Growth Momentum

Kim wants to maintain her growth momentum. Yet the present setup doesn't give her a lot of room to do so. Including the salary she takes from the business, Kim calculates that she is receiving approximately 18 percent of sales (after debt service) and that the current store is rapidly reaching its limit of sales growth. At best, it can generate an additional 20 percent sales volume, assuming no entry of major competitors.

The Private Line

The private-label manufacturer wants to implement a similar program for the men's line at Fashion Focus. Kim has established a fine rapport with this man, and she believes they could work well together toward a common goal. If he can design and make garments that customers consider equal to or better than brand names, sales and profits should increase, given her direct marketing efforts and the exceptional skills of her staff. Even if sales remain constant, the margin this manufacturer offers is approximately 5 percent greater than what is being generated from the established brand names.

Options

In spite of Kim's initial success, her banker accuses her of having "expansion fever." Moreover, some of her close friends, including her mentor, are sceptical about expansion because of the time pressures of a multiunit operation and the importance of owner identity in each market. Fashion Focus has developed a store personality that has much to do with Kim's leadership and the contribution that she has made to the Vancouver community by serving as a campaign chairperson for hospital fund-raising.

Kim Webber has considered these comments, yet she believes that business survival has been achieved and that expansion must be a key pursuit in the near future. She sees the following options for growth:

- Enlarge her existing store and expand the merchandise assortment.

- Open new stores on her own or with a partner.

- Develop a number of franchise stores in western Canada.

- Market the line of private-label clothing to retail stores.

Focal Topics

1. What are the major reasons for the success of Fashion Focus up to now?

2. Analyze the options for growth that Kim has spotted along with others that should be considered.

3. What strategy would you recommend that would contribute to the growth of the retail business? Design an implementation program for this strategy.

13

Distributing Goods

In this chapter, you will learn:

- What activities are involved in physical distribution.

- How companies use a total physical distribution concept.

- The basic decisions involved in warehousing.

- The goals of inventory management.

- How managers decide on the amount of inventory to carry.

- How companies keep track of inventory.

- The modes of transportation the physical distribution manager can evaluate.

- How companies that are too small to own or lease their own means of

  transportation can move goods economically.

"Mr. Christie, You Make Good Cookies!"

The headline describes how Christie Brown & Co. want their products and organization to be perceived by the consumer. It is a corporate objective.

In order to achieve and maintain that objective, the company must pay the strictest attention to quality at every step in the production and distribution process. Its many products include Oreo®, Chips Ahoy!®, Dad's®, Peek Freans®, and David® cookies plus Ritz®, Triscuit®, and Premium Plus® crackers.

Control of these products through the distribution channel has been a major reason for the company's success in the marketplace. From five bakeries located in Ontario and Quebec, Christie Brown & Co. distributes its cookies and crackers to eleven company-operated sales branches across Canada. CN's Intermodal Services carries the bulk of Christie Brown & Co. products, delivering almost 40 000 tonnes each year. CN's delivery service must provide damage-free goods on a time-sensitive basis to meet Christie Brown & Co. standards. Each sales branch then distributes to retail stores in a defined geographical area, using a company-operated delivery fleet. This system enables Christie Brown & Co. to guarantee daily delivery, improve turnover at the retail level, control the product quality, and respond quickly to sales variations. Common carriers are used only to service customers in remote locations where delivery frequency cannot justify the costs of operating the private fleet.

Another advantage of the Christie Brown & Co. private fleet is the advertising impact that the trucks' striking, four-colour graphics have on thousands of people along the way. It is a creative, cost-effective way to make an impression.

All goods-producing firms must find reliable and economical ways to move their products to their customers. This chapter addresses the decisions involved in getting products from manufacturers to customers.

What Is Physical Distribution?

Preceding chapters discuss how the ownership of products changes hands. The exchange may be a simple one involving just a buyer and a seller. Or, it may be a more complex transaction with several levels of wholesalers and retailers. All of the participants in the exchange make up a marketing channel.

This chapter concentrates on the physical handling and movement of goods, not ownership, although the two usually go together. People who are preparing themselves for a business career must understand all of the functions of physical distribution and the challenges and opportunities that exist when evaluating alternative systems.

Making products available where customers want them is a necessary first step to their exchange. Few realize how much effort the first step requires.

Consider buying a candy bar. The ownership exchange is simple: coins are deposited into a vending machine and, with luck, the candy drops out and the exchange is completed. But a staggering number of other activities make that transaction possible.

Wholesale intermediaries usually stock the machine. The candy probably reaches them by a roundabout route. The wholesale customer places an order with a manufacturer. After checking inventories, the manufacturer may discover a shortage of stock and order a start-up of production. A warehouse full of raw materials transported from distant places — sugar from the West Indies, almonds from California, chocolate from Ghana — will feed the production process. Another warehouse, perhaps closer to the wholesale intermediary, may receive and store the finished product from the factory. Warehouse workers then draw up billing and shipping papers, load a truck with the amount ordered, and ship it to the wholesale customer's own warehouse. From there, wholesalers make deliveries to the hundreds of outlets they supply, including the vending machine.

Whoever named a candy product the "100 Thousand Dollar Bar" was not far off. A substantial investment in labour, storage facilities, and transportation is necessary to supply this one simple product to Canadian consumers. The wise management of that investment is the job of those involved in physical distribution.

Physical distribution, or logistics, includes all those activities required to move finished goods along marketing channels, including storing the goods along the way. The objective of a physical distribution system is well described in 3M Canada's logistics mission statement: "To manage the procurement, storage, and transfer of materials and products from source to customers ensuring their expectations in terms of accuracy, timeliness, and reliability, are consistently maintained."[1]

Physical Distribution
The process of storing and moving products along marketing channels.

412

The six most important activities in this element of the marketing mix are:

1. *Warehousing*

   - In-plant — organizing the raw materials and finished goods inventories within the maufacturing facility.

   - Field warehousing — organizing the warehouse network to best serve customers.

2. *Inventory management* — optimizing inventory levels to minimize costs while meeting customer-service demands.

3. *Transportation*

   - Shipping—organizing the loading and transportation of goods to the customer.

   - Receiving—organizing the transportation and unloading of raw materials for production.

4. *Order processing*—communicating customer orders to the physical distribution system; includes providing proper documentation (quantity desired, shipping papers, destination specification, invoicing).

5. *Administration* — organizing the procurement of materials from suppliers.

6. *Packaging* — choosing the most economical package to ensure proper labelling, handling protection, and merchandising.[2]

Service and nonprofit organizations may also have some interest in physical distribution. For example, banks are concerned with the supply of money on hand, and hospitals must know the number of beds available for patient care — both inventory problems. This topic is addressed in Chapter 18.

All members of a marketing channel are involved in physical distribution to some extent, but whoever controls the channel usually has major responsibility. This chapter focuses on the manufacturer's role in the physical distribution of goods. In the past ten years, management ideas about that task have changed considerably.

The Growing Focus on Physical Distribution

Traditionally, management directed its cost-reduction efforts to improving production efficiency. With the adoption of the marketing concept, however, the focus of firms changed to satisfying consumer wants, and what consumers wanted was more convenience in purchasing. Firms began to realize the implications of the fact that a physical distribution system creates time utility and place utility through transportation serv-

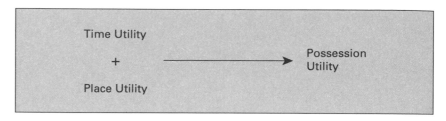

Figure 13.1 Physical Distribution Creates Utility

ices (see Figure 13.1) and that the objectives of such a system must be to achieve the service level desired by customers at the lowest possible cost. Canada Dry's distribution network, for example, proved key to the success of a nationwide promotion (see Marketing Today 13.1).

As more and more outlets were opened in the suburbs, the job of supplying them grew. That job was complicated by increases in the number of products offered to consumers. Keeping track of inventories and handling and shipping orders has become an immense challenge.

Moving more goods to more outlets raised the cost of physical distribution. When distribution charges began to influence a company's bottom line significantly, management was forced to pay attention.

Total Physical Distribution Concept
Principle that all management functions related to moving products to buyers must be fully integrated.

The Total Physical Distribution Concept

The new imperatives led many firms to adopt the **total physical distribution concept,** which states that all management functions related

Marketing Today 13.1

Canadian Tire: Definitely More Than Just Tires!

The trend in the food industry to greater crossover between food and nonfood items explains why you might have come across a "wall" of fruit drinks beside the camping display in a Canadian Tire retail outlet. With the number of single-person households on the rise in Canada, there is a growing demand for the convenience of one-stop shopping.

In August 1987, the Canadian Tire promotion of Canada Dry's C-Plus orange and tropical fruit drinks in the 250-millilitre tetra packages was held throughout the company's 370 outlets. Critical to the success of the promotion was Canada Dry's unique distribution network.

The firm has licensing agreements with more than 50 independent bottlers, who produce Canada Dry soft drinks and distribute them directly to supermarkets, retail outlets, and convenience stores, using their own trucks. This "store-door" system enabled Canada Dry to get the product to customer outlets across the country quickly, which is crucial in a national advertising program.

Many retail opportunities like this exist for food items in traditionally nonfood outlets since they meet consumer expectations for convenience shopping.

Source: Adapted from "Food and Drink in Surprising Places," *Canadian Beverage Review* (Fall, 1988), p. 24.

to moving products to buyers must be fully integrated. The organization chart of a firm that adopts the concept may look like Figure 13.2. Distribution is a department equal to marketing and production, and it is responsible for the six major distribution activities.

Integrating these activities is not an easy task. Each area involves an immense number of details that no one person could hope to keep track of. However, the development of the computer has made the concept a practical one. Indeed, quite simple computer uses can have an excellent effect. For example, Johnson and Johnson improved the efficiency of its order entry system by issuing laptop computers to its sales force.[3]

Implementing the Concept

Using the total physical distribution approach means considering the total cost of *all* the activities involved in a physical distribution system. For instance, eliminating all field storage facilities will reduce the warehousing component of the total distribution cost. To maintain the same level of customer service, all products may have to be shipped by air, a method that is, of course, expensive. Yet it is quite likely that the net effect of the increase in transportation costs would outweigh the cost savings achieved by eliminating the warehouses.

In making such decisions, the physical distribution manager must balance two objectives: (1) minimizing costs to the firm as a whole and (2) providing a satisfactory level of customer service (see Figure 13.3). Table 13.1 is a typical job description outlining the duties of a modern distribution manager.

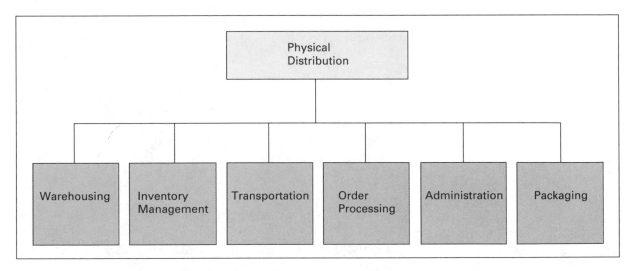

Figure 13.2 Management Organization under the Total Physical Distribution Concept

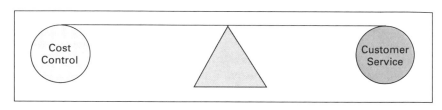

Figure 13.3 The Physical Distribution Balancing Act

Minimizing Costs

Visible Costs
Direct and indirect costs that show up on a profit and loss statement.

Hidden Costs
Costs of doing business — for example, a cancelled order — that do not show up on a profit and loss statement.

Minimizing costs is a difficult task for two reasons. First, many costs must be considered, some of which are not obvious. Marketers refer to visible and hidden costs. **Visible costs,** which show up on a profit and loss statement, include the direct expenses of running warehouses and hiring transportation, as well as the indirect costs of insuring goods and paying property taxes. **Hidden costs,** which accountants cannot record, include losses that result from a customer's failing to order or cancelling an order if an item is out of stock. It is difficult to know when costs are minimized if only some of the costs are specified exactly.

Second, it is the total cost that must be kept down. Common sense suggests that the way to minimize total costs is to do things in the cheapest possible way in each area of physical distribution. But, as already suggested, a cost increase in one area of the distribution system

Table 13.1 Wanted: Distribution Manager

Responsibilities

1. Plan, implement, and control Canadian distribution network
   ■ Determine transport modes and equipment
   ■ Interview and select transportation suppliers
   ■ Negotiate rates
   ■ Ensure quality in service standards

2. Manage tractor-trailer fleet that distributes frozen products
   ■ Negotiate equipment leases
   ■ Plan and load for equipment schedules
   ■ Supervise contract drivers
   ■ Optimize backhauls

3. Contract outside warehousing as required   ■ Negotiate term rates and quality standards for public storage of both frozen and dry products

4. Prepare freight and warehousing budgets
   ■ Involve suppliers in forecasting and planning
   ■ Plan wage increases for fleet drivers
   ■ Plan for equipment replacement

Source: Adapted from Lynne Calderwood, '''Balance' is key to success,'' *Materials Management and Distribution*, May 1990, p. 33.

will sometimes be more than offset by a cost saving in another. Marketing specialists call this a **cost trade-off.**

The most frequent trade-offs are between transportation and storage costs. For example, an automaker could make sure that every car dealer has all the necessary auto parts for every possible repair. In this way, the company would avoid the expense of having to rush parts to a dealer, but the cost of carrying all those parts would be burdensome.

The cost trade-off may also involve storage and manufacturing costs. If a company stores enough of a product to handle peak demand periods, it will avoid filling expensive rush orders, but the cost of storage will be greater.

Another trade-off is between packaging and other costs. If the company tries to save money by using the cheapest possible packaging, it might find itself incurring additional expenses to replace damaged merchandise or paying extra for special handling.

Companies therefore evaluate the total cost of distribution to find the best balance. For example, increased costs of fleet truck operations forced Unox Foods to change its product offering from fresh to frozen wieners. This move enabled it to use distributors and to ship to strategically located warehouses, thus reducing overall costs.

For help in the task of minimizing costs, some companies are turning to computer systems. AMP of Canada, which supplies electrical connectors and devices to electronic equipment manufacturers, recently introduced an on-line computer network that distributors can dial direct to obtain Canada-wide price and delivery information. This network, which reduces the time needed to respond to customer requests, is part of an overall effort by AMP Canada to minimize activities in its marketing organization that do not add value to its products.[4]

Providing Customer Service

In finding ways to lower costs, marketers must weigh the effects of cost savings on customer service. In some cases, customers may look elsewhere for a product that must be back ordered for several weeks or that arrives in poor condition. A summary of services that customers expect appears in Table 13.2, along with examples of the kinds of standards companies set in an effort to live up to expectations.

Sometimes customers will pay extra for superior distribution. A farmer's market, for example, sells tomatoes that have remained on the vine longer than is typical for tomatoes sold in supermarkets. This means that the grower must get them to market faster, but many customers are willing to pay more for the riper, fresher produce. Likewise, users of courier services are willing to pay a higher price for faster delivery. A letter that costs $0.40 to send from Toronto to Vancouver by first-class mail will cost $9.95 for next-day delivery by Canada Post's Priority Post Courier. To attain the minimum cost objective while delivering consistent customer service, the company must have an in-depth knowledge of all areas of physical distribution. Market factors such as account

Cost Trade-Off
Practice of allowing costs to increase in one business area to bring down costs in another.

location, order frequency, lead times for delivery, and product factors such as shelf life, durability, and weight must all be considered when formulating a physical distribution strategy. As part of the marketing

Table 13.2 Customer Service Standards

Service Factor	Model Standard
Speed of delivery	Delivery overnight, within three days, or within the limits set by competitors
Reliability of delivery	Delivery within X days, 90 percent of the time
Availability of items ordered	97 percent of orders for item X filled from stock
Accuracy in order filling	98 percent accuracy for all orders placed
Receipt of goods in undamaged condition	97 percent of goods received undamaged

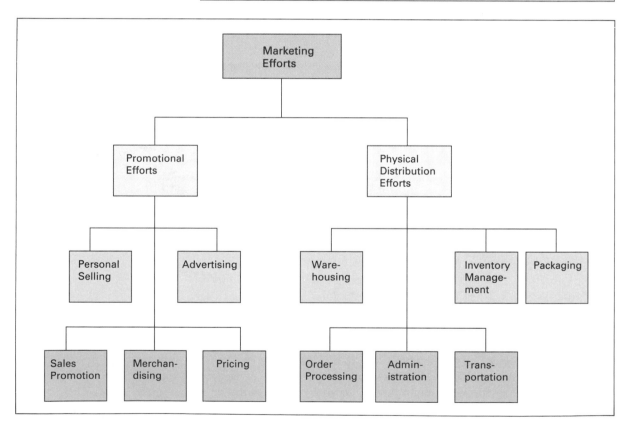

Figure 13.4 Marketing Activities: Promotional and Physical Distribution

Source: Keith G. Hardy and Allan J. Magrath, *Marketing Channel Management: Strategic Planning and Tactics* (Glenview, IL: Scott Foresman and Company, 1988), p. 215.

effort, physical distribution efforts service the demand created by the promotional efforts (see Figure 13.4). Since warehousing, inventory control, and transportation account for most of the costs of physical distribution (see Figure 13.5), this chapter looks at each of those areas more closely.

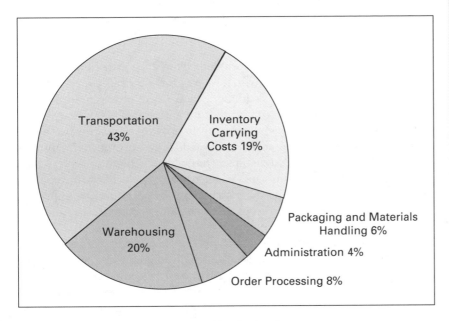

Figure 13.5 Relative Costs of Physical Distribution Components

Source: Herbert W. Davis, ''Physical Distribution Costs: Performance in Selected Industries — 1980,'' *Annual Proceedings of the National Council of Physical Distribution Management*, 1980, p. 35.

Warehousing

Significant opportunities for savings, without lessening customer service, exist in the area of warehousing. That is why it is the focus of a good deal of management attention today. Three matters in particular are of interest: (1) what type of warehouse to operate, (2) whether to own or rent facilities, and (3) where to locate them.

Types of Operations

Warehouses are distinguished mainly by the functions they perform. The storage warehouse and the distribution centre warehouse are the two main types.

Storage Warehouses

When most people think of a warehouse, it is usually the **storage warehouse** they have in mind. In this type of facility, goods are stored for

Storage Warehouse
Facility in which goods are stored for weeks, months, c years until they are needed.

weeks, months, or years until they are needed. Dofasco, a steel company located in Hamilton, Ontario, devotes almost 18 hectares of real estate to storage![5] Companies may decide to store goods for several reasons.

Some companies produce goods that are in demand only seasonally. For example, most toys are sold during the Christmas season. Most toy companies could not possibly meet all of the demand for their products by producing only in the month of December. Instead, they spread production through the year and store goods in warehouses until they are needed.

Other firms have the opposite problem. They face year-round demand but can produce only seasonally. Del Monte, for example, cans enormous quantities of peaches in the summer when supplies are plentiful and then stores them until demand catches up with supply.

The ups and downs of the business cycle provide companies with still another reason for storing goods. In periods of high inflation, manufacturers stock up on raw materials so they will not have to buy at even higher prices later. By contrast, when prices are declining, producers may hold back goods from the market until the situation improves. Farmers who store bumper crops of wheat and corn are a common example.

Automated Warehouse
Facility with advanced materials handling systems under control of a central computer.

In the past, storage warehouses were often older, multistory structures that depended on labour, rather than equipment, for moving goods. Recently, however, single-story **automated warehouses,** with advanced materials-handling systems under the control of a central computer and sophisticated radio communication devices, have begun to replace the older facilities. Although they may cost as much as $10 to $20 million to build, they are much more efficient and can be operated with only a few employees.[6]

High-tech systems can be useful in a variety of warehousing situations. Bell Canada, for example, introduced bar-coding into its cable-cutting operation as a means of inventory control. The result was improved accuracy, greater timeliness of inventory records, and increased ability to track and control cable reels. The system paid for itself in two years through savings in paperwork and increased productivity.[7]

Distribution Centre Warehouses

Distribution Centre Warehouse
Facility that serves primarily as a temporary way-station before the goods are rapidly moved to customers.

In contrast to the storage warehouse, the **distribution centre warehouse** is established primarily as a temporary way-station prior to the very rapid movement of goods to customers. Thus, while storage warehouses hold goods back from markets for long periods of time, distribution centres discharge goods quickly, usually within a week's time.

The concept of the distribution centre was developed after World War II. Goods in storage do not make money for a company, but they add to expenses. The slower that goods move, for example, the more a company must pay for insurance against spoilage or damage and for security precautions. For example, General Motors, in Oshawa, Ontario, has calculated that each extra turnover of inventory saves it $1 million in expenses.[8] Distribution centres decrease the cost of storage.

They also decrease other costs. Because goods move through distribution centres faster than through traditional warehouses, customers can be served through fewer facilities. Transportation costs also may be lowered because the company ships to fewer locations. The loads are larger, and bulk loads are cheaper to transport than smaller loads.

Lower costs are not the only advantage of distribution centres; they are also more efficient than storage warehouses, primarily because they are usually more modern. All are one-story structures that eliminate the need for elevators and permit the use of modern equipment. Most are also automated, and many use computers to keep track of the flow of goods in and out of the warehouse.

Ownership

After physical distribution managers determine the type of warehouse that suits their needs, they must decide whether to use a private or public facility. The main feature of a **private warehouse** is that the building, equipment, and labour are company owned or controlled. A **public warehouse,** on the other hand, is controlled by an independent, can be rented by anyone needing space for a short time, and is usually shared by a number of companies.

Each has advantages and disadvantages. The chief advantage of a private warehouse is that the owner has total control over operations and personnel. For example, a product such as wine may need special handling, which a public facility cannot guarantee.

If a company does not produce enough goods to keep a warehouse constantly stocked or cannot predict sales, using public facilities may make better sense. Public warehouses issue receipts that allow companies to borrow from banks, using the stored goods as collateral.

Public warehouses may offer a variety of additional services. These include filing monthly inventory status reports, preparing transportation documents, weighing shipments, monitoring loss and damage from transportation, and assisting the company in filing claims for such losses. These services contribute to the popularity of public warehouses.[9]

The choice between private and public warehouses is often a matter of trade-offs, and some companies use both. Kellogg's Canada, for example, owns and operates its own warehouses in London and Rexdale, Ontario, near its manufacturing plants and distribution centres. But it uses public warehousing in the major centres of British Columbia, Alberta, Saskatchewan, and Nova Scotia to improve its customer service by shortening the order cycle to the major retail and food service accounts.

Location

In general, physical distribution managers have three options in deciding where to locate a warehouse. A business can position a warehouse

Private Warehouse
Storage centre owned or controlled by the company that uses it.

Public Warehouse
Storage centre controlled by an independent, available for rent for a short time, and usually shared by a number of companies.

(1) near the company's factory, (2) close to the market, or (3) at an intermediate point between the two.

Factory-positioned warehouses may be used for two purposes. They may store raw materials and fabricated parts until they are needed for manufacture, or they may serve as traditional warehouses or distribution centres for finished products. The latter is especially favoured by multiproduct companies that cannot economically store all of their product line near all of the markets they serve.

Market-positioned warehouses are designed to collect the products of one or more manufacturers in or near the market served before shipping the goods short distances to customers. When such warehouses are owned by a manufacturer, their purpose is simply to prevent having to ship in small quantities over long distances to many customers. Retailers often make use of market-positioned warehouses.

Intermediate-positioned warehouses are usually chosen by manufacturers with several plants and widely scattered markets. The warehouses gather the products of the various plants and mix them for shipment.

Location decisions are complex. After a general strategy for positioning a warehouse is decided on, specific sites must be chosen. Many factors should be weighed when choosing a site, including (1) availability of transportation, (2) quantity and quality of labour, (3) cost of land, (4) taxes, and (5) services provided by the local government. Computers now aid physical distribution managers in making the location decision.

Marketing Today 13.2 describes some of the physical distribution challenges faced by Labatt as it expands to serve the global market.

Inventory Control

To manage inventory successfully, physical distribution managers must start with the company's goals for minimizing costs while maintaining a specified level of customer service. With those objectives in mind, the managers can then determine the proper inventory size and set up a system to keep track of it.

Goals of Inventory Management

In general, inventory managers pursue two goals: (1) to provide an adequate level of customer service by avoiding out-of-stock situations and (2) to minimize a company's investment in inventory.

Avoiding Stockouts

Items that are not available for shipment are referred to as *stockouts*. Back orders and stockouts are not well accepted in today's marketplace and can be very costly to a company. Customers easily become disen-

Factory-Positioned Warehouse Facility used to store raw materials and fabricated parts until they are needed for manufacture or one that serves as a traditional warehouse or distribution centre for finished products.

Market-Positioned Warehouse Storage place designed to collect the products of one or more manufacturers in or near the market served before shipping goods short distances to customers.

Intermediate-Positioned Warehouse Storage place that serves manufacturers with several plants and widely scattered markets by gathering products of various plants and mixing them for shipment.

Marketing Today 13.2

Labatt's Blue Goes Abroad

Labatt Brewing Company Ltd., of London, Ontario, is Canada's largest brewer. It holds 42 percent of the domestic beer market, and its international division is responsible for delivering beer to customers all over the world.

The distribution system has responded well to some interesting challenges placed on it by the international markets. Japan is Labatt's second-largest export market with approximately 14 percent of its export sales. (Only the United States buys more.) Each month, six to ten 12-metre containers leave for Japan. Eighty percent of the shipments are Labatt's Blue.

In 1985, when the Japanese received their first shipment of Blue, Labatt was faced with an unusual problem associated with its packaging in four-packs. In some oriental cultures, the word for the number four means death.

As a result, the introduction of "death packs" of Labatt's Blue met some resistance. In time, however, the convenience of the four-packs outweighed superstition and they were accepted.

Labelling requirements, which differ among countries, also provide challenges for exporting beer. Japan requires that all ingredients be listed on the label along with the data of production. Products marketed in Australia, on the other hand, must have the expiry date printed on the label.

The shipment period presents other difficulties. Export beer is double filtered to increase its shelf life to twelve months. Still, precautions must be taken to prevent the beer from freezing during transit and from spoiling because of overexposure to heat as it might in countries such as Israel.

The domestic distribution system has its own challenges. Labatt has three breweries in Ontario and one in each of the other nine prov-

inces. It uses its own fleet of trucks to serve the domestic market. Truckload-size orders are cost-effective to ship. Smaller customers, however, challenge the customer service and shipping departments to provide quality service while keeping costs down. One way transportation costs are reduced is by pooling shipments. A collection of pallet-size orders will fill a truck, which is scheduled to make all of the deliveries on the same day.

Labatt's network extends outside Canada with breweries located in the United States, England and Italy. Plans are underway to expand into Africa and Iceland. The Soviet Union has also contacted Labatt. What's to become of Labatt's Blue in a country where the colour symbolizing something good is *red*?

Source: Adapted from "Japan Keeps Labatt in the Black with Blue Orders," *Transportation Business* 10 (July 1990), p. 11.

chanted and turn to competitors. One lost sale can mean the permanent loss of a large customer. On the other hand, maintaining an inventory large enough to fill nearly all orders from stock on hand puts pressure on a firm's cash flow by reducing available working capital.

There is no hard-and-fast rule governing the percentage of orders that should be filled from stock. A well-known principle of inventory management is that usually about 20 percent of the products a company carries account for the majority of sales. Products with the largest sales should always be available so that nearly 100 percent of orders can be filled from stock. Lower levels of stock may be kept for less important products.

A technique called **ABC analysis** identifies items with the biggest sales payoffs. Items are listed by sales volume, as shown in Table 13.3.

ABC Analysis
Inventory technique for identifying items with biggest sales payoffs by listing them by sales volume. Best sellers (A products) must be stocked at all times.

Table 13.3   ABC Analysis

Class and Item		Sales Dollars		Percentage of Total Dollars	Percentage of Product Line
A	1 2	$20 000 18 000	$38 000	56%	20%
B	3 4 5 6	8 000 6 000 5 000 4 000	23 000	34	40
C	7 8 9 10	3 000 2 500 1 000 500	7 000	10	40
			$68 000		

Source: Edward W. Smykay, *Physical Distribution Management*, 3rd ed. (New York: Macmillan, 1973), p. 208.

Those that account for the largest percentage of sales are classified as A products — those that must be stocked at all times. Lower levels of stock can be maintained for B and C products.

Cost Considerations

Two costs are of particular concern in inventory management — acquisition costs and carrying costs.

Acquisition costs are expenses incurred in preparing for manufacturing or in buying the product to put in inventory. For the manufacturer, these are the costs of setting up production of the goods. For retailers and wholesalers, they are the expenses of recordkeeping and handling the paperwork for each order. They may run from a few dollars to several hundred dollars per order.

Carrying costs are the expenses involved in holding goods over a period of time. These costs vary, but they may range from 10 to 35 percent of the total costs of the goods. Thus, if a company stocks $100 000 worth of goods, it must spend $10 000 to $35 000 to hold them in storage. Table 13.4 lists the major types of carrying costs and the percentage of the total each often represents.

The table shows that the chief carrying cost is often interest, a term that deserves some explanation. If the goods stored are purchased with borrowed funds, interest must be paid to a bank. But even if goods are purchased with company funds, the company is paying "interest" for that investment. The company that keeps $100 000 in inventory does not have that money to invest elsewhere to gain income. (In other words, it incurs an opportunity cost equal to the income it does not earn). Thus, every dollar in inventory represents an expense — in interest paid on borrowed money or interest lost by not investing elsewhere.

Acquisition Cost
Expense incurred in preparing for manufacturing or in buying product for inventory.

Carrying Cost
Expense of holding goods over a period of time.

Table 13.4   Typical Carrying Costs

Type	Percentage of Total Cost
Interest	4–15
Obsolescence and deterioration	2– 8
Storage	2– 5
Insurance	1– 4
Taxes	1– 3
Total	10–35

Another consequence of high inventory levels is increased danger of obsolescence. Technological advances can make a product obsolete while it is sitting on the shelf. With car models changing each year, a GM production plant must match inventory levels very closely with production requirements or be forced to carry surplus materials for a long time once the changeover begins for production of the next model year.

Because carrying costs and acquisition costs are so high, physical distribution managers have a stake in keeping down total inventory size. Avoiding stockouts while keeping inventory costs down is a delicate balancing act that requires some trade-offs.

Determining Inventory Size

To discover the correct inventory size, managers make assumptions about upcoming demand. These assumptions are really sales forecasts (discussed in Chapter 4). In general, the more accurate a company's forecast is, the less money it must tie up in excess inventory.

Physical distribution managers use sales forecasts to project the amount of inventory they need to order when it is time to replenish stock. The technical name for the amount to be reordered is the **economic order quantity (EOQ)**. It is that amount of stock that costs the least to keep on hand in order to meet the average level of demand. A simple example will show how the economic order quantity is determined.

Suppose owners of a retail store know from sales forecasts that the store can sell 5000 chairs in a year, but they do not know how many it can afford to keep in stock. A graph, similar to that in Figure 13.6, can be constructed showing acquisition and carrying costs for orders placed only once or an increasing number of times. The figure shows that acquisition costs increase as more orders are placed. The reason is simple: paperwork must be repeated for each order. By contrast, carrying costs decrease as more orders are placed because fewer chairs must be stored in costly facilities. One cost must be traded off against the other to find the optimum order size.

In the example, the most economical number of orders per year is five.

Economic Order Quantity (EOQ)
Amount of stock that costs the least to keep on hand in order to meet the average level of demand.

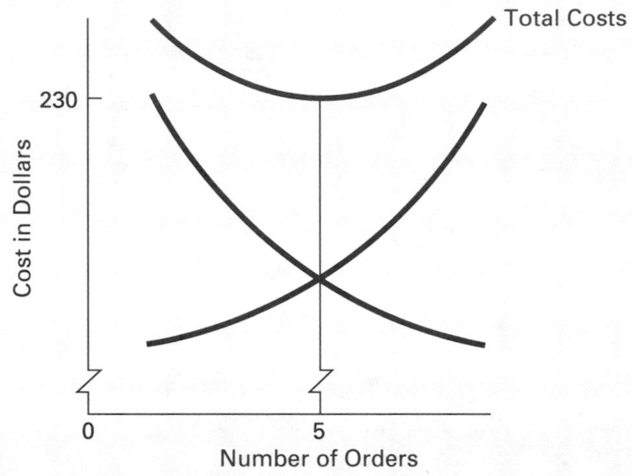

Figure 13.6 EOQ Model for Chairs

Number of Orders	Acquisition Costs	Carrying Costs	Total Costs
1	$ 20.00	$650.00	$670.00
2	40.00	325.00	365.00
5	100.00	130.00	230.00 ← EOQ
10	200.00	65.00	265.00
20	400.00	32.50	432.00

At that point, total cost (acquisition costs plus carrying costs) is the smallest. If the store owners know from a sales forecast that the store can sell 5000 chairs, then it may be calculated that after each order period, the store should have on hand 1000 chairs (5000 ÷ 5); that is, to meet the average level of demand at the least cost, the store should carry 1000 chairs.

The economic order quantity specifies only the stock needed to meet average demand. If the sales forecast is wrong and if there is a sudden surge in demand, a stockout may result in losing customers. To guard against this, companies usually also maintain a **safety stock,** or an amount above the basic stock level, to handle emergencies.

The Japanese have developed a different approach to distribution and inventory management called **just-in-time (JIT)**, which has been adopted in Canada by some manufacturers including General Motors. The JIT concept is to have parts and raw materials arrive at the production centre just as they are needed, thus significantly reducing inventory levels. There is no room for defective parts or unreliable delivery schedules in this system. Careful control of input material supply is crucial.[10]

Safety Stock
Amount above the basic stock level to handle emergencies.

Just-in-Time (JIT)
Inventory control procedure whereby raw materials arrive at the production centre just as they are needed.

Keeping Track of Inventory

Knowing how fast stock is moving is important in determining how much inventory to keep on hand. For example, the chair retailer must monitor the stock level to know if the calculations of the economic order quantity were actually equal to demand. Records of the amount of stock on hand and its rate of depletion must be kept. The two most common record-keeping methods are physical counts and perpetual inventory.

A **physical count,** as the name implies, involves analyzing products on hand at a specific time. Most retailers and wholesalers conduct such a physical count at least twice a year. By comparing the results with those of the previous count, the operation can identify areas of system malfunction.

The physical inventory count tells little about the day-in, day-out flow of goods, however. For that, a firm needs a record of **perpetual inventory,** a list of all goods in stock that is updated frequently. New goods are entered on the list as they arrive. Whenever goods are sold or used, they are subtracted. Manufacturers, in particular, must keep careful perpetual inventory records to know the rate of use of materials.

Until recently, most retailers could not effectively use a perpetual inventory system. Their large merchandise assortment would have made the recordkeeping operation too expensive. But computerized cash registers have changed that situation. They enable managers of large retail stores like Sears and The Bay to know, on a daily basis, which merchandise is moving and which requires reordering. The sale of an item in retail stores can prompt an automatic reordering from distribution centres or suppliers through the computer network, if the item in question is no longer in stock. Retail stores that keep a perpetual inventory may still take a physical count. Any discrepancy between the perpetual count and the physical count may indicate a shoplifting problem.

Transportation

The physical storage and inventorying of goods are important responsibilities, but transportation is often the single biggest headache of the physical distribution manager. For one thing, it is usually the largest expense of the three. Despite its cost, transportation is often a neglected area of physical distribution, and problems result. Failure to plan for transportation can result in late deliveries, excessive freight costs, and damaged merchandise, which will erode profits.

The physical distribution decision maker must be concerned with

- Meeting customer delivery requirements.

- Ensuring that the quality and quantity of goods that arrives meets customer expectations.

Choosing the right method to ensure that the products arrive at their

Physical Count
Inventory practice of totalling the number of items of each line on hand at a regular interval.

Perpetual Inventory
Frequently updated list of all goods in stock.

destination on time can result in a comparative service advantage over a competitor.

Table 13.5 is a glossary of terms used today in the transportation industry.

Transportation Modes

Five modes of transportation link producers and consumers: (1) railways, (2) motor carriers, (3) water transportation, (4) air transportation, and (5) pipelines. Some modes are more popular than others because they meet more of the requirements shippers look for in transportation. Figure 13.7 ranks each form of transport by five important characteristics. A closer look at the transportation alternatives will reveal the reasons behind the ranking.

Railways

Rail transportation, while generally cheaper than many other alternatives over the long run, is hampered by certain limitations. First, trains generally must be used with other transportation modes to provide door-to-door service, which increases handling costs. Second, boxcars are slow, averaging only about 30 kilometres an hour.[11] Trains do carry a wide variety of products (especially bulky products such as coal, metal, lumber, and grain), and they are the preferred means of transportation over long distances between cities.

Spurred by the prospect of capturing a larger percentage of the traffic in manufactured and high-value products, the railways have introduced several services.[12] Among the most familiar is *piggyback*—transporting truck trailers on rail cars. This technique combines the efficiency of long-haul rail transportation with the flexibility of trucking.

Another innovation is the use of *unit trains* for high-volume shipments. These trains are loaded with one commodity, such as coal, and travel nonstop between two points. When they have unloaded their cargo at

Table 13.5 Transportation Terms and Abbreviations

Abbreviation	Term
B/L	Bill of lading
COFC	Container on flat car
LCL	Less than carload
T/C	Tank cartage
T/L	Truckload
FOB	Free on board
TOFC	Trailer on flat car
LTL	Less than truckload
L&D	Loss and damage

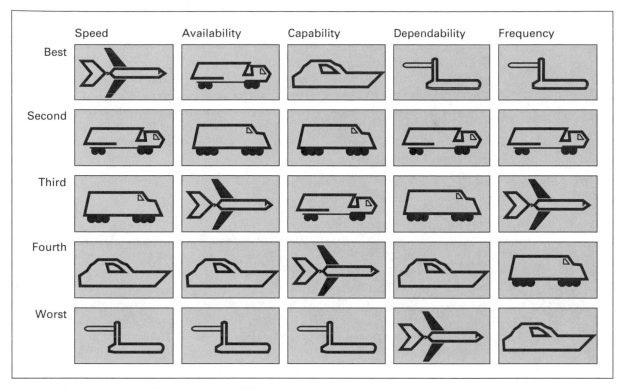

	Speed	Availability	Capability	Dependability	Frequency
Best					
Second					
Third					
Fourth					
Worst					

Figure 13.7 Comparing the Five Basic Forms of Transportation

the destination point, they return to the starting point to reload. Canadian National operates a unit train delivering coal from the interior of British Columbia to Vancouver for Japanese steel companies.

A third innovation is called ACI (Automatic Car Identification). All rail cars are equipped with an identification label that can be read by scanners at locations throughout Canada at speeds of 130 kilometres per hour. The information is transmitted to a central computer that communicates the exact location and status of their shipments.[13]

Motor Carriers

Because of Canada's well-developed highway system, trucks can service most major areas of Canada from coast to coast. They also rank high in the frequency and dependability of their scheduling. Trucks are often the fastest way of shipping goods over moderate distances because they ship directly, with no intermediate unloading onto another mode of transportation. For these reasons, truck transport is the preferred mode of shipment for machinery, nonperishable food products, and compact goods such as furniture.

But trucks do have some drawbacks. They cannot economically carry bulk goods like steel because of weight load limitations. Also, truck transport is expensive. It can be five times as costly as rail for some heavy goods of little unit value, such as coal.

Many truckers feel that future profitability will come from linking their services with other forms of transport to offer shippers an efficient and economical package and from improving their own efficiency. With the introduction of deregulation the Canadian trucking industry, many carriers may be forced out of business. TNT Canada Inc., of Mississauga, a dominant carrier in the market, has eliminated its less-than-truckload (LTL) business. A comparison of American and Canadian trucking costs in 1990 reveals that U.S. firms have a significant advantage. Canadian operating costs are approximately 20 percent more than those of the American firms.[14]

Water Transportation

By far, water transportation provides the cheapest way of carrying bulky goods over a long distance. Ocean-going vessels mainly carry oil; inland ships and barges usually transport minerals and agricultural and forestry products.

The one obvious disadvantage of water transportation is that not all buyers and sellers are on a major waterway. Ships also travel very slowly, and their scheduled runs are less frequent than other transportation modes.

Air Transportation

Air transportation is very important to the movement of some products. When speedy delivery over long distances is essential, as it is with perishables like flowers and fruit, airplanes cannot be matched. Goods that require special handling, such as electronic equipment and optical instruments, often go by air as well. Firms may also rely on air cargo shipments as part of JIT inventory management. Northern Telecom Canada ships approximately 90 percent of its international orders by air.[15]

Cost is the major disadvantage of air. It is 20 times more expensive than rail. In addition, not all areas have airports, which limits availability. Furthermore, plane service can easily be disrupted by weather conditions.

Still, air transport appeals to an increasing number of shippers because of cost trade-offs — for example, as noted earlier, they may allow a firm to carry less inventory. Air Canada and Canadian Airlines International have been adding to their fleets to expand their freight business. Many shippers have adopted the approach of using containerization over pallets to improve the speed and control of freight movement.[16] (Shipments loaded in sealed containers cannot be separated and misdirected at transfer points during loading and unloading, as might happen to goods loaded on individual pallets.)

Pipelines

The use of pipelines has increased tremendously since the 1950s. They transport not just oil and gas but ground coal carried in a liquid (called slurry). Dependability and low cost of operation are the main advantages of pipelines.

But pipelines are expensive to build and to maintain. The Alaska pipeline, completed in 1977, cost more than $7 billion to construct. Shipping the product to where it is needed is also a problem. Another drawback is that a pipeline has only one speed—slow. Liquids move through a pipeline at a leisurely five to six-and-a-half kilometres an hour.

Classes of Carriers

Transportation companies are classified in three categories: common carriers, contract carriers, and private carriers. Some carriers are subject to strict regulation, and some are bound by no laws at all. The amount of government supervision depends on the class of carrier.

Common carriers include all those transport companies that must serve the general public. The government requires that members of this class operate only with the permission of the appropriate regulatory authority. The rates and services of all makes of common carriers are regulated to some extent, even in these days of deregulation.

Contract carriers are less regulated because they serve only a limited number of customers, not the general public. They may negotiate different rates with different customers, but they must publicly make known what they charge. The rates and conditions of service are specified in a contract, which usually covers no less than a six-month period. Most contract carriers are truckers.

Finally, the class of **private carriers,** which includes all transportation owned by an individual company that is not primarily in the transportation business, is free from federal regulation. The private fleet of trucks owned by Sears to make deliveries to its customers is an example. Most private carriers are truckers, although a few oil companies own their own pipelines, and some manufacturers own a 25 or 30 kilometre railway running between plants.

Savings in Transportation

Small manufacturers that cannot afford to own or lease their own transportation have a serious problem if they do not produce in quantities large enough to warrant a full load. It is expensive to ship by common carrier in less than full truckloads or boxcar loads. Even large manufacturers may have this problem sometimes. But there is a solution.

Freight forwarders are transportation intermediaries that collect

Common Carrier
Transport company that must serve the general public.

Contract Carrier
Means of transport that serves only a limited number of customers and may negotiate different rates for different customers.

Private Carrier
Transportation owned by an individual company that is not primarily in the transportation business.

Freight Forwarder
Company that consolidates small shipments from a number of companies for transport in full loads.

small shipments from a number of companies, consolidate them for transport in full loads, and then see that the goods reach their final destination. They earn a portion of the savings realized by shipping in full loads. Manufacturers benefit because they pay less with faster delivery service than they would if they shipped on their own in smaller loads. They are also relieved of most of the required paperwork.

Trends in Physical Distribution

As noted previously, the total physical distribution concept has spurred marketers to think of the whole, rather than the separate parts, of an operation. The major trends in transportation concern achieving more efficiency by combining various modes.

Intermodal transportation refers to co-ordinating two or more transportation modes to minimize the disadvantages and maximize the strong points of each. Several combinations are possible. The three most common are:

1. *Piggyback*—a truck-railroad combination.

2. *Fishyback*—a joining of truck and ship.

3. *Birdyback*—a truck and air service.

Though attempts to combine transportation modes were made in the 1920s, intermodal transportation became popular only in the 1960s, when containers were introduced. **Containers** are large, standard-size metal boxes into which goods are placed for shipping and then sealed. They eliminate the need to load and unload individual goods each time merchandise is shifted to a new mode of transport.

Containers save time and money. Consider the savings in a typical fishyback operation, when goods are transferred from ship to truck. It used to take about 200 workers a week's time to unload a large freighter. Today, 20 or 30 dock hands using a crane can unload large containers from a ship in a day's time. Damage to goods and loss from theft are minimized because the containers are sealed.

By the year 2000, significant changes in physical distribution systems are expected to bring about more economical and efficient movement of goods from manufacturer to consumer. For example,

- Advances in vehicle tracking systems will enable carriers to respond to problems more quickly and meet delivery times more consistently.

- Through improved design, transportation equipment will become more fuel-efficient and be capable of higher payloads.

- Double-stack trains will have a major impact on shipping costs.

- Electronic data interchange (EDI) will directly link manufacturer, carrier, and supplier, saving all of them time and paperwork and improving productivity. It will accomplish this through computer-to-

Intermodal Transportation
Co-ordination of two or more transportation modes to minimize the disadvantages and maximize the strong points of each.

Container
Large, standard size metal box into which goods are placed for shipping and which is sealed.

computer exchange of business information without human intervention. More than 1000 Canadian companies are already using EDI.[17]

All of these changes will come about partly because of tighter environmental-protection legislation from the federal and provincial governments. As the 1990s progress, societal concerns will emerge as a more significant factor in corporate decision making.

For Canadian trucking companies, the picture is less optimistic. The cumulative effect of the goods and services tax (GST), the Canada–U.S. Free Trade Agreement, and the deregulation of the trucking industry could hurt it severely. Government-imposed costs are making it impossible for Canadian companies to remain competitive with those in the United States, which are expected to dominate the North American trucking industry if the situation remains unchanged.[18]

For shippers, however, all these changes present great opportunities, both in achieving cost savings and in developing new markets.

Chapter Replay

1. **What activities are involved in physical distribution?**
   Physical distribution includes all the activities required to move finished goods along marketing channels. This involves warehousing, inventory control, and transportation.

2. **How do companies use a total physical distribution concept?**
   Companies practising the total physical distribution concept integrate all management functions related to moving products to buyers. The person responsible for these activities is the physical distribution manager. The manager must balance the objective of minimizing costs with the objective of providing customer service.

3. **What are the basic decisions involved in warehousing?**
   The physical distribution manager must decide what type of warehouse is appropriate, whether to rent or own the facility, and where the warehouse should be located.

4. **What are the goals of inventory management?**
   Inventory managers pursue two goals: to provide the specified level of customer service by avoiding out-of-stock situations and to minimize the company's investment in inventory.

5. **How do managers decide on the amount of inventory to carry?**
   Physical distribution managers use sales forecasts to project how much inventory they will need. They weigh the acquisition costs and carrying costs to determine an economic order quantity. Besides the stock needed to meet average demand, companies usually also maintain a safety stock. Some managers use a distribution and inventory management system called just in time, or JIT, ensuring materials arrive just when needed.

6. **How do companies keep track of inventory?**
   Companies do physical counts of inventory and also keep perpetual inventory records.

7. **What modes of transportation can the physical distribution manager evaluate?**
   The manager can select from among railways, motor carriers, water transportation, air transportation, and pipelines.

8. **How can companies that are too small to own or lease their own transportation move goods economically?**
   Small manufacturers can use freight forwarders.

Key Terms

ABC analysis	intermodal
acquisition cost	transportation
automated warehouse	just-in-time (JIT)
carrying cost	market-positioned
common carrier	warehouse
container	perpetual inventory
contract carrier	physical count
cost trade-off	physical distribution
distribution centre	private carrier
warehouse	private warehouse
economic order quantity	public warehouse
(EOQ)	safety stock
factory-positioned	storage warehouse
warehouse	total physical distribution
freight forwarder	concept
hidden costs	visible costs
intermediate-positioned	
warehouse	

Discussion Questions

1. What decisions are involved in implementing the total physical distribution concept?

2. Which of the following goods would be better kept in a storage warehouse? Which would be better kept in a distribution centre warehouse? In each case, explain your answer.

   a. Fresh tomatoes on their way to grocery stores.

   b. Large quantities of tomatoes that have been canned at the end of the summer.

3. Why might a company want to use a private warehouse? What are some advantages of using a public warehouse?

4. Stan Salesperson was exasperated. He just lost an order for 200 desk chairs because the company had only 150 in stock. The customer didn't want to wait for the additional 50 chairs. "We should always keep enough inventory to fill all our orders," complained Stan. "It doesn't seem like we ever have enough for our peak period." Is Stan's complaint legitimate? If not, explain why not. If it is, describe how the company could do a better job of inventory control.

5. Sally Storekeeper runs a shoe store. Every year, she shuts down for a day to take a count of inventory. Besides this physical count, how else can Sally keep track of inventory? What kinds of information can Sally obtain from each technique?

6. Which mode of transportation best meets each of the following requirements?

   a. A steady, dependable supply of natural gas.

   b. Economical delivery of a large load of lumber over a long distance.

   c. Rapid delivery of replacement parts from a company that emphasizes customer service.

   d. Carrying furniture from a warehouse to consumers in the metropolitan area serviced by that warehouse.

7. What is the difference between a common carrier and a contract carrier? Why are common carriers regulated, while private carriers are not?

8. Larry Woodsmith runs a small company that makes dining room tables, which he sells in the Maritimes. His company doesn't make enough furniture to warrant a full truckload every time he needs to fill orders. How can Larry afford to ship his tables to his customers?

Novacor Chemicals

CASE 13.1

Novacor Chemicals, based in Calgary, Alberta, entered the polyethylene manufacturing business in 1984. Novacor began with a plant in mid-central Alberta, which still produces linear low-density polyethylene. It expanded in 1987 by acquiring, from Union Carbide, a Sarnia, Ontario, plant that produces low- and high-density polyethylene.

Source: Case developed by Bill Crowe, St. Lawrence College, Kingston, Ontario, and Mark Siemonsen, marketing consultant, from information supplied by Novacor Chemicals Ltd., Calgary, Alberta.

Novacor is unique as a Canadian-owned manufacturer of polyethylene (similar Canadian firms are subsidiaries of U.S. corporations). It competes with giants such as Dow, Dupont, Exxon, Chevron Quantum USI, and Union Carbide. Novacor supplies customers in both Canada and the United States from Canadian plant locations.

Background

Physical Distribution

The principal method of distribution for the polyethylene industry is rail; specially designed, jumbo hopper cars take bulk loads to strategically located rail-to-truck transfer facilities. Bulk trucks are used to serve customers within cost-competitive distances directly from plants or rail transfer facilities. Polyethylene resin is sometimes packaged in bags or boxes and delivered by closed vans from plants or storage warehouses to customers who do not have bulk storage capability. Containers are used for intermodal shipping of export goods outside North America.

The Market

Canada consumes only 15 percent of the plastics produced in North America. Therefore, Novacor, the sixth largest petrochemical company in North America, must aggressively pursue a niche in the larger U.S. market, where it competes for market share with the U.S. giants in their own backyard.

Novacor's polyethylene resins are a bulk commodity with few product advantages to differentiate them from similar resins offered by competitors. Competitive advantage can be gained through improved customer service.

The Decision

Realizing its dependence on providing customer service, Novacor recently undertook an extensive marketing research program on the needs of each customer. It identified several areas of physical distribution that could be improved to increase the level of customer service. Progress in those areas is seen as a key element in gaining competitive advantage. Close communication and co-operation with customer and carrier are going to be vital to Novacor's success.

Novacor immediately negotiated agreements with carriers, especially railways, that included guaranteed transit times. Customers can now depend on delivery times given at the time of order.

Novacor is also developing in-house programs to monitor delivery time and other service components of customer orders. Implementation of control systems such as EDI are planned for the future.

Focal Topics

1. Do you think that Novacor can sustain a service advantage over its competitors with customers in the United States?

2. What distribution alternatives can Novacor use to reduce costs further?

3. If the deregulation of the Canadian trucking industry results in disrupting the east-west shipping corridor across Canada, what strategy should Novacor use to serve the domestic market?

CAMI Manufacturing

CASE 13.2

The CAMI auto manufacturing plant, which manufactures the Tracker and Swift automobiles, has been operating in Ingersoll, Ontario, since 1989. It is an example of state-of-the-art logistical efficiency, combining just-in-time production methods, the advances of EDI, and a four-point philosophy, adopted from Japan, based on team spirit, empowerment, constant improvement, and open communications.

Teamwork is essential to the operation at CAMI. Each individual takes full responsibility for his or her part in the realization of team goals. The successful implementation of JIT production at CAMI means the firm requires minimum storage capacity. Furthermore, inventory control is simplified by reduced size.

How It Works

The implementation of CAMI's philosophy extends beyond its own personnel to its carriers and raw material suppliers. Responsibility for ensuring the scheduled delivery of parts rests on the supplier. This includes choosing the mode of transportation, organizing customs clearance and freight payments, and taking care of any other event that might arise during the shipment of goods. "CAMI is strictly a manufacturer of automobiles," says John Sinclair, assistant traffic manager.

CAMI's transportation and materials handling departments are, however, thoroughly involved with suppliers and carriers in determining supply and delivery scheduling in order to maintain the firm's JIT production schedules. CAMI will, for example, help to organize a "milk run" route in which a dedicated driver picks up from four or five suppliers. The EDI system issues delivery schedules and shipping notices to the driver and receiver. The file is then transferred to the finance

Source: Case developed by Bill Crowe, St. Lawrence College, Kingston, Ontario, and Mark Siemonsen, marketing consultant, with information from J.D. Corcoran, "Japanese Management Philosophy Pays Off for CAMI," *Transportation Business* 10 (July 1990).

department to begin billing procedures. Ninety-five percent of the volume of CAMI's material is delivered daily from 70 percent of its more than 100 suppliers.

Inbound materials at CAMI are delivered exclusively by truck. Intermodal transportation is used for parts and assemblies, such as power trains, that are manufactured in Japan. Shipping lines bring parts to the west coast, where connection is made with railway to move the goods east. Each shipping line has a trucking company that delivers the parts directly to CAMI from the rail yard and then backhauls the containers.

CAMI's yard has a capacity of 50 containers and takes deliveries of approximately 100 containers per week during full production. The arrival of containers from as far as Japan is scheduled only three to four days before the material is needed for production.

With markets becoming increasingly more global, many North American producers will have to follow CAMI's example in order to be competitive.

Focal Topics

1. List all of the physical distribution advantages that CAMI has realized with the implementation of JIT production and EDI.

2. How might the presence of unions and independent truckers in CAMI's physical distribution system jeopardize the stability of its supply?

3. What foreseeable developments in transportation would further reduce CAMI's costs?

Murphy's Snack Foods

Murphy's Snack Foods began in 1979. For a decade it was a small fry in Canada's $600-million-a-year potato chip and corn snack industry. It competed only in the corn snacks segment of the industry (see the accompanying table), using a single plant in Concord, Ontario, to produce items for other snack food companies and for some private label brands for chain stores, such as Loblaws (no-name products) and Marks and Spencer.

The Canadian Potato Chip and Corn Snack Industry

Product	% of Retail Sales
Potato chips	75%
Corn Snacks	
Extruded corn*	5
Popcorn	3
Tortilla chips	12
Corn chips	5

*Cheese twists, cheese balls, and so on.

The situation changed drastically in April 1989, when Murphy's acquired a Frito-Lay plant in nearby Kitchener and the rights to six of that well-known firm's brand names in Canada.

The reason for the change began in January 1988, when Hostess Food Products Ltd., a wholly owned subsidiary of General Foods Inc., and the Frito-Lay Division of Pepsi-Cola Canada Ltd. announced plans for a merger. Hostess was the industry leader in Canada; Frito-Lay ranked fourth with a market share of 9.4 percent. The Competition Tribunal reviewed the merger, under the Competition Act, and concluded that it would reduce competition if allowed to proceed as planned. The tribunal approved a restructured deal that included divesting part of Frito-Lay to Murphy's Snack Foods. In April 1989, Murphy's Potato Chips acquired the plant, six brand names (O'Grady's, Laurentide, Adams, Ridgies, Jacks, and Tostitos), and a fleet of delivery trucks.

For the once-tiny firm, the acquisition meant a huge commitment of resources, both financial and human. The risk seems to be paying

Source: Case developed by Bill Crowe, St. Lawrence College, Kingston, Ontario, and Mark Siemonsen, marketing consultant. Information and photo (page 339) supplied by Murphy's Potato Chips, Kitchener, Ontario.

off (see the accompanying sales history), but the rapid transition has left problems, many of which involve distribution and production levels.

Recent Sales History of Murphy's Snack Foods

Year	Gross Sales
1985	$ 2 500 000
1986	3 000 000
1987	4 000 000
1988	5 500 000
1989	32 000 000
1990	35 000 000

Channels of Distribution

Moving to the sale of brand-name products required Murphy's to change its channels of distribution. It also had to develop new packaging and truck maintenance systems while addressing all the issues associated with running a larger organization.

Before

Before April 1989, Murphy's usual way of doing business in Ontario was to take customer orders over the phone and arrange for either customer pick-up or drop shipment. A small portion of sales went to wholesale merchants, which serviced the smaller stores. In Quebec, a distributor placed truckload orders and warehoused them until they were sold. These methods were cost-effective, although they eliminated customers that required merchandising assistance.

With the 1984 introduction of Murphy's Good Value Snacks line, sold primarily to small chains and department stores such as Kmart and Zellers, came a significant increase in sales volume. Nevertheless, Murphy's traditional distribution channels continued to satisfy the needs of its customers.

After

The accepted industry practice for branded products is a route sales distribution system (rack jobbers). To survive at this level, Murphy's was forced to change channels to serve its new market.

Murphy's had only a few months to develop a sales team, including 75 route salespeople, and the routes and remuneration packages. It also had to restructure its accounting system to handle route sales. Frito-Lay had used a manual system; Murphy's opted to move immediately to an automated system with computerized hand-held order-entry units.

Murphy's has continued to use drop shipments for situations in which merchandising is not required or permitted. (Chain stores such as Loblaws, A&P, and IGA have union restrictions against merchandising by a supplier.)

Physical Distribution System

Murphy's Potato Chips services a market located primarily (about 95 percent) in Ontario, with the remainder spread among Quebec, Newfoundland, and the Maritimes. After it acquired the Frito-Lay brands, its physical distribution system changed significantly.

Before

All production for Murphy's corn snacks items used to originate from its Concord plant, and all distribution was handled from one warehouse there for customer pick-up or for delivery by one of Murphy's two trucks. Once orders were delivered, the responsibility for organizing stock and reordering was left with the customer.

Orders were taken over the phone for delivery from stock, typically within two days. Production was scheduled to maintain stock levels which were dictated by the sales history of the various products. Producing to stock created no problems with the main sellers (cheese balls and cheese twists) since inventory turnover was high. For the slower moving items, however, production was scheduled each ten-day period to allow larger production runs. This cost-minimizing procedure sometimes resulted in stockouts or in overstocks in which the product became stale and had to be rejected.

Murphy's production volume required the full capacity of its two delivery trucks. The trucks were not fully utilized, however. Inefficiencies developed because of the improper supervision of drivers, the inability to plan shipments to maximize truck use (since notice was often very short), and the necessity of short-shipping customers because of stockouts. It was often necessary to hire expensive carriers to make additional deliveries.

After

Since acquiring the Frito-Lay brands, Murphy's has moved all production to the facility in Kitchener, where the production scheduled is based on orders. A one-week lead time for shipment is now required. Salespeople, who visit their accounts weekly or biweekly, service the racks, remove stale products, and replenish the stock.

Within the plant, the inventory turns over in less than a week. Ideally, goods move out of production straight onto a truck. The firm has a total of 11 highway trailers and 75 route sales vans, as well as its two original delivery trucks.

Under the April 1989 plan, most of which Murphy's adapted from Frito-Lay, shipments would go to two kinds of distribution facilities:

- Warehouses, in Ottawa, Scarborough (an eastern borough of Toronto), and Concord, sites central to sizeable populations. Each such facility can service the needs of six to eleven route salespeople. All are operated by a warehouse manager, who is responsible for maintaining stock levels.

- Bin locations, in areas of fairly low population density. Each bin is a smaller facility, with one or two sales people operating out of it. These salespeople are responsible for all goods delivered to their bin as well as for stock replenishment. The original plan called for 25 bins.

With this seemingly well-organized system in place, Murphy's distribution costs have proved to be approximately 300 percent of the industry standard. The firm attributes part of this high cost to the fact that the acquired fleet of trucks needed major repairs and some even had to be replaced. Furthermore, the organization of the warehousing system was not optimal, but when Murphy's took over the operations at Kitchener there was no time to analyze its efficiency. Since then, the warehouse in Concord has been closed and another facility opened in Mississauga (a western suburb of Metropolitan Toronto). Five bins have been closed in the Hamilton and Kitchener districts and replaced by two centrally located warehouses.

At the Retailer

Before Murphy's acquired major brands, it was essentially a production facility supplying low-end product lines to retailers and wholesalers. Its customers did not require, and it was not structured to provide, merchandising services such as stock reordering, stock rotation, or display maintenance. New merchandising has become critically important—hence its use of rack jobbers to maintain displays. Struggling to keep sales at levels that justify its greatly enlarged production facilities has become a treadmill that management has not found a way to get off.

The Battle for Shelf Space

Gaining shelf space is an important part of competition at this level of the industry. The major supermarket and convenience store chains, such as Loblaws, A&P, and Beckers, negotiate shelf space at the head office level. By industry custom, a seller may offer:

1. *Superior service* — which stresses that the physical distribution system be able to supply all of a chain's outlets.

2. *Listing allowances*—which are payments for the opportunity to put the product on the shelf.

3. *Selling price incentives* — which are "off invoice" deals such as

- Case allowances—a fixed allowance per case for promoting the product. For example, if the item normally retails at $1.99 per bag, it will sell at $1.79 with a case allowance of $0.20 a bag.
- Volume rebates.
- Co-op advertising.

Case allowances are the most important of these tactics since chips are very price sensitive. About 75 percent of the total sales volume sells at less than retail price. Sometimes there are bidding wars to secure space during special occasions, such as New Year's and Superbowl Sunday.

Murphy's Tactics

This game is hardball, and Murphy's management sometimes wonders if it has the money to play. So far it has managed to avoid listing allowances, which are very costly. It cannot avoid case allowances, given their importance, but it has chosen to be selective about who gets them when. This approach has dangers, however. Since its sales volume is lower than that of its competitors, which use case allowances, Murphy's is continually at risk of losing shelf space (or its position on the shelf).

Murphy's is also trying some other tactics. It has introduced products that no one else can provide. It is, for example, the sole Canadian distributor of Cape Cod chips, manufactured by Eagle Snacks in the United States. Finally, it is pursuing chains' private-label business, which is very low margin but brings up production volumes and gives leverage for negotiating shelf space for the branded products.

Sales to Independent Stores

Murphy's approach to mom and pop and convenience stores must be a bit different. Product approval is gained through selling at head office to convenience store chains, but it is the individual operators that decide how much of a product to order. These sales have a higher margin (more small bags and higher selling prices), but they require more work from the route salespeople, who make the actual sales. It is thus important to design the right remuneration package to motivate the sales force properly.

Some case allowances are used, but there are rarely volume rebates or co-op advertising deductions.

For stores in which Murphy's has not obtained shelf space, salespeople are encouraged to set up temporary cardboard displays for an initial trial. If it is successful, the store owner may decide to grant shelf space for the product. Another method Murphy's is using is the introduction of the bonus bag (25 percent more). Promotions appeal to the retailer and also to the salespeople, who now have something new to offer.

A Catch-22 Situation

Murphy's is continually faced with the problem of acquiring and maintaining shelf space for all its products. Its financial position does not allow for a national advertising program. Neither can it offer case allowances to the extent of its competitors. Yet it must increase its sales volumes if it is to operate the Kitchener production facility efficiently. Its managers feel they are in a Catch-22 situation.

Focal Topics

1. What do you think Murphy's should do to utilize its delivery trucks more effectively?

2. What channel strategies should Murphy's employ to expand to the western Canadian market?

3. What effect might requiring a one-week lead time for delivery or a minimum order quantity have on the efficiency of the distribution system? What are some of the risks?

4. Evaluate the risks Murphy's faced at the time of the acquisition.

5. Distribution costs are the highest component in the price of snack foods. With the increasing costs of operating fleet trucks and increasing demand for more and better service by retailers, what can Murphy's do to reduce physical distribution costs?

6. Why are snack foods so price sensitive?

7. What recommendations can you give Murphy's for increasing sales volumes?

8. What do you see as the future of Murphy's Snack Foods?

Promotion Strategy

Chapter 14

Marketing Communication: The Promotional Mix

In this chapter, you will learn:

- The activities involved in promotion of a company's product.

- How communication occurs.

- Some sources of misunderstanding in the communication process.

- Advantages of communication through advertising.

- The major advantage and disadvantage of personal selling.

- Some functions of packaging.

- Types of promotional strategies.

- How marketers budget for promotion.

- How marketers measure the effectiveness of a promotional campaign.

The Power of the Package

If you never thought that packages could help sell the products inside them, consider the last time you went to the grocery store to pick up a loaf of bread. If you're like many shoppers, you left with more than bread. According to recent studies, more than two-thirds of buying decisions are made in the store — where they presumably are influenced by packaging.

While such impulse buying may sound ideal for the makers of those products, they have run into a problem. With so much effective packaging competing for your attention, marketers have to keep coming up with more attractive ideas.

One way they are doing this is by appealing to consumers' desire for convenience. For food products, this often means food that can be cooked or reheated in a microwave oven. Increasingly, makers of frozen dinners and entrees are switching from aluminum trays to microwavable plastic plates. Campbell, for example, is testing soup packaged in a plastic bowl ready to heat and serve.

Consumers are also seeing an increasing number of squeezable plastic containers. Such containers are used for a variety of products, including ketchup, barbecue sauce, jelly, mayonnaise, and salad dressings. The squeezable containers are not only convenient; they are also safer to handle than glass jars. Before introducing jelly in these containers, Welch Foods conducted research and learned that many consumers were willing to pay a little extra for jams and jellies sold in plastic containers.

Milk outside refrigerated dairy cases is becoming

another common sight. Packaging in aseptic cartons keeps milk fresh for up to three months. The challenge to marketers is to convince shoppers that this milk is the real thing, not a synthetic or watered-down product. Dairymen Inc. addressed this potential problem for its Farm Best milk with a design suggesting freshness. The carton features the Farm Best logo framing a quiet country scene. A banner labels the milk ''freshly packed.''

The job of convincing a shopper to buy a product typically ends with the packaging. But before that, marketers use a variety of other methods to convince people to buy a good, a service, or an idea. This chapter provides an overview of the activities involved.

Sources: Kate Bertrand, ''The 6 Hottest Trends in Food Packaging,'' *Packaging*, January 1986, pp. 24–30, 32; Nancy L. Croft, ''Wrapping Up Sales,'' *Nation's Business*, October 1985, pp. 41–42; Lori Kesler, ''Successful Packages Turn Medium into Message,'' *Advertising Age*, October 13, 1986, pp. S-2–S-3; and Herbert M. Meyers, ''Package Design,'' *Art Product News*, July/August 1986, pp. 30 + .

Promotion as Communication

It is a mistake to assume that promotion is the same as advertising. While advertising is one of the most important — and perhaps the most visible — elements of a promotional strategy, it is hardly the only one. Consider these examples:

- The telephone company buys advertising space in newspapers and on television to persuade and encourage people to phone long distance more often. Such paid *advertising* in mass media can be an effective element in the communication and sales of products.

- Shortly after *Return of the Jedi* opened in movie theatres across North America, Burger King offered customers drinking glasses emblazoned with scenes from the film with every purchase of Coke. Burger King's intent was not to advertise the movie but to sell soft drinks and hamburgers to accompany them. The glasses were a device in a strategy known as *sales promotion*.

- Approximately every eighteen months McDonald's restaurants throughout Canada donate $1 from the sale of every Big Mac to a children's charity called Ronald McDonald House. Local celebrities and media personalities help to cook and serve the Big Macs. McDonald's promotional strategy is to obtain free media attention, a form of promotion known as *publicity*.

- A stylishly dressed young couple stop to admire a new Nissan 300 ZX prominently displayed in a dealer's parking lot. As they examine the various options listed on the window sticker, a salesperson ambles over. "Want to take it for a spin?" he asks. *Personal selling* is another element of the promotional mix.

- You tell your roommate that you're going to make lasagne for dinner, but when you get to the store, you realize that you're not sure exactly what goes into it. Printed on one of the boxes of lasagne noodles is a recipe that looks good and pretty simple to make. So you buy that brand of pasta even though it costs seven cents more. Since *packaging* is often called on to sell a product directly from the shelf, it is frequently included among the elements of the promotional mix.

Together these methods — advertising, sales promotion, publicity, personal selling, and packaging — make up the part of the marketing mix known as **promotion**. Promotion is that marketing communications activity that attempts to inform and remind individuals and persuade them to accept, resell, recommend, or use a product, service, idea, or institution. Three points may be made about this definition.

First, promotional communication has a triple purpose: to inform,

Promotion
Marketing communication that attempts to inform and remind individuals and persuade them to accept, resell, recommend, or use a product, service, idea, or institution.

remind, and persuade. Most people do not object to the informational content of promotion because it serves to spread the word quickly about innovations. Consider how long it would have taken consumers to become aware of the availability of videocassette recorders without promotion. Similarly, most people welcome occasional reminders about products that they are already familiar with. Jell-O has been around for years, but homemakers like to see magazine ads for the product with new recipe suggestions.

The persuasive aspect of promotion, however, has been the subject of some criticism. Some would argue that such promotional messages manipulate people to want what they do not have, usually through emotional appeals. But not all persuasion is manipulative. Few would object to an ad that tried to sell a car by an appeal to its sporty looks or to a clerk's compliment on how fine one looks in a new pair of shoes. Compliments and phrases like "sporty looks" are persuasive, not informational, messages. Most marketers believe persuasion is a valid communication technique.

A second point is that not all promotion is directed to the ultimate consumer. Some is addressed to manufacturers or institutions, some to intermediaries who specialize in resale, and some to opinion leaders who are in a position to recommend usage. Each of these markets requires a different message to be effective. A consumer may be impressed by no-drip bottles of maple syrup, but a supermarket manager is likely to be more interested in ease of shelving or amount of profit to be made on the product.

Finally, the definition implies that promotion is a useful tool for both profit and nonprofit organizations. At Your Service 14.1 describes ways of marketing a free service to the community.

Moreover, although promotion is often used to sell a product or service, it is being increasingly accepted in the marketing of political candidates, government institutions, and ideas. The 88 Winter Olympics campaign in Alberta made extensive use of promotion to stimulate tourism. The Advertising Council runs advertisements with the messages "Cocaine. The big lie" and "Just Say 'No' to Drugs" to sell the idea of staying away from drugs.

Developing Effective Promotional Communication

The one thing that all of the examples cited above have in common is that they attempt to communicate, that is, to transmit information. A marketing communication is a specific form of information transmittal. It is one in which a seller attempts to transmit information to a buyer.

Promotion is not the only element of the marketing mix that communicates information. A product's design may convey a quality or a bargain-basement image. A price is set to reinforce the image. An exclusive or intensive distribution strategy further underlines the product quality

At Your Service 14.1

Marketing Crisis Lines

Crisis telephone lines are an important and growing public service, but they work only if people know about them and use them when they are needed. For this reason, any group running a crisis line has to be involved in marketing it.

The first challenge is getting information out. It is essential for the public to be made aware that the service exists, that they need it, and how to access it. Since the usefulness of crisis lines is not limited to one segment of the population, they should be marketed broadly — to every level of society.

That means using the mass media: newspapers, radio, TV, and billboards.

Publicity can be very effective. Newspapers are often willing to describe how the service works or do a biographical sketch of a volunteer. Staff or volunteers can appear on open-line radio shows.

A crisis line's own printed material can also be helpful, especially if it is used thoughtfully. Bookmarks with the pertinent information can replace business cards. Brochures can be put in many places throughout the city.

Complementing these efforts should be networking with other agencies — Boys' and Girls' Clubs, the Elizabeth Fry Society, the Addiction Research Foundation — as well as hospitals, clinics, and religious groups.

Ultimately, the best referrals come from word of mouth. That means having volunteers who practise good listening skills, making it inviting for callers to phone back. To encourage high-quality people to volunteer, it is essential that the contribution of volunteers be recognized on a continuing basis. It is also important to have a good training program. Such a program can, in turn, be marketed to the public, generating not only income but also community interest and awareness.

message. Why, then, is there a need for one branch of marketing — promotion — to specialize in communication? The answer is that promotion is needed to make explicit what the other elements of the marketing mix only imply. The slogan "The quality goes in before the name goes on," featured in Zenith's advertising messages, makes consumers aware of the television's technical excellence, which they might otherwise have missed.

But communication only works if the receiver of the information (in this case, the potential buyer) *understands* what the sender (for our purposes, the seller) is trying to say. That may not seem like a particularly dramatic revelation, but consider an example.

In the late 1970s, Anheuser-Busch tried to market a nonalcoholic adult soft drink called Chelsea that would provide a "socially acceptable substitute for alcohol." The product looked and was packaged like beer, although it contained less than 0.5 percent alcohol. Chelsea's advertising proclaimed it "the not-so-soft drink." Instead of understanding the slogan to mean a nonalcoholic beverage designed for adult tastes, neoprohibitionists saw the drink as "a pernicious attempt to predispose children toward beer drinking." After a storm of negative publicity and boycotts, Anheuser-Busch withdrew Chelsea from its test markets.[1]

Transmitting information is not always as simple as it may seem. For a communication to be effective, it must:

1. Gain the attention of the receiver.

2. Be understood by both the receiver and the sender.

3. Stimulate the needs of the receiver and suggest an appropriate method of satisfying those needs.[2]

How Communication Works

Many theorists have concluded that promotional communications, like all forms of communication, can take place because an orderly way of transmitting a message, similar to a telephone circuit, exists.[3] A simplified model of how communication occurs is shown in Figure 14.1. The basic elements of this communication circuit are: (1) the **source**, or originator of the message; (2) the **receiver**, the ultimate destination of the message; and (3) the **medium of transmission**, the means by which the message moves from sender to receiver. Some very important processes must occur, however, for the message to be understood. The message must be **encoded**, or put into understandable form by the source. At the opposite end, the receiver must **decode**, or retranslate the message into understandable terms. Finally, the receiver must signal the understanding by **feedback** to the source.

Some Complications

The message may not be understood at all, or it may be understood in a way quite different from that intended. Recall the party game in which a group of people sit in a circle. The first person whispers a message ("Savvy businessmen wear blue suits") to the person sitting next to the first person. The game continues until the last receiver announces the message heard ("Your grandmother wears combat boots"). The garbled message usually bears little resemblance to the original. Many firms have had similar experiences. The message originally sent is unrecognizable by the time the consumer receives it. Many factors can complicate the communication model.

Source
Originator of a message.

Receiver
Ultimate destination of a message.

Medium of Transmission
Means by which a message moves from sender to receiver.

Encoding
Putting a message into understandable form by the source.

Decoding
Retranslating a message into terms the receiver understands.

Feedback
Understanding signalled by the receiver to the source.

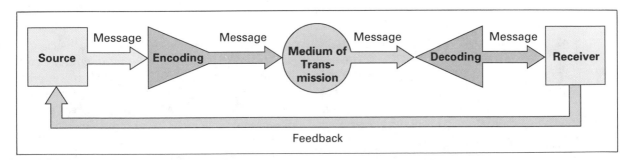

Figure 14.1 Model of the Communication Process

Source Effect
Distortion of a communication resulting from the reputation of the source of a message.

Source Effect

Sometimes the reputation of the source affects the way a message is received. This phenomenon is known as the **source effect**. For example, one study of the effect of consumer knowledge of brands showed that if a company does not market the leading brand, it really does have to try harder to get a favourable sales response from its ads. Ad copy was prepared for three brands, two of them market leaders and the other relatively unknown. When the ad copy did not identify the brands, selected consumers judged the ads equally effective in motivating them to buy. When brand names were mentioned in the copy, however, the advertising effectiveness of the least-known brand dropped noticeably.[4]

The source effect impeded the unknown brand's message, but it also helped the leading brands to communicate their strengths. Using the credibility of the sender to add persuasiveness to the message is a common marketing strategy. Salespeople use their company's name, if it is well known, to gain access to buyers. And TV ads for products often lean on the credibility of people who appear in them. Candid interviews with homemakers discussing the merits of various laundry detergents are thought to be more believable than a company spokesperson's touting the benefits of a brand.

Multiple Transmitters

Many mistake the words of a message, whether spoken or in print, for the whole message. In fact, most messages are transmitted through more than words. Sales representatives, for example, are often very much aware of their body language. Posture, facial expression, and tone of voice can heighten a presentation or torpedo it.

Multiple transmitters also exist in print communications. The layout of an advertisement often conveys as much as the words. A discount store's ads are likely to be cluttered with notices of bargains, whereas an exclusive department store's ads may feature few words and much white space. Both approaches are effective in underlining the message. The first conveys the excitement of a sale, the second the elegance associated with quality goods.

Decoding Errors

Receivers do not always get the message that a source sends out. A classic example is the angry response that a Xerox television commercial aroused. The commercial showed a chimpanzee running off copies on a new machine and delivering them to the boss. The intended message was the machine's simplicity of operation. What some viewers saw — especially secretaries and reproduction clerks — was a put-down of their jobs. Xerox withdrew the advertisement.

Many decoding errors arise from selective perception and interpretation. People often see or hear only what they want. But another related problem is **noise**, interference that is either deliberately or accidentally introduced and blocks or distorts transmissions. There are three types of noise:[5]

1. *Internal noise* is the kind that characterizes the message itself. A message transmitted in a vocabulary unknown to the receiver creates such noise, as do preconceptions, word of mouth, and culture. Marketing Today 14.1 describes how one company overcame a problem with internal noise.

2. *External noise* is introduced accidentally from outside the communication process. Commercials telecast to viewers in barrooms have little chance of being heard.

3. *Competitive noise* is deliberately introduced by another source to gain a competitive advantage. A maker of bubble gum at one time attempted to break into the eastern market by conducting a large ad campaign. Almost as soon as the gum was introduced, however, rumours spread among youngsters in the area that the gum contained spider eggs or caused cancer. The suspicion was that the product's competitors had started the rumour.[6]

Inadequate Feedback

Lack of sufficient feedback to the source can stand in the way of future communications. Political parties routinely spend thousands of dollars

Noise
Interference that is either deliberately or accidentally introduced and blocks or distorts transmissions.

Marketing Today 14.1

A Novel Marketing Technique

Creative Output faced a difficult hurdle in promoting its manufacturing-scheduling software. The software, called Optimized Production Technology (OPT), had a number of competitors, was a complicated product, and met with suspicion because it handled a common problem in an unusual way.

The company would send representatives into the factory to guide users, but as soon as the reps left, the users would revert to their former way of scheduling. And the software therefore failed to live up to its promise.

So Eli Goldratt, head of Creative Output, looked for an inexpensive, attention-getting way to explain and sell his product. His solution was to write a steamy novel, a manufacturing romance titled *The Goal, Excellence in Manufacturing*. The book tells the story of Alex Rogo, a division manager for UniCo, whose plant and marriage are both about to fold. Thanks to the OPT-style advice of an old college professor, Alex manages to placate his boss and hold onto his wife.

The novel was a smashing success. Visitors to trade shows snapped it up, trade magazines serialized it, and Waldenbooks carried it. Following up on the success of the novel, Creative Output introduced a computer game using the principles of OPT. As a result of the novel and the game, potential clients started telling each other about OPT and Creative Output, and business is rolled in. Says Goldratt, "We almost don't have to do any selling. The client is calling us before we have the chance to call him."

Source: Adapted from Craig R. Waters, "One of a Kind," *Inc.*, July 1986, pp. 107–108.

on polls during the course of their campaigns to determine how they are doing with various segments of the population. Inadequate feedback presents great difficulties for advertising executives. As John Wanamaker, a famous department store founder, once lamented, "Half my advertising dollars are wasted; I just don't know which half."

Elements of the Promotional Mix

In review, the major types of promotional activity are advertising, personal selling, sales promotion, publicity, and packaging. Most organizations tend to rely on either advertising or personal selling to carry most of their message and use the other tools as supplements. As forms of communication, all have important points in common. Before considering similarities, it is important to distinguish how they differ from one another. Chapters 15 and 16 discuss the various forms of promotion in more detail.

Advertising

Advertising
Any paid form of nonpersonal presentation and promotion of ideas, goods, or services by an identified sponsor.

The American Marketing Association defines **advertising** as "any paid form of nonpersonal presentation and promotion of ideas, goods, or services by an identified sponsor."[7] The key words are "nonpersonal" and "paid by an identified sponsor." Instead of communicating with customers face to face, companies that advertise ordinarily use a mass medium —television, newspapers, radio, billboards, or other well-known means of communication. When ads appear in media with editorial or program content, they are set off and clearly identified as messages paid for by a sponsor.

The cost of advertising varies by medium, but it is one of the cheapest ways to reach people. For example, at $1.1 million a minute in 1986, a television advertisement during the Super Bowl might sound expensive. But consider that those advertisements were expected to reach many millions of people.[8] The cost of reaching each viewer was actually relatively small.

Efficiency is not the only advantage of advertising. Advertising captures attention because it is often quite creative. Some even claim that they enjoy ad messages more than the programs and articles that accompany them. A television commercial for the California Raisin Advisory Board features a conga line of sneaker-wearing animated raisins singing and dancing to "I Heard It through the Grapevine." On Halloween of the year the commercials hit the screen, the "in" costume was the raisin outfit. The ad was so popular that people even wrote in to say it had persuaded them to buy raisins.[9]

Another advantage of advertising is that it allows perfect reproduction of the desired message.[10] No intermediary, such as a salesperson, stands between the promoter and the potential customer to garble the message.

Of course, in another way, this advantage can turn into a disadvantage. Without the personal touch, a consumer's attention can wander and the message may be lost. The advantages of advertising apparently far outweigh the disadvantages, however. Advertising expenditures in 1987 exceeded $7 billion in Canada.[11]

Personal Selling

According to Employment Canada, about 1.2 million Canadian workers are engaged in sales occupations ranging from the selling of encyclopedias door-to-door to the selling of computer systems to the Canadian government. Selling, unlike advertising, involves a one-to-one relationship with a customer. **Personal selling** is the oral presentation of a tangible or intangible product by a seller to a prospect for the purpose of completing an exchange.

The obvious advantage of a direct oral presentation is that it allows the salesperson to judge the reaction of customers to the sales talk. By gauging the response, the salesperson can tailor the message to the customer's needs. The price of this custom fitting is expensive, however. The cost of a sales call on a consumer has risen to more than $100, and the cost of a call in the industrial market to more than $250. In terms of the number of people reached, this is vastly more expensive than an advertisement that costs $0.5 million but reaches millions of potential buyers. However, since products requiring a personal sales effort are usually more expensive than those that depend on advertising, the extra cost of selling may be worthwhile.

Publicity

In November 1983, ABC-TV aired a controversial television film, *The Day After*, a story about the effects of nuclear war on civilians. The actual screening of the movie was almost anticlimactic. For months prior to the telecast, ABC had been building an enormous publicity campaign about the program. Taped copies were leaked into circulation and were being screened for nuclear-freeze sympathizers as early as the previous July. As its air date approached, *The Day After* was being discussed on every newscast, morning talk show, and newspaper in North America—and a fair share of those abroad.[12] Following the broadcast, ABC ran a special edition of *Viewpoint*, anchored by Ted Koppel, in which notable public figures were called on to respond to issues raised in the TV movie.[13]

The network had scheduled the movie during a "sweeps week," a time when the A. C. Nielsen Company carefully monitors audience viewing habits. The American network that leads in the Nielsen rating can then charge advertisers the highest prices. Despite some compelling programming on the other networks, ABC's strategy paid off. *The Day After* was watched by 100 million, making it the highest-rated made-for-TV movie.[14]

Personal Selling
Oral presentation of a tangible or intangible product to a prospect for the purpose of completing an exchange.

Publicity
Any information relating to a manufacturer or its products that appears in any medium on a nonpaid basis.

Public Relations
Activities that attempt to generate a favourable attitude toward a company among employees, shareholders, suppliers, and the government, as well as among customers.

Sales Promotion
Promotional activities besides selling, advertising, and publicity that stimulate purchases or aid dealer effectiveness.

ABC's promotional efforts were a form of **publicity**, "any information relating to a manufacturer or its products that appears in any medium on a nonpaid basis."[15] This definition distinguishes publicity from advertising, which is paid for and clearly set off from news in the media. Publicity has two chief advantages over advertising. It is believable, because it appears as news rather than as a commercial message. It also costs comparatively little; the chief cost is the salaries of publicists. However, firms cannot control publicity in the same way they can control paid advertisements.

Publicity is only one part of a much larger task called **public relations**, which attempts to generate a favourable attitude toward a company among employees, shareholders, suppliers, the government, and customers. When a trust company contributes heavily to the United Way, sponsors a showing of local art, or allows employees to donate some of their work time to community service, it has these publics in mind. Public relations, which also includes activities such as institutional advertising and corporate contributions to the community, is business's recognition of the necessity of maintaining a favourable public image.

Sales Promotion

All the other promotional activities of a firm that stimulate consumer purchases or aid dealer effectiveness fall into the category of **sales promotion**. Coupons, music videos, free glasses, publishers' sweepstakes, and cosmetic demonstrations are just a few examples of the many forms that sales promotion may take.

In the 1980s, sales promotion activity increased markedly in importance because it was necessary to stimulate consumer buying in a sluggish economy. Sales promotion techniques are effective in doing this because they are extremely visible, often appeal to the "something for nothing" instincts in people, and usually bring about an immediate buying response. One sales promotion executive noted, "When you want awareness, you advertise. When you want immediate action, you promote."[16] Sales promotion can also be used to stimulate dealer interest. The main drawback of sales promotion techniques is that competitors tend to copy them, cancelling their effectiveness.

Packaging

Packaging has become increasingly important as a promotional tool. When there is no advertising budget, a package sometimes must bear the weight of the entire promotional message.

As many marketers have discovered, the importance of packaging cannot be overestimated. Think of some of the world's great packages:

the original Coke bottle, the Whitman's Sampler, or the cylindrical Quaker Oats box. Consider, too, how different the perception of a product would be if, for example, an expensive perfume came packaged in a milk carton or if a gift of Valentine candies arrived in a shabby brown box.

Marketers are so concerned with packaging that it has become a $9 billion-a-year industry in Canada. Innovations in packaging are, in fact, responsible for the success of some products. Marlboro cigarettes introduced its flip-top box in 1954, and its sales jumped from 0.3 billion cigarettes to 14.3 billion in two years' time. The advent of the aerosol can gave birth to a whole industry — hair sprays.[17] At the beginning of this chapter, you read about some more recent innovations.

Packaging has become so plentiful that in recent years many people have begun to preach that we have much too much of a good thing. This social question is explored at the end of the chapter. First, however, it is necessary to understand why so much packaging is used today.

The Functions of Packaging

Fifty years ago, the main function of packaging was to provide a means of transport for a product between a neighbourhood store and the home. Grocers scooped sugar into brown paper sacks and barkeepers filled a bucket with beer. A packaging revolution has occurred since then. Today, packages are expected to perform many functions. These include:

1. *Packages offer protection to the product and consumer.*   Egg cartons, plastic wrap around record albums, and dark green wine bottles are examples of packages that serve primarily to protect products from damage and spoilage.

   In addition to protecting the product, some packages protect the consumer. One reason shampoo is sold in plastic rather than glass bottles is to avoid broken bottles in bathrooms. Manufacturers have been using increasingly sophisticated packaging to reduce the likelihood that products will be tampered with or sampled. Typical safeguards include tamper-rings on jars of nuts, heat-shrink neck bands on ASA bottles, and shrink wrapping around ice cream cartons. One expert has suggested using hologram seals on bottles. These seals would be hard for a would-be tamperer to duplicate, and they would look unusual enough for consumers to notice whether they were there.[18]

2. *Packages increase the use of the product.*   Marketers want consumers not just to try a product, but to continue to use it in greater quantities. Packaging can help. Through colourful packaging in differently shaped boxes, the makers of facial tissues have expanded use of their products from the bedroom or bathroom into other rooms of the house.

3. *Packages increase sales by adding a reuse value.*   A number of pack-

ages are designed to allow package reuse for other purposes. Margarines are now sold in plastic tubs that serve as containers for leftovers when the contents are used up. Avon Products is a master at such packaging. Recent catalogue offerings included bubble bath for children in a decanter shaped like a popular movie character, compass-shaped soap in a fancy tin box, and eggnog-flavoured gum in a plastic gum holder.

4. *Packages promote the product.*   A recent trend is toward self-service in retail stores. Discount and variety stores offer sales help only when requested, and supermarkets do not offer sales personnel. Products must sell themselves—an increasingly difficult task. This role of packaging is so important that many marketers conduct tests of packaging in an attempt to determine whether the packaging helps sales of the product. The tests consider what the package "says" about the product and how it can do it, given the selling environment—the store and the product's competition.[19]

A skilfully designed package will reinforce the information a consumer has already absorbed about the product through advertising, sales promotion, or publicity.

In some cases, packaging alone can change the way consumers feel about a product. Hanes, for example, managed by the clever packaging of L'Eggs panty hose to reverse a long-standing impression that all hosiery sold in supermarkets was of inferior quality. The egg-shaped L'Eggs package elicited perceptions of a fragile yet protected product. It also connoted fashion and sex appeal. Backed by a skilful advertising campaign, L'Eggs became the first supermarket panty hose success story.[20]

Packages might also provide a variety of other benefits:

- *Informing consumers about product benefits:*   The package for a roll of Scotch transparent tape reads "Stays Clear!"

- *Offering suggestions or recipes:*   Boxes of Chex cereals often carry a recipe for Party Mix, a snack made with those cereals. Packaging for adjustable pliers, such as Vise Grips, might show various possible uses for this tool.

- *Announcing special value:*   Two cassette tapes might be wrapped in a package labelled, "Buy Two, Get One FREE!"

- *Selling other items in the same line:*   For example, some books contain a list of other books written by the same author. A box of Great Crisps! crackers shows a picture of the different flavours available.

- *Assuring protection:*   Many medicine packages contain a label such as "safety sealed for your protection."

- *Highlighting special product features:*   An example is toothpaste in a box labelled "Maximum Fluoride Protection."

Package Design

For a package to serve many functions, it must be well designed. The task is more difficult than it may seem. Packaging is fairly standard for given types of products. Foil and plastic wrap, although tube-shaped, come in a rectangular box. How, then, can a package designer of a particular brand of foil or plastic wrap distinguish one company's products from others on the same shelf?

Colour   One way is to use colour effectively. Psychologists have shown that people react to certain colours in predictable ways. For impulse items, red is an effective colour because it motivates people to act. As makers of expensive chocolates have discovered, gold and silver are good choices for an elegant specialty good. Men seem to buy anything that is packaged in brown, including cosmetics, perhaps because it evokes outdoor images.[21] When the Campbell Soup Company introduced Le Menu gourmet frozen dinners, it was careful to package the product in a modern-looking, sandstone-coloured box. The company's goal was to eliminate the 1950s image associated with TV dinners.

Style   Style can also serve to individualize packages. Two different styles are currently in vogue: one frequently dubbed "North American Country" and the other a sleek, contemporary look.

The design of some natural cereals, picturing rural scenes of the nineteenth-century on box panels, conveys a nostalgic feeling. On the other hand, products such as Avon's *Odyssey* fragrance collection are packaged in a vertical, sculptured bottle. Avon designed it specifically for "women of today [who] approach life as an adventure, journeying into new and unexplored places, propelled by an inner energy."[22]

Copy   Package copy — both words and pictures — can also help distinguish a product from its competitors. In one survey, brand names were removed from packages, and people were asked to identify the product. The words "squeezably soft" on one package alerted 97 percent of those surveyed that the product was Charmin tissue. Mr. Clean's bald head and gold earring won recognition from 68 percent of those tested.[23]

Form   Some variation in package form within a product category is acceptable, but not very much. When Ipana toothpaste came out with an aerosol dispenser a few years ago, it failed to catch on. The environmental danger of certain kinds of packaging is a major issue today as discussed at the end of the chapter. Also, retailers resist odd shapes and sizes as much as consumers. They object to packages that take too much space, topple over, or cannot be conveniently stacked. Clearly, the requirement that packages be both attention-getting and functional puts a heavy burden on designers.

Packaging is much too critical a promotional device to be treated casually. As more and more marketers wake up to the importance of packaging, the industry has mushroomed into a multibillion-dollar business. While the development of new products accounts for a significant portion of this figure, marketers of established brands account for twice the business of new items.[24]

Promotional Objectives and Strategies

The various elements of the promotional mix have the same objectives as all other marketing activities: to bring about an exchange. But an exchange may not always be a sale. Marketers may wish to influence viewing habits ("Watch CTV"), choice of vacation sites ("Discover Canada"), or fondness for political candidates. They may also wish to promote an idea—even if it seems contradictory to their goal of selling a product.

Less than a year after the repeal of Prohibition in the United States, Jos. E. Seagram & Sons launched an advertising campaign with copy that began "We who make whiskey say: 'Drink Moderately.'" Since then, Seagram's has continued to promote moderation in drinking and has led the way among distillers in urging its customers not to drive if they have been drinking.[25]

The broader goal of promotion, then, may be to communicate between a producer and a public. Frequently, communication is meant to elicit an immediate and traditional exchange—a sale; at other times the goal may be more oblique—to create a favourable impression of a company, to raise consciousness for an idea, or to influence legislation that would favourably affect an industry.

Whether the desired response is concrete (redeem this coupon) or more abstract (don't be scared of computers), the promotion should be planned. This plan should map out just what is to be accomplished and how each promotional element will be used. That involves setting objectives, or goals, and then designing strategies to meet those objectives.

Objectives

Overall company and marketing goals discussed in Chapter 2 must be translated into promotional goals. This process should occur in two steps. An organization must first set very general communications objectives and then, after research, quantify them for each promotional tool used.

Marketers set general communications objectives rather than specific sales goals because it is nearly impossible to measure the results of a promotional campaign by sales results. Several general communications goals may be pursued. One theory suggests that the goals of promotion coincide with the stage of product knowledge of a prospective buyer. Thus, promotion may:

1. Create *awareness,* or knowledge of the existence of a product, service, or idea.

2. Arouse *interest* in the product, service, or idea.

3. Create *desire* for the product by showing consumers how it can satisfy their needs.

4. Stimulate *action,* which may be either a purchase or the adoption of an idea.

The stages are frequently referred to by the acronym AIDA: *a*wareness, *i*nterest, *d*esire, and *a*ction. These sequential steps are the usual path that most consumers follow before making a purchase decision. Figure 14.2 shows the relationship between the four stages of AIDA and the effectiveness of four of the five promotional methods. Advertising, for example, is highly effective in creating awareness but less effective in stimulating action. The reverse is true for personal selling. Publicity may also serve to familiarize the public with a product, but it has little value in spurring action.[26]

To see these principles in action, consider a bank with a branch located near campus. It has decided to build business by offering a special chequing account for students who get their student loans through the branch. First, the bank wants to build *awareness,* so it sends the school newspaper press releases describing the bank's involvement with post-secondary education, its special programs for students, and financial information of interest to students.

When students begin to grow more aware of the bank's programs, it begins its efforts to develop *interest.* It runs ads about the new chequing accounts in the school paper, and it posts signs around campus. The branch then tries to build *desire* by mailing each student a brochure detailing the advantages of opening an account with it. Finally, to stimulate *action,* the branch hosts a series of lectures during which a bank

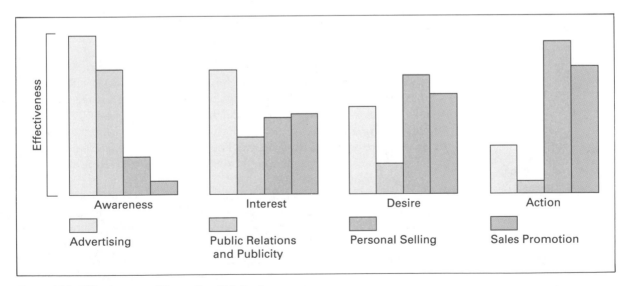

Figure 14.2 Effectiveness of Promotional Methods

representative describes what the bank can offer students, answers questions, and distributes new-account forms.

Most marketers agree that these general goals should be quantified so that results can be measured. An advertising objective for the chequing account might have been "to increase brand awareness by 15 percent among students within 12 weeks" — a clear statement that could be measured by research. Similar quantitative goals could be set for the other promotional tools. All goals should be consistent with overall company and marketing objectives.

Strategies

Promotional objectives give marketers a goal; strategies tell them how to get there. Promotion managers may use either a push strategy or a pull strategy, or they may employ some combination. The major difference is in the type of promotion stressed. Figure 14.3 illustrates the differences.

The Push Strategy

Push Strategy
Urging members of a market channel to sell a product or give it adequate display.

Push strategy got its name because it involves pushing, or urging, members of a market channel to sell a product or give it adequate display. Both personal selling and trade promotion are used by each channel member to promote the product to the channel below. Producers, for example, promote to wholesalers, wholesalers to retailers, and retailers to consumers. Producers may offer special advertising allowances or prizes to dealers to gain their support.

The Pull Strategy

Pull Strategy
Creating demand for a product within a channel of distribution by appealing directly to the consumer.

An ad in *Stickers!* magazine, a publication aimed at children who collect stickers as a hobby, offered kids a chance to win free stickers if they took the entry blank featured on the page to their favourite sticker store. The ad went on to say, "With their order from us, they'll get a 10% discount and you'll be entered in a FREE sticker drawing." Promoters of this product are using a **pull strategy**. They are attempting to create demand for a product within a channel of distribution by appealing directly to the consumer. Advertising, rather than personal selling, is the primary promotional tool used for this strategy. Companies that concentrate on convenience goods, such as Procter & Gamble, specialize in this strategy, often using coupons or samples to build demand for their products. However, a pull strategy has been employed successfully by industrial goods companies as well. For instance, the Farr Company, manufacturer of air filters for engines, created a demand for its product among buyers and users of trucks and locomotives, which forced equipment manufacturers to buy Farr's filters.

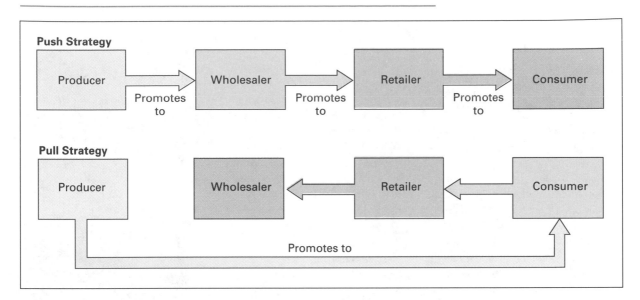

Figure 14.3 Push and Pull Promotional Strategies

The Combination Strategy

Most familiar consumer goods companies use a balance of selling, advertising, and other promotional techniques in a **combination strategy** to achieve their goals. For example, to promote Chaz, a line of cologne, after-shave, soap, and talc for men, Revlon ran a $150 000 "Grand Prix" Sweepstakes. Tom Selleck, star of *Magnum P.I.*, was hired as spokesperson, and a Ferrari sports car was offered as a grand prize.

Ads featuring Selleck were run in *Newsweek, Playboy,* and *Sports Illustrated* for a combined circulation of 16 million. Each ad featured an instant-winner, scratch-off game piece as a bind-in card that required participants to visit the store to determine their prize—a sales promotion technique.

A separate sweepstakes was conducted for retailers with matching prizes (excluding the Ferrari), and salespeople were motivated to exceed selling quotas with additional prizes.

Revlon received 1 502 000 sweepstakes entries, and sales increased 35 percent as a result of the promotion.[27]

Combination Strategy
Balance of selling, advertising, and other promotional techniques combining push and pull strategies to achieve sales goals.

Choosing the Right Strategy

The choice of a strategy is made by weighing many factors. The most important considerations are product type, the customers in the target market, and the strategy of competitors. Marketing Today 14.2 describes how Rolls-Royce takes these into account.

Marketing Today 14.2

Selective Promotion for Rolls-Royce

Rolls-Royce Motor Cars Inc. does not have a central advertising strategy. The company explains that this is because their cars are perceived differently in each market, and buying patterns and attitudes vary. In addition, the quality image of Rolls-Royce Motor Cars is so strong that many observers suggest the company may not need to do much advertising to sustain its brand identity.

Instead, Rolls-Royce focuses on dealers. It gives local dealers incentives to spend a preset amount on advertising. Dealers also make heavy use of promotional activity — typically social occasions for potential customers, ranging from fashion shows to clay-pigeon shoots and polo matches. Once potential customers are brought together, the dealership can use direct selling to encourage sales.

A major Rolls-Royce Motor Cars dealership is the one in Beverly Hills, California. This dealership has used an ad budget of $400 per car, combined with a variety of promotional and publicity activities. The dealership sponsored a weekly classical music radio program, participated in several charities, and hosted periodic parties known as "Rolls-Royce of Beverly Hills Happenings." One of these events took place to celebrate the opening of the dealership's new service department; at this "happening," Princess Margaret was the guest of honour.

Rolls-Royce Motor Cars Inc.

Source: Adapted from Brian Oliver, "Rolls-Royce Rides on Reputation, Not Ads," *Advertising Age,* June 16, 1986, pp. S-30–S-31.

What Product Type?

Some products, such as small appliances or food items, are relatively simple to promote, while others, including most industrial goods, require specialized knowledge for installation, operation, or maintenance. In general, the more complex a product, the more appropriate a push strategy. Sales personnel are the key element in IBM's business computer promotion strategy because they are needed to explain computer capabilities and to engage in the long negotiations required to close sales. No such personal effort is needed to sell an Almond Joy candy bar; a pull strategy utilizing mainly advertising is far more effective.

Some consumer products, particularly shopping goods such as clothing, autos, or large appliances, do require some selling effort because they are more costly and consumers compare values before buying. A combination strategy, therefore, is most effective. A Maytag advertisement pulls customers into stores. But Maytag sales reps are also needed to convince retailers to stock their products, and floor salespeople may be given a bonus (called "push money" or "spiffs") to put forth a special effort to sell the machines. Table 14.1 shows the relative importance of

Table 14.1 Advertising-to-Sales Ratios, 1982

Industry	Ad Dollars as Percentage of Sales
Phonograph records	13.0%
Toys and amusement, sporting goods	10.5
Perfumes, cosmetics	8.4
Drugs	8.2
Distilled beverages	7.9
Malt beverages	7.0
Soaps and detergents	6.9
Candy	6.1
Household appliances, retail	5.7
Jewellery	5.0
Books	4.6
Food products	4.2
Real estate	3.0
Heating equipment and plumbing fixtures	2.2
Industrial measuring instruments	2.0
Engines and turbines	1.8
Farm machinery	1.4
Surgical and medical instruments	1.2
Manifold business forms	0.7
Cement, hydraulic	0

Source: Schonfeld & Associates, Inc., 2550 Crawford Ave., Evanston, Ill., as seen in *Advertising Age*, August 15, 1983, p. 20.

advertising to sales for different types of products. The table confirms the observation that a pull strategy (emphasizing advertising) is far more common for convenience goods than for industrial goods, and a combination strategy is more typical for shopping goods.

What Customers?

A firm's customers may be few and geographically concentrated or numerous and widely dispersed. Firms selling to a small, concentrated market generally rely more on personal selling — a push technique — than organizations that make a mass appeal. Thus, sellers of automotive parts can use a small sales force to cover Ontario and Quebec, the provinces where automobile manufacturers cluster. Manufacturers of toaster ovens, on the other hand, must use sales promotion to move their products through wholesale and retail channels and advertising to create demand.

Other customer characteristics also influence the choice of a strategy. Professional purchasing agents or buyers of rare antiques, both of whom have special knowledge, are more likely to respond to a message delivered through a salesperson than through an impersonal mass medium such as a magazine.

What About Competition?

Competitors affect all marketing efforts, and promotion is no exception. In most cases, it would be suicidal to neglect advertising if it is commonly used by competitors or to ignore intermediaries if a strong sales effort is required.

Rheingold Beer, a New York-based firm, discovered this the hard way when it attempted to break into the market on the West Coast of the United States in the 1950s. Beer sales generally depend on a combination strategy, but Rheingold chose to ignore the combination of sales effort and advertising usually used in the area. The firm bypassed the traditional wholesale distributors and tried to pull customers directly into retail outlets by ads. Moreover, their ads were placed in newspapers and magazines, not on radio and TV, which were then more commonly used for advertising beer in the area. The campaign failed, and Rheingold withdrew from the market.[28]

Exceptions exist to every rule, of course. Sometimes strategists succeed by ignoring conventional ways of doing things. Most encyclopedias, for example, rely on a push strategy, with heavy emphasis on door-to-door selling. But when Random House introduced its one-volume encyclopedia in the United States in 1977, the president of the company went on a publicity tour, and the product was heavily advertised—both pull techniques. By all accounts, this campaign was a success. Random House shipped 110 000 copies to stores during the campaign, a record for a one-volume encyclopedia.[29]

Budgeting for Promotion

Developing a workable strategy is complex, but it is by no means the only job a promotional manager must perform. Plans must be drawn up to carry out the strategy, and controls must be established. Budgeting plays a major role in both tasks. A budget guides a manager in purchasing the selling, advertising, and other services needed. It also supplies a measuring stick for quantifying progress, detecting flaws in strategy, and making comparisons with past performance.

How much should a firm spend on promotion? Economists say that a firm should spend only up to the point of diminishing returns. Unfortunately, managers find it quite difficult to determine when money spent is beginning to become counterproductive. More common are the other more practical methods of setting an overall budget and allocating funds discussed here.

Percentage-of-Sales Budgeting
Sales approach that fixes amount to be spent for promotion as a percentage of the previous year's sales or of anticipated sales for the coming year.

The Percentage-of-Sales Approach

The widely used **percentage-of-sales** approach fixes the amount to be spent for promotion as a percentage of last year's sales or of anticipated sales for the coming year. Both figures are arrived at by looking at company records. Thus, if a firm generally spends 7 percent of sales revenues on promotion and it expects to sell $5 million next year, it will allocate $350 000 for promotion.

Although this approach is simple, it has problems. Making advertising dependent on sales is putting the cart before the horse. If sales decline, promotion funds will also decline, although more promotion may be just what is needed to increase demand for the product. The firm is tied to spending a certain amount even though market conditions may warrant a reduction or an increase.

The Fixed-Sum-per-Unit Method

Sometimes a promotional budget is established by putting aside a specified amount for each unit produced — the **fixed-sum-per-unit** method. This can be a useful approach when a firm produces many different brands, each of which requires a different promotional effort. For example, a manufacturer of laundry detergent might apply a figure of 45 cents per case for promoting its best-selling brand. Weaker brands might receive 70 cents and a new brand, $1.50 per case.

The advantage of this method is that the manufacturer knows the promotional cost per unit in advance — an aid in setting the price. The disadvantage is that this method uses the past as an inflexible guide to future promotional expenditures.

Fixed-Sum-per-Unit Budgeting
Allocating a specified amount for each unit produced.

The Competitive Comparison Method

Meeting competition — spending as much on promotion as the leading firms do — is the essence of the **competitive comparison** method. Although firms generally do not publicize how much they spend, trade association studies of industry averages are available.

This method is somewhat more sophisticated than the percentage-of-sales approach because the percentage figure used comes not just from one company's records but from those of a whole industry. However, both methods rely on the past as a predictor of the future. An added disadvantage of competitive comparison budgeting is its false assumption that all companies in an industry operate under the same conditions. To cite one variation, a new firm in an industry may have to spend more on promotion than an established company. Comparisons can be misleading and thus should always be thought of as rough guides.

Competitive Comparison Budgeting
Plan to spend as much on promotion as leading firms do.

The Objective and Task Method

The major problem with all of the methods discussed thus far is that they are backward-looking. By contrast, the **objective and task** method

Objective and Task Budgeting
Strategy that emphasizes setting goals and then fixing costs of meeting those goals for each promotional task used.

recognizes that promotion leads to future sales. To be effective, therefore, promotion must be tied to future objectives, not to past sales.

The method works in the following way. After promotional objectives are set, the tasks necessary to reach those objectives and their costs are worked out for each form of promotion to be used. Other costs, such as those for research, are then added in, and all costs are totalled to arrive at a budget. Consider a promotion for a new kind of frozen pizza. Assume that one objective is to increase brand awareness by 15 percent through advertising within six months. The tasks to accomplish this and their costs (in an extremely simplified form) might look like this:

50 network television announcements	$500 000
40 full-colour pages in national magazines	228 000
Research costs	50 000
Administrative costs	150 000
Total	$928 000

This list could include publicity, sales promotion, and selling tasks if they support this effort.

From a business point of view, the approach of building up the amount to be spent on promotion makes a great deal of sense. It orients management toward the future by emphasizing goals, and it eliminates rote spending justified by past budgets. Also, objective and task budgeting provides a standard for control. If the goal of increasing brand recognition is not reached, the tasks can be reinvestigated to discover their weaknesses.

Of course, determining which tasks are most effective in reaching goals can be very difficult. In the case of advertising, for example, many choices must be made. What media should be used? What appeals should be made? When should they be scheduled? These and other questions must be answered for each task. For a multiproduct firm that uses all forms of promotion, the job is enormous. Increasingly, firms are looking to the computer to analyze data in a way that helps them in their budgeting decisions.

Evaluating and Controlling Promotion

In practice, showing which tasks fail and why is complicated and, in some cases, impossible. Measuring the effectiveness of a certain outlay by sales results may fail for several reasons, but three in particular stand out.[30] First, in good promotional programs, the tools work together. It is difficult to determine which promotional effort created the desired effect. For example, a woman who buys a new Chevrolet would be hard-pressed to say which element of promotion influenced her decision most. It could have been a television commercial, a direct-mail piece sent by a local dealer, or a persuasive car salesperson. Or, none of these may have influenced her; she may simply have liked the look of her neighbour's new Chevrolet.

Another reason why measuring the effectiveness of advertising by sales results is difficult is that outside factors complicate measurement. Sometimes, no matter how much promotion is used, uncontrollable factors determine the success or failure of a campaign. Consider the weather. Officials at Toro Company, a manufacturer of snow throwers, found that among U.S. consumers the biggest barrier to buying a machine was the fear that there would not be enough snow to justify the cost. The previous year's mild winter made it likely that people would hold off buying a snow thrower until they were convinced it would be necessary. To counter the psychological resistance, Toro marketers devised a promotional gimmick that faced the issue head on. Toro promised to refund the entire price of any of its machines purchased before December 10 if the winter's snowfall amounted to less than 20 percent of the average where the machine was bought. To protect themselves, Toro executives took out weather insurance. The scheme worked. The promotion increased sales by several thousand, and fortunately for the insurer, the northern United States had a very white winter.[31]

Weather is not the only uncontrollable factor. Producers can spend millions on promotion, but if retailers do not stock the item, their efforts are wasted. One author reported that in spite of all his local appearances during one month, the sales figures for his book did not increase because local stores had not ordered his best-selling novel.

Finally, measurement is difficult because almost all promotional efforts suffer from time lag. Managers plan promotional expenditures to have an immediate impact, but what they accomplish or fail to accomplish may have resulted from a previous campaign. Advertising professionals call this phenomenon *carryover.* Part of the reason many companies switch advertising agencies frequently is a failure to recognize that a new approach takes time to penetrate and an old approach takes time to wear off. Carryover obviously complicates the task of singling out the effect of a particular commercial, coupon offer, or sales pitch.

Indirect Measurement

It would be wrong to conclude that because measuring the effect of promotion on sales is complex, no attempt should be made. Promotion managers, like other managers, must justify what they spend. Although they may not be able to say that *x* dollars in promotion produced *y* dollars in additional sales, they can measure indirect effects — the number of consumers exposed to an ad or sales talk, the number who recall what they saw or heard, and so forth. Such indirect effects can be measured before, during, or after a promotional campaign is launched.

Pretesting — measuring a promotional campaign's effectiveness before spending on a large scale — involves testing an organization's communications on a small segment of the market. For example, as part of its strategy to upgrade the image of its snacks, Austin Foods Company

Pretesting
Measuring a promotional campaign's effectiveness before spending on a large scale.

changed its package design. Designers created a new logo, a red mill to symbolize product wholesomeness. In addition, red bands on the labels bear the message that the products — peanut-butter- and cheese-filled crackers and cream-filled cookies—contain 100 percent vegetable shortening and no preservatives. The company showed the packages to potential consumers and found that people did in fact perceive the product as of higher quality than the competition.[32]

Information secured while a promotional effort is under way, called **concurrent testing**, is also valuable. Sales reps are usually required to submit weekly, and sometimes daily, reports to managers. For measuring advertising, perhaps the most famous concurrent testing device is the Nielsen audiometer, an instrument for measuring how many viewers are tuned in to a television program and its commercials.

Posttesting, which takes place after a full-scale campaign has been completed, is commonly conducted. Sales analysis, discussed in Chapter 4, is a form of posttesting that measures the results of the sales force's effort. Many of the same measures used in concurrent testing are used in the posttesting phase for other types of promotion.

Except for publicity, the measurement of all forms of promotion is a developing art. Table 14.2 lists some of the tests used for each promotional tool. Chapters 15 and 16 discuss several tests in greater detail.

The Role of Social Responsibility in Promotion

Techniques for managing promotional tools are important for those planning a career in marketing, but they are by no means the only aspect of promotion deserving attention. Promotion has a social dimension. It is the part of the marketing mix most visible to the public. Consequently, it is the area most open to criticism. Those employed in sales, advertising,

Concurrent Testing
Securing information while a promotional effort is under way.

Posttesting
Measuring the effectiveness of a full-scale campaign after it has been completed.

Table 14.2 Indirect Measurement of Promotion

	Pretesting	Concurrent Testing	Posttesting
Personal Selling	Screening and testing of potential sales reps; field testing of sales approach	Sales reports, management field trips	Quotas, sales analysis
Advertising	Checklists, consumer juries, split runs	Consumer diaries, Nielsen people meter, traffic counts	Readershp surveys, repeat of concurrent tests
Sales Promotion	Test mailings, test markets	Coupon and entry monitoring; counts of the number of displays set up	Final counts of orders, entries, inquiries, redemptions
Publicity	—	—	Count of number of requests for reprints or inquiries
Packaging	Focus groups may discuss proposed package	Nielsen and consumer group surveys	Sales analysis, monitor customer response by mail, phone

or public relations positions may at times experience a conflict between professional and personal beliefs.

Chapter 3 discusses some of the social issues marketers must keep in mind. Chapter 15 looks more closely at how the advertising community addresses its social responsibilities. Before closing this chapter, it is worth looking at one more example of a social issue facing marketers that demonstrates just how complex these problems can be.

In recent years, modern packaging practices have come under increasing attack from environmentalists and consumer groups. Both maintain that the packaging revolution has had harmful side effects. Their charges have focused public attention on the packaging industry.

Environmentalists complain that modern packaging wastes resources and pollutes the environment. Is it really necessary, they ask, to wrap slices of cheese individually? How is society to dispose of the waste materials created by overpackaged cereals?

The environmentalists have a point. The cost of collecting and disposing of packaging materials is over $500 million a year. A particularly acute problem is the disposal of plastics. Many plastics resist decay, and some, like polyvinyl chloride, emit poisonous gases when burned.

Packaging experts are now paying more attention to environmentalist complaints. But consumers themselves sometimes impede their efforts. Bottlers, for example, use many returnable bottles. But the modest deposit fees are often not enough to motivate users to return them, and some bottlers are actually losing money.

But sometimes apparent "overpackaging" serves an important function. In the wake of the deaths in the United States caused by cyanide-laced Tylenol capsules in 1982, Johnson & Johnson quickly devised a triple safety-sealed package for protection against product tampering.

Much still remains to be done in the area of waste avoidance and economical disposal, but marketers are now more influenced by social pressures to find solutions. The problem is often one of reconciling conflicting demands for efficient, safe, yet convenient packaging. At Globe '90, an international conference on business and the environment held in Vancouver, the Canadian environmental ministers reached an agreement on standards to help clean up the environment. They agreed to work to reduce packaging by half by the year 2000. "Fifty percent of packaging is not necessary, it's useless," said Lucien Bouchard, the then federal minister of the environment. He warned that legislation is being prepared to back up the agreement.[33]

Packaging is one obvious area in which there is room for many conflicting opinions, but it is by no means the only one. Other questions regarding marketers' social responsibilities are even more controversial. For example:

1. How much information should promotion convey? The whole truth — including a product's flaws? If not, how much can be omitted without deception?

2. Should promotion, and especially advertising, be aimed at vulner-

able groups (such as children) who cannot distinguish between the persuasive and informational parts of a message?

3. In light of world shortages, should marketers promote less consumption of material goods?

These questions are raised now so that they will be kept in mind while the tools of promotion are studied in more depth. There are no easy answers. But marketers of the future should know that people on the various sides of such issues raise valid points. The challenge lies in finding a solution that takes into account the needs of individuals, businesses, and society.

Chapter Replay

1. **What are the activities involved in promotion of a company's product?**
   Promotion includes advertising, sales promotion, publicity, personal selling, and packaging.

2. **How does communication occur?**
   The source encodes the message, putting it into understandable form. The source sends the message through a medium of transmission. The receiver decodes the message and signals understanding by providing feedback to the source.

3. **What are some sources of misunderstanding in the communication process?**
   The reputation of the source can affect the way a message is received. The multiple transmitters involved in sending a message may conflict with one another. The receiver may make decoding errors, interpreting a message in an unintended way. Inadequate feedback can cause future messages to suffer.

4. **What are some advantages of communication through advertising?**
   Advertising is relatively inexpensive, measured as the cost to reach each viewer. It can be creative and can therefore be an effective way to capture attention. It also allows perfect reproduction of the desired message.

5. **What are the major advantage and disadvantage of personal selling?**
   The major advantage is that it allows the salesperson to match the sales effort to the customer. The major disadvantage is the high cost of this personalized approach.

6. **What are some functions of packaging?**
   Packages protect the product and the consumer. They increase the use of the product, and they increase sales if they add a reuse value.

They promote the product by describing special benefits or values or by selling related items.

7. **What are the major types of promotional strategies?**
Promotional strategies include a push strategy, in which the producer promotes to intermediaries, and a pull strategy, in which the producer promotes to the consumer. Many marketers use a combination of these strategies.

8. **How do marketers budget for promotion?**
Marketers allocate funds using the percentage-of-sales approach, the fixed-sum-per-unit method, the competitive comparison method, or the objective and task method.

9. **How do marketers measure the effectiveness of a promotional campaign?**
Marketers can measure effectiveness by evaluating sales results, although this method is difficult to use accurately. Often, marketers use indirect measurement through pretesting, concurrent testing, or posttesting of the promotional effort.

Key Terms

advertising	**percentage-of-sales**
combination strategy	**budgeting**
competitive comparison	**personal selling**
budgeting	**posttesting**
concurrent testing	**pretesting**
decoding	**promotion**
encoding	**public relations**
feedback	**publicity**
fixed-sum-per-unit	**pull strategy**
budgeting	**push strategy**
medium of transmission	**receiver**
noise	**sales promotion**
objective and task	**source**
budgeting	**source effect**

Discussion Questions

1. How does the communication process work? What can interfere with this process?

2. The Good Life Insurance Company runs ads on television and also has a sales force of 256 salespeople, who call on prospective and current customers. If Good Life can reach a million people with $1 million in advertising, why would it want to spend $100 a sales call

for personal selling? How might the company combine these two approaches?

3. Companies have little control over the message when they use publicity as a promotional tool. Why would a company want to use publicity?

4. Bright Eyes, Inc., sells eye drops. In designing a package for the product, what issues should the company consider?

5. Tom Tremulous and Steve Subarious are preparing to open a bed and breakfast inn near a beautiful provincial park. Steve said, "We need to plan how to promote our inn." Tom replied, "I know, and I've got it all figured out. I'll show you my idea for some great advertisements." What steps should Tom and Steve take before planning advertisements?

6. Compare the relative merits of the different methods for developing a promotion budget.

7. Last April, Alicia Aloysius tried her first promotional campaign for her combination Italian/Mexican restaurant. She obtained publicity by sponsoring a spaghetti-eating contest, and she ran coupons for a free order of guacamole in the local newspaper. In May, her sales receipts were twice as much as her April receipts. Alicia declared her promotional campaign a success. What are some shortcomings of Alicia's evalution?

8. Consider the promotional campaign described in Question 7. How might Alicia Aloysius measure the effectiveness of this campaign indirectly?

9. Brand X Pizza Company has reformulated its pizza recipe. Now its sausage pizzas contain sausage made out of soybeans and a cheese substitute made out of tofu. The company wants to produce a promotional campaign based on the slogan, "New Improved Brand X Pizzas Are Lower in Calories." Should the company mention the changes in its ingredients, even though its research suggests that fewer people would buy a pizza made from soybeans and tofu? Explain your answer, indicating the amount of information you think the company should be responsible for conveying.

CASE 14.1

Second Harvest

Second Harvest is a charitable organization that locates, collects, and delivers edible surplus food to agencies and organizations that provide food to people in need in Metropolitan Toronto. Recently, these agencies

Source: This case was written by Professor F. G. Crane, Dalhousie University, and Professor T. K. Clarke, Sonoma State University, 1988.

have been unable to keep up with the increasing demand for emergency food assistance.

The Situation

Close to 100 000 people make use of emergency food outlets in Toronto every month. However, the number of people who are in need of food in Toronto is estimated at 400 000. Ironically, while people are going hungry, more than 20% of all food produced in North America is wasted. Second Harvest started in 1985 with a non-existent budget and a few volunteers. The objective of Second Harvest was to redistribute surplus food, at no charge, to qualified agencies feeding hungry people. These agencies include soup kitchens, shelters, drop-in centres, and subsidized housing developments. Second Harvest retrieves the surplus food from any industry, group, or individual who regularly or occasionally has excess food, including food producers, farmers, retailers and wholesalers, restaurants, hospitals, production houses, and organizers of special events.

Second Harvest's Record

In its first year of operation, Second Harvest had redistributed more than 250 000 pounds of food from seven food donors to seven agencies. By the end of 1986, Second Harvest had redistributed over 550 000 pounds of food valued at close to $1 million. The cost to redistribute the food was estimated at less than 7% of the total food value. The food came from 110 donors and went to more than 50 agencies. Currently, the organization redistributes over 1 million pounds of food, which translates into enough food for 5000 meals a day. Second Harvest continues to rely heavily on volunteers as the main distributors, although it now has three trucks with paid drivers.

Communications Problem

One of the major problems faced by Second Harvest is the lack of knowledge at the governmental and community level about the extent of the hunger problem. The role of Second Harvest is often attacked as a band-aid solution at best and at worst a contributor to the forces that perpetuate poverty. They are also accused of letting the government off the hook. But Second Harvest maintains that its very existence has put government policy on the hook as being inadequate or non-existent. The organization and its service is, according to Second Harvest, an emergency response by a caring community until government policy can be adapted to the realities that have created this problem. The organization has made a concerted advocacy and public relations effort concerning its mandate and the plight of the hungry, not just in Toronto, but all across Canada.

Focal Topics

1. What kind of a communications program should Second Harvest develop to inform the various publics? What should Second Harvest be saying to them?

2. How would you recommend that Second Harvest evaluate the effectiveness of its communications program?

3. What activities, other than an advocacy and public relations effort, would you recommend that Second Harvest undertake in the area of communications?

CASE 14.2

Kransco

R. John Stalberger, Jr., injured his knee in 1970 before trying out for the university football team. To rehabilitate his knee after the injury, he invented what is today known as the Hacky Sack® footbag. Created as an exercise aid, the product has spawned a company, various footbag games, and a players' association. The ultimate goal of the association is to see footbagging become an internationally recognized sport and therefore an Olympic event.

Background Information

Stalberger developed a kicking game using a small object made of hand-stitched leather, called a Hacky Sack footbag. Because of his background in baseball, football, and other sports, he saw the game as a good off-season training and warm-up exercise. It enhanced bilateral control and versatility. Stalberger, who also has a background in physical therapy, knew that such a workout for the heart and lungs was important for fitness. He wanted to develop the game as a conditioning exercise.

Stalberger poured all of his energies into developing the Footbag Game. He was determined to make it a nationally accepted exercise game and sport. The Footbag Game is the modern version of ancient kicking games. It differs from all similar games in two main areas. First, using the body above the waist as a striking surface is prohibited (except

Source: Hacky Sack is a registered trademark of and is patented by Wham-O, Inc., a Kransco Group Company. This case has been edited from the original case, which appeared in *Cases for Analysis in Marketing*, by W. Wayne Talarzyk. Copyright © 1985 by CBS College Publishing. Reprinted by permission of Holt, Rinehart and Winston, Inc. Additional information provided by Kransco.

in freestyle play). Second, the method of play utilizes five basic kicks that dictate the equal use of both feet.

Marketing Activities

Over the years, Hacky Sack has been promoted directly to consumers through advertisements in publications such as *National Lampoon, Sports Illustrated,* and *Boys' Life Magazine.* In a campaign in *Scholastic Coach* and *Athletic Directory,* Hacky Sack is presented to physical education teachers as an important training device for soccer, pre-sports warm-up, and other activities.

The company has also marketed its product to the sporting goods industry by participating in various trade shows and by advertising in specialized publications such as *Sporting Goods Business, The Sporting Goods Dealer, Sports Retailer*, and *Sports Merchandiser.* To support individual retailers in promoting the product, the company has developed a series of advertising slicks. Retailers can add their names and addresses to the copy and then run the advertisements in local newspapers. In addition to general themes for Hacky Sack, the company has developed segmented advertising slicks that tie the product to conditioning for other sports such as soccer, running, football, and skiing. On occasion, the company also sends Hacky Sack footbag demonstrators to retail stores for promotional programs. A Hacky Sack footbag with a book on how to play with it costs about $9.

Additional Dimensions

In connection with Frisbee, another of its products, Kransco planned to offer festivals in 50 major markets during the spring. These Hacky Sack/ Frisbee Festivals, which have been run for three years, are free skill clinics and expert demonstrations. The festivals are supported by advertisements on cable television, spot television markets (top 10 markets with the highest concentration of 12- to 24-year-old males), and youth-oriented radio stations.

Focal Topics

1. What dimensions could the company use to segment the market for Hacky Sacks?

2. Which market segments do you think would be best for Kransco to pursue? Why?

3. What marketing strategies would you recommend to reach those segments?

Chapter 15

Advertising, Sales Promotion, and Publicity

In this chapter, you will learn:

- The kinds of advertising marketers can use.

- Reasons for advertising.

- The kinds of organizations that employ the most people in the field of advertising.

- The steps involved in developing an ad campaign.

- Creative styles for presenting advertising messages.

- The major media that advertisers use.

- How advertisers and the government have responded to criticisms of advertising.

- How sales promotion can increase sales.

- Advantages and disadvantages of using publicity.

- Activities typically included in a public relations program.

Commercial Creativity

Cable TV and videocassette recorders are changing the style of television advertising. Television viewers are increasingly able to avoid commercials or to ''zap'' through the ones on videotaped programs. Advertising executive Jane Fuller predicts that by the year 2000 about 60 percent of television viewers will be tuning out ads. With viewers no longer a captive audience, advertisers are looking for ways to convince people to watch.

This often means commercials have a more subtle sales pitch. Hard sells and annoying jingles are being replaced with ads that try to entertain. Some are styled after music videos, while others tell mini-stories. Many use special effects. One source of the creativity is use of successful movie directors to make the advertisements. Some who have done so include Adrian Lyne *(Flashdance)*, Hugh Hudson *(Chariots of Fire)*, and Ridley Scott *(Alien)*.

One of the most popular of the new breed of advertisements is the California Raisin Advisory Board's dancing raisins. One woman reported that it was the only commercial she had ever gone back into the room to watch. Viewers are attracted to the Labatts' Kokanee beer ads, which depict a small dog named Brew, who is used as a mascot and a deliverer of the

product to beer drinkers. The Kokanee beer ads frequently centre on mythical characters, such as the abominable snowman and the sasquatch.

While not all commercials are entertaining, this style of advertising may continue to grow in popularity. As the number of commercials grows along with the opportunities for avoiding them, the job of the advertiser requires ever more creativity. This chapter discusses principles of advertising. Then it describes how marketers can reach customers through sales promotion and publicity.

Sources: Adapted from ''America's Favorite Campaigns,'' *Adweek*, March 2, 1987, p. 24; and Barbara Rosen, ''And Now, a Wittier Word from Our Sponsors,'' *Business Week*, March 24, 1986, p. 90.

One observer of the advertising business has noted that recent graduates with advertising degrees may be in for a culture shock of sorts. Trained in the sophisticated, computer-driven world of the modern college or university, these graduates often find that the real world of advertising can be less sophisticated. Nevertheless, advertising and marketing majors find they also have much to learn about putting principles to work in creative ways. The industry observer suggests that students benefit most from learning analytical tools and ways of approaching tasks.[1] This chapter attempts to begin laying that foundation.

The Nature and Growth of Advertising

Advertising as we know it today began with industrialization and the inventing of the printing press. Because of mass production, goods were produced faster than they could be consumed. Advertising grew to inform the public and increase consumption. Printers found advertising to be profitable and began to solicit and encourage it.

Advertising continues to grow in our own era. Statistics Canada reports that net advertising revenue was $5.0 billion in 1983. Only three years later the amount was $6.8 billion—a 35-percent rise.[2]

The principal reasons for the growth are more consumer income, greater consumer willingness to spend on services and pleasures, more competition, more products and outlets for shopping, and a movement to self-service retailing. The top ten national advertisers from 1988 are listed in Table 15.1.

Table 15.1 Canada's Top Ten National Advertisers, 1988

Rank 1987	Rank 1988	Advertiser	Total Advertising (in Thousands of Dollars)
1	1	Government of Canada	$91 317.2
2	2	Procter & Gamble Inc.	58 624.2
3	3	General Motors of Canada Ltd.	52 512.1
102	4	Gulf and Western Inc.	44 627.1
8	5	R.J.R. Inc.	42 291.3
5	6	John Labatt Limited	42 106.0
9	7	The Molson Companies	41 172.1
4	8	The Thomson Group	40 184.5
337	9	Cineplex Odeon Corporation	38 851.5
10	10	Government of Ontario	37 935.7

Source: *The Blue Book of Canadian Business*, 1989, Media Measurements Services, Inc., p. 703.

Selective or Brand Advertising

Most people associate advertising with messages that try to increase consumer preference for a particular firm's product. Advertisers refer to this as **selective or brand advertising,** because its aim is to convince consumers to "select" Wheaties, say, over Kellogg's Corn Flakes. This form of advertising is the oldest, and outwardly it has not changed much in a hundred years. In 1890, for example, the leading advertisers sold drugs, household goods, clothes, and food and drink.[3]

The theory behind most selective advertising is that a product in the mature stage of its life-cycle (see Chapter 9) must be kept before the public to maintain its market share. Selective advertising also works for services, from dry cleaners to lawyers.

Primary Demand Advertising

Besides promoting a particular firm's products or services, advertising may also increase the total demand for products without distinguishing between brands.[4] **Primary demand advertising,** as it is called, is used mainly for innovative products in the first stages of their life-cycle. Mazda's first ads for its cars, for example, stressed the benefits of the rotary engine rather than the brand name. Such ads are also effective for older products that already command a large market share.

Association advertising is a special way of increasing primary demand. Members of a trade association may pool funds to promote a class of products or services. The Canadian Association of Orthodontists urges adults to seek orthodontic treatment by promoting the benefits of healthy gums and teeth. Telecom Canada advertises "make someone happy" in order to encourage people to phone long distance more often.

Institutional Advertising

A paid message designed to build long-range goodwill for a firm, rather than to sell specific goods, is termed **institutional** (or **corporate**) **advertising.** A strong corporate image is advantageous in the marketplace. Hallmark's advertising motto, "When you care enough to send the very best," has helped to make it the dominant force in the greeting card industry for more than 20 years.

Controversy is another reason for using such advertising. RJR/Nabisco, for example, runs advertising suggesting ways that smokers can behave responsibly and considerately. The ads are designed to improve the company's image among nonsmokers. Similarly, Petro-Canada runs advertisements about issues such as environmentalism.

Other forms of institutional advertising are less controversial. Mobil Oil sponsors *Masterpiece Theater* and Gulf Oil underwrites the National Geographic Specials. Corporate advertising is also used to communicate

Selective or Brand Advertising
Messages that try to increase consumer preference for a particular firm's product.

Primary Demand Advertising
Advertising aimed at increasing the total demand for products without distinguishing between brands.

Association Advertising
Advertising sponsored by a trade association to promote a class of products or services.

Institutional (or Corporate) Advertising
Paid message designed to build long-range goodwill for a firm rather than to sell specific goods.

with prospective or present employees, to signal a company's new direction or name change, or to wake up the investment community to a company's earnings potential. It may also be used to air gripes about governmental policies.[5]

Noncommercial Advertising

Advertising by nonprofit organizations, **noncommercial advertising,** is relatively new and rapidly growing. Philanthropic causes such as CARE are long-time advertising users. Today, however, other social and political groups are finding that it pays to advertise. The four chief users are (1) public-interest groups, (2) federal and provincial governments, (3) hospitals and universities, and (4) political parties. Nonprofit organizations account for about 10 percent of all money spent for advertising.

Why Advertise?

The specific reasons for advertising are as varied as the organizations that sponsor it. Most advertisers, however, seek to accomplish a few general goals.

Informing and persuading the public are among the primary reasons most companies advertise. The mixture of information and persuasion varies with the type of advertising and the stage in a product's life-cycle. Primary demand and institutional advertising are usually more informative than selective advertising. Furthermore, newly introduced products usually require more informative advertising than products in the maturity phase of their life-cycle.

Some experts believe that regardless of the amount of information an ad contains, ultimately it must seek to persuade its audience to buy a car or contribute to CARE. People need information, but they also need to be prodded to act. Recall from Chapter 14 that all communication, including advertising, aims not only to create awareness and arouse interest but also to create desire and stimulate action.[6]

In addition to informing and persuading, ads also work for firms by (1) reminding consumers of a company's products or services and (2) reassuring buyers they have made the "right" purchase. Consumers must be reminded because they can remember only about a thousand bits and pieces of ads they have seen and, as they learn new bits, they forget the old.[7] They require reassurance because buyers often experience anxiety about their decision after making a large purchase.

Ads also back up the sales force. A shopper who has seen an ad promoting a Kitchen Aid dishwasher is a better sales prospect than one who walks into an appliance dealer's showroom without having seen the ad.

Ads can also provide leads for salespeople if they contain coupons that interested prospects can fill in and return. This is particularly true for industrial advertising, although magazines such as *PC Magazine* and

House & Garden's Building and Remodeling Guide often include bound-in cards enabling readers to send for booklets about products. Those requesting information may then be contacted by salespeople from the company that provided the booklet. In industrial advertising, such coupons may help identify people in a firm who influence purchasing decisions.

Ads can also help industrial salespeople gain entrance to a firm by building the reputation of the company for which they work. (See Figure 15.1.) Lanier Business Products, makers of dictating equipment, started as an unknown company but became widely recognized because of its ads in business magazines and its radio spots featuring the comedy team of Stiller and Meara.

Figure 15.1 Industrial Advertising as an Aid to Personal Selling

Source: Courtesy of Lanier Business Products, a Harris Company.

The Organization of Advertising

Advertising is an exciting field for a career. The common belief that only those with creative talent in writing or art are good prospects for advertising careers is not true. The advertising industry employs market researchers, broadcast production managers, account executives who act as liaisons between clients and agencies, media buyers, and fashion stylists, as well as people in traditional business fields such as accounting, personnel, and finance. The industry also employs jingle writers, arrangers, singers, actors, and even dogs.

The two organizations that employ the most people in the field are advertising departments and agencies.

The Advertising Department

Advertising departments operate within profit and nonprofit organizations. They are always responsible for setting the advertising objectives of a campaign and its budget. In many large retail stores, they also plan and execute the campaign. In most other organizations, however, independent advertising agencies take over these jobs, and the department reviews their work.

As Figure 15.2 shows, ad departments may be organized by function, media, product, end-user, or geographical location. All are headed by an advertising manager, who usually reports to the chief marketing executive for the co-ordination of advertising activities with other marketing mix elements. The advertising manager's job is to oversee the planning of all campaigns, to act as a go-between in ad agency–company relations, and to control expenses.

Firms like Procter & Gamble that produce many different products have replaced the advertising manager with the product, or brand, manager. The latter has many other jobs besides advertising. The change was made because it was felt that advertising managers lack the specialized expertise needed to promote a large number of products effectively. Product managers usually oversee a few advertising specialists who give advice and work with ad agencies to create campaigns.

The Advertising Agency

According to Statistics Canada, the country had more than 2300 advertising agencies in 1987.[8] Agencies are useful because they bring together highly skilled specialists. Advertisers today often prefer to work through agencies because they provide greater objectivity than an internal department and they often cost less.

The agencies themselves may specialize in handling consumer goods, industrial goods, financial services, or international business. Other

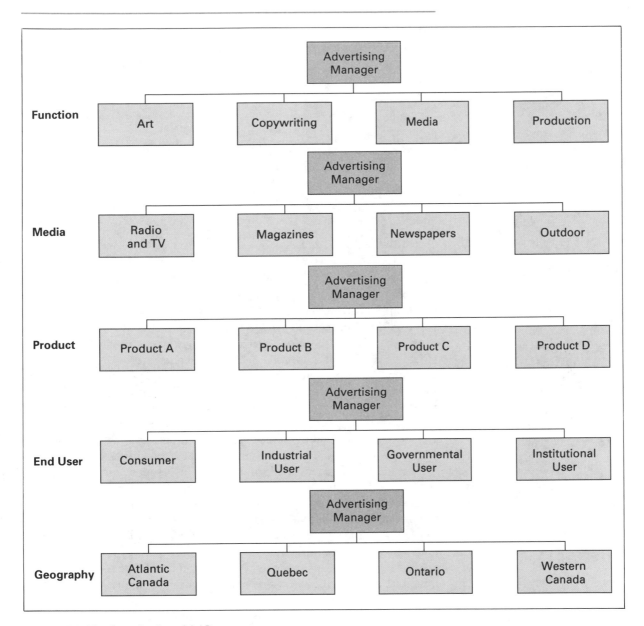

Figure 15.2 The Organization of Ad Departments

agencies specialize in one of the two official languages, or in reaching minority target markets. The ten largest agencies, listed in Table 15.2, handle mainly consumer goods.

Traditionally, the large established advertising agencies are paid by commission, usually 15 percent of the dollar value of the media they purchase for a company. For example, an agency may purchase $20 000 worth of space in *Maclean's* magazine. The magazine will bill the agency $17 000 ($20 000 − 15 percent commission), and the agency will bill the client the full $20 000.

Table 15.2   Canada's Leading Agencies, 1987

Agency	Billings (in Millions of Dollars)
FCB Ronalds Reynolds Ltd.	$178.1
MacLaren Advertising	163.4
J. Walter Thompson Company	162.0
McKim Advertising Ltd.	160.0
Ogilvy & Mather Advertising	145.0
The BCP Group Inc.	128.0
Saffer Advertising Inc.	125.0
Vickers & Benson Ltd.	122.4
Baker Lovick Ltd.	122.0
Cossette Communication Marketing	120.7

Source: *Marketing*, December 14, 1987, p. 21.

Besides placing the ad, the agency may perform a number of other functions for its commission, including marketing research, product testing, and the creation and production of ad material.

As an example of how an advertising agency works, consider the efforts of Ogilvy & Mather, a large U.S. agency, to obtain the AT&T Advanced Information Systems account. First, the company's executive vice-president and creative head assembled a team of 12 managers, account supervisors, researchers, and creative directors to develop a proposal. They, in turn, guided more than a hundred writers, artists, and producers. Ogilvy & Mather had little more than two months in which to compete with nine other agencies in convincing AT&T that it had the best idea.

The company demonstrated its strengths in a credentials meeting with AT&T. While Ogilvy had little experience in the communications field, it presented eight case histories of other clients with problems similar to those of AT&T. The agency also met with a telecommunications expert to learn about the field. The agency's research department assembled a glossary of telecommunications terms for the agency's staff to refer to.

After the credentials meeting, AT&T provided the agency with a document asking specific questions about how the company should launch Advanced Information Systems. The media department drew up plans for placing advertisements. Team leaders met in strategy sessions and developed a campaign emphasizing product benefits. Copywriters and artists went to work. The best ideas were sorted out. The team that would present the proposal rehearsed it carefully, practising responses to tricky questions. The final presentation was a success; the agency got the account.

Managing the Ad Campaign

We can all cite a commercial that stuck in our mind despite the fact that we saw it for only 30 seconds or glanced at it casually in a magazine.

People screen out a great many of the ads they see, so breaking through their attention barrier is a real feat. (See Marketing Today 15.1.) The brief message we receive may be the product of months of work.

Among the questions that must be addressed before creating an ad that captures attention are: (1) What is the objective of this advertising campaign? (2) What is the budget? (3) How should this product be positioned? (4) What message should be used to promote it? (5) In what media should it run? and (6) How will the ad's effectiveness be measured?

Setting Advertising Objectives

Whether a company's advertising is handled in-house in an advertising department or through an independent agency, the objectives of any campaign must be in keeping with the broader promotional objectives set by the company.

There may be different goals for different types of advertising. The objective of an institutional ad may be to stimulate investor interest, while the objective of a selective or brand ad may be to encourage brand switching. In each case, goals should be quantified both in terms of degree and of time.

Establishing a Budget

Once objectives are set, a budget must be established. To determine how much of a budget should be allotted for advertising, certain factors should be taken into account. The nature of the company is probably the

Marketing Today 15.1

Advertisements That Work

Spending a lot of money doesn't guarantee that an advertisement will get results. A researcher called Video Storyboard Tests confirmed this in a recent survey of television viewers. It compared how much companies spent to advertise a product with how many people remembered the ads. The result was the "cost per memory."

An example of an advertising success was the "Lee, Lee, Lee, Lee, Lee Sensation" campaign for Lee's jeans. While Lee spent less than Levi's and Wrangler, more people remembered its advertisements. But Chic, which spent the least per week to advertise, actually spent the most per thousand retained impressions.

Among credit cards, Visa was most efficient, with its "Everywhere you want to be" theme. For each thousand retained impressions, it spent only $9.10. At the other extreme was Discover, which spent $88.18 for each thousand. Discover had the hardest task, though, because it was a new product.

Source: Adapted from "The Fourth Annual Measure of Efficiency," *Adweek,* March 2, 1987, pp. F.C. 22–F.C. 23+.

foremost consideration. Advertising is far less important to industrial companies than to those specializing in consumer goods. The nature of the product is also significant. Producers of soft drinks, toys, cosmetics, and tobacco products typically spend a far greater percentage of their total budgets on advertising than companies manufacturing clothing, furniture, or greeting cards. The stage in the product life-cycle and the company's financial resources must also be considered. Once a budget has been agreed upon, the challenge of creating the ad can begin.

Positioning

Positioning
Theory holding that to sell a product, a company must create a unique niche or position for it in the consumer's mind.

Many advertisers today accept the theory of **positioning**. The theory states that to sell a product, a company must create a niche or position for the product in the consumer's mind that is unique relative to competitive products. In other words, positioning involves defining a class of competitors and finding a way to distinguish the product in that class. Marketers must match the product attributes to the needs and perceptions of the market segment. If customers are to form an effective product image, certain attributes must be stressed. Crest toothpaste became successful by emphasizing the reduction of cavities, while Molson's beer effectively positioned itself as the "lite beer."

Effective product positioning or the finding of an unsatisfied need in the marketplace allows the marketer to reduce the need to cut prices or become involved in head-to-head competition. 7-Up greatly increased its sales when it positioned itself as the "uncola." The emphasis on the clean, clear taste allowed 7-Up to be noticed.

Are competitors really a matter of choice rather than a given? In many cases, yes. Before 1970, for example, the rule of thumb was that one drank red wines with red meats and white wines with chicken and fish. Instead of going along with this accepted rule, the agency for Blue Nun, a German white wine, positioned it as a wine that was correct with every dish. The strategy was so successful that other companies adopted it. The company then switched its positioning to "Blue Nun Goes Everywhere," suggesting that people take the wine on picnics and to the beach. Later Schiefflin & Company, the wine's importer, again repositioned Blue Nun, this time in a by-the-glass promotion.[9]

Sometimes all the competitors in a certain class are very much alike, and one firm dominates. It may not pay to meet the competition head on. RCA discovered this when it tried to enter the computer field against IBM and failed miserably. Positioning can help to avoid direct competition. Ad agencies try to find a selling proposition that distinguishes the product. Thus, to compete with similar brands of aerobics shoes, all made of leather, Avia advertised the extra shock absorption provided by its double-wedge heel. B. F. Goodrich's campaign against Goodyear ("We're the other guys — without the blimp") was one of the most successful of all time for the company.

Creating the Message

For a successful campaign, it is not enough to find a unique position for a product. In the 1960s, for example, NoCal set itself up against Coke and Pepsi as the only sugar-free soft drink, but it soon lost out when Tab and Diet Pepsi came on the scene. The reason, according to one analyst, was that its advertising messages were bland.[10] In the hotly competitive advertising business, the message is just as important as the position for success.

Over the years, several creative styles for presenting messages have evolved. Some of them have established the reputations of today's largest agencies.

The Image Sell

One of the best-known approaches, the image sell, stresses the importance of creating an exclusive image for a product in ads. David Ogilvy, of the Ogilvy Group, is noted for this approach in the selling of Schweppes mixers. In his ads, he featured the elegant figure of Commander Whitehead, Schweppes' president.[11] The quality image is still with the product today, more than 30 years after it was first introduced. At Your Service 15.1 describes the creation of an image for The Travelers insurance group.

In some cases, a successful company image in one market may be a handicap in another. IBM, for example, had built a blue-chip name in the world of office equipment, but in the mass market it was perceived as cold and efficient. To launch its first mass-market product, the Personal Computer (PC), IBM knew it had to humanize its image. The company decided to use Charlie Chaplin's Little Tramp, with his baggy trousers and ever-present red rose, to make the company—and the product—seem less threatening. (See Figure 15.3.) The strategy worked. By combining its traditional aggressive marketing with low-cost production and a new, friendly image, IBM, in two years' time, rocketed to number one in sales in the personal computer industry.[12]

The Direct Sell

The opposite of the image sell is the direct sell. This approach, advocated by Ted Bates Worldwide, relies on uncovering one unique product benefit (or "unique selling proposition") and then hammering it home through repetition. A well-known example of this format is the ad for M&Ms, "the candy that melts in your mouth, not in your hands." The direct sell also lends itself to product demonstrations, such as absorbency tests for paper towels.

The Humorous or Soft Sell

Ads that joke about the product were the rage of the late 1960s and early 1970s. Among the most famous were Alka-Seltzer's spots ("Try it, you'll

At Your Service 15.1

Travelers Puts Its Image on Canvas

When The Travelers insurance group wanted to create an image for its organization, it turned to Bill Richards, a New York artist. The company commissioned a painting that interprets its well-known logo of a red umbrella. Richards painted in front of television cameras and an enthusiastic live audience.

According to the advertising agency's creative director, Bob Joseph, showing the creator, the process of creation, and the creation itself is a visual symbol of The Travelers' ability to "turn the business of investment into an art." By showing Richards at work on various stages of the painting, the ad equates the nurturing of investments with the slow grace of the painter.

The finished painting hangs in the company's headquarters.

Source: Adapted from Chuck Reece, "Travelers Turns Investment into Art," *Adweek*, July 14, 1986, p. 24.

like it"; "I can't believe I ate the whole thing"). The ad slogans became part of everyday speech, but they did little to sell the product. In fact, sales actually declined.

Later Alka-Seltzer spots were based on in-depth marketing research, which showed that heavy users of antacids are largely middle-income, upwardly mobile people. Alka-Seltzer's agency repositioned the product as an upbeat remedy for "the symptoms of stress that can come with success."[13]

Humour seems to be making a comeback in advertising, although in a new form. The newer advertising is based on a kind of humour that focuses on life's most anxious moments.

Figure 15.3   IBM's Dramatic Departure from Its No-Nonsense Image

Source: Courtesy of International Business Machines Corporation.

The Competitive Sell

Comparative advertising, as the competitive sell is also known, is the creative style that uses the names of competitors. The Scali, McCabe, Sloves Agency popularized the technique after a U.S. regulatory commission ruled in 1972 that naming competitors was in the public interest. The commission reasoned that ads identifying only "Brand X" offered too much freedom to set up imaginary competition. The battle between competitors got under way in earnest when Pepsi attacked Coke in its Pepsi Challenge taste tests and Coke counterattacked.

A similar battle broke out when Burger King launched a campaign claiming that its broiled burgers are better than those of McDonald's, which are fried. McDonald's sued immediately, a response that backfired. The battle made network news, resulting in enormous free publicity for Burger King and better sales growth than for McDonald's.[14]

When competing soft drinks started advertising that they contain fruit juice, Orangina countered with comparative advertising, billing itself

Comparative Advertising Creative style that uses names of competitors.

as "The soft drink with juice you can taste." For the company to be able to run these ads on network television, it first had to prove the difference by using focus groups. The advertisements featured crowds of angry people, rock singers, and a sad young woman, all complaining that they couldn't taste the juice in Orangina's competitors. The advertising agency's creative director explained that the ads told Orangina drinkers, "You're smarter than other people, hipper, and you understand what's bogus in this world."[15]

Are consumers really better served by naming names? Critics say no. They maintain that citing names contributes only to information overload. Consumers remember that two names were mentioned, but they do not remember which claimed to be better. Moreover, the information one competitor uses against another may be selective, providing data only in areas in which the brand excels.[16] But defenders maintain that consumers do benefit from comparisons. After Datril challenged Tylenol in ads, the price of Tylenol came down. And in a Brillo versus SOS controversy, the brand under attack changed its soap content.[17]

Selecting the Media

A campaign can fail, despite accurate positioning and a highly creative message, if an advertisement does not reach the right audience. Media selection therefore is usually given over to experts. As used in promotion, **media** are all the different means by which advertising reaches its audience.[18]

In some ways, media experts have an easier job today. In the 1890s, for example, there was a craze for placing ads in unusual places—on the sides of elephants at a circus, for example, or even on low-hanging clouds via a projector.[19] Today, there are only six major media — newspapers, magazines, television, radio, direct mail, and outdoor/transit signs. The division of the advertising dollar among them is shown in Table 15.3.

Advertisers also look for ways besides the major media to draw attention to products. For example, Pepsi has tried advertising at the beginning of the videocassette version of *Top Gun.* Likewise, Target Vision uses video billboards to broadcast on U.S. campuses via closed-circuit television. It features editorial material on the weather, entertainment, and campus activities. Advertisers buy time on these billboards.[20]

Although the number of major media is small, deciding which to use can be complex. Many factors must be considered. The nature of the product or service is one. Radio, for example, is unsuitable for conveying the features of fashion goods—they must be seen. The size of the advertising budget is another factor. A small retailer would be hardpressed to advertise on an expensive medium like television.

Media experts also look at the strengths and weaknesses of the media themselves. There are five qualities that help distinguish them:

1. *Selectivity*—whether a medium reaches only those who are potential buyers.

Media
All the different means by which advertising reaches its audiences.

Table 15.3 Advertising Expenditures by Media, 1986

Medium	Amount (in Millions of Dollars)
Newspapers	$2 116 587
Television	1 095 320
Miscellaneous*	1 587 884
Radio	611 540
Magazines	865 996
Outdoor**	545 000

*Includes direct mail, directories, catalogues, and so on.

**Includes transit advertising.

Source: Statistics Canada.

2. *Flexibility*—how much time in advance an ad must be placed.

3. *Life span*—the length of time the audience is exposed to a message.

4. *Production quality*—how many human senses are engaged and how well.

5. *Reputation*—the credibility and prestige of the medium.

Some media are stronger in some of these qualities than in others, as a closer look at each will show.

Newspapers

Canada's 111 daily and some 1150 weekly newspapers reach approximately 60 percent of the population. Most of these papers are local, but a few, such as the *Financial Post* and *The Globe and Mail* are national.

The geographic selectivity of newspapers is one of their advantages. Local retailers need not waste advertising money on those who cannot reach their stores. Newspapers also have a reputation for credibility among the many people who read them daily. That asset is generally transferred to the advertising that appears in them. One study found that in making day-to-day purchases, consumers relied on newspapers more than any other form of advertising. (See Table 15.4.) One further advantage is that ads can be placed in newspapers almost overnight.

Newspapers get poor marks on life span and production quality, however. They are read very quickly and are saved only for about a day. Reproduction of illustrations has been poor, although modern methods of printing have lessened this problem.

Magazines

Thirteen business publications and more than 60 consumer magazines sold in Canada have a circulation of more than 20 000. Despite this large

Table 15.4 Rating Ads by Media

When making day-to-day purchases, do you rely a great deal, some, or very little on information provided by advertising in the following media?

Media	Responses*
Newspapers	66%
In-store	58
TV	55
Magazines	53
Yellow pages	51
Radio	42
Direct mail	33

*Percentage of responses indicating "a great deal" or "some."

Source: *Advertising Age*, October 24, 1983, p. 18.

overall audience, most magazines are highly targeted because they appeal to special interests (fashion, sports, specific hobbies). Even mass-circulation magazines like *Maclean's*, *Time*, and *Reader's Digest* have regional editions so that advertisers can select the areas where they want their messages to appear. In addition, magazines are strong where newspapers are weak. They have a comparatively long life span (as well as a high pass-along rate), and they offer high-quality illustrations for products like fashion and food.

The quality that magazines lack most is flexibility. Monthly magazine ads, for example, must be placed 60 to 90 days in advance. Magazines also appeal to only the sense of sight, which limits their effectiveness for some products.

Television

The reasons for advertising on TV are clear: more Canadian homes are equipped with a television set than with a bathtub, and the average set is on about seven hours a day. Although television is a mass medium, it can be selective. Ads may be placed nationally on one of the networks, in specific geographic areas (or "spots"), or locally on one station. In addition, the programming guarantees some demographic selectivity (for example, *Degrassi High* appeals primarily to teenagers, *Golden Girls* to women). Television also scores high on production quality. It is excellent for product demonstrations because it reproduces both pictures and the human voice. The skilful advertiser can benefit from the flexibility of being able to combine words, graphics, actors, and music. For example, research has suggested that the use of background music can affect how certain viewers respond to television commercials.[21]

For television, however, national advertisements usually must be booked months in advance, although local stations are more flexible.

The life of a TV commercial is at most 60 seconds, and usually only 30. And, finally, television commercials are expensive. The cost of a TV commercial grew 230 percent between 1970 and 1982 — far more than costs in any other medium. A typical 30-second spot costs more than $13 000 on CTV's *Bill Cosby Show*. Add to that the cost of producing the commercial itself, which has exceeded $1 million, and it is clear that television is a medium ordinarily affordable only by larger advertisers. (National advertisers spent nearly $8.5 million on TV in 1986, according to Statistics Canada.[22])

One response to skyrocketing television advertising costs has been the birth of the "split 30." Under this arrangement, one advertiser can run commercials for two different products as long as the ad's total length is no more than 30 seconds. Alberto-Culver, for example, could buy one time slot and advertise Alberto VO5 shampoo and Sugar Twin sweetener. Advocates claim split 30s are the only way to cope with rising costs. Critics say they only create unmanageable commercial clutter, lead to less creativity in advertising, and sell products less effectively.[23] Advertisers fear the increase in "zapping," whereby viewers with remote control devices simply change stations when commercials appear. Nevertheless, some advertisers have tried even shorter, 10-second ads.

Despite its disadvantages, television advertising is expected to grow in the future. Some advertisers have begun to sponsor low-budget programs on cable TV, whose content often fits neatly with a sponsor's products. While the audiences for these shows are much smaller than for network programming, they have the advantage of being highly targeted. An audience of car enthusiasts is virtually guaranteed, for example, for "STP's Pitstop" show, which runs during stock-car races on a sports cable channel.[24]

Radio

Radio is experiencing one of the most innovative and competitive periods in its history. Satellite transmission means that local stations can tap into a broad range of national programming. AM stations, while they are struggling to regain lost market share,[25] can broadcast in stereo. Computers are being used to transmit fast-breaking news stories. There are approximately 700 radio stations in Canada.

Radio is attractive to advertisers for many reasons. In drawing power, radio dominates television through most of the day. Radio's audience is broad. Nearly all Canadian homes have radios — indeed, approximately 30 percent have four or more.[26] Radio is also far more selective than TV. Most programs originate locally, and special formats (all-news, talk, rock music, country music) help segment the audience. Scheduling is generally more flexible for a radio commercial as well, and total cost is also usually less.

Radio commercials, like television's, are brief. But their chances of being heard may be greater because there are millions of radios in cars alone, and many of those are tuned in during "drive time," the period spent commuting to and from work. In addition, many now own some form of walkabout radio, so potential consumers may hear an advertiser's message while out jogging, walking the dog, or working on a tan at the beach.

With television ad prices becoming astronomical, many analysts believe that radio will emerge as an even stronger medium in the future.

Direct Mail

In 1988, nearly $2 billion was spent on various forms of direct mail, including sales letters, catalogues, postcards, and house organs (periodicals published by organizations), among others. Direct mail is the second largest advertising medium in Canada in terms of dollar expenditures.[27]

Direct mail combines many of the qualities that advertisers look for in a medium. With the aid of computers, potential customers can be targeted in an infinite variety of ways, and messages can be personalized.

Direct mail is also flexible. With the help of a co-operative printer and first-class postage (rarely used, however, because of the expense), a rush campaign could take only days from conception to a consumer's mailbox. Direct mail is also the medium in which it is easiest to track results. Given a generous budget, direct mail can incorporate magazine-quality art—or even a sample of the product.

Among its drawbacks are its association with "junk mail" and its relatively high cost. In addition, its growing popularity among marketers has led to such an increase in volume that it is easy for one company's message to be lost among those of so many competitors jamming a consumer's mailbox.

Direct mail is big business. Increasingly, companies are looking to the international market as a vast, relatively untapped area for expansion.

Outdoor/Transit Media

Outdoor advertising may include billboards, blimps, joggers' T-shirts, taxicabs, and more. During 1986, advertisers spent an estimated $5.5 million to put their messages on billboards.[28]

Besides being relatively inexpensive, outdoor media are selective of local audiences, and they have a long life span—often 30 days or more. However, traffic jams aside, passersby are generally exposed to billboards for only about five to ten seconds, which limits the message they can carry.

The San Diego Zoo has overcome this limitation by using a series of three billboards with a simple message. (See Figure 15.4.) The first board shows a snake that flicks its tongue as it slithers toward a birthday cake. About 400 metres away, another board shows the same snake, mouth open and closer to the cake. Another 400 metres down the road, the snake has swallowed the cake, and now-curious motorists see a message

Figure 15.4 A Series of Billboards That Tell a Story

Source: Client: San Diego Zoo; Agency: Philips-Ramsey. Used with permission.

that explains the pictures: "Celebrate the San Diego Zoo's 70th Birthday."

Some firms are trying novel ideas for outdoor advertising that go far beyond run-of-the-road billboards. One company makes inflatable advertising pieces in the shape of corporate products and characters—sometimes as high as nine metres tall. Its clients include McDonald's and Coca-Cola.[29] Another enterprising advertiser affixes message-carrying, two-and-a-half-metre-long, blimp-shaped balloons to mopeds, and has riders cruise the highways simulating moving billboards.[30]

Testing Advertising Effectiveness

The cost of producing—writing, casting, filming, and editing—a single uncomplicated TV commercial can run to $100 000. Added to that is the cost of purchasing time. Magazines can be expensive as well. A single-page four-colour ad in *Maclean's* magazine, for example, can cost more than $20 000.

With that kind of money at stake, advertisers want some assurance that their messages will bring results. Advertisers try to measure such things as whether the intended audience was exposed to, is aware of, or can recall their messages. A few common ways of testing effectiveness are noted in Table 15.5.

Advertising: Criticisms and Constraints

Creating a major advertising campaign is a complex process, involving a good measure of art, an equal dose of science, a hefty amount of money, and a small army of people. At its best, advertising can be an amusing, informative, creative, and cost-effective way of communicating information about a product. But because it is such a powerful means of delivering a message, it has also been the focus of a great deal of criticism.

Advertising has been accused of being deceptive, manipulative, wasteful, and irritating. Critics say that advertising often degrades women, insults men, and takes advantage of children who are too young to distinguish between programming and commercials.

The advertising community is understandably concerned about these charges. To counter what it feels is unfair criticism, it has mounted several advertising campaigns of its own to attempt to change consumer perceptions about advertising. One such campaign featured an advertisement with the heading "This ad is full of lies." The advertisement went on to provide arguments against the "lies" that advertising makes people buy things they don't want, makes things cost more, helps bad products sell, and is a waste of money.

Individual advertisers have also responded to complaints. For example, a single father wrote to Sears to complain about brochures for cleaning products that were explicitly directed to "mother." The director of public affairs at Sears wrote to the unhappy father, promising that the company would henceforth try to substitute the word *parent* for *mother* or *father*.[31]

But many of the criticisms leveled against advertising are more serious than simply an unpopular public image. In the past, some advertising has been deceptive, and some downright false. As noted in Chapter 3, the Canadian advertising industry has formed self-regulating bodies— the Canadian Advertising Advisory Board (CAAB) and la Confédération générale de la publicité (COGEP)—to help guard against such abuses. In addition, various governmental groups have the power to regulate

Table 15.5 Techniques for Measuring Advertising Effectiveness

Pretesting

Evaluation of advertising before the campaign.

Opinion and Attitude Tests

Consumer juries — carefully selected panels of people are asked to rate the effectiveness of various ads.

Theatre-type tests — test TV commercials are screened by an audience who indicate likes and dislikes by pressing buttons.

Attitude scales — respondents are asked to rate their feelings toward a particular advertisement on an attitude rating scale.

Mechanical Laboratory Methods

Tachistoscopes — a mechanical device that measures how long it takes respondents to get the point of an illustration, a headline, etc.

Eye camera — a camera that photographs the movement of people's eyes while they read an ad to gain information on the placement of a headline, the length of the copy, etc.

Psychogalvanometer — similar to a lie detector, this instrument measures a subject's emotional reaction to an ad.

Pupillometer — this device measures a subject's pupil size while viewing an ad; wider pupils indicate interest or emotional involvement.

Projective Techniques

Depth interviewing — a trained interviewer probes a respondent about underlying feelings about an ad, for example, "What does this ad tell you about yourself?"

Word association and sentence completion tests — a researcher selects certain words or phrases from an ad to test consumer reaction to their meaning.

Concurrent Testing

Evaluation of TV and radio advertising at the time it is aired.

Nielsen Audimeter — electronic device used to record audience tuning of TV sets.

Consumer diaries — booklets in which members of a representative sample record what they are actually viewing or listening to.

Posttesting

Evaluation of advertising after it has appeared in various media.

Readership (recognition) tests — at a certain point after the receipt of a magazine, an interviewer asks a reader to go through the publication and indicate which ads were read.

Recall tests — similar to a readership test, but respondents are asked to tell what they remember about an ad without having the magazine before them.

Attitude change measures — a survey of the change in consumer attitudes about a product following an advertising campaign by using a similar precampaign study as a benchmark.

advertising. The most powerful is Consumer and Corporate Affairs Canada, which administers the Federal Competition Act.

While there is no denying that many of the criticisms of advertising have been justified, the general public still seems to think that the benefits of advertising outweigh its possible hazards. A recent U.S. study showed that 93 percent of respondents agreed or strongly agreed that advertising is an important part of the economy; 59 percent said they enjoyed the advertising they read, saw, or heard; and a surprising 53 percent said they would like their children to be employed in the advertising business.[32]

The Role of Sales Promotion

Sales promotion covers promotional efforts that cannot be classed as personal selling, advertising, or publicity. Factory tours, cents-off coupons, trade show exhibits, and message-bearing beer mugs are all examples of the forms sales promotion can take.

As they do with advertising, marketers should begin a sales promotional campaign by establishing objectives and a budget. For the consumer market, objectives might include encouraging brand switching, attracting new users, or getting established customers to buy greater quantities. For intermediaries, objectives might include encouraging retailers to carry a new product line or a higher level of inventory, building brand loyalty, or offsetting a competitor's promotion. For the sales force, objectives might include building support for a new product or model, encouraging more sales calls, or stimulating off-season sales.[33]

Sales promotion often is designed to assist the efforts of the sales force. In some cases, the aid is direct, as when it paves the way for a sales rep's call. For example, American Telecom Inc., a low-profile supplier of telecommunications equipment, developed a sweet way to introduce potential distributors to its new line. Instead of sending them the usual telegram, brochure, or pamphlet, the company sent each dealer a box containing a 1500-gram solid chocolate telephone, a sample contract, some introductory literature, and the business card of the ATI regional sales manager. The cost of the mailing was high — $50 per piece — but the response more than justified the expenditure. Every single dealer expressed interest in handling the new line, and ATI found itself in the enviable position of being able to pick the dealers it wanted to form its distributor network.[34]

Like ATI's gift, many sales promotion tools are aimed at intermediaries. The theory is that a wholesaler or retailer deals with thousands of products and must be offered an extra incentive to "push" those of a particular firm. But sales promotions can also be directed toward consumers and the sales force. When consumers are the target, the producer tries to pressure intermediaries indirectly by creating consumer demand (a "pull strategy"). When the target is the sales force, the purpose is to fire up enthusiasm or keep members informed.

Table 15.6 lists the tools of sales promotion by target audience, and Figure 15.5 shows the relative importance of some of them.

Table 15.6 Types of Sales Promotion

For Sales Reps	*For Intermediaries*	*For Consumer*
Sales meetings	Sales meetings	In-store demonstrations
Sales manuals	Contests	Premiums
Product demonstration models	Push money	Samples
Contests and incentive campaigns	Dealer gifts	Coupons
Sales letters and bulletins	Point-of-purchase materials	Trading stamps
	Trade shows and exhibits	Refunds
	Advertising allowances	Contests and games
	Business catalogues	Direct mailings

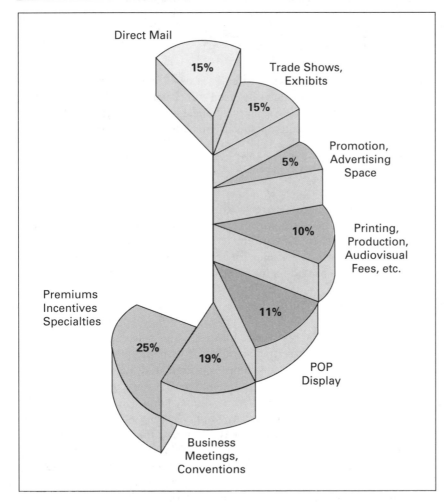

Figure 15.5 The Importance of Selected Promotional Tools

Source: Adapted from Roger A. Strang, ''Sales Promotion — Fast Growth, Faulty Management,'' *Harvard Business Review*, July–August 1976, p. 118.

Promoting to the Sales Force

Perhaps the most common form of sales promotion to the sales force is the annual sales meeting. Here new product lines are introduced and selling techniques refreshed. Since salespeople who sell directly to consumers encounter more rejections than others, their meetings are often more like pep rallies.

Besides sales meetings, contests and incentive campaigns are common promotional motivators. Each year, for example, Ciba-Geigy Corporation, a pharmaceutical company, gives distinguished performance awards to its top sales reps. Winners get pewter bowls, publicity in the *Journal of the American Medical Association* (which is read by their physician customers), and a three-day vacation. Increases in sales of about 20 percent are common during such campaigns.[35]

Promoting to the Intermediary

Some promotional tools aimed at sales reps — including sales meetings, contests, and gifts — can also be used effectively with intermediaries. Others — such as trade shows, point-of-purchase materials, and advertising allowances — are targeted specifically for wholesale intermediaries and retailers.

Trade Shows

Every year many manufacturers exhibit their goods at **trade shows** to large audiences. The main purpose of these expositions is to allow salespeople to display their new products to dealers, to make new contacts, and to develop mailing lists for future use. In some industries, such as apparel, they also provide a marketplace where sales are made.

Point-of-Purchase Materials

Posters and signs, display racks, banners, and price cards are some of the promotional tools classified as **point-of-purchase (POP) materials.** Some POP materials today are more sophisticated, incorporating materials such as interactive video and displays that emit product aromas.[36]

North American marketers spend billions of dollars each year on POP displays. Perhaps the largest array of such displays is found in supermarkets. With thousands of products competing for consumer attention, an impressive POP device can give a product a competitive edge. Surveys have shown that the addition of POP materials to an advertising program can increase awareness of the entire program by up to 50 percent.[37]

Today, a growing trend is for retailers to take control of POP displays. Many retailers have been disappointed over the quality of some POP materials, so they use materials they generate themselves. These materials guide customers through the store and have a unified design. In

Trade Show
Exposition that allows salespeople to display their new products to dealers, to make new contacts, and to develop mailing lists for future use.

Point-of-Purchase (POP) Materials
Promotional tools such as posters, display racks, and price cards.

response, some manufacturers are working closely with retailers to design POP materials. The aim is to prepare materials that work most effectively for both the manufacturer and the retailer.[38]

Advertising Allowances

Frequently retailers, and sometimes wholesalers, are reimbursed in part by a manufacturer for running the company's ad in a newspaper or on local broadcast media. Such **advertising allowances** are commonly given to department stores by appliance manufacturers and cosmetics companies. "Co-operative advertising," as it is also known, can be very attractive to dealers. Often the added business that the ads bring in will cost retailers much less because of the money refunded by the manufacturer for running the ad.

Advertising Allowance
Reimbursement by a manufacturer for part of the cost of local advertising run by retailers and wholesalers.

Promoting to Consumers

Sales promotions to consumers are often dated to encourage an immediate impact on sales or on a company's competitive position. Unfortunately for the initiator, most sales incentives are easily duplicated, and therefore may have only a short-term effect before competitors' defensive manoeuvres erode any sales increases.

Coupons

A **coupon** offers consumers a certain amount off the price of an item. In 1988, Canadian manufacturers issued approximately 15 billion coupons and only approximately 220 million coupons were redeemed.[39]

Most coupons are distributed through the mail, in newspapers and magazines, within a package, or on the back of cash register tapes. Large food-processing companies such as General Mills and Pillsbury are among the largest providers of coupons to the public.

One reason coupons have been popular among manufacturers is the increasing costliness of advertising rates. Coupons enable manufacturers to maintain a price while stimulating sales with a price break. Coupons also can be effective in inducing consumers to try a new product. They are relatively flexible and easy to use, consumers find them appealing, and they are suitable for a number of marketing objectives.

One drawback of coupons is that they may be redeemed fraudulently by people who didn't actually buy the product. While manufacturers have tried to fight the problem in various ways, including the use of decoy coupons, the problem persists.[40] In addition, persistent use of coupons can "train" consumers to wait for a price break before buying.[41]

Coupon
Sales promotion tool aimed at consumers that offers a certain amount off the price of an item.

Samples and Premiums

Manufacturers offer **samples,** or giveaways in a trial size, for products whose benefits cannot be fully conveyed through advertising. Computer

Sample
In promotion: Giveaway in a trial size for products whose benefits cannot be fully conveyed through advertising.

software companies, for example, sometimes have demonstration disk-ettes bound into issues of computer magazines such as *PC World.* This enables subscribers to sample new programs.

Samples may also be mailed, given away in stores, or handed out on streets. They are expensive, but they gain attention.

Premiums are items offered free or at a low cost as a reward for buying a product. They may keep customers loyal and, if properly selected, reinforce the product's image. One Chevy Oldsmobile dealer used pre-miums that generated a lot of attention. The dealership had trouble selling five Toronados, so it advertised that consumers who bought a Toronado would get a free Yugo. Within a month, all five Toronados were off the lot. Some people who looked at the cars came from 325 kilometres away.[42]

Blending Sales Promotion Tools

The strongest sales promotion programs tie together the tools aimed at various groups. Revlon cosmetics offers an excellent example. In a typ-ical large department store such as Eaton's, Revlon's program might employ the following promotional tools:

1. Bonuses for retail sales personnel.

2. Training for in-store demonstrators.

3. Co-operative advertising funds.

4. Installation of cosmetic counters and fixtures.

5. Consumer gifts with purchases.

6. Special clinics for teenagers.

Revlon's program includes something for everyone—sales personnel, store owners, and consumers. Any one of the elements listed may help to increase sales. Working together, however, they produce a whole that is greater than the sum of its parts.

Marketers can also blend sales promotion tools with other types of product promotion. For example, Charles of the Ritz combines free sam-ples with advertising. In ads for eye shadow, readers can pull back tabs to find samples of the makeup to try on immediately. Some observers are optimistic that this technique will give a big boost to makeup sales.[43]

The Role of Publicity

When Grete Waitz crossed the finish line as the women's champion of the 1983 New York Marathon, millions of people were watching. It was no coincidence that prominently displayed on Ms. Waitz's uniform were the words "Team Xerox." Subsequent photos of Ms. Waitz in the press

Premium
Item offered free or at a low cost as a reward for buying a product.

and on television news broadcasts carried the Xerox message to millions of additional viewers. While the company paid the runners to wear the uniform, it didn't have to pay for the media coverage.

After studying their potential customer base, Xerox marketers had determined that sponsorship of sports events was an efficient way to reach the market they had targeted. Marathon running seemed a natural tie-in with their new line of photocopiers. The company decided to sponsor 15 major marathon events around the world. It also assembled "Team Xerox," consisting of world-class runners Grete Waitz, Bill Rogers, and Rob de Castella, who agreed to wear Team Xerox uniforms whenever allowed.[44]

The company carefully reinforced the marathon tie-in by running advertising for the photocopier featuring a marathon runner in the business press. Xerox demonstrated a skilful use of publicity, both for its new product line and for the company's corporate image.

Publicity, as defined in Chapter 14, refers to any information relating to a manufacturer or its products that appears in any medium on a nonpaid basis. This definition hints at the major differences between publicity and advertising, which are summarized in Table 15.7. For one thing, because the medium providing the coverage doesn't charge for the time or space, publicity is less controllable than advertising. A 300-word publicity release submitted to a newspaper may be cut to 50 words or run on a slow news day instead of on the day the publicist preferred. Also, unlike advertisements, which can be repeated until the public recalls them, a publicity item usually appears only once.

Despite these disadvantages, publicity can be a valuable promotional tool used in conjunction with advertising or by itself. It appears as news and therefore is as believable as news. An advertisement by Imperial Oil saying that it is doing its best to find new energy sources may be met with scepticism. A news item prepared by an Imperial Oil publicist that tells the story of a new oil find and its importance may be a more effective way of helping the company's image. Because publicity is highly believable, organizations and professionals who would normally not advertise have found it an effective means of promotion.

In addition to news releases, which are usually 300-word pieces sometimes accompanied by a photograph, there are four other publicity tools:

1. *Feature articles*—500- to 3000-word articles that often appear in the business and family-living sections of newspapers.

Table 15.7 Major Differences between Advertising and Publicity

Advertising	Publicity
Paid for	No charge for media coverage
Selling slant	News slant
Sometimes lacks credibility	High credibility
Ads scheduled close together	Items infrequently used more than once
Placer has complete control	Media share control

2. *Press conferences and personal appearances*—Businesses use these for major announcements, such as executive changes.

3. *Records and films*—Radio and television stations often need "fillers."

4. *Editorials*—Firms sometimes supply editors with material for their editorial pages.

These forms of publicity may be used alone or in combination for maximum effectiveness.

Besides publicity, which is often part of a broader communication strategy, an organization's public relations program may include:

- *Opinion research*—amassing information regarding public attitudes that may be used in drafting speeches, making decisions regarding operating policies, preparing news releases, or taking a stand on legislation.

- *Lobbying*—promoting legislative or administrative action for an organization or against an adverse interest. It can also include obtaining government co-operation of sponsorship for a cause (such as National Fire Prevention Week).

- *Public affairs*—promoting an organization's total concept of corporate citizenship. This function is usually confined to large corporations and conglomerates.

- *Fund raising and membership drives*—primarily the province of private health, education, and welfare agencies that depend on contributions for their survival.[45]

At Your Service 15.2 describes how some companies are using toll-free numbers as part of their programs.

Like other forms of promotion, a publicity program should begin with objectives consistent with an overall marketing program. These may be to generate sales inquiries, to promote a new product image, to gain visibility for new applications for a mature line, or to promote new distributors.[46]

Measuring the effectiveness of a public relations campaign can be difficult. Although numbers of news stories, photographs, and personal appearances can be counted, it is often difficult to determine if all that coverage really had an impact. In some cases, publicity programs can use the same tactics as other forms of promotion to measure results:

1. *Controlled market comparisons*—sales results can be compared in test markets where public relations was included as part of the marketing mix versus those where it was not.

2. *Direct response*—public relations can sometimes generate cost-effective, direct customer response. Mensa, an organization for people with high IQs, succeeded in placing an "IQ Quiz" in *Reader's Digest* that drew 75 000 inquiries.

3. *Communication with the sales force* — by providing the sales force with reprints of publicity for merchandising to customers, and then surveying salespeople for customer response, a public relations department can get an idea of the effectiveness of a campaign.[47]

Chapter Replay

1. **What kinds of advertising can marketers use?**

   The various types of advertising include selective or brand advertising, primary demand advertising, institutional advertising, and noncommercial advertising.

2. **What are some reasons for advertising?**

   Advertisers inform the public and try to persuade them to buy certain products. Ads remind consumers of an organization's products and reassure buyers that they have made the right purchase. Ads also back up the sales force and provide leads for salespeople.

3. **What kinds of organizations employ the most people in the field of advertising?**

   The organizations that employ the most people are advertising departments, which operate within for-profit and nonprofit organizations, and advertising agencies, which prepare most ads and which may specialize in certain kinds of advertising.

4. **What steps are involved in developing an ad campaign?**

   In developing an advertising campaign, marketers must set objectives, determine a budget, define a positioning strategy, decide on a message, choose media, and develop ways to measure the effectiveness of the campaign.

5. **What are some creative styles for presenting advertising messages?**

   Advertisers can use an image sell, a direct sell, a humorous or soft sell, or a competitive sell.

6. **What major media do advertisers use?**

   The six major media are newspapers, magazines, television, radio, direct mail, and outdoor/transit signs.

7. **How have advertisers and the government responded to criticisms of advertising?**

   Individual advertisers try to modify messages that consumers find objectionable. As a whole, the advertising community prepares messages describing the benefits of advertising. The government has passed laws regulating advertising, which are administered by Consumer and Corporate Affairs Canada.

8. **How can sales promotion increase sales?**

   Through contests, sales meetings, and incentives, sales promotion can motivate the sales force and intermediaries. Through coupons, point-of-purchase materials, samples, and premiums, it can also stimulate consumers to act.

9. **What are some advantages and disadvantages of using publicity?**

   The user of publicity pays nothing for the media coverage. In addition, publicity offers a news slant and high credibility. But publicity items are rarely used more than once, and the organization generating the publicity gives up some control to the media.

10. **What activities are typically included in a public relations program?**

    An organization's public relations program may include publicity, opinion research, lobbying, public affairs, and fund raising and membership drives.

Key Terms

advertising allowance
association advertising
comparative advertising
coupon
institutional (or
  corporate) advertising
media
noncommercial
  advertising
point-of-purchase (POP)
  materials

positioning
premium
primary demand
  advertising
sample
selective or brand
  advertising
trade show

Discussion Questions

1. Why might an organization use primary demand advertising rather than brand advertising?

2. Brand Z Corporation uses a highly trained sales force to sell pharmaceuticals to doctors and hospitals. Why would the company want to advertise when it already spends a lot of money on salespeople?

3. What activities do advertising agencies typically perform for their clients?

4. In general terms, describe how a chain of fast-food restaurants might use an image sell. How might it use a direct sell? A competitive sell?

5. Rita Jones is responsible for advertising for her company, which sells tents and sleeping bags. She determines that the company can afford either to advertise in magazines that appeal to campers or to buy mailing lists from those magazines and send out brochures to the readers. Based on the information in this chapter about magazines and direct mail, which of these approaches would you recommend? Why?

6. Why are some manufacturers reluctant to use coupons extensively? Besides coupons, what sales promotion methods do manufacturers use to reach consumers?

7. The Big Museum of Natural History has been dissatisfied with its publicity program. For the last few years, the museum has sent out press releases every month or so but rarely receives media coverage. The Big Museum therefore hired a new publicity director, Paul Plum. What publicity techniques might Paul use besides press releases?

8. What are some ways of measuring the effectiveness of a public relations campaign?

CASE 15.1

Exxon Office Systems

Given the uncertainties of the world market for oil and gas, Exxon, for a number of years, had been looking for new sources of long-term earnings growth. It is estimated that the company put $1 billion into synthetic fuels research and development before curtailing investments in the area. An additional $1 billion went to acquiring Reliance Electric Company, an investment that has been filled with problems and has shown disappointing returns. Major sums also went into mining and nuclear fuels, where a number of business lines have shown profitable returns.

One significant investment outside the area of oil was in office automation systems. Several hundred million dollars have been invested in building an office systems business. The company's three major office product lines — the Qwip telephone facsimile transmission unit, Qyx electronic typewriter line, and Vydec word processor line—were merged in 1981 to form Exxon Office Systems (EOS).

Initial Communications Effort

In 1981, after its organization, EOS spent almost $5 million in an advertising campaign designed to bring instant recognition and credibility to the new company. Some industry observers felt that the campaign fell short of the mark. In fact, there were many rumours that Exxon was going to cut its losses and get out of the office automation business. Exxon management repeatedly denied the rumours.

During the first half of 1982, the company spent $500 000 on a one-month print campaign designed to reinforce the fact that Exxon was still aggressively pursuing the word processing market and planned to develop new technology. The advertisements, developed by Marsteller, Inc., featured statements of commitment by various EOS officers in the headlines. In the initial advertisement, the president of EOS was quoted as saying, "Remember . . . when you buy our word processing systems . . . you buy our commitment to your future." The company's other advertising activities for various new and existing products utilized television and direct mail, as well as the print media.

Another Campaign

In many people's minds, Exxon was still not firmly established as an office automation company. At the same time, EOS had received some

Source: Adapted from Robert Raissman, "Exxon Out to Boost Its Sagging Office Unit," *Advertising Age,* June 28, 1982, p. 50; and Edward D. Sheffe, "Campaign: Getting Away from Gas Pumps," *Madison Avenue,* September 1983, pp. 60–66.

unfavourable responses from the trade press. One publication implied that some of the firm's earlier products had become outmoded and expensive. The situation posed two immediate challenges for the company: (1) to establish popular awareness among its target audience and (2) to overcome the unfavourable comments about its products and future in the marketplace.

New Products

The first issue was addressed by a series of new-product introductions, carefully designed and timed to create and maintain excitement in the marketplace. A basic objective was to get the proper message about EOS to the industry consultants. The company actively participated in trade shows and pursued major consultants in the industry. At the same time, efforts were under way to develop an aggressive advertising campaign to try to fix the "tigers-and-gasoline" image problem.

Advertising

While many of the office automation firms were directing their communications to departmental or individual user levels, EOS people felt that the decision-making authority was moving up the organization, especially as systems representing significant capital investments were considered. The objective was perceived as getting Exxon's message across to middle- and senior-level managers in larger companies—people who might not be highly technically oriented. Once it was decided to focus on network television as the primary vehicle, animation was considered as the logical choice for the campaign. Such an approach had the key elements of universal appeal, flexibility, and even credibility if done right.

Marsteller created three 60-second and five 30-second television spots. They focused on EOS's corporate identity, the Exxon 500 series information processor, the Qwip facsimile, the new Exxon 965 Ink Jet Printer, and the communications capabilities and integration of the products. Three of the spots specifically stressed the theme, "At Exxon Office Systems, we bring the high-tech office down to earth." An animated executive, created by Arnie Levin, a well-known *New Yorker* cartoonist, was shown strolling through an office with information processors growing out of the top of each desk. The stylized machines were very much in evidence, but the emphasis was more on smiling, productive people. Narrated by John Huston, the assurance throughout the commercials was that Exxon Office Systems is here to stay and can help ease the trauma as people and companies make the transition to "The Future . . . without the shock."

The commercials ran in major markets from October through November and April to mid-June 1983. To reinforce the broadcast media, an ongoing print campaign ran in national and local newspapers and in general business, trade, and office publications.

Focal Topics

1. Why do you believe the earlier campaigns for Exxon Office Systems did not create the desired position in the marketplace?

2. How would you measure the effectiveness of EOS's later advertising campaign?

3. From Exxon's perspective, the initial results of the second campaign were favourable. The key question is whether the campaign will have staying power. What are your advertising recommendations to Exxon, if and when the campaign seems to have run its course? Be specific about objectives, creative themes, and media selection.

CASE 15.2

Detyzco, Inc.

"Pet 88 is a nutritionally balanced, frozen dessert for your dog—fortified with vitamins and minerals. Your dog will love it!" are the words used on the package to describe Detyzco's new product aimed at dog lovers. The firm has achieved selected distribution in Southwestern Ontario for its products and would like to attain national market coverage.

Product Development

About three years ago, Peter DeMarco, a poultry science student working at a pet store, casually asked his employer, "Why isn't there a good nutritional ice cream for dogs?" C. Dale Cook, owner of the Pet Palace, responded that he did not know why, but thought that such an idea might be "just crazy enough to sell." With some interest and mostly curiosity they asked William Tyznik, a recognized animal nutritionist at a local university, about the possibility of such a product.

After many trials and experiments over a period of nine months, Tyznik, working with DeMarco, came up with the basic formula at the laboratory level. Cook, who had formerly worked with a major contract research organization, began to get more involved with the process with the objective of taking the product from the laboratory to the marketplace.

The product was tested and retested on dozens of dogs during most of 1986. It was then necessary to develop the production capability to manufacture and package such a product. In 1987, a patent was sought for the product and later that year the product was introduced in the market. The three men involved formed Detyzco, a solely owned corporation, to manufacture and market the product. Their joint resources amounted to a modest $75 000.

Source: From *Cases for Analysis in Marketing*, 3rd ed., by W. Wayne Talarzyk, pp. 19–22. Copyright 1985, CBS College Publishing. Reprinted by permission of CBS College Publishing.

Product Description

Pet 88 Frozen Dog Dessert is packaged in a six-serving carton. Each individual serving is in a four-ounce plastic cup. The product can be served to dogs in its frozen state or thawed in the refrigerator and served as a creamy pudding.

Pricing

The product is currently retail priced at $1.39 per six-pack carton. At this price retailers have a margin of about 25 to 30 percent. Food distributors receive a markup of 15 percent for handling the product from Detyzco to the retailer.

Promotion

To introduce Pet 88 Frozen Dog Dessert to the market, Detyzco produced a 30-second television advertisement.

A "new business package" consisting of forty 30-second spots and costing a total of $2000 was purchased from a major metropolitan television station. These advertisements were "run of schedule," meaning that the station could fit them into its schedule throughout the broadcasting day as space was available.

The primary purpose of this series of advertisements was to provide credibility to the company and its product in order to help convince retailers to carry the product. It was hoped that customers would ask retailers for the product if it was not on display.

Detyzco also developed a point-of-purchase poster for the product along with a counter card to help promote the product. The same graphic logo was used in all promotional materials, including packaging, to provide continuity to the product presentation.

After initial distribution was achieved, the firm utilized a few radio commercials (following the same general theme of the television advertisements). Copy for these radio commercials was read live by the announcers in an attempt to achieve an individual touch with more spontaneity. Sales for the first quarter amounted to $18 000.

Focal Topics

1. Discuss your evaluation of the advertising plan presented here.

2. What creative themes, other than those described, would you use in television and radio commercials? Support your recommendations.

3. What other media could be used as part of the advertising program? Which, if any, would you recommend?

4. How would you measure the effectiveness of the advertising plan?

Chapter 16

Personal Selling and Sales Management

In this chapter, you will learn:

- The circumstances under which personal selling is most important in the marketing mix.

- Basic types of sales jobs.

- The decisions an organization must make with regard to its sales force.

- How the sales manager can organize the sales force.

- How companies screen applicants for sales positions.

- The tasks of the sales manager.

- The stages of the selling process.

- How salespeople are compensated.

- How sales managers evaluate the performance of salespeople.

Selling the Corporate Caterer

If you're having lunch at your desk, you might want to send out to Fisher & Levy, a corporate caterer that specializes in delivery. Instead of corned beef on rye, you'll be able to enjoy, say, a chicken provençale sandwich attractively presented along with specially printed napkins and packaged mints.

The owners of Fisher & Levy are Doug Levy, a chef, and Chip Fisher, the marketing department. Fisher started a sales career upon graduating from Harvard with a degree in English. At that time, he took a position selling computers for IBM. He wanted to work for IBM because he thought selling for that company was an excellent marketing position. Working there taught him a lot about selling a premium product for a premium price.

Selling is Fisher's forte. About every six weeks he heads out to drum up new business. Starting with a briefcase full of menus, he goes door to door in the city's office buildings. He starts at the top of each building, because he finds the wealthiest clients there.

Fisher has polished sales tactics. He dresses to look like a young professional and walks into buildings with the air of someone heading to an appointment. That way, he minimizes the chance that a building manager or security guard will discover he's soliciting and ask him to leave. For the same reason, he avoids being seen on different floors by the same person.

For most salespeople, the receptionist is a hurdle, but for Fisher this person is a prospect. He explains, "I guess 90 percent of the people in offices go to the receptionist for information about where to get food." After a polite, friendly introduction, he drops off a few menus and then heads for the next office.

Evidently, Fisher's selling technique is working. In the two years between 1984 and 1986, Fisher & Levy's sales doubled.

Personal selling is often crucial to a company's success. This chapter takes a more detailed look at how companies can make the most of this important marketing function.

Source: Adapted from Bill Kelley, "Gourmet to Go," *Sales and Marketing Management*, January 1987, pp. 43–44.

Personal Selling's Place in the Promotional Mix

A firm may have an outstanding product that it offers at a competitive price, an efficient distribution system, award-winning advertising, eye-catching sales promotional displays, and headline-making publicity. But, as the late Red Motley, an outstanding sales trainer, once said, "Nothing happens until somebody sells something." The salesperson is the sparkplug that keeps our industrial society going.

In the increasingly self-service world of retailing, the role of personal selling is not always immediately apparent. Nonetheless, it is still an essential part of any firm's marketing plan. While Nabisco's sales force, for example, may not be lurking in the cookie aisle of the local supermarket urging shoppers to sample their new line, they are probably a very real presence to the store's owner or manager. In fact, Nabisco fields a small army of salespeople who regularly visit supermarkets to inspect and position the baked goods.[1] And back at the company's headquarters, many other personal sales must take place before one cookie can come off a conveyor belt. Someone had to sell Nabisco flour, chocolate chips, plant machinery, transportation services, warehousing facilities, advertising assistance, tax advice, office forms, typewriters, and soap for the washrooms.

All this activity makes a sales career one that can be both financially rewarding and practically recession-proof. Canadian firms spend heavily on their thousands of salespeople. Many new college and university graduates become salespeople every year. Marketing Today 16.1 describes attitudes of students toward selling careers.

As discussed in Chapter 7, personal selling is generally the most important element in the promotional mix of industrial marketers. The other circumstances in which personal selling is of primary importance are summarized in Table 16.1.

Types of Sales Jobs

Despite dramatic changes in the way products are now sold, selling still suffers from the negative stereotypes of its occasionally disreputable past. Certainly the snake-oil salesmen who roamed the frontier and Arthur Miller's tragic play *Death of a Salesman* have done little to make selling seem an appealing profession. But today's salesperson is likely to be part of a sophisticated team of professionals, highly skilled in the demands of a particular field, a creative problem solver rather than product pusher, and an important source of information for clients.

Many of the misconceptions about selling arise because of failure to recognize the variety of jobs included under the heading "sales." A

Marketing Today 16.1

Student Interest in Selling

While women have played an important role in marketing, they have been underrepresented in the field of personal selling. Recently, two researchers tried to determine whether this reflected a lack of interest. They surveyed 296 students at three universities, asking them to rate ten marketing careers on a five-point scale from 1 (least preferred) to 5 (most preferred).

Although the study was conducted in the American Midwest, its findings seem applicable to Canada.

The male and female respondents gave significantly different answers. Women were more interested than men in public relations, advertising, and retail management. Men were more interested than women in wholesale sales, manufacturer sales, industrial buy-

ing, distribution management, and product management.

When asked about the attributes of sales careers, women were more likely to agree with statements that a sales career entails responsibility, requires high-pressure sales tactics, and has too little monetary reward. Men were more likely to agree that sales careers require much travel and high skills and that salespeople are money-hungry. In explaining these differences, the researchers noted that more women than men indicated that their contact with salespeople has mostly been limited to sales clerks. The authors suggest that recruiters might emphasize female role models for sales positions.

While women expressed less interest in a sales career, neither group was particularly enthusiastic. Thus, sales managers must make extra efforts to attract qualified graduates to sales positions.

Phyllis Woloshin

Source: Adapted from Robert W. Cook and Timothy Hartman, "Female College Student Interest in a Sales Career: A Comparison," *Journal of Personal Selling and Sales Management* 6 (May 1986): 29–34.

Table 16.1 Factors Affecting the Importance of Personal Selling in the Promotional Mix

	Personal Selling is likely to be more important when	Advertising is likely to be more important when
Consumer is:	geographically concentrated, relatively small in numbers	geographically dispersed, relatively large in numbers
Product is:	expensive, technically complex, custom-made, special handling required, trade-ins frequently involved	inexpensive, simple to understand, standardized, no special handling, no trade-ins
Price is:	relatively high	relatively low
Channels are:	relatively short	relatively long

Source: Louis E. Boone and David L. Kurtz, *Contemporary Marketing*, 5th edition (Hinsdale, Ill.: The Dryden Press, 1986), p. 436. Copyright 1986 by The Dryden Press, a division of CBS College Publishing. Reprinted by permission.

widely accepted classification of selling jobs by Robert McMurry shows how diverse selling is. His classification, which distinguishes sales jobs by the degree of creativity they involve, include the following categories of sales personnel:[2]

Merchandise Deliverer
Salesperson who sees that buyers receive their purchases.

Order Taker
Salesperson whose main function is to write or ring up orders.

Missionary
Salesperson whose role is to build goodwill or to educate potential customers rather than to make a direct sale.

Technical Salespeople
Technicians in sales positions who act as consultants and sometimes help to design products or systems to meet a client's needs.

Creative Salespeople
Individuals charged with determining customers' needs, helping them solve problems, and getting orders.

1. **Merchandise deliverers.** People in this category have no responsibility for creative selling, but they provide essential support to the sales effort by seeing that buyers receive their purchases. Truck wholesalers, such as those who sell and deliver bakery products directly to supermarkets, fall into this category.

2. **Order takers.** Salespeople who may suggest an article for purchase but whose main function is to write or ring up orders are called order takers. "Inside" order takers may work within a store or take telephone orders at direct-mail firms or sales offices. "Outside" order takers work in the field. For instance, the junior sales reps for Del Monte check grocery displays and shelves and reorder when supplies of the canned products are low. They also gather information on competitive products and feed it back to headquarters.

3. **Missionaries.** These are salespeople whose job is to build goodwill or to educate potential customers rather than to make a direct sale. Drug companies like Upjohn send missionary salespeople (often called "detailers") to doctors to describe the uses of new drugs and leave free samples. Other manufacturers sometimes use missionaries to supplement the efforts of independent wholesale distributors who handle their products.

4. **Technical salespeople.** Technicians in sales positions who act as consultants and sometimes help to design products or systems to meet a client's needs are technical salespeople. They are high on the creativity scale. Reynolds Aluminum once used members of its sales staff with engineering backgrounds to convince Ford to switch from steel to aluminum bumpers. The deal was closed after three years when the sales staff came up with a model strong enough to withstand banging by Ford negotiators but light enough to be lifted with one hand.[3]

5. **Creative salespeople.** Those charged with determining customer needs, helping them solve problems, and getting orders are properly called "creative" salespeople. They may work within a company or in the field, and they may sell tangible products or intangible services. New products require a large measure of creative selling, since potential customers must be made to see how an innovation can solve their problems. Many trainees start as order takers or missionaries, but their goal is to reach senior positions that involve creative selling.

Of course, not all jobs fit neatly into one of the categories listed here. Clothing salespeople at a retail store, for example, may write orders, but they are also responsible for creating customer goodwill; in addition, they may have enough technical knowledge of clothing design to advise a customer on a well-made coat. It is useful to classify them as order takers because they spend the largest part of their time processing orders. But all selling jobs, if well done, may involve a degree of creativity.

As might be expected, the more knowledge, creativity, and responsibility a sales job requires, the greater its compensation will be. In general, those who sell services earn most, followed by industrial goods and consumer goods salespeople. Postsecondary graduates taking sales positions start, on average, at more than $20 000.[4] At the other extreme, top commission-only salespeople earned an average of more than $185 000 in 1985, four times the figure paid to the top salary-only salespeople.[5] A sales career can clearly offer much satisfaction in the area of personal achievement—and an opportunity for substantial financial rewards.

Making Sales Force Decisions

Once a company decides to field a sales force — for any of the reasons cited—many decisions must be made. Among them are: (1) the goals of the sales force; (2) the size force the company requires; and (3) how the sales force should be structured.

Establishing Sales Force Objectives

The first step in determining the role of the sales force is to set objectives. This process is less evident than it may seem. While selling products is any sales force's foremost objective, it is often not the only one. Other objectives may include presales activity, such as identifying new customers and educating them about a company's products and services, and postsales activity, such as offering technical assistance and further problem-solving advice. At the time of the sale, a salesperson may help to arrange financing and assist with the mechanics of delivery. Some of these goals—such as providing technical assistance—are hard to quantify. But whenever possible, sales organizations try to specify objectives as precisely as possible. One company may set a goal, for example, of increasing overall sales by 6 percent within a year or propose that each salesperson open two new accounts monthly.

Finally, one of the most valuable functions of a sales force is to provide feedback from customers on the effectiveness of an advertising or promotion campaign, the success—or problems—of a new product, and the activities of competitors. In their travels, salespeople may pick up ideas for new products or suggestions for improvements on old ones. A marketing organization that uses its sales force effectively can find it an invaluable source of information.

Determining Sales Force Structure

Once objectives have been set, a sales manager must determine how to organize the sales force for maximum efficiency. Structures include organizing by:

1. *Territory.* Most textbook publishers, for example, have divisions in the Atlantic provinces, Quebec, Ontario, the Prairies, and British Columbia.

2. *Product.* Because Dow Chemical manufactures a diverse line of technically complex products, the company's sales reps specialize in selling chemicals, plastics, metal products, medical products, consumer products, or packaging.

3. *Market.* Eastman Kodak, maker of photographic equipment, organizes its sales force around a business system market and a consumer market.

4. *A combination.* If a company sells many products to different types of customers over a wide geographical area, it may choose to organize the sales force by a combination of methods. For example, in one company, a sales representative may be responsible for selling a certain product throughout the country. Another company may further organize its sales force so that each representative sells a certain product line to a specified market in a well-defined territory.

Within the framework of this overall work force design, sales managers must answer the question, how much territory can an individual salesperson cover effectively? The answer depends on many factors, including the nature of the product, the number and location of buyers, and the type of selling required. For example, an IBM computer sales rep may cover only a few city blocks in Toronto because the product is complex, potential customers — large business firms — are densely clustered, and the job requires creative selling. The situation of a sales rep for Union Carbide's agricultural pesticides is just the opposite. The territory may cover three or four western provinces because farms are widely scattered and the product may not require as much creative selling.

Some sales managers also must consider how the salesperson's time should be spent. Technical and creative salespeople usually allocate their own time, but the routes and schedules of order takers and missionary salespeople may be determined at headquarters. Regular routes and schedules mean that repeat buyers get service they can rely on and that the sales force's time is being used efficiently.

Decisions regarding sales force structure have taken on great importance as the cost of an average sales call has skyrocketed. Sharp increases in the cost of meals, lodging, and gasoline have pushed the average cost to more than $250.[6]

Managing efficient use of time and territory is critical to a salesperson's success. Executives surveyed in over 400 industries indicated that, for the future, sales managers will emphasize the importance of time and territory management to their sales personnel. The way salespeople invest available sales time may well be one of the most critical factors influencing territory sales/cost ratios.[7]

Staffing the Sales Force

A company now has the broad outlines of the sales force sketched in. What remains is as much an art as a science: recruiting and selecting the best possible sales force.

Are Creative Salespeople Born or Made?

Much has been written about whether good salespeople are born or made. Most of the research has centred on drawing up lists of traits common to all good salespeople. The result: no two researchers seem to agree on the qualities that ensure superior selling ability. Some researchers stress a high level of energy and self-confidence as common to all good salespeople; others think superior selling ability springs from a feeling of being unwanted and unloved and the need to overcome that feeling.[8] (See Figure 16.1.)

Such obvious disagreement seems to discredit the notion that an individual must be born with certain characteristics to succeed in selling. Because there is such a diversity of selling jobs, the qualities that make for a good salesperson in one field may not work in another. The intellectual and psychological requirements desirable for selling computers may not be so desirable for selling encyclopedias. One job may require an MBA and problem-solving ability, while the other may be filled by someone with little formal education but a great deal of perseverance. Companies attempt to screen out those who are obviously unsuitable for the kinds of selling they require. They then supply those selected with extensive training.

The Screening Process

Sales trainees are recruited from a number of sources. They may come from nonselling jobs within a company or be "pirated" from competing companies. More frequently today they are recruited from college and university campuses because of the degree of technical ability most professional sales jobs require. Many companies do not insist on technical backgrounds, however. The personnel director of IBM has noted, "We search for individuals who are intelligent, quick learners, problem solvers. We don't look for specific academic backgrounds. We've hired some music majors, because they have very logical minds"[9]

Companies use a wide variety of tools to sort out the qualifications of applicants. Sales managers rely heavily on application forms and job

What motivates the super salesperson? One study of several thousand top produ- cers isolated motives common to most:

Need for Status—The best salespeople seek recognition as proof of their ability and performance. They enjoy power and authority and are strongly aware of image and reputation.

Need for Control—Successful sellers like people, enjoy being with them, and delight in influencing them. They seldom care deeply whether others like them, a trait that enables them to use emotion without falling prey to it.

Need for Respect—They want to be seen as experts on what is right, best or appropriate. They regard themselves as well-intentioned people, willing to help and advise others.

Need for Routine—Contrary to the popular belief that top salespeople are impulsive and somewhat undisciplined, most like routine and hate having it interrupted.

Need for Accomplishment—Material comforts—a nice house, expensive clothing, a fancy car—are only the beginning. Money starts as a prime motivator, but the top salespeople earn so much that one said,"Money loses its ability to inspire you." The superstars constantly create new challenges and go after the "impossible sales" to maintain their enthusiasm.

Need for Stimulation—Top producers are normally calm, relaxed people who thrive on challenge. They have more physical energy than most people and welcome outside stimulation as a way to channel their energy in satisfying ways.

Need for Honesty—The best salespeople have such a strong need to believe in the product that they will switch jobs if the company's reputation slips or if they have serious doubts about a new product line. They are not rigidly moralistic; experience has taught them to accept imperfections, in people and products, of the real world.

Figure 16.1 Do You Have What It Takes to Be a Superstar?

Source: Donald J. Moine, "The Fire Within." Reprinted with permission from *Psychology Today*, March 1984, p. 44. Copyright 1984 American Psychological Association.

interviews. The biographical data that these tools reveal help match the backgrounds of job applicants and customers. In the field of life insur- ance, for example, a study in the 1960s demonstrated a relationship between similarity in the buyer's and seller's ages and success in making a sale.[10]

Companies may also use various tests to determine if candidates have the traits that spell success. One approach many experts recommend is to give a company's top salespeople tests that measure the traits usually found in people who do well in selling. The results are then used to build a profile of the characteristics most important in that particular sales field. Candidates for sales jobs can then be measured against that profile.[11]

Few companies rely solely on test scores for hiring, however. Almost all intelligence, personality, and vocational interest tests have been found to be poor predictors of good performance in sales work. This fact seems to bear out the notion that training rather than innate sales ability has more to do with selling success.

Companies take the job of hiring salespeople seriously. The process is not only time-consuming, but expensive. One electronics firm estimated that the cost of hiring a salesperson was well in excess of $25 000. Out-of-pocket expenses for the first six months included:

Advertising costs	$ 1 500
Base salary (first 6 months)	12 000
Samples and equipment	2 000
Initial training	750
Miscellaneous expenses	1 500
	$17 750

Add to that the cost of management time spent in the hiring process and sales and profits lost while a territory is inadequately covered, and the costs become enormous.[12]

A company must make its selections carefully for at least one other reason: damage done to customer relations and company reputation by a poor salesperson can take years to overcome.

Managing the Sales Force

With the sales force in place, work can begin on translating the goals and objectives set by management into results. The responsibility for that job usually falls to a sales manager. With so much riding on sales force performance, its management is a crucial task. **Sales management** involves recruiting, selecting, and training salespeople, supervising and motivating them on the job, and evaluating their performance. Why is sales management so important? Because without proper training, efficient assignment of work, and adequate incentives, the sales force drifts aimlessly. Block Drug, makers of Polident denture cleanser and Tegrin shampoo, found that out the hard way.

Twenty-five years ago, Block, lacking competition, regarded its sales reps mainly as order takers. But when Procter & Gamble entered the market with Head & Shoulders, and Warner-Lambert with Efferdent, Block had to alter its strategy. Instead of depending mainly on advertising, the company tried a new push strategy that required an increased sales effort to retailers. Cast in their new roles as creative salespeople, Block's reps floundered. There were three problems. First, they had never been trained in the skills necessary for creative selling. Second, their schedules called for them to maintain a six-calls-a-day average, even though they were assigned more duties. Third, although the company wanted them to increase sales by penetrating a new market—mass merchandising outlets such as discount stores—it offered no pay incentives. The results were disastrous. Sales declined, and shelf space and market share decreased.

Sales Management
Marketing function that embraces recruiting, selecting, and training salespeople, supervising and motivating them, and evaluating their performance.

When Block discovered its mistake, it attacked the problem systematically. The company divided its 10 000 accounts into two groups—large orders and small. Sales reps were assigned to cover only the top 3750 customers; the rest would be contacted by mail. This action freed the sales force to seek out new accounts. But before doing that, sales reps were called in for retraining. Their base pay was increased, and they were given bonuses for meeting management objectives. The new program succeeded. Block reported a 20 percent increase in sales and a 10 percent increase in profits after its reorganization.[13]

The Block example shows how management's involvement and support of sales staff efforts can make the difference in an entire firm's success in the marketplace.

Training

In general, all applicants who are hired go through a formal or informal training program. The length of the program may vary from a few weeks to many months, depending on the complexity of the product or service being sold. Dow Chemical's training program for its industrial sales reps lasts 25 to 30 weeks. At IBM, a training program can take as long as two years. Regardless of the type of company, training is expensive, costing tens of thousands of dollars. The sheer size of a company's investment in training is a good indication of how high a regard managers have for the selling job.

Training can take place on or off the job. Good training programs like Dow's combine the two. One unusual on-the-job program, that of Roche Laboratories, a drug company, requires missionary sales reps to spend two weeks in a hospital learning the regimen of interns and physicians. Training off the job ordinarily occurs in a classroom setting, although learning by doing is stressed. The Xerox Corporation uses **role playing**, in which one person acts the part of the salesperson and the other the customer. The scene is videotaped, so that trainees can evaluate their performance. Some companies also use tapes and cassettes for home self-instruction. Marketing Today 16.2 describes some training programs for telephone sales reps.

During the training program, companies try to impart both knowledge and sales skills. Three sorts of factual information are stressed:

1. *Knowledge of the company* — its history, objectives, sales policies, officers, and organizational setup.

2. *Knowledge of the product* — its physical features and manufacture and the benefits customers can expect.

3. *Knowledge of the competition* — product strengths and weaknesses, price, and the promotional support it receives.

Salespeople must develop the proper attitude about their selling career, the company they work for, the products they sell, the people

Role Playing
Training method for salespeople in which one person acts the part of the salesperson and the other takes the part of the customer.

Marketing Today 16.2

**Training for
Telephone Sales**

Telemarketing is increasingly popular in light of the high cost of sales calls. But many companies are finding that people who sell on the phone could be doing a lot better. To improve performance, they are turning to sales trainers.

One company that offers training in telemarketing is Dylnamics. This company emphasizes relationship building. The nine-hour Dylnamics

workshop trains telemarketers in the principles of behavioural science. They learn specific skills for making positive initial contacts with potential customers and for following up to build receptiveness, interest, and involvement. After the sessions, the salespeople can receive additional counselling — by phone, of course.

Another company, Learning International, teaches courses called Professional Telephone Selling Skills and Telephone Prospecting. These courses combine

written exercises, interactive video and audio, role playing, games, discussions, and self-instructional follow-up. The goal is to teach techniques for overcoming a potential customer's resistance to spending time on the phone with a salesperson and ways to control the conversation.

Sources: Adapted from ''Communication Key to Training TSRs,'' *Marketing News,* August 1, 1986, p. 12; and ''Selling You by Phone,'' *INC,* April 1986, p. 99.

---

they work with, and their customers. Enthusiasm is essential to be successful at selling. Because salespeople work with little supervision and their assets are time and talent, they must also develop good work habits such as planning, effective time management, and maintenance of thorough records. Pointers are often provided in training sessions.

In addition, sales reps are also expected to learn a general approach to selling. Two approaches are often taught—the AIDA theory of selling and the want-satisfaction theory.

The AIDA Theory

Chapter 14 described the communication theory, which suggests that promotional goals be keyed to the stage of product knowledge of a prospective buyer. This theory can also be used to guide a prospect through the various stages (*a*wareness, *i*nterest, *d*esire, and *a*ction) leading to a purchase decision. Some companies prepare a standard presentation for trainees—including prescribed phrases and appropriate pauses and gestures for each stage—which is why the theory is often referred to as the "canned approach."

This approach to selling allows a great deal of company control over the sales message, which means less chance for misunderstanding. But in concentrating on the salesperson's message, it neglects the customer. Not all customers, for instance, pass through all of these stages. Some may already be aware of the product and have an interest. A sales representative who insists on points aimed at bringing the buyer through all four stages may be wasting his time and the customer's. Firms that cannot afford long training periods or that have customers with similar needs and no special problems may find this approach satisfactory, however. Door-to-door salespeople are often trained using this approach.

The Want-Satisfaction Theory

Want-Satisfaction Approach
Sales theory that stresses that the salesperson must first determine what a buyer really wants or needs before launching a sales talk.

Unlike the AIDA theory, the **want-satisfaction approach** stresses that the salesperson must first determine what a buyer really wants or needs before launching a sales talk. This requires skilful questioning and, above all, an ability to listen. Office equipment salespersons, for example, may be accustomed to stressing the operating ease of the photocopiers they are selling. However, they may find after some probing that certain office managers are more concerned with copy quality. If they had pursued their preconceived notion of what buyers wanted, they might have lost an important sale.

Prospects will buy only what is in their self-interest. They are not interested in the product's features — only in the benefits that they will gain from the product. To discover what the prospect wants, the salesperson must use empathy: "To sell Bill Bell what Bill Bell buys, you must see Bill Bell through Bill Bell's eyes."

For most creative and technical selling jobs, training in the want-satisfaction theory is probably best. At this level, salespeople can expect to encounter a wide range of customers with different problems. A formula approach simply may not work. Also, the high-calibre person attracted to such selling positions may be turned off by a pre-established pattern of selling. The want-satisfaction method takes longer to master, but it usually results in more profitable sales.

Job Performance

Selling is a skill like running. Both require training, but no amount of it can substitute for the proving ground — the race for the runner and the sales situation for the salesperson.

A company can enhance the performance of its salespeople by providing them with the proper tools; increasingly, this means computers. Hewlett-Packard, for example, gave its salespeople an edge by equipping each of them with a portable personal computer and software selected to address their top concerns. The software includes a time management program and *Lotus 1-2-3* to help salespeople keep track of accounts. The company is also planning to make greater use of programs that give sales reps access to information that helps them prepare bids, contact the office, and obtain leads on hot prospects.

HP expects that the computers will accomplish three goals:

1. Increase the amount of time salespeople spend with customers instead of doing paperwork and visiting the office.

2. Increase the company's visibility — customers will remember Hew-

lett-Packard as the company whose sales reps use computers.

3. Improve motivation among salespeople by giving them tools that make them feel more professional.

Initial results suggest that HP is meeting all of these goals.[14]

No two sales are exactly alike in the problems encountered, but the process of selling itself does not vary. It consists of six stages. (See Figure 16.2.) The actual meeting of buyer and seller takes place in the four middle stages—the approach, presentation, handling of objections, and the close. However, the preparation for that meeting in the prospecting stage and the follow-up afterward can be crucial.

Prospecting and Qualifying

Rarely do the builders of better mousetraps find lines waiting outside their doors. They must actively seek out buyers, which is termed **prospecting**. Even order takers in retail stores sometimes prospect. For example, the salespeople in exclusive department stores such as Abercrombie & Fitch keep records of customers who might be interested in seeing designer clothing as it comes in. Finding new accounts is absolutely essential to field sales reps.

There are many new ways of finding new prospects. Sales reps from

Prospecting
Actively seeking out buyers.

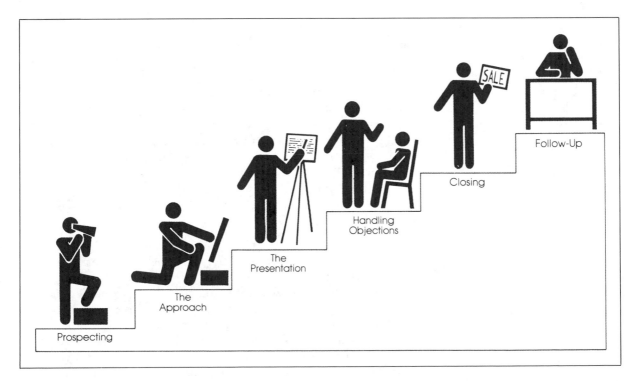

Figure 16.2 The Selling Process

Fuller Brush may use the cold-canvass method of going from door to door. Insurance sales agents and other field personnel often use a less hit-and-miss approach: asking present customers or acquaintances for referrals. Trade association mailing lists and business magazine ads by manufacturers aid salespeople who sell to industry. Some salespeople offer rewards to anyone whose lead develops into a sale.

Not all prospects turn into buyers, however. Consumers may not have the money, or industrial contacts the authority, to purchase. To avoid wasting time in visiting them, salespeople **qualify** prospects. That means they determine whether prospects have the authority to buy and the money to pay for purchases. Qualifying prospects may involve making preliminary phone calls, checking credit, or simply chatting with secretaries. Keeping records on file cards or in other ways is useful if repeat business is expected. If a prospect looks promising, an appointment is made.

The Approach

The sales presentation begins with the **approach**, or **warm-up**. The purpose of the approach is first to secure attention and then to establish rapport and credibility with the client. At Your Service 16.1 describes two approaches to selling personal services.

One unique attention getter used by a very successful insurance salesman involves handing the prospect a $50 bill and informing him that he may keep it if he cannot save at least that much by switching insurance firms. The salesman reports that he has never lost the money. The device is effective because it appeals to curiosity. The offer of a free sample by a door-to-door Avon salesperson has the same effect. A less flashy but still serviceable attention-getting device is dropping the name of a mutual friend or a firm that is known and respected by the client.

Besides getting attention, the approach should also establish rapport between seller and buyer by involving the prospect in the sale. Sometimes this can be accomplished by a pertinent question to the prospect. For example, a sales representative for a jewellery manufacturer might inquire of a retailer, "That display in your front showcase is eye catching, but has it increased sales?"

An approach that is both attention getting and involving is ideal. Consider the following anecdote:

> A timid-appearing young insurance agent entered the office of a dynamic sales manager, shyly approached the desk, and then softly uttered, "You don't want to buy any life insurance, do you?" "No!" snarled the manager. "That's what I was afraid of," sighed the embarrassed agent, starting to leave. "Just a minute," demanded the aggressive manager. "I've been dealing with salespeople all my life, and you, without a doubt, are the worst I've ever seen. Don't you realize that you have to inspire confidence, and that to do it you must have confidence in yourself? To help you gain that confidence to

Qualifying
Determining whether prospects have the authority to buy and the money to pay for the purchases.

Approach (Warm-Up)
Beginning of sales presentation intended to secure attention and to establish rapport and credibility with the client.

The Perils of Selling Yourself

The classic case of selling oneself is through a resume or in a job interview. Selling unusual services requires a more unusual approach — and can introduce some unusual perils.

Ann Haggerty started a service called Rent a Wife, which performs a variety of the tasks that traditional wives have performed: shopping, ironing, planning parties, running errands, watering the plants. Explains Haggerty, ''We do anything to save people time, to make their lives a little nicer, the way things were 40, 50 years ago when home was really home . . . because people had time to do things that enhanced their lives.''

Unfortunately, some people have inferred from the company's name that it performs some intimate services that are not offered. Heavy breathers will be disappointed to find that Rent a Wife installed an answering machine.

Rent-a-Nerd offers quite a different service. Mike MacDonald modelled his service after a Halloween character he invented named Hornby K. Fletcher. Hornby wears outrageous clothes and taped horn-rim glasses, and he fills his pockets with at least 100 pennies, five combs, calculator, transparent ruler, two slide rules, dental floss, styptic pencil, tape, rubber bands, extra shoestring, and a couple of 50-millimetre screws removed from his ankle following a bicycle accident. Who would hire a nerd? Many people seem to need one for parties, bar mitzvahs, office events, and other occasions.

Sources: Adapted from Clarence Petersen, ''Rent a Wife — Up to a Point,'' *Chicago Tribune,* February 8, 1987, sec. 3, p. 1; and ''Rent-a-Nerd Transforms

Mary Herlehy

Former Programmer into the Life of Your Party,'' *Advertising Age,* February 16, 1987, pp. 46–47.

make a sale, I'll sign for a $40,000 policy.'' As he signed, the manager advised, ''You have to learn some effective techniques for approaching customers and then use them.'' ''Oh, but I have,'' replied the young agent enthusiastically. ''I have an approach for almost every kind of businessperson. The one I just used on you was my standard approach for sales managers.''[15]

The agent's approach certainly gained attention. But more important, it involved the prospect by offering him a rather imaginative benefit: the ability to show off his own sales ability by helping the young man out.

The Presentation

On average, a salesperson has between ten minutes and half an hour to convince a prospect to buy.[16] To make maximum use of that time, he or

Presentation
Stage of selling process during which a salesperson translates the features of a product into benefits the customer can understand.

she must plan a **presentation**. The AIDA approach to selling obviously requires planning, but so does the want-satisfaction method. Even if the sales talk is not memorized, the seller can prepare a list of benefits that may interest the customer.

One way of doing this is to jot down the product's features and to translate each of these into a benefit that the client may derive from the feature.[17] For example, an automobile salesperson may translate the product feature "fuel injection system" into the customer benefit "savings on gasoline bills." After doing so for a number of product features, the salesperson can establish an order of importance, draw up a checklist or outline, and commit it to memory. In the sales presentation, the salesperson may choose not to follow the outline, but he or she will remember the points.

In addition to planning what to say, a salesperson should also think of a way to demonstrate the product. *Sales and Marketing Management* once did a survey showing that after three days, people remember only 10 percent of what is said to them; however, they recall 65 percent of what is both told and shown them. Besides aiding memory, demonstrations also help maintain interest during the presentation by inviting the prospect's participation. The salesperson can use demonstration materials as a jumping-off point for questioning the prospect's understanding of a product's benefits. Booklets, flip-charts, slides, movies, and product samples are often used to help make a sales presentation.

More and more today, old-fashioned sample cases are giving way to VCRs or compact portable computers that can be used to display products. The new electronic sales tools often serve two purposes. On the one hand, video presentations can quickly and precisely show off a complicated product's assets—often more dramatically than a salesperson can. On the other hand, some companies have begun using video equipment to give a presentation the "something extra" that distinguishes its product from those of the competition. Said one marketing executive of a soft-drink company, "The ability to interact in a sales meeting is an attention-getting device. It's much better than flopping an old printout on the bottler's desk."

But most companies agree that video presentations are no replacement for personal contact. "I'd be fooling myself if I thought the customer was going to stand up and give the salesman an order because of the tape I made," said one senior product specialist. "It's just one part of the [sales] puzzle."[18]

Handling Objections

Someone once defined selling as the art of getting used to the unexpected. Objections are the unexpected in selling. The more experienced the salesperson, the more easily objections can be handled. Five categories of objections are identifiable:

1. *Delay or time objections:* "I have to talk it over with my wife."
2. *Product objections:* "I don't care for that brand."

3. *Vendor objections:* "We always deal with the Squibb Company."

4. *Product service objections:* "You don't have enough service centres for this imported bicycle."

5. *Price objections:* "I can't afford to pay that much for a suit."

For the most part, objections are a healthy sign: they show a prospect is listening. Moreover, they can be overcome. If an objection comes early in the presentation, a salesperson can sidestep it by saying, "I'm coming to that." Sometimes an objection can be turned into a sales point. A prospect who objects to the price of a product may be convinced that its durability is worth the extra cost. In general, it is wise to avoid arguing. Experienced salespeople use the "Yes, but" technique: "I can understand why you feel that way; however. . . ." That technique offers assurance without arousing hostility. Coming to a sales presentation armed with a few answers to the most common objections is also a good idea.

Closing

The point at which a prospect agrees either to buy or not to buy is called the **closing**. Despite the name, a closing does not have to occur at the end of a sales presentation. Salespeople should begin closing from the beginning. They do not sell, the customer buys; therefore, the salesperson should attempt to close after describing each benefit. In order to determine when to close, the salespeople must learn to ask questions to get the prospect's opinions, to check the prospect's reaction, and to determine understanding. Skilful salespeople must become effective listeners as well as empathic talkers.

Salespeople have been known to talk themselves out of a sale by speaking too long. When prospects are ready to buy, they will give a signal. It may be a physical action such as reading the order form. Or it may be a simple statement or question: "When can you make delivery?" The signal is not always clear, so a salesperson may have to make several trial closes during the course of the transaction. Some well-tested closing techniques are listed in Table 16.2.

Not all closes are equally successful with every customer. And some customers may turn down the offer to purchase flatly. According to one source, the typical encyclopedia salesperson suffers 179 turndowns for every sale.[19] A ratio of five refusals to one sale is much more common.

Follow-Up

A survey to determine why people did not return to the dealer who had sold them their last car revealed that over two-thirds left because they felt the salesperson did not care.[20] The moral: repeat business requires continuing contact with customers. The **follow-up**, as such contact is called, can serve a number of purposes. Customers often experience doubt after a major purchase; they may need reassurance. Also, if special terms were agreed to, such as a rush delivery, the salesperson is respon-

Closing
Point of the selling process at which a prospect agrees to buy or decides not to buy.

Follow-Up
Stage of the selling process during which a salesperson checks to see that orders have been filled and the customer is satisfied.

Table 16.2 Closing Techniques

Technique	Description	Example
Direct approach	Ask for the order	When would you like that delivered?
Preference close	Give the prospect a choice	Will that be cash or charge?
Multiple acceptance approach	Obtain a series of agreements	So you like the colour? And the fit seems all right? Would you like me to box it for you?
Special offer close	Provide an inducement	If you order today, I can have it for you by the end of the week.
Last-chance offer	Use when supply is limited	By next week we expect to be out of this special purchase.
List of features close	Summarize the benefits	The machine can produce twice the output of your present equipment and in the long run will save you money.
Fair-minded approach	Compare advantages and disadvantages	You may have to sacrifice now to pay for this house, but you'll pay no more rent and someday the house will be yours.
Assumption close	Assume the buyer will purchase	To save us time, I've written up this order.

Tickler File
Reminder file, often composed of cards, containing data on a sale and times to call back.

sible for checking them. And, for a servicing problem, the sales rep is often the customer's only contact in the company. So the follow-up call, a few days or a few weeks after the sale, can solve problems and create goodwill. To remind themselves, salespeople sometimes keep a **tickler file,** composed of cards containing data on the sale and times to call back.

Follow-up calls can also be useful in determining why a sale was lost. One marketing director at Sperry Rand, after losing a major sale of computers, returned to the buyer. He discovered that the sale had fallen through because he had failed to make clear how the buyer's present equipment could be converted to work with the new computers. As a result of the follow-up, Sperry Rand developed a series of conversion tools for their sales reps aimed at solving the problem.[21]

To keep customers, a salesperson must know the customers well, handle complaints promptly, serve customers thoroughly, and show appreciation of their business.

Compensation

Good salespeople are among any company's greatest assets. Consequently, developing a compensation plan that attracts and motivates effective sales personnel, and then keeps them from seeking greener pastures elsewhere, is one of a sales manager's most important responsibilities. Sales personnel are usually compensated in one of three ways: straight salary, commission, or some combination.

Straight Salary
Pay plan under which salespeople are guaranteed a regular income.

About 17 percent of all companies use a **straight salary** plan that guarantees salespeople a regular income.[22] It is widely used in industries in which a salesperson has to perform functions other than creative selling. For example, a salesperson for Chanel perfumes may be charged with the task of arranging attractive displays in major department stores. An order taker in the field, such as a beer wholesaler who must cover a great number of stores and whose main function is restocking rather than finding new accounts, may also receive a straight salary. Straight salaries are relatively easy for management to administer, but they may not motivate salespeople to do their best.

Sellers who are expected to create new business may work solely on **commission**, receiving a percentage of sales. The selling staff of clothing manufacturers commonly receives commissions for displaying and selling sample lines. Commissions spur sales and help control costs. A firm with a 5 percent commission plan is assured that its selling costs will approximate 5 percent of sales. But straight commissions are not widely favoured by sales reps themselves because most want more financial stability.

When salespeople must divide their time equally between selling and nonselling activities, a salary plus commission or bonus is best. A commission represents payment on a percentage of sales, whereas a bonus is paid as a flat fee. Most industries use a combination plan of some sort, typically 80 percent salary and 20 percent commissions.[23] When Green Giant converted to sales plus bonus, it offered its food brokers bonus points for exceeding quotas of cases sold. At the end of the year, points were converted into sizeable lump-sum payments. The plan was an effective motivator.[24]

Selling is one of the few careers in which the amount of effort expended is most clearly reflected in a person's paycheque. In some industries the top salespeople routinely earn six-figure incomes—often more than the company's president.

Besides compensating employees with money, companies can reward them in other ways. They can offer benefits such as insurance, paid vacations, a company car, and a pension. In addition, compensation can include such intangibles as self-respect, opportunity for advancement, and recognition inside and outside the organization.[25]

Commission
Pay plan under which salespeople are paid a percentage of the sales they close.

Motivation

Selling can be exhilarating or deflating. The high of closing a large sale may be followed by weeks of depressing, flat refusals. The effort of catering to other people's needs can be exhausting. Conventional wisdom has often held that "the key to motivating salespeople is money," but recent studies have shown that the task is not that simple.[26]

While no one would deny that a compensation plan that rewards sales performance is a powerful motivating factor, other psychological issues are also important. Because good salespeople typically have strong needs for accomplishment, it is critical that they be able to see the correlation

Sales Task Clarity
The visible relationship between a salesperson's efforts and sales results.

between their efforts and sales results. This relationship has been termed **sales task clarity**. Designing a system in which sales tasks are clear often presents a real challenge to even the most able sales manager.

A drug company salesperson, for example, spends a great deal of time calling on doctors to educate them about the advantages of a new medicine. But without a later audit of prescriptions written by those doctors for that product and competing ones, it is hard to determine if a sale was ever made. This can be extremely frustrating to a salesperson who has no way of knowing if sales efforts are bearing fruit.

Recognizing this problem, sales managers should strive to find ways in which to set goals that are as concrete as possible. Even in ambiguous situations, such as those faced by drug retailers, it is possible to set specific objectives and enhance feedback. Salespeople might be asked to add five new qualified prospects to an account list each month, for example, or computerized systems might be designed to track sales more effectively.

Sales task clarity has been found to be 50 percent more important in determining motivation than innate personality traits such as need for achievement. And it is nearly three times as important as the type of pay plan a company offers.[27]

Once salespeople meet the objectives set out for them, they should be recognized and rewarded. Sales contests, "salesperson of the month" and "most interesting sale of the week" awards are ways some companies recognize and motivate salespeople.

Evaluation

Salespeople lead independent lives. Still, they need guidance, and their performance must be evaluated to determine who deserves rewards and who requires help. Both sales reps and managers have a role in measuring performance.

The Sales Manager's Role

Sales Quota
Quantitative measure of the effectiveness of salespeople.

Sales quotas are quantitative measures of the effectiveness of salespeople. They may be expressed as goals to be reached, levels of minimum performance, or ceilings not to be exceeded. Sales managers establish quotas on the basis of past records and sales forecasts. Table 16.3 describes common types of sales quotas, with examples.

In the past, sales-volume quotas expressed in dollar amounts were the standard measuring stick. Managers discovered, however, that large sales do not always mean large profits. Some products may cost a great deal to sell in relation to what they return. Sales personnel who sell many products that return different rates of profit are now given gross-profit quotas instead. Gross-profit quotas encourage them to sell high-profit products rather than low-profit items that may be easier to sell.

Table 16.3   Measurements of Sales Effectiveness

Type	Description	Example
Sales-volume quota	Sets amount to be sold in dollars or units	Sales rep will sell $100 000 or 5000 cases
Gross-profit quota	Measures profitability of goods sold	Sales rep will return $50 000 in profit
Activity quota	Sets number of calls to be made, orders to be gotten, displays set up, and so on	Sales rep will make 4 calls a day, bring in 2 new orders a week, set up 6 special displays, and so on
Expense quota	Limits the amount sales rep can spend	Sales rep can spend up to $10 000 in travel, lodging, food, and so on this year

The two other quotas in Table 16.3 — activity and expense quotas — also aid in the evaluation of the sales force. But they should not be used alone to measure effectiveness. Sales reps can make their records look better by increasing calls per day, for example, but the added calls may produce no further sales and may actually hurt sales by preventing the reps from giving their existing accounts adequate attention.

The Salesperson's Role

Quotas can be gross exaggerations or reasonable measures of what a salesperson can be expected to produce. Effective sales managers keep in touch with field sales reps so that they know what is reasonable. Reports are one way of doing so. Most field sales personnel are required to file, on a weekly or monthly basis, call reports of their visits to prospects and expense reports detailing costs of meals, hotels, transportation, and so forth. Some salespeople also file reports on product complaints, lost orders, and market conditions.

The number one complaint of sales forces has been that there is too much paperwork. New technology seems destined to make that complaint obsolete. As more companies invest in computer systems that are capable of "talking" to one another, "paperless ordering" is becoming more common.[28]

In other companies, salespeople can update computer records daily by making a simple phone call from the field. The computer can then analyze the cost of each call, the cost of each customer, the cost of serving each territory, and the relationship between the cost of a particular sales call and the profit it generates. This can help a sales manager decide which customers to concentrate on, how frequently to call on them, and how much money to spend servicing an account.[29]

Part Five Promotion Strategy

Chapter Replay

1. **Under what circumstances is personal selling most important in the marketing mix?**

   Personal selling is likely to be most important when consumers are geographically concentrated and relatively few; when the product is expensive, technically complex, custom-made, requires special handling, and involves trade-ins; when the price is relatively high; and when the marketing channels are relatively short.

2. **What are the basic types of sales jobs?**

   Classified by degree of creativity, sales jobs include merchandise deliverers, order takers, missionaries, technical salespeople, and creative salespeople.

3. **What decisions must an organization make with regard to its sales force?**

   The organization must establish goals for the sales force, decide what size force the company requires, and determine how the sales force should be established.

4. **How can the sales manager organize the sales force?**

   The manager can organize the sales force by territory, by product, by market, or by some combination of these. In so doing, the manager must consider how much territory each salesperson can cover effectively.

5. **How do companies screen applicants for sales positions?**

   To screen applicants, companies use application forms, job interviews, and various tests.

6. **What are the tasks of the sales manager?**

   The sales manager recruits, selects, and trains salespeople; supervises and motivates them on the job; designs compensation plans that will attract and keep effective personnel; and evaluates the sales force's performance.

7. **What are the stages of the selling process?**

   The stages of the selling process are prospecting and qualifying, the approach, the presentation, handling objections, closing, and follow-up.

8. **How are salespeople compensated?**

   Sales personnel are usually compensated with straight salary, straight commission, or — most commonly — some combination of the two. In addition, companies offer salespeople benefits and intangible rewards.

9. **How do sales managers evaluate the performance of salespeople?**

   Managers measure the salesperson's performance against quotas, including sales-volume quotas, gross-profit quotas, activity quotas, and expense quotas.

Key Terms

approach (warm-up)	qualifying
closing	role playing
commission	sales management
creative salespeople	sales quota
follow-up	sales task clarity
merchandise deliverer	straight salary
missionary	technical salespeople
order taker	tickler file
presentation	want-satisfaction
prospecting	approach

Discussion Questions

1. For each of the following products, identify whether personal selling or advertising is likely to play a more important role in the promotional mix.

    a. Specialized accounting and tax preparation software that is geared to a doctor's or lawyer's private practice and, among other things, prepares tax returns.

    b. Relatively unsophisticated spreadsheet software that competes on the basis of price and adaptability to many situations (which also means that the user has to work harder to apply it to a situation).

    c. Soft drinks.

2. What are the types of sales positions? Which type would a company likely hire to sell an innovative financial service it has just developed?

3. A trust company is planning to hire telephone sales reps to sell individual retirement accounts. Besides a goal for the volume of new accounts, what other objectives might the bank establish for the sales reps?

4. How do companies use test scores in screening applicants for sales positions?

5. Liza Dooalot is the new sales manager for Long Life Insurance Company. Her boss, Jack Cracker, gave her information about two sales training programs and suggested that she select one of these for training the company's salespeople. One of the training programs uses the AIDA theory; the other uses the want-satisfaction theory. Which would you recommend that Liza use?

6. John Dough got a summer job selling encyclopedias. He practised

his presentation over and over until he could deliver it flawlessly. He researched neighbourhoods and picked one in which he thought sales would be best. Then he rang his first doorbells. When someone answered the door, John would say, "Hi! Please let me show you these encyclopedias." After a number of days of trying, John found that no one would give him a chance to deliver his presentation. What in John's technique might account for his lack of success? How might he improve his technique?

7. What are some signs that a prospect is interested in buying? What is likely to happen if a salesperson keeps trying to push a product after that point?

8. The sales reps for Acme Business Forms are paid a straight salary. Lately, sales have declined somewhat, and Acme's sales manager suspects that the problem is the motivation of the sales force. In what ways might the sales manager use compensation and other factors to better motivate the sales reps?

9. Why shouldn't managers use activity quotas and expense quotas alone to evaluate performance?

CASE 16.1

Educational Marketing Associates, Inc.

Educational Marketing Associates, Inc. (EMA) is an organization that sells advertising for desk pads that are distributed free of charge to college and university students. Eric Kingson, founder and president of EMA, realizes that the salespeople have a difficult product to sell. Kingson, faced with a high turnover rate of salespeople, is looking for ways to improve selection, training, motivation, and compensation to decrease turnover.

The Situation

Desk Pad Description

The desk pads distributed by EMA are about 45 by 55 centimetres. Each pad includes a perforated topsheet of coupons to be torn off and kept for use throughout the term and ten identical sheets that actually make up the desk pad. The sheets are fastened to the desk pad base on three sides to prevent corners from curling up.

Approximately one-third of the space on the ten sheets is blank and can be used by the students for reminders or doodling. The remaining two-thirds is used for advertising. An average of 30 advertisers appear on each desk pad. A calendar and sports schedules for the term are also printed on the desk pad.

The Selling Environment

EMA salespeople have a difficult selling job. They are not selling a tangible product such as a computer. The company itself does not have an image comparable to a firm such as IBM. Many of the companies EMA sales representatives call on are small businesses. Often it is difficult to convince the proprietor of a small business that the advantages of participating outweigh the initial cost. Furthermore, many of the businesses in a campus environment come and go, which makes it difficult for a salesperson to establish a stable customer base.

The hours that an EMA salesperson works may be long and unpredictable. For example, many pizza places do not open until the dinner hour. Thus, the salesperson not only has to call on the potential client after normal business hours, but the client may be too busy preparing pizzas to discuss advertising. In fact, the salespeople are constantly faced with discouragement. As many as ten calls may be made before a sale is obtained.

Eric Kingson thinks that the selling situation is partly responsible for EMA's high turnover of salespeople. He has tried to combat the turnover problem by recruiting individuals who could handle frequent rejection and training the recruits to sell this particular product. Furthermore, he has tried to motivate the salespeople effectively and to compensate them adequately to encourage them to stay with the job. However, Kingson has never been satisfied with the results of efforts in any of these areas. The following section describes what he has done or has thought about doing in terms of recruitment, training, compensation, and motivation.

Managing the Sales Force

Kingson has recruited salespeople directly out of school, with limited sales experience, with work experience but not sales experience, and with extensive sales experience. He has interviewed potential sales representatives from campus placement offices and employment agencies. He has placed ads in the newspaper for salespeople and has a bonus program for current employees who bring in recruits who are later hired.

Kingson has experimented with a variety of training programs such as (1) field training — where the trainee observes the supervisor, the supervisor observes the trainee, and a combination of both; (2) a three-day classroom training program, with the trainee then going into the field with or without supervision; and (3) a week-long, intensive training session with video presentations, role playing, and other techniques.

Kingson has tried several methods of compensation, including straight commission, no draw; draw against commission; straight salary; and salary plus bonus. Kingson has never given salespeople expense accounts, but he has tried car allowances, car and food allowances, and company cars.

Kingson believes that one of the useful methods of motivating salespeople is through recognition. EMA, therefore, publishes a weekly newsletter to publicize the performance of the top salesperson of the week. Each week, the best performing salesperson wins a gift certificate to a local restaurant. Monthly contests are also held. The salesperson of the month, the super salesperson of the month, and the sales trainee of the month are all recognized and awarded prizes.

Focal Topics

1. What are the advantages and disadvantages of the compensation alternatives Eric Kingson has tried? Which compensation plan do you recommend (you may develop a new plan)?

2. Suggest several ways to improve the morale and motivation of the sales force at EMA.

3. Give your recommendations on how recruiting and training procedures at EMA might be improved.

CASE 16.2

Hyde-Phillip Chemical Company

Michael Claxton, a recent marketing graduate, has been assigned the task of evaluating Hyde-Phillip Chemical Company's methods of selling the firm's products. Hyde-Phillip currently utilizes a mix of company salespersons, merchant wholesalers, and agent wholesalers to present its products to current and potential users. While this combination of selling forces is somewhat unusual, it reflects the orientation of management over time to the relative values of alternative forms of sales representation. Claxton's challenge is to review the data that has been gathered on the three types of sales efforts, determine if additional information is needed, and make recommendations as to what changes, if any, should be made in the firm's approach to sales representation.

Information on the Company

Hyde-Phillip was formed in the early 1960s through the merger of Hyde Industrial Chemicals and Phillip Laboratories. Both firms had a broad range of experience in the development and production of certain types of chemicals and related supplies for a variety of industrial users. While the two firms had a few overlapping product lines, each brought to the merger some exclusive product offerings. The resulting combination of the two firms yielded a new organization capable of marketing a com-

Source: This case has been edited from an earlier one that appeared in *Cases for Analysis in Marketing*, by W. Wayne Talarzyk. Copyright © 1985 by CBS College Publishing. Reprinted by permission of Holt, Rinehart & Winston, Inc.

plete line of chemicals for industrial use.

Prior to the merger, Hyde Industrial Chemicals had utilized a group of industrial distributors (merchant wholesalers) to market its products. Phillip Laboratories, on the other hand, had several manufacturers' agents (agent wholesalers) who sold its product offering. The new firm, after the merger, retained some of the industrial distributors and some of the manufacturing agents and then began to develop its own sales force.

Today, Hyde-Phillip serves 30 sales territories within three regions, using its own sales force of 50 individuals (6 women and 44 men), 9 industrial distributors, and 9 manufacturers' agents. The 50 salespeople are about evenly allocated across 12 of the sales territories. Each of the industrial distributors and manufacturers' agents has exclusive selling rights in one of the 18 remaining sales territories. Individual distributors and agents have 5 to 30 people working for them and many represent other noncompeting manufacturers. The 30 sales territories were originally established to represent areas of approximately equal sales potential for Hyde-Phillip's products.

Data on Sales Territories

As a first step in beginning his analysis, Claxton asked his assistant to compile the available information on each of the 30 sales territories. This information is presented in coded form in the accompanying table.

In terms of level of sales, 9 territories have annual sales in excess of $2 million, 15 have sales between $1 and $2 million, and 6 have sales less than $1 million. As already indicated, in 12 of the territories the firm is represented by its own sales force, and industrial distributors and manufacturers' agents each represent the company in 9 territories.

Based on estimates provided by the sales support department, 12 of the territories make extensive use of the available sales support programs, 12 are moderate users, and 6 are light users. Each of the firm's territories falls into one of three geographic divisions—Eastern, Central, and Western. As indicated in the table, each of these divisions includes 10 sales territories.

Claxton's initial reaction was that the firm should consider replacing part of its own sales force and the manufacturers' agents with more industrial distributors. He is concerned, however, with what other variables should be taken into account to more fully analyze and evaluate Hyde-Phillip's current approach to sales representation.

Focal Topics

1. From the perspective of Hyde-Phillip, discuss the relative advantages and disadvantages of each of the following forms of sales representation: company sales force, industrial distributors, and manufacturers' agents.

Available Data on Sales Territories

Territory Number	Level of Sales (millions of dollars)	Type of Representation	Use of Sales Support	Geographic Location
1	$1–2	Company	moderate	Eastern
2	<$1	Company	light	Eastern
3	$1–2	Ind. distributor	extensive	Western
4	>$2	Company	extensive	Western
5	$1–2	Mnfrs' agent	extensive	Western
6	$1–2	Company	moderate	Western
7	<$1	Mnfrs' agent	moderate	Eastern
8	>$2	Ind. distributor	extensive	Central
9	$1–2	Company	moderate	Central
10	$1–2	Company	moderate	Eastern
11	>$2	Ind. distributor	extensive	Western
12	>$2	Company	extensive	Central
13	$1–2	Ind. distributor	moderate	Central
14	$1–2	Mnfrs' agent	moderate	Western
15	>$2	Company	moderate	Eastern
16	$1–2	Mnfrs' agent	moderate	Central
17	$1–2	Company	light	Western
18	>$2	Ind. distributor	extensive	Central
19	$1–2	Mnfrs' agent	moderate	Central
20	<$1	Company	light	Central
21	>$2	Mnfrs' agent	extensive	Eastern
22	$1–2	Ind. distributor	extensive	Eastern
23	<$1	Mnfrs' agent	extensive	Western
24	<$1	Company	light	Central
25	<$1	Ind. distributor	light	Western
26	>$2	Ind. distributor	extensive	Central
27	$1–2	Company	moderate	Central
28	>$2	Ind. distributor	extensive	Eastern
29	$1–2	Mnfrs' agent	light	Eastern
30	$1–2	Mnfrs' agent	moderate	Eastern

2. Based upon the data in the case, which form of sales representation seems "best" for Hyde-Phillip at this time?

3. Based on your analysis of the case, what would be your specific recommendations to the company at this time?

Case for Part Five

Chrysler Corporation

"He's an American legend, the tough-talking, straight-shooting businessman who brought Chrysler back from the brink and in the process became a media celebrity, a newsmaker, and a man many have urged to run for President." This description appears on the front flap of the cover of *Iacocca, An Autobiography*. This man, when removed as president of Ford Motor Company, was told by his wife, Mary, "Don't get mad, get even."

As part of the revival of Chrysler, and, in some ways as part of getting even, Lee Iacocca signed many of Chrysler's print advertisements and appeared in many of the company's television advertisements.

Spokesperson Iacocca

In his autobiography, Iacocca states that he was asked to personally appear in television advertisements shortly after he came to Chrysler. At that time, several companies were using their presidents as company spokespersons. But acting on instinct and professional advice from friends, Iacocca declined. He did not feel that the time was appropriate.

About a year later, after he had signed some of Chrysler's print advertisements, the firm's advertising agency, Kenyon & Eckhardt, asked him to reconsider appearing in the television advertisements. Their logic: "Everyone thinks Chrysler's going bankrupt. Somebody has to tell them you're not. The most believable guy to do that would be you. First, you're well known. And second, the viewers know very well that after you make the commercial, you have to go back to the business of making the cars you touted. By appearing in these ads, you're putting your money where your mouth is."

At first, Iacocca only delivered tag lines to the commercials, such as "I'm not asking you to buy one of our cars on faith, I'm asking you to compare" and "If you buy a car without considering Chrysler, that'll be too bad—for both of us."

Sources: Lee Iacocca with William Novak, *Iacocca, An Autobiography* (Bantam Books, 1984); "100 Leading National Advertisers," *Advertising Age*, September 4, 1986, pp. 63+; Michelie Krebs, "Chrysler Credit To Test Two Plans," *Automotive News*, March 24, 1986, p. 32; and Raymond Serafin and Patrick Strnad, "Iacocca Back in Pitchman Seat for '87," *Advertising Age*, September 22, 1986, pp. 50+.

Later his statements became bolder: "You can go with Chrysler, or you can go with someone else — and take your chances." In one line, which was his own creation and which has been parodied in many ways, he said, "If you can find a better car — buy it." As conditions continued to improve at Chrysler, Iacocca began to do fewer television commercials and finally stopped completely.

Promotional Activities

Over the years, Chrysler has used a variety of promotional activities to reach consumers. Some examples include the following:

- At one point when sales were low, Chrysler's advertising agency came up with: "We want to get you to consider a Chrysler product. Come in and test-drive one of our cars. If you do, and if you then end up buying a car from one of our competitors, we'll give you fifty bucks just for considering us."

- Another marketing first: "Buy one of our cars, take it home, and within thirty days, if you don't like it *for any reason*, bring it back and we'll refund your money." The only catch was a depreciation charge of $100, since the car could not be resold as new. The total number of returns worked out to less than two-tenths of 1 percent.

- The company placed major emphasis on its five-year, 80 000-kilometre warranty program, with emphasis on "setting new standards of performance."

- In July 1986, the company set new sales incentives of 5.5 percent financing or up to $1500 rebates on most models.

- Chrysler Credit Corporation, the automotive financing arm of Chrysler, tested two financial programs: balloon note financing and variable-rate financing. With balloon note financing, the buyer makes monthly payments that are lower than with traditional financing for a specified number of months. A lump sum (or balloon payment) is due at the end of the period. The consumer has the choice of paying the lump sum and keeping the car or turning it over to the financial institution. With variable rate financing, the interest rate on the loan is adjusted periodically, based on market conditions, with the number of monthly payments increased or reduced.

Recent Advertising

In the fall of 1985, Chrysler continued the theme, "All the Japanese you need to know," to advertise its 1986 vehicles imported by Mitsubishi Motors. The objective was to set its captive imports apart from its domestically built cars by positioning them as Japanese.

Colt four-door sedans and a new, four-wheel-drive Colt Vista received extra television and print advertising that was aimed predominantly at women.

According to *Advertising Age*, "Chrysler's September-breaking ads for 1986 models were patriotic and comparative. The positioning reflected thinking that Chrysler faces a long-term competitive disadvantage against imports. Chrysler used more daytime and prime-time TV, radio, and cable TV in 1986."

In terms of its overall corporate objective, Chrysler's aim was to "be the best." Plymouth's theme was "Born in America," and Dodge focused again on being "An American Revolution." Advertisements for Chrysler stated, "Chrysler technology makes 'Made in America' mean something again." The Canadian arm of Chrysler initiated an indigenous marketing campaign and one of its most memorable slogans was "Chrysler Canada. Changing the landscape."

Iacocca Returns

To show that the company is not "resting on our laurels," chairman Lee Iacocca returned as spokesperson for Chrysler's 1987 advertising program. In one advertisement for a 1988 luxury model, Iacocca said, "It ain't cheap but neither is caviar." The Maserati-built Chrysler luxury coupe was priced at around $30 000.

Specific corporate advertising that featured Iacocca focused on the new Chrysler LeBaron coupe and convertibles, new compacts Plymouth Sundance and Dodge Shadow, new mid-size pickup Dodge Dakota, and the restyled Dodge Daytona.

"Best-built, best-backed American cars and trucks" remained as the basic advertising theme in all corporate and divisional print advertisements. Corporate advertisements used these lines: "Working together to be the best" and "Fastest-growing car and truck company in America."

Focal Topics

1. How important do you think Iacocca's presence in Chrysler's advertising was in turning the company around?

2. What are the main reasons a consumer chooses one automobile over another?

3. How important do you think advertising is for Chrysler at the corporate level, at the divisional level, and at the dealer level?

4. What advertising-promotion recommendations would you make to Chrysler?

5. Do you think it is a good move for Chrysler to again use Iacocca for its advertising? Why, or why not?

Special Marketing

Chapter 17

In this chapter, you will learn:

- The differences between foreign trade, foreign marketing, and multinational

  marketing.

- Ways in which businesses can penetrate foreign markets.

- Economic characteristics marketers consider in evaluating international markets.

- Some cultural differences marketers must be aware of.

- How governments affect a marketer's involvement in a country.

- Limitations on researching foreign markets.

- Issues marketers must consider in developing products for international markets.

- The pricing decisions international marketers must make.

- The major types of intermediaries Canadian companies use to place their products

  in foreign markets.

- Reasons marketers may have to modify promotions for foreign markets.

Bombardier Goes Global

In 1965, when Laurent Beaudoin became president of Bombardier Inc., the company was so small that he could stand at his office door and watch snowmobiles coming off the assembly line. Bombardier then employed 700 people at Valcourt, Quebec, and company engineers called Beaudoin ''the test pilot'' because he usually tried a newly designed machine before approving production. Now, Bombardier employs 20 000 people in five countries and manufactures products that include aircraft, railcars and military vehicles, as well as snowmobiles. Beaudoin, the architect of that growth, says that his goal has been to convert a family firm into a major force in the world. ''Most of our market has always been outside Quebec,'' adds Beaudoin. ''That has expanded the horizons of our people and given us the opportunity to think on a global basis.''

Beaudoin says that Bombardier's success has inspired other Quebeckers to enter business. He also maintains that Bombardier is one of the few Canadian companies positioned to take advantage of the economic unification of Europe in 1992. The company acquired a Belgian manufacturer of railway cars in 1986. Then, in June 1989, Bombardier purchased Belfast-based Short Bros. PLC, an aircraft manufacturer and Northern Ireland's largest employer.

Bombardier grew out of a Valcourt automobile garage founded by J. Armand Bombardier, a remarkable inventor who began building powered sleds as a teenager in the 1920s. He built a succession of tracked all-terrain vehicles in the 1930s. By the 1950s, the Bombardier Ski-Doo had established the company as a world leader in its field.

Its diversification strategy has made Bombardier the largest manufacturer of mass-transit vehicles in North America. It acquired the Belgian company, Constructions ferroviares et métalliques (BN), in order to penetrate the European rail-vehicle market, which is four times larger than North America's. It entered the

Brian Willer/Maclean's

aerospace industry in 1986 by purchasing Canadair Inc. of Montreal, which produces the Challenger corporate jet, from the Canadian government. Short Bros. gives Bombardier a foothold in the European aerospace industry.

Beaudoin says that the company now wants to expand into Asia, in conjunction with its new global push, but wants also to remain an independent, Quebec-based company. The roots of Bombardier remain in the village of Valcourt, where Ski-Doos are still manufactured. But Beaudoin now works on the seventeenth floor of a downtown Montreal office tower and, from there, he has a new view of the world.

Companies in many industries have found their future in foreign markets. This chapter describes some of the issues marketers confront in selling across national boundaries.

Source: Adapted from ''Building for the Future with a World-wide View,'' *Maclean's*, December 25, 1989, p. 20.

Marketing Abroad

Anyone familiar with pocket calculators knows the name Hewlett-Packard. The firm specializes in producing the Cadillacs of electronic devices. The company was founded 45 years ago by two young men with only $538 and a garage for working space. Today, it designs over 3000 products in 22 plants. An important reason for the firm's success is its expansion into overseas markets.

Hewlett-Packard's international marketing activity began in the late 1940s when the firm exported a few products outside North America. Overseas exports grew until they reached 10 percent of sales volume ten years later. Sensing a vast, untapped market in Europe, the company then increased its foreign commitment by setting up a marketing headquarters in Geneva, Switzerland, with its own sales force. To supply the increased demand, the firm also established factories in Germany and England. By 1980, foreign sales—many of them from German-developed products—were larger than domestic sales.[1]

Hewlett-Packard's experience is typical of those firms that engage in **international marketing**, or the performance of marketing activities across national boundaries.[2] Most international companies start as domestic producers, gradually explore export markets, and eventually begin production inside foreign markets.

Global exports of goods and services have grown much faster than the value of total production in all industrial countries in the postwar period.[3] In 1988, world trade in goods alone exceeded $3.24 trillion (Cdn.).[4] Services are an important and rapidly growing area of international trade (unfortunately, statistics about the international exchange of services are scanty).

The Canadian Situation

International trade is exceedingly important to the Canadian economy. In 1988, the value of Canadian exports totalled $134 billion, representing 27 percent of its gross national product. By contrast, the United States exported 8.4 percent of GNP, the United Kingdom 23.5 percent of GNP, and Japan 12.9 percent of GNP.[5]

The vast majority of Canadian exports—$97.9 billion or 73 percent—went to the United States. Exports to our second largest trading partner, Japan, represented only 6.6 percent of the total, and those to all nations in the European Community totalled $10.7 billion or 8.4 percent. Figures 17.1 and 17.2 illustrate Canada's export and import trade. Canada trades an enormous amount of both goods and services. It has maintained a surplus trade in goods, primarily because of its huge exports of natural resources and semimanufactured goods. This surplus has been offset

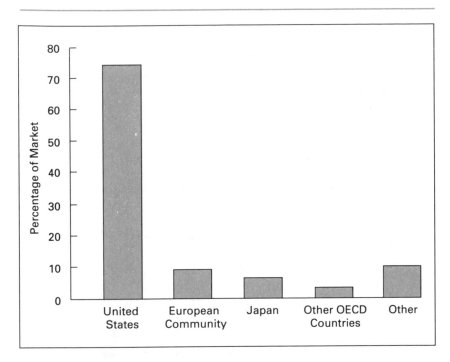

Figure 17.1 Destination of Canadian Exports, 1989

Source: Statistics Canada, *Summary of Canadian International Trade (H.S. Based)*, 1989, cat. no. 65-001, February 1990.

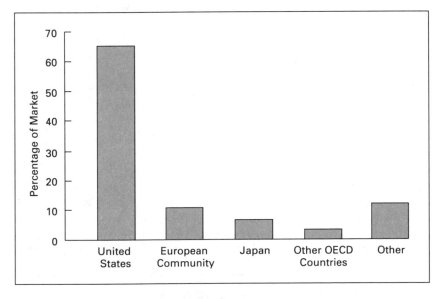

Figure 17.2 Source of Imports, 1989

Source: See Figure 17.1.

recently, however, by a growing deficit of trade in services and the out-flow of profits to foreign investors (for example, nonmerchandise exports). Figure 17.3 graphically depicts the trend of Canada's overall trade balance. Government is placing increasing emphasis on the development of foreign markets for Canadian goods and services in order to reverse this trend.

Reasons for International Marketing

Firms seek markets overseas for two reasons: because they are pushed out of their home markets or because they are pulled by promising market prospects abroad.[6]

Many factors push companies out of domestic markets. Heavy compe-

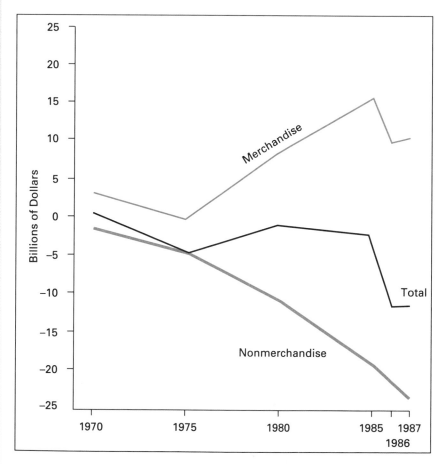

Figure 17.3 Canada's Overall Trade Balance, 1970–1987

Source: See Figure 17.1, November 1988.

tition at home is one of them. Fast-food outlets are found at nearly every North American intersection, so the companies look to Europe and Asia, where they are still a novelty. Some of that competition comes from abroad. For example, as imported automobiles gained popularity in Canada and the United States, the response of North American automakers included increased development of overseas markets.

Another push can come from unfavourable government policies. High corporate taxation and minimum-wage laws have contributed to the decisions of Canadian manufacturers to establish plants abroad. Finally, excess production capacity at home may push firms into selling abroad. Canadian farmers engage in international marketing because of surplus production.

The major force pulling manufacturers abroad is the market potential of other countries. Canadian companies have a very small domestic market. In order to create economies of scale and expand profits, they seek export markets for their products. The easiest and least expensive market for Canadians to penetrate is the U.S. market, which represents 25 percent of the world's purchasing power.[7]

Export markets in less-developed regions can extend product life-cycles. Canadian tobacco manufacturers, faced with a declining domestic market, have found the demand for cigarettes growing in some Third World countries as disposable incomes rise in those countries. Concurrently, the relative affluence and large number of North American buyers leads many foreign marketers to target North American markets (see Figure 17.4 for an advertisement targeted to U.S. consumers).

Modes of International Marketing

International marketing is a complex field because it can encompass a number of activities.[8] The term used to be a synonym for **foreign trade**, which involves home production and the export of products across national boundaries. When Hewlett-Packard first started selling abroad, its international marketing was limited to foreign trade.

But many companies, including Hewlett-Packard, have discovered that both sales and profits can be improved by operating within the foreign country where goods are to be sold. This mode of international marketing is known as **foreign marketing**. Firms that engage in foreign marketing generally have a serious international commitment, and their organizational structure usually expands to reflect this.

A company that decides to market in one foreign country usually expands to several countries eventually. At this point, international marketing activities must be co-ordinated for maximum efficiency. Integrating marketing activities carried out in a number of countries is referred to as **multinational marketing**. The difference between firms that engage in foreign trade and foreign marketing, on the one hand, and those involved in multinational marketing, on the other, is worth emphasizing.

Foreign Trade
Home production and the export of products across national boundaries.

Foreign Marketing
Operating within the foreign country where goods are to be sold.

Multinational Marketing
In contrast to foreign marketing: Integrating marketing activities carried out in a number of countries.

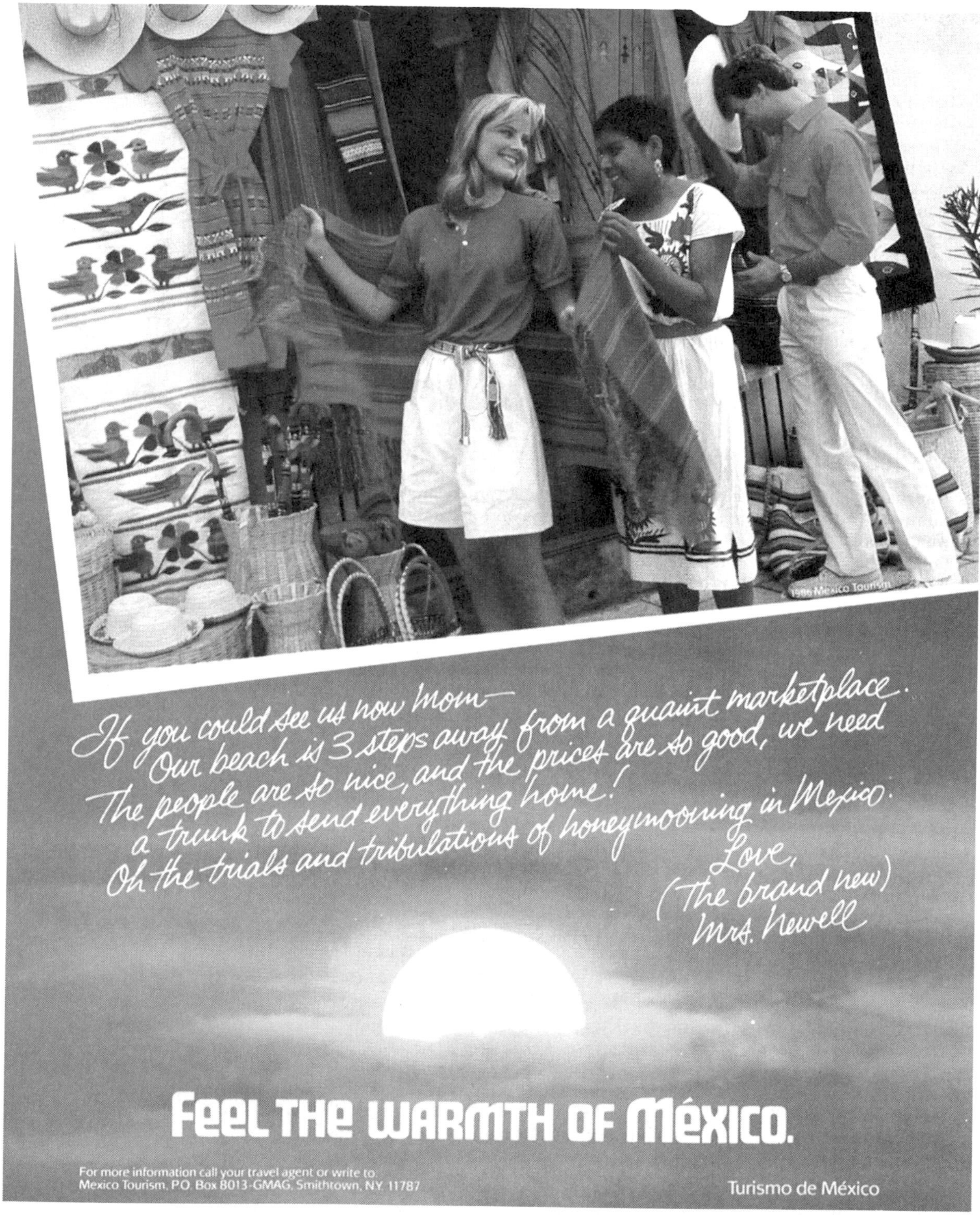
1986 Mexico Tourism
If you could see us now Mom—
Our beach is 3 steps away from a quaint marketplace.
The people are so nice, and the prices are so good, we need
a trunk to send everything home!
Oh the trials and tribulations of honeymooning in Mexico.
Love,
(The brand new)
Mrs. Newell
FEEL THE WARMTH OF MÉXICO.
For more information call your travel agent or write to:
Mexico Tourism, P.O. Box 8013-GMAG, Smithtown, NY 11787
Turismo de México

Secretaria de Turismo

Figure 17.4 Targeting a Relatively Affluent Market — U.S. Consumers

Multinational corporations not only trade with but operate out of several countries and obtain much of their profit from such operations. Furthermore, they make decisions based on alternatives available anywhere in the world. For example, they convert their cash on hand into currencies that are strongest. And they produce component parts wherever costs are lowest. Thus Ford assembles its cars in the United States, but it produces engines in Germany, electrical systems in Canada, and transmissions in England.

True multinational corporations no longer emphasize the distinction between home and foreign markets, although most have a national identity. Because the United States enjoyed such rapid economic expansion in the 1950s and 1960s, many of the best-known multinationals are based in that country—examples include General Motors, Exxon, and Hewlett-Packard. About half of all sales by multinationals in the mid-1980s were made by U.S.-based firms. But there are many giant non-U.S. multinationals including Bombardier (Canadian), Sony (Japanese), Shell (British and Dutch), Bayer (German), and Nestlé (Swiss).

Japanese corporations, unlike Canadian and American corporations, have massive funds available for investment and are now buying up companies and real estate around the world, including North America. Ironically, the United States is resisting this perceived threat to its sovereignty in much the way Canadians resisted American investment in the 1960s. Sony's purchase of Columbia Pictures in late 1989 struck deep into the American heart.

Multinational companies are receiving increasing attention. It is important to keep in mind, however, that their mode of operation represents only one type of involvement in international marketing.

Routes of Expansion Abroad

In addition to distinguishing the types of involvement in international marketing, most experts also differentiate the ways that businesses can penetrate foreign markets. The routes of expansion abroad include exportation, licensing, joint ventures, and direct investment. Foreign trade is usually associated with exportation alone. But both foreign trade and foreign marketing can take place by any one or all of those means.

Marketers choose a route based on a variety of considerations, including the amount of time and resources they want to commit and the level of risk they are willing to bear. The different routes also give organizations different degrees of control over the marketing activity abroad. As Figure 17.5 shows, exportation provides a company with the least amount of control and risk, whereas direct investment allows maximum control, increased risk, and the potential for maximum profits.

Exportation

Exporting is usually the first step in international marketing, because it requires the smallest financial commitment. For example, firms with

Stong Control   **Weak Control**

Direct Investment	Joint Venture	Licensing	Exporting (Directly to Buyers)	Exporting (indirectly through Intermediaries)

Figure 17.5   Routes of Entry and Degree of Control

surplus production find exporting a convenient way of ridding themselves of the excess while picking up a contribution to their costs. Or a company that detects a demand for its products overseas may find it worthwhile to hire additional workers or add another shift.

Trading House
Commercial intermediary linking domestic producers and foreign-based purchasers or consumers.

Indirect Export   Firms that engage in exporting may do so indirectly or directly. Those with the least amount of exporting experience usually start indirectly, by using **trading houses**, commercial intermediaries that link domestic products and foreign purchasers or consumers.

Trading houses are very important to the Canadian economy. They handle a sizeable percentage of all the country's exports (13 percent in 1983) and almost half of its exports to countries other than the United States (40 percent in 1983).[9] Trading houses can act as merchants, purchasing goods for their own account, or as agents, receiving a commission or fee for their services. The marketing functions trading houses offer Canadian manufacturers may include market and buyer identification, price negotiation, financial arrangements, shipping arrangements, promotion abroad, and protection against export risks such as unfavourable shifts in exchange rates and political factors. An example of a trading house is Mitsubishi, which purchases Canadian goods for export to Japan. The Canadian manufacturer deals locally with Mitsubishi Canada and treats the transaction as a domestic sale.

Direct Export   Direct exporting occurs when a company takes responsibility for marketing its own products abroad, as Hewlett-Packard did in the opening example. It actively seeks export opportunities and in doing so commits the firm to directing a portion of its resources to serving foreign markets. The firm's risk increases, but so does its control over marketing functions.

Licensing

Licensing
Arrangement under which a company (the licensor) grants a foreign firm (the licensee) the rights to patents, trademarks, and the use of technical processes in exchange for a royalty or fee for use.

A company with a limited amount of money to invest but a need for greater control over marketing may try **licensing**. In this arrangement, a company (the licensor) grants a foreign firm (the licensee) the rights to patents, trademarks, and the use of technical processes in exchange for a royalty or fee for use. Usually the licensor will also agree to provide management assistance.

Some companies use licensing extensively. An automotive equipment manufacturer had almost 500 different licensing agreements in foreign countries, which brought in millions of dollars in royalties and were the source of valuable technical developments.[10] Franchising is a form of licensing that is becoming increasingly popular.

The main advantages of licensing are that a firm risks no capital in granting a licence and that it gains direct access to foreign markets. The latter is especially important, since governments often limit the number of goods from abroad, blocking access to markets by exportation.

One drawback is that control over quality may be limited. Government-owned companies in Egypt produce Pepsi-Cola under licence, and dealers complain it lacks the flavour of beverages produced by private companies.[11] Another disadvantage is that after a time the licensee may adapt the licensed product and become an independent competitor. Japanese companies have done so in the past with transistor radios and are now challenging North Americans in producing power tools, microwave ovens, and outboard motors. Other entry routes are sometimes safer.

Joint Ventures

Companies wishing even more control over marketing may choose a **joint venture**, or partnership with a foreign firm. Both partners invest money and share ownership and control in proportion to their investment. McDonald's Restaurants of Canada Ltd. opened the first McDonald's in the Soviet Union in early 1990. The outlet is operated as a 50-50 joint venture between the Canadian company and Moscow city council's food service administration.[12]

There are also many joint ventures operating in Canada with foreign partners. Quinette Coal in northeastern British Columbia is partially owned by the Japanese steel companies it supplies, and it raised some of its funding from Japanese banks.

A joint venture allows a company to pool expertise and to share risks with another company or to take advantage of another company's existing lines of distribution. Also, because a joint venture can enter a market faster than a new company alone, this arrangement can give a company a head start or at least allow it to keep up in a fast-changing environment. Pooling resources is also important in industries with soaring costs, such as the aircraft industry.

Despite these advantages, not all joint ventures work out well. Dow Chemical Company and Germany's BASF set up a joint venture in the United States; BASF provided the technology to make chemical raw material and fibres, and Dow provided the marketing expertise. Even though the enterprise was making a profit, the partners dissolved it; BASF wanted to expand, while Dow was reluctant to invest further in a venture that made a product—fibres—outside of its main business of chemicals.[13]

This example illustrates one of the major drawbacks of a joint venture: conflicting objectives. Other major disadvantages are the lack of total control and the risk of investment loss. And one partner may use its

Joint Venture
Partnership with a foreign firm under which both partners invest money and share ownership and control in proportion to their investment.

experience in the venture to improve its ability to compete with the other partner.

Nevertheless, firms sometimes are forced into agreeing to partial ownership by government decree. For example, India and the Soviet Union deny foreigners majority ownership of any venture in their countries. Firms may accept such a restriction if they feel a local firm can provide them with needed knowledge of an unfamiliar marketplace.

Direct Investment

Direct Investment
Total control of production and sales of goods in a foreign country.

The highest level of commitment a firm can give to foreign markets is **direct investment** — the establishment of a wholly owned subsidiary providing total control of the production and sale of goods in a foreign country. Firms undertake foreign manufacturing for many reasons including:

1. Sidestepping trade barriers, such as tariffs as well as quotas and other nontariff barriers (all of which are defined later in this chapter).

2. Taking advantage of cheaper labour or materials abroad.

3. Reducing transportation costs.

The United States has invested heavily in foreign countries since World War II. Many of Canada's largest companies, such as General Motors of Canada and Ford Motor Co. of Canada, are wholly owned subsidiaries of U.S. firms.

Up to 1988, U.S. direct investment abroad totalled $327 billion compared to Canadian direct investment abroad of $61 billion.[14] Now Japan is challenging the United States as a world investor. In 1988, direct Japanese investment in Canada was $600 million, while in the United States it amounted to $64 billion, a whopping 52-percent increase over that of the previous year.[15]

Direct investment allows a company superior control over operations. On the other hand, it also exposes a company to expropriation, or seizure, of facilities if hostility develops between the host country and the foreign company. Firms must weigh both benefits and risks before deciding on this route for expanding abroad.

The Environment of Marketing Abroad

In deciding whether to market abroad, a company needs to consider the opportunities and limitations of the international marketplace. This includes the conditions within countries, as well as the broader issues of marketing internationally.

The principles of analyzing the international marketplace are basically the same as those involved in learning about the domestic external environment. The marketer examines economic, cultural, and political/

legal characteristics of the marketplace to identify opportunities and select target markets. Canadian companies marketing to the United States find similarities between the two countries makes the task relatively easy. Nevertheless, in marketing to other countries the process may be more complex. For example, Canadian companies marketing abroad typically have to contend with trade restrictions and agreements, a language barrier, competition among national interests, and attitudes toward foreign companies in general. Thus, the following discussion of economic, cultural, and political/legal characteristics applies some familiar principles to some new situations.

Economic Differences

The world population has passed the 5-billion mark. Fewer than 7 percent of all these people live in North America. Moreover, the population of most of the rest of the world is growing at a faster rate than the North American population. Typically, the more developed and affluent the country, the lower the birth rate. The fastest growth is occurring in oil-producing countries of the Middle East.[16]

But people are considered part of a market only if they have purchasing power. One way to measure this is to use **per-capita income**, which is a country's gross national product divided by its population. Per-capita income figures vary widely among nations. Canada and the United States are among the wealthiest, with a 1987 per-capita income of $15 080 and $18 430 respectively (all figures in U.S. dollars). Switzerland did even better with a per-capita income of $21 250. At the other extreme were Ethiopia at $120 and Chad at $150. According to the World Bank, about half of the world's population live in countries with per-capita incomes of less than $500.[17]

Per-Capita Income
A country's gross national product divided by its population.

This breakdown is important to marketers. If markets are people with money, more than half the world is unattractive for marketing. Some trading in raw materials and agricultural products between less-developed countries and the rest of the world does go on. But direct investment for manufacturing and selling abroad is confined to about a dozen industrialized countries and a handful of other countries that are developing industrially.

Developing countries may, in fact, become increasingly important to marketers in the future. Competition in industrialized countries is becoming so intense that certain developing countries, among them Egypt, Spain, Chile, and China, are beginning to look like attractive and less-crowded markets. That is why Canada Dry, 7-Up, and Coca-Cola are challenging Pepsi-Cola's dominance in Egypt. The market is, as one executive put it, "like a sponge," and it may offset some of the losses soft-drink companies expect to suffer at home because of the shrinking youth market.[18]

Per-capita income should be evaluated with care, as it often hides extremes. In addition, marketers should consider other measures of economic differences. One common classification divides countries according to their industrial structure:[19]

- *Subsistence economies,* in which most people engage in simple agriculture and consume most of their output.

- *Raw-material-exporting economies,* which are rich in natural resources and receive most of their revenue from exporting them.

- *Industrializing economies,* in which manufacturing accounts for about 10 to 20 percent of the economy and a small middle class is forming.

- *Industrial economies,* which are major exporters of manufactured goods and investment funds and have large middle classes.

In considering a classification such as this, marketers assess the kinds of products demanded in the different economies, the prospects for growth, and the likelihood that an economy is shifting from one type to another. As an example, industrializing economies provide a market for selling raw materials to manufacturers and selling luxury goods to those who have become wealthy from the manufacturing. Notably, some industrializing nations — South Korea, for example — also are becoming an important source of competition for manufacturers in industrial economies.

Besides data on income and industrial structure, marketers must also study a country's **economic infrastructure**. That refers to facilities such as paved roads, communication and transportation services, banks, and distribution organizations that make marketing possible.

Outside North America, even in largely industrial countries, the infrastructure is not always well developed. For example, Canadian marketers commonly facilitate sales by allowing customers to charge purchases on credit cards. But in many countries, few consumers have credit cards. This has hampered the expansion of home shopping via cable television.[20]

Economic Infrastructure
Facilities such as paved roads, communication and transportation services, banks, and distribution organizations that make marketing possible.

Cultural Differences

Marketers sometimes assume that the beliefs, values, and customs most familiar to them apply everywhere. When they enter a foreign market, they find themselves in culture shock.

When the Campbell Soup Company first entered the Dutch market, it neglected to notice a difference in customs. Dutch housewives were familiar with canned soups, but not condensed soups, which require adding a can of water. Many failed to read the cooking instructions on the can and complained of the soups' bitter taste. Campbell lost millions in sales before it discovered the problem and ran informational ads.[21]

Failure to take account of cultural differences is responsible for many, if not most, marketing failures abroad. Language, aesthetic perceptions, social organization, and values differ widely from country to country.

Language

Most marketers are aware of language differences when they enter a foreign market. But they are sometimes less conscious of the difficulties of translating expressions from one language to another.

Examples of translation errors are numerous. When the advertising agency for a U.S. chicken processor tried to translate the slogan "It takes a tough man to make a tender chicken" into Spanish, it came out, "It takes a sexually excited man to make a chicken affectionate." And breweries have had their share of problems with Spanish translations. One claimed to sell "the beer that would make you more drunk," and a light beer boasted that it is "Filling. Less delicious."[22] Translating into Asian languages can be particularly challenging, and the mistakes startling. Coca-Cola, for example, once found that it was promoting itself with Chinese characters that translated to "bite the waxy tadpole."[23]

Language can be a very difficult problem when marketers must sell in multilingual countries. The situation is bad enough in a bilingual country like Canada, where labels and packages must be in both English and French. But imagine the problems of marketing in India, where 203 languages and dialects are spoken.

Aesthetic Perceptions

Ideas concerning beauty and good taste are almost as internationally varied as languages. These aesthetic differences also influence marketing.

Consider the meanings people give to various colours. White, often a symbol of joy in this country, is usually associated with mourning in the Far East and is therefore unsuitable for packaging. Major marketing errors have resulted from ignoring the importance of colour. For example, a yellow cologne failed to sell in Africa because consumers associated it with animal urine. Only when the product was tinted green did it succeed.[24]

People's ideas about beauty in design also may vary. One marketing expert has observed that many consumer products have universal appeal in North America, Japan, and the European Community—the countries that account for most of the demand for these goods. Higher education levels and exposure to television have led citizens of these countries to develop similar tastes. Nevertheless, modifications are needed at times. For example, piano interiors are basically the same, but preferences for the exterior vary. In North America, consumers like wood grains, but in Japan, where pianos are used for children's education, consumers prefer black enamel. In contrast, watches and motorcycles sold around the world can have universal designs.[25]

Social Organization

All societies have families in some form, but roles within the family may differ markedly from culture to culture.

Women seldom enjoy equality with men outside industrialized countries, and that can affect marketing. For example, in some less-developed countries, men do the shopping because women are confined to the home. Advertising must therefore appeal to men. Even in many industrialized and developing countries, women's activities outside the home are limited. Thus, in Spain or Turkey, marketers might not be able to draw together a group of working-class women for panel discussions on products.[26]

The role of children in the family also varies from country to country. In North America, because children have a voice in some purchasing decisions, advertising can be directed at them. But in England, children have a more limited role and advertising aimed at them is considered inappropriate.

The social revolution that affects women and the family is, however, beginning to spread worldwide. Therefore, some of the generalizations about social organization that are valid today may break down in the near future. Marketers must be alert to such changes.

Values

The term *value* can refer to a religious or moral belief or merely a practical attitude that sums up a person's experience. Values are perhaps the most variable cultural item discussed thus far, and they too can affect marketing success.

Wendy's would probably have little or no success in India because of the Hindu prohibition against eating beef. Similarly, until recently a drug firm selling contraceptives would encounter difficulties in Latin America, with its large Roman Catholic population. (Now, the threat of AIDS is developing a condom market even in previously restricted areas.) Religious or ethical values sometimes restrict certain kinds of advertising.

The unwitting violation of another culture's beliefs is one sort of dilemma marketers face. A quite different problem arises when marketers are confronted with values their culture finds unethical. For example, in many foreign countries, bribery of officials to cut through red tape is an accepted way of life.

Political and Legal Differences

Regulations governing business vary widely around the world, depending on the political climate of each country. In many countries, the regulations governing business are even more restrictive than Canadian laws. Firms must be aware of political and legal differences before marketing abroad.

Government Policy

Government policies can affect a marketer's involvement in a country. Governments control marketing activities through four major protectionist measures:

1. By imposing **tariffs**—taxes on imports.

2. By setting **import quotas** — restrictions on the number of particular kinds of goods entering a country.

3. By imposing **currency controls** — restrictions on the money that can be taken out of a country.

4. By establishing **nontariff barriers (NTBs)**—invisible tariffs that effectively limit trade without stating a specific excise tax that can be challenged. The numerous examples of NTBs include restrictive health regulations, labelling laws, customs documentation and clearance procedures, and advertising laws.

Tariff
Tax on imports.

Import Quota
Restriction on the number of goods entering a country.

Currency Controls
Government-imposed restrictions on currency leaving the country.

Nontariff Barrier (NTB)
Invisible tariff that effectively limits trade.

These restrictions to trade are intended to make goods and services produced within the country more competitive with imports. Presumably, they make the country's businesses more profitable and increase its level of employment; unfortunately, they also can increase prices paid by consumers.

Canada is a trading nation and generally supports the reduction of trade barriers. The government does not hesitate, however, to impose **countervailing duties** — a duty on imports designed to counteract an unfair subsidy paid by another country to its producers for export, thereby giving them an unfair advantage over Canadian producers. For example, corn exports were being subsidized by the U.S. government and adversely affecting Canadian corn producers. In 1988, the Canadian government assessed a countervailing duty, which was upheld by an international review process. Conversely, the United States asserted that British Columbia exports of softwood lumber were government-subsidized through unrealistically low stumpage fees. It assessed a countervailing duty to protect the American softwood lumber industry.

Countervailing Duty
A duty on imports designed to counteract unfair subsidies paid to producers by foreign governments.

Occasionally foreign firms have been accused of **dumping** their products into Canada — selling their products here at prices less than those charged in their own domestic market. B.C. apple growers have charged Washington State producers with dumping apples into Canada on several occasions and have received protection from antidumping duties. It should be noted that domestic producers must be adversely affected for antidumping duties to be assessed. California producers of lettuce often dump excess production into Canada. If Canadian lettuce is not in season, the Canadian consumer benefits from very low retail prices, but Canadian producers are not harmed.

Dumping
Practice of selling goods overseas at a lower price than a company charges in its own home market.

Governments may restrict exports as a matter of foreign policy. For example, Canada severely restricts the sale of uranium for nonpeaceful purposes. Governments can also encourage trade. In early 1990, the Mexican government sent a high-level delegation, including seven cabinet ministers, to Ottawa to encourage investment in Mexico by Canadian businesses and to improve bilateral trade between Canada and Mexico.

Canadian firms marketing abroad are bound both by laws governing international trade and the federal Competition Act. A company can be held in violation of the Competition Act if it commits an action abroad that affects business activities in Canada.

Political Life Abroad

Marketers must learn two important facts of life about marketing overseas. First, government participation in economic affairs is far greater in most countries than in Canada and the United States. Second, many countries are politically unstable, which makes marketing there a risky venture.

In countries where the government owns the means of production, the government may be the only customer. This affects marketing planning. For example, in the People's Republic of China, technical experts and state planners decide what products will be imported. Chinese trade experts recommend that all advertising contain technical information rather than persuasive appeals.[27]

Sometimes, no matter what a government does to encourage marketing interest, violence erupts and marketers caught in the turmoil lose their investments. One company that provides political risk insurance for U.S. investors in developing countries, for example, had to pay out more than $14 million in claims to businesses hurt in the 1979 Iranian revolution. The IT&T Corporation claimed losses of $92.5 million when the Chilean government took over its properties.[28]

Marketers must try to evaluate the risk of outbreaks before entering new markets. To do so, they may use both subjective means, such as talks with political and business leaders and assessments by educated experts, and objective means, including extrapolation from past events.[29] A company interested in investing in Indonesia, for example, might undertake a study of past trends of political instability in that country and then prepare a forecast of future risk. If the risk of political upheaval seemed too high, the company might then reconsider its plans for expansion.

International Law and Agreements

While there is no international law-making body, police force, or court system (with the limited exception of the World Court in The Hague), international "laws" do exist in the form of treaties, conventions, and agreements among nations. For example, the United Nations has been working on development of an international commercial code. Several current trade agreements have far-reaching implications for Canadian marketers.

Large multinational companies have legal staffs that keep up with this vast and expanding body of laws. Marketers must stay on top of legal developments. Their success in the marketplace often depends on their doing so.

Canada–U.S. Free Trade Agreement The Canada–U.S. Free Trade Agreement came into effect January 1, 1989. Its goals include the eventual elimination of barriers to trade in goods and services between Canada and the United States, encouragement of fair competition, liberalization of cross-border investment, and establishment of a dispute-resolution mechanism.

The agreement is intended to benefit Canadian and U.S. citizens by increasing economic activity and employment while reducing the cost of consumer and industrial goods.[30] There is, however, extensive debate in Canada as to whether or not the agreement is a good one for the country. It will be several years before the results can be properly assessed.

The schedule for elimination of Canada–U.S. tariff barriers is based on the readiness of particular industries to compete internationally. For example, all tariffs were eliminated on computers, animal feeds, skis, and motorcycles in January 1, 1989. Other industries, such as paper, paints, furniture, and most kinds of machinery, will have tariffs eliminated over five years ending January 1, 1994. The remaining tariffs — those on goods such as steel, most agricultural products, textiles and apparel, and softwood lumber — will be eliminated over ten years.[31]

In order to qualify for duty-free treatment, goods must either originate in Canada or the United States or have substantial value added to them there. The purpose of these origin rules is to prevent offshore producers from avoiding one country's tariffs by shipping goods through the other.

GATT An agreement that is particularly important for North American marketers is the General Agreement on Tariffs and Trade (GATT), an international trade agreement designed to reduce the level of tariffs.[32] More than 120 nations are members or associates of the GATT, which is based on two main principles:

1. *Nondiscrimination* — GATT members grant others the same tariff rate.

2. *Consultation* — GATT provides a forum for discussing trade disagreements. Since 1947, GATT has sponsored several major tariff negotiations, resulting in reduced tariff rates for tens of thousands of items.

The European Community — Europe 1992 The European Community consists of 12 member countries: namely, Belgium, France, [West] Germany, Luxembourg, Italy, the Netherlands, Denmark, Ireland, the United Kingdom, Greece, Spain, and Portugal. Its goal is a truly unified European market in which goods, people, and capital can move freely.[33] The target date for substantial completion of the economic unification is December 31, 1992—thus the term "Europe 1992."

For Canada, Europe 1992 means development of a single market serving 325 million consumers — over 75 million more than in the United States. Trading regulations will be simplified for Canadian exporters because goods will have to pass through only one customs point for distribution to the 12 member states.

Some marketers worry that the European Community will develop into a "fortress" excluding goods from nonmember nations. Europe's traditional position as a global trading region makes this concern appear largely unfounded.[34]

Strategic Planning for International Markets

Environmental analysis makes marketers aware of the difficulties they may encounter in several possible markets worldwide. With that kind of background knowledge, marketers can plan the strategy they wish to pursue. (See Marketing Today 17.1 for a description of the global strategies of two soft-drink companies.) As noted in Chapter 2, planning marketing strategy is a two-step process involving (1) selection of the target market and (2) design of the marketing mix.

Marketing Today 17.1

Coke and Pepsi Seek Global Appeal

Around the world, consumers enjoy soft drinks. Cola makers have responded to this broad appeal by adopting a global strategy, selling the same product, packaging, and upbeat message in many nations. For the two leading brands — Coca-Cola and Pepsi — the competition has been stiff, resulting in aggressive promotion.

Worldwide volume for Coca-Cola is double that for Pepsi. Consequently, Pepsi has responded by competing selectively. For example, the company promoted heavily in Canada and edged out Coke here. When Coke introduced Cherry Coke in Canada, Pepsi countered with Cherry Pepsi. Pepsi's advertising campaign uses the theme "We Got the Taste," a message designed to communicate flavour superiority. Pepsi also acquired Seven-Up International (which does not include U.S. operations), to give the company greater muscle and enable it to compete with Coca-Cola's Sprite.

Coke's global brand strategy is based on "availability, affordability, and acceptability." Coke sees its biggest opportunity as growth in per-capita consumption of its product. North American consumers drink about eight times as much as the overseas market. To take advantage of the growth opportunity, Coca-Cola positions its brands not merely as the most satisfying

soft drink, but as the most satisfying beverage. This means that in Japan, for example, Coke's biggest competition isn't Pepsi, it's tea.

Source: Adapted from Jeffry Scott, "The Cola Wars Go Global," *Adweek,* September 22, 1986, p. B.R. 18.

Uzzle/ARCHIVE

Targeting relates to selection of the market or markets a company can serve best. To do that, marketers must engage in research to determine the demographic, sociological, and psychographic characteristics of potential customers. On the basis of such research, product, price, placement, and promotion policies can be tailored to meet the needs of customers.

Researching Foreign Markets

The goals and methods of research are the same for both the domestic market and foreign markets. But research of international markets can be more difficult.

Market research, as noted in Chapter 4, usually begins by gathering secondary data. Published information about market size and customer behaviour is not always as available for other countries as for Canada and the United States. Possible sources of information include the federal and provincial governments, Canadian embassies abroad, foreign consulates and embassies in Canada, the U.S. Department of Commerce, and international organizations such as the United Nations and the International Monetary Fund. More data are likely to be available for industrialized countries than for developing or less-developed countries.

All secondary data must be evaluated carefully. National pride sometimes stands in the way of statistical accuracy, and information about income level or demand for a product may be exaggerated. Another difficulty is that data collected from various sources are not always comparable. For example, collecting statistics on alcohol consumption in Europe may be complicated by the fact that beer is considered an alcoholic beverage in the north, whereas in the south it may be categorized with soft drinks.[35]

When secondary data are unavailable or questionable, primary data must be collected. But difficulties also arise in this area. One researcher noted the following typical problems:

- Telephone research is nearly impossible, even in industrialized countries such as England and [West] Germany, where only about one-third of all households have phones.

- Mail surveys are not easily conducted in countries with high illiteracy rates such as Italy and Spain.

- Long questionnaires are not acceptable in Hong Kong, which is a rush society, but even short questionnaires may turn out to be long in Brazil because citizens are conscientious answerers.[36]

Educational and cultural differences make primary research difficult but not impossible. In increasingly competitive international markets, such research is becoming an absolute necessity.

Multinational Marketing
In contrast to global marketing: Adjusting the marketing mix to meet the specific needs of each nation or group of nations.

Global Marketing
Developing one marketing mix to service all world markets.

Selecting Target Markets

Information gleaned from market research helps the organization select target markets. The organization may choose to engage in **multinational marketing**—that is, to develop a marketing mix aimed at certain nations or groups within nations and adjust it to meet the specific needs of each. Or it may decide on **global marketing** — preparing a single marketing mix to appeal to a broad segment of the world marketplace.

With global marketing, the organization tries to identify needs held in common around the world and to design a single marketing mix to meet those needs. Some observers have noted that American companies more typically plan a product for the U.S. market and then try to sell it internationally, making modifications if deemed necessary. This is not global marketing, because it starts with a single country's needs and preferences, rather than identifying commonalities among nations.[37]

True global marketing can require more creativity, because marketers must go beyond the differences in what people say they want; instead they try to identify underlying needs. Buyers may be willing to change their expectations if the marketer offers a product at a lower price than they pay for existing products. Standardized products that have sold successfully around the world include automobiles, agricultural commodities, banking and insurance services, McDonald's hamburgers, and Hollywood movies.[38]

After examining a number of researchers' reports, one marketing expert has concluded that a global strategy is most appropriate for firms with less ambitious sales goals, a greater emphasis on cost control, fewer production plants, and fully owned subsidiaries overseas. By contrast, the organizations most likely to benefit from a multinational strategy are those with ambitious goals for sales and market share, operations in many foreign markets, extensive financial and managerial resources, a global production network, and significant joint-venture operations.[39]

When the organization has selected its international target markets, it is ready to plan the elements of the marketing mix.

Product Planning

Marketers must determine whether to sell the same product abroad as at home, modify it for the new market, or develop an entirely different product. At Your Service 17.1 describes a company that helps marketers make decisions of this nature.

The tactic of selling the same product around the world is practical if culture has no influence on the way the product is used or prepared. Many consumer products, such as soft drinks and cosmetics, are the same no matter where they are sold. For example, Oil of Olay is formulated the same for American and European markets, and commercials have shown beautiful women around the world praising the product in their native language.

In the case of food products and many other consumer or industrial products, however, modifications must be made for a variety of reasons. For example, Exxon reformulates its gasoline to meet climatic conditions; Nestlé sells dozens of varieties of coffee to meet local taste preferences; and Burroughs, an office equipment manufacturer, adapts the voltage of its machines to the electrical power systems of various countries.[40]

Sometimes a product must be redesigned entirely to meet the needs of a population. For example, Ford has developed a type of model-T truck appropriate for low-income Asian countries, and Coca-Cola markets a protein- and vitamin-fortified drink to sell to markets in need of a diet supplement.[41]

The physical makeup of a product is, of course, only one aspect of the total product. Service, another consideration, is especially important in selling a foreign product. Singer sewing machines have an excellent reputation in Europe because of the company's liberal service policy.

In addition to the service component, branding is a significant part of the total product. Brand-name choice is a difficult problem. Some firms such as Coca-Cola believe it is important to establish a worldwide image for a product by using the same name. Other firms feel that a national name in foreign markets may arouse hostility. Kodak dropped its brand name in Latin American markets because of high nationalist sentiment there.[42]

Of course, the tactic of downplaying an international brand name can backfire. One American firm in Mexico picked a Spanish name for its product, assuming Mexicans would prefer a product identified with their country. In fact, the market for the product was highly class conscious and preferred the status that goes with buying American-made goods.[43]

Pricing Strategies

Marketing managers face a variety of pricing problems, depending on what mode of international marketing activity they select. Two common areas of concern are how to price exports and how to price component parts or goods transferred between a company and its foreign subsidiary.

Export Pricing

Chapter 10 notes that prices can be set on a cost-plus basis or on the basis of demand. Ideally, costs and the amount of consumer demand should both be considered.

Marketers must determine whether to charge the same price at home and abroad, or whether to charge a higher or lower price. Seldom are the costs of selling at home the same as the costs of selling overseas. Higher prices abroad might be justified because (1) there may be additional taxes in the form of tariffs, (2) special packaging and documentation may be required, (3) the costs of distribution may be greater, or (4) inflation may be higher abroad.

On the other hand, exporting does not always mean higher costs. Sometimes domestic sales may be sufficient to cover research and overhead costs, so that any sales made abroad may be looked on as "gravy" — a contribution to profit. A lower price, therefore, may be justified. In some cases it may even be required, if competition abroad charges less than the home market price or the foreign government controls prices. Companies selling goods overseas at a lower price than they charge in their own home markets may, however, be accused of dumping. Many countries, like Canada, prohibit the practice if it significantly harms home competitors.

Transfer Pricing

When a company establishes marketing operations abroad, it must decide how much to charge subsidiaries for goods or parts shipped to or from them. This pricing within the corporate family is known as **transfer pricing**, and it is controversial.

Some experts claim that multinational corporations use transfer pricing to better their profits. For example, transfer pricing can be used to evade high taxes. Thus, if Canadian corporate income taxes are higher than Switzerland's tax rate, a Canadian company may underprice what it sells to its Swiss subsidiary or overprice what it buys from it in order to minimize profits and its resulting tax bill in Canada. Many governments have passed laws against pricing aimed specifically at avoiding taxes.

Companies are expected to follow an **arm's-length policy** in transfer pricing. Such a policy requires the subsidiary to charge or be charged the same price available to any buyer outside the firm. When there are no outside buyers to provide a standard price, problems may arise. Also, the means to police whether companies are actually charging the same price are sometimes absent. For these reasons, many countries are now calling for stiffer international controls to prevent abuses.[44]

Transfer Pricing
Pricing within a corporate family, perhaps used to avoid taxes.

Arm's-Length Policy
Policy that requires a firm's subsidiary to charge or be charged the same price available to any buyer outside the firm.

Placement Decisions

Firms can choose a number of arrangements to place their products in foreign markets. Several factors are involved in the decision, including degree of control desired. Firms that need special control to provide servicing may set up their own sales force abroad as Singer does. Other organizations prefer to sell franchisees the right to use their name, as H&R Block does.

Some companies prefer to work through trading houses, which, as already noted, serve as commercial links between Canadian-based producers and foreign consumers. Marketers are likely to prefer such intermediaries when first entering the export market, when selling products that are susceptible to heavy competition, and when operating in non-Western markets (that is, the ones with which they are least familiar).[45]

The major types of trading houses that link Canadian manufacturers and foreign markets are:

1. Buyers resident within Canada who work for foreign firms.

2. Overseas representatives of foreign firms.

3. Independent intermediaries who either buy goods for sale abroad (merchant wholesalers) or arrange to bring buyers and sellers together (agents).

Some companies that sell many different types of products use several of these routes.

The relative size and number of wholesalers varies greatly from country to country. In general, the industrialized nations have large wholesaling organizations serving many retailers, while wholesaling in developing countries is likely to be fragmented. A notable exception to this rule is Japan, where wholesalers sell to other wholesalers. Because wholesaling in most countries is more fragmented and operates on a smaller scale than in North America, wholesalers elsewhere often provide less service.

Retailing, too, may vary. The customary size of retail outlets varies from country to country. Retailers may provide fewer services and may expect wholesalers to extend credit over lengthy periods.

The problem of inefficient channels of distribution is often worsened overseas by poor physical distribution facilities. Transportation is especially troublesome in less-developed countries. In Zaire, for example, a typical shipment of goods must be loaded and unloaded four times to reach the African interior because of a disjointed transportation system.[46] Warehousing is a problem everywhere, even in industrialized countries. Storage facilities may be small, old-fashioned, and ill-equipped. Inadequate transportation or warehousing adds to costs and may even stand in the way of successfully marketing products abroad.

Besides getting products to customers, placement involves extending credit to facilitate a purchase. Because governments generally want to promote exports, they may help companies that want to extend credit on exports. For Canadian companies, this help comes from the Export Development Bank.

Extending credit internationally can be quite risky. Not only individuals and corporations, but even many nations have had trouble keeping up with debt payments. Exporters that want to extend credit may buy special insurance policies to protect themselves against the risk that the foreign debtor will be unable to pay because of certain commercial and political risks. In Canada such insurance is available from the Federal Business Development Bank.

Promotional Considerations

The purpose of promotion is communication. But because communication takes place within a culture, promotional programs in different countries may require widely varying approaches. To reach the target audiences, messages must be varied, one perhaps stressing an emotional theme and the other making a more rational appeal. Media and timing of messages also vary with the target audiences. Many companies turn for help to agencies that specialize in promoting to foreign markets. (See At Your Service 17.2.)

Not all companies try for a unique message in different markets. For example, jeans manufacturer Levi Strauss keeps ads uniform from country to country, believing that Levi customers speak a common language —the language of youth.[47] Similarly, ads for General Motors' Corvette

At Your Service 17.2

Ad Agencies Help Marketers Sell in China

Selling in China involves so many cultural differences that many companies find they need more than the usual services from advertising agencies. Advertising agencies in China help clients find their way through the bureaucratic maze and advise them about the bewildering differences in culture, language, and media. Agencies also guide companies in translating their name and trademark into a Chinese dialect understood by the target market.

In sum, agencies serve as advisers, helping their clients create a positive image and avoid blunders. Cultural blunders in advertising include misusing the colour white and the number four (both associated with death), as well as preparing ads that refer to politics or sex or overtly promote Western life-styles.

When Sperry and Burroughs merged to form Unisys, they turned to DYR/Beijing for help with promotion in China. Rather than merely translating the American ad into Chinese, the agency started by making sure the Chinese staff really understood the themes of the ad: brain power, world power, staying power, and "the power of two [companies combined]." The agency spent a lot of time discussing the meaning of the concepts and then rewrote them to make them understandable to a Chinese audience. In selecting a name for the company, Unisys settled on a rough translation of United Information Systems. Finally, the ad was rewritten so that it rhymed, an elegant practice by Chinese standards.

Sources: Adapted from Karen Singer, "The China Card: A Giant Reawakens to Advertising," *Adweek*, February 23, 1987, p. 17; and Karen Singer, "Commerce in China Requires an Eye toward Custom," *Adweek*, March 2, 1987.

are carefully designed to be able to cross international markets with only a change in language. While the wording in the ad shown in Figure 17.7 may be in Arabic, Dutch, English, French, German, or Spanish, the background is purposely vague. It could be a desert or a misty morning on the Highlands. Furthermore, no human models are used.[48]

Standardized campaigns are not always possible, however. Ad messages may have to be changed for a number of reasons. Language, mentioned earlier, is one. The "Un-Cola" slogan of 7-Up could not be translated into other languages and still retain its special meaning.[49] Differing values and attitudes also sometimes stand in the way of a common message. Club Méditerranée finds that it must vary its message to appeal to different segments of the European market. The Swiss don't like to vacation with their children, so Club Med puts less emphasis on family ambience in its Swiss ads. The resort chain promotes sunny beaches to the Germans, but not to Italians, who have sunny beaches at home and are more attracted by the activities Club Med offers.[50]

The media used to convey the messages may also have to be locally tailored. Media availability and impact vary widely. For example:

■ TV is present in most industrialized countries, but commercial time is often severely limited. The Scandinavian countries have banned commercials altogether, although this is beginning to change somewhat.[51]

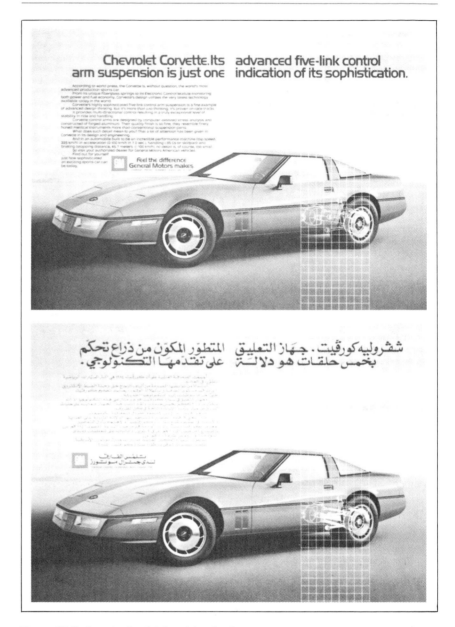

Figure 17.7 Standardized Advertising for Corvette

Source: Courtesy of General Motors Corporation and McCann-Erickson, Inc.

- Newspapers are fragmented along political lines in much of Europe, requiring marketers to place ads in a dozen papers to achieve the coverage of one or two newspapers in North America.

- Unusual media, such as movies featuring commercials, are often required to reach illiterate audiences in developing countries.[52] In Thailand, a highly successful campaign to promote vasectomies used slogans painted on the hides of water buffalo.[53]

When media are restricted or unavailable, sales promotion techniques become important. Free samples, coupons, and contests have been used to arouse product interest abroad. But sometimes governments have acted to restrict the use of these techniques as well. In Greece, Colgate was once sued for giving away razor blades with its shaving cream.[54]

Different national attitudes toward advertising and sales promotion carry over to the field of personal selling. In Europe, smiling Avon callers are not well received because European women regard at-home sales calls as an intrusion. On the other hand, European industrial buyers do not like to be seen with salespeople in public. At trade shows, costly floor space must be set aside for private compartments where customers can deal out of view of competitors.[55] Marketers may find adaptations such as this a nuisance, but in many cases they are absolutely necessary to carry on a successful marketing program.

Packaging is also a significant part of the total promotional mix. Packaging must conform not only to the aesthetic preferences of customers, but also to their income limitations and shopping habits. Large economy-size packages may be practical in affluent Canada, where many customers shop once a week, but smaller packages are needed in other countries where poverty or custom dictates that people shop daily.

Standardizing or Adapting the Marketing Mix

The preceding review of marketing mix elements may make a global marketing strategy sound impossible. But that is not the case. Differences have been stressed because marketers have tended to ignore them in the past. Where circumstances are similar, however, marketing managers would be foolish to introduce unnecessary adaptations. Just as in selecting target markets, international marketers may choose between multinational marketing and global marketing, in selecting marketing strategy they can make a similar choice.

Standardization—the practice of transferring all parts of a successful marketing mix from one country to another—may be desirable to keep costs down, to make products easily identifiable among travellers, and to simplify planning and control.

When cultural, economic, and legal differences make complete standardization undesirable or impossible, a **modified standardization approach**, changing one or more elements of the marketing mix, may be more appropriate. For example, the same product may be sold worldwide, but different advertising approaches may be used.

While a standardized approach to marketing is often the most cost efficient, it should not be used indiscriminately. What works fine in St. Paul may be disastrous in São Paulo, as even the U.S. retailing giant Sears, Roebuck learned to its chagrin. Sears withdrew its entire opera-

Standardization
Practice of transferring all parts of a successful marketing mix from one country to another.

Modified Standardization Approach
Practice of changing one or more elements of the marketing mix.

tion from Brazil after a series of marketing mistakes. As retail marketing became fiercely competitive in Brazil, Sears ceased to innovate. The apparel it offered was widely regarded as lacking style. Its store sites, chosen in the 1950s and 1960s, were no longer choice locations, and its advertising was inappropriate to the local customs. In Brazil, even kitchen stoves and blenders are featured in lively and amusing television commercials. Sears failed to use television, and its print ads were unexciting. According to one São Paulo shopper, the ads "were filled with weird gray drawings of little things like vegetable drainers and pea podders on sale that week." One analyst observed that Sears, more than most multinationals, is run from its U.S. headquarters, with little local input: "[Marketing] solutions are sent by telex from Chicago. It's 'send down promotion package No. 84.' " To add further insult to injury, Sears' stores featured shelving at American heights—although Brazilians are several inches shorter than the average North American. And Sears failed to offer financing, although Brazilians, accustomed to triple-digit inflation, prefer to finance everything from irons to television sets in 24 monthly payments. After watching its sales slide steadily for several years, Sears decided to sell out to a Dutch conglomerate.[56]

International marketing is a complex task. In devising marketing strategies, managers must consider both similarities and differences between their own country and the country they wish to penetrate. Shortcuts based on unresearched assumptions are the surest road to market failure. But, as McDonald's, Coca-Cola, Levi Strauss, and many other companies have shown, when handled properly, international marketing can be an area of boundless opportunity.

Chapter Replay

1. **What are the differences between foreign trade, foreign marketing, and multinational marketing?**

   Foreign trade involves producing goods or services at home and exporting them. Foreign marketing involves operating within the foreign country where goods are to be sold. Multinational marketing refers to integrated marketing activities carried out in a number of countries.

2. **In what ways can business penetrate foreign markets?**

   The routes of expansion abroad include direct or indirect exportation, licensing, joint ventures, and direct investment.

3. **What economic characteristics do marketers consider in evaluating international markets?**

   Marketers compare different countries' per-capita income, industrial structure, and economic infrastructure.

4. **What are some cultural differences marketers must be aware of?**

   Marketers must take account of differences in language, aesthetic perceptions, social organization, and values.

5. **How do governments affect a marketer's involvement in a country?**

   Governments control marketing activities by imposing tariffs, by setting import quotas, by restricting the flow of currency, and by setting price ceilings. Governments may restrict imports to protect domestic businesses or restrict exports to protect national security. In addition, marketers are subject to international trade agreements such as the General Agreement on Tariffs and Trade and to bilateral agreements such as the Canada–U.S. Free Trade Agreement.

6. **What are some limitations on researching foreign markets?**

   Published secondary information is not always available or accurate. Information from different sources is not always comparable. Educational and cultural differences make primary research difficult.

7. **What issues must marketers consider in developing products for international markets?**

   Marketers must consider whether to sell a single version of a product or to modify it for various submarkets. The company must give special attention to service and choose brand names that are understandable and positive in foreign markets.

8. **What pricing decisions must international marketers make?**

   International marketers must decide whether to charge a different price for exports than for products sold domestically. They also must decide how much to charge foreign subsidiaries for goods or parts shipped to or from them.

9. **What are the major types of trading houses or intermediaries Canadian companies use to place their products in foreign markets?**

   The major types of trading houses are resident buyers within Canada who work for foreign firms, overseas representatives of foreign firms, and independent intermediaries who either buy goods for sale abroad or arrange to bring buyers and sellers together.

10. **What are some reasons marketers may have to modify promotions for foreign markets?**

    Messages may have to differ to overcome language barriers, to adapt to differing values and attitudes, to reflect the availability and impact of various media, to respond to differing national attitudes toward advertising and selling, and to accommodate income limitations and shopping habits.

Key Terms

arm's-length policy
countervailing duty
currency controls
direct investment
dumping
economic infrastructure
foreign marketing
foreign trade
global marketing
import quota
international marketing
joint venture
licensing

modified standardization
  approach
multinational marketing
  (in contrast to foreign
  marketing; in contrast
  to global marketing)
nontariff barriers
per-capita income
standardization
tariff
trading house
transfer pricing

Discussion Questions

1. When Canadian farmers have a bumper crop, they look for foreign buyers. Are they engaging in foreign trade, foreign marketing, or multinational marketing? Besides surplus production, what other forces lead companies to enter foreign markets?

2. Pretty Smile Inc. runs a chain of dental care centres offering emergency care and checkups without appointments. Because competition in the dental care business is so stiff in Canada, the company is thinking of expanding to some foreign markets. What routes to expansion are available to the firm? Which do you recommend it use? Why?

3. The per-capita income of Country Z, an industrializing nation, is only $1630 (compared to $15 080 for Canada). Does this mean that a manufacturer of luxury goods shouldn't bother trying to sell in Country Z? Why, or why not?

4. What are some sources of cultural differences that marketers should be aware of?

5. What are some reasons governments regulate imports and exports? What are some actions governments take to encourage international trade?

6. When Wondrous Cleaning Products wants to add to its line of home-cleaning products in Canada, it researches the market by conducting a telephone poll and holding a focus group interview of homemakers. Why might these research techniques fail when Wondrous expands operations into Turkey?

7. What are some advantages of selling a single product globally? When is this approach appropriate?

8. NiftyTek Computers sells computers through its own distribution network in Canada and the United States but relies on independent intermediaries for its sales in Indonesia. What might account for the different placement strategies?

9. Bob Baxter, owner of Big Bus Tours, is planning to set up bus tours in the capitals of the world's 15 largest nations. Bob and Big Bus's marketing director, Lynette Long, meet with a marketing consultant, Pat Prognosticator. Pat uses elaborate diagrams to illustrate her view that Big Bus Tours should hire 15 advertising agencies — one in each city — to devise 15 different advertising campaigns. "You have to meet the unique needs of each marketplace," explains Pat.

    After Pat leaves, Lynette exclaims, "That's crazy! All we need to do is hire our usual agency in Montreal to prepare some ads. That will give us English and French versions. Then we'll get some translators to translate the words into other languages. Pat's ideas would cost us a fortune."

    Who is right — Pat or Lynette? Why?

Hard Rock Cafe

CASE 17.1

On November 22, 1986, the Dallas edition of the Hard Rock Cafe opened with much fanfare. Dan Aykroyd, a partner in the company, reunited the original Blues Brothers Band for the black-tie party that marked the opening. Commenting on the Dallas location, Aykroyd said, "If the New York Hard Rock is the Grand Central, this baby is the Supreme Court of rock 'n' roll."

Background

The original Hard Rock Cafe was created in 1971 in London by Issac Tigrett of Jackson, Tennessee, who, along with his partners, felt that Europe should sample the best of American cooking — "the best down-home, righteous meals at reasonable prices." That location, in the fashionable area of Mayfair and just around the corner from Buckingham Palace, showed a first-year net profit of $7000. Today it grosses some $2 million a year and is the third British restaurant company ever to be listed on the London Stock Exchange.

Hard Rock Cafes have been added in such cities as Toronto, New York, Stockholm, Dallas, Houston, Boston, and Chicago. A sister company has restaurants in Los Angeles and San Francisco. More locations are planned. All cafes are based on the philosophy of genuine value for

Source: Edited from Richard David Story, "Hard Rock Story," *USA Today*, November 20, 1986, pp. 01+, and *Hard Rock Cafe Hall of Fame Guide* from original London location.

money, along with a simple spiritual message — "Love All — Serve All" — with each meal.

Restaurant Atmospherics

The Hard Rock Cafe represents what *People* magazine called "The Smithsonian of rock 'n' roll." According to Sotheby, the cafes feature "Truly the largest collection in the world of musical memorabilia." Among the most famous items are Elvis Presley's velvet suit, John Lennon's first stage suit, Elton John's psychedelic piano, Keith Richards' five-string guitar, B. B. King's "Lucille" guitar, and over 200 authentic Gold Albums awarded to the Beatles, the Beach Boys, and other famous recording groups. The collection circulates among the various restaurant locations.

"From the very beginning, rock was the uniting force," Tigrett says. The total collection of rock memorabilia on walls, ceilings, and floors of Hard Rock Cafes is estimated at close to $3 million.

Music is a constant companion at each Hard Rock Cafe. For example, the Dallas location features a $700 000 sound system with 32 amplifiers. The resulting 3000 amps makes the restaurant a rock 'n' roll haven.

The Offering

Along with the rock 'n' roll atmosphere, Hard Rock Cafes offer what are billed as the most reasonably priced hamburgers, french fries, milkshakes, pig (barbequed pork) sandwiches, and T-bone steaks. The Dallas restaurant also serves *fajitas* and buffalo stew.

Individual restaurants sell a variety of personalized clothing items. Students on college and university campuses around the world wear T-shirts, sweatshirts, jackets, caps, and other items that carry the Hard Rock Cafe emblem along with the city of origin.

Focal Topics

1. How would international markets differ from domestic markets for Hard Rock Cafes?

2. How would you explain the success of the Hard Rock Cafe in London?

3. What do you see as the greatest potential problems facing Hard Rock Cafes as they move into more international markets? How can the company best cope with these problems?

Franklin International (C)

As indicated in part A of this case (Case 2.2), Franklin was started in 1935 as a manufacturer of animal glues for the furniture industry. The Industrial Division (originally the Franklin Glue Company) was the first manufacturer of synthetic aliphatic resin glues to be used in the furniture manufacturing process.

Background

The superior technical ability of its salespeople has always been a key differentiating factor in comparing Franklin to the competition. In addition, a substantial application and research laboratory has provided backup and analysis for the customer's use of Franklin's products. Eleven warehouses throughout the country inventory products and provide pickup service when desired. The Industrial Division has also been able to provide customers with a special product when needed, such as adding a coloured dye to the adhesive in order to match the wood or finish being used.

Because of these additional services, the Industrial Division has always positioned itself as the quality, premium-priced adhesive producer in the marketplace. Management determined some time ago that it did not want to participate in markets that were based only on price and that if satisfactory margins were not available from a product, then it would not carry that product.

Some of the major market segments that the Industrial Division serves are:

- Household furniture—assembly of components and complex furniture pieces.

- Wood dimension—laminating edge and face pieces to main material surfaces.

- Fingerjointed stack—gluing smaller pieces of wood together to form wider, thicker, or longer pieces.

- Replacement truck flooring—assembly of wood pieces to replace worn floors in trucks.

- Modular housing fabrication — using adhesive products in the production of mobile and manufactured housing.

- Polyfoam laminating—gluing various insulating materials to various surfaces.

International Dimensions

Franklin International has never had a major export operation. As recently as 1980, the firm sold only thirteen 55-gallon drums of its products overseas. Those were delivered to Central America. By 1983, however, the international demands for the company's products had increased significantly but still represented a very small component of total industrial sales.

Imports have become an increasing factor in furniture marketing in North America. In some cases, completed pieces of furniture are shipped. In other instances, components are assembled in foreign countries and then shipped to the United States for final assembly and finishing. Some of the assembly facilities are owned by U.S. firms; others are owned by foreign companies that do component assembly outside the United States. Franklin found that many of the foreign firms were interested in using Franklin adhesives to assemble the components or complete furniture pieces.

In analyzing its export sales, Franklin found that about 75 percent were going to European countries. Yugoslavia, site of the 1984 Winter Olympic Games, turned out to be the major purchaser. In that country, individual wood furniture consortiums were purchasing the glues primarily to assemble furniture components. Franklin reached the European market through a Yugoslavian agent who has dual citizenship and lives in New York City. Franklin would like to expand the distribution of its products into Poland, Romania, and Czechoslovakia. The company is also thinking about developing a warehouse facility in Trieste. By shipping to such a location, the products could then be forwarded to other locations at lower tariff rates.

The other 25 percent of Franklin's export sales were going to Asian countries, such as Singapore and Korea, and to Taiwan. To reach those markets, the company worked through agents in California who serve local representatives in the various countries. Furniture manufacturers in those countries are typically involved in producing case goods (bedroom and dining room furniture) and knocked-down furniture that is assembled by the ultimate consumer.

Franklin is exploring the option of selling directly to the representatives in Southeast Asian countries. In addition, the company may have an interesting opportunity to engage in a barter relationship with a chemical plant that is being developed in Taiwan. That plant will produce, among other chemicals, vinyl acetate monomer and polyvinyl alcohol, both basic components in the manufacture of the polymer that is used in the manufacture of adhesive products. Franklin possibly could trade its finished products for the raw materials.

Focal Topics

1. What do you see as the possible advantages and disadvantages of Franklin's expanding the export of its adhesive products?

2. What alternative ways are available for Franklin to increase its international sales? Which do you recommend that it use?

3. What is your overall evaluation of the potential to barter with the chemical facility in Taiwan?

18

Chapter 18

In this chapter, you will learn:

- The basic types of nonprofit marketing.

- How nonprofit organizations market ideas.

- Major categories of nonprofit organizations.

- Ways in which nonprofit organizations differ from businesses.

- The major similarities of nonprofit and for-profit organizations.

- Why environmental analysis is especially important for nonprofit organizations.

- Characteristics of the marketing mix for nonprofit organizations.

- The major ways to measure marketing success in the nonprofit sector.

The Fine Art of Marketing Culture

"Museums can't be marketed like a bar of soap." Not so long ago, that was a typical response of museum directors who scorned the idea of promoting their institutions with crass sales techniques. But in the face of massive cutbacks in government funding and a slower economy in some regions, museums and other cultural institutions are embracing marketing zealously. The results are often a pleasant surprise.

Consider a few examples:

- The Vancouver Symphony Orchestra was facing another season in the red until it took the symphony to the people. One event that sold out was its symphony in the mountains. The VSO played outdoors high up in the mountains of Whistler village.

- The Shaw Festival, held during the summer months in Niagara-on-the-Lake, markets its festival all year round by selling crafts incorporating the Shaw Festival logo.

- The Ontario Science Centre in Toronto promotes its features to business travellers, encouraging them to bring their families on their next business trip and extend their stay in the city and take in the wonders of the Centre.

HARD HAT ART.

It's only to be enjoyed at the Art Gallery, now through December 1991.
You'll see not only great art, but construction workers creating their own works of art. Each visit promises something new. The great art of building at 317 Dundas Street West, Toronto.
Or call (416) 977-0414. You'll see why it's hats off to the AGO.

AGO
Art Gallery of Ontario
THE ART OF BUILDING

Young & Rubicam Advertising Ltd.

Forces other than funding cutbacks have combined to persuade cultural institutions that they must market more aggressively or lose their audiences. The same is true for many other kinds of nonprofit organizations. This chapter examines how the general principles of marketing apply to the specific needs of the nonprofit sector.

Sources: Alan Rosenthal, "Museums Jump into the Marketing Game," *Advertising Age*, September 27, 1982, p. M-2.

The Scope of Nonprofit Marketing

Most of this book concentrates on organizations that operate for profit. But an important part of the Canadian economy —some say as much as 20 percent—operates for some other reason besides making a profit. Included in the nonprofit sector are religious organizations, human services organizations, museums, private libraries, public, separate, and private schools, hospitals, colleges and universities, symphony orchestras, labour unions, government bodies, political parties, and other organizations incorporated under the various provincial society acts. These organizations employ a variety of service workers and professionals.

What do the United Way, the Charlottetown Festival, the National Gallery of Canada, and the Red Cross have in common? All of those nonprofit organizations face serious problems that can be solved, at least in part, by the application of marketing principles. The existence of problems in the nonprofit sector is not hard to document:

- Police departments nationwide face growing public fear of crime at a time when their employees must ask for higher wages from taxpayers. They have a serious public relations problem.

- Charities and cultural institutions are hard-pressed for funds because people now give less, as a percentage of their annual income, than in previous years, and there are now more charities and cultural institutions competing for donations than ever before.

- Hospitals and medical professionals are limiting the care they can provide patients because of the lack of beds available and surgical room staff.

These people and resource problems are the kinds of problems marketing people can help solve.

The idea of applying marketing to nonprofit organizations is comparatively recent. The marketing concept took hold in the business world in the late 1950s and early 1960s. As business managers began to be called upon to volunteer their time in the nonprofit sector, they started to see the usefulness of the marketing discipline outside business.

Theorists such as Robert Bartels and Richard Bagozzi gave a sound conceptual basis to business volunteers' intuition by defining marketing as "exchange." As explained in Chapter 1, exchange is a broader concept than buying and selling. When a product and money change hands, that is one type of exchange. But another kind of exchange occurs when political promises are traded for votes or when volunteer labour is offered for a feeling of doing good.[1]

Whenever an exchange occurs — whether or not it involves money — marketing principles can be applied. This chapter explores the usefulness of marketing in not-for-profit situations.

Types of Nonprofit Marketing

In the nonprofit sector, marketers apply their skills mainly to organizations. But persons and ideas can also be "sold" by using marketing techniques.

Person Marketing

Person marketing involves "an effort to cultivate the attention, interest, and preference of a target market toward a person."[2] An interesting example of this was the Vancouver lumber executive who was forced into early retirement and after some fruitless months of hunting for a senior executive job, placed an ad in his local paper "husband for rent." His advertisement detailed his experiences with lawn cutting, plumbing, and general fix-it-yourself projects. He received so many responses that he now has four other displaced senior executives happily employed.

> **Person Marketing**
> Efforts directed toward cultivating the attention, interest, and preference of a target market toward a person.

More typical examples of person marketing occur in the job market everyday. As students enter the job market, they are advised by their marketing professors to consider themselves as "packages." They are a product that has strengths and weaknesses. Their clothes, their manner, their intellect are all characteristics that the employer will assess before making an offer of employment.

Other person marketing occurs in the political arena. In 1968, Pierre Trudeau developed an "image" for himself that swept him into power with a large majority for his Liberal party. Politicians now hire professional advertising people to build media campaigns that substantially differentiate themselves and their image from the competition. When Trade Minister John Crosbie criss-crossed the country selling the Canada–U.S. Free Trade Agreement, he discussed the issues that were important to whichever province he was in.

Political advertising has often received criticism. Some legislators have even tried to limit the kinds of advertising a candidate may run. But whether advertising is manipulative of voters is subject to debate. The candidate who spends the most on ads is not always the winning candidate.

Besides advertising, political marketing uses promotional materials such as campaign buttons and bumper stickers, informational brochures, and efforts to obtain publicity by staging media events. In addition, campaigners conduct marketing research to determine voters' interests and to measure the success of promotional efforts.

Idea Marketing

Idea Marketing
Offering a cause in exchange for public acceptance.

The essence of **idea marketing** is the offering of a cause in exchange for public acceptance. It might be argued that all marketing is idea marketing, whether it be to promote the idea that getting sunburned is bad and that Coppertone Shade can help, or that encouraging a child's creativity is good and Crayola products will do the trick. One particular type of idea marketing is **social marketing.** Social marketing is the use of marketing techniques to increase the acceptability of a social idea, cause, or practice in a target group.[3]

Social Marketing
Use of marketing techniques to increase the acceptability of a social idea, cause, or practice in a target group.

Many causes are marketed to the Canadian public, including positions both for and against legalized abortion and ownership of hand guns, pressure against drunk drivers (see Figure 18.1), and promotion of women's rights in the work force. The Broadcasters of British Columbia sponsor a campaign of discouraging drugs amongst high school students.

Marketing an idea is not synonymous with promotion, though that is an important tool. Other marketing mix variables such as price (the "cost" of acceptance by the target group) and even placement (convenient locations for the public to appreciate fully the offer being promoted) must also be carefully considered. The use of the various elements of the marketing mix to market ideas is discussed at greater length later in this chapter.

Organization Marketing

Organizational Marketing
Activities that attempt to influence others to accept the goals of, receive the services of, or contribute in some way to an organization.

The biggest share of nonprofit marketing can be classified as **organizational marketing,** which attempts to influence others to accept the goals of, receive the services of, or contribute in some way to an organization. There are countless types of nonprofit organizations, but they can be classified in three categories.[4]

One category is composed of **service organizations.** These are institutions, such as hospitals, colleges, and museums, that provide a service for clients, sometimes in exchange for a fee. However, because the price charged for the service does not cover costs, these organizations usually must depend on others—contributors—to make up the difference. Service organizations thus have at least two large markets to reach—clients (patients, students, museum-goers, and so on) and donors.

Service Organization
Institution, such as a hospital, college, or museum, that provides a service for clients, sometimes in exchange for a fee.

A second category of nonprofit organizations consists of **mutual benefit associations.** Political parties, unions, clubs, and churches fall into this category. These associations are organized for the benefit of members, not outsiders. Marketing activities are carried on primarily to increase membership, although they are also sometimes performed to win the support of outsiders. For example, the International Ladies' Garment Workers' Union's (ILGWU) campaign—"buy Canadian"—was designed to urge Canadians to buy Canadian-made clothing and to persuade the federal government to pass legislation limiting imports.

Mutual Benefit Association
Association organized for the benefit of members, not outsiders.

The final category of nonprofit organizations includes **government**

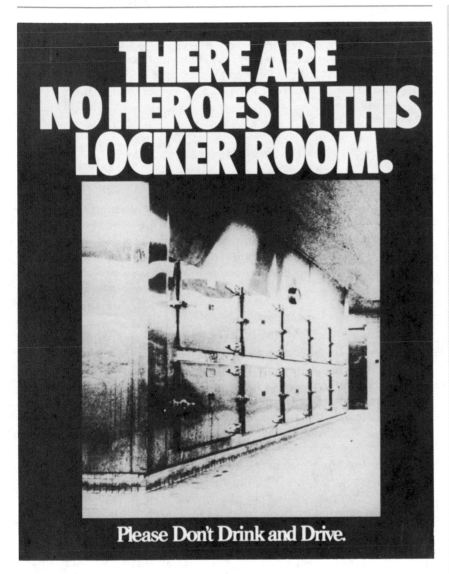

THERE ARE NO HEROES IN THIS LOCKER ROOM.

Please Don't Drink and Drive.

Figure 18.1 Promotion of a Cause

Source: Reader's Digest

organizations, which serve the interests of the public at large. All government agencies, including military services and police and fire departments, need professional marketing to win goodwill and improve their operations. For example, the Canadian Forces use marketing to encourage enlistment. According to Canadian Armed Forces recruiters, advertising with the slogan "Chose a Career, Live the Adventure" has had broad appeal. Other elements of the marketing mix are important, too. An attractive element of the product that the military offers to recruits has been the Canadian Forces Community College Program with headquarters at Seneca College in Ontario and the Regular Officers

Government Organization
Nonprofit agency that serves the interests of the public at large.

Training Program available from the three military universities in Victoria, Kingston, and Saint-Jean, Quebec.

Organization marketing is the focus of much of the rest of the chapter, but it is important to keep in mind that what is said also applies to the other two kinds of nonprofit marketing — person marketing and idea marketing.

Marketing for Profit and Nonprofit Organizations: A Comparison

General Motors and General Foods produce vastly different products, but both companies use the principles described in this text to market their products. The gap between what General Motors offers the public and what a community college provides may seem even wider. Yet the same principles apply. There are some differences, however.

Differences

The most obvious difference between General Motors and a postsecondary institution is the dissimilarity in marketing objectives. An organization like General Motors exists to make a profit for its shareholders, and it does so by stimulating as much demand for its auto models as possible. By contrast, a university or college's main purpose is to provide a service — education — and its existence would be threatened if it took in as many students as wanted that service. That is why there are admission standards. In general, nonprofit organizations work with limited resources and cannot afford to stimulate as much demand as possible. Only in very rare cases are profit-making organizations similarly constrained over the long run.

A second difference is noticeable in the markets served. General Motors meets its profit-making objectives by marketing to a single public —the buying public. But a community college and many nonprofit organizations must consider several markets. The student body is an important market for all schools, but so are alumni and legislators who may provide funds, and parents and teachers who may influence students' choices of school. Those who directly use the "product" exchanged by nonprofit organizations are called **client publics,** and those who have an indirect interest are referred to as **general publics.**[5] Not all nonprofit organizations have two or more distinct markets or publics to serve. But many do, and that complicates the marketing task.

Nonprofit organizations, moreover, have a more difficult time than profit-making organizations in setting control standards. General Motors has sales data and market share figures to guide it in knowing whether it is meeting objectives, for example. Sometimes nonprofit organizations have difficulty finding similar measures.

The difficulty is not unconquerable. A community college may have

Client Public
Those who directly use the product exchanged by nonprofit organizations.

General Public
Those who have an indirect interest in a nonprofit organization's goods or services.

as its objective "to provide a quality education for students"—a standard not subject to exact measurements. But it can substitute indirect measures (such as achievements of students or accreditation of the school). Control may be more difficult in nonprofit organizations, but it is not impossible.[6]

Similarities

Nonprofit and profit-making organizations are more similar than dissimilar. The major similarities may be stated as follows:

1. Both need to plan objectives and analyze their environments to operate efficiently. Chapter 2 points out that objectives tell an organization where it is going, and environmental analysis lists the obstacles to getting there. Businesses need such planning to avoid being sidetracked and to anticipate trouble. Operating with more limited funds, nonprofit organizations need such planning even more.

2. Both need to know their clients to serve them well. By engaging in target-market analysis, businesses decide whether to serve the mass market or to cater to one or more segments. Nonbusiness organizations can benefit from the same kind of analysis. Complaints about "government bureaucracy" or "unresponsive churches" arise from the failure to analyze publics and their needs.

3. Both work with the same marketing elements—the four "Ps"—in serving customer needs. In the case of a nonprofit organization, the product may be more intangible, the price of exchange nonmonetary, the distribution channels more direct, and the promotional effort more dependent on publicity and volunteer salespeople. Still, all four elements are present.

4. Both need to check whether objectives are being reached and marketing programs implemented. As noted previously, measuring results may be more difficult for nonprofit organizations, but they must try to check on public satisfaction.[7]

This abstract statement of similarities is more convincing when applied to actual situations. The remainder of the chapter will explore some of these similarities.

Marketing Objectives and Environmental Analysis

Generally speaking, the objectives of business organizations named in Chapter 2 are not the same as those of nonbusiness organizations because profit is not central to the latter's purpose. Nevertheless, nonprofit organizations must have clear objectives, and, like businesses, they must evaluate how realistic their objectives are in light of environmental conditions.

Nonprofit Organizational Objectives

As noted in Chapter 2, two kinds of objectives interest marketers: (1) general organizational objectives, which direct the organization as a whole; and (2) marketing objectives, which state what marketers can do to support the overall objectives. Table 18.1 lists a few hypothetical examples of both types for a hospital, and a union.

Note that the organizational objectives listed in the table are stated not in terms of a product or service offering but of a public to be served. Organizations that are product oriented may become locked in to limited objectives and disappear as conditions change. Firms that are public oriented may adapt to a changing world.

The Council of Forest Industries in British Columbia provides an interesting example of how a nonprofit organization adapted its purpose to meeting changing times. In the early 1960s, COFI was primarily concerned with lobbying the provincial government to ensure that its members' position on taxes, stumpage rates, and logging rights were well represented. Now in the 1990s, COFI's work is more with an environmentally aware public, and it positions the forest industry as "Managing the forests forever."

After flexible organizational objectives are determined, marketing objectives to meet overall goals can be set. Whenever possible, marketing objectives should be quantified. As Table 18.1 shows, fund-raising or recruiting goals may be conveniently assigned a dollar or number value. Other goals, such as convincing or informing the public, are harder to attach numbers to, but some effort should be made.

The Environment of Nonprofit Organizations

Recall that three distinct environmental levels must be analyzed to determine whether objectives are realizable. The internal, operating,

Table 18.1
Objectives of Typical Nonprofit Organizations

Organization	General Organizational Objectives	Marketing Objectives
Hospital	To deliver quality medical care to the community.	To become recognized in the treatment of multiple sclerosis among 65 percent of Canadian physicians. To attract x dollars for research next year.
Union	To raise the living standard of members.	To increase consumption of union goods by 20 percent over 2 years. To recruit x new members in 6 months.

and general environments affect the operation of profit-making and non-profit organizations alike. In a sense, nonprofit organizations must be even more environmentally sensitive than businesses because their existence often depends on the goodwill of donors and taxpayers as well as the public they serve.

The Internal Environment

The internal environment, consisting of the tangible and intangible resources an organization needs to operate, can make or break the marketing efforts of a nonprofit organization.

Like businesses, many nonprofit organizations have tangible resources such as buildings and financial reserves. For example, the National Aviation Museum in Ottawa includes in its assets 100 aircraft and the three World War II hangars it uses to display the museum collection. Likewise, a religious organization's assets may include its house of worship, its educational facilities, and the money currently available to it.

Such tangible assets are important because they determine the kinds of programs the organization can pursue. But most nonprofit organizations are restricted in the amount of money available to them in a given year. Organizations such as the United Appeal fund all of their programs in one year from money raised in the preceding year. They cannot borrow or issue new stock, as businesses can. That is why fund-raising is so important.

Intangible resources can be as important as tangible ones. If a college happens to have a strong engineering program, it might want to consider such opportunities as starting a forestry program or an evening credit program in specialized technical disciplines for a market that seeks updating of skills. The school might also consider providing these classes closer to places where it is convenient for potential students to take advantage of the instruction.

The Operating Environment

The factor of most concern in the operating environment of nonprofit organizations is competition. It has intensified for many reasons. For example, the lowered birth rate of the 1970s has resulted in a fierce battle by U.S. colleges and universities to recruit a reduced number of student candidates. Religious organizations are trying a variety of approaches to attract new members, offering special services and renting their facilities for concerts and plays.

Another reason for increased competition in the nonprofit sector is changing values. Religious congregations are especially affected. Churchgoers of all denominations are "shopping" for a congregation they find more spiritually nourishing. This practice has led to big gains in some congregations—and big losses in others. Since a church's operating expenses are generally funded by donations from members, a decline in membership can have dire effects. Some churches, responding to this competition, have begun improving the "product" they offer and actively promoting livelier services (see Figure 18.2), which sometimes incorporate guitar music, slide shows, interpretive dance, laity participation, and altar girls. As one professor noted, "It's no longer a case of building a better mousetrap; now we have to market our product."

In the past, nonprofit organizations tended to ignore the importance of competition, believing it to exist only among businesses. But the federal and provincial governments' budget cutbacks have brought home to organizations the fact that the supply of funding is limited. Any exchange relationship involves potential gains or losses to participants. Organizations that can promise and deliver more benefits, whether tangible or intangible, are likely to win a greater following.

The General Environment

The four most important factors in the general environment are economic developments, technological advances, legal and governmental actions, and social expectations and values. Nonprofit organizations, like businesses, must evaluate all of these.

Economic forces can affect demand. Inflation, for example, has had a negative effect on college and university enrolment by driving up the cost of tuition. It has also hurt charitable fund-raising since the segment

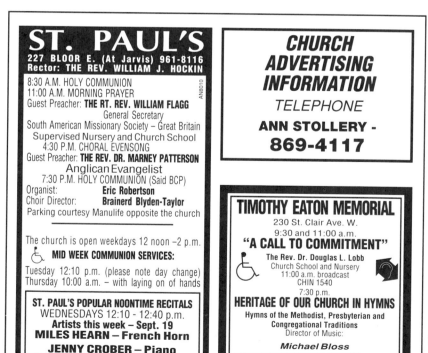

Figure 18.2 Promotion of Churches

that accounts for 50 percent of all giving (those with incomes below $20 000) is hardest hit. Cultural organizations (museums, symphonies, and so on) may not be as hard hit because they are supported mainly by those in the highest income bracket, who can manage to stay ahead of inflation. In the province of Alberta, which depends heavily on the oil industry, the decline in oil prices in the latter half of the 1980s dried up funds for a wide variety of nonprofit organizations.

Technological developments must also be considered in the nonprofit sector. Technological advances in computer equipment have allowed organizations such as the Variety Club to use television fund-raising and then to follow up on pledges, thus realizing a greater return on their efforts. Hospitals across the country are interested in technological advances that help fight disease because well-equipped hospitals attract top physicians and donors.

Legal developments may seem unimportant because most consumer laws that restrict business marketing practices are not applicable in the nonprofit sphere. Government actions can affect nonprofit organizations, however. In its 1990 budget, the federal government severely reduced the amount of funding it would provide provincial governments to help offset their costs for health care and education. Laws affecting the tax status of charitable organizations and those on donations to political parties are two more examples of the influence of the legal environment on the nonprofit sector.

Equally important to the survival and prosperity of most nonprofit organizations is the social climate in communities where they operate. Occasionally, nonprofit marketing programs are controversial. Abortion clinics meet opposition from local church groups. Agencies charged with building nuclear power plants may face opposition in some communities. Environmental analysis allows marketers to anticipate such problems and cope with them through marketing programs.

Target Marketing

Chapter 4 introduced target marketing, which consists of determining (1) whether to treat all members of the market the same or to distinguish various segments and (2) if segments are distinguished, whether to market to one or a number of them. The decisions are the same in the profit and nonprofit spheres.

For most nonprofit organizations, it pays to distinguish market segments. In fact, for those nonprofit institutions that cater to both a client public and a general public, it is absolutely necessary. U.S. public television stations serve an educated viewing public but raise most of their operating funds from businesses, the federal government, and private foundations. They must have separate marketing objectives and strategies for the viewing public and the giving public.

But even for organizations supported by the same members they serve, it pays to consider segmentation if members have different needs. A nonprofit organization can choose to concentrate its marketing effort on one segment or on many segments, as can a business. At Your Service 18.1 describes how one non-profit organization used a targeted strategy.

Marketing Mix Variables

Nonprofit marketers work with the four "Ps" just as business marketers do. For example, marketers for a political candidate can see their task as offering a product (the candidate), at a price (the electorate's vote), by various promotional means (television ads, publicity releases, the candidate's personal appearances), and through various outlets (all-candidates meetings, small clubs, social events, work sites, television debates). The meaning of the four "Ps" varies somewhat, but many of the same considerations apply.

Product Considerations

A product is a complex entity, even in a business setting. In nonbusiness organizations, a product can be still more difficult to define. Often what is offered for exchange is completely intangible. A symphony offers a musical performance. A charity may offer its donors a good feeling. Of course, not all the products of a nonprofit organization are so intangible. A library provides books, and a family-planning clinic offers contraceptives.

At Your Service 18.1

Target Marketing of Forests

Environmentalists are the target market for a special service provided by MacMillan Bloedel Ltd. The ongoing arguments between the forest companies of British Columbia and environmental groups have led to a new M&B program in which special tours are being conducted in areas of major controversy. Through an extensive use of TV and newspapers ads, users of the forest are encouraged to contact the company, which directs them to a specific area of their concern. M&B personnel then conduct the tour in the forest and provide explanations in some detail on the companies' policies of forest management. This program allows the company to reach those people who are directly concerned with a message that is both educational and factual.

Source: Information provided by MacMillan Bloedel Ltd., Vancouver.

CARMANAH

Adrian Dorst/CWCW

When the product is highly intangible, as in the case of an idea, marketers may try to embody it in a more concrete form. The idea of safe driving, marketed by Young Drivers of Canada, for example, is "sold" in such tangible forms, or "packages," as defensive driving courses and lower-premium insurance policies for good drivers.[8] In promoting its mission — health of body, mind, and spirit — the YMCA offers a wide variety of programs: child care, aquatics, youth employment, health and fitness, camping, youth sports, international exchange, and other volunteer and family activities. (See Figure 18.3.)

Many of the concepts introduced previously about business products apply to nonbusiness products as well. For example, Procter & Gamble provides a broad mix of products for the market (from Pampers to Pringle's to Dove), but so does the Vancouver Art Gallery, which offers a permanent collection of works by Emily Carr, special shows of classic European painters, slide shows for children, and art reproductions for sale in its shop.[9] In this respect, the agencies of the federal government offer perhaps the widest mix of goods and services in the nonprofit sector.

Another product concept application in both the business and nonbusiness spheres is the product life-cycle — the notion that all goods and services move through stages that call for a different marketing strategy. A good example in the nonprofit sector is the TOEFL test taken by many foreign students as one of the entry requirements for Canadian colleges and universities. This test, while adequate in the 1960s and 1970s, no longer meets all the needs of Canadian postsecondary institutions. The test has reached the decline stage and must be remarketed to gain new life. As part of its concern for keeping the product acceptable to the marketplace, the nonprofit group that runs the TOEFL is studying large-scale revisions and updates. (See Figure 18.4.)

The products of nonprofit organizations may also require demarketing when they go into a decline. A university, for example, may want to phase out a resource-draining graduate school and concentrate on undergraduate education. It may accomplish this by offering graduate courses on only one campus.

Pricing Considerations

The concept of price varies depending on what is being marketed in the nonprofit sector. When ideas are marketed, the price is often nonmonetary. The price of commitment to the idea of equal rights for women may be simply a letter to an MP. Some ideas that are marketed extract a psychological price as well. A "quit smoking" campaign calls on the public to pay for better health by giving up the perceived pleasure of that habit.

In the marketing of organizations, the notion of price can also have varied meanings. Mutual benefit associations, such as unions and clubs, often charge dues or membership fees that must cover the cost of services

The YMCA has a way of changing people's lives.
And it doesn't seem to matter if you're young, old, or somewhere in between.
For example, with our fitness programs you might have a change in your body. Or because of our youth, family and volunteer programs, you might feel a change inside, about yourself and your relationship with others.
In any case, the Y affects different people in many ways. With all kinds of different programs and activities. Yet one thing doesn't seem to change. And that is, when you go into the YMCA, you don't come out the same. You come out a little *better.*

The YMCA. It's for all of you.

Figure 18.3 Promotion of an Intangible Product: Fitness

to members. The price for the services of a government organization is the tax citizens pay.

Service organizations, which have both donor and client markets, charge both a monetary and nonmonetary price. Frequently the monetary charge to clients does not cover costs. Symphonies and museums charge admission fees but do not run solely on those funds. Benefactors make up the difference. The nonmonetary charge by service organizations is often psychological or intangible. The Canadian Cancer Society asks its donors for a personal commitment of time as well as money.

Setting prices when both monetary and nonmonetary considerations are involved is difficult.[10] The goal in determining the nonmonetary price

Figure 18.4 Update to the TOEFL Test

is to encourage involvement; therefore, the psychological costs must be minimized. In setting the monetary price, the goal is usually to cover costs.

Occasionally, however, nonprofit pricing is demand oriented rather than cost oriented. Some organizations charge a high price and try to stimulate demand. Or the price is set to encourage or discourage demand. Public libraries have a difficult time collecting fees for overdue books. Some are now increasing these fees—say, from 5 cents to 10 cents a day. The result is fewer overdue accounts and increased revenue from those borrowers who continue to remain tardy.

Placement Considerations

Since most of the products marketed by nonprofit organizations are ideas or services, their distribution (or placement in the consumer's hands) tends to be direct, without the use of intermediaries.

For ideas, the channels of distribution are the same as the media used to communicate them. Channel width is an important consideration: How many different media should be used to make people aware of the idea? A "save the whales" campaign may be handled best by an exclusive distribution strategy, using only direct mailings to members of conservationist organizations. By contrast, to promote causes such as Foster Parents Plan of Canada (see Figure 18.5), these organizations would want to reach a broad national audience. So they would choose many media, such as television and publications like *Chatelaine* and *Maclean's*.

The placement of services is similar to the distribution of goods in many respects. Services must be delivered through retail-like outlets. Thus, Simon Fraser University distributes its educational services through its main Burnaby campus, and also through its downtown Vancouver campus. In general, sites must be selected carefully in order to reach the maximum number of customers. Charities usually set up chapters in major metropolitan areas in order to take advantage of the large number of volunteers and major donors usually found there.

The Canadian Medical Association uses more diverse distribution channels for its product (information). The CMA aggressively promotes its research results and makes them available by publishing articles and books. The president makes personal trips to Ottawa to bring information directly to Parliament. In addition, members sit on high-profile government committees, become spokespersons in their areas of expertise, and make themselves available to the media. The greater the visibility, the higher the prestige, which in turn attracts new members and interests donors to the CMA's research work.

Promotional Considerations

All of the means of promotion used by business—personal selling, advertising, publicity, and sales promotion — can be used by nonprofit marketers as well. Some variation in emphasis is noticeable, however.

In the nonprofit sector, the most important promotional element is often personal selling. Some organizations, particularly larger ones, hire experts to raise funds, recruit members, or sell ideas or services. Another approach is to recruit people with high status or income to participate on a board of advisers or board of directors. These board members can then tap friends or colleagues in high places and ask for their support. Many people are willing to help but are waiting to be asked directly. Sometimes a direct request can bring a substantial contribution.

Nonprofit organizations are making increased use of telemarketing.

Figure 18.5 Foster Parents Plan of Canada

The Variety Club raises more than $1 million each year with its telethon.

In an unusual twist to telephone selling, the San Antonio Zoo took advantage of a common April Fool's joke: leaving a co-worker a message to call, say, a Ms. Ella Funt or a Mr. G. Raffe at the number of the zoo. When such calls came in, the zoo's telephone operator would ask, "Who gave you that note?" and suggest playing a trick on that person. The trick was for the zoo to call the prankster and ask him or her to match the donation of the original caller. In 1987, the zoo raised $11 000 in pledges that way.[11]

Volunteers are an important part of the sales force in the nonprofit sector. They help not just in soliciting funds but in attracting clients. For example, Alcoholics Anonymous uses its rehabilitated members to explain their experiences to alcoholics. Personal contact work requires training, supervision, and motivation. Training may be more informal and supervision less close than in business. And psychological motivators are more important than monetary rewards, although some charities offer prizes to their most successful fund-raisers.

Besides personal selling, nonprofit marketers have found advertising to be a highly effective way of communicating with the public. Many cities and provinces are discovering just how powerful advertising is. Aggressive tourism advertising by cities such as Toronto, Montreal, and Vancouver attracts millions of visitors who spend millions of dollars with happy merchants. New York State's "I Love New York" campaign, which has been running since 1977, is considered among the most successful advertising campaigns for any product. In a six-year span, the revenue attributed to tourism in New York more than doubled, from $5.5 billion annually to $11.5 billion, and the promotion launched a host of imitators.

Some of the advertising available to nonprofit organizations is free. Advertising agencies volunteer their services through the Advertising Agency Association of Canada (AAAC), and the media run the resulting campaigns at no charge. The United Appeal is successful in taking the generosity of free help one step further. Recognizing the importance of using as many different media as possible, United Appeal volunteers from the advertising agencies ask their clients to donate billboard and air time to the current campaign. Advertising of this sort resembles publicity in that it is nonpaid. Other forms of publicity—including press conferences and news releases — are very important to nonprofit marketers with limited funds.[12]

Sales promotion tools are also valuable instruments to gain public attention. Exhibits, leaflets, and dramatic events are the principal tools of sales promotion for nonprofit organizations. In recent years, for example, the Canadian Cancer Society has sponsored the Cold Turkey Day, when smokers are encouraged to quit. The Canadian government has communities across the country competing in an annual fitness challenge.

The most effective promotional strategy co-ordinates all the tools mentioned here. The Globe '90 conference, jointly sponsored by the federal government and private firms, was designed to address the global environmental crisis. For one week, newspapers, TV, and radio put out reams of free information all over the world. More than 600 businesses displayed products and services that are helping to solve the ecological problem all nations are facing. Federal ministers and environmentalists shared the same platform and many solutions were agreed on. Volunteers worked endless hours and advertising specialists gave willingly of their talents and advice.

Government itself is perhaps the largest nonprofit marketer. Recently, the federal government has promoted Participaction, the goods and services tax, and national parks, to name just a few. Provincial and municipal governments, even school boards, also promote a long list of services. A more troubling question than the degree of success of government's promotional programs is whether the government should be involved in promotion at all. Some critics charge that promotion, and especially advertising, by the government lends itself to abuse of power and wasteful spending. Each year Canada Post spends millions to remind us to mail early, and yet critics say the Crown corporation charges more and more and provides less and less service. On the other hand, promotion of an issue such as literacy is commendable for such an organization. (See Figure 18.6.) Since the government is such an important part of

Figure 18.6 Canada Literacy Symbol

the nonprofit sector, its marketers must give serious consideration to this issue and many others as they prepare government promotional campaigns.

Marketing Control

Even a well-planned marketing program can fail if marketers ignore controls. The process of control involves four steps: (1) setting well-defined objectives, (2) measuring actual results against planned results, (3) finding reasons for deviation from the plan, and (4) taking corrective action.

Objectives established in the planning phase set goals to be reached. For nonprofit marketers, the most difficult job in the control phase is to find measurements that indicate progress toward objectives. The kinds of measures needed in the nonprofit sector are not so different from those needed by business.[13] The most important measures are:

1. *Total marketing response.* In business, this refers to additional sales resulting from a marketing program. In the nonbusiness sector, it could mean increased patronage for a symphony or museum or additional funds raised by a charity in response to the marketing strategy.

2. *Market share.* This is actually a measure of how well an organization is doing relative to its direct competitors. Not all nonprofit organizations have direct competitors. A city police department has no direct competitors, though it certainly competes for limited funds with other city agencies. Charitable organizations, on the other hand, do compete and must measure their performance against competitors. Slippage in dollars raised while other organizations are experiencing an increase might indicate a marketing failure.

3. *Cost per dollar of marketing response.* In the process of meeting objectives, marketing programs should not financially strain an organization. Costs must be weighed carefully against results. For example, if a new marketing approach is going to add additional costs of 15 percent, the response rate should increase by approximately 30 percent.

4. *Marketing attitudes.* Measuring customer satisfaction is important. Businesses sometimes make return sales calls, or they survey panels of product users. Nonbusiness marketers can use similar checking techniques. Canada Post, for example, checks on customer satisfaction by making available cards that postal users can fill out with complaints or remarks about service.

One or more of these measures can be used to gauge progress toward objectives. If total market response or market share falls short of plans, if costs run too high in relation to public response, or if customer attitudes are negative, reasons must be found for the failure and corrective action must be taken.

Corrective action by the post office, for example, consists of forwarding every complaint received on its customer service cards to the local postmaster for action. The postmaster must explain how the problem was resolved to a consumer affairs bureau in Ottawa. The Ottawa bureau spot checks complaints to see if follow-up action was actually taken. Since an important marketing objective of Canada Post is to raise its public image, the control program is a key to meeting that objective. Other nonprofit organizations might benefit from imitating the example.

Chapter Replay

1. **What are the basic types of nonprofit marketing?**
   Nonprofit marketing includes person marketing, idea marketing, and organization marketing.

2. **How do nonprofit organizations market ideas?**
   They use social marketing — they apply marketing techniques to increase the acceptability of a social idea, cause, or practice in one or more selected target groups.

3. **What are the major categories of nonprofit organizations?**
   Nonprofit organizations include service organizations, mutual benefit associations, and government organizations.

4. **In what ways do nonprofit organizations differ from businesses?**
   Nonprofit organizations usually have limited resources, often serve general publics as well as client publics, and may have more difficulty establishing control standards.

5. **What are the major similarities of nonprofit and for-profit organizations?**
   Both need to plan their objectives and analyze their environments in order to operate efficiently; both need to know their markets; both work with the same elements of the marketing mix; and both need to keep track of whether they are meeting objectives.

6. **Why is environmental analysis especially important for nonprofit organizations?**
   It is important because the existence of nonprofit organizations often depends on the goodwill of donors and taxpayers as well as the public they serve.

7. **What are the characteristics of the marketing mix for nonprofit organizations?**
   The elements of the marketing mix are the same as for business marketing. In the nonprofit sector, the product may be a person, an

idea, or an organization. The price may be monetary, nonmonetary, or a combination of the two. Distribution channels are usually direct. Promotion often relies heavily on personal selling, which may depend on volunteers. Advertising may be nonpaid.

8. **What are the major ways to measure marketing success in the nonprofit sector?**
   The most important measures of marketing success are total marketing response, market share, cost per dollar of marketing response, and marketing attitudes.

Key Terms

client public	organizational marketing
general public	person marketing
government organization	service organization
idea marketing	social marketing
mutual benefit association	

Discussion Questions

1. What kinds of products do nonprofit organizations market?

2. What are the major differences between nonprofit and business organizations? What are the similarities?

3. Revise the following proposed marketing objectives to quantify them.

   a. For a community college: Attract good students.

   b. For a community organization: Start a day care centre.

   c. For a mass transit system: Increase ridership.

4. In deciding whether to add a new wing, what are some characteristics of the environment that an art museum should consider?

5. To sell season's tickets, a local opera company is considering placing an advertisement in the entertainment section of a local newspaper, running ads on a radio station that plays classical music, or sending a brochure to the mailing list of people who bought symphony orchestra tickets last year. The budget allows for only one of these approaches. Which do you recommend? Why?

6. A group of lawyers started a legal aid clinic to provide services in a neighbourhood where most people have low to middle incomes. The goal of the clinic is to make legal services available to people who otherwise could not afford them. In setting prices, should the lawyers use a demand-oriented or a cost-oriented strategy? Why?

7. Personal selling is a major part of promotion for many nonprofit organizations. Who are the salespeople in a nonprofit organization?

8. How can a nonprofit organization measure the success of its marketing efforts?

9. Is it ethical for an organization such as a charity or a church to spend money on a radio or newspaper ad when it could be spending the money on helping the needy? Why, or why not?

March of Dimes Birth Defects Foundation

CASE 18.1

The National Foundation for Infantile Paralysis was founded in 1938 by U.S. President Franklin D. Roosevelt. It was set up as a permanent, nonstock, nonprofit organization, incorporated under the Membership Corporation Law of New York. It spread quickly across the United States and also to Canada. The organization worked hard to combat the dreaded disease and its effects.

In the 1950s, polio was conquered by the Salk and Sabine vaccines. Now the National Foundation was faced with a decision of how best to utilize the knowledge, experience, and volunteer leadership developed over a 20-year period. Extensive analysis indicated that the foundation's specialized programs in research, patient services, and professional and public health education could address another major health concern — the vast and, at the time, largely unexplored field of birth defects.

The March of Dimes, a name initially coined for the annual fundraising campaign of The National Foundation, had become so closely identified with the organization that it was adopted in 1979 as the formal corporate name—the March of Dimes Birth Defects Foundation.

The mission of the March of Dimes, conducted in Canada by the Kinsmen Mothers March, is to unify, lead, and direct the fight to prevent birth defects and their consequences. In its efforts to protect the unborn and the newborn, the approaches it employs to attain its goals remain the same as in the effort against polio:

1. Research seeks causes of birth defects; faster, and more accurate, diagnostic methods; and more effective treatment and prevention techniques.

2. Health services strive to improve delivery of health care and programs of prevention related to genetic disorders, low-birthweight babies, and high-risk pregnancies.

3. Professional education disseminates knowledge gained through research and trains health professionals to improve and expand maternal/newborn health care.

4. Community services implements chapter programs to inform and educate the North American public about birth defects prevention, and to develop volunteer leadership and advocacy initiatives.

Professional Education

The March of Dimes attains its goals through a partnership of medical professionals and volunteers. It fights birth defects with a broad spectrum of programs supported by voluntary contributions. The national organization and its local chapters are leaders in educating health professionals and lay people about developments in the prevention and treatment of birth defects.

Varied, innovative professional education programs make research and health services results available to a wide range of health care professionals. Up-to-date information about birth defects, genetics, and perinatal health are reported in such publications as the *March of Dimes Reprint Series* and the *Original Article Series.* Other printed and audiovisual materials on outreach education, adolescent pregnancy, nutrition, nursing research, newborn behaviour, and intensive care are also disseminated.

The March of Dimes supports the International Clearinghouse for Birth Defects Monitoring Systems, a resource for reporting and exchanging information on birth defects incidence among a score of countries. The foundation sponsors medical conferences, symposia, and seminars to transmit and encourage discussion and exchanges of information and ideas concerning the study and treatment of birth defects.

Public Education through Community Services

Community services programs inform and educate the public about risks posed by birth defects and low birthweight to the unborn and newborn. Since early, regular prenatal care is recognized as the most important factor in the health of a mother and baby, every effort is made to communicate this to all sectors of society. Community services programs use print materials, audiovisuals, and exhibits to support group and individual behaviour patterns conducive to healthy childbearing. Grants are awarded to schools, hospitals, and community agencies to assist in preventive health education programs.

The March of Dimes takes a leading role in developing the public health education campaign of a coalition of government, professional, and voluntary health agencies. It also offers prenatal health education programs in the workplace to reach potential parents, particularly the increasing number of working women. In addition, the March of Dimes maintains a continuing effort to communicate its preventive message through the media, including news releases, feature articles, public service announcement campaigns, and video news reports, on risks during pregnancy and how to minimize them. The goal of all community service and publicity efforts is to achieve maximum awareness and understanding of birth defects and the need for their prevention and treatment.

Fund-Raising

Many of the ways in which the March of Dimes raises money annually are linked to its informational and educational prevention programs. Fund-raising activities are a primary way of informing the public about the need to prevent birth defects. Through an initial involvement with fund-raising, volunteers are recruited for service and community programs. As a result, the March of Dimes over the years has chosen not to participate in the United Way or other locally oriented campaigns. In its early years, the foundation adopted this policy to assure its independent ability to launch emergency appeals for funds during polio epidemics.

March of Dimes fund-raising events are conducted nationally and locally and depend on volunteer involvement for planning and execution. National events include the telethon, which carries the message of prevention coast-to-coast while raising millions of dollars annually. Similar events include the annual Mothers March and WalkAmerica. Chapters sponsor a broad range of other fund-raising events to fund national programs and others at the community level.

Focal Topics

1. What basic marketing concepts are being used by, or could be helpful to, the March of Dimes?

2. What advantages and disadvantages result from the Foundation's conducting its own separate campaign for support instead of joining a local organization such as the United Way? How can these advantages be maximized and disadvantages be minimized?

3. Indicate what strategy the organization should use to communicate its objectives, projects, results, and needs to its public.

Simpson Road Church

CASE 18.2

In early 1984, Simpson Road Church observed its fiftieth anniversary. A variety of worship services, guest speakers, church dinners, and special ceremonies and events were held to celebrate the occasion. The membership was proud of its church and the many accomplishments realized during its first 50 years.

As the pastor and leaders of the church began to think about the future of Simpson Road Church, however, they realized that it needed a plan, a set of goals and objectives, or some sort of strategy as it entered its second half-century of religious service. Toward that end, a Vision Committee was formed to help develop an understanding of where Simpson

Source: Much of the information here is based on an actual church. The name and certain facts have been modified.

Road Church was at that time and where it should be headed in the future.

Church Characteristics

As a prelude to developing a set of plans and objectives for Simpson Road Church, the Vision Committee compiled a list of salient characteristics of the church.

- It is in the downtown area of a major metropolitan community with a population of some 900 000.

- The present church structure is about 40 years old, has been fairly well maintained, but is in need of some major renovations to minimize future maintenance problems.

- As shown in the accompanying table, the church's 1983 membership, according to its rolls, was 526. Average attendance at morning worship was 169 for the year, while average attendance at Sunday school was 109.

- Also, as shown in the table, financial contributions decreased in 1983 after showing increases in the previous three years.

- Present seating capacity of the church, including a currently closed balcony, is for 825 people.

- During the week, the church makes its facilities available to local organizations for meetings. Some of the organizations using the facilities include Boy Scout groups, Lamaze classes, and some inner-city counselling groups.

- The church has an annual budget of just over $105 500, with approximately 80 percent coming from contributions to the church and the remaining coming from interest on the church's endowment fund and memorial gifts.

- A variety of programs is provided for all age groups—men's monthly prayer breakfasts, weekly meetings for various women's groups, and

Membership, Attendance, and Offering Statistics, 1977–1983

Year	Total Members	Members Gained	Members Lost	Worship Average	Sunday School Average	Total Offerings
1983	526	25	9	169	109	$84 672
1982	511	32	16	175	113	86 366
1981	495	5	8	156	104	72 641
1980	498	9	20	165	101	68 894
1979	509	8	16	168	108	69 525
1978	517	17	15	185	121	74 726
1977	515	10	22	210	133	76 220

an active youth program including Sunday evening sessions along with monthly special activities. Individual Sunday school classes also hold special studies and social get-togethers several times a month.

■ The church supports an active ministry in the downtown area. Through it, individuals and families in need can receive food, clothing, and temporary shelter.

Proposed Membership Research

In developing plans for the future, the Vision Committee considered it essential to have information on the attitudes, feelings, and understandings of its members toward the church and its activities. A special subcommittee, chaired by George McCormick, was formed to design, implement, and interpret a comprehensive research study of Simpson Road's membership.

George, in preparing for the first subcommittee meeting, looked to the book of Hebrews: "Consider how we may spur one another toward love and good deeds . . . do not give up meeting together . . . but to encourage one another" (Hebrews 10:24,25). This led him to the conclusion that the purpose of the research would be to obtain information that would help the church continue its goal of building up the church body. He felt that a good approach to gathering the needed membership input would be to design a detailed questionnaire to be completed by each person in the church 12 years and older. Specific information to be compiled included the members' feelings, attitudes, and understanding of the church for its members and the community.

Focal Topics

1. Do you believe that it is appropriate to use marketing concepts in religious organizations? Why, or why not?

2. What marketing concepts might be appropriate for Simpson Road Church to use in planning for the future?

3. How would you design the membership survey form? Be specific about types of questions and ways of asking them.

Case for Part Six

Live Aid

In retrospect, it was the largest, single-day fund-raising event in history. On July 13, 1985, fans sweated and cheered — 90 000 in Philadelphia and 72 000 in London — and an estimated 1.5 billion people tuned in via television through the magic of satellite television. Live Aid, the brainchild of Irish rock musician Bob Geldof, raised more than $60 million for famine relief in Ethiopia and other African countries.

Background

In 1984, Bob Geldof, lead singer of the Boomtown Rats, recruited other British recording artists to tape the hit song, "Do They Know It's Christmas/Feed the World." Proceeds, which exceeded $11 million, were used for African famine relief by the organization British Band Aid. Not to be outdone, a galaxy of American pop music stars got together and recorded an overwhelmingly well-received, "We Are The World," the proceeds from which went to USA for Africa. Meanwhile Canadian artists recorded "Tears Are Not Enough" for the Northern Lights for Africa Society.

Geldof then had the vision of bringing together the world's greatest rock musicians for a huge, live benefit concert. An organization called Worldwide Sports and Entertainment, formed to put together mega-events, got the massive concert idea rolling.

The Event

The international, 16-hour rock 'n' roll extravaganza was held on July 13, 1985. Artists performed live on stages in Philadelphia and London. By connecting together 13 satellites to reach more than 128 countries simultaneously and shipping four hours of videotaped highlights to 22 additional countries, Live Aid was delivered to audiences of more than 1.5 billion people, more than a third of the world's population.

Some 56 acts performed during the concert. Among the artists were Mick Jagger; Paul McCartney; Tina Turner; Duran Duran; Joan Baez; Bob Dylan; and Peter, Paul, and Mary.

Sources: Michael Goldberg, "Live Aid Take May Hit $60 Million," *Rolling Stone,* August 29, 1985, pp. 17 + ; and Allan Dodds Frank, "It's Only Rock 'n' Roll but They Like It," *Forbes,* September 23, 1985; p. 140.

The Results

Estimated costs to put on the Live Aid concert came to a little more than $4 million. Total revenue from all sources was expected to reach more than $60 million, leaving some $56 million for famine relief in Africa.

MTV broadcast the entire 16 hours in the United States and donated all of its $750 000 advertising revenue to the relief fund. ABC paid about $1.5 million for the rights to run its three-hour special, and a syndicate of 105 independent television stations paid about $2.5 million in rights fees and revenue for advertising. According to ABC, as many as 40 million people saw at least part of its broadcast. An additional $6 million came in from television rights fees from other countries.

The biggest portion of Live Aid revenue, roughly $36 million, came from the telethons that were held in some 22 countries. Amounts from selected countries included $1.4 million (Canada), $18.9 million (the United Kingdom), $10 million (United States), $2.0 million (New Zealand), $4.9 million (Ireland), and $3.5 million (Australia). In the United States, the average amount contributed per call during the telethon was $30.

Ticket sales and merchandising activities accounted for an additional $9.5 million in Live Aid revenue. Four corporate sponsors—AT&T, Pepsi, Kodak, and Chevrolet—contributed a total of $5 million for exposure during the concert, including having their names displayed on banners across the stage for all of the world to see.

John Costello, Pepsi's senior vice-president of marketing, estimates that his soft-drink company received 350 million favourable impressions in the United States alone for about one-third the cost of reaching that audience in prime time. That exposure was from the 26 minutes of advertising that Pepsi bought on MTV and various syndicated broadcasts.

The Future

Expenditure of Funds

Various organizations involved with Live Aid established relationships with most of the reputable agencies already at work in the famine-stricken countries and asked them to submit funding requests for needed projects. Some of the money raised was used to purchase food and supplies to be distributed through the established relief agencies. Funds were also used to obtain and distribute medical supplies and equipment. Trucks and other vehicles were purchased to transport the food and supplies to the areas of need.

Much of the money raised was devoted to longer-term projects in an effort to prevent the African tragedy from happening again. Investments were made in agricultural development projects, including water-drilling rigs to help with irrigation.

Additional Events

The success of Live Aid led to a number of other large-scale fund-raising events. Farm Aid was designed to assist financially stricken farmers in the United States. A worldwide torch relay race, First Earth Run, was held in September 1986 to raise funds for UNICEF. Live Aid sequels called Sport Aid and Farm Aid II were also held in 1986.

On May 25, 1986, the Los Angeles-based USA for Africa sponsored "Hands Across America." This event, involving more than 6 million people and a number of corporate sponsors, sought to have individuals standing in a line that stretched from New York to Los Angeles link hands at a specified moment. The objective was to raise money to aid the hungry and homeless in the United States.

While these and other similar events seemed to be well received by individuals and corporate sponsors, some questions are beginning to be raised. Might the sheer number of such events, coupled with a fatigue factor, undermine interest in the massive fund-raisers?

Focal Topics

1. What do you think are the reasons that made Live Aid so successful?

2. Beyond the aid recipients, who else benefits from such fund-raising events? In what ways do they benefit?

3. How would you promote an event like Live Aid to get more people around the world to watch it?

4. What suggestions do you have for additional ways to generate revenue from an event like Live Aid?

5. What do you see as the future for massive international fund-raising events?

Figure A.1 A Decision Tree

Source: Copyright Hallmark Cards Inc.

Career Resource Guide

The purpose of this appendix is to help students target their ambitions in selecting an entry-level position in the field of marketing. We will describe some of the most prevalent entry-level jobs in the areas of sales, advertising, sales promotion, public relations, marketing research, retailing, wholesaling, telemarketing, and entrepreneurship. We will also explain how internships help students become more qualified in the job market.

Sales

According to surveys, many students graduating with diplomas or degrees in marketing join the work force in sales positions. Selling jobs are plentiful, and some are especially attractive to graduating students.

Wholesale Sales

Wholesale selling involves the sale of goods and services to intermediaries who in turn resell the goods to others for a profit. Examples include selling to retailers, wholesalers, and industrial and commercial firms. A *wholesaler representative* would be responsible for selling to retailers while working for a wholesaler, jobber, and/or distributor. Wholesale selling often involves selling a vast number of products—in some cases up to 50 000 items. This is accomplished by selling from a catalogue or series of catalogues because there are too many items to memorize. A wholesaler rep usually represents more than one supplier or manufacturer and, in some cases, may represent competitors in the marketplace. For many years wholesale reps were considered order takers, but with increasing competition in the field, they have become order seekers through their sales efforts. Among their objectives are communicating enthusiasm to the prospective buyers and helping them feel the need to carry a new or improved product.

A *merchandising salesperson* sells to retailers. The main area of responsibility for these salespeople is developing a territory that will produce the maximum volume of business for a particular product. Their job description might include the following tasks: checking inventory to find out exactly what the customer needs; discussing and taking regular orders, including recommending the amount of product the customer

Moving Up

**Jo Foxworth
Founder
Jo Foxworth
Advertising, Inc.**

A Mississippi native, Jo Foxworth received a journalism degree from the University of Missouri and began her career selling advertising for a newspaper in McComb, Mississippi, for $10 a week. Following that she worked in retailing and advertising in Louisville and at Nan Duskin in Philadelphia before moving to New York in 1955.

In New York, she began her advertising career in earnest with a job at J. M. Mathes and soon after moved to McCann-Erikson, where she worked as a copywriter on the Coca-Cola, Westinghouse, Nestlé, and Liggett & Myers accounts. After stints at a few other agencies, she decided to start her own shop with D'Agostino supermarkets as her first client. Soon after, J. C. Penney, Celanese Corporation, and United Fruit Company were added to the roster.

Jo Foxworth is probably best known for a speech she gave in which she set forth the "Nine Commandments for Women in Business." Among them:

"Thou shalt try harder; thou need not be only number two."

"Thou shalt know when to zip thy lip and listen quietly."

"Thou shalt watch thy language; there may be gentlemen present."

Source: Adapted from Bart Cummings, "The Benevolent Dictators," *Advertising Age*, February 20, 1984, pp. M-4–5, M-51.

Meifert & Heal

needs to take care of business on a regular basis; showing customers the monthly and quarterly specials offered by the companies represented; and presenting special sales to get the companies' goods on display or in the dealers' advertising.

Industrial Sales

In the area of industrial sales, a *manufacturers' representative* works directly for and is employed by the manufacturer. These salespeople call on wholesalers, dealers, and distributors. They are also contact and promotional people, sales supervisors, complaint handlers, adjusters, and public relations people. Entry-level positions in this area of selling are scarce and are filled by assertive, innovative, and emotionally well-adjusted people who must be able to manage time and accept rejection. They must be knowledgeable about the company and its products and services; they should also know all areas of marketing, including product and product development, pricing and discount policies, physical distribution, promotion, and sales promotion. The manufacturers' representative relays customers' needs to the firm's research and development department so new products may be planned and developed for the marketplace. This job usually involves a great deal of travelling.

Moving Up

**Lenore Cooney
Account Supervisor
Dudly-Anderson-
Yutzy Public
Relations**

"What can you say about a 100-year-old bridge in need of refurbishment?" Lenore Cooney asked herself the day she got the Brooklyn Bridge account. Plenty, as it turned out. The hundredth birthday party for the bridge on May 24, 1983, became such an extravaganza that one reporter called it "this year's version of the royal wedding."

Behind all this hoopla was Lenore Cooney, who had spent 18 months researching stories, finding angles, providing photographs, filling airtime, and otherwise servicing the insatiable media monster.

By the time the last fireworks display had vanished into the New York night sky, the stack of newspaper clippings about the event had reached two metres, articles had appeared in every magazine from *Life* to *Popular Mechanics*, total U.S. television coverage had run to 18 hours, and TV crews from Canada, Brazil, Japan, and five

European countries had covered the event.

While selling the Brooklyn Bridge seems like a singular marketing challenge, according to Cooney it wasn't much different from selling bananas or pain relievers or floppy disks. Public relations success in any of these areas, says Cooney, requires that a marketer find a theme, develop the news angles, and "then follow up, follow up."

Source: Adapted from Curtis Hartman, "Selling the Brooklyn Bridge," *Inc.*, November 1983, p. 58.

Retail Sales

Generally speaking, the *retail salesperson* positions are not sought out by college and university graduates. The main reason for this is because most of these positions are minimum wage jobs and offer limited chance for advancement. If advancement is to come, it usually takes a very long time. A good professional retail salesperson can be a great asset to a retail company and usually is paid on a commission basis. This type of sales position would normally involve a "big ticket" item such as furniture, appliances, fences, and floor coverings.

Direct Sales

Our discussion of direct sales positions is limited to the most common types. Let's begin with the *account executive trainee* in an advertising agency. Trainees frequently receive formal training, some on the job and some in a classroom. They work in various departments of the agency, including media, creative, production, traffic, customer service, and customer relations. Their tasks may be menial, but they are exposed to all aspects of the agency and have contact with successful account executives. Trainees also work with assistant account executives. By so doing, they make client contact, help put ideas together, "chase" material and people, and contribute to decision making.

Moving Up

Ivan Fellegi
Chief Statistician
Statistics Canada

A career civil servant, Ivan Fellegi joined Statistics Canada, the government agency that manages the census and other government surveys and data keeping, as a "superclerk" in 1957. He studied nights at Ottawa's Carleton University, where he earned his M.Sc. and Ph.D., while he worked his way up through the StatsCan ranks. Today, he runs the agency, which, to him, is like managing any business.

As chief statistician, Fellegi is hard at work bringing StatsCan into step with modern times. In addition to the census every five years, the agency conducts some 500 surveys and releases hundreds of publications. As the bulk of StatsCan's raw data comes from telephone interviews and written surveys, Fellegi is keen to reduce the paperwork burden on respondents and to increase efficiency.

Fellegi is excited about the growing interchange between the private sector and the agency that has immersed itself in Canadian lives for almost 70 years. The federal government buys more than $15 billion a year in services from the private sector. Fellegi says he'd be happy to sell back information worth 1 percent of that amount. His message to the StatsCan legions from Ottawa headquarters

is simple: "We run a world-renowned shop here. Talk to business and tell them we've got a great product."

Source: Adapted from "Profile, Ivan Fellegi — Managing Canada's Largest Database," in Steven H. Appelbaum, M. Dale Beckman, Louis E. Boone, and David L. Kurtz, *Contemporary Canadian Business*, 3rd ed. (Toronto: Holt, Rinehart and Winston of Canada, 1990), p. 402.

A *specialty advertising salesperson* works for a company that sells specialty advertising items such as calendars, T-shirts, caps, pens, pencils, and rulers. The selling includes making cold calls and servicing repeat business. The salesperson's objective is to encourage customers to "get their name out before their buying public." One specialty advertising salesperson said, "If you can get the item to hold still for 30 seconds, we'll get your name on it and you can give it to your customer."

The key to successful specialty advertising selling is first to develop the customer's need for a specialty item and then to develop a plan for the distribution of that item. Developing a distribution plan is especially important: many repeat sales have been lost because the item never got into the hands of the person who made the buying decision. Because there are about 15 000 different specialty advertising items, the salesperson must be able to suggest those items that would be most appropriate to deliver the customer's message. Roger Shuneson began his career in specialty advertising as a salesman for Brown & Bigelow, one of the largest firms in the business. After five years of selling, he was promoted to district manager and then regional manager. According to Shuneson, go-getters do well in the business. He says, "There's always a need for talented salespeople who want to make a lot of money."

Moving Up

Michael Bregman
Creator and Chairman
Mmmuffins Inc.

Building and buying food companies wasn't always what Michael Bregman envisioned for himself. Although both his father and grandfather had been involved in such work, following in his father's footsteps did not initially appeal to Bregman. "My attitude was that the bakery business was a declining one," he says. As a Harvard MBA student, he pictured a career in management consulting or perhaps investment banking.

During the 1970s, Bregman worked as an assistant to Dave Nichol, then president of Loblaw Companies Ltd. One of his assignments was in Loblaw's bakery departments. Witnessing the customer response to such new items as oversized muffins, Bregman sensed an opportunity. "The consumer had never stopped demanding high-quality baked goods, but the industry had forgotten how to

provide them," he says "That meant there was a big niche that hadn't been exploited."

With the help of his wife, Barbara, who tested recipes, loans of around $425 000, and some good advice from his father, Bregman opened his first mmmarvelous mmmuffins store in Toronto's Eaton Centre in 1979. Business was slow during the first few weeks, but within six months he had achieved twice his projected weekly sales for the first year.

Bregman quickly launched a second concept, the Michael's Baguette chain, which specialized in French bread and croissants. He later entered into a partnership with the founders of the Coffee Tree stores, which specialize in roasting coffee beans right on the premises. Mmmuffins Inc. now boasts 120 outlets in Ontario with more to come in other parts of Canada.

Bregman intends to be a major player in the Canadian food industry. Undoubtedly, there will be

more retail developments, and he sometimes thinks about overseas expansion. A clear focus on understanding the customer and his or her needs plus having an obsessive commitment to execute in the best way possible are some of the main reasons for the success of mmmuffins.

Source: Adapted from "Profile, Michael Bregman — The Mmmuffin Man Finding New Market Opportunities," Steven H. Appelbaum, M. Dale Beckman, Louis E. Boone, and David L. Kurtz, *Contemporary Canadian Business*, 3rd ed. (Toronto: Holt, Rinehart and Winston of Canada, 1990), p. 286.

Real estate selling is another direct sales area that rewards those with initiative. Many *real estate salespeople* have made a fortune. Some have even gone on to start their own firms. Selling real estate involves more than just listing and selling houses, vacant lots, and businesses. An important part of the job is developing a list of prospects. This may be done in many ways, from receiving calls made to the real estate company for a particular house listed to making cold calls in a neighbourhood that has the potential for profitable sales. In the trade, the latter is known as "farming" a neighbourhood, whereby salespeople make themselves known to the residents of an area by making calls, introducing themselves, and letting the residents know of the services they provide.

Real estate selling is a career in which the recent graduate can excel

Moving Up

**Sylvia Rempel
Creator of
Sun Ice Designs**

As a teenage refugee from Kassel, West Germany, in the early 1950s, young Sylvia Rempel worked with other members of her family in the sugar beet fields of Alberta to help repay their ocean fare from Europe. Rempel has worked hard ever since. In the ensuing years she married, raised four children and found time to create a multimillion-dollar sportswear company — Sun Ice Ltd. — whose sports clothes and leisurewear are now stocked by stores throughout Canada and the United States. Sun Ice was chosen to provide outfits for about 10 000 Canadian athletes, officials, and volunteers at the Calgary Winter Olympics.

Rempel's achievement demonstrates that a well-designed and well-marketed product can surmount the distance from major markets. An important factor in marketing Sun Ice products has been the national pride shown by the company. It has supplied top Canadian athletes with the company's distinctive gear. The members of three climbing teams on Mount Everest wore Sun Ice clothing, and the outstanding Canadian downhill skiing team of Steve Podborski, Ken Read, and Gerry Sorensen displayed the Sun Ice logo on the slopes of the international circuit.

The origins of Sun Ice were modest. Married at 20 to Calgary schoolteacher Victor Rempel, Sylvia began making outfits for her family and a growing number of neighbourhood clients. Then a local ski shop owner stocked some of Rempel's outfits. As sales grew, she moved the fledgling company from her basement through a series of locations and finally expanded into a modern $3-million factory where 200 employees work on a computer-controlled production line.

After penetrating the U.S. market, the company has plans for Japan and Europe. In the meantime, the company's president is as dedicated to work as ever. She still designs most of the styles in the Sun Ice collection and personally makes sure that the company's reputation for quality is upheld. "I'm always around the production floor," says Rempel. "They call me Eagle Eye."

Source: "Profile, Sylvia Rempel — Creator of Sun Ice Designs, Products to be Shown to the World," in Steven H. Appelbaum, M. Dale Beckman, Louis E. Boone, and David L. Kurtz, *Contemporary Canadian Business*, 3rd ed. (Toronto: Holt, Rinehart and Winston of Canada, 1990), p. 308.

from the time he or she gets a licence and generate an excellent income. Compensation is usually on a straight commission basis. Because most real estate salespeople are independent contractors, they do not receive many of the benefits of company employees. This means that they are responsible for their own benefits, such as insurance. They also take full responsibility for making their own tax payments (there is no withholding) and Canada (or Quebec) Pension Plan contributions; they are not eligible for unemployment insurance.

Some salespeople specialize in certain areas such as residential, commercial, or industrial real estate. All selling, however, requires a people orientation and a desire to serve clients. Satisfying clients is especially important in selling real estate because new business is often generated from referrals. Lynne Van Deventor, a realtor associate at a Century 21 office in Lansing, Michigan, attributes her success to a good referral business and customer follow-up. Van Deventor is one of many women who have prospered in this field of selling. In a recent year she sold over $12 million of residential, commercial, industrial, and vacant land real estate and has been the leading salesperson in her office for the past 11 years.

Advertising

An *assistant art director* has a general knowledge of marketing and an art background. Creativeness is essential, even though the assistant often begins in the composition room, putting together advertisements. Communication skills are also important because the assistant interacts with the art director, copywriters, and production people. The assistant art director graphically projects what the copywriter has written. Assistants may be assigned to a small account, working under the supervision of the art director. Some of their time may be spent with a photographer or illustrator and in brainstorming sessions for innovative ideas.

A *sales promotion assistant* can work for an advertising agency or a wholesaler. Sales promotion is one of the most important links in the marketing process: it gets the product or service into the distribution process and the sell-through process.

Sales involves interfacing with different vendors for promotion ideas. The other part of the job is sales merchandising, which entails sending bulletins to the field on current promotions. A third part of the position involves helping brand groups when they need assistance in the selection of promotional pieces by developing various promotional materials and screening outside ideas that come in.

Public Relations

Working with the public relations staff, an *assistant public relations reporter or writer* assists in gathering important information, interpreting the information, and then writing press releases from this data. An assistant usually compiles and checks press lists, helps set up and confirm arrangements for public relations events, researches background facts and figures for a supervisor, and develops a network of contacts, which is a valuable source of information. This area of marketing requires excellent verbal and writing skills as well as the ability to communicate with clients, other staff members, and the media. Developing good relationships with media personnel is especially important because they publish or air the message about a company's product, service, or image. An assistant could be promoted to a public relations officer or director of public relations.

Marketing Research

Collecting information is the primary task of a *marketing research assistant.* Most of the information is collected through telephone calls. An assistant might also work with an assistant marketing analyst in compiling information for a project. For this, familiarity with computers and computer reports is necessary. Advancement in marketing research requires at least a bachelor's and preferably a master's degree.

Retailing

Most graduates begin their careers in retailing as *executive trainees*. Trainees are often assigned to a buyer and a group manager so they are exposed to both the merchandising and the managerial aspects of retailing. Initial tasks might include assisting the assistant buyer to ensure that correct merchandise has been received and is moved to the proper selling area at the right time, and working on temporary price changes.

In moving up the retail ladder, a trainee could become an assistant buyer, a buyer, a divisional merchandise manager, and finally a general manager. Those who advance quickly are bright and innovative and have a lot of ambition and desire to keep on learning.

Executive trainees can also move into sales management positions. A *sales manager* is responsible for a small number of classifications under the divisional group manager's authority. The sales manager organizes and staffs the department and handles financial planning, quota setting, and territory management. The sales manager must constantly train and evaluate the sales force, motivating them to excel through appropriate incentives and compensation.

Wholesaling

One entry-level position in the physical distribution area of marketing is an *order processing rate clerk,* whose main task is processing orders. This involves identifying the appropriate storage and transportation rates, examining new equipment purchase details, and performing routine financial and inventory control. Clerks frequently use computers to perform these functions. They also assist the terminal manager with planning and analysis, customer service, traffic and transportation, warehouse operation, and inventory control. This experience helps prepare them for a promotion to terminal manager and then regional manager.

Another entry-level position is a *traffic scheduler,* who is responsible for comparing transportation costs and then processing the necessary paperwork to accomplish this task. The job includes scheduling, customer service, selecting a carrier (on a limited basis), and tracing shipments. The traffic scheduling person would assist the traffic manager in his or her main responsibility, cost savings. They must find the most dependable, accessible, least expensive carrier that can deliver the goods on time and in the quantity needed.

Another wholesaling job available to graduating students is that of the *production or warehouse line.* People work with the inventory co-ordinator by moving the product upward through the channels as rapidly as possible. This position includes writing and expediting orders, handling manufacturing relations, and maintaining records on inventory counts. Establishing good communications with the channel members is a top priority. Promotions may lead to inventory co-ordinator and then inventory control manager.

An *assistant brand manager* works with sales promotion managers in developing theories, strategies, techniques, and credibility for the brand. For the consumer goods wholesaler and manufacturer, the assistant brand manager assists the sales promotion manager in trying to develop appropriate promotions that will improve the business of the brand groups. They perform creative tasks similar to those of an advertising agency. They often recognize an opportunity, approach the brand group with an idea, and then work with the necessary support groups to develop, implement, and measure the success or failure of the promotional event. An assistant brand manager may be promoted to a promotional assistant and then a planning co-ordinator.

Telemarketing

The fastest-growing business in North America, according to some studies, is telemarketing. There are many jobs for *telemarketers,* who sell everything from newspapers to computers. The owner of a telemarketing business says telemarketers must have a good voice and maintain excellent voice techniques. A good command of the English language and proper grammar usage are essential; bilingual skills are even better. Telemarketers study product characteristics and learn sales scripts. They must be sincere and capable of conveying the excitement of the product they are selling without the benefit of face-to-face contact with prospective buyers.

Entrepreneurship

A classroom survey revealed that over 50 percent of students studying business would like to become entrepreneurs.[1]

With this amount of interest, it is important to address the possibilities of owning a business after graduation. During a recent interview with Ms. Priscilla Peterson, manager of Management Recruiters and owner of Office Mates in Lansing, Michigan, she stated, "I came here to become a *management recruiter executive.* I liked the business so well I became the manager and then started my own business called Office Mates." In Office Mates, office support people are placed around the immediate area, "usually not over 50 miles from Lansing," says Ms. Peterson. "This is known as a 'head hunting' business," Ms. Peterson goes on to say, "and it would be a very good experience for a college graduate to become a business owner." In this business they try and match possible employees with companies that need talented individuals. The management recruiter would be responsible for the development of client companies and the servicing of those companies by finding people to fill their needs. Their duties and responsibilities include the following: 1) develop new client companies through telephone calls; 2) write orders; 3) recruit, when necessary, to fill openings for clients; 4) interview applicants; 5) present job openings to qualified candidates; 6) reference check applicants; 7) arrange interview dates and times; 8) prepare applicants for job interviews; 9) follow up interviews with applicants and employers; 10) close and finalize placements; 11) make necessary "key accounts" visits; 12) plan the next day's activities during the planning hour; and 13) keep records on daily statistics of placements.

Ms. Peterson states, "For one to be acceptable in this business, one should possess several traits. Among these are enthusiasm, positive attitude, internal motivation, good self-image, some kind of previous success, a curious mind, common sense, good listening skills, and integrity." She went on to say, "Ninety percent of this job is telemarketing." This is an attractive business that a college or university graduate may well be qualified to run.

Internships

An excellent way to become familiar with many entry-level marketing jobs is to become an intern. An internship is a co-operative arrangement between businesses and colleges or universities whereby students work part-time and receive school credit for their on-the-job training. Interning gives students the opportunity to determine whether or not they are suited to a certain type of job.

About 50 percent of all intern students are hired by the companies they worked for during their college years. An internship can be a vital part of an education. It gives students a chance to practise what they have learned in the classroom, it exposes them to the workplace and teaches them how to function in a controlled setting, and it provides them with an opportunity to develop interpersonal skills and attitudes involving relationships with others. Internships also help students to develop proficiency in judgement and decision making, to understand the functions of marketing and management, and to realize the importance of dependability, appearance, and promptness.

Internships are available in many areas of marketing — selling, marketing research, retail sales, telemarketing, and office management.

Appendix B

Marketing Arithmetic

Many decisions that marketers make are based on an analysis of their company's financial statements. To arrive at these business decisions, marketers must be able to perform some basic marketing arithmetic.

Marketing arithmetic deals with simple arithmetical ideas, such as percentages and ratios. This appendix presents three major areas of marketing arithmetic: the operating statement, analytical ratios, and pricing.

The Operating Statement

The *operating statement* can also be called the profit-and-loss statement, or the income statement. This statement, which is one of the major tools for analyzing a company's financial performance, presents a summary of a company's sales and expenses *over a specific period of time*—a month, a quarter, or a year.

Another important financial statement is the *balance sheet,* which shows the assets, liabilities, and net worth of a company *at one point in time.* Both of these financial statements are used by marketers to arrive at decisions.

For the marketer, however, the operating statement is the more important of the two financial statements. Besides showing whether a company had a net profit or net loss, it provides much of the information needed to figure the analytical ratios used in marketing decision making.

Table B.1 shows the December operating statement for Jones & Smith Clothiers, Inc., a small retail company. This is the type of operating statement that a company would provide to its marketers. It has six main parts: gross sales, net sales, cost of goods sold, gross margin, operating expenses, and net profit before taxes.

Gross sales are the total sales revenue received by a company during a specific period of time. In the case of Jones & Smith, gross sales were $54 000 for the month of December.

Net sales are the revenue retained by a company after subtracting the amount paid to customers for sales *returns* and *allowances.* If a customer returns merchandise and receives a refund or credit, this is considered a sales return. If a customer returns a damaged item and is given a price reduction on the item, this is considered an allowance. The net sales for Jones & Smith in December were $51 000.

Cost of goods sold is the total amount that a company paid for the merchandise it sold. Jones & Smith's cost of goods sold was $26 800. This

Table B.1   A Sample Operating Statement

Jones & Smith Clothiers, Inc. *Operating Statement* *for December*			
Revenues			
Gross sales		$54 000	
Less: Sales returns and allowances	$ 3 000		
Net sales			$51 000
Cost of goods sold			
Beginning inventory, December 1 (at cost)		$10 000	
Gross purchases during year	$25 000		
Less: Purchase discounts	1 000		
Net purchases	$24 000		
Plus: Freight in	800		
Net purchases (total delivered cost)		24 800	
Cost of goods available for sale		$34 800	
Less: Ending inventory, December 31 (at cost)		8 000	
Cost of goods sold			$26 800
Gross margin			$24 200
Operating expenses			
Selling expenses			
Sales salaries and commissions	$ 6 000		
Advertising	2 000		
Delivery charges	2 000		
Total selling expenses		$10 000	
General expenses			
Office salaries	$ 4 000		
Rent and utilities	3 000		
Miscellaneous general expenses	1 000		
Total general expenses		$ 8 000	
Total operating expenses			$18 000
Net income before taxes			$ 6 200

figure was determined by first adding the *beginning inventory,* or goods on hand at the beginning of December, to the net purchases (including transportation cost) and then subtracting the ending inventory amount.

If Jones & Smith were a manufacturing company instead of a retail company, the purchases section of the operating statement would be replaced by a cost of goods manufactured section. This section includes the cost of raw materials, labour, and factory overhead (light, heat, power). It is important to remember that for retailers the cost of goods sold is the cost of merchandise purchased for resale.

The next line on the operating statement is *gross margin,* or gross profit. This figure is obtained by subtracting the cost of goods sold from net sales. Jones & Smith's gross margin was 24 200. Gross margin is the total amount that a company has to cover operating expenses and to provide a net profit.

Operating expenses are all the expenses, other than the cost of goods, that a company has during the time covered by the operating statement. Included in this part of the operating statement are selling expenses and general expenses. Some companies also list administrative expenses separately within this section. Selling expenses are sometimes listed as marketing expenses.

Jones & Smith Clothiers' selling expenses included salaries and commissions for sales personnel, advertising, and delivery charges. General expenses covered office salaries, rent and utilities, and miscellaneous expenses such as office supplies and insurance. By adding the total selling expenses of $10 000 to the total general expenses of $8000, Jones & Smith Clothiers find that total operating expenses were $18 000.

Total operating expenses are then subtracted from gross margin to determine *net income before taxes,* or net profit before taxes. This part of the operating statement is often referred to as the "bottom line." If a company has a loss rather than a profit for the operating period, the bottom line reads:

Net Income (Loss) before Taxes

Jones & Smith's net income before taxes was $6200. This amount is used to cover taxes as well as profits for owners or shareholders. Net income *before* taxes is important because a company's operating performance is evaluated on this basis.

The Jones & Smith operating statement is an example of a *multistep* statement. This is the form of statement that marketing personnel within a company would use to analyze the company's performance. Another type of operating statement, the *single-step* statement, arrives at net profit before taxes in one step: expenses are subtracted from net sales; no other information is provided. Companies use the single-step form in their reports to shareholders or in other public documents.

Analytical Ratios

In addition to showing a company's net sales and net profit, the operating statement provides data for figuring important *analytical ratios*, or performance ratios. These ratios enable marketers to evaluate their company's performance by comparing it with their performance in previous operating periods or with the performances of similar companies in their industry. Statistics Canada, the various Financial Post services, Dun & Bradstreet Canada, and various trade associations are sources for these kinds of comparative data.

Operating Ratios

Operating ratios are analytical ratios obtained by dividing each item on the operating statement by the amount of net sales. These ratios are expressed as a percentage of net sales, with net sales as a base of 100 percent. Although an operating ratio can be calculated for each line on the operating statement, the most important and most commonly used operating ratios for marketers are gross margin ratio, operating expense ratio, and net profit ratio. The formulas for calculating these ratios and other marketing ratios are given in Table B.2.

The *gross margin ratio* shows the percentage of net sales dollars available to cover operating expenses and to provide a profit after paying for the cost of goods sold. Using the information from Table B.1, the gross margin ratio for Jones & Smith is calculated as follows:

$$\text{Gross Margin Ratio} = \frac{\text{Gross Margin}}{\text{Net Sales}}$$

or

$$\frac{\$24\,200}{\$51\,000} = .475 \text{ or } 47.5\%$$

The higher the gross margin ratio, the more dollars a company has left for expenses and profit.

The *operating expense ratio* indicates the percentage of each net sales dollar needed to cover total operating expenses. If this ratio is high, it means that the company is spending a great deal on salaries, commissions, and advertising. The marketer can then calculate the ratio for each item within the operating expenses section to determine which expenses were too high.

Jones & Smith's operating ratio is figured as follows:

$$\text{Operating Expense Ratio} = \frac{\text{Total Operating Expenses}}{\text{Net Sales}}$$

or

$$\frac{\$18\,000}{\$51\,000} = .353 \text{ or } 35.3\%$$

The *net profit ratio* reveals the percentage of each net sales dollar that is left *after* all expenses have been paid but *before* payment of income taxes. Some companies, however, figure net profit ratio *after* taxes have been deducted. When comparing the net profit ratios of several similar companies, marketers must know whether the ratios were calculated before or after taxes.

Net profit ratios vary widely from one industry to another. Thus marketers should know the industry average before evaluating their company's net profit ratio. For example, a 1 percent net profit ratio is average in the supermarket industry but low in the retail clothing industry.

Jones & Smith's net profit ratio is figured as follows:

$$\text{Net Profit Ratio} = \frac{\text{Net Income before Taxes}}{\text{Net Sales}}$$

or

$$\frac{\$\ 6\,200}{\$51\,000} = .122 \text{ or } 12.2\%$$

Question 1 If a company had net sales of \$110 000, gross sales of \$112 000, gross margin of \$55 800, and expenses of \$43 000, what would the gross margin ratio, expense ratio, and net profit ratio be?

Stock Turnover Rate

Another kind of analytical ratio that helps measure a company's performance is the *stock turnover rate*. This is the number of times that a company's average inventory is sold, or turns over, during a specified period of time — usually a year. Average inventory can be figured by adding beginning and ending inventories, then dividing by 2.

$$\text{Average Inventory} = \frac{\text{Beginning Inventory} + \text{Ending Inventory}}{2}$$

Stock turnover rate can be computed in three different ways, depending on the kind of figures available. The formulas for computing stock turnover rate are:

$$\text{Stock Turnover Rate} = \frac{\text{Cost of Goods Sold}}{\text{Average Inventory at Cost}}$$

$$\text{Stock Turnover Rate} = \frac{\text{Net Sales}}{\text{Average Inventory at Selling Price}}$$

$$\text{Stock Turnover Rate} = \frac{\text{Sales in Units}}{\text{Average Inventory in Units}}$$

Table B.2 Analytical Ratios Commonly Used in Marketing

Ratio	Formula
Gross Margin Ratio (Percentage)	$\frac{\text{Gross Margin}}{\text{Net Sales}} = \text{Gross Margin \%}$
Operating Expense Ratio (Percentage)	$\frac{\text{Total Operating Expenses}}{\text{Net Sales}} = \text{Expense \%}$
Net Profit Ratio (Percentage)	$\frac{\text{Net Income before Taxes}}{\text{Net Sales}} = \text{Net Profit \%}$
Stock Turnover Rate (STR) (Based on Cost)	$\frac{\text{Cost of Goods Sold}}{\text{Average Inventory at Cost}} = \text{STR}$
	$\frac{\text{Average}}{\text{Inventory}} = \frac{\text{Beginning Inventory} + \text{End Inventory}}{2}$
Return on Investment (ROI)	$\frac{\text{Net Profit}}{\text{Net Sales}} \times \frac{\text{Net Sales}}{\text{Investment}} = \text{ROI}$
Markup Percentage (Based on Selling Price)	$\frac{\text{Dollar Markup}}{\text{Selling Price}} = \text{Markup \%}$
Markdown Ratio (Percentage)	$\frac{\text{Markdown} + \text{\$ Allowance}}{\text{Net Sales for Item}} = \text{Markdown \%}$

The most commonly used formula is based on cost of goods sold because all the data are easily available on the operating statement. By using the first formula and information from Jones & Smith's operating statement, the stock turnover rate is calculated as follows:

$$\text{Average Inventory at Cost} = \frac{\$10\,000 + \$8\,000}{2} = \$9\,000$$

$$\text{Stock Turnover Rate} = \frac{\$26\,800}{\$\,9\,000} = 2.98$$

This means that Jones & Smith's inventory turned over 2.98 times during the year.

Average stock turnover rates, like net profit ratios, also vary from one industry to another and from one department to another in the same company. For example, the turnover rate of a grocery store should be much higher than the turnover rate of a furniture store. Within the grocery store, the meat department should have a much higher turnover rate than the canned goods department.

Usually, a high stock turnover rate shows that a company's management is efficient and is turning a profit. However, if the stock turnover rate is too high, it might mean that a company is maintaining too low an average inventory. A reduced stock turnover rate from one year to the next shows that a company is carrying some unpopular items in its inventory. Thus the stock turnover rate is an important figure for evaluating a company's performance.

Question 2 Compute the stock turnover rate for a company whose cost of goods sold was $54\,200, with beginning inventory of $26\,000 and ending inventory of $24\,000.

Return on Investment

Return on investment (ROI) is an analytical ratio that compares a company's profits with the amount of investment the company needs to make or sell a product. *Investment* is a company's total assets, such as land, factory or store, equipment, and inventory, minus the firm's liabilities. The ROI shows how well a company has used its assets to generate sales and make a profit. Thus it is an important ratio for marketers.

To figure a company's ROI, a marketer needs both the balance sheet and the operating statement. The amount of investment is obtained from the company's balance sheet. The operating statement provides the net sales and net profit before taxes figures. The formula for calculating ROI follows:

$$\text{ROI} = \frac{\text{Net Profit}}{\text{Net Sales}} \times \frac{\text{Net Sales}}{\text{Investment}}$$

If Jones & Smith's balance sheet for December 31, 1983, showed

$30 000 for total investment, the ROI would be figured in this way:

$$ROI = \frac{\$6\,200}{\$51\,000} \times \frac{\$51\,000}{\$30\,000}$$

$$= .1215 \times 1.7 = .2066 \text{ or } 20.66\%$$

Question 3 By using this formula a company can determine how to increase its ROI either by increasing its net profit or decreasing its investment. If Jones & Smith increased sales to $75 000, how would the ROI be affected? Would this happen no matter how much sales were increased? Now figure Jones & Smith's ROI, with sales of $75 000 and investment reduced to $25 000. Then figure Jones & Smith's ROI using the original figures, but increasing the net profit to $10 000.

Pricing

Another major area of marketing arithmetic involves pricing. Marketers should know how to calculate selling prices using the formulas for markups and markdowns. Both markups and markdowns are expressed as percentages.

Markups

A *markup* is the dollar amount added to the cost of goods to determine the selling price. Markup is closely related to gross margin because both are expected to cover operating expenses and net profit. Markups can be figured as either a percentage of cost or as a percentage of selling price:

$$\frac{\text{Markup Percentage}}{\text{Based on Cost}} = \frac{\text{Dollar Markup (Amount Added to Cost)}}{\text{Cost}}$$

$$\frac{\text{Markup Percentage}}{\text{Based on Selling Price}} = \frac{\text{Dollar Markup (Amount Added to Cost)}}{\text{Selling Price}}$$

If Jones & Smith bought ties at a cost of $6 a piece and set a selling price of $10 for them, the markup would be $4. The markup percentage could be figured in these two ways:

$$\frac{\text{Markup Percentage}}{\text{Based on Cost}} = \frac{\$4.00}{\$6.00} = 66.67\%$$

$$\frac{\text{Markup Percentage}}{\text{Based on Selling Price}} = \frac{\$4.00}{\$10.00} = 40\%$$

Although the *dollar* markup used in both formulas is the same, the *percentage* of markup differs because one formula was based on cost and the other formula was based on selling price.

For marketers to make valid comparisons between markups on identical items from one store to another, they must know what the markup percentage was based on. For this reason, *markup percentages are usually stated as percentage of selling price*—unless indicated otherwise.

Suppose Jones & Smith bought suits at $90 a piece and knew that their usual markup based on selling price is 40 percent. The selling price could be determined by using the following formula:

$$\text{Selling Price} = \frac{\text{Cost in Dollars}}{100\% - \text{Markup Percentage Based on Selling Price}}$$

or

$$\text{Selling Price} = \frac{\$90.00}{100\% - 40\%} = \frac{\$90.00}{60\%} = \$150.00$$

Sometimes marketers wish to convert the markup percentage from one base—cost or selling price—to the other. This can be done by using one of the following formulas:

$$\frac{\text{Markup Percentage}}{\text{Based on Cost}} = \frac{\text{Markup Percentage Based on Selling Price}}{100\% - \text{Markup Percentage Based on Selling Price}}$$

$$\frac{\text{Markup Percentage}}{\text{Based on Selling Price}} = \frac{\text{Markup Percentage Based on Cost}}{100\% + \text{Markup Percentage Based on Cost}}$$

If Jones & Smith had calculated only one markup percentage for the ties, they could convert that markup percentage in one of the following ways:

$$\frac{\text{Markup Percentage}}{\text{Based on Cost}} = \frac{40\%}{100\% - 40\%}$$

$$= \frac{40\%}{60\%} = 66.67\%$$

$$\frac{\text{Markup Percentage}}{\text{Based on Selling Price}} = \frac{66.67\%}{100\% + 66.67\%}$$

$$= \frac{66.67\%}{166.67\%} = 40\%$$

Most marketers, however, have tables to convert one markup percentage to another.

Markup percentages are sometimes affected by the stock turnover rate of particular items. For example, high turnover rates for fresh food items in a supermarket mean a lower markup percentage, but lower turnover rates for cosmetics in the same supermarket mean a higher markup percentage.

Markdowns

When customers will not buy an item at its original selling price, the marketer must *mark down*, or reduce, the selling price. Markdowns may be made for soiled or damaged goods, for end-of-season clearances, or for a special sales promotion. Often, however, markdowns are made because the store's buyer bought items that required too high a markup. For this reason, the markdown ratio is an important measure of a company's operating efficiency.

Markdowns and sales allowances are similar because in both instances an item's price is reduced. To compute a markdown ratio, the dollar amount of markdown is added to the dollar amount of allowances and then divided by net sales for that item only. The markdown formula is as follows:

$$\text{Markdown Percentage} = \frac{\text{Dollar Markdown} + \text{Dollar Allowances}}{\text{Net Dollar Sales per Item}}$$

If Jones & Smith priced ten suits at $150 each, sold four suits at the original selling price, marked down the remaining six suits to $110 and sold four of them, and gave an allowance of $15 on one of the originally priced suits, the markdown ratio would be computed as follows:

$$\begin{aligned}
\text{Markdown} \atop \text{Percentage} &= \frac{(\$40.00\,\text{Markdown} \times 6\,\text{Suits}) + \$15.00\,\text{Allowances}}{(\$150.00 \times 4\,\text{Suits}) + (\$110.00 \times 4\,\text{Suits})} \\[2mm]
&= \frac{\$240.00\,\text{Markdown} + \$15.00\,\text{Allowances}}{\$300.00 + \$440.00} \\[2mm]
&= \frac{\$255.00}{\$740.00} = 34.46\%
\end{aligned}$$

Thus the markdown ratio included all ten suits — the four that sold at the original selling price, the four that sold at the markdown price, and the two that remained unsold. The total markdown ratio was 34.46 percent.

Summary

Effective marketers should be able to analyze their company's operating statements and balance sheets in order to make sound marketing decisions. By computing analytical ratios based on data from the operating statement, marketers are able to measure their company's performance in relation to industry averages.

The stock turnover rate tells marketers whether or not management is efficiently turning a profit. By calculating the return on investment (ROI) ratio, marketers can measure how well their company has used its assets to generate sales and to make a profit. Determining markup and markdown percentages is also a task for the marketer.

Answers to Questions

Question 1

$$\text{Gross Margin Ratio} = \frac{\$55\,800}{\$110\,000} = 50.7\%$$

$$\text{Expense Ratio} = \frac{\$43\,000}{\$110\,000} = 39.1\%$$

$$\text{Net Profit Ratio} = \frac{\$12\,800}{\$110\,000} = 11.6\%$$

Question 2

$$\text{Average Inventory at Cost} = \frac{\$26\,000 + \$24\,000}{2} = \frac{\$50\,000}{2} = \$25\,000$$

$$\text{Stock Turnover Rate} = \frac{\$54\,200}{\$25\,000} = 2.168$$

Question 3

ROI with sales increased to $75 000:

$$\text{ROI} = \frac{\$\,6\,200}{\$75\,000} \times \frac{\$75\,000}{\$30\,000} = .0826 \times 2.5 = .2065 \text{ or } 20.65\%$$

ROI with investment reduced to $25 000:

$$\text{ROI} = \frac{\$\,6\,200}{\$75\,000} \times \frac{\$75\,000}{\$25\,000} = .0826 \times 3 = .2478 \text{ or } 24.78\%$$

ROI with net profit increased to $10 000, sales of $51 000, and investment of $30 000:

$$\text{ROI} = \frac{\$10\,000}{\$51\,000} \times \frac{\$51\,000}{\$30\,000} = .1960 \times 1.7 = .3332 \text{ or } 33.32\%$$

Appendix C

Marketing for Small Businesses

Studies of marketing often cite the strategies of large corporations as examples. Product positioning at firms such as General Motors, Molsons, and IBM illustrates marketing strategy. Professional marketing research departments are often described as an essential part of the corporate staff, while research and development of new products is viewed as an ongoing process.

Although the activities of large corporations serve as excellent examples, students should realize that proper marketing is essential for small businesses as well as large ones. This section is provided to illustrate the contribution of small business to the marketing environment and to provide an example of the marketing activities of one small firm.[1]

Small businesses provide many benefits to the marketing environment that typically go unnoticed by the general public. More than 500 000 new businesses are started each year, each attempting to provide consumers with a new product, better service, or a more convenient location. Occasionally, completely new industries have germinated through the efforts of entrepreneurs like Steven Jobs, who invented the personal computer. New products such as Softsoap and herbal decaffeinated tea were developed by individuals who acted upon their ideas.

Small businesses often provide goods and services to markets the large corporations consider too small. For example, one entrepreneur developed and marketed K-9 Cola, a nutritious soft drink for dogs. Although the product may have a sales potential sufficient to provide the entrepreneur with an excellent income, large pet food manufacturers such as Ralston Purina may consider the market too small to be of interest.

Small businesses also provide goods and services to large corporations. For example, General Motors purchases goods and services from more than 30 000 small businesses. Similarly, large aircraft manufacturers such as Canadair, McDonnell Douglas, Boeing, and Lockheed subcontract with thousands of small machine shops to provide them with necessary products and services.

Small businesses, then, contribute much to the marketing environment, but they face many problems that large corporations do not. Small businesses often have very limited financial and human resources. They must compete effectively without adequate funds to complete research projects or run a sufficient amount of advertising. The entrepreneur is often the marketing manager, as well as the manager of personnel, finance, and production. The entrepreneur is often not prepared for this overwhelming burden; while good decisions bring rewards, bad decisions can be catastrophic.

The following case provides an example of one entrepreneur's new business and her marketing strategies. Like most successful small businesses, her firm fills a niche in the market that large business have neglected. Her customers appreciate her quality products and service, and therefore return to her shop to make their purchases.

The K&K Aquarium and Pet Centre: A Case Study

As Kathy Fessler walked around her shop, she gently stroked a snake that coiled around her arm. The snake contentedly rested its head near Kathy's wrist, seemingly unaware of the activity around it. Kathy explained that although someone had expressed interest in purchasing the snake, she had become so attached to it she may no longer have wanted to sell it.

For Kathy Fessler, whose home is also home to horses, dogs, rabbits, cats, and a variety of other animals, owning a pet shop is a natural extension of daily activities. Her pet shop developed from her hobby of breeding tropical fish, which she began approximately six years ago. As a member of the local Aquarium Society, she won several awards for the quality and colour of her fish. Eventually, she had 27 tanks in her basement and spent all day each Saturday cleaning them. As the fish multiplied, she began to sell the offspring to local pet shops, using the income to offset the cost of her expanding hobby. In 1984, Kathy and her twin sister Karen started K&K Aquarium Maintenance, selling and maintaining aquariums in offices and private homes.

Growth

Although the business grew and prospered, K&K found its sales limited because the maintenance service was operated out of the entrepreneurs' homes and offered no opportunity to display aquariums. For the business to grow, a retail outlet seemed essential. In January 1986, Kathy and Karen opened K&K Aquariums and Pet Centre, a retail outlet. Although the business is legally a partnership, Karen is not actively involved in the management of the store.

The company mission of K&K Aquariums and Pets, as described by Kathy, is to help people enjoy their pets. This is accomplished by providing people with the healthiest pets possible and teaching the customers about proper care for the animals. Kathy's philosophy is that a sale is not as important as ensuring correct pet care. In keeping with this philosophy, employees are instructed not to rush customers, not to sell unnecessary products, and to provide customers with complete instructions.

Products and Services

The company now consists of both a retail outlet and the maintenance service. The retail outlet sells a variety of pets including cats, birds, tropical fish, hamsters, guinea pigs, snakes, and iguanas. Pet supplies are also available, as are books on the proper care of specific animals. The outlet sells many name-brand products including Tetra fish products, Science Diet dog and cat food, and Victory Veterinary Formula flea products. Kathy purchases both name-brand and less well-known products for her inventory, as long as the products meet her high standards of quality. A 48-hour guarantee is offered on all animals, and customer satisfaction is guaranteed on all purchases. However, few customers return products or animals. The time spent with customers prior to the purchase often helps to ensure that they make the correct purchase.

A layaway plan is also available to allow customers to finance major purchases. This plan is often used by customers purchasing animals for gifts since it can be timed to have the purchase paid off immediately before the gift is needed. This ensures that the customer's choice of a specific animal will not be sold to anyone else and that the animal will receive proper care until the customer wishes to pick it up.

The aquarium maintenance service provided by K&K includes cleaning and general tank maintenance, emergency visits for sick fish, and moving and setting up tanks for people who relocate within the metropolitan area. General tank maintenance consists of two visits per month to each customer during which the water is changed, purified, and checked for the proper pH level. The fish are checked for diseases and any necessary medication is administered. All equipment such as filters, air stones, and so forth are checked and replaced if they are not functioning properly.

Customer Groups

The store serves a wide variety of customers of all ages, but they do fall into several general categories. Customers for the retail outlet include families, hobbyists, and gift purchasers. The constant stream of parents and small children into the store is one indication that families are a major customer group for K&K.

Hobbyists also are a major group of customers. K&K offers a 15-percent discount to members of animal and fish clubs, such as the Aquarium Society, in an attempt to promote better animal health care and awareness of the pet industry. Many hobbyists purchase animals and supplies at K&K because of the high quality of the products and expert advice.

Gift purchasers also represent a customer group. Birthdays, anniversaries, Christmas, and Mother's Day are a few of the special occasions for which purchases are made. Many gift certificates are also purchased by customers who are unsure of making correct choices.

Families, hobbyists, and gift purchasers are also customer groups of the aquarium maintenance service. Many families and hobbyists enjoy owning tropical fish but do not wish (or lack the time) to maintain the aquariums. K&K will visit the customers' homes to provide the necessary service. An aquarium maintenance contract can also be purchased as a gift, if desired.

The maintenance service has one additional customer group. Organizations and businesses often purchase aquariums and maintenance contracts for offices, retail outlets, and so forth. The aquariums are displayed to provide a diversion for customers who must wait for service. An accounting firm that had an aquarium maintained by K&K found that customers are more relaxed and don't mind waiting if they can watch the fish in the aquarium. Similarly, a retail outlet found that the aquarium makes children calmer and more patient while their parents are shopping. The maintenance service is also available to these firms so that the care of the fish does not become burdensome.

Competition

K&K's competition for the maintenance service comes primarily from two companies, Tanks A Lot and Aquarium Maintenance. Although several other firms provide similar services, Kathy believes they are not strong competition. K&K's competitive advantage consists of two factors. For the first, K&K will clean any size tank, at a price based on the number of litres it holds. Many competing firms do not want to clean smaller tanks because it is more cost effective to clean larger ones.

K&K's second competitive advantage is its use of a diatom, a piece of equipment for cleaning the tanks. Although a tank can be cleaned in other ways, the diatom results in a noticeable improvement immediately. Kathy believes that the use of a diatom convinces the customer that the tank is well cared for and therefore helps maintain customer satisfaction.

The competition for retail sales consists primarily of the Fenton Pet Shop, located approximately four kilometres from Kathy's outlet, and the Kmart store, located three kilometres in the other direction. Although Kmart sells fish and birds at lower prices than K&K, Kathy does not try to compete on price. K&K's competitive advantage over Kmart comes from quality products, total pet care, and as much help and instruction as needed. Many customers come to Kathy's shop to purchase an animal after they have visited Kmart and decided they want more instructions, better quality pets, and continued support after the purchase. K&K's competitive advantage over the Fenton Pet Shop is location. Traffic in the Fenton shopping district where Fenton Pet Shop is located is congested, and residents often seek more accessible stores.

Environmental Factors

Numerous environmental factors affect the operation of a pet shop. These factors include both legal considerations and technological changes.

Many legal restrictions have been established to ensure the proper care of animals. For example, K&K does not sell dogs because local zoning laws require special enclosures and ventilation. Because these additional fixtures would have resulted in much higher startup costs, Kathy decided not to sell dogs.

The government also has laws regulating the sale of any wildlife. To sell animals such as crayfish, snakes, birds, and fish that live naturally in the area, a retail outlet must have a bill of sale from a licensed dealer. This prevents a pet shop owner from selling an animal taken from its natural habitat.

Technological changes have also helped to improve the care of pets. In the tropical fish industry, better filters, tank cleaning tubes, and water testing kits have improved the care and breeding of fish. Because of research on cats, dogs, and a variety of other animals, better flea-control products and more nutritious foods have been developed. Research, technology, and law interact to improve the pet industry and ensure the highest standards of quality. The pet shop owner must be aware of all of the factors and constantly monitor the changes that occur.

Suppliers

K&K uses many suppliers in an effort to obtain quality animals at reasonable prices. Suppliers for tropical fish include Beltz Aquarium, a large wholesaler about 25 kilometres distant, and Fritz's, which is located nearby. Kathy prefers to pick up inventory from these wholesalers because, although both of these wholesalers will deliver, they offer a 10-percent discount if delivery is not requested.

K&K has also started ordering from Eastside Hatchery, some 125 kilometres away. Kathy believes Eastside, although not so conveniently located, offers better prices and delivery while also providing larger, higher-quality fish. The owner of Eastside Hatchery will replace any of his fish lost because of diseases or other factors, while Beltz and Fritz's give only a 48-hour guarantee. Kathy believes Eastside gives better service because it is a smaller business and Kathy's account is important to the company.

K&K uses local private breeders to supply many of the other animals such as hamsters, guinea pigs, and parakeets. Use of local suppliers eliminates the need to ship animals long distances. This is important because the stress of shipment results in a high loss rate. Many of the local breeders can also provide very high quality animals. For example, one breeder who raises parakeets for shows sells K&K the birds that do not meet show quality. Although many birds do not meet show quality standards, they are still excellent birds. Customers of K&K have become aware of these birds and are willing to wait to get one. Proof of customer loyalty became evident when the supplier went out of town for a short time, and K&K sold all of its parakeets. By the time the supplier came back to town, K&K had a waiting list of customers.

K&K also has established a working relationship with Bentley Animal Hospital, located a few blocks away. When medical supplies or advice are needed, Kathy calls the veterinarians at Bentley. Similarly, if a customer comes to the shop to purchase supplies for a sick animal, Kathy will call Bentley (or refer the customer to them) for a serious problem.

Company Strengths

Location

K&K is located in a suburban community of approximately 2800 people and 500 businesses; the unincorporated area around the municipality includes many other residents and businesses. The city includes densely populated residential areas, as well as a few farms and industrial parks. The area has many middle-income families with young children, one of the major target markets of K&K.

K&K Aquarium and Pet Centre was one of the first businesses to open in Brookwood Centre, a neighbourhood shopping centre in a heavily residential area just off a major highway. The access road, which passes the shopping centre, has a daily traffic count of 19 410. The cross-street behind the centre has a daily traffic count of 13 240 and was recently widened to handle the increasing traffic volume. There are plans to widen the access road. Many new shopping centres are planned for the surrounding area to help meet the needs of the increasing population.

Before deciding on Brookwood Centre, Kathy and Karen looked at many other sites, many with lower rental costs. However, they chose Brookwood Centre because of the high traffic counts and good accessibility. They leased a 165-square-metre space at the third storefront from the end of the shopping centre. They chose this space because it is near the road and has excellent visibility. Although they would have preferred the storefront at the very end (because it has even better visibility), it had already been leased by a video tape rental store. Kathy is pleased with her location and believes that the continued growth of the area will be a definite advantage for her store.

Knowledge and Reputation

Kathy's knowledge of pet care and the store's reputation for quality products and complete service are the primary intangible resources for the firm. Kathy's willingness to take as much time as necessary with each customer has helped to establish the reputation of caring, not just selling.

Kathy's contacts with others in the industry also have helped to establish a network for exchanging information. Her membership in the Aquarium Society, friendly relationships with competitors, and a referral system with Bentley Animal Hospital all serve to increase her knowledge of the industry and her awareness of the changes that are occurring.

The store's reputation for high-quality products and knowledgeable service is also a major intangible strength of the company. Many customers visit the store because they were referred by another satisfied customer. This reputation is one of the factors that helps differentiate K&K from its competitors.

Goals

Long-Term Goals

One of Kathy's goals for her store is to increase the products and services offered. She hopes eventually to carry more salt water fish, and to add puppies to her product line. She would also like to offer a dog grooming service to help generate revenue during the summer months when aquarium sales generally decline. She has considered expanding into the storefront next to hers (if the current tenant moves) in order to accomplish these goals.

Eventually, Kathy hopes to own more than one shop. This would give her more buying power with suppliers and help increase her profit margin. She also believes that this would help her to get the best advertising for her money, because with several outlets radio advertising would be cost-effective.

Short-Term Goals

Kathy's more immediate goals are to expand the number of customers for the aquarium maintenance service, to increase productivity in the store so that sales per employee increase, and to try to obtain the greatest effectiveness for the advertising dollars that she spends. These goals will help increase revenue and profit and lead to future expansion.

Like many small business owners, Kathy is knowledgeable about the industry but has no formal business background. Therefore, one of her short-term goals is to learn more about all aspects of business management. Kathy believes that more knowledge of business management will also help to increase the productivity and profits of the store.

Promotion

K&K has no specific advertising budget, although Kathy believes one should be developed. Most advertising runs in local publications that are distributed free of charge to consumers. These publications include two TV program guides, *The TV Weekly* and *TV Fanfare*, both distributed free at the local supermarkets. *TV Fanfare* is a small weekly publication with a distribution of 500 per month. Advertising rates are affordable, with a front cover ad costing only $20. *The TV Weekly* has a distribution of 22 000 per week. Advertising rates range from one-eighth of a page at $42 per week to a full page for $150 per week. Another publication that K&K uses periodically is *The Green Apple*, which is distributed door to door to homes in the area. *The Green Apple* is primarily an advertising circular. It provides coupons and promotional information from local businesses to 112 000 homes. Advertising rates vary with the placement and frequency of the ad; however an average cost for a 75 by 125 millimetre ad is $70.

Of all of these advertising methods, Kathy prefers *The TV Weekly*, not only because of its good response rate, but also because the staff at *The TV Weekly* provides assistance in ad design. Often if Kathy has an idea for a specific type of promotion, she can just explain the idea and the employees at *The TV Weekly* then design an effective ad. Kathy is very pleased with the publication's use of eye-catching phrases and pictures, which help to improve the ad's effectiveness. For Kathy, who must handle so many other responsibilities, this assistance with advertising is invaluable.

Ads run all year long, even though the business is very seasonal. Kathy uses advertising to capitalize on the peak season and offset slow periods. The busiest months come in winter when people spend more time inside and have time to devote to their hobbies. In the summer months, when sales usually decline, Kathy uses promotional efforts to generate customer traffic. This helps to maintain a more consistent monthly volume.

K&K often runs institutional advertising to publicize the company, the product lines available, and the quality image of the store. These ads feature the company name along with the brand name products and the discounts offered to members of animal and fish clubs. These ads are designed to appeal to customers, often hobbyists, looking for a high-quality store.

K&K also runs sale ads and product ads to appeal to the families in the area. These ads may feature a specific animal, such as a "Snake Sale," or a "Ferret Sale," or they may announce discounts or "buy one, get one free" specials.

All ads give the company name, location, and phone number. Many ads list the store hours, product guarantee policy, and the availability of the lay-a-way payment plan. (Figure C.1 provides examples of two K&K ads.)

One of the best forms of advertising for K&K is generated by the store's reputation for quality and service. Referrals from previous customers are a major source of promotion. This not only helps to generate business from local residents but also brings customers from other areas. It is not uncommon for out-of-province customers to come to the shop when they are visiting relatives in town merely because it was highly recommended by a family member.

Like many business owners, though, Kathy is baffled by consumer behaviour. An ad run at two different times often generates an excellent response one time and almost no response the next. In addition, customer

Figure C.1   K&K Aquariums Advertisement

response is often delayed, making measurement more difficult. Kathy once ran a snake special that generated no immediate customers. Three weeks after the ad ran, however, many customers came in to buy snakes. For a small business owner with no access to formal market research, this type of consumer behaviour can be frustrating.

Current advertising is designed primarily for families, hobbyists, and gift purchasers. Advertising and promotion will be developed in the future to create more awareness among the organizational customer group. This promotion will include direct mail literature about aquariums and the maintenance service as well as direct sales calls by K&K staff members. Kathy believes that this major promotional effort to companies should only be undertaken after personnel are completely trained and knowledgeable and have developed sales skills. Only then can a highly professional, quality image be conveyed to other businesses.

Conclusion

Like all small-business owners, Kathy faces many challenges in trying to operate her store. It is not easy for Kathy to find employees who know enough about pet care and meet her standards of quality. In addition, the need for Kathy to be a jack-of-all-trades and manage many different factors is sometimes overwhelming. However, Kathy sees many opportunities for growth and is optimistic about the future of the pet industry in general and her business in particular.

Focal Topics

1. What are the major factors contributing to K&K's success?

2. For a small business like K&K that lacks a marketing research department, what is the best way to develop effective advertising?

3. K&K currently has no specific advertising budget. Why should one be developed?

4. In addition to developing a budget, what additional planning should be done concerning promotional efforts?

Notes

Chapter 1

[1]Peter Drucker, *The Practice of Management* (New York: Harper & Row, 1954), p. 38.

[2]LeRoy C. Blake, "t'Marketing': What's in a Name?" *Industrial Marketing*, March 1983, p. 110.

[3]"AMA Board Approves New Marketing Definition," *Marketing News*, March 1, 1985, p. 1.

[4]Philip Kotler, "A Generic Concept of Marketing," *Journal of Marketing*, April 1972, p. 48.

[5]Explanation adapted from Richard P. Bagozzi, "Marketing as Exchange," *Journal of Marketing*, October 1974, pp. 77–81.

[6]Louis E. Boone and David L. Kurtz, *Contemporary Business*, 5th ed. (Hinsdale, Ill.: The Dryden Press, 1987), p. 332.

[7]The classic study of how marketing benefited the toy industry is Robert Steiner, "Economic Theory and the Idea of Marketing Productivity" (Working Paper, Marketing Science Institute, Cambridge, Mass., December 1974).

[8]This list of marketing functions is similar to one proposed by Edmund McGarry, "Some Functions of Marketing Reconsidered," in *Theory of Marketing*, edited by Reavis Cox and Wroe Anderson (Homewood, Ill.: Irwin, 1950), pp. 269–273.

[9]Adapted from Appelbaum, Beckman, Boone, Kurtz, *Contemporary Canadian Business*, Third Edition, Holt, Rinehart and Winston of Canada, Limited, Toronto, 1990, pp. 19–20.

[10]The history of changing business philosophies is traced in Richard R. Weeks and William J. Marks, "The Marketing Concept in Historical Perspective," *Business and Society*, Spring 1969, pp. 24–32.

[11]The evolution of The Pillsbury Company's business philosophy is traced by Robert J. Keith, "The Marketing Revolution," *Journal of Marketing*, January 1960, pp. 35–38.

[12]Louis E. Boone and David L. Kurtz, *Contemporary Marketing*, 5th ed. (Hinsdale, Ill.: The Dryden Press, 1986), p. 12.

[13]Eric N. Berkowitz, Roger A. Kerin, and William Rudelius, *Marketing* (St. Louis, Mo.: Times Mirror/Mosby College Publishing, 1986), p. 17.

[14]Marvin Bower, "The Role of Marketing in Management," in *Handbook of Modern Marketing*, edited by Victor Buell (New York: McGraw-Hill, 1970), pp. 1–7.

[15]Blake, " 'Marketing': What's in a Name?"

[16]This and other studies on brand loyalty are cited in Thomas Exter, "Looking for Brand Loyalty," *American Demographics*, April 1986, pp. 32–33, 52–56.

[17]Frederick E. Webster, Jr., "Top Management's Concerns about Marketing: Issues for the 1980s," *Journal of Marketing*, Summer 1981, p. 15.

[18]Berkowitz et al., *Marketing*, p. 83.

[19]Peter F. Drucker, *Management: Tasks, Responsibilities, Practices* (New York: Harper & Row, 1973), p. 64.

[20]"The Soda Wars: Citrus Takes on Caffeine," *Newsweek*, September 15, 1986.

[21]Franklin S. Houston, "The Marketing Concept: What It Is and What It Is Not," *Journal of Marketing* 50 (April 1986): 82.

[22]Ibid., pp. 81–87.

[23]Roger C. Bennett and Robert G. Cooper, "The Misuse of Marketing: An American Tragedy," *Business Horizons*, November–December 1981, p. 52.

[24]Blake, "t'Marketing': What's in a Name?"

[25]"Japan vs. America: Same Goal, Different Tactics," *Sales and Marketing Management*, October 1986.

[26]See Philip Kotler, *Marketing Management: Analysis, Planning, and Control*, 5th ed. (Englewood Cliffs, N.J.: Prentice-Hall, 1984), p. 29; and Andrew Takas, "Societal Marketing: A Businessman's Perspective," *Journal of Marketing*, October 1974, pp. 2–7.

[27]Jerry W. Anderson, Jr., "Social Responsibility and the Corporation," *Business Horizons*, July–August 1986.

Chapter 2

[1]William M. Bell, "Marketing — More than Selling," in 1974 *Combined Proceedings of the American Marketing Association*, edited by Ronald C. Curhan (New York: AMA, 1975), p. 527.

[2]See O. C. Ferrell and William M. Pride, *Fundamentals of Marketing* (Boston: Houghton Mifflin, 1982), pp. 401–403.

[3]Yoplait examples are based on information from Andrew C. Brown, "The Many Uses of Hot Air," *Fortune,* January 12, 1981, p. 106; Beatrice Trum Hunter, "Yogurt," *Consumers' Research Magazine,* January 1980, pp. 30–32; and *Progressive Grocer,* June 1983, pp. 39–40.

[4]These differences are discussed in greater detail in Kenneth R. Davis, *Marketing Management,* 5th ed. (New York: Wiley, 1985).

[5]The problem of defining company mission too narrowly is discussed by Theodore Levitt, "Marketing Myopia," in *Modern Marketing Strategy,* edited by Edward C. Bursk and John F. Chapman (Cambridge, Mass.: Harvard University Press, 1964), pp. 24–48.

[6]See Peter Vanderwicken, "What's Really Wrong at Chrysler?" *Fortune,* May 1975, pp. 176–178ff.

[7]William J. Hampton, "The Next Act at Chrysler," *Business Week,* November 3, 1986, pp. 66–69, 72.

[8]This section borrows heavily from Scott, Warshaw, and Taylor, *Introduction to Marketing Management,* 5th ed. (Homewood, Ill.: Irwin, 1985), pp. 19–38.

[9]Robert Ball, "Volkswagen's Struggle To Restore Its Name," *Fortune,* June 27, 1983, pp. 100–104.

[10]"New fizz in old bottles" in *Time* (Canadian Edition), 6 August 1990, p. 36.

[11]Ann M. Morrison, "The General Mills Brand of Managers," *Fortune,* January 12, 1981, pp. 99–100.

[12]"Airlines in Turmoil," *Business Week,* October 10, 1983, pp. 98–102.

[13]Gay Jervey, "Parker Bros. Puts Its Chips on New Boards," *Advertising Age,* August 22, 1983, pp. 4, 52–53.

[14]Community Relations" in Canadian Business, January 1990, p. 55.

Chapter 3

[1]For a more in-depth analysis of the market types, see E. Jerome McCarthy and William D. Perreault, Jr., *Essentials of Marketing* (Homewood, Ill.: Irwin, 1985), pp. 100–104.

[2]Louis E. Boone and David L. Kurtz, *Contemporary Business,* 5th ed. (Hinsdale, Ill.: The Dryden Press, 1987), p. 15.

[3]Philip Kotler and Gary Armstrong, *Marketing: An Introduction* (Englewood Cliffs, N.J.: Prentice-Hall, Inc., 1987), p. 295.

[4]Julie Franz and Brian Lowry, "Produce Marketers Take Fresh Approach," *Advertising Age,* October 13, 1986, pp. 4, 92.

[5]For a more in-depth discussion, see George A. Steiner and John F. Steiner, *Business, Government, and Society* (New York: Random House, 1985), pp. 438–470.

[6]Stephen Koepp, "Pul-eeze! Will Somebody Help Me?" *Time,* February 2, 1987, pp. 48–55.

[7]"Eyelashes at 20 Paces," *Time,* September 15, 1986, p. 57.

[8]Scott Hume and Patricia Strnad, "Consumers Go 'Green,'" *Advertising Age*, September 20, 1989, p. 3.

[9]See Steiner and Steiner, *Business, Government, and Society,* pp. 212–214.

[10]GE and Whirlpool models for social responsibility are discussed in Lawrence P. Feldman, *Consumer Protection: Problems and Prospects* (New York: West, 1976), pp. 250–251.

[11]Bernice Kanner, "Stale Mallomars and Other Outrages," *New York,* September 5, 1983, pp. 16–20.

[12]C. Jackson Grayson, cited by Judson Gooding, "It's No Easy Trick To Be the Well-Informed Executive," *Fortune,* January 1973, p. 87.

[13]"The Squeeze on the Product Mix," *Business Week,* January 5, 1974, p. 50.

[14]Philip Elmer-DeWitt, "The Wall Comes Tumbling Down," *Time,* February 2, 1987, p. 68; and Bill Howard and William G. Wong, "Compaq Leads the Way to Speed and Compatibility," *PC Magazine,* November 25, 1986, pp. 134–139.

[15]John D. Baxter, "#1 Lead Indicator Is Consumer Spending," *Iron Age,* November 19, 1982, pp. 27–29.

[16]"How We've Changed," *The Royal Bank Reporter*, Winter 1986, p. 3.

[17]Statistics Canada, *Income Distribution by Size in Canada,* 1985, cat. no. 13-207 , table 1.

[18]Marilyn Ronald, "Average Families' Real Income Unchanged in 1988 from 1980," *The Globe and Mail,* December 5, 1989, p. B5.

[19]"High Tech Temps in Growing Demand," *High Technology,* February 1987, p. 9.

[20]John W. Wilson, "The Chip Market Goes Haywire," *Business Week,* September 1, 1986, pp. 24–25.

[21]Alicia Hills Moore, "Where the U.S. Stands," *Fortune,* October 13, 1986, pp. 28–37.

[22]Ibid., p. 28.

Chapter 4

[1]M. Dale Beckman, David L. Kurtz, and Louis E. Boone, *Foundations of Marketing*, 4th Cdn. ed. (Toronto: Holt, Rinehart and Winston of Canada, 1988), p. 129.

[2]GM's story is documented in Daniel J. Boorstin, *The Americans: The Democratic Experience* (New York: Vintage Books, 1973), pp. 551–555.

[3]Russell I. Haley, "Benefit Segments: Backwards and Forwards," *Journal of Advertising Research* 24 (February/March 1984): 19–25.

[4]Information provided by Toronto Transit Commission, January 1990, on its annual survey, performed by Environics Research Group.

[5]Haley, "Benefit Segments."

[6]George Miaoulis and Michael D. Kalfus, "Benefit Segmentation Analysis Suggests Marketing Strategies for MBA Programs," *Marketing News*, August 5, 1983, p. 14.

[7]Haley, "Benefit Segments."

[8]Philip Kotler, *Principles of Marketing*, 3rd ed. (Englewood Cliffs, N.J.: Prentice-Hall, 1986), p. 173.

[9]An application of this method is described in Haley, "Benefit Segments," pp. 22–24.

[10]"How Colgate Brand Managers Applied Psychos to Market and Media for Irish Spring," *Media Decisions*, December 1976, pp. 70–71ff.

[11]Jack A. Lesser and Marie Adele Hughes, "The Generalizability of Psychographic Market Segments across Geographic Locations," *Journal of Marketing* 50 (January 1986): 18–27.

[12]Robert Haas discusses use of such sources in detail in "SIC System and Related Data for More Effective Market Research," *Industrial Marketing Management*, 1977, pp. 429–435.

[13]"Variations on a Theme," *Inc.*, May 1984, p. 148.

[14]Ellen Paris, "Massacre on the Miracle Mile," *Forbes*, April 26, 1982, pp. 40–41.

[15]Patricia Winters, "Crush Fails To Fit on P&G Shelf," *Advertising Age*, July 10, 1989, Front cover and pp. 42–43.

[16]See Eric N. Berkowitz, Roger A. Kerin, and William Rudelius, *Marketing* (St. Louis, Mo.: Mosby College Publishing, 1986), pp. 208–215; and John C. Chambers et al., "How To Choose the Right Forecasting Technique," *Harvard Business Review*, July–August 1971, pp. 45ff.

[17]See Berkowitz, Kerin, and Rudelius, *Marketing*, pp. 208–215; and John C. Chambers et al., *An Executive's Guide to Forecasting* (New York: Wiley, 1974), p. 16.

[18]For subjective methods of demand estimation, see Donald S. Tull and Del I. Hawkins, *Marketing Research*, 3rd ed. (New York: Macmillan, 1984).

[19]For a more in-depth discussion of time-series projection, see Steven P. Schnaars, "Situational Factors Affecting Forecast Accuracy," *Journal of Marketing Research* 21 (August 1984): 290–297.

Chapter 5

[1]Kim Foltz, "What's in a Name?" *Newsweek*, October 21, 1985, p. 64.

[2]This and many of the following examples are based on Donald F. Cox and Robert E. Good, "How To Build a Marketing Information System," *Harvard Business Review*, May–June 1967: p. 146.

[3]Darrell E. Owen, "SMR Forum: Information Systems Organizations — Keeping Pace with the Pressures," *Sloan Management Review* 27 (Spring 1986): 59–68.

[4]Robert Levy, "Scanning for Dollars," *INC.*, September 1986, pp. 63–64.

[5]Philip Kotler, *Principles of Marketing*, 3rd ed. (Englewood Cliffs, N.J.: Prentice-Hall, 1986), p. 86.

[6]"Skil Finally Breaks the Profit Barrier," *Business Week*, November 25, 1972, pp. 50–54.

[7]Cox and Good, "How to Build a Marketing Information System," p. 146.

[8]Robert L. Yeager, "Engineering the Customer-Oriented Marketing Strategy," *Business Marketing*, November 1985, pp. 66, 68.

[9]"Key Role of Research in Agree's Success Is Told," *Marketing News*, January 12, 1979, pp. 14–15.

[10]Stephen A. Greyser, "Research-Management Partnership Proves Best," *Advertising Age*, November 14, 1985, p. 34.

[11]Herbert L. Aist and Bayne Sparks, "Market Research," *H & H*, May 1972, p. 102.

[12]Alexa Smith, "Researchers Must Control Focus Group — and Those behind the Mirror as Well," *Marketing News*, September 12, 1986, pp. 33–34, 36.

[13]Amanda Bennett, "Once a Tool of Retail Marketers, Focus Groups Gain Wider Usage," *The Wall Street Journal,* June 3, 1986, p. 31.

[14]Eugene H. Fram, "How Focus Groups Unlock Market Intelligence: Tapping In-House 'Researchers,'" *Business Marketing,* December 1985, pp. 80, 82.

[15]Kotler, *Principles of Marketing,* pp. 97–98.

[16]William G. Zikmund, *Exploring Marketing Research,* 2nd ed. (Hinsdale, Ill.: The Dryden Press, 1986), pp. 145–154.

[17]This case is presented in full in Robert S. Wheeler, "Marketing Tales with a Moral," *Product Marketing,* April 1977, p. 41.

[18]Julian L. Simon, *Basic Research Methods in Social Science: The Art of Empirical Investigation* (New York: Random House, 1969), p. 4.

[19]Frederick C. Klein, "Researcher Probes Consumers Using Anthropological Skills," *The Wall Street Journal,* July 7, 1983, p. 21.

[20]Roy G. Stout, "Developing Data to Estimate Price-Quantity Relationships," *Journal of Marketing,* April 1969, pp. 34–36.

[21]Mason Haire, "Projective Techniques in Marketing Research," *Journal of Marketing* 14 (April 1950): 649–656.

[22]Philip Kotler and Gary Armstrong, *Marketing: An Introduction* (Englewood Cliffs, N.J.: Prentice-Hall, 1987), p. 100.

[23]E. Jerome McCarthy and William D. Perreault, *Essentials of Marketing,* 3rd ed. (Homewood, Ill.: Irwin, 1985), p. 122.

[24]For more detail on survey methods, see Rena Bartos, "Qualitative Research: What It Is and Where It Came From," *Journal of Advertising Research* 26 (June/July 1986): RC-3–RC-6; Charles S. Mayer, "Data Collection Methods: Personal Interview"; Paul L. Erdos, "Data Collecting Methods: Mail Surveys," and Stanley L. Payne, "Data Collecting Methods: Telephone Surveys," in *Handbook of Marketing Research,* pp. 2-82–2-123; and Charles Overholser, "Quality, Quantity, and Thinking Real Hard," *Journal of Advertising Research* 26 (June/July 1986): RC-7–RC-12.

[25]Lee Adler, "Confessions of an Interview Reader," *Journal of Marketing Research* (May 1966): 194–195.

[26]For more information on the theory of sampling, see Paul B. Sheatsley, "Survey Design," in *Handbook of Modern Marketing,* especially pp. 17–76; Thomas T. Semon, "Basic Concepts," in ibid., pp. 217–229; and Zikmund, *Exploring Marketing Research,* pp. 436–437.

[27]These statistical techniques are discussed at length in *Handbook of Marketing Research,* pp. 2-307–2-498.

[28]The case is reported in Chester R. Wasson, "Use and Appraisal of Existing Information," in *Handbook of Marketing Research,* p. 2–12.

Chapter 6

[1]The definition of the scope of consumer behaviour comes from Leon G. Schiffman and Leslie Lazar Kanuk, *Consumer Behavior,* 3rd ed. (Englewood Cliffs, N.J.: Prentice-Hall, 1983).

[2]For a good overview of the contribution of these disciplines to marketing, see James F. Engel, Roger D. Blackwell, and Paul W. Miniard, *Consumer Behavior,* 5th ed. (Hinsdale, Ill.: The Dryden Press, 1986), pp. 15–17.

[3]The uses and users of consumer behaviour studies are explored in David W. Cravens et al., *Marketing Decision Making,* rev. ed. (Homewood, Ill.: Irwin, 1980), pp. 370–371.

[4]Philip Kotler, *Marketing Management,* 5th ed. (Englewood Cliffs, N.J.: 1984).

[5]The material in the section on culture is adapted from T. K. Clarke and F. G. Crane, *Consumer Behaviour in Canada: Theory and Practice* (Toronto: Harcourt Brace Jovanovich Canada, 1990). pp. 63–67, 71, 75–77.

[6]This material is adapted from N. K. Dhalla, *These Canadians* (Toronto: McGraw-Hill, 1966); Frederick Elkin and Mary B. Hill, "Bicultural and Bilingual Adaptations in French Canada: The Example of Retail Advertising," *Canadian Review of Sociology and Anthropology,* 1965, 132–48.

[7]This material is adapted from Douglas J. Tigert, "Can a Separate Marketing Strategy for French Canada Be Justified: Profiling English-French Markets Through Life Style Analysis," in Thompson and Leighton, *Canadian Marketing*; Jean-Charles Chebat and George Henault, "The Cultural Behavior of Canadian Consumers," in *Cases and Readings in Marketing,* ed. V. H. Kirpalani and R. H. Rotenberg (Toronto: Holt, Rinehart and Winston, 1974); and M. Saint-Jacques and B. Mallen, "The French Market Under a Microscope," *Marketing,* 1981.

[8]This material is adapted from Marcel Boisvert, "Is the French-Canadian Consumer Really Different?" *Sales and Marketing Management in Canada* 24, no. 2 (February 1983): 10–11.

[9]Joan Kron, *Home Psych: The Social Psychology of Home Decoration* (New York: Clarkson Potter, 1983).

[10]Good overviews of class differences in consumption behaviour are found in Engel et al., *Consumer Behavior*, Chapter 14; and Schiffman and Kanuk, *Consumer Behavior*.

[11]See Francis S. Bourne, "Group Influence in Marketing and Public Relations," in *Some Applications of Behavioral Research*, edited by Renais Likert and S. P. Hayes (Paris: UNESCO, 1957), pp. 208–224; and Engel et al., *Consumer Behavior*, pp. 318–319.

[12]M. Wayne DeLozier, *The Marketing Communication Process* (New York: McGraw-Hill, 1976), pp. 158–159.

[13]Paul F. Lazarsfeld et al., *The People's Choice* (New York: Duell, Sloan & Pearce, 1948).

[14]Engel et al., *Consumer Behavior*, pp. 543–546, devote more attention to these differences.

[15]For further discussion of the differences in purchase behaviour in each phase and alternatives to the traditional stages, see ibid., pp. 277–292.

[16]Thayer C. Taylor, "Markets That Marketers Pursue Are a Changin'," *Sales and Marketing Management*, July 28, 1980, p. A-19.

[17]Clarke and Crane, *Consumer Behaviour in Canada*, pp. 44, 45.

[18]See Harry L. David and Benny P. Rigaux, "Perception of Marital Roles in Decision Processes," *Journal of Consumer Research*, June 1974, pp. 51–62.

[19]See Scott Ward and Daniel Wackman, "Purchase Influence Attempts and Parental Yielding," *Journal of Marketing Research*, August 1972, pp. 316–319.

[20]*Publishers Weekly*, September 23, 1983, p. 16; Jeffrey A. Trachtenberg, "Big Spenders: Teenage Division," *Forbes*, November 3, 1986, pp. 201, 204.

[21]Richard Kern, "USA 2000," *Sales and Marketing Management*, October 27, 1986, p. 12.

[22]Ernst & Young, *Tomorrow's Customers*, 22nd ed. (Toronto, 1989), pp. 9–11.

[23]See Abraham Maslow, *Toward a Psychology of Being* (New York: Van Nostrand, 1968), pp. 189–215.

[24]Kenneth E. Runyon, *Consumer Behavior*, 2nd ed. (Columbus, Ohio: Charles E. Merrill, 1980), p. 209.

[25]C. Glenn Walters, *Consumer Behavior: Theory and Practice*, 3rd ed. (Homewood, Ill.: Irwin, 1978), p. 237.

[26]Reported in Engel et al., *Consumer Behavior*, p. 235.

[27]Ibid., pp. 115–116.

[28]Elaine Donelson, *Personality: A Scientific Approach* (Pacific Palisades, Calif.: Goodyear, 1973), p. 3.

[29]Jack A. Adams, *Learning and Memory: An Introduction* (Homewood, Ill.: Irwin, 1976), p. 6.

[30]E. Jerome McCarthy and William D. Perreault, Jr., *Basic Marketing*, 8th ed. (Homewood, Ill.: Irwin, 1984), p. 204.

[31]See Wayne DeLozier, *The Marketing Communications Process* (New York: McGraw-Hill, 1976), pp. 56–61.

[32]The description of VALS is based on Del Hawkins, Roger J. Best, and Kenneth A. Coney, *Consumer Behavior*, 3rd ed. (Plano, Tex.: Business Publications, Inc., 1986), pp. 429–445.

[33]The following discussion relies on that presented in Shiffman and Kanuk, *Consumer Behavior*.

Chapter 7

[1]Richard E. Plank, "Industrial Marketing Education: Present Conditions and Future Prospects," working paper, Montclair State College, Upper Montclair, N.J., July 1982.

[2]M. Dale Beckman, David L. Kurtz, and Louis E. Boone, *Foundations of Marketing*, 4th Cdn. ed. (Toronto: Holt, Rinehart and Winston of Canada, 1988), p. 236.

[3]Ibid.

[4]This chapter draws heavily from Michael D. Hutt and Thomas W. Speh, *Industrial Marketing Management*, 2nd ed. (Hinsdale, Ill.: The Dryden Press, 1984). This section is from Chapter 2.

[5]Ibid.

[6]Donald R. Lehmann and John O'Shaughnessy, "Difference in Attribute Importance for Different Industrial Products," *Journal of Marketing*, April 1976, pp. 36–42; Lowell E. Crow and Jay D. Lindquist, "Impact of Organizational and Buyer Characteristics on the Buying Center," *Industrial Marketing Management*, February 1985, pp. 49–58. See also Lehmann and O'Shaughnessy, "Decision Criteria Used in Buying Different Categories of Products," *Journal of Purchasing and Materials Management*, Spring 1982, pp. 9–14.

[7]Thomas V. Bonoma and Gerald Zaltman, eds., "Introduction," in *Organizational Buying Behavior* (Chicago: American Marketing Association, 1978), p. 8.

[8]See Paul F. Anderson and Terry M. Chambers, "A Reward/Measurement Model of Organizational Buying Behavior," *Journal of Marketing* 49 (Spring 1985): 7–23; and Michael Kutschker, "The Multi-Organizational Interaction Approach to Industrial Marketing," *Journal of Business Research* 13 (October 1985): 383–403.

[9]Thomas V. Bonoma, "Major Sales: Who Really Does the Buying?" *Harvard Business Review*, May–June 1982, p. 111.

[10]H. Lazo, "Emotional Aspects of Industrial Buying," in *Proceedings of the American Marketing Association*, edited by R. S. Hancock (Chicago: American Marketing Association, 1960), p. 265.

[11]"Computer Shock Hits the Office," *Business Week*, August 8, 1983, p. 46.

[12]Ibid., p. 53.

[13]Bonoma and Zaltman, *Organizational Buying Behavior*, pp. 3–4.

[14]This section is drawn from Philip Kotler and Gary Armstrong, *Marketing: An Introduction* (Englewood Cliffs, N.J.: Prentice-Hall, Inc., 1987), pp. 185–186.

[15]F. E. Webster and Yoram Wind, "A General Model for Understanding Organization Buyer Behavior," *Journal of Marketing*, April 1972, p. 17.

[16]For more discussion of this point, see Jean-Marie Choffray and Gary Lilien, "Assessing Response to Industrial Marketing Strategy," *Journal of Marketing*, April 1978, pp. 29–30.

Chapter 8

[1]Philip Kotler, *Principles of Marketing*, 3rd ed. (Englewood Cliffs, N.J.: Prentice-Hall, 1986), p. 6.

[2]"New Products: Still Rising . . . Finding a Winner . . . Hassles," *The Wall Street Journal*, November 3, 1983, p. 27.

[3]Lisa Miller Mesdag, "The Appliance Boom Begins," *Fortune*, July 25, 1983, pp. 52–57.

[4]For refinements of the consumer product classification system, see Louis P. Bucklin, "Retail Strategy and the Classification of Consumer Goods," *Journal of Marketing*, January 1963, pp. 50–55; and Leo V. Aspinwall, "The Marketing Characteristics of Goods," in *Four Marketing Theories* (Boulder: University of Colorado, 1961).

[5]"Crayola Draws a New Image," *Marketing and Media Decisions*, November 1981, pp. 70–71, 108–109.

[6]Pat Sloan, "Benetton Readies Its First Fragrance," *Advertising Age*, October 6, 1986, p. 34.

[7]Pamela G. Hollie, "Monopoly Loses Its Trademark," *New York Times*, February 23, 1983, p. D1; and Joani Nelson Horchler, "Is the Trademark 'Monopoly' Doomed?" *Industry Week*, March 21, 1983, pp. 70–71.

[8]See Laurie Freeman, "Battle for Shelf Space," *Advertising Age*, February 28, 1985, p. 16; and Bill Saporito, "Has-Been Brands Go Back to Work," *Fortune*, April 28, 1986, pp. 123–124.

[9]Freeman, "Battle for Shelf Space."

[10]"Generics Now Hurting Private Label," *Supermarket Business*, September 1982, p. 8.

[11]Mary McCabe English, "Calm after the Storm," *Advertising Age*, March 15, 1982, p. 18.

[12]Martha R. McEnally and John M. Hawes, "The Market for Generic Brand Grocery Products: A Review and Extension," *Journal of Marketing* 48 (Winter 1984): 75–83.

[13]B. Portis, T. Deutscher, and J. Rasmussen, "Trial and Satisfaction with Generic Products in Canada," in *Proceedings of the Administrative Sciences Associations of Canada Vol. 1*, edited by Vernon J. Jones (ASAC, 1980), pp. 280–288.

[14]Bill Kelley, "Zenith Labs on a New Product High," *Sales and Marketing Management*, October 1986, pp. 42–45.

[15]Ibid., p. 44.

[16]Kotler, *Principles of Marketing*, p. 267.

[17]See M. Ven Venkatesan, "Characteristics of Services Necessitate a Different Approach than Product Marketing," *Marketing News*, May 27, 1983, p. 14.

[18]William J. Winston, "Topic: Internal Marketing—Key to a Successful Professional Service Marketing Program," *Journal of Professional Services Marketing* 1 (Fall 1985/Winter 1985–86): 15–18.

[19]George Russell, "Where the Customer Is Still King," *Time*, February 2, 1987, p. 56.

[20]Many of the concepts summarized here are expanded in G. Lynn Shostack's excellent article, "Breaking Free from Product Marketing," *Journal of Marketing*, April 1977, pp. 73–80.

[21]Dan R. E. Thomas, "Strategy Is Different in Service Businesses," *Harvard Business Review* (July–August 1978): 158–165.

[22]"Accountants to Zoologists," *Time,* February 2, 1987, p. 52.

Chapter 9

[1]*New Product Management for the 1980s,* Booz Allen & Hamilton, 1982. p. 8.

[2]Hiotaka Takeuchi and Ikujiro Nonaka, "The New New Product Development Game," *Harvard Business Review,* January–February 1986, p. 137.

[3]Peter Finch, "Intrapreneurism: New Hope for New Business," *Business Marketing,* July 1985, pp. 32–34.

[4]Anastasia Toufexis, "Going Crazy over Calcium," *Time,* February 23, 1987, pp. 88–89.

[5]See Nariman K. Dhalla and Sonia Yuspeh, "Forget the Product Life Cycle!" *Harvard Business Review,* January 1976, pp. 102–112, for the view that generalizations about the average length of life-cycles are useless and may mislead managers into killing off brands prematurely. For an opposite view, see John E. Smallwood, "The Product Life Cycle: A Key to Strategic Marketing Planning," *MSU Business Topics,* Winter 1973, pp. 29–35; Ben M. Enis et al., "Extending the Product Life Cycle," *Business Horizons,* June 1977, pp. 46–56; and "Keeping Products Alive and Well in the Market," *Product Marketing,* November 1977, pp. 46–53.

[6]E. Jerome McCarthy and William D. Perreault, Jr., *Essentials of Marketing,* 3rd ed. (Homewood, Ill.: Richard D. Irwin, 1985), p. 242; and Sak Onkvisit and John J. Shaw, "Competition and Product Management: Can the Product Life Cycle Help?" *Business Horizons,* July/August 1986, pp. 51–62.

[7]Joshua Hyatt, "Cat Fight," *Inc.,* November 1986, pp. 82 + .

[8]Takeuchi and Nonaka, "The New New Product Development Game."

[9]Neil Ulman, "Sweating It Out: Time, Risk, Ingenuity All Go into Launching New Personal Product," *The Wall Street Journal,* November 17, 1978, pp. 1, 41.

[10]John A. Prestbo, "At Procter & Gamble Success Is Largely Due to Heeding Customers," *The Wall Street Journal,* April 29, 1980, p. 1.

[11]Hyatt, "Cat Fight."

[12]"The Lower Birthrate Crimps the Baby Food Market," *Business Week,* July 13, 1974, p. 47.

[13]Shelby H. McIntyre and Meir Statman, "Managing the Risk of New Product Development," *Business Horizons,* May/June 1982, pp. 51–55.

[14]Philip Kotler, *Marketing Management: Analysis, Planning, and Control* (Englewood Cliffs, N.J.: Prentice Hall, 1984), p. 205.

[15]Caryn James, "Publishers' Confessions — Rejections I Regret," *New York Times Book Review,* May 6, 1984, pp. 1, 34–37.

[16]Lawrence Incrassia, "There's No Way to Tell If a New Food Product Will Please the Public," *The Wall Street Journal,* February 26, 1980, pp. 1, 23.

[17]"Test Marketing: The Most Dangerous Game in Marketing," *Marketing Insights,* October 9, 1967, p. 16.

[18]Richard Edel, "New Graphics Energize Magazines' Appeal," *Advertising Age,* October 17, 1983, p. M46.

[19]O. C. Ferrell and William M. Pride, *Fundamentals of Marketing* (Boston: Houghton Mifflin, 1982), p. 194.

[20]Judann Dagnoli, "Walking Shoes May Open Gait to Big Profits," *Advertising Age,* July 7, 1986, pp. 12, 47.

[21]Charles D. Schewe and Reuben M. Smith, *Marketing Concepts and Applications* (New York: McGraw-Hill, 1983), p. 315.

[22]"Home Computer Firms," *The Wall Street Journal,* September 12, 1983, p. 1.

[23]Theodore Levitt, *Marketing for Business Growth,* 2nd ed. (New York: McGraw-Hill, 1974), pp. 162–165.

[24]Ann M. Morrison, "The General Mills Brand of Managers," *Fortune,* January 12, 1981, pp. 99–107.

[25]"Dannon Expands on the Diet Market," *Marketing and Media Decisions,* November 1981, pp. 74–75, 130–131..

[26]See Carl R. Anderson and Carl P. Zeithaml, "Stage of the Product Life Cycle, Business Strategy, and Business Performance," *Academy of Management Journal* 27 (March 1984): 5–24; Roger A. Kevin et al., "Cannibalism and New Product Development," *Business Horizons,* October 1978, pp. 25–31; and Onkvisit and Shaw, "Competition and Product Management."

[27]This example is from Chester R. Wasson, *Product Management: Product Life Cycles and Competitive Marketing Strategy* (St. Charles, Ill.: Challenge Books, 1971), pp. 183–184.

[28]See Philip Kotler, "Harvesting Strategies for Weak Products," *Business Horizons,* August 1978, pp. 15–22.

[29]Ferrell and Pride, *Fundamentals of Marketing,* p. 198.

Chapter 10

[1]*Marketing News,* November 11, 1983, p. 1.

[2]Philip Kotler, *Principles of Marketing,* 3rd ed. (Englewood Cliffs, N.J.: Prentice-Hall, 1986), p. 366.

[3]D. V. Shiner, "Analysis of the Nova Scotia Foodservice Industry — 1990," Nova Scotia Department of Agriculture and Marketing, unpublished report, May 1990. p. 17.

[4]"The More Expensive a Product, the Better the Quality, Right?" *The Wall Street Journal,* December 22, 1977, p. 1.

[5]Eitan Gerstner, "Do Higher Prices Signal Higher Quality?" *Journal of Marketing Research* 22 (May 1985): 209–215.

[6]"The Price TI Is Paying for Misreading a Market," *Business Week,* September 19, 1983, pp. 61–64; "Round Two for Computer Makers," *Business Week,* September 19, 1983, pp. 93–95; and "Why TI Will Return to Home Computers," *Business Week,* November 14, 1983, pp. 48–49.

[7]David W. Cravens, Gerald E. Hills, and Robert B. Woodruff, *Marketing Decision Making: Concepts and Strategy,* rev. ed. (Homewood, Ill.: Irwin, 1980), Chapter 14.

[8]Daniel J. Boorstin, *The Americans: The Democratic Experience* (New York: Vintage Books, 1973), p. 108.

[9]Cravens et al., *Marketing Decision Making,* p. 326.

[10]*The T. Eaton Company Limited* v. *The Queen* (1973), II C.C.C. (2d) 74, 10 C.P.R. (2d) 36 (Ontario Provincial Court).

[11]*Competition Act,* 1988, section 56.

[12]"Sears, FTC Settle Case on 'Bait and Switch,'" *Advertising Age,* March 8, 1976, p. 3.

[13]Gerald Badler, director of the Strategy Planning Institute, as quoted in "Flexible Pricing," *Business Week,* December 12, 1977, p. 80.

[14]Jeffrey H. Birnbaum, "Pricing of Products Is Still an Art, Often Having Little Link To Costs," *The Wall Street Journal,* November 25, 1981, p. 29.

[15]George P. Sproles, "New Evidence on Price and Product Quality," *Journal of Consumer Affairs,* Summer 1977, pp. 69–73.

[16]This point is made by Martin R. Schlessel in "Pricing in a Service Industry," *MSU Business Topics,* Spring 1977, pp. 37– 48. The author studied the pricing of exterminator services and concluded that most firms price with the market. However, some industry members got away with above-market pricing because buyers lacked objective criteria for judging the quality of service before the purchase.

[17]Laura Landro, "Technology, Competition Cut Prices of Electronics Gear as Quality Rises," *The Wall Street Journal,* December 1, 1981, p. 37.

[18]The classic article discussing new product pricing is Joel Dean, "Pricing Policies for New Products," reprinted in *Harvard Business Review,* November–December 1976, pp. 141–153. See also the chapter on pricing in Richard H. Buskirk and Percy J. Vaughn, Jr., *Managing New Enterprises* (New York: West, 1976).

[19]See Kent Monroe, *Pricing: Making Profitable Decisions* (New York: McGraw-Hill, 1979), Chapter 13.

[20]See "Airline Takes the Marginal Route," *Business Week,* April 20, 1963, pp. 111–112 +; and Brenton Walling, Jr., "Why Price-Cutting Backfires in the Airline Industry," *Business Week,* October 10, 1977, pp. 116, 118.

[21]David J. Rachman and Michael H. Mescon, *Business Today* (New York: Random House, 1982), p. 289; and George W. James, "Airline Deregulation: Has It Worked?" *Business Economics,* July 1985, pp. 11–14.

[22]Rachman and Mescon, *Business Today,* p. 289.

[23]Ibid.

[24]Ibid.

[25]For the arguments that cost-plus pricing is also competitively smart and socially fair, see Philip Kotler, *Marketing Management,* 5th ed. (Englewood Cliffs, N.J.: Prentice-Hall, 1984), p. 517.

[26]Jeffrey Birnbaum, "Location, Volume, Marketing Make Prices Vary Widely in NYC," *The Wall Street Journal,* December 3, 1981, p. 31.

[27]See Louis W. Stern and Adel I. El-Ansary, *Marketing Channels* (Englewood Cliffs, N.J.: Prentice-Hall, 1977), pp. 339–340.

[28]H. J. Maidenberg, "Misadventures of Cocoa Trade," *New York Times,* February 25, 1979, pp. F1, 41; Hershey Foods Corporation.

[29]See "Consumers Find Firms Are Paring Quantities to Avoid Price Rises," *The Wall Street Journal,* February 15, 1977, pp. 1, 21.

[30]Dik Warren Twedt, "Does the '9 Fixation' in Retail Pricing Really Promote Sales?" *Journal of Marketing,* October 1975, pp. 54–55.

[31]Birnbaum, "Pricing of Products Is Still an Art," p. 29

Chapter 11

[1]Tevana Traders Corp., "Initial Public Offering Prospectus," Toronto, pp. 11, 12.

[2]Kenneth G. Hardy and Allan J. Magrath, *Marketing Channel Management: Strategic Planning and Tactics* (Glenview, IL: Scott, Foresman and Co., 1987), pp. 6, 7.

[3]Michael Lauzon, "Superwood To Recycle Multimaterial Boxes," *Plastics News,* June 11, 1990, pp. 1, 20.

[4]Tim Falconer, "Kids Play: Using Parties To Sell Toys," *Canadian Business,* March 1987, p. 31.

[5]"Industry Update," *Plant Engineering and Maintenance* 13 (April 1990), p. 41.

[6]David W. Cravens, Gerald E. Hills, and Robert B. Woodruff, *Marketing Decision Making: Concepts and Strategy,* rev. ed. (Homewood, Ill.: Irwin, 1980), pp. 287–288.

[7]See Robert E. Weigand, "Fit Products and Channels to Your Markets," *Harvard Business Review,* January–February 1977, pp. 95–105, for a complete discussion. Some of the examples used here are from that article.

[8]James D. Hlavacek and Tommy J. McCuistion, "Industrial Distributors — When, Who, and How?" *Harvard Business Review,* March–April 1983, pp. 96–101.

[9]M. Dale Beckman, David L. Kurtz, and Louis E. Boone, *Foundations of Marketing,* 4th Cdn. ed. (Toronto: Holt, Rinehart and Winston of Canada, 1988), pp. 440–441.

[10]Morton Ritts, "The Big Push," *Canadian Business,* June 1987, p. 52; and Brandt Louie, "The West: Industry Leaders Speak Out," *Canadian Grocer,* April 1990, p. 53.

[11]Bruce Mallen, "Conflict and Cooperation in Marketing Channels," *Progress in Marketing,* edited by L. George Smith (New York: American Marketing Association, 1964).

[12]Robert W. Little, "The Marketing Channel: Who Should Lead This Extra Corporate Organization?" *Journal of Marketing,* January 1970, pp. 31–38.

[13]Montrose S. Sommers, James G. Barnes, William J. Stanton, and Charles Futrell, *Fundamentals of Marketing,* 5th Cdn. Ed. (Toronto: McGraw-Hill Ryerson, 1989), pp. 429–431.

[14]Hardy and Magrath, *Marketing Channel Management,* p. 100.

[15]These techniques are discussed more thoroughly in Mallen, "Conflict and Cooperation in Marketing Channels." See also "Distributor Incentive Programs — You Both Should Win," *Sales and Marketing Management,* September 8, 1975, pp. 45–48.

[16]The advantages of vertical marketing systems are discussed at length in Bert C. McCammon, Jr., "Perspectives for Distribution Programming," in *Vertical Marketing Systems,* edited by Louis P. Bucklin (Glenview, Ill.: Scott, Foresman, 1970), p. 44.

[17]Philip Kotler, Gordon H. D. McDougall, and Gary Armstrong, *Marketing,* Cdn. ed. (Toronto: Prentice-Hall, 1988), p. 305; and Sommers et al., *Fundamentals of Marketing,* p. 419.

[18]"Selling Sung," *Canadian Business* 59 (September 1986): 23–31, 147–150.

[19]Director of Investigation and Research, Competition Act, Consumer and Corporate Affairs Canada, *Annual Report,* March 31, 1989, p. 12.

[20]Phillip Bagozzi, *Principles of Marketing Management* (Chicago: Science Research Associates, 1986), pp. 575–576.

Chapter 12

[1]Philip Kotler, *Principles of Marketing,* 3rd ed. (Englewood Cliffs, N.J.: Prentice-Hall, 1986), p. 444.

[2]Jan DeForest, "Economic Woes May Benefit Radio," *Marketing,* January 8, 1990, p. 19.

[3]"Satisfaction of Consumer Needs," in Raymond A. Marquardt, James C. Makens, and Robert G. Roe, *Retail Management,* 3rd ed. (Hinsdale, Ill.: The Dryden Press, 1983), p. 237.

[4]Martin Mehr, "Sears Debating Pricing Policies," *Marketing,* September 25, 1989, p. 24.

[5]Louis W. Stern and Adel I. El-Ansary, *Marketing Channels,* 2nd ed. (Englewood Cliffs, N.J.: Prentice-Hall, 1982).

[6]Allison Dawe, "S&R Workers Join Union — Workers Can Expect Raise, Union Says," *The Whig-Standard* (Kingston, Ontario), July 6, 1990.

[7]Kenneth Wylie, "A Perspective on Today's Grocer," *Advertising Age,* October 10, 1983, pp. M9–M10.

[8]See Danny N. Bellenger, Thomas J. Stanley, and John W. Allen, "Food Retailing in the 1980s: Problems and Prospects," *Journal of Retailing,* Fall 1977, pp. 59–70; and Larry Edwards, "Soft Sales Challenge Food Marketers," *Advertising Age,* October 30, 1978, pp. 27, 103.

[9]The Royal Bank, *Annual Report 1989*, p. 13.

[10]This section draws from information in Lisa Gubernick, "Stores for Our Times," *Forbes,* November 3, 1986, pp. 40–42; and Jeremy Schlosberg, "The Demographics of Convenience," *American Demographics*, October 1986, pp. 36–40.

[11]George Benson, "Gas and a Whole Lot More," *Marketing*, January 22, 1990, p. 32.

[12]Mark Evans, "The Old Milk Store — Evolving into a 1 Stop Shop," *Financial Post*, October 30, 1989, p. 47.

[13]Anna Sobczynski, "Cashing in on the Best of Both Worlds," *Advertising Age,* October 10, 1983, p. M-22.

[14]Annetta Miller, "Filling a Tooth at the Grocer: Off to the Hypermarket," *Newsweek*, November 10, 1986, p. 59.

[15]Philip Kotler and Gary Armstrong, *Marketing: An Introduction* (Englewood Cliffs, N.J.: Prentice-Hall, 1987), p. 366.

[16]Mark Evans, "Bargain Chains Busting Out," *Financial Post*, September 25, 1989, p. 9.

[17]"Playing the Department Store Game," *Chain Store Age,* August 1983, pp. 65–68.

[18]Colin Lanquedoc, "Ikea Plotting Expansion in Fun Furniture Outlets," *Financial Post*, July 27, 1987, p. 13.

[19]Ibid., p. 13.

[20]"Why Analysts Like Catalog Showrooms," *Business Week,* October 10, 1977, p. 105; Kotler and Armstrong, *Marketing: An Introduction*, p. 369; and David J. Rachman and Michael H. Mescon, *Business Today* (New York: Random House, 1982), p. 329.

[21]William Dunn, "Edmonton's Eighth Wonder of the World," *American Demographics*, February 1986, p. 20.

[22]"Shopping Center Futures," *Stores,* May 1983, pp. 28–30.

[23]Dean Rotbart and Laurie P. Cohen, "The Party at Mary Kay Isn't Quite So Lively, as Recruiting Falls Off," *The Wall Street Journal,* October 28, 1983, pp. 1, 18.

[24]Suzy Hagstrom, "Consumers' Turn of Page Fuels Catalog Sales Picture," *Sentinel Star,* February 23, 1982, pp. 1E, 8E.

[25]Lanquedoc, "Ikea Plotting Expansion."

[26]Lori Kesler, "Marketing's Stepchild Comes into Its Own," *Advertising Age,* November 28, 1983, p. M-9.

[27]Don Hogarth, "Loonie Fuels Vending Fortunes," *Financial Post*, November 27, 1989.

[28]Rifka Rosenwein, "Whir, Click, Thanks: Merchandisers Turn to Electronic Salesmen in 24-Hour Kiosks," *The Wall Street Journal,* June 23, 1986, p. 23.

[29]Some independents have branch operations, but having several stores does not qualify an organization as a chain.

[30]"The Purchasing Power of a 10,000 Seat Restaurant," *Ontario Restaurant News*, April 1989.

[31]See Thomas J. Murray, "Franchising Comes of Age," *Dun's Review,* August 1977, pp. 58–60; "Things Are Looking Up for Franchises," *U.S. News and World Report*, May 10, 1976, p. 65; and Shelby D. Hunt, "The Trend toward Company-Operated Units in Franchise Chains," *Journal of Retailing*, Summer 1973, pp. 3–12.

[32]Mark Cohen, "Canada Slow on Franchise Legislation — Many Provinces Have a Wait and See Attitude," *Canadian Foodservice and Hospitality*, February 1988.

[33]Irving Burstiner, "A Three-Way Mirror," *Journal of Retailing*, Spring 1974, pp. 24–36 + .

[34]"The Wall Group — A Point of Purchase Success Story," *Marketing*, January 23, 1990.

[35]See Philip Kotler, "Atmospherics as a Marketing Tool," *Journal of Retailing*, Winter 1973–1974, pp. 48–64. For examples of the use of fashion videos, see Pat Sloan, "Fashion Videos Dress for Work," *Advertising Age,* July 28, 1986, p. 36.

[36]The issue is discussed by William R. George in "The Retailing of Services — A Challenging Future," *Journal of Retailing*, Fall 1977, pp. 85–97. See also Richard M. Bessom and Donald W. Jackson, Jr., "Service Retailing: A Strategic Marketing Approach," *Journal of Retailing*, Summer 1975, pp. 75–84.

[37]For a more detailed discussion, see Stanley C. Hollander, "The Wheel of Retailing," *Journal of Marketing*, July 1960, pp. 37–42.

[38]This hypothesis has been developed by several writers. See Bert C. McCammon, Jr., "Future Shock and the Practice of Management," in *Attitude Bridges the Atlantic*, edited by Philip Levine (Chicago: American Marketing Association, 1975), pp. 84–86; and William R. Davidson, Albert D. Bates, and Stephen J. Bass, "The Retail Life Cycle," *Harvard Business Review*, November–December 1976, pp. 89–96.

[39]Jim McElgunn, "A New Plan for Woodward's," *Marketing*, December 11, 1989.

Chapter 13

[1]"3M Mission," *Transportation Business* 10 (July 1990), p. 2.

[2]Kenneth G. Hardy and Allan J. Magrath, *Marketing Channel Management: Strategic Planning and Tactics* (Glenview, IL: Scott, Foresman and Co., 1987), pp. 198–205.

[3]Andrew Tausz, "There's a Promised Land of Better Communication and Increased Efficiency," *Modern Purchasing*, March 1989, p. 31.

[4]Barrie Whittaker, "Increasing Market Share through Marketing Excellence," *Canadian Business Review* 17 (Spring 1990), pp. 35–37.

[5]Joe Terrett, "Forging a World Class Team — Purchasing's Role in World Class Steel Production," *Modern Purchasing*, October 1989, pp. 14, 17.

[6]Philip Kotler, *Principles of Marketing*, 3rd ed. (Englewood Cliffs, N.J.: Prentice-Hall, 1986), p. 435.

[7]Adapted from Richard Rix, "Bell Gives Codes Ringing Endorsements," *Materials Management and Distribution*, July 1990, p. BCQ7.

[8]GM's Move to J.I.T. Production — General Motors Gears Up for the Future with Its Oshawa, Ontario Autoplex," *Modern Purchasing*, May 1990, pp. 22, 23.

[9]Jack W. Farrell, "Computers Cut Distribution Network Down to Size," *Traffic Mamagement*, February 1986, p. 64.

[10]Michael R. Leenders, Harold E. Fearon, and Wilbur B. England, *Purchasing and Materials Management*, 8th ed. (Homewood, IL: Irwin, 1984), pp. 182–185.

[11]Bill Paul, "Freight Transportation Is Being Transformed in an Era of Deregulation," *The Wall Street Journal*, October 20, 1983, pp. 1, 18.

[12]Ibid., p. 18.

[13]M. Dale Beckman, David L. Kurtz, and Louis E. Boone, *Foundations of Marketing*, 4th ed. (Toronto: Holt, Rinehart and Winston of Canada, 1988), p. 515.

[14]Andrew Tausz, "Transborder Trucking Shakeout," *Modern Purchasing*, March 1990, pp. 29, 32.

[15]Andrew Tausz, "Shipping by Air," *Modern Purchasing*, November 1988, pp. 29, 31.

[16]Andrew Tausz, "Air Cargo Takes Off," *Modern Purchasing*, May 1990, p. 15.

[17]"A Changing Scene," *Materials Management and Distribution*, June 1990, p. C14.

[18]"Departing Traffic Manager for Dofasco Predicts Gloomy Future for Canadian Transportation," *Transportation Business* 10 (July 1990), p. 8.

Chapter 14

[1]"Felled by a Head of Foam," *Fortune,* January 15, 1979, p. 96.

[2]Wilbur Schramm, *The Nature of Communication between Humans,* rev. ed. (Urbana: University of Illinois Press, 1971), pp. 3–53.

[3]See, for example, Wilbur Schramm, ed., *The Process & Effects of Mass Communications* (Urbana: University of Illinois Press, 1955), pp. 3–26; and John Ball and Francis C. Byrnes, eds., *Principles and Practices in Visual Communications* (Washington, D.C.: National Education Association, 1960).

[4]Marjii F. Simon, "Influence of Brand Names on Attitude," *Journal of Advertising Research*, June 1970, pp. 28–30.

[5]These types of noise are discussed in James A. Constantin et al., *Marketing Strategy and Management* (Dallas: Business Publications, Inc., 1976), p. 361. See also Terrence Shimp and M. Wayne DeLozier, *Promotion Management and Marketing Communication* (Hinsdale, Ill.: The Dryden Press, 1986), pp. 27–28.

[6]"Ballooning Fortunes of Bubble Yum," *New York Times,* March 25, 1977.

[7]Ralph S. Alexander, ed., *Marketing Definitions* (Chicago: American Marketing Association, 1964), p. 9.

[8]"Super Bowl XX: Who Bought the Million-Dollar Minutes," *Business Week,* February 3, 1986, p. 94.

[9]Charlyne Varkonyi, "Raisins Gain Day in Sun," *Chicago Tribune,* January 22, 1987, sec. 7, p. 10.

[10]This feature is discussed by James U. McNeal in "Promotion: An Overview." See his collection *Readings in Promotion Management* (New York: Appleton-Century-Crofts, 1966), p. 5.

[11]The Canadian Media Directors Council Media Digest, 1989–90, p. 10

[12]"The Nightmare Comes Home," *Time,* October 24, 1983, pp. 84–86.

[13]Craig Reiss, "ABC the Big Victor," *Advertising Age,* November 28, 1983, pp. 1, 104.

[14]Diane Mermigas, " 'Day' Blasts ABC to Top," *Advertising Age,* November 28, 1983, p. 2.

[15]David J. Rachman and Michael H. Mescon, *Business Today,* 3rd ed. (New York: Random House, 1982), p. 308.

[16]Leo LeFort, "We've Come a Long Way, Baby," *Advertising Age,* August 22, 1983, p. M-12.

[17]For other packaging advances, see Walter Stern, "The Top Ten Packaging Advances Since 1927," *Modern Packaging,* July 1977, pp. 44 m +. See also the articles cited in the opening vignette for this chapter.

[18]Cynthia Crossen, "Tamperproof Packaging: Inventors Say It Can't Be Done — but They Keep Trying," *The Wall Street Journal,* February 26, 1986, p. 27; and Melissa Larson, "Food Packagers Add Tamper-Evident Features," *Packaging,* January 1986, pp. 62–64, 66.

[19]John Lister, "To Research or Not to Research," *Advertising Age,* September 22, 1986, p. 80; and William H. Motes and Arch G. Woodside, "Field Test of Package Advertising Effects on Brand Choice Behavior," *Journal of Advertising Research* 24 (February/March 1984): 39–45.

[20]"Packaging Remains an Underdeveloped Element in Pushing Consumers' Buttons," *Marketing News,* October 14, 1983, p. 3.

[21]Colour as a motivational tool in packaging is discussed in Walter P. Margulies, *Packaging Power* (New York: The World Publishing Company, 1970), pp. 110–118.

[22]Denise Lenci, "Packaging Is Key As Avon Fragrance Scores," *Drug and Cosmetic Industry,* November 1982, p. 50.

[23]Walter Margulies, "How Many Brands Can You Spot with Names Off Packages?" *Advertising Age,* August 21, 1972, pp. 37–40. For other examples of good package design, see Roy Parcels, "Ten Steps to Profitable Packages," *Advertising Age,* September 5, 1977, pp. 31 +; Lori Kesler, "Successful Packages Turn Medium into Message," *Advertising Age,* October 13, 1986, pp. S-2–S-3; and Herbert M. Meyers, "Package Design," *Art Product News,* July/August 1986, pp. 30–31, 34.

[24]Bernice Kanner, "Wrapping It Up," *New York,* June 6, 1983, p. 12.

[25]"Liquor's Other Campaigns," *Advertising Age,* August 15, 1983, p. M-40.

[26]Charles D. Schewe and Reuben M. Smith, *Marketing: Concepts and Applications,* 2nd ed. (New York: McGraw-Hill, 1983), p. 488. For research into the relationship of the factors leading to action, see David W. Stewart, "The Moderating Role of Recall, Comprehension, and Brand Differentiation on the Persuasiveness of Television Advertising," *Journal of Advertising Research,* April/May 1986, pp. 43–47.

[27]William S. Robinson, "Best Promotions of the Year," *Advertising Age,* May 9, 1983, p. M-54.

[28]This case is discussed in detail in Thomas Berg, *Case Histories of Marketing Misfires* (New York: Doubleday, 1970), pp. 132–156.

[29]Reported in *Sales and Marketing,* January 1978, p. 38.

[30]These three reasons are discussed in Rolie Tillman and C. A. Kirkpatrick, *Promotion: Persuasive Communication in Marketing* (Homewood, Ill.: Irwin, 1972). See also Motes and Woodside, "Field Test of Package Advertising Effects on Brand Choice Behavior"; Simon Broadbent and Stephen Colman, "Advertising Effectiveness: Across Brands," *Journal of the Market Research Society* 28 (January 1986): 15–24.

[31]Bill Richards, "Executives at Toro Are Dreaming of a White Winter — Very White," *The Wall Street Journal,* December 20, 1983, p. 27.

[32]Nancy L. Croft, "Wrapping Up Sales," *Nation's Business,* October 1985, pp. 41–42.

[33]Glen Bohn, "Feds to Help Pay Cost of Expoland Cleanup," *Vancouver Sun,* March 22, 1990, p. D8.

Chapter 15

[1]Bob Lauterborn, "What Should Ad Majors Learn?" *Advertising Age,* January 19, 1987, pp. 18, 20.

[2]The Canadian Media Directors Council Media Digest, 1989–90, p. 10.

[3]A list of the early leading advertisers can be found in Maurice I. Mandell, *Advertising,* 2nd ed. (Englewood Cliffs, N.J.: Prentice-Hall, 1974), p. 37.

[4]David J. Rachman and Michael H. Mescon, *Business Today,* 3rd ed. (New York: Random House, 1982), p. 297.

[5]Cecilia Reed, "Reading the Board Room Message Right," *Advertising Age,* January 23, 1984, p. M-9.

[6]For more on the persuasive function of advertising, see C. H. Sandage, "Basic Functions of Advertising," in *Issues in Advertising,* edited by Robert E. Karp (New York: MSS Information Corp., 1972), pp. 14–30.

[7]Harry D. Wolfe and Dik Twedt, *Essentials in the Promotional Mix* (New York: Appleton-Century-Crofts, 1970), p. 54.

[8]Statistics Canada, Business Services, 1985–87, cat. no. 63-232, table 1.

[9]"Shiefflin Tests Dual-Positioned Red Wine," *Marketing News,* November 11, 1983, p. 4.

[10]Leo Greenland, "No, This Is Not the Era of Positioning," *Advertising Age,* July 10, 1972, pp. 43–44, 46.

[11]For an account of Ogilvy's other image sells, see his *Confessions of an Advertising Man* (New York: Atheneum, 1964).

[12]"Softening a Starchy Image," *Time,* July 11, 1983, p. 54.

[13]Bernice Kanner, "The Fizz Bizz," *New York,* January 16, 1984, pp. 10–16.

[14]For more information on this battle, see Bill Abrams, "Some New Ads May Rekindle Burger Battle," *The Wall Street Journal,* March 4, 1983, pp. 1, 31; "The Fast Food War: Big Mac under Attack," *Business Week,* January 30, 1984, pp. 44–46; and Anna Sobczynski, "Serving Up a Variety of Choices," *Advertising Age,* November 21, 1983, pp. M-9–M-10.

[15]Debbie Seaman, "Orangina Spots May Start 'Juice Wars,' " *Adweek,* August 4, 1986.

[16]See Gordon H. G. McDougall, "Comparative Advertising: Consumer Issues and Attitudes," in *Contemporary Market-*

ing Thought: 1977 Educators' Proceedings, edited by Barnett Greenberg and Danny Bellenger (Chicago: American Marketing Association, 1977), pp. 286–291; Edmond M. Rosenthal, "Comparative Ad — Weapon or Fad?" *Marketing Times,* September–October 1976, pp. 10–15; and Edwin McDowell, "Oh, for the Good Old Days of Brand X," *New York Times,* April 22, 1979, pp. F1, F9.

[17]These claims were made by a spokesperson for the U.S. Federal Trade Commission, speaking on the "MacNeil/Lehrer Report," August 10, 1977.

[18]Rachman and Mescon, *Business Today,* p. 298.

[19]For more unusual "media," see Ed Brennan, *Advertising Media* (New York: McGraw-Hill, 1951), pp. 210–211.

[20]"Do Top Guns Swig Diet Pop?" *Time,* March 9, 1987, p. 65; Dottie Enrico and Mary Huhn, "Target Vision Aims for Travelers, Students," *Adweek,* September 15, 1986, p. 62.

[21]C. Whan Park and S. Mark Young, "Consumer Response to Television Commercials: The Impact of Involvement and Background Music on Brand Attitude Formation," *Journal of Marketing Research* 23 (February 1986): 11–24.

[22]Statistics Canada, Radio and Television Broadcast, 1986, cat. no. 56-204, p. 38.

[23]Bill Abrams, "Planned Rise in TV Ads Stirs Debate," *The Wall Street Journal,* December 1, 1983, p. 31; Craig Reiss, "Opponents of Split 30s Fear Basic Change in TV," *Advertising Age,* October 31, 1983, pp. 3, 96.

[24]Nancy E. Marx, "Sponsors Start Making Shows to Plug Goods on Cable TV," August 25, 1983, p. 17.

[25]Andrew Jaffe and Jua Nyla Hutcheson-Brewster, "Radio Biz Eyes Anti-Drug Push," *Adweek,* September 15, 1986, p. 17.

[26]Statistics Canada, Radio and Television Broadcast, 1986, cat. no. 56-204, Text Table 1, p. 13.

[27]Adele Weder, "How the junk mail purveyors are turning up the volume" in *Financial Times,* 20 November 1989, p. 7.

[28]Statistics Canada, Business Services, 1985–87, cat. no. 63-232, p. 16.

[29]Bill Johnson, "Advertiser Thrives by Making Inflatables of Firms' Products," *The Wall Street Journal,* September 26, 1983, p. 25.

[30]Laurie P. Cohen, "Thought Goodyear Had the Corner on This Market? Keep Looking Up," *The Wall Street Journal,* September 26, 1983, p. 25.

[31]Jack Feuer, "Activists, Industry Rethinking Men's Place in Ads," *Adweek,* September 29, 1986, pp. 56, 60.

[32]Nancy Millman, "Consumers Rate Advertising High," *Advertising Age,* October 24, 1983, pp. 1, 18.

[33]Philip Kotler, *Principles of Marketing,* 3rd ed. (Englewood Cliffs, N.J.: Prentice-Hall, 1986), pp. 528–529.

[34]"Sweet Sell Garners 100% Response for Phone Equipment Manufacturer," *Marketing News,* April 1, 1983, p. 3.

[35]Sally Scanlon, "Let's Hear It for Recognition," *Sales and Marketing Management,* April 12, 1976, p. 44; see also James O'Hanlon, "Even a Millionaire Couldn't Buy Something Like That," *Forbes,* November 1, 1977, pp. 88–90.

[36]J. Max Robins, "Making Point of Purchase More Pointed," *Adweek,* November 10, 1986, pp. P.G. 8, P.G. 10.

[37]"Cosmetics Display Walls Spearhead Boom in Point-of-Purchase Media Use," *Marketing News,* February 18, 1983, p. 18.

[38]Robins "Making Point of Purchase More Pointed," p. P.G. 10.

[39]Media Measurement Services Ltd., a division of A. C. Nielsen Co. of Canada Ltd., *Small Business,* February 89, p. 47.

[40]Jennifer Alter and Nancy Giges, "Industry Losing $350 Million on Coupon Misredemption," and Nancy Giges, "New Coupon Trap Set," both in *Advertising Age,* May 30, 1983, pp. 1, 57.

[41]Joanne Lipman, "Firms Bid to Cut Sales Coupons, Other Incentives."

[42]Timothy K. Smith, "Buy One Car, Get One Free: Marketers Experiment with Freebies on Grand Scale," *The Wall Street Journal,* March 16, 1987, p. 23.

[43]Bernice Kanner, "Teaser Strips," *New York,* March 17, 1986, pp. 24, 27.

[44]"Marathon Sponsorship Is Promotion Centerpiece for Xerox Photocopier Line," *Marketing News,* February 17, 1984, pp. 1, 10.

[45]This section is based on Scott H. Cutlip and Allen H. Center, *Effective Public Relations,* 5th ed. (Englewood Cliffs, N.J.: Prentice-Hall, 1982), pp. 8–11.

[46]David P. McClure, "Publicity Should Be Integrated in Marketing Plan," *Marketing News,* December 10, 1982, p. 6.

[47]Roy R. Bumsted, "How to Measure Effectiveness of PR Campaign," *Marketing News,* March 18, 1983, p. 13.

Chapter 16

[1]Gay Sands Miller, "Nabisco Sees Its Sales Force Providing Promotional Services for Other Firms," *The Wall Street Journal,* April 21, 1980, p. 20.

[2]Robert N. McMurry, "The Mystique of Super-Salesmanship," *Harvard Business Review,* March–April 1961, p. 114.

[3]"How a Salesman Urges Auto Companies To Use More Aluminum Parts," *The Wall Street Journal,* June 13, 1977, p. 1.

[4]"1987 Survey of Selling Costs: Compensation," *Sales and Marketing Management,* February 16, 1987, pp. 51–59.

[5]"Top Commission-Only Reps' Average Take: 185 Gs," *Sales and Marketing Management,* October 1986, pp. 26–27.

[6]"Why Telemarketing?" in Encyclopedia of Telemarketing. (Prentice-Hall: Englewood Cliffs, 1987), p. 5.

[7]Charles Futrell, *Sales Management: Behavior, Practice, and Cases* (Hinsdale, Ill.: The Dryden Press, 1981), p. 147.

[8]See, for example, McMurry, "The Mystique of Super-Salesmanship," for the notion that self-confidence is essential to successful selling. The opposite view is forwarded by Gerard W. Ditz, "Status Problems of the Salesman," *MSU Business Topics* (Winter 1967), especially p. 77. A more recent assessment of needed traits is found in Lawrence M. Lamont and W. J. Lundstrom, "Identifying Successful Industrial Salesmen by Personality and Personal Characteristics," *Journal of Marketing Research,* November 1977, pp. 517–529.

[9]William B. Mead, "The Life of a Salesman," *Money,* October 1980, pp. 117–124.

[10]Franklin B. Evans, "Selling as a Dyadic Relationship—A New Approach," *American Behavioral Scientist,* May 1963, pp. 76–79.

[11]John Wolfe, "How To Hire the Best Possible Sales Force," *INC.,* November 1980, p. 120.

[12]Ibid.

[13]"Block Drug Takes the Cure," *Sales and Marketing Management,* June 14, 1976, pp. 33–35.

[14]Thayer C. Taylor, "Hewlett-Packard Gives Sales Reps a Competitive Edge," *Sales and Marketing Management,* February 1987, pp. 36–38 +.

[15]Stan Kossen, *Creative Selling Today* (San Francisco: Canfield Press, 1977), p. 140.

[16]"What Makes a Good Presentation? It Depends on Where You Sit," *Sales and Marketing Management,* January 22, 1973, p. 45.

[17]More detail on this suggestion can be found in W. J. E. Crissy et al., *Selling and the Personal Force in Marketing* (New York: Wiley, 1977), pp. 247–250.

[18]"Rebirth of a Salesman: Willy Loman Goes Electronic," *Business Week,* February 27, 1984, pp. 103–104.

[19]Marvin A. Jolson, "Direct Selling: Consumer vs. Salesman," *Business Horizons,* October 1972, pp. 87–95.

[20]Cited in David L. Kurtz et al., *Professional Selling* (Dallas: Business Publications, Inc., 1976), p. 238.

[21]"The New Supersalesman — Wired for Success," *Business Week,* January 6, 1973, p. 48.

[22]William J. Stanton and Richard H. Buskirk, *Management of the Sales Force,* 7th ed. (Homewood, Ill.: Irwin, 1987), p. 326.

[23]John A. Byrne, "Motivating Willy Loman," *Forbes,* January 30, 1984, p. 91.

[24]Some firms use a "draw against commission" combination. They pay their salespeople a fixed amount regularly, but the amount is deducted from commissions they make. Salespersons whose draws regularly exceed their commissions are, of course, not long for the sales force.

[25]Stanton and Buskirk, *Management of the Sales Force,* pp. 301, 325.

[26]John Wolfe, "How To Hire the Best Possible Sales Force," p. 121.

[27]Benson P. Shapiro and Stephen X. Doyle, "Make the Sales Task Clear," *Harvard Business Review,* November–December 1983, pp. 75–76.

[28]"Rebirth of a Salesman."

[29]Yovovich, *Advertising Age,* June 14, 1983, p. M-22.

Chapter 17

[1]Hewlett-Packard's story is told at length in George Leroy, *Multinational Product Strategy: A Typology for Analysis of Worldwide Product Innovation and Diffusion* (New York: Praeger, 1976), pp. 74–77. See also Vern Terpstra, *International Marketing,* 4th ed. (Hinsdale, Ill.: The Dryden Press, 1987), p. 307.

[2]Terpstra, *International Marketing,* p. 4.

[3]*The Canada–U.S. Free Trade Agreement — An Economic Assessment* (Ottawa: Department of Finance, 1988), p. 3.

[4]International Monetary Fund, *International Financial Statistics Yearbook* (Washington, D.C.: IMF, 1989).

[5]Ibid.

[6]Terpstra, *International Marketing,* p. 9.

[7]Ibid.

[8]We are grateful to Professor J. J. Boddewyn of Baruch College for the distinctions made in this section.

[9]External Affairs Canada, *Export Markets: The Trading House Connection* (Ottawa: Department of External Affairs, 1989).

[10]Terpstra, *International Marketing,* pp. 360–363.

[11]"Egypt an Oasis for Soft Drinks," *New York Times,* August 1, 1978, p. D1.

[12]John Daly, "The 'Big Mak' Attack," *Maclean's,* February 12, 1990, p. 50.

[13]"Are Foreign Partners Good for U.S. Companies?" *Business Week,* May 28, 1984, p. 59.

[14]Tom Kierans, "Fear of Foreigners," *Canadian Business,* February 1990, p. 37.

[15]John Demont et al., "Investing Japanese Style," *Maclean's,* November 20, 1989, pp. 58–60.

[16]Terpstra, *International Marketing,* p. 55.

[17]The World Bank Atlas, 1988. (Washington, D.C.: The World Bank, 1988), pp. 5–6.

[18]See "Egypt an Oasis for Soft Drinks," p. D4; and Fox Butterfield, "The China Trade: Companies Mob Peking," *New York Times,* February 4, 1979, sec. 12, p. 58.

[19]Philip Kotler and Gary Armstrong, *Marketing: An Introduction* (Englewood Cliffs, N.J.: Prentice-Hall, 1987), pp. 478–479.

[20]Judann Dagnoli, "Home Shopping Beams to Japan," *Advertising Age,* January 19, 1987, p. 8.

[21]José de la Torre, "Product Life Cycle as a Determinant of Global Marketing Strategies," *Atlanta Economic Review,* September–October 1975, p. 14.

[22]Joshua Hyatt, "Bad Translations Turn Ads from Mild to Spicy," *INC.,* November 1986, p. 18.

[23]Karen Singer, "Commerce in China Requires an Eye toward Custom," *Adweek,* March 2, 1987.

[24]Eliyahu Tal, "Advertising in Developing Countries," *Journal of Advertising* (Spring 1974): 21.

[25]Perry Pascarella, "In Search of Universal Designs," *Industry Week,* July 22, 1985, pp. 47, 49, 52.

[26]A. Graeme Cranch, "Modern Marketing Techniques Applied to Developing Countries," *1972 Proceedings of the Spring and Fall Conference of the American Marketing Association,* edited by Boris W. Becker and Helmut Becker (Chicago: American Marketing Association, 1972), pp. 183–186; and Lee Adler, "Special Wrinkles in International Marketing Research — Part I," *Sales and Marketing Management,* July 12, 1976, p. 63.

[27]See Gerry Semmel, "Developing Trade with the People's Republic of China," *Industrial Marketing,* July 1976, pp. 70–72.

[28]Clyde H. Farnsworth, "Easing a Company's Risks Overseas," *New York Times,* April 25, 1982, sec. 3, 6:3.

[29]R. J. Rummel and David A. Heenan, "How Multinationals Analyze Political Risk," *Harvard Business Review,* January– February 1978, pp. 67–76. See also Frank Vogl, "Protection against Political Upheaval," *New York Times,* January 28, 1979, sec. 3, pp. 1, 12.

[30]*The Canada–U.S. Free Trade Agreement.* (Ottawa: Department of Finance, 1988).

[31]Ministry of External Affairs, *The Canada–U.S. Free Trade Agreement: Synopsis* (Ottawa: Department of External Affairs, 1988).

[32]For a more in-depth discussion of GATT, see Terpstra, *International Marketing,* pp. 34–35.

[33]*The European Community and Canada* (Ottawa: Delegation of the Commission of the European Communities in Canada, 1989).

[34]*1992: Implications of a Single European Market* (Ottawa: Secretary of State for External Affairs, 1989).

[35]Adler, "Special Wrinkles in International Marketing Research," p. 63.

[36]For other types of marketing research problems, see Charles S. Mayer, "The Lessons of Multinational Marketing Research," *Business Horizons,* December 1978, pp. 7–13.

[37]Theodore Levitt, "The Globalization of Markets," *Harvard Business Review,* May–June 1983, pp. 92–102; and Perry Pascarella, "In Search of Universal Designs," p. 49.

[38]Levitt, "The Globalization of Markets."

[39]Peter G. P. Walters, "International Marketing Policy: A Discussion of the Standardization Construct and Its Relevance for Corporate Policy," *Journal of International Business Studies,* Summer 1986, pp. 55–69.

[40]Terpstra, *International Marketing,* p. 244; Ulrich Weichman, "Integrating Multinational Marketing Activity," *Columbia Journal of World Business,* Winter 1974, pp. 12–13; and Norris Willatt, "How Nestlé Adapts Product to Its Markets," *Business Abroad,* June 1970, pp. 31–33.

[41]Richard D. Robinson, *International Business Management* (New York: Holt, Rinehart & Winston, 1973), p. 27; and Edwin McDowell, "Coke's Hi-C Aims to Raise Food Value of Soft Drinks," *New York Times,* April 24, 1978, pp. D1–D2.

[42]Terpstra, *International Marketing,* pp. 254–255.

[43]S. B. Prasad and Y. Krishna Shetty, *An Introduction to Multinational Management* (Englewood Cliffs, N.J.: Prentice-Hall, 1976), p. 155.

[44]See Terpstra, *International Marketing,* pp. 539–545; and Stephan H. Robock et al., *International Business and Multinational Enterprises* (Homewood, Ill.: Irwin, 1977), pp. 465–468.

[45]Erin Anderson and Anne T. Coughlan, "International Market Entry and Expansion via Independent or Integrated Channels of Distribution," *Journal of Marketing* 51 (January 1987): 71–82.

[46]Terpstra, *International Marketing,* p. 408.

[47]Ibid., p. 445.

[48]Ralph Gray and Jessee Snyder, "GM Mapping Future on Truly Global Scale," *Advertising Age,* March 12, 1984, pp. 3, 64.

[49]David I. McIntyre, "Multinational Positioning Strategy," *Columbia Journal of World Business,* Fall 1975, p. 109.

[50]Claire Wilson, "Going European: Club Med Tries for Broader Appeal with New Pan-Regional Campaign," *Advertising Age,* January 19, 1987, p. 50.

[51]Jack Burton, "Swedish Shops Using PSA Spots to Improve Ad Quality," *Advertising Age,* January 19, 1987, p. 50.

[52]See Christine D. Urban, "A Cross-National Comparison of Consumer Media Patterns," *Columbia Journal of World Business,* Winter 1977, pp. 53–64; and Cranch, "Modern Marketing Techniques Applied to Developing Countries," p. 414.

[53]Mary McKinney, "McCann-Erickson Gets Thai Birth Control Account," *Advertising Age,* February 6, 1984, p. 35.

[54]Prasad and Shetty, *An Introduction to Multinational Management,* p. 159.

[55]Douglas and Dubois, "Looking at the Cultural Environment for International Marketing Opportunities," p. 107; and Blair R. Gettig, "Some Basic Lessons for the U.S. Adman Whose Company Is Going Multinational," *International Marketing,* November 1976, p. 70.

[56]Laurel Wentz, "Marketing Errors Doomed Sears in Brazil," *Advertising Age,* May 16, 1983, p. 32.

Chapter 18

[1]See Chapter 1. See also Philip Kotler, "A Generic Concept of Marketing," *Journal of Marketing,* April 1972, pp. 46–54; Robert Bartels, "The Identity Crises in Marketing," *Journal of Marketing,* October 1974, pp. 73–76; and Richard P. Bagozzi, "Marketing As an Exchange," *Journal of Marketing,* October 1975, pp. 32–39.

[2]Philip Kotler, *Marketing for Nonprofit Organizations* (Englewood Cliffs, N.J.: Prentice-Hall, 1975), p. 365.

[3]Philip Kotler, *Principles of Marketing,* 3rd ed. (Englewood Cliffs, N.J.: Prentice-Hall, 1986), p. 693.

[4]The categories are those of Peter M. Blau and W. Richard Scott, *Formal Organizations* (San Francisco: Chandler, 1962), pp. 45–58.

[5]Kotler, *Marketing for Nonprofit Organizations,* p. 19.

[6]These differences are discussed more fully in George Wasem, "Marketing for Profits and Nonprofits," *Banker's Monthly Magazine,* March 15, 1975, pp. 23–24; and Franklin S. Houston and Richard E. Homans, "Public Agency Marketing: Pitfalls and Problems," *MSU Business Topics,* Summer 1977, pp. 36–40.

[7]For a more detailed discussion, see Wasem, "Marketing for Profits and Nonprofits," pp. 25–27; and Ray O'Leary and Ian Iredale, "The Marketing Concept: Quo Vadis?" *European Journal of Marketing,* 1976, pp. 146–157.

[8]See Philip Kotler and Gerald Zaltman, "Social Marketing: An Approach to Planned Social Change," *Journal of Marketing,* July 1971, p. 7.

[9]Other examples of the widening product mix of museums can be found in Roger Ricklefs, "Museums Merchandise More Shows and Wares to Broaden Patronage," *The Wall Street Journal,* August 14, 1975, p. 1.

[10]A good summary of the complexities of pricing for nonprofit organizations is found in Benson P. Shapiro, "Marketing for Nonprofit Organizations," *Harvard Business Review,* October 1973, p. 130.

[11]Andrea Rothman, "Ms. Buffy Lowe and Friends Made a Tidy Profit on April Fool's Day," *The Wall Street Journal,* April 3, 1987, p. 29.

[12]See Kotler, *Marketing for Nonprofit Organizations,* pp. 211–213.

[13]The measures discussed are suggested by Kotler in *Marketing for Nonprofit Organizations,* pp. 250–251.

Appendix A

[1]Based on surveys in marketing, sales, and sales management classes at Lansing Community College and in an advertising class at Michigan State University.

Appendix C

[1]*Small business* has been defined in many ways by various organizations. The Small Business Administration, a government agency, classifies businesses as small according to number of employees and sales volume. The specific guidelines vary though, depending on the industry. For example, a construction company is small if sales do not exceed $12 million. In contrast, a retail variety store must have sales of less than $2.5 million in order to be considered small. Some manufacturing plants are considered small only if they have less than 500 employees, while others can have as many as 1,000. "Small business," then, includes the mom-and-pop store, but also many other firms.

Glossary

ABC Analysis
Inventory technique for identifying items with biggest sales payoffs by listing them by sales volume. Best sellers (A products) must be stocked at all times.

Accessory Equipment
Less expensive industrial product necessary to the final product's manufacture though not part of it—for example, hand tools and office equipment.

Acquisition Cost
Expense incurred in preparing for manufacturing or in buying product for inventory.

Administered System
Vertical marketing system in which one member secures agreement from other members of a channel on certain plans concerning price, display, and advertising.

Advertising
Any paid form of nonpersonal presentation and promotion of ideas, goods, or services by an identified sponsor.

Advertising Allowance
Reimbursement by a manufacturer for part of the cost of local advertising run by retailers and wholesalers.

Agent
Wholesale intermediary who merely arranges for the buying and selling of goods but never actually acquires ownership or possession of them.

Approach (Warm-Up)
Beginning of sales presentation intended to secure attention and to establish rapport and credibility with the client.

Arm's-Length Policy
Policy that requires a firm's subsidiary to charge or be charged the same price available to any buyer outside the firm.

Aspirational Group
Reference group with which a person may want to be identified.

Association Advertising
Advertising sponsored by a trade association to promote a class of products or services.

Atmospherics
Marketing task of creating certain effects in buyers by designing store environments.

Attitude
State that includes a person's beliefs about and feelings toward some object, combined with a tendency to behave in a certain way with respect to that object.

Attitude Scale
Technique for measuring consumer attitudes that poses statements about which respondents are asked to indicate the intensity of their agreement or disagreement.

Auction Company
Agent wholesaler that works on a one-time basis for a commission; may send catalogues to prospective buyers and take bids at time of auction.

Automated Warehouse
Facility with advanced materials handling systems under control of a central computer.

Average Markup
Single percentage used to determine the selling price of each item in a given product line.

Bait Pricing
Illegal practice of advertising a "special" at a cut-rate price with no intention to sell at the price advertised.

Benefit Segmentation
Division of a market into classes on the basis of benefits that members of each class seek.

Breakeven Analysis
Way for price setters to determine what will happen to profits at various price levels.

Broker
Agent wholesaler who brings buyers and sellers together, acting on behalf of one or the other and used on a one-time basis.

Business Analysis
Process of estimating future sales and profit potential of a new product.

Buyer
Person, often called purchasing agent, with the formal responsibility of placing orders.

Buyer Behaviour
Study that provides marketing managers with an understanding of what is behind the decision to spend money, time, and effort on consumption-related items.

Buyer's Market

Market in which there is an abundance of goods and services.

Buying Centre

Group involved in purchasing for an industrial market.

Cannibalization

Process by which a company's new product takes sales away from existing products in the same company's line.

Carrying Cost

Expense of holding goods over a period of time.

Cash-and-Carry Wholesaler

Limited-function merchant wholesaler who does not provide financing or delivery services.

Cash Discount

Reduction from list price made for early payment.

Catalogue Showroom

Retail discount business based on catalogue promotion and showrooms that display a limited selection of the items in the catalogue. Customers receive goods from an adjacent warehouse.

Census

Complete canvass of every member of a population under study.

Central Business District

Downtown shopping area of most cities, consisting of large department stores and specialty stores.

Chain Store

Group of stores centrally owned and managed that sell similar goods.

Channel Captain

Member of a marketing channel with power or ability to set and enforce policy.

Channel Length

Number of links (intermediary types) in a particular marketing chain.

Channel Member Type

Kind of wholesaling intermediary and retailer in a marketing channel.

Channel Number

Quantity of different marketing channels used to reach buyers.

Channel Width

Number of outlets or individual firms employed at each level in a channel.

Client Public

Those who directly use the product exchanged by nonprofit organizations.

Closing

Point of the selling process at which a prospect agrees to buy or decides not to buy.

Cluster Sampling

Probability sampling in which the population under study is divided into subgroups and then parts of the group are chosen at random to be sampled.

Combination Store

Combination of a supermarket and a drugstore under a single roof.

Combination Strategy

Balance of selling, advertising, and other promotional techniques combining push and pull strategies to achieve sales goals.

Commission

Pay plan under which salespeople are paid a percentage of the sales they close.

Commission Merchant

Agent wholesaler who markets the output of small farmers for a commission; may store goods but does not take title.

Common Carrier

Transport company that must serve the general public.

Comparative Advertising

Creative style that uses names of competitors.

Competitive Comparison Budgeting

Plan to spend as much on promotion as leading firms do.

Concentrated Marketing

Practice of dividing the market into market segments and selecting only one segment to serve with a marketing mix.

Concurrent Testing

Securing information while a promotional effort is under way.

Consumer Market

Individuals who buy either for their own or for their family's personal consumption.

Consumer Products

Goods sold to individuals or households for their personal use.

Consumer Responsibility

Buyers' obligation to know their rights and to make informed judgements.

Consumerism

Movement to increase the influence, power, and rights of consumers in their dealings with institutions of all types.

Container

Large, standard size metal box into which goods are placed for shipping and which is sealed.

Contract Carrier

Means of transport that serves only a limited number of customers and may negotiate different rates for different customers.

Contractual System

Vertical marketing system based on a formal agreement among channel members to co-operate on such matters as buying, advertising, accounting practices, and other functions. Forms are franchises, retail-sponsored co-operatives, and wholesale-sponsored voluntaries.

Contribution (Incremental) Pricing

Special type of cost-plus pricing that allows companies to produce unprofitable items to cover variable costs.

Convenience Goods

Products that individuals buy quickly and often.

Convenience Sample

Nonprobability sample in which subjects are chosen on the basis of convenience to the researcher.

Convenience Store

Small retail outlet that provides snack food and staple groceries quickly and conveniently.

Corporate System

Vertical marketing system in which one channel member fully or partially owns the business operations of two or more channel levels.

Correlation Analysis

Statistical method of forecasting used to find factors that change in advance of changes in product demand.

Cost-Benefit Analysis

System for weighing economic costs against economic benefits.

Cost-Plus Pricing

Policy of setting prices by totalling costs and adding a margin of profit.

Cost Trade-Off

Practice of allowing costs to increase in one business area to bring down costs in another.

Countervailing Duty

A duty on imports designed to counteract unfair subsidies paid to producers by foreign governments.

Coupon

Sales promotion tool aimed at consumers that offers a certain amount off the price of an item.

Creative Salespeople

Individuals charged with determining customers' needs, helping them solve problems, and getting orders.

Culture

A people's shared customs, beliefs, values, and artifacts that are transmitted from generation to generation.

Cumulative Discount

Policy that permits a customer to total up consecutive orders to qualify for the discount.

Currency Controls

Government-imposed restrictions on currency leaving the country.

Customary Pricing

Pricing some types of products—usually small-value items—at a certain level to avert consumer resistance at higher levels.

Customer Sampling

Survey conducted to sample customers' intentions to buy.

Data Bank

Marketing information system's storehouse of information gathered from internal and external environments and used to retrieve data selectively; also called a data base.

Decider

Manager with authority to make the final choice.

Decline Phase

Stage of product life-cycle during which products start losing a significant number of customers without replacing them.

Decoding

Retranslating a message into terms the receiver understands.

Demarketing

Promotion aimed at persuading the public that there are valid economic reasons for withdrawing a product.

Demographic Segmentation

Division of a market into classes on the basis of geographic proximity or some shared socioeconomic trait.

Department Store

Store that brings together a number of items under one roof.

Depression

Phase of the business cycle characterized by a radical drop in business activity and consequent high unemployment and business failure.

Derived Demand

Demand by industrial users that depends on consumer demand for the finished product.

Differential Advantage

Special edge over competition an organization may have or develop by working with the elements of the marketing mix.

Differentiated Marketing

Practice of marketing to many market segments, each with a different marketing mix.

Direct Investment

Total control of production and sales of goods in a foreign country.

Discount

Deduction made from the list price and offered to wholesalers and retailers.

Discount Store

Store that sells fast-moving branded merchandise at cut-rate prices.

Discretionary Income

Any money remaining from disposable income that a family or individual is free to spend for luxuries or save.

Disposable Income

Any money that remains after taxes are paid.

Dissociative Group

Reference group from which a person may want to dissociate himself or herself.

Distribution

Activity directed toward placing goods and services where they are needed and when they are wanted.

Distribution Centre Warehouse

Facility that serves primarily as a temporary way-station before the goods are rapidly moved to customers.

Drop Shipper

Limited-function merchant wholesaler who neither maintains a warehouse nor carries inventories but who takes title to goods and is responsible for billing and collecting payment.

Dumping

Practice of selling goods overseas at a lower price than a company charges in its own home market.

Economic Forecast

Prediction of how the economy will fare as a whole in light of changes in the national and international business climate.

Economic Infrastructure

Facilities such as paved roads, communication and transportation services, banks, and distribution organizations that make marketing possible.

Economic Order Quantity (EOQ)

Amount of stock that costs the least to keep on hand in order to meet the average level of demand.

Elastic Demand

Relationship that holds between price and revenue if total revenue increases with a price drop or decreases with a price rise.

Elasticity of Demand

Rate at which demand changes in response to price changes.

Emergency Items

Products bought when an unexpected need arises.

Encoding

Putting a message into understandable form by the source.

Environmental Analysis

Examination of the environment and identification of the circumstances and conditions that can cause the greatest problems or offer the greatest opportunities.

Exchange

Process by which two or more parties freely give something of value to one another to satisfy needs and wants.

Exclusive Distribution

Selling a product through only one wholesaler or retailer in a given area.

Executive-Panel Survey

Means for sales forecasting using opinions of company officials.

Experimentation

Research method that establishes cause-and-effect relationships.

FOB Pricing

Practice of having the buyer choose and pay for transportation at some point ("free on board"). The buyer takes title at that time.

Factory-Positioned Warehouse

Facility used to store raw materials and fabricated parts until they are needed for manufacture or one that serves as a traditional warehouse or distribution centre for finished products.

Fad

Product with a short life-cycle, usually no more than two years.

Family Brand

Brand that covers many products under one brand name.

Family Life-Cycle

Traditional stages through which families pass, from the unmarried state through child rearing, empty nest, and loss of a spouse.

Feedback

Understanding signalled by the receiver to the source.

Fixed Costs

Costs that do not vary with a firm's output; also called overhead.

Fixed-Sum-per-Unit Budgeting

Allocating a specified amount for each unit produced.

Flanker Product

Item related to an already established product and bearing the same brand name.

Fluctuating Demand

Demand in the industrial sector that may vary widely in response to changing economic conditions or changes in consumer tastes.

Focus Group Interview

Method of determining customer attitudes by interviewing a relatively homogeneous group assembled to discuss a topic.

Follow-Up

Stage of the selling process during which a salesperson checks to see that orders have been filled and the customer is satisfied.

Forecasting

Predicting demand in the marketplace over a given period of time.

Foreign Marketing

Operating within the foreign country where goods are to be sold.

Foreign Trade

Home production and the export of products across national boundaries.

Form Utility

Value added to a product by converting raw materials into a finished good.

Four "Ps"

Elements of the marketing mix, which are product, price, promotion, and placement.

Franchise

Agreement whereby an independent businessperson sells the products or services of another company, uses its name, adopts its policies and otherwise operates it in accord with the methods prescribed by the head office.

Freight Forwarder

Company that consolidates small shipments from a number of companies for transport in full loads.

Full-Service Merchant Wholesaler

Wholesale intermediary who performs a wide variety of distribution tasks such as assembly, storage and delivery, and financing, and may provide market information.

Gatekeeper

Organizational member who controls the flow of information into the buying centre.

General (Macro) Environment

Economic, technological, legal, and social forces that are largely outside the control of marketers and that affect the success or failure of marketing plans.

General Public

Those who have an indirect interest in a nonprofit organization's goods or services.

Generic Product

Product that is unbranded and marketed with minimal advertising.

Global Marketing

Developing one marketing mix to service all world markets.

Goals

Organizational objectives that have been made specific with regard to size and time.

Goods

Tangible objects exchanged in marketing.

Government Organization

Nonprofit agency that serves the interests of the public at large.

Growth Phase

Stage of product life-cycle during which product availability and marketing efforts expand and sales and profits surge upward.

Halo Effect

Transfer of goodwill from one product in a company's line to another.

Heterogeneous Shopping Goods

Products that a consumer will buy only after making a comparison of the style or quality of brands—for example, a dress or suit.

Hidden Costs

Costs of doing business—for example, a cancelled order—that do not show up on a profit and loss statement.

Home Improvement Centre

Large-scale hardware store that offers one-stop shopping for around-the-house needs at prices that may be somewhat lower than those at smaller hardware stores.

Homogeneous Shopping Goods

Products that a consumer buys only after making price comparisons among sellers—consumers see them as essentially the same.

Hypermarket

Giant mass merchandiser that offers a broad selection of hard and soft goods and grocery items at discount prices on a self-serve basis.

Hypothesis

Educated guess about the relationship between things or what will happen in the future.

Idea Marketing

Offering a cause in exchange for public acceptance.

Import Quota

Restriction on the number of goods entering a country.

Impulse Items

Products bought on the spur of the moment.

Incubation Phase

Stage of product life-cycle during which a product is conceived, developed, and tested.

Independent Store

Store owned and managed by a single person, partnership, or corporation, usually a one-unit operation.

Individual Brand

Distinct name given to each product a company produces.

Industrial Distributor

Wholesaler who sells to the industrial market.

Industrial Market

Businesses, governments, and organizations that buy goods and services for resale or for use in producing other goods and services.

Industry Forecast

Prediction of likely sales for a class of products.

Inelastic Demand

As it relates to consumer behaviour: Demand that remains relatively constant despite price changes.

Inelastic Demand

As it relates to price setting: Relationship that holds between price and revenue if total revenue increases with price rises or decreases with price cuts.

Influencer

One who can affect the decision process by assisting in evaluating alternative products.

Innovator

Person who is first to find out about and use a new product.

Input

Facts not in a consumer's control that may affect decisions to buy.

Installation

Large, expensive, industrial product necessary for the production of final products but not a part of those goods—for example, industrial plants and major equipment.

Institutional (or Corporate) Advertising

Paid message designed to build long-range goodwill for a firm rather than to sell specific goods.

Intensive Distribution

Selling a product through almost all available wholesale or retail outlets.

Intermediate-Positioned Warehouse

Storage place that serves manufacturers with several plants and widely scattered markets by gathering products of various plants and mixing them for shipment.

Intermodal Transportation

Co-ordination of two or more transportation modes to minimize the disadvantages and maximize the strong points of each.

Internal (Micro) Environment

Factors in an organization (such as financial resources and employees) capable of being influenced but not totally controlled by marketing managers.

International Marketing

Performance of marketing activities across national boundaries.

Intrapreneurship
Entrepreneurial activity within an organization.

Introductory Phase
Stage of product life-cycle during which a company brings a new product to the marketplace.

Joint Demand
Market condition when demand for one product will be affected by the availability of another product with which it is used.

Joint Venture
Partnership with a foreign firm under which both partners invest money and share ownership and control in proportion to their investment.

Judgement Sample
Nonprobability sample composed of subjects who are specially qualified in the area of interest of a study.

Just-in-Time (JIT)
Inventory control procedure whereby raw materials arrive at the production centre just as they are needed.

Law of Demand
Economic rule that states more goods generally are sold at a lower price than at a higher one.

Learning
Any change in an individual's response or behaviour resulting from practice, experience, or mental association.

Legal Environment
Laws that compel businesses to operate under competitive conditions and to observe specified consumer rights.

Licensing
As it relates to business in general: Process by which designer or character names or identities are leased to businesses for use on their products in exchange for royalties.

Licensing
Arrangement under which a company (the licensor) grants a foreign firm (the licensee) the rights to patents, trademarks, and the use of technical processes in exchange for a royalty or fee for use.

Life-Style
Person's pattern of living expressed in activities, interests, and opinions.

Limited-Function Merchant Wholesaler
Merchant wholesaler who provides only a few services for customers.

List Price
Selling price quoted to buyers.

Loss Leader
Item priced below cost to attract customers.

Mail Order Firm
Company that provides a wide range of goods ordered by customers from catalogues and shipped directly to them by mail.

Mail-Order Wholesaler
Limited-function merchant wholesaler who does not engage in personal selling; sales catalogues are sent to retail firms or other wholesalers.

Manufactured Materials (Manufactured Parts)
Industrial goods that have in some way been shaped or finished and are incorporated into another product.

Manufacturers' Agent
Agent wholesaler who handles marketing in areas a manufacturer chooses not to cover with its own sales force.

Market
For business, those who are willing to buy a firm's output and have the purchasing power to do so. For nonprofit firms, those who have an interest in a product and are willing to exchange something in return (whether monetary or nonmonetary).

Market Potential
Total of all sales that might be generated in a market segment.

Market Segment
Group of individuals, groups, or organizations in a market sharing similar characteristics that cause them to have similar wants or needs.

Market Share
Percentage of total industry sales that a particular firm can claim.

Marketing
Activities performed by individuals, businesses, and not-for-profit organizations that satisfy needs and wants through the process of exchange.

Marketing Concept
Business philosophy emphasizing that (1) companies should produce only what customers want; (2) management must integrate all company activities to develop programs to satisfy those wants; and (3) long-range profit goals should guide management decisions.

Marketing (Distribution) Channel

The people and organizations involved in making a product available to a user.

Marketing Information System (MIS)

Orderly procedure for regular collection of raw data internally and externally and conversion of those data into information for use in making marketing decisions.

Marketing Manager

Chief marketing executive who co-ordinates the work of the members of a marketing department.

Marketing Mix

Plan that specifies what will be offered to customers (the product) and how (its price, promotion, and placement).

Marketing Objectives

Stated goals of the marketing department that specify quantitatively how marketing will contribute to meeting overall organizational objectives.

Marketing Research

Method for collecting, on a one-time basis, data pertinent to a particular marketing problem or opportunity.

Marketing Strategy

Concrete plan for achieving marketing objectives by using a specified marketing mix to reach a specified target market.

Market-Positioned Warehouse

Storage place designed to collect the products of one or more manufacturers in or near the market served before shipping goods short distances to customers.

Markup

Difference between the cost of an item and its selling price.

Markup Percentage

Markup expressed as a percentage.

Mass Marketing

Practice of directing the marketing mix at all potential buyers rather than a particular subgroup.

Maturity Phase

Stage of product life-cycle during which the number of buyers continues to grow, but more slowly, until sales level off.

Media

All the different means by which advertising reaches its audiences.

Medium of Transmission

Means by which a message moves from sender to receiver.

Membership Group

Reference group to which a person may belong — for example, family, friends, neighbours.

Merchandise Deliverer

Salesperson who sees that buyers receive their purchases.

Merchant Wholesaler

Independent who buys goods from manufacturers, takes physical possession of them, and sells them to other intermediaries.

Missionary

Salesperson whose role is to build goodwill or to educate potential customers rather than to make a direct sale.

Modified Rebuy

Repurchase in which the buyer wants to modify product specifications, prices, terms, or suppliers.

Modified Standardization Approach

Practice of changing one or more elements of the marketing mix.

Monopolistic Competition

Situation in which there are many sellers in a market who rarely engage in price competition but compete by trying to establish brand preferences among consumers.

Monopoly

Situation in which one company is the exclusive provider of a product or service.

Motivation

Inner state that activates or moves people toward goals.

Multinational Marketing

In contrast to foreign marketing: Integrating marketing activities carried out in a number of countries.

Multinational Marketing

In contrast to global marketing: Adjusting the marketing mix to meet the specific needs of each nation or group of nations.

Multiple Brand Strategy

Corporate practice of promoting individual brands that compete with one another.

Mutual Benefit Association

Association organized for the benefit of members, not outsiders.

National Brand

Branded item distributed by a national manufacturer.

Needs Hierarchy

Theory of Abraham Maslow that there is an order in which

human needs arise. When one need is at least partially satisfied, the need at the next highest level arises.

New Product

Good or service new to the company producing it.

New-Product Committee

Group of top-level executives and representatives of several departments that meets regularly to consider new products.

New-Product Department

Permanent committee that works on new-product ideas on a day-to-day basis.

New-Product Venture Team

Group that usually assumes total responsibility for a new product from conception through decline.

New Task

Purchase of a good or service for the first time.

Noise

Interference that is either deliberately or accidentally introduced and blocks or distorts transmissions.

Noncommercial Advertising

Paid message sponsored by nonprofit organizations.

Noncumulative Discount

One-time reduction for larger-than-usual order.

Nonprobability Sample

Sample that involves personal judgement in the selection of sampled items.

Nontariff Barrier (NTB)

Invisible tariff that effectively limits trade.

Objective and Task Budgeting

Strategy that emphasizes setting goals and then fixing costs of meeting those goals for each promotional task used.

Observation

Research method that involves either the personal or mechanical viewing of subjects or physical phenomena.

Odd Pricing

Retail practice of adjusting prices to end with an odd number or just under a round number (for example, $7.99).

Oligopoly

Situation in which a few firms dominate the market, set similar prices, and make entry by other firms difficult.

One-Price Policy

Policy of offering goods purchased at the same time and in the same quantity at a single price to all.

Operating Environment

Individuals and organizations outside a firm (such as dealers and competitors) that help shape marketing plans and can, in turn, be shaped by them to some extent.

Opinion Leader

Member of a group who is capable of influencing others in it.

Order Taker

Salesperson whose main function is to write or ring up orders.

Organizational Marketing

Activities that attempt to influence others to accept the goals of, receive the services of, or contribute in some way to an organization.

Organizational Objectives

Overall goals a firm pursues, such as increasing sales or maintaining a quality image.

Output

Actual purchase and postpurchase evaluation by a consumer.

Ownership Group

Type of department store organization in which stores keep their separate name but are owned by a corporation that centrally provides some buying and management functions.

Ownership Utility

Value added to a product by giving consumers a way to obtain ownership of it.

Penetration Pricing

Policy of setting initial price for a new product very low in order to achieve the largest possible market share quickly.

Per-Capita Income

A country's gross national product divided by its population.

Percentage-of-Sales Budgeting

Sales approach that fixes amount to be spent for promotion as a percentage of the previous year's sales or of anticipated sales for the coming year.

Perception

Process by which an individual becomes aware of the environment and interprets it so that it fits into his or her frame of reference.

Perpetual Inventory

Frequently updated list of all goods in stock.

Person Marketing

Efforts directed toward cultivating the attention, interest, and preference of a target market toward a person.

Personal Selling

Oral presentation of a tangible or intangible product to a prospect for the purpose of completing an exchange.

Personality

Sum of characteristics that make a person what he or she is and distinguish each individual from every other individual.

Physical Count

Inventory practice of totalling the number of items of each line on hand at a regular interval.

Physical Distribution

The process of storing and moving products along marketing channels.

Place Utility

Value added to a product by making it available where buyers want it.

Placement

Means of delivering a product; also called distribution.

Point-of-Purchase (POP) Materials

Promotional tools such as posters, display racks, and price cards.

Positioning

Theory holding that to sell a product, a company must create a unique niche or position for it in the consumer's mind.

Posttesting

Measuring the effectiveness of a full-scale campaign after it has been completed.

Premium

Item offered free or at a low cost as a reward for buying a product.

Presentation

Stage of selling process during which a salesperson translates the features of a product into benefits the customer can understand.

Pretesting

Measuring a promotional campaign's effectiveness before spending on a large scale.

Price Collusion

Joint fixing of prices by competitors.

Price Discrimination

Price cuts that are not offered equally to every buyer.

Price Leader

Dominant member of an industry that announces pricing policies other companies often follow.

Price Lining

Practice of grouping merchandise into classes by means of price.

Price

Value placed on a product.

Pricing Objectives

Long-range goals that managers wish to pursue in their pricing decisions.

Pricing Policies

Pricing plans for dealing with situations in the future that generally recur.

Primary Data

Original information gathered for a specific research project.

Primary Demand Advertising

Advertising aimed at increasing the total demand for products without distinguishing between brands.

Private Carrier

Transportation owned by an individual company that is not primarily in the transportation business.

Private (Distributor) Brand

Product sold under the name of a retailer or wholesale intermediary.

Private Warehouse

Storage centre owned or controlled by the company that uses it.

Probability Sample

Sample in which each member is selected from a given population on some objective basis not controlled by the researcher.

Procompetitive Legislation

Laws that sustain and protect competition.

Product

Anything that can be offered to a market for attention, acquisition, use, or consumption that might satisfy a want or need.

Product Life-Cycle

Five phases through which a product passes: (1) incubation, (2) introduction, (3) growth, (4) maturity, and (5) decline.

Product Position

Image that a product has in consumers' minds, especially in relation to competing products.

Product Positioning

Decisions marketers make to create or maintain a certain product concept in consumers' minds.

Production Orientation

Business philosophy emphasizing that (1) anything that can be produced can be sold; (2) the most important managerial task is to keep the cost of production down; and (3) a company should produce only certain basic products.

Profit

What remains for a business after expenses are deducted from revenues or income.

Promotion

Marketing communication that attempts to inform and remind individuals and persuade them to accept, resell, recommend, or use a product, service, idea, or institution.

Prospecting

Actively seeking out buyers.

Prosperity

Period in business cycle of generally high income, employment, and business growth.

Psychographic Segmentation

Division of the market into classes on the basis of the lifestyles of members.

Public Relations

Activities that attempt to generate a favourable attitude toward a company among employees, shareholders, suppliers, and the government, as well as among customers.

Public Warehouse

Storage centre controlled by an independent, available for rent for a short time, and usually shared by a number of companies.

Publicity

Any information relating to a manufacturer or its products that appears in any medium on a nonpaid basis.

Pull Strategy

Creating demand for a product within a channel of distribution by appealing directly to the consumer.

Pure Competition

Situation in which there are many sellers, no seller dominates a market, and the products sold are interchangeable.

Push Strategy

Urging members of a market channel to sell a product or give it adequate display.

Qualifying

Determining whether prospects have the authority to buy and the money to pay for the purchases.

Quantity Discount

Reduction in list price to intermediaries for buying in large volume.

Quota Sample

Nonprobability sample composed of subjects chosen on the basis of characteristics thought pertinent to a study.

Rack Jobber

Full-service merchant wholesaler who supplies grocery and other retail stores with nonfood items on display racks and who owns the goods and racks.

Random Sample

Probability sample in which each member of a population under study has an equal chance of being selected.

Raw Material

Natural resource such as crude oil or a cultivated product such as wheat used in the production of finished products.

Recall

Power of certain government agencies to require manufacturers to notify customers that a product may be hazardous and may be exchanged or repaired.

Receiver

Ultimate destination of a message.

Recession

Phase of the business cycle characterized by decreasing income, employment, and growth rate.

Reciprocity

In industrial marketing, the relationship between buyer and seller that influences purchasing decisions rather than economic or performance factors.

Recovery

Upswing in the business cycle characterized by a gradual rise in business and consumer economic well-being.

Reference Group

Group that serves as a model for an individual's behaviour and frame of reference for decision making.

Research Design

Method for carrying out a marketing study.

Retail Life-Cycle

View that retail stores, like products, have life-cycles that consist of phases: innovation, accelerated development, maturity, and decline.

Retailer

Intermediary who sells directly to consumers.

Retailing

All activities involved in selling goods or services directly to final consumers for their personal, nonbusiness use.

Role

In sociology, a kind of specialization of task. Family roles include those concerning decisions that may be wife-dominated, husband-dominated, or autonomous (either spouse may decide).

Role Playing

Training method for salespeople in which one person acts the part of the salesperson and the other takes the part of the customer.

Safety Stock

Amount above the basic stock level to handle emergencies.

Sales Analysis

Breakdown of a company's sales data by product or customer demand, territorial volume, and salesperson performance.

Sales Branch

A manufacturing firm's service centre and stock storehouse.

Sales-Force Survey

Means for sales forecasting using estimates of company salespeople.

Sales Forecast

Prediction of actual sales a company can expect to make in a certain market or segment.

Sales Management

Marketing function that embraces recruiting, selecting, and training salespeople, supervising and motivating them, and evaluating their performance.

Sales Office

Headquarters for a sales force away from a company's plant.

Sales Orientation

Business philosophy emphasizing that (1) finding buyers for products is management's chief concern; and (2) convincing buyers to purchase a firm's output is management's chief task.

Sales Promotion

Promotional activities besides selling, advertising, and publicity that stimulate purchases or aid dealer effectiveness.

Sales Quota

Quantitative measure of the effectiveness of salespeople.

Sales Task Clarity

The visible relationship between a salesperson's efforts and sales results.

Sample

In promotion: Giveaway in a trial size for products whose benefits cannot be fully conveyed through advertising.

Sample

In research: Limited canvass of a representative part of a population under study.

Scrambled Merchandising

Practice, by previously specialized retailers, of selling many unrelated lines of goods.

Screening

First attempt to separate ideas worth pursuing from those that are not.

Seasonal Discount

Special price for buying out of season.

Secondary Data

Information that exists before a particular study is conducted and that was collected for another purpose.

Selective or Brand Advertising

Messages that try to increase consumer preference for a particular firm's product.

Selective Distribution

Use of more than one but fewer than all firms that might carry a product.

Selective Exposure

Process of filtering out information that is not of interest.

Selective Perception

Process of filtering out or modifying information that conflicts with one's ideas or beliefs.

Selective Retention

Memory of only what supports one's ideas or beliefs.

Seller's Market

Market in which there is a shortage of goods and services.

Selling Agent

Agent wholesaler who handles marketing for the entire output of small manufacturers.

Service

Intangible benefit exchanged in marketing.

Service Organization

Institution, such as a hospital, college, or museum, that provides a service for clients, sometimes in exchange for a fee.

Shopping Centre

Group of stores planned, owned, and managed as a unit and with ample parking, usually in a suburban area.

Shopping Goods

Products that a consumer buys only after making comparisons among competing stores.

Skimming

Pricing policy under which new products are often priced high, and their price is gradually lowered as they mature.

Social Class

Group distinguished by characteristics such as occupation, education, possessions, and values.

Social Environment

Climate of public opinion that affects marketers' practices.

Social Marketing

Use of marketing techniques to increase the acceptability of a social idea, cause, or practice in a target group.

Social Responsibility

Moral obligation of businesses to consider the effects of their decisions on society and to accomplish social benefits.

Societal Marketing

Concept that balances concern for profits with concern for satisfying individual wants and societal needs.

Source

Originator of a message.

Source Effect

Distortion of a communication resulting from the reputation of the source of a message.

Specialty Goods

Products that a consumer is willing to make a special effort to obtain.

Specialty Store

Store that concentrates on selling a selection of only one line of merchandise.

Standard Industrial Classification (SIC) Code

Numbering system followed by the Canadian government for categorizing businesses by economic activity.

Standardization

Practice of transferring all parts of a successful marketing mix from one country to another.

Staple Items

Products bought through habit—for example, milk.

Storage Warehouse

Facility in which goods are stored for weeks, months, or years until they are needed.

Straight Rebuy

Repurchase without any modifications to the product, terms, or suppliers.

Straight Salary

Pay plan under which salespeople are guaranteed a regular income.

Strategic Marketing Planning

Process of establishing an organization's goals, assessing opportunities, and developing marketing objectives; results in marketing strategies.

Stratified Sampling

Probability sampling in which subgroups are identified and then randomly sampled.

Subculture

Subgroup within a larger culture that has distinctive lifestyles, values, norms, and beliefs.

Supermarket

Retail food store that carries dry groceries, dairy products, and fresh produce and allows customers to make their own selection.

Superstore

Large store that carries a broad selection of one type of product at low prices. Sometimes called "category killer."

Supplies

Industrial products needed for the maintenance or repair of equipment or for the operation of a business.

Survey Research

Study using direct or indirect interviews.

Target Market

Market segment an organization designs its marketing mix to reach because that segment is considered likely to demand the product being marketed.

Target Marketing

Practice of dividing the market into segments and devising a marketing mix to appeal to one or more targeted market segments.

Target Rate of Return
Goal stated as a certain percentage of return on sales or investment.

Tariff
Tax on imports.

Technical Salespeople
Technicians in sales positions who act as consultants and sometimes help to design products or systems to meet a client's needs.

Technology
Application of principles of science to the solution of practical problems.

Telemarketing
Direct selling in which salespeople telephone potential customers.

Test Marketing
Trial marketing in a limited area chosen as representative of an entire market.

Theory of Conditioned Learning
View holding that learning takes place by association.

Theory of Instrumental Learning
View that people learn to act in a certain way when some responses are rewarded (or reinforced) and others are punished.

Tickler File
Reminder file, often composed of cards, containing data on a sale and times to call back.

Time-Series Projection
Statistical method for forecasting sales based on past patterns projected into the future.

Time Utility
Value added to a product by making it available when buyers need it.

Total Physical Distribution Concept
Principle that all management functions related to moving products to buyers must be fully integrated.

Trade Discount
Reduction to "the trade" (wholesalers and retailers) from list price.

Trade Show
Exposition that allows salespeople to display their new products to dealers, to make new contacts, and to develop mailing lists for future use.

Trading House
Commercial intermediary linking domestic producers and foreign-based purchasers or consumers.

Transfer Pricing
Pricing within a corporate family, perhaps used to avoid taxes.

Transfer Principle
Principle that all functions of the marketing channel are vital and when not performed by one channel member must be taken over by another.

Truck Wholesaler
Limited-function merchant wholesaler who performs all the functions of full-service organizations except financing; operates by selling and making deliveries directly from a truck.

Turnover
Number of times average inventory is sold during a given period.

Uniform-Delivery Pricing
Practice of quoting a single price to all sellers regardless of location, reached by averaging the transportation charges of all buyers and adding that figure to the selling price.

Usage-Rate Segmentation
Division of a market into classes on the basis of the rate at which members buy and use products.

User
Member of a buying centre who works with the products purchased.

Utility
Want-satisfying power of goods or services.

Value Added
The increase in value of input material when transformed into semifinished or finished goods.

Variable Costs
Costs that increase or decrease with the amount of output.

Variable-Price Policy
Policy that allows special prices for different customers.

Vending Machine
Device that dispenses products automatically after money is inserted.

Vertical Marketing System (VMS)
System in which one channel member owns, controls, or coordinates the operations of other channel members.

Visible Costs

Direct and indirect costs that show up on a profit and loss statement.

Want-Satisfaction Approach

Sales theory that stresses that the salesperson must first determine what a buyer really wants or needs before launching a sales talk.

Warehouse Store

No-frills store that emphasizes lower prices over atmosphere and customer service.

Wheel of Retailing

Theory that all retail innovators start as low-cost, low-price stores, improve services and raise prices at maturity, and decline when new types of low-cost stores challenge them.

Wholesale Intermediary

An intermediary that sells to retailers, other wholesaling intermediaries, or industrial users.

Wholesale Merchant

Full-service merchant wholesaler who supplies mainly retailers or institutions.

Wholly Owned Wholesaler

Distribution arm of manufacturer that sets it up. Can be manufacturers' sales branches or sales offices.

Zone-Delivery Pricing

Policy under which sellers divide the country or market into two or more zones, charging the same rate within a zone but different rates among zones.

Index

Words appearing in boldface type are glossary terms defined in text. The boldface page numbers indicate the pages on which the key terms are defined.

To the Owner of this Book

We are interested in your reaction to *Marketing Today* by Ross Crain and David Rachman. Through feedback from you, we may be able to improve this book in future editions.

1. What was your reason for using this book?
   _____college course
   _____university course
   _____continuing education
   _____other (please specify)

2. If you used this text for a program, what was the name of that program?

3. Which chapters or sections were omitted from your course?

4. Have you any suggestions for improving this text?

Fold here

- -